Emerging Economies and the Transformation of International Business

NEW HORIZONS IN INTERNATIONAL BUSINESS

Series Editor: Peter J. Buckley
Centre for International Business,
University of Leeds (CIBUL), UK

The New Horizons in International Business series has established itself as the world's leading forum for the presentation of new ideas in international business research. It offers pre-eminent contributions in the areas of multinational enterprise – including foreign direct investment, business strategy and corporate alliances, global competitive strategies, and entrepreneurship. In short, this series constitutes essential reading for academics, business strategists and policy makers alike.

Emerging Economies and the Transformation of International Business

Brazil, Russia, India and China (BRICs)

Edited by

Subhash C. Jain

University of Connecticut, USA

NEW HORIZONS IN INTERNATIONAL BUSINESS

Edward Elgar

Cheltenham, UK • Northampton, MA, USA

Published by
Edward Elgar Publishing Limited
Glensanda House
Montpellier Parade
Cheltenham
Glos GL50 1UA
UK

Edward Elgar Publishing, Inc.
William Pratt House
9 Dewey Court
Northampton
Massachusetts 01060
USA

A catalogue record for this book
is available from the British Library

Library of Congress Cataloguing in Publication Data

Emerging economies and the transformation of international business :
Brazil, Russia, India and China / edited by Subhash C. Jain.
       p. cm.
   Includes bibliographical references and index.
   1. International trade. 2. Strategic planning—Developing countries—Case studies. I. Jain, Subhash C. (Subhash Chandra), 1938–
   HF1379.E47 2006
   338.8′8—dc22   2006005605

ISBN-13: 978 1 84542 597 5
ISBN-10: 1 84542 597 9

Printed and bound in Great Britain by MPG Books Ltd, Bodmin, Cornwall

A UCONN CIBER SUPPORTED RESEARCH INITIATIVE

CIBER is a program of the US Department of Education.
The CIBER program's mandate is to enhance US competitiveness in
the global business arena through activities involving US businesses,
educators and students.

Contents

Contributors

Preet S. Aulakh holds the Pierre Lassonde Chair in International Business at the Schulich School of Business, York University, Canada. He has done extensive research on various international business areas, including foreign entry modes, managing cross-border alliances and partnerships, structuring international distribution channels, international licensing agreements, international strategies and performance of firms from emerging economies, among others.

Jack N. Behrman is Lurther Hodges Distinguished Professor Emeritus at the University of North Carolina's Kenan-Flagler Business School. His expertise lies in the areas of international economics & business, transnational corporations (TNCs), international business–government relations, ethics, comparative management, science and technology, and creativity and innovation.

Robert C. Bird is an Assistant Professor of Legal Studies at the University of Connecticut. Robert received his JD and MBA from Boston University. Robert's research interests include employment law and intellectual property law.

Zhiwu Chen is Professor of Finance at Yale School of Management, Yale University. He is an expert on finance theory, securities valuation, emerging markets, and China's economy and capital markets. In the last few years, he has been actively doing research on market development and institution-building issues in the context of China's transition process and other emerging markets.

Stephen Coelen holds several positions: Professor in Residence in Economics at the University of Connecticut; Research Associate in both the Connecticut Center for Economic Analysis (CCEA) and the Center for International Business Education and Research (CIBER); and Adjunct Professor and chief international advisor to the University of Fort Hare in the Republic of South Africa.

Igor Filatotchev is a Professor of International Strategic Management at King's College London. His research interests are focused on corporate governance effects on entrepreneurship development, strategic decisions and organizational change. He earned his PhD in Economics from the Institute of World Economy and International Relations (Moscow) in 1985.

Robert Grosse has taught international finance in the MBA programs at the University of Miami, University of Michigan, and Instituto de Empresa (Madrid, Spain). He has also taught in many Latin American universities, where he is a leading author on international business. He is currently President of the Business Association of Latin American Studies.

Mohsin Habib is Associate Professor of Management at the University of Massachusetts-Boston. He teaches global management and ethics at the undergraduate and MBA levels. His research interests include the role of corruption in international business, FDI, and country-level competitiveness.

Subhash C. Jain is a Professor of International Marketing, Director of the Center for International Business Education and Research (CIBER) funded by the US Department of Education, and Director of the GE Global Learning Center endowed by General Electric Company, in the School of Business, University of Connecticut.

William H.A. Johnson is an Assistant Professor of Operations and Technology in the Management Department of Bentley College in Waltham, MA. His research is diverse and multidisciplinary, examining issues of cooperative innovation including initiatives in subsidiary innovation, use of options thinking in strategic innovation and processes in new product development and R&D projects.

Prashant Kale is in the faculty of Corporate Strategy and International Business at the Stephen M. Ross School of Business, University of Michigan. His research focuses on the role and management of strategic alliances and acquisitions in the context of both emerging technologies and emerging economies.

Ben L. Kedia is Robert Wang Professor of International Business at the University of Memphis in Memphis, TN, and Director of the Memphis CIBER. His research focuses on emerging economies, international outsourcing, and knowledge transfer among multinational corporations.

Somnath Lahiri is advanced doctoral student in Management at the University of Memphis, TN. His research interests include emerging economies and international outsourcing.

Daniel J. McCarthy is the Alan S. McKim and Richard A. D'Amore Distinguished Professor of Global Management and Innovation at the College of Business Administration, Northeastern University, Boston, MA. He is a Fellow at the Davis Center for Russian Studies at Harvard University, and is one of the top two scholars internationally in business and management in Russia, based on a study of publications in leading journals from 1986 to 2002.

Hemant Merchant is the Dean's Endowed Research Fellow and Associate Professor of International Strategy at Simon Fraser University (Vancouver, Canada). He is the recipient of the 2005 and 2006 Douglas C. Mackay Outstanding Paper Awards in International Business.

Debmalya Mukherjee is advanced doctoral student in Management at the University of Memphis, TN. His research interests include emerging economies and cross-border knowledge transfers.

Sheila M. Puffer is a Professor of International Business at Northeastern University, Boston, MA. She has been recognized as the number 1 scholar internationally in business and management in Russia based on a study of publications in 12 leading academic journals from 1986 to 2002. She is a Fellow at the Davis Center for Russian Studies at Harvard University.

Roopa Purushothaman is a global economist at Goldman Sachs, covering global thematic issues as a member of the global research team.

Ravi Sarathy is a Professor of Management and International Business in the College of Business Administration at Northeastern University. His major interests are in international business and international marketing and global strategy.

Karl P. Sauvant is the Executive Director of the Columbia Program on International Investment (a joint undertaking of Columbia Law School and the Earth Institute), Lecturer in Law at Columbia Law School, Special Advisor to the UN Millennium Project and Guest Professor at Nankai University, China.

Camille P. Schuster is a Professor of Marketing and International Business at California State University San Marcos. She received her PhD from The Ohio State University and her MA from Arizona State University.

Dominic Wilson is a senior global economist at Goldman Sachs. He works on global thematic issues as a member of the global research team.

Linda Yueh is Fellow in Economics, Pembroke College, Oxford University, and is also appointed to the Department of Economics, LSE. Her research areas include globalization, the Chinese economy, and economic development and growth as well as aspects of international law and economics.

Leon Zurawicki is a Professor of International Marketing at the University of Massachusetts-Boston. He is an author of four books and numerous articles. Dr Zurawicki's research interests center on corruption in international business.

Foreword

The twenty-first century may well be the time when the balance of power shifts to Brazil, Russia, India and China, nations collectively referred to as BRICs. These nations constitute the shape of the future, giving rise to a new world economy. Leaders in BRICs are frenetically laying the groundwork for decades of new growth. Predictions are that in less than 50 years, the BRICs economies, if things go right, could be larger than those of the G6 (the United States, Japan, Germany, the UK, France and Italy).

If the BRICs meet the projections cast for them, there will be significant implications for the US economy. As the developed nations become a shrinking part of the global market, the evolving markets in BRICs could provide tremendous opportunities for many US companies. Thus, it is imperative for our companies to be invested in and involved in the BRIC markets. This is an extremely important strategic choice for many firms.

Are we ready to face the challenges that the BRICs might pose? Perhaps not. While the opportunities in China are well understood, I suspect the potential in India, Russia and Brazil is not. Extensive education is needed to make our business leaders of today and tomorrow aware of the relative importance of BRICs as an engine of new demand growth and spending power.

Different educational opportunities are available to US managers to learn about global markets. The CIBER (Center for International Business Education and Research) program of the US Department of Education is uniquely relevant in assisting US firms to become globally aware and learn to compete in BRICs and other emerging markets. Thirty business schools that receive the CIBER grant organize a variety of programs geared toward enhancing US competitiveness in global markets through undertaking educational, outreach and research programs. The BRIC Conference at the University of Connecticut, held in spring 2005, is an example of a CIBER program. The conference was organized by the University of Connecticut CIBER and was co-sponsored by CIBERs at Columbia University, University of Memphis, Thunderbird, the Galvin School of Management and the University of Wisconsin.

The BRIC Conference highlighted the emergence of Brazil, Russia, India and China as significant future players in the global economy. It was an impressive gathering of scholars from all over the world presenting their views on the rise of BRICs and what America must do to compete with these nations. I am glad that the conference papers have been assembled to be issued as a book. It should be interesting and necessary for both college students and professionals to learn about BRICs and how to cope with the challenges that their growth generates.

I am grateful to the US Department of Education, especially Program Specialist Susanna Easton, who has strongly backed our CIBER in this and its other endeavors. Her gifted leadership has gone a long way in promoting internationalization of business schools throughout the country.

I want to commend Subhash C. Jain, the Director of UCONN CIBER, for the excellent idea of holding the BRICs Conference. He and his staff deserve applause for the superb job of organizing the conference.

I must recognize the co-sponsoring CIBERs at Columbia, Memphis, Thunderbird and Wisconsin that teamed up with UCONN to support the event financially. Finally, I want to thank Subhash Jain for asking me to write the Foreword, and wish the contributing authors success in their future research.

William C. (Curt) Hunter, Dean
School of Business
University of Connecticut

Preface

After the collapse of the Soviet Union, the US became the lone superpower of the world. But it may not be able to hold this dominant position for long. The rapid transformation of BRICs means the US must prepare for a far different future, one where it must learn to share economic power as never before. The US must craft fresh strategies that will allow her to thrive in the shifting economic environment. US companies must train their current and future managers to compete with firms in the BRICs.

The BRIC Conference at the University of Connecticut in spring 2005 was held to examine what the US must do to compete with BRICs. Nineteen scholars from the US and abroad presented papers to examine various aspects of the ascendancy of BRICs. This book comprises the collection of these papers. The book presents what Americans need to know now about Brazil, Russia, India and China that will transform the global economy. It delves into the massive power of the BRICs and how they will reshape the global economy; it examines what could occur to slow their growth; it studies their strengths and weaknesses; and asks what the US should do to maintain its lead in terms of both government policies and firm strategies.

This book, which is the output of the BRIC Conference, would not be possible without the active support of a number of individuals whom I must recognize. First, I am grateful to all the colleagues from different parts of the world for traveling to the University of Connecticut to participate in and speak at the conference. Without their commitment this book would not be feasible. Second, I want to thank CIBER Directors at Columbia University, University of Memphis, Thunderbird, the Galvin School of Management and the University of Wisconsin for co-sponsoring the BRICs Conference. Third, I am indebted to Dean William C. (Curt) Hunter, University of Connecticut, for writing the Foreword to this book despite his heavy commitments and frequent travels. Fourth, the CIBER colleagues at UCONN: Associate Director Kelly Aceto, and Student Manager of the program Alla Remen deserve my sincere thanks for their support in pursuing the BRIC program. Alla worked hard to coordinate the program with the speakers, while Kelly took care of the minutest logistical details. Along with them, I want to convey my thanks to graduate assistant Stephen Petretto and office staff Regina Forker and Diksha Gagrani for their wholehearted help and support. Lastly, I want to thank my wife for putting up with me working late hours for several weeks before and during the conference. Her intellectual and moral support keep me going.

As in the past, it has been a pleasure working with the people at Edward Elgar Publishing. Both Acquisition Editor Alan Sturmer and Production Editor Kate Emmins have been extremely helpful in making this book possible. I owe them a large debt of thanks.

Subhash C. Jain
1 September 2005

PART I

Introduction

1. Dreaming with BRICs: the path to 2050

Dominic Wilson and Roopa Purushothaman

Over the next 50 years, Brazil, Russia, India and China – the BRICs economies – could become a much larger force in the world economy. Using the latest demographic projections and a model of capital accumulation and productivity growth, we map out GDP growth, income per capita and currency movements in the BRICs economies until 2050.

The results are startling. If things go right, in less than 40 years, the BRICs economies together could be larger than the G6 in US dollar terms. By 2025 they could account for over half the size of the G6. Currently they are worth less than 15 percent. Of the current G6, only the US and Japan may be among the six largest economies in US dollar terms in 2050.

About two-thirds of the increase in US dollar GDP from the BRICs should come from higher real growth, with the balance through currency appreciation. The BRICs' real exchange rates could appreciate by up to 300 percent over the next 50 years (an average of 2.5 percent a year).

The shift in GDP relative to the G6 takes place steadily over the period, but is most dramatic in the first 30 years. Growth for the BRICs is likely to slow significantly toward the end of the period, with only India seeing growth rates significantly above 3 percent by 2050. And individuals in the BRICs are still likely to be poorer on average than individuals in the G6 economies, with the exception of Russia. China's per capita income could be roughly what the developed economies are now (about US$30 000 per capita).

As early as 2009, the annual increase in US dollar spending from the BRICs could be greater than that from the G6 and more than twice as much in dollar terms as it is now. By 2025 the annual increase in US dollar spending from the BRICs could be twice that of the G6, and four times higher by 2050.

The key assumption underlying our projections is that the BRICs maintain policies and develop institutions that are supportive of growth. Each of the BRICs faces significant challenges in keeping development on track.

This means that there is a good chance that our projections are not met, either through bad policy or bad luck. But if the BRICs come anywhere close to meeting the projections set out here, the implications for the pattern of growth and economic activity could be large.

The relative importance of the BRICs as an engine of new demand growth and spending power may shift more dramatically and quickly than expected. Higher growth in these economies could offset the impact of graying populations and slower growth in the advanced economies.

Higher growth may lead to higher returns and increased demand for capital. The weight of the BRICs in investment portfolios could rise sharply. Capital flows might move further in their favour, prompting major currency realignments.

Rising incomes may also see these economies move through the 'sweet spot' of growth for different kinds of products, as local spending patterns change. This could be an important determinant of demand and pricing patterns for a range of commodities.

As today's advanced economies become a shrinking part of the world economy, the accompanying shifts in spending could provide significant opportunities for global companies. Being invested in and involved in the right markets – particularly the right emerging markets – may become an increasingly important strategic choice.

The list of the world's ten largest economies may look quite different in 2050. The largest economies in the world (by GDP) may no longer be the richest (by income per capita), making strategic choices for firms more complex.

DREAMING WITH BRICS

The world economy has changed a lot over the past 50 years. Over the next 50, the changes could be at least as dramatic.

We have highlighted the importance of thinking about the developing world in our recent global research, focusing on key features of development and globalization that we think are important to investors with a long-term perspective. A major theme of this work has been that, over the next few decades, the growth generated by the large developing countries, particularly the BRICs (Brazil, Russia, India and China) could become a much larger force in the world economy than it is now – and much larger than many investors currently expect.

In this piece, we gauge just how large a force the BRICs could become over the next 50 years. We do this not simply by extrapolating from current growth rates, but by setting out clear assumptions about how the process of growth and development works and applying a formal framework to generate long-term forecasts. We look at our BRICs projections relative to long-term projections for the G6 (the US, Japan, the UK, Germany, France and Italy).[1]

Using the latest demographic projections and a model of capital accumulation and productivity growth, we map out GDP growth, income per capita and currency movements in the BRICs economies until 2050. This allows us to paint a picture of how the world economy might change over the decades ahead.

The results of the exercise are startling. They suggest that if things go right, the BRICs could become a very important source of new global spending in the not too distant future. Figure 1.1 shows that India's economy, for instance, could be larger than Japan's by 2032, and China's larger than the US by 2041 (and larger than everyone else as early as 2016). The BRICs economies taken together could be larger than the G6 by 2039.

Our projections are optimistic, in the sense that they assume reasonably successful development. But they are economically sensible, internally consistent and provide a clear benchmark against which investors can set their expectations. There is a good chance that the right conditions in one or another economy will not fall into place and the projections will not be realized. If the BRICs pursue sound policies, however, the world we envisage here might turn out to be a reality, not just a dream.

The projections leave us in no doubt that the progress of the BRICs will be critical to how the world economy evolves. If these economies can fulfill their potential for growth, they could become a dominant force in generating spending growth over the next few decades.

A DRAMATICALLY DIFFERENT WORLD

We start with some key conclusions that describe the way the world might change by 2050. The big assumption underlying all of these projections is that the BRICs maintain growth-supportive policy settings. The figures and tables throughout the text illustrate these points. Our conclusions fall under five main topics: (1) economic size; (2) economic growth; (3) incomes and demographics; (4) global demand patterns; and (5) currency movements.

Economic Size

In less than 40 years, the BRICs economies together could be larger than the G6 in US dollar terms. By 2025 they could account for over half the size of the G6. Currently they are worth less than 15 percent (see Figure 1.2 and Figure 1.3).

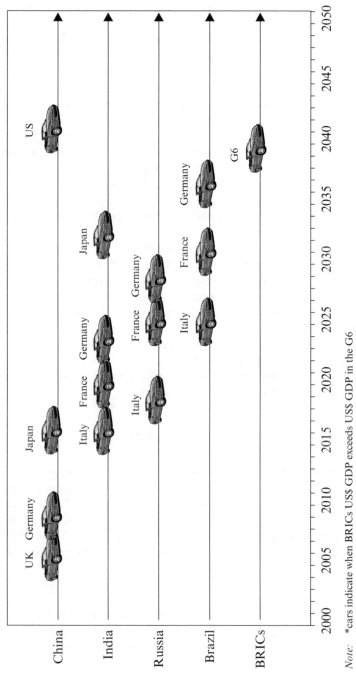

Note: *cars indicate when BRICs US$ GDP exceeds US$ GDP in the G6

Figure 1.1   Overtaking the G6: when BRICs' US$ GDP would exceed G6

GDP
(2003 US$bn)

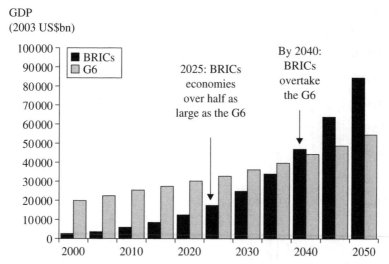

Figure 1.2   BRICs have a larger US$ GDP than the G6 in less than 40 years

GDP
(2003 US$bn)

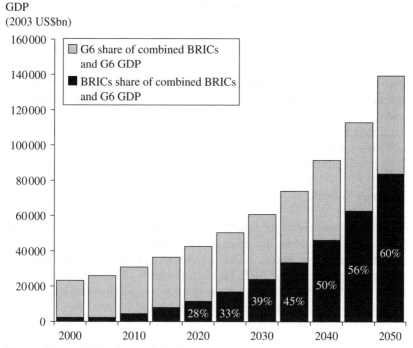

Figure 1.3   BRICs share of GDP rises

GDP
(2003 US$bn)

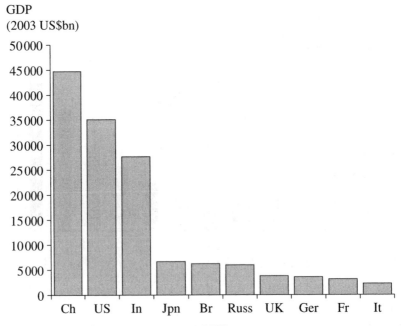

Figure 1.4   The largest economies in 2050

In US dollar terms, China could overtake Germany in 2008, Japan by 2015 and the US by 2039. India's economy could be larger than all but the US and China in 30 years. Russia would overtake Germany, France, Italy and the UK.

Of the current G6 (US, Japan, Germany, France, Italy, UK) only the US and Japan may be among the six largest economies in US dollar terms in 2050 (see Figure 1.4).

Economic Growth

India has the potential to show the fastest growth over the next 30 and 50 years. Growth could be higher than 5 percent over the next 30 years and close to 5 percent as late as 2050 if development proceeds successfully.

Overall, growth for the BRICs is likely to slow significantly over this time frame. By 2050, only India on our projections would be recording growth rates significantly above 3 percent (Figure 1.5 and Figure 1.6).

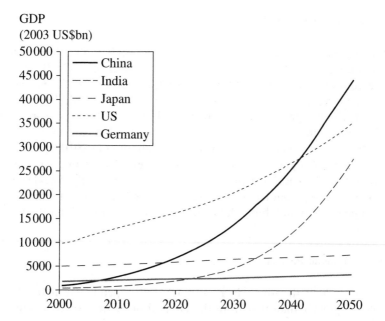

Figure 1.5   China overtakes the G3; India is close behind

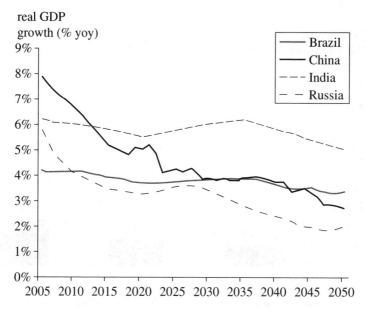

Figure 1.6   India shows most rapid growth potential of the BRICS

Incomes and Demographics

Despite much faster growth, individuals in the BRICs are still likely to be poorer on average than individuals in the G6 economies by 2050. Russia is the exception, essentially catching up with the poorer of the G6 in terms of income per capita by 2050. China's per capita income could be similar to where the developed economies are now (about US$30 000 per capita). By 2030, China's income per capita could be roughly what Korea's is today. In the US, income per capita by 2050 could reach roughly $80 000.

Demographics play an important role in the way the world will change. Even within the BRICs, demographic impacts vary greatly. The decline in working-age population is generally projected to take place later than in the developed economies, but will be steeper in Russia and China than India and Brazil.

Global Demand Patterns

As early as 2009, the annual increase in US dollar spending from the BRICs could be greater than that from the G6 and more than twice as much in dollar terms as it was in 2003. By 2025 the annual increase in US dollar spending from the BRICs could be twice that of the G6, and four times higher by 2050 (Figure 1.7).

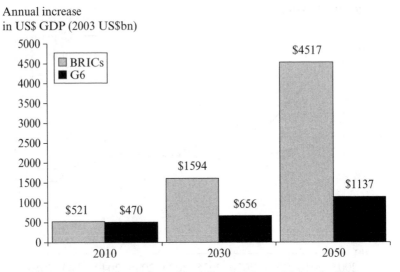

Figure 1.7   Incremental demand from the BRICs could eventually be quadruple G6 demand

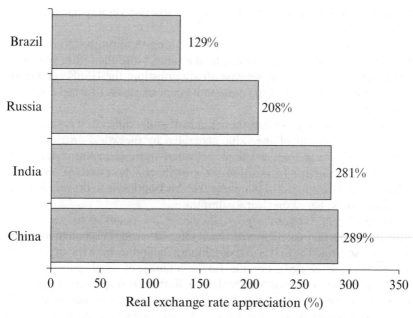

Figure 1.8   BRICs exchange rates could appreciate by close to 300%

Currency Movements

Rising exchange rates could contribute a significant amount to the rise in US dollar GDP in the BRICs. About one-third of the increase in US dollar GDP from the BRICs over the period may come from rising currencies, with the other two-thirds from faster growth.

The BRICs real exchange rates could appreciate by up to 300 percent over the next 50 years (an average of 2.5 percent a year) (see Figure 1.8). China's currency could double in value in ten years' time if growth continued and the exchange rate were allowed to float freely

HOW COUNTRIES GET RICHER

Our predictions may seem dramatic. But over a period of a few decades, the world economy can change a lot. Looking back 30 or 50 years illustrates that point. Back in the 1950s, Japan and Germany were struggling to emerge from reconstruction. Thirty years ago, Korea was just beginning to emerge from its position as a low-income nation. And even over the last decade, China's importance to the world economy has increased substantially.

History also illustrates that any kind of long-term projection is subject to a great deal of uncertainty. The further ahead into the future you look, the more uncertain things become. Predictions that the USSR (or Japan) would overtake the US as the dominant economic power turned out to be badly off the mark.

While this makes modeling these kinds of shifts difficult, it is still essential. Over 80 percent of the value generated by the world's major equity markets will come from earnings delivered more than ten years away. Developing strategies to position for growth may take several years and require significant forward planning. The best option is to provide a sensible framework, based on clear assumptions.

As developing economies grow, they have the potential to post higher growth rates as they catch up with the developed world. This potential comes from two sources. The first is that developing economies have less capital (per worker) than developed economies (in the language of simple growth models they are further from their 'steady states'). Returns on capital are higher and a given investment rate results in higher growth in the capital stock. The second is that developing countries may be able to use technologies available in more developed countries to 'catch up' with developed country techniques.

As countries develop, these forces fade and growth rates tend to slow towards developed country levels. In Japan and Germany, very rapid growth in the 1960s and 1970s gave way to more moderate growth in the 1980s and 1990s (see Figure 1.9). This is why simple extrapolation gives silly answers over long time frames. As a crude example, assuming that China's GDP growth continued to grow at its current 8 percent per year over the next three decades would lead to the prediction that China's economy would be three times larger than the US by 2030 in US dollar terms and 25 times larger by 2050.

Countries also grow richer on the back of appreciating currencies. Currencies tend to rise as higher productivity leads economies to converge on purchasing power parity (PPP) exchange rates. There is a clear tendency for countries with higher income per capita to have exchange rates closer to PPP. The BRICs economies all have exchange rates that are a long way below PPP rates. These large differences between PPP and actual exchange rates come about because productivity levels are much lower in developing economies. As they develop and productivity rises, there will be a tendency for their currencies to rise towards PPP. The idea that countries experiencing higher productivity growth tend to appreciate is an important part of both our GSDEER and GSDEEMER models of equilibrium exchange rates (see Figure 1.10).

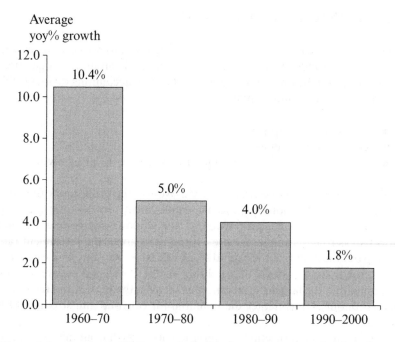

Figure 1.9   Japanese GDP growth declined as the economy developed

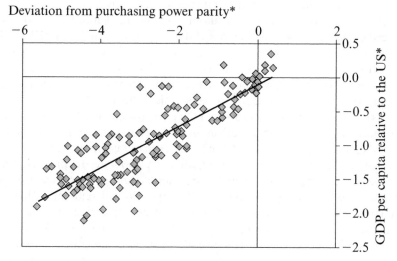

Note: expressed in logs

Figure 1.10   Higher income per capita moves exchange rates closer to PPP

BREAKING DOWN GROWTH

To translate these two processes into actual projections, we need to develop a model. The model we use is described in more detail in the Appendices but the intuition behind it is quite simple. Growth accounting divides GDP growth into three components:

- growth in employment
- growth in the capital stock
- technical progress (or total-factor productivity (TFP) growth).[2]

We model each component explicitly. We use the US Census Bureau's demographic projections to forecast employment growth over the long term, assuming that the proportion of the working-age population that works stays roughly stable. We use assumptions about the investment rate to map out the path that the capital stock will take over time. And we model TFP growth as a process of catch-up on the developed economies, by assuming that the larger the income gap between the BRICs and the developed economies, the greater the potential for catch-up and stronger TFP growth.

We then use the projections of productivity growth from this exercise to map out the path of the real exchange rate. As in our GSDEER framework, we assume that if an economy experiences higher productivity growth than the US, its equilibrium exchange rate will tend to appreciate.

By varying the assumptions about investment, demographics or the speed of catch-up, we can generate different paths for annual GDP, GDP growth, GDP per capita (in local currency or US dollars), productivity growth and the real exchange rate (see Table 1.1).

Because both the growth and currency projections are long-term projections, we ignore the impact of the economic cycle. Effectively, the projections can be interpreted as growth in the trend (or potential growth) of the economy and the currencies' path as an equilibrium path. Where economies peg their exchange rates (as in China), it is even more important to view the exchange rate projections as an equilibrium real rate. In practice, real exchange rate appreciation might come about through a combination of nominal appreciation and higher inflation, with different mixes having different implications. We abstract from inflation, expressing all of our projections in real terms (either 2003 local currency or 2003 US dollars).[3]

Generally speaking, the structure of the models is identical across the four economies. We make two minor alterations. We assume that the 'convergence speed' of TFP in Brazil and India is slower than in Russia and China for the first 20 years, largely because of lower education levels

Table 1.1   BRICs real GDP growth: 5-year period averages

%	Brazil	China	India	Russia
2000–2005	2.7	8.0	5.3	5.9
2005–2010	4.2	7.2	6.1	4.8
2010–2015	4.1	5.9	5.9	3.8
2015–2020	3.8	5.0	5.7	3.4
2020–2025	3.7	4.6	5.7	3.4
2025–2030	3.8	4.1	5.9	3.5
2030–2035	3.9	3.9	6.1	3.1
2035–2040	3.8	3.9	6.0	2.6
2040–2045	3.6	3.5	5.6	2.2
2045–2050	3.4	2.9	5.2	1.9

and poorer infrastructure (more on these factors below), but gradually rises from 2020 onwards (as these structural problems are addressed) so that all of the BRICs are 'running' at the same convergence speed. We also assume that China's investment rate gradually declines from its current levels of around 36 percent to 30 percent (close to the Asian average) by 2015. We use GS forecasts until 2004 and begin the simulations in 2005.

A MORE DETAILED LOOK AT THE BRICS' POTENTIAL

We have already highlighted some of the most striking results, though there are many other intriguing aspects. The tables and figures set out the key features of the projections, summarizing them in five-year blocks. They show average GDP growth rates, income per capita in US dollars, the real exchange rate and the main demographic trends.

In each economy, as development occurs, growth tends to slow and the exchange rate appreciates. Both rising currencies and faster growth raise US dollar GDP per capita gradually and the gap between the BRICs and developed economies narrows slowly.

The impact of demographics varies, with labor force growth contributing relatively more to growth in India and Brazil and detracting from growth in Russia, where the US Census projections show the labor force shrinking quite rapidly. Where labor force and population growth is rapid, income per capita tends to rise more slowly as higher investment is needed just to keep up with population growth.

% of total
population

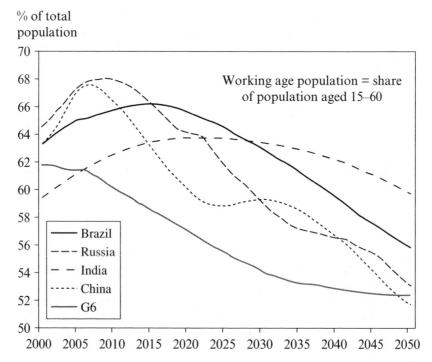

Figure 1.11   Working-age population projected to decline

To illustrate the shift in economic gravity, we also make comparisons with the G6. To do that, we use a less sophisticated version of the same model to project G6 growth. We assume a common 2 percent labor productivity growth rate across the G6, so differences in projected GDP growth are purely a function of demographics (and real exchange rates remain roughly stable). A shrinking working-age population appears to be the biggest issue in Japan and Italy, whose growth rates are lower than the others, and the smallest issue in the US, which maintains the fastest growth (see Figure 1.11).

Our G6 projections allow us to compare the paths of GDP and GDP per capita in the BRICs with that of the more advanced economies in a common currency. The shift in GDP relative to the G6 takes place steadily over the period, but is most dramatic in the first 30 years. The BRICs overtake the G6 through higher real growth and through the appreciation of BRICs' currencies. About one-third of the increase in US dollar GDP from the BRICs over the period may come from rising currencies, with the other two-thirds from faster growth (see Table 1.2, Table 1.3 and Table 1.4).

Table 1.2   Projected US$ GDP

2003 $USbn	BRICs				G6						BRICs	G6
	Brazil	China	India	Russia	France	Germany	Italy	Japan	UK	US		
2000	762	1078	469	391	1311	1875	1078	4176	1437	9825	2700	19702
2005	468	1724	604	534	1489	2011	1236	4427	1688	11697	3330	22548
2010	668	2998	929	847	1622	2212	1337	4601	1876	13271	5441	24919
2015	962	4754	1411	1232	1767	2386	1447	4858	2089	14766	8349	27332
2020	1333	7070	2104	1741	1930	2524	1553	5221	2285	16415	12248	29928
2025	1695	10213	3174	2264	2095	2604	1625	5567	2456	18340	17345	32687
2030	2189	14312	4935	2980	2267	2897	1671	5810	2649	20833	24415	35927
2035	2871	19605	7864	3734	2445	2603	1708	5882	2901	23828	34064	39668
2040	3740	26439	12367	4467	2668	3147	1788	6039	3201	27229	47013	44072
2045	4794	34799	18847	5156	2898	3381	1912	6297	3496	30956	63596	48940
2050	6074	44453	27803	5870	3148	3603	2061	6673	3782	35166	84201	54433

Table 1.3 Projected US$ GDP per capita

2003 US$	BRICs				G6					
	Brazil	China	India	Russia	France	Germany	Italy	Japan	UK	US
2000	4 338	854	468	2 675	22 078	22 814	18 677	32 960	24 142	34 797
2005	2 512	1 324	559	3 718	24 547	24 402	21 277	34 744	27 920	39 552
2010	3 417	2 233	804	5 948	26 314	26 877	23 018	36 172	30 611	42 926
2015	4 664	3 428	1 149	8 736	28 338	29 111	25 086	38 626	33 594	45 835
2020	6 302	4 965	1 622	12 527	30 723	31 000	27 239	42 359	36 234	48 849
2025	7 781	7 051	2 331	16 652	33 203	32 299	28 894	46 391	38 479	52 450
2030	9 823	9 809	3 473	22 427	35 876	33 898	30 177	49 944	41 194	57 263
2035	12 682	13 434	5 327	28 749	38 779	37 087	31 402	52 313	44 985	63 017
2040	16 370	18 209	8 124	35 314	42 601	40 966	33 583	55 721	49 658	69 431
2045	20 926	24 192	12 046	42 081	46 795	44 940	36 859	60 454	54 386	76 228
2050	26 592	31 357	17 366	49 646	51 594	48 952	40 901	66 805	59 122	83 710

Table 1.4   Projected US$ GDP per capita growth: 5-year averages

Average %yoy	BRICs				G6					
	Brazil	China	India	Russia	France	Germany	Italy	Japan	UK	US
2000–2005	−9.8	9.2	3.7	7.0	2.2	1.4	2.7	1.1	3.0	2.6
2005–2010	6.3	11.2	7.5	10.3	1.5	2.0	1.6	0.9	1.9	1.7
2010–2015	6.4	9.2	7.4	8.1	1.5	1.6	1.7	1.2	1.9	1.3
2015–2020	6.2	7.8	7.2	7.5	1.6	1.3	1.7	1.8	1.6	1.3
2020–2025	4.6	7.3	7.4	6.1	1.6	0.9	1.2	1.8	1.2	1.4
2025–2030	4.7	6.9	8.2	6.2	1.6	0.9	0.9	1.5	1.3	1.7
2030–2035	5.2	6.5	8.9	5.2	1.6	1.7	0.8	1.0	1.7	1.9
2035–2040	5.3	6.3	8.9	4.3	1.9	2.0	1.3	1.2	2.0	2.0
2040–2045	5.0	5.9	8.3	3.6	1.9	1.9	1.8	1.6	1.8	1.9
2045–2050	4.9	5.4	7.6	3.4	2.0	1.8	2.1	2.0	1.7	1.9

We also look explicitly at where new demand growth in the world will come from. While it takes some time for the level of GDP in the BRICs to approach the G6, their share of new demand growth rises much more rapidly (see Figure 1.12). Because it is incremental demand that generally drives returns, this measure may be particularly useful to assess the extent of opportunities in these markets. We measure that new demand growth as the change in US dollar spending power in the various economies, so again it incorporates both growth and currency effects. On these measures, the BRICs come to dominate the G6 as a source of growth in spending power within ten years.

Taking each of the economies in brief:

- Brazil: over the next 50 years, Brazil's GDP growth rate averages 3.6 percent. The size of Brazil's economy overtakes Italy by 2025; France by 2031; UK and Germany by 2036.
- China: China's GDP growth rate falls to 5 percent in 2020 from its 8.1 percent growth rate projected for 2003. By the mid-2040s, growth

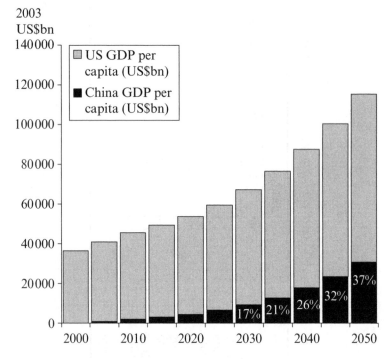

*Figure 1.12   China's income per capita growing share of US income
              per capita*

slows to around 3.5 percent. Even so, high investment rates, a large labor force and steady convergence would mean China becomes the world's largest economy by 2041.

- India: while growth in the G6, Brazil, Russia and China is expected to slow significantly over the next 50 years, India's growth rate remains above 5 percent throughout the period. India's GDP outstrips that of Japan by 2032. With the only population out of the BRICS that continues to grow throughout the next 50 years, India has the potential to raise its US dollar income per capita in 2050 to 35 times current levels. Still, India's income per capita will be significantly lower than any of the countries we look at (see Figure 1.13)
- Russia: Russia's growth projections are hampered by a shrinking population (an assumption that may be too negative). But strong convergence rates work to Russia's benefit, and by 2050, the country's GDP per capita is by far the highest in the group, and comparable to the G6. Russia's economy overtakes Italy in 2018; France in 2024; UK in 2027 and Germany in 2028.

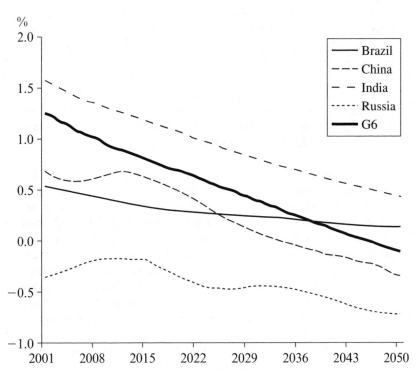

Figure 1.13   Projected population growth rates

Although we focus on the BRICs, as the four largest developing economies, we do not mean to suggest that development elsewhere is not important. In Box 1.1, we look at what our approach says for South Africa and the African region and other larger developing economies could also become important.

BOX 1.1 SOUTH AFRICA AND THE CHALLENGE FOR THE AFRICAN CONTINENT

With Asia, Europe and Latin America represented in the BRICs profile, some readers will notice Africa's absence. The BRICs are chosen because they are the four largest developing economies currently. Still, it is interesting and important to look beyond at the potential for Africa, and particularly South Africa, the largest economy in the region, to play a part in the same kind of process.

We have already published a ten-year outlook on South Africa using detailed econometric work to project the same components of growth (employment growth, capital stock growth and technical progress) that underpin our methodology here (see *Global Economics Paper #93, 'South Africa Growth and Unemployment: A Ten-Year Outlook'*). The study showed that South Africa could achieve 5 percent growth over the next decade if the right policies were put in place (see Figure 1.14). The emphasis on getting the conditions for growth right is one that is important for the BRICs also.

To provide comparison, we applied our projection methods for the BRICs to South Africa. The method is simpler than that in our paper on South Africa, but does provide a longer-term outlook. Table 1.5 sets out the main results in terms of growth. Projected growth over the next decade is a little lower than the 5 percent projected in our more detailed study (around 4 percent here), but the main thrust of the outlook is similar. The differences arise largely because the demographic projections we assume much sharper shrinkage in the labor force (around 1 percent per year) than did the more detailed exercise. Both in South Africa, and in the region more generally, the challenge of AIDS and the impact it will have on labor force and population dynamics is an important risk and challenge that has no direct counterpart elsewhere.

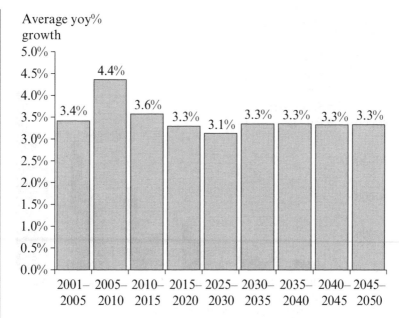

Figure 1.14   South Africa projected real GDP growth

Table 1.5   Projected US$ GDP levels

2003 US$bn	South Africa	Brazil	China	India	Russia
2000	83	762	1 078	469	391
2010	147	668	2 998	929	847
2020	267	1 333	7 070	2 104	1 741
2030	447	2 189	14 312	4 935	2 980
2040	739	3 740	26 439	12 367	4 467
2050	1 174	6 074	44 453	27 803	5 870

Our longer-term projections show South Africa growing at an average rate of around 3.5 percent over the next 50 years, comparable to our predictions for Russia and Brazil (see Table 1.5). With declining population growth rates, per capita incomes under these projections would rise significantly more rapidly. We find under these projections that South Africa's economy would be significantly smaller than the BRICs in 2050 (around US$1.2 billion compared to US$5.9 billion for Russia, the smallest of the

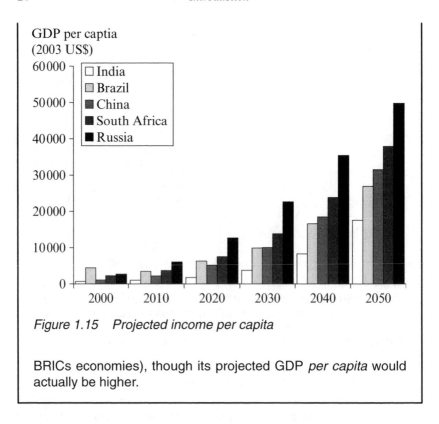

GDP per captia
(2003 US$)

Figure 1.15   Projected income per capita

BRICs economies), though its projected GDP *per capita* would actually be higher.

ARE THE RESULTS PLAUSIBLE?

The projection of a substantial shift in the generation of growth towards the BRICs is dramatic. Is it plausible? We have looked at three main ways to cross check the forecasts, all of which give us broad comfort with the results.

First, the forecasts for GDP growth in the next ten years are not out of line with the IMF's assumptions of potential growth in these economies (roughly 5 percent for Russia, 4 percent for Brazil, 8 percent for China, 5–6 percent for India). With the exception of Brazil, our projected growth rates are also close to recent performance. Brazil's performance would have to improve quite significantly relative to the past.

Second, although the implied changes in GDP and currencies may look dramatic on an absolute basis, they are significantly less spectacular than what some economies actually achieved over the last few decades. In Japan, between 1955 and 1985 real GDP increased by nearly eight times (from initial levels of income per capita not unlike some of the BRICs) and real industrial production increased tenfold. Between 1970 and1995 – the yen appreciated by over 300 percent in nominal terms against the US dollar. In the more recent past, Korea's GDP in 2000 increased by nearly nine times between 1970 and 2000. Next to these experiences, our projections look quite tame. Although the projections assume that economies remain on a steady development track, they do not assume 'miracle-economy' growth.

As a final check on our estimates, we applied an entirely different approach to generate long-term growth projections based on cross-country econometric research. We took a well-known existing econometric model from Levine and Renelt (LR) that explains average GDP growth over the next 30 years as a function of initial income per capita, investment rates, population growth and secondary school enrollments.[4]

Although the technique employed is very different and a year-by-year path cannot be generated, the model has close parallels to our own approach. Initial income per capita drives our productivity catch-up, investment drives capital accumulation, and the level of education can be thought of as helping to determine the speed of convergence. Projections using the LR equation are not identical to our own, but are close enough to reassure us that we are making sensible assumptions. Our own models are a bit more optimistic about growth prospects in general, but not by much.

A LOOK BACK IN TIME: WHAT WOULD WE HAVE SAID IN 1960?

We mentioned earlier that the world has changed a lot in the last fifty years. One further check on the plausibility of our projections is to go back in time, apply the same methods that we have used here, and look at how our projections of GDP growth then would have compared with subsequent reality.

To do that, we looked at a set of 11 developed and developing countries (the US, the UK, Germany, France, Italy, Japan, Brazil, Argentina, India, Korea and Hong Kong) starting in 1960 and projecting their GDP growth for the following 40 years (data availability meant we could not easily do a full 50-year projection).

We applied the same methodology, modeling capital stock growth as a function of the starting level of capital and investment and technical progress as a catch-up process on the US (see Table 1.6). Because we did not have demographic projections for 1960 (as we do now for the next 50 years), we used actual population data for the period as the basis for our labor force growth assumptions (effectively assuming that this part of the exercise was predicted perfectly).

Table 1.6   Comparing our projections with the Levine-Renelt model

30 year average real GDP growth	Our Projections	Levine-Renelt Model
Brazil	3.7	3.3
Russia	3.9	3.5
India	5.8	5.3
China	5.6	5.8

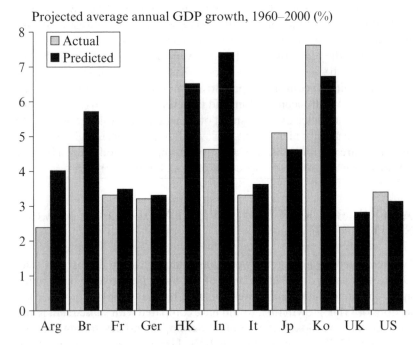

Figure 1.16   How our model fares in guaging growth 1960–2000

The results of that exercise are generally encouraging. In general, the projected average growth rates over the period are surprisingly close to the actual outcomes (see Figure 1.16). For the more developed countries, where the growth path has been steadier (France, Germany, the UK, the US, Italy) the differences between projected and actual growth rates are small.

For the developing countries (and Japan, which in 1960 was a developing country that was significantly poorer than Argentina) the range of outcomes is wider. For those countries where policy settings were not particularly growth-supportive – India, Brazil and Argentina – actual growth fell below what we would have projected. But for the Asian economies that had an unusually favorable growth experience, our method would have under-predicted actual growth performance in some cases quite significantly.

Overall, the results highlight that our method of projection seems broadly sensible. For the BRICs to meet our projections over the next 50 years, they do not need 'miracle' performance – though it is important that they stay on the right track in maintaining broadly favorable conditions for growth.

ENSURING THE CONDITIONS FOR GROWTH

This historical exercise highlights a critical point. For our projections to be close to the truth it is important that the BRICs remain on a steady growth track and keep the conditions in place that will allow that to happen. That is harder than it sounds and is the main reason why there is a good chance that the projections might not be realized. Of the BRICs, Brazil has not been growing in line with projections and may have the most immediate obstacles to this kind of growth. It provides a good illustration of the importance of getting the necessary conditions in place.

Research points to a wide range of conditions that are critical to ensuring solid growth performance and increasingly recognizes that getting the right institutions as well as the right policies is important.[5] These are the things that the BRICs must get right (or keep getting right) if the kinds of paths we describe are to be close to the truth. The main ingredients (more detailed discussion of the evidence is provided in Box 1.2:

- Sound macroeconomic policies and a stable macroeconomic background. Low inflation, supportive government policy, sound public finances and a well-managed exchange rate can all help to promote growth. Each of the BRICs has been through periods of macroeconomic instability in the last few decades and some face significant macroeconomic challenges still. Brazil for instance has suffered greatly from the precariousness of the public finances and the foreign borrowing that it brought about (see Box 1.3).
- Strong and stable political institutions. Political uncertainty and instability discourages investment and damages growth. Each of the BRICs is likely to face considerable (and different) challenges in political development over the next few decades. For some (Russia most obviously), the task of institution-building has been a major issue in recent growth performance.

BOX 1.2   THE CONDITIONS FOR GROWTH

A set of core factors – macroeconomic stability, institutional capacity, openness and education – can set the stage for growth. Robert Barro's influential work on the determinants of growth found that growth is enhanced by higher schooling and life expectancy, lower fertility, lower government consumption, better maintenance of the rule of law, lower inflation and improvements in the terms of trade. These core policies are linked: institutional capacity is required to implement stable macroeconomic policies, macro stability is crucial to trade, and without price stability a country rarely has much success in liberalizing and expanding trade. We briefly view some of the most recent findings on these ingredients here:

Macro Stability

An unstable macro environment can hamper growth by distorting prices and incentives. Inflation hinders growth by discouraging saving and investment. Accordingly, a key focus is price stability, achieved through fiscal deficit reduction, tighter monetary policy and exchange-rate realignment. Within the BRICs, macroeconomic indicators reflecting policy divergence show wide swings: through the 1990s, Brazil, averaged an inflation rate of 548 percent and a government deficit of 21.2 percent of GDP, against China's average inflation rate of 8 percent and government deficit of 2.3 percent of GDP.

Institutions

Institutions affect the 'efficiency' of an economy much in the same way as technology does: more efficient institutions allow an economy to produce the same output with fewer inputs: Bad institutions lower incentives to invest, to work and to save. 'Institutions' in this broad sense include the legal system, functioning markets, health and education systems, financial institutions and the government bureaucracy. Recent research argues that poor political and economic policies are only symptoms of longer-run institutional factors – a line of reasoning that could not help explain the disappointing results of developing countries' adoption of macroeconomic policy reforms in the 1990s.

Openness

Openness to trade and FDI can provide access to imported inputs, new technology and larger markets. Empirical studies of trade and growth fall into three buckets. First, country studies document the economic and political consequences of import-substitution policies and export promoting policies. Second, much work uses cross-section or panel data to examine the cross-country relationship between openness and growth. This had produced mixed evidence, but in general it demonstrates a positive relationship between openness and growth. Third, sector, industry and plant-level studies investigate the effects of trade policy on employment, profits, productivity and output at a micro-economic level. There appears to be a greater consensus here than in the cross-country work about the productivity-enhancing effects of trade liberalization.

Education

As economies grow rapidly, they may face shortages of skilled workers, meaning that more years of schooling are a prerequisite for the next stage of economic development. Enrolment rates have increased dramatically over the past 30 years, on average over 5 percent per year, particularly in higher education (around 14 percent). Among the BRICs, India receives low marks for education indicators, particularly at the primary and secondary levels. Many cross-country studies have found positive and statistically significant correlations between schooling and growth rates of per capita GDP – on the order of 0.3 percent faster annual growth over a 30-year period from an additional one year of schooling.

BOX 1.3   BRAZIL: CHALLENGES IN SETTING THE CONDITIONS FOR SUSTAINED GROWTH

Of the BRICs, Brazil is the only one where recent growth experience has been significantly lower than our projected growth rates. This suggests that more needs to be done to unlock sustained higher growth in Brazil than is the case elsewhere, and that our convergence assumptions for Brazil (though already lower than in China and Russia) may still prove too optimistic without deeper structural reforms.

Over the last 50 years, Brazil's real GDP growth rate amounted to 5.3 percent, but Figure 1.17 shows that growth has been declining sharply since the debt crisis of the 1980s. Following a growth

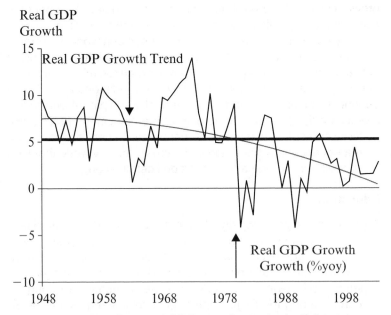

Figure 1.17   Brazil's trend GDP growth rate is declining

surge between the late 1960s and the early 1970s on the back of economic liberalization, growth rates fell – in part because of a series of external shocks combined with poor policy response amidst a political transition from a military regime to a democracy.

Over the last decade, real GDP growth amounted to 2.9 percent, compared to an average of 5.3 percent since 1950. The excessive reliance on external financing and domestic public debt during the oil crisis and during the Real plan has rendered this adjustment effort particularly difficult, in part explaining the marked drop in growth rates.

The adjustment process has also reduced investment, which contributed to a depreciation of the capital stock, particularly in infrastructure, with important consequences for productivity. Even so, temporary surges in external financing or statistical rebounds may push growth higher temporarily, but for Brazil to break the historical downward trend in GDP growth and attain the kind of path set out in our projections here will take more.

The Lula administration is making some progress. Macro stabilization is a key precondition of successful reform and is now clearly under way. The result of that stabilization is likely to be an improvement in growth over the next year or two that is reflected in our current forecasts of about 3.5 percent a year. On its own, though, stabilization will be insufficient to raise and sustain Brazil's growth rate to the kinds of levels that are set out in the projections in this chapter. If that goal is to be achieved, substantial structural reforms will also be needed.

Comparing Brazil with China and the other Asian economies gives a sense of the relatively larger obstacles that Brazil currently faces:

- Brazil is much less open to trade. The tradable goods sector in China is almost eight times larger than in Brazil, when measured by imports plus exports.
- Investment and savings are lower. Savings and investment ratios are around 18–19 percent of GDP compared to an investment rate of 36 percent of GDP in China and an Asian average of around 30 percent.
- Public and foreign debt are much higher. Without a deeper fiscal adjustment and lower debt to GDP ratio (currently at 57.7 percent of GDP on a net basis and 78.2 percent of GDP on a gross basis), the private sector is almost completely crowded out from credit markets. China's net foreign debt and public debt are both significantly smaller.

Unless significant progress is made in removing or reducing these obstacles, the projections set out here (which still show much lower growth than Brazil's post-war average) are unlikely to be achievable and the slide in trend growth could continue.

- Openness. Openness to trade and foreign direct investment has generally been an important part of successful development. The openness of the BRICs varies, but India is still relatively closed on many measures.
- High levels of education. Higher levels of education are generally helpful in contributing to more rapid growth and catch-up. The LR growth estimates above are based on a strong connection between secondary schooling and growth potential. Of the BRICs, India has the most work to do in expanding education.

HOW DIFFERENT ASSUMPTIONS WOULD CHANGE THINGS

In our models, the effect of these conditions for growth can be thought of as operating through our assumptions about the investment rate and the rate of catch-up in TFP with the developed economies. If the BRICs economies fail to deliver the kinds of conditions that are broadly necessary for sustained growth, our assumptions about investment and convergence will prove too optimistic. For Brazil and India, in particular, if they succeed more quickly than we expect, investment rates might actually be higher than our projections and convergence more rapid.

To illustrate in a simple way the point that the assumptions that we have made – and the underlying conditions that determine them – are important, we show briefly what happens if we change them:

- Catch-up: because the convergence rate captures a broad range of factors that determine the ability to 'catch up', altering it can make a significant difference to projections. For example, if we lower China's 'convergence rate' by a third, our projections of average GDP growth rate over the 50-year period fall to 4.3 percent from 4.8 percent and our projected 2050 US dollar GDP level drops by 39 percent. In our baseline model, rates of convergence are generally slower for India and Brazil than for China and Russia. If we raised our convergence rates in India and Brazil to those of China and Russia, India's 2000–2030 average GDP growth rate would rise to 7.4 percent, against 5.8 percent originally. Brazil's GDP growth rate would rise as well: to 4.3 percent from 3.7 percent.
- Investment: the assumed investment rates are less important, but substantial differences from our assumptions would certainly alter the main conclusions. Lowering our assumptions of China's investment rate by 5 percentage points slightly lowers China's average 2000–2030 GDP growth rate to 5.5 percent from 5.7 percent. Cutting 5 percentage points off investment rates across the BRICS would reduce their GDP levels on average by around 13 percent by 2050.
- Demographics: the demographic assumptions may also turn out to be incorrect. For instance, Russia's demographics might not turn out to be as negative as the US Census projections, and declining fertility and rising mortality may turn out to have been a temporary feature of the transition from communism. Shifting demographic trends might also be partly offset by attempts to raise participation or to extend working ages, neither of which we currently capture.

Sensitivity to these kinds of assumptions clearly means that there is significant uncertainty around our projections. The advantage of the framework that we have developed is that we now have the tools to look at these and other questions in much more detail. We also have a clear baseline against which to measure them.

IMPLICATIONS OF THE BRICs ASCENDANCY

Each of the BRICs faces very significant challenges in keeping development on track. This means that there is a good chance that our projections are not met, through either bad policy or bad luck.

Despite the challenges, we think the prospect is worth taking seriously. After all, three of these markets – China, India and Russia – have already been at the top of the growth charts in recent years. They may stay there.

If the BRICs do come anywhere close to meeting the projections set out here, the implications for the pattern of growth and economic activity could be very large indeed. Parts of this story – the opportunities in China, for instance – are well understood. But we suspect that many other parts – the potential for India and the other markets and the interplay of ageing in the developed economies with growth in the developing ones – may not be.

We will be using the tools developed here to look in detail at different kinds of scenarios and to flesh out the links between our growth projections and investment opportunities, but we set out some brief conclusions here:

- The relative importance of the BRICs as an engine of new demand growth and spending power may shift more dramatically and quickly than expected under the right conditions. Higher growth in these economies could offset the impact of graying populations and slower growth in today's advanced economies.
- Higher growth may lead to higher returns and increased demand for capital in these markets – and for the means to finance it. The weight of the BRICs in investment portfolios could rise sharply. The pattern of capital flows might move further in their favor and major currency realignments would take place.
- Rising incomes may also see these economies move through the 'sweet spot' of growth for different kinds of products, as local spending patterns change. This could be an important determinant of demand and pricing patterns for a range of commodities.
- As the advanced economies become a shrinking part of the world economy, the accompanying shifts in spending could provide significant opportunities for many of today's global companies.

Being invested in and involved in the right markets – and particularly the right emerging markets – may become an increasingly important strategic choice for many firms.

- The list of the world's ten largest economies may look quite different in 50 years time. The largest economies in the world (by GDP) may also no longer be the richest (by income per capita), making strategic choices for firms more complex.
- Regional neighbors could benefit from the growth opportunities from the BRICs. With three out of the four largest economies in 2050 potentially residing in Asia, we could see important geopolitical shifts towards the Asian region (see Figure 1.18). China's growth is already having a significant impact on the opportunities for the rest of Asia. Sustained strong growth in the other BRICs economies might have similar impacts on their major trading partners.

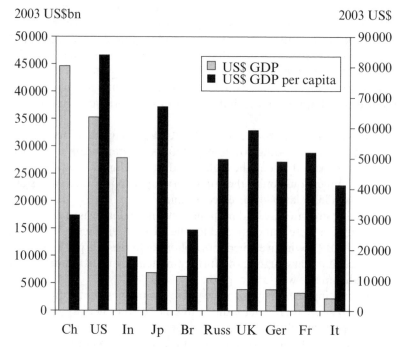

Figure 1.18   GDP size and relative income per capita levels will diverge over time

NOTES

1. Any decision to limit the sample of countries is to some extent arbitrary. In focusing on the G6 (rather than the G7 or a broader grouping), we decided to limit our focus to those developed economies with GDP currently over US$1 trillion. This means that Canada and some of the other larger developed economies are not included. Adding these economies to the analysis would not materially change the conclusions.
2. We do not explicitly allow for increases in human capital (education), which are implicitly picked up in the technical progress/TFP term in our model.
3. Higher inflation in the BRICs would raise nominal GDP forecasts in local currencies and nominal exchange rates, but would not change the forecasts of real GDP or of US dollar GDP under the standard assumption that higher inflation would translate into an offsetting depreciation in the currency.
4. Levine, Ross and David Renelt (1992). 'A Sensitivity Analysis of Cross-Country Growth Regressions,' *American Economic Review*, **82**(4), 942–63.
5. Because of this, the catch-up process is often described as a process of 'conditional convergence', where the tendency for less-developed economies to grow more rapidly is only evident after controlling for these conditions.

APPENDIX 1.I   A LONG-TERM MODEL OF
GROWTH AND EXCHANGE RATES

Growth Model

We provide detail on the underlying assumptions of our models. The model relies on a simple formulation of the overall level of GDP (Y) in terms of (1) labour (L); (2) the capital stock (K); and (3) the level of 'technical progress' (A) or total factor productivity (TFP).

We assume that GDP is a simple (Cobb-Douglas) function of these three ingredients:

$$Y = AK^a L^{1-a}$$

where a is the share of income that accrues to capital.

We then needed to describe the process by which each of the different components (labour, the capital stock and TFP) change over time:

- For L, we simply use the projections of the working-age population (15–60) from the US Census Bureau.
- For K, we take the initial capital stock, assume an investment rate (investment as a percentage of GDP) and a depreciation rate to calculate the growth in the capital stock:

$$K_{t+1} = K_t(1 - \delta) + \left(\frac{I_t}{Y_t}\right) Y_t$$

- For A, the description of technical progress, we assume that technology changes as a part of a process of catch-up with the most developed countries. The speed of convergence is assumed to depend on income per capita, with the assumption that as the developing economies get closer to the income levels of the more developed economies, their TFP growth rate slows. Developing countries can have faster growth in this area because there is room to 'catch up' with developed countries:

$$\frac{A_t}{A_{t-1}} = 1.3\% - \beta \ln \left(\frac{Incomepercapita_{DC}}{Incomepercapita_{US}}\right)$$

where β is a measure of how fast convergence takes place and 1.3 percent is our assumed long-term TFP growth rate for the US.

The assumptions needed to generate the forecasts are summarized below:

- Labour force and population, from the US Census Bureau projections.
- Depreciation rate (δ) assumed to be 4 percent as in the World Bank capital stock estimates.
- Investment rate assumptions based on recent history, for Brazil (19%), for India (22 percent) for Russia (25 percent) for China (36 percent until 2010, declining to 30 percent thereafter).
- Income share of capital assumed to be 1/3, a standard assumption (α) from historical evidence.
- US long-run TFP growth assumed to be 1.33 percent, implying steady-state labour productivity growth of 2 percent our long-run estimate.
- Convergence speed for TFP (β) assumed to be 1.5 percent within the range of estimates from academic research.

Exchange Rate Model

Our model of real exchange rates is then calculated from the predictions of labour productivity growth. Specifically, we assume that a 1 percent productivity differential in favour of economy A relative to the US will raise its equilibrium real exchange rate against the US dollar by 1 percent, where our long-run assumption for US productivity growth is again 2%.

$$\Delta \ln(e) = \Delta \ln\left(\frac{Y}{L}\right) - 0.02$$

This assumption that the relationship is one-for-one underpins our GSDEER models and the coefficient on relative productivity terms in our GSDEEMER models is generally also clustered around 1. We make the simplifying assumption that over the long term, only productivity differentials play a large role in determining real exchange rates.

APPENDIX 1.II OUR PROJECTIONS IN DETAIL

Table 1A.1 Projected US$ GDP

2003 US$ bn	BRICs				G6						BRICs	G6
	Brazil	China	India	Russia	France	Germany	Italy	Japan	UK	US		
2000	762	1078	469	391	1311	1875	1078	4176	1437	9825	2700	19702
2001	601	1157	466	383	1321	1855	1093	4032	1425	10082	2607	19808
2002	491	1252	474	379	1346	1866	1114	4358	1498	10446	2595	20628
2003	461	1353	511	430	1387	1900	1155	4366	1565	10879	2754	21253
2004	435	1529	554	476	1455	1966	1212	4366	1647	11351	2994	21998
2005	468	1724	604	534	1489	2011	1236	4427	1688	11697	3330	22548
2006	502	1936	659	594	1520	2059	1257	4498	1728	12041	3691	23104
2007	539	2169	718	654	1547	2102	1277	4536	1762	12348	4079	23572
2008	579	2422	782	716	1572	2141	1297	4556	1797	12656	4499	24019
2009	622	2699	853	780	1597	2178	1317	4573	1836	12966	4953	24466
2010	668	2998	929	847	1622	2212	1337	4601	1876	13271	5441	24919
2011	718	3316	1011	917	1649	2246	1358	4638	1918	13580	5962	25389
2012	771	3650	1100	990	1677	2282	1381	4683	1960	13883	6512	25866
2013	828	4002	1196	1068	1706	2317	1403	4736	2004	14184	7094	26349
2014	888	4371	1299	1149	1736	2352	1425	4795	2046	14486	7707	26840
2015	952	4754	1411	1232	1767	2386	1447	4858	2089	14786	8349	27332
2016	1019	5156	1531	1322	1799	2418	1469	4925	2130	15106	9028	27847
2017	1091	5585	1659	1417	1832	2448	1492	4999	2170	15427	9752	28367
2018	1167	6041	1797	1518	1865	2476	1513	5074	2209	15750	10524	28887
2019	1248	6538	1945	1626	1897	2502	1534	5146	2247	16083	11357	29410
2020	1333	7070	2104	1741	1930	2524	1553	5221	2285	16415	12248	29928
2021	1397	7646	2278	1829	1963	2544	1571	5297	2321	16765	13150	30462
2022	1465	8250	2470	1924	1996	2562	1588	5372	2355	17133	14109	31006

2023	1537	8863	2682	2028	2029	2577	1603	5443	2389	17518	15110	31559
2024	1613	9517	2916	2141	2062	2591	1615	5509	2422	17918	16187	32117
2025	1695	10213	3174	2264	2095	2604	1625	5567	2456	18340	17345	32687
2026	1781	10947	3459	2395	2128	2619	1634	5641	2491	18803	18582	33316
2027	1873	11732	3774	2533	2163	2634	1644	5696	2528	19293	19913	33958
2028	1971	12555	4123	2679	2198	2652	1653	5740	2567	19801	21327	34611
2029	2076	13409	4508	2828	2233	2672	1662	5778	2607	20319	22821	35271
2030	2189	14312	4935	2980	2267	2697	1671	5810	2649	20833	24415	35927
2031	2308	15260	5407	3131	2300	2727	1678	5835	2692	21371	26107	36603
2032	2436	16264	5930	3283	2333	2763	1686	5851	2740	21946	27911	37319
2033	2572	17317	6508	3434	2367	2806	1692	5861	2791	22554	29830	38072
2034	2716	18428	7147	3585	2404	2854	1699	5869	2845	23187	31877	38858
2035	2871	19605	7854	3734	2445	2903	1708	5882	2901	23828	34064	39668
2036	3033	20845	8621	3881	2490	2953	1719	5902	2961	24492	36380	40516
2037	3201	22152	9453	4028	2535	3002	1733	5930	3023	25168	38833	41389
2038	3374	23522	10352	4175	2580	3051	1748	5961	3085	25852	41423	42276
2039	3554	24949	11322	4321	2625	3100	1767	5998	3144	26542	44147	43175
2040	3740	26439	12367	4467	2668	3147	1788	6039	3201	27229	47013	44072
2041	3932	28003	13490	4613	2711	3192	1810	6086	3258	27929	50038	44987
2042	4128	29589	14696	4756	2754	3238	1834	6136	3317	28654	53171	45933
2043	4336	31257	15989	4891	2801	3285	1859	6187	3377	29399	56473	46908
2044	4560	33003	17371	5022	2849	3333	1885	6239	3437	30170	59955	47913
2045	4794	34799	18847	5156	2898	3381	1912	6297	3496	30956	63596	48940
2046	5031	36636	20421	5289	2946	3428	1941	6362	3554	31761	67378	49993
2047	5276	38490	22099	5417	2995	3473	1971	6431	3611	32592	71281	51074
2048	5527	40420	23886	5552	3045	3516	2001	6506	3668	33437	75385	52173
2049	5789	42408	25785	5701	3097	3559	2031	6586	3725	34297	79684	53296
2050	6074	44453	27803	5870	3148	3603	2061	6673	3782	35165	84201	54433

Note: GS BRICs Model Projections.

Table 1A.2 Projected US$ GDP per capita

2003 US$	BRICs				G6					
	Brazil	China	India	Russia	France	Germany	Italy	Japan	UK	US
2000	4338	854	468	2675	22078	22814	18677	32960	24142	34797
2001	3381	910	457	2633	22143	22545	18895	31775	23860	35373
2002	2726	979	458	2611	22461	22659	19224	34297	25003	36312
2003	2530	1051	486	2976	23047	23059	19920	34322	26042	37470
2004	2364	1181	520	3305	24080	23856	20881	34290	27333	38735
2005	2512	1324	559	3718	24547	24402	21277	34744	27920	39552
2006	2668	1478	602	4142	24968	24986	21629	35292	28509	40346
2007	2835	1646	647	4570	25321	25512	21960	35587	28986	41004
2008	3015	1827	695	5013	25650	25998	22300	35751	29492	41655
2009	3209	2023	748	5470	25975	26452	22649	35917	30043	42304
2010	3417	2233	804	5948	26314	26877	23018	36172	30611	42926
2011	3640	2453	864	6453	26682	27312	23407	36516	31201	43550
2012	3875	2682	929	6981	27069	27767	23816	36942	31808	44142
2013	4124	2922	998	7540	27470	28224	24234	37442	32413	44715
2014	4387	3171	1071	8126	27892	28674	24656	38016	33007	45283
2015	4664	3428	1149	8736	28338	29111	25086	38626	33594	45835
2016	4957	3696	1233	9389	28807	29534	25522	39292	34161	46440
2017	5226	3981	1321	10092	29282	29936	25964	40.032	34700	47035
2018	5594	4283	1416	10845	29762	30321	26407	40795	35218	47630
2019	5939	4613	1516	11655	30242	30678	26833	41561	35731	48247
2020	6302	4965	1622	12527	30723	31000	27239	42359	36234	48849
2021	6562	5346	1739	13212	31211	31296	27628	43186	36709	49496
2022	6838	5747	1867	13959	31709	31572	27995	44023	37154	50182
2023	7133	6153	2007	14777	32208	31824	28335	44845	37593	50902

2024	7 447	6 587	2 161	15 674	32 701	32 058	28 628	45 648	38 031	51 652
2025	7 781	7 051	2 331	16 652	33 203	32 299	28 894	46 391	38 479	52 450
2026	8 136	7 542	2 517	17 697	33 718	32 555	29 152	47 287	38 958	53 348
2027	8 514	8 068	2 723	18 809	34 251	32 830	29 413	48 037	39 466	54 306
2028	8 919	8 621	2 949	19 983	34 796	33 135	29 671	48 709	40 013	55 297
2029	9 352	9 198	3 199	21 194	35 339	33 483	29 922	49 350	40 585	56 294
2030	9 823	9 809	3 473	22 427	35 876	33 898	30 177	49 944	41 194	57 263
2031	10 320	10 454	3 776	23 674	36 406	34 378	30 417	50 483	41 823	58 281
2032	10 852	11 138	4 110	24 926	36 938	34 938	30 657	50 966	42 534	59 384
2033	11 421	11 859	4 477	26 191	37 493	35 605	30 884	51 400	43 301	60 560
2034	12 030	12 623	4 882	27 470	38 101	36 332	31 126	51 826	44 124	61 786
2035	12 682	13 434	5 327	28 749	38 779	37 087	31 402	52 313	44 985	63 017
2036	13 364	14 293	5 808	30 030	39 518	37 857	31 730	52 868	45 898	64 292
2037	14 075	15 201	6 326	31 323	40 278	38 628	32 116	53 499	46 858	65 581
2038	14 813	16 157	6 884	32 636	41 049	39 408	32 548	54 180	47 827	66 875
2039	15 576	17 159	7 482	33 966	41 834	40 195	33 036	54 924	48 758	68 165
2040	16 370	18 209	8 124	35 314	42 601	40 966	33 583	55 721	49 658	69 431
2041	17 191	19 315	8 810	36 684	43 363	41 727	34 169	56 591	50 569	70 713
2042	18 037	20 443	9 544	38 057	44 151	42 499	34 787	57 507	51 509	72 040
2043	18 935	21 635	10 326	39 386	44 998	43 291	35 442	58 448	52 470	73 401
2044	19 904	22 892	11 160	40 706	45 893	44 110	36 133	59 419	53 434	74 805
2045	20 926	24 192	12 046	42 081	46 795	44 940	36 859	60 454	54 386	76 228
2046	21 964	25 530	12 988	43 463	47 706	45 759	37 627	61 583	55 331	77 680
2047	23 040	26 891	13 988	44 832	48 640	46 559	38 430	62 774	56 275	79 171
2048	24 152	28 321	15 050	46 280	49 601	47 346	39 237	64 035	57 211	80 677
2049	25 318	29 810	16 174	47 871	50 589	48 142	40 061	65 376	58 169	82 196
2050	26 592	31 357	17 366	49 646	51 594	48 952	40 901	66 805	59 122	83 710

Note: GS BRICs Model Projections.

Table 1A.3   Projected real GDP Growth

%yoy	BRICs				G6*					
	Brazil	China	India	Russia	France	Germany	Italy	Japan	UK	US
2000	4.2	8.0	5.4	10.0	4.2	2.9	3.3	2.8	3.1	3.8
2001	1.5	7.3	4.2	5.0	2.1	0.6	1.7	0.4	2.1	0.3
2002	1.5	8.2	4.7	4.3	1.2	0.2	0.4	0.1	1.9	2.4
2003	1.1	8.1	5.6	6.1	0.5	0.0	0.6	2.7	1.8	2.7
2004	3.5	8.4	5.9	4.4	2.9	1.9	2.4	1.7	2.9	3.5
2005	4.2	7.9	6.2	5.8	2.3	2.3	2.0	1.4	2.4	3.1
2006	4.1	7.6	6.2	5.3	2.1	2.4	1.7	1.6	2.4	2.9
2007	4.1	7.3	6.1	4.8	1.8	2.1	1.6	0.8	2.0	2.6
2008	4.1	7.1	6.1	4.5	1.6	1.9	1.5	0.4	2.0	2.5
2009	4.2	6.9	6.1	4.3	1.6	1.7	1.5	0.4	2.2	2.5
2010	4.2	6.6	6.1	4.1	1.6	1.5	1.6	0.6	2.2	2.4
2011	4.1	6.4	6.0	4.0	1.7	1.6	1.6	0.8	2.2	2.3
2012	4.1	6.0	6.0	3.8	1.7	1.6	1.6	1.0	2.2	2.2
2013	4.0	5.8	5.9	3.7	1.7	1.6	1.6	1.1	2.2	2.2
2014	4.0	5.5	5.9	3.6	1.8	1.5	1.6	1.3	2.1	2.1
2015	3.9	5.2	5.8	3.5	1.8	1.4	1.6	1.3	2.1	2.1
2016	3.9	5.1	5.8	3.4	1.8	1.3	1.5	1.4	2.0	2.2
2017	3.8	4.9	5.7	3.4	1.8	1.2	1.5	1.5	1.9	2.1
2018	3.8	4.8	5.7	3.3	1.8	1.2	1.5	1.5	1.8	2.1
2019	3.7	5.1	5.6	3.3	1.7	1.0	1.4	1.4	1.7	2.1
2020	3.7	5.0	5.5	3.3	1.7	0.9	1.3	1.4	1.7	2.1
2021	3.7	5.2	5.6	3.3	1.7	0.8	1.2	1.5	1.6	2.1
2022	3.7	4.9	5.7	3.3	1.7	0.7	1.0	1.4	1.5	2.2
2023	3.7	4.1	5.7	3.4	1.7	0.6	0.9	1.3	1.4	2.2

Year									
2024	3.8	4.2	5.8	3.5	1.6	0.5	0.7	1.2	1.4	2.3
2025	3.8	4.2	5.8	3.6	1.6	0.5	0.6	1.0	1.4	2.4
2026	3.8	4.1	5.9	3.6	1.6	0.6	0.6	1.3	1.4	2.5
2027	3.8	4.3	5.9	3.6	1.6	0.6	0.6	1.0	1.5	2.6
2028	3.8	4.1	6.0	3.6	1.6	0.7	0.6	0.8	1.5	2.6
2029	3.8	3.9	6.0	3.5	1.6	0.8	0.5	0.7	1.6	2.6
2030	3.9	3.9	6.1	3.4	1.5	0.9	0.5	0.6	1.6	2.5
2031	3.9	3.8	6.1	3.3	1.5	1.1	0.5	0.4	1.6	2.6
2032	3.9	3.9	6.1	3.1	1.4	1.3	0.4	0.3	1.8	2.7
2033	3.9	3.8	6.2	3.0	1.5	1.6	0.4	0.2	1.9	2.8
2034	3.9	3.8	6.2	2.9	1.6	1.7	0.4	0.1	1.9	2.8
2035	3.9	3.9	6.2	2.8	1.7	1.7	0.5	0.2	2.0	2.8
2036	3.9	3.9	6.1	2.7	1.8	1.7	0.6	0.3	2.0	2.8
2037	3.8	3.9	6.1	2.6	1.8	1.7	0.8	0.5	2.1	2.8
2038	3.8	3.9	6.0	2.5	1.8	1.6	0.9	0.5	2.1	2.7
2039	3.7	3.8	5.9	2.5	1.8	1.6	1.0	0.6	1.9	2.7
2040	3.6	3.7	5.8	2.4	1.7	1.5	1.2	0.7	1.8	2.6
2041	3.6	3.8	5.8	2.3	1.6	1.4	1.3	0.8	1.8	2.6
2042	3.5	3.4	5.7	2.2	1.6	1.4	1.3	0.8	1.8	2.6
2043	3.5	3.5	5.6	2.1	1.7	1.4	1.4	0.8	1.8	2.6
2044	3.6	3.5	5.5	2.0	1.7	1.5	1.4	0.8	1.8	2.6
2045	3.5	3.3	5.4	2.0	1.7	1.4	1.5	0.9	1.7	2.6
2046	3.4	3.1	5.4	1.9	1.7	1.4	1.5	1.0	1.7	2.6
2047	3.4	2.8	5.3	1.8	1.7	1.3	1.5	1.1	1.6	2.6
2048	3.3	2.9	5.2	1.9	1.7	1.2	1.5	1.2	1.6	2.6
2049	3.3	2.8	5.1	2.0	1.7	1.2	1.5	1.2	1.6	2.6
2050	3.4	2.7	5.1	2.1	1.7	1.2	1.5	1.3	1.5	2.5

Notes: GS BRICs Model Projections.

APPENDIX 1.III   DEMOGRAPHIC PROJECTIONS: THE COHORT COMPONENT METHOD

We have used the US census population estimates, which are based on the cohort component population projection method, which follows each cohort of people of the same age throughout its lifetime according to mortality, fertility and migration.

First, fertility rates are projected and applied to the female population in childbearing ages to estimate the number of births every year (see Figure 1AIII.1). Second, each cohort of children born is also followed through time by exposing it to projected mortality rates. Finally, the component method takes into account any in-migrants who are incorporated into the population and out-migrants who leave the population. Migrants are added to or subtracted from the population at each specific age.

In setting levels for mortality and fertility, available data on past trends provide guidance. For mortality, information concerning programs of public health are taken into account. For fertility, factors such as trends in

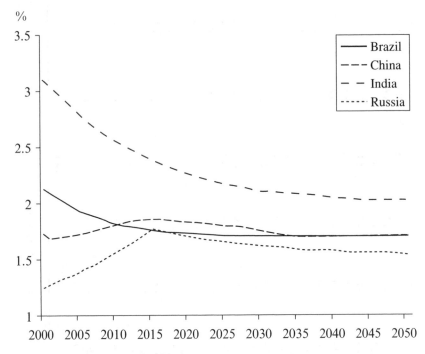

Figure 1AIII.1   Total fertility rate

age at marriage: the proportion of women using contraception: the strength of family planning programs; and any foreseen changes in women's educational attainment or in their labor force participation are factored into the analysis. Assumptions about future migration are more speculative than assumptions about fertility and mortality. The future path of international migration is set on the basis of past international migration estimates as well as the policy stance of countries regarding future international migration flows.

2. BRIC economies: earlier growth constraints, contemporary transformations and future potential, and key challenges

Ben L. Kedia, Somnath Lahiri and Debmalya Mukherjee

INTRODUCTION

In recent years, considerable attention has been devoted to the growing prominence of a few developing nations. Collectively these nations have come to be referred to as emerging economies or emerging markets (Akbar and Samii, 2005; Hoskisson et al., 2000; London and Hart, 2004). It is widely argued that these economics will alter the competitive landscape of the global market place, and they show considerable promise in becoming dominant players in years to come. In this regard, two countries that have consistently merited academic attention are China and India (Mistry, 2004; Saran and Guo, 2005; Tan and Peng, 2003). Two other nations frequently mentioned are Brazil and Russia (Rezende, 1998; Hitt et al., 2004). Together these four economies – collectively referred to as BRIC (acronym for the nations' names) – are seen as being the future leaders of global economy (Khanna et al., 2005; Wilson, 2005).

Today's interest in BRIC economies has been largely fuelled by a research paper titled 'Dreaming with BRICs: The Path to 2050' (Goldman Sachs, 2003). The research projected that the list of ten largest economies of the world may look very different in the near future from what it is now. Specifically, the paper predicted that the BRIC nations will become much larger economic forces by 2050, collectively (and individually in some cases) surpassing some of the established powers like the USA, the UK, Germany, Japan, France and Italy. For example, it is projected that the economy of Brazil will overtake that of Italy in 2025 and that of France by 2031. Japan's GDP is projected to be outstripped by India by 2032.

Figure 2.1 shows that in the coming years the percentage shares of world GDP will be dominated by the BRIC nations while the share of USA will remain relatively stable. Specifically, it shows that in 2025, BRIC nations will account for 25 percent of the world GDP and USA will account for 27 percent. By 2050, the share of BRIC will rise to 60 percent, while USA's share will go down to 25 percent, and rest of the world will account for 15 percent.

Although such a transformation in the global economic scenario is indeed interesting to follow and research, it is of no less importance, if not more, to witness how these nations overcome some of the challenges in their bid to attain the projected world dominance (Venkitaramanan, 2003). Two relevant questions that merit consideration in this context are: (1) why were the BRIC nations not deemed earlier to be so promising? and (2) what subsequent changes have taken place within these countries that have propelled the current surge of interest? Our purpose in this chapter is to attempt to answer these two questions. We will also highlight some of the major obstacles or challenges that these nations need to address if the optimistic estimates of the Goldman Sachs paper (hereinafter referred to as GS research) and other researchers are to come true. In doing so, we do not desire to sound pessimistic regarding the growth of BRIC nations. In the course of our elaboration, we will continue to use the terms, 'nations' and 'economies' interchangeably.

In the next section, we will discuss how the four BRIC nations grew over the years and what prevented them from being considered as powerhouses of the future until recently. Much of the information and data presented here have been referenced from authentic sources such as the CIA World Book (http://www.cia.gov/cia/publications/factbook/) and World Bank Report. Appendix Table 2A.1 provides an overview of major issues.

BRIC ECONOMIES: EARLIER GROWTH CONSTRAINTS

Brazil

Brazil became an independent nation in 1822 following three centuries of Portuguese rule. It is by far the largest and most populous country in South America. A first surge of industrialization took place during the years of World War I, but it was only from the 1930s onwards that Brazil reached a level of modern economic behavior. The industrialization process from the 1950s to the 1970s led to the expansion of important sectors of the economy such as the automobile industry, petrochemicals and steel, as well as to the initiation and completion of large infrastructure projects. Brazil's

Percentage of World GDP: 2004

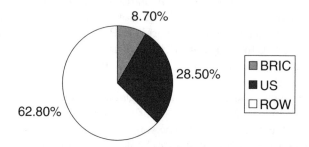

Percentage of World GDP: 2025

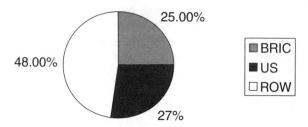

Percentage of World GDP: 2050

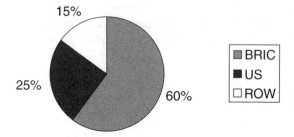

Notes:
Estimates of World GDP were derived from several sources.
World GDP 2004 US$40.8 trillion estimated from World Bank data http://www.worldbank.org/data/databytopic/GDP.pdf.
World GDP 2025 US$68 trillion estimated from GS research (2003) and *Business Week*, 22–29 August, 2005.
World GDP 2050 US$140 trillion estimated from World Bank report http://www1.worldbank.org/devoutreach/fall02/article.asp?id=175.

Figure 2.1   Percentage of world GDP: BRIC, USA and rest of the world (ROW)

gross domestic product (GDP) increased at an average rate of 8 percent per annum from 1970 to 1980 despite the impact of the 1970s world oil crisis. Per capita income rose fourfold during the decade, to US$2200 in 1980.

Brazil had to overcome more than 50 years of military intervention in the governance of the country until 1985 when the military regime was replaced by civilian rule. The 1980s were years of disruption for the national economy. In the early 1980s, a sudden, substantial increase in interest rates in the world economy coincided with lower commodity prices, and precipitated Latin America's debt crisis. Brazil was forced into strict economic adjustment. In addition, there were the negative impacts of the second oil shock in the early years of the decade, a deep recession, and an inflationary upsurge.

These unstable domestic conditions and opportunities turned investors away from productive applications of capital in Brazil. The overall tax ratio in the 1980s came down to 22 percent of GDP – almost ten percentage points below the peak of the mid-1970s. Brazil's yearly growth rates of GDP showed wide fluctuations. For example, the average growth rate in the 1950s was 7.15 percent, in the 1960s it was 6.12 percent, 8.84 percent in the 1970s, 2.93 percent in the 1980s and 1.6 percent between 1990 and 1995 (Sweetwood, 2002).

A disastrous administrative reform, coupled with a demoralizing wage policy for public servants in the early 1990s, led to unprecedented levels of inefficiency in public administration and deterioration in performance. In 1990, inflation hit 5000 percent. Between 2001 and 2003, Brazil's real wages fell and the national economy grew, on average, only 2.2 percent per year. During this period, the country absorbed a series of domestic and international economic shocks. The currency depreciated sharply in 2001 and 2002, which contributed to a dramatic current account adjustment in 2003 and 2004. However the current economic resilience of Brazil is attributed to the policies of former president Cardoso and current president Lula Da Silva.

The government's national exchequer remained strained as domestic debt increased steadily from 1994 to 2003. Moreover, Brazil's foreign debt (a mix of private and public debt) has remained large in relation to its small (but growing) export base. Additionally the country suffered (and still does) from poverty, illiteracy, disease, crime, income inequality, deteriorating health care and education systems, and environmental despoliation.

Russia

Russia got disintegrated from the erstwhile Soviet Union in the August of 1991. Its economy experienced a dramatic transformation in the 1990s – the dismantling of the centrally planned economy that was a hallmark of the Soviet Union, followed by its replacement with an economy operating on the basis of market forces and private property. Since then, the country has struggled in its efforts to build a democratic political system and market economy to replace the strict social, political and economic controls of the soviet communist period. While some progress has been made on the economic front, recent years have seen a recentralization of power under President Putin and erosion in nascent democratic institutions. Overall, Russia's movement towards becoming a powerful nation was earmarked by decentralized political control, fewer central policies, and lack of a strong national system to invoke the policies that were adopted.

Russia remained plagued by a dilapidating manufacturing base, a weak banking system, a poor business climate that discouraged both domestic and foreign investors, corruption, and widespread lack of trust in institutions. Oil, natural gas, metals and timber accounted for the major portion of exports, leaving the country vulnerable to swings in world prices. In addition, a string of investigations launched against a major Russian oil company (named Yukos), culminating with the arrest of its CEO in the fall of 2003, have raised concerns by some observers that President Putin is granting more influence to forces within his government that desire to reassert state control over the economy.

Transition in Russia has not been very methodical. The central government did not establish clear directions about the types of joint ventures it would like to encourage, and has generally been unable to compel firms to follow the few policies it has established (Shleifer and Treisman, 2000). In 1992 and 1993, the government expanded the money supply and credits at explosive rates that led directly to high inflation and to deterioration in the exchange rate of the currency. Official Russian economic statistics indicate that from 1990 to the end of 1995, Russian GDP declined by roughly 50 percent, far greater than the decline that USA experienced during the Great Depression (http://www.answers.com/topic/economy-of-russia). A number of factors, including a heavy tax burden that encouraged non-compliance, and an inefficient and corrupt tax collection system resulted in the revenue shortage of 1996. Economic growth slowed down in the second half of 2004 and the Russian government could forecast growth of only 4.5 percent to 6.2 percent for 2005 (http://www.indexmundi.com/ russia/economy-profile.html).

The large-scale discontinuous changes in Russia produced wholesale revisions in its institutional structure. Despite that, it has often been argued that real economic reform was never tried in Russia, given that it was quickly subverted by actors outside the government's control, such as the Central Bank, ministries, regional governments and industrial managers.

The abusive governance practices came in several forms like share dilution, asset stripping, corporate graft and pure thuggery (Metzger et al., 2002). Thus several issues like excessive government control, political instability, inefficient economic policy, and policy handling contributed towards Russia's image as a less-than-powerful global player.

India

India represents one of the world's oldest civilizations. It obtained independence from British rule in August 1947. Much of India's population resides in villages, whose economy is largely isolated and self-sustaining. Agriculture has been the predominant occupation of the populace. Despite impressive gains in economic investment and output, India faces pressing problems such as the ongoing territorial dispute with neighboring Pakistan, overpopulation, environmental degradation, poverty, and ethnic and religious strife. Significant economic reforms, beginning in 1991, have transformed India into one of the fastest-growing economies in the world.

Although India had a vibrant democracy all along, several factors such as bureaucratic governments, inefficient and ineffective control systems, and corruption in high places prevented desired levels of growth for decades. India's diverse economy encompasses traditional village farming, modern agriculture, handicrafts, a wide range of modern industries, and a multitude of services. After independence, India embarked upon an economic strategy based on socialism, self-sufficiency and central planning. From around 1950, it pursued an import-substitution industrialization policy, by which it restricted imports to protect its own manufacturers from foreign competition, maintain self-sufficiency and industrialize its economy. Especially during the period between 1956 and 1980, the command and control industrial policy regime, popularly known as the 'license raj,' was in operation in India (Mazumder, 2004).

By 1980, India's share of international trade had fallen from 2.5 percent at independence to less than 0.5 percent. Its annual economic growth rates averaged a mere 3.6 percent from 1950 to 1980 while the population grew at an average annual rate of 3.1 percent, resulting in negligible per capita income growth. For the most part, India experienced a lower rate of return on financing owing to investments in large, long-gestating, capital-intensive projects, such as electric power, irrigation and infrastructure. Moreover, delayed completions, cost overruns and underuse of capacity were contributing factors (Sheth, 2004).

Increased borrowing from foreign sources in the late 1980s helped fuel economic growth but led to pressure on the balance of payments. Privatization of government-owned industries proceeded slowly, and continues to generate political debate. Moreover continued social, political and economic rigidities held back needed initiatives. The huge and growing population of India has been the fundamental social, economic and environmental problem. At present, China has a larger population than India, but many demographers expect India to overtake China in this first half of this century.

China

China, the last nation in BRIC list, is a large storehouse of natural and human resources and like India has abundance of cheap labor. Moreover, it is rapidly evolving as a manufacturing base not only for the US customers but for the global consuming community. But the country's dominance in the world stage is not really new. For centuries China stood as a leading civilization, remaining ahead of the rest of the world in the areas of arts and sciences (Witzel, 2005). However, in the nineteenth and early twentieth centuries, the country was beset by civil unrest, major famines, military defeats and foreign occupation.

The People's Republic of China, or simply China, was founded in 1949. China's controlling state was unable to provide the flexibility needed for a more decentralized system to develop, one that could sustain high economic growth. The nation periodically had to backtrack, retightening central controls at intervals. The government struggled for long to sustain adequate job growth for millions of workers laid off from state-owned enterprises, migrants, and new entrants to the workforce. A huge challenge for the nation had been to reduce corruption and other economic crimes and keep afloat the large state-owned enterprises, many of which had been shielded from competition by subsidies and had been losing ability to pay full wages and pensions.

After World War II, the Communists under Mao Zedong (1893–1976) established an autocratic socialist system that ensured China's sovereignty and imposed strict controls over everyday life. In 1958, Mao launched the 'Great Leap Forward', a plan that intended to serve as an alternative model for economic growth and contradicted the Soviet model of heavy industry that was advocated by others in the Communist Party. Under this economic program, Chinese agriculture was to be collectivized and rural small-scale industry was to be promoted. The Great Leap began with tremendous success, with agricultural and steel production running very high. However, the plan was stalled by inefficient management, and by 1959 the Great Leap had become a disaster for the nation. Although the steel production quotas were reached, much of the steel produced was useless, as it had been made from scrap metal. National politics were divided between moderates, radicals and Maoists. In 1960 there was withdrawal of all Soviet aid.

China, as a nation, has not always been immutable and solid, and the specter of chaos has hung over it several times. Several issues digressed attention of the government over the years. Muslim unrest and Tibetan nationalism have been near-constant sources of tension for the country's leadership. Similarly, China's relationship with Taiwan, often referred to as one of Asia's most dangerous potential flash points, has been far from good. The nation failed to achieve a sustained growth in per capita food production primarily because population growth was encouraged in the 1950s and 1960s; and the industrialization policy of the Great Leap Forward failed. However, from the late 1970s, China began reforming the economic system.

In the preceding paragraphs, we discussed how the BRIC nations developed over the years and what factors kept their growth levels (economic and non-economic) to a minimum at worst and a modest at best. Certainly during this period of early development, these economies were not considered to hold much future promise. There was not much positive thinking that these nations may one day surpass some of the highly developed and powerful countries in the world, except in the arena of population growth.

In the next section, we will highlight some of the issues that help to explain why the BRIC nations are currently being regarded highly in terms of their respective potentials to emerge as future world powers. In the process, we will try to address the second relevant question that arises in the context of BRICs, that is, what has caused the recent surge of interest in these nations?

BRIC ECONOMIES: CONTEMPORARY TRANSFORMATIONS AND FUTURE POTENTIAL

Brazil

Currently, Brazil has the tenth-largest economy in the world and it is already in the process of opening itself up in a big way to international capital. The country possesses large and well-developed agricultural, mining, manufacturing and service sectors. Brazil's economy outweighs those of all other South American countries and it is fast expanding its presence in world markets. The three main focus areas of Brazil's economic program are a floating exchange rate, an inflation-targeting regime and tight fiscal policy – all reinforced by a series of IMF programs.

From 1992 to 1997 Brazilian exports increased from US$35.7 billion to US$53 billion. In 1997, there was an overall increase of 10.5 percent in the nation's exports. Moreover, there has been a steady increase in overall investments – both inward and outward. The investment ratio rose to 18 percent of GDP, a level that will enable the economy to move to higher rates of growth. Arthur Andersen, Chicago, in its 2001 survey indicated broad economic optimism among Brazil's business leaders. In January 2001, Standard & Poor raised Brazil's credit rating substantially. In 2004, Brazil enjoyed more robust growth that yielded increases in employment and real wages. The GDP growth of more than 5 percent in 2004 remains the fastest expansion in ten years. Brazil also had record trade surpluses and exhibited its first current account surpluses since 1992. There was also a surge in exports, particularly in agriculture, leading to high productivity gains. One of the reasons for this growth is the gradual reduction in trade barriers. Overall, there is much optimism that Brazil has promise for the future. 'Brazil seems to finally be heading down the right path in the financial world' (Sweetwood, 2002).

Russia

Russia finally achieved some political stability after it moved from a communist dictatorship to a multi-party democracy. There are signs of economic rebound and the nation now appears to be on a sustained growth path. Since the financial crisis of 1998, Russia has maintained six years of growth, averaging 6.5 percent annually. It is also clear that since 2000, investment and consumer-driven demand have played a noticeably increasing role. Real fixed capital investments have averaged gains greater than 10 percent between 2000 and 2005, and real personal incomes have realized average increases over 12 percent. Russia has also improved its international financial position since the 1998 financial crisis, with its foreign debt declining from 90 percent of GDP to around 28 percent. In 2001, the nation's economy was the second fastest growing in the world. Currently, Russia accounts for about 3 percent of the European Union's trade.

Oil and gas production have long been supportive activities for the Russian economy. It is estimated that Russia has the largest reserves of natural gas in the world. Now this sector is even more productive, and responsible for much of the strong economic performance, especially with the cooperation and investment by world energy companies, and also with the bonanza of high fuel prices. Strong oil export earnings have allowed Russia to increase its foreign reserves from only $12 billion in 1998 to some $120 billion at the end of 2004. These achievements, along with a renewed government effort to advance structural reforms like reduction in tax rates, have raised business and investor confidence in Russia's economic prospects.

Like China, Russia is an economy in transition – from plan to market. Russia's strength lies in its three main assets: natural resources (particularly fuel and petrochemicals), new markets and efficiency. After the nation underwent radical economic reforms in the last decade it seems that it is poised to become a powerful nation in the years to come. Recent reforms in the Russian corporate and securities laws and regulations are deemed to address the severe corporate abuses of earlier years.

India

Despite many obstacles like bureaucratic governments, inefficient governance, high tax regimes, burdensome regulations and a burgeoning population, the nation has managed to sustain economic growth since the 1980s. Between 1980 and 1989, the economy grew at an annual rate of 5.5 percent, or 3.3 percent on a per capita basis. National industry grew at an annual rate of 6.6 percent and agriculture at a rate of 3.6 percent. A high rate of investment was a major factor in improved economic growth. In the early 1990s, considerable progress was made in loosening government regulations, especially in the area of foreign trade (Saran and Guo, 2005). In fact, in 1991 the national economy was liberalized by the then government which allowed for 100 percent foreign equity and full convertibility of the rupee on the current account. Many restrictions on private companies were lifted, and new areas were opened to private capital. Since 1994, the Indian economy has posted an excellent average growth rate of 6.8 percent and has managed to reduce poverty by about 10 percentage points. In fact, India belongs to the select group of the 17 fastest-growing economies among the world's 132 (Rao, 1996).

Although two-thirds of the Indian workforce is in agriculture, services constitute the major source of economic growth. The present union government has committed to furthering economic reforms and developing basic infrastructure to improve the lives of the rural poor and boost economic performance. Government controls on foreign trade and investment have been reduced in some areas, but high tariffs (averaging 20 percent in 2004) and limits on foreign direct investment are still in place. The central government has also indicated that it will promote liberalized investment in civil aviation, telecom and insurance sectors in the near-term. India has become a major exporter of software services and software workers by capitalizing on its large numbers of well-educated people skilled in the English language. Over a short span of time, India has emerged as the major outsourcing destination for nations including USA and UK. India's dominance in software and IT-related services has resulted in a constant inflow of foreign funds, but one needs to see how far the real gains from the IT sector can be channeled back into the domestic economy to enhance productivity gains. Interestingly, some soybean-growing Indian farmers are known to use IT services in making their harvesting decisions. To get daily quotes on the Chicago Board of Trade, these farmers log in from their field operations (Klein, 2004).

There is another reason to be optimistic about India's economic performance. A large and effective Indian education system has produced thousands of highly qualified Indian professionals who have migrated to many parts of the world and have achieved financial success. This phenomenon is spread over diverse fields as education, business, medicine etc. The financially sound migrants have strong ties with their homeland. Like the overseas Chinese, these non-resident Indians are investing in modern India on a sufficiently large scale to make a positive economic impact.

China

After Mao's death in 1978, the Chinese leadership began moving the sluggish, soviet-styled planned economy to a more market-oriented system. Although the movement operated within a political framework of strict communist control, the economic influence of non-state organizations and individual citizens steadily increased. With the signing of the 1984 Sino-British Joint Declaration, China set a course towards economic reconstruction. However, political reform was almost negligible and general dissatisfaction with the communist Party, soaring inflation and increased demands for democracy led to widespread social unrest.

China's evolutionary economic transition has been closely guided by the government. The authorities switched to a system of household and village responsibility in agriculture in place of the old collectivization and increased the authority of local officials and plant managers in industry. The government also permitted a wide variety of small-scale enterprises in services and light manufacturing, and opened the economy to increased foreign trade and investment. Jiang Zemin's leadership charted a new course based on economic growth; overseeing the admission of China into the World Trade Organization (WTO) in 2001. The result has been a quadrupling of GDP since 1978.

Foreign investment remains a strong element in China's remarkable economic growth. For the last two decades, China's economy has ranked 6.1 percentage points above the world average in annual growth rate. Agriculture and industry posted major gains. Accession to the WTO helped strengthen its ability to maintain strong growth rates but has put additional pressure on the hybrid system of strong political controls and growing market influences. China has benefited from a huge expansion in computer internet use, with 94 million users at the end of 2004. China significantly improved in the arenas of technology absorption, its prominence in world trade, and alleviation of poverty.

China has also embarked on an aggressive program of converting departmental enterprises into corporations and privatizing government companies. Between June 1999 and December 2001, China has raised over US$23 billion, mainly through the initial public offering (IPO) route. The country's rapid economic growth has become a key component in the world's economy. While much of China's economic growth has come from exports – most of them to Western consumer markets – the Chinese domestic economy also continues to grow as prosperity spreads throughout the country's economy. Measured on a purchasing power parity (PPP) basis, China was the second-largest economy in the world in 2004 after the US.

Thus China is held as the leading hot prospect in international business for the coming decades. With its strong indigenous developments, persistent and heavy foreign direct investment, large consumer base and expanding opportunities, China is seen as a huge potential player in the future global market.

Although the GS research mentions that each of the four BRIC nations do face 'very significant challenges in keeping development on track' (Goldman Sachs, 2003, p. 16), we need a better idea of how strong these challenges are. This brings us to the last section of the chapter. In the succeeding paragraphs, we will discuss some of the challenges that lie ahead of the BRIC nations. As we highlight some of their economic, social and individual challenges, we emphasize that the dreams of the BRICs can be fulfilled through serious consideration of how these challenges can be overcome or at least minimized.

BRIC ECONOMIES: KEY CHALLENGES

BRIC: Economic Challenges

Let us look at Table 2.1. The table shows data (for 2010, 2025 and 2050) on GDP, GDP per capita and GDP growth rate of the BRIC nations along with those of the G6 nations. These are the projected estimates that appear in the GS research. As seen in the table, China is projected to attain the highest GDP in 2050, followed by USA and India. Although GDP is traditionally used as a robust measure of a country's economy, the real impact of a national economy is reflected in the GDP per capita measure

Table 2.1 *Projections by Goldman Sachs*

Country	GDP[1]			GDP[2] (per capita)			GDP[3] (growth)		
	2010	2025	2050	2010	2025	2050	2010	2025	2050
Brazil	668	1 695	6 074	3 417	7 781	26 592	4.2	3.8	3.4
Russia	847	2 264	5 870	5 948	16 652	49 646	4.1	3.6	2.1
India	929	3 174	27 803	804	2 331	17 366	6.1	5.8	5.1
China	2 998	10 213	44 453	2 233	7 051	31 357	6.6	4.2	2.7
France	1 622	2 095	3 148	26 314	33 203	51 594	1.6	1.6	1.7
Italy	1 337	1 625	2 061	23 018	28 894	40 901	1.6	0.6	1.5
USA	13 271	18 340	35 165	42 926	52 450	83 710	2.4	2.4	2.5
UK	1 876	2 456	3 782	30 611	38 479	59 122	2.2	1.4	1.5
Germany	2 212	2 604	3 603	26 877	32 299	48 952	1.5	0.5	1.2
Japan	4 601	5 567	6 673	36 172	46 391	66 805	0.6	1.0	1.3

Notes:
1. 2003 US$ bn
2. 2003 US$
3. % yoy

(for a discussion on the Indian context, see Dasgupta, 2004). To this end, USA is seen to retain first ranking in 2050, followed by Japan, UK and France. Notice that the BRIC nations rank 9th, 5th, 10th and 8th respectively amongst the ten nations considered. However, in the arena of GDP growth in 2050, India ranks 1st, followed by Brazil, China, USA and Russia.

Let's see what has been happening in reality and what the near-term projections are. As seen in Table 2.2, the average annual growth of BRIC nations' GDP and GDP per capita between 1993 and 2003 has not been unimpressive relative to those of the G6 countries. GDP figures show that China had the highest growth (8.6 percent) followed by India (5.9 percent). Only two nations of the G6 had figures higher than Brazil's. However, the growth for Russia has been only 1.4 percent, meaning that it ranks close to the lowest (Japan) amongst the ten nations shown in the table.

Likewise, when growth of GDP per capita is considered, China (7.6 percent) has the highest rate of all the ten countries, followed by India (4.1 percent). Interestingly, the growth data for Russia are better than those of Brazil and Japan – both had a 1 percent growth rate and figured in the bottom portion of the list. In the columns that show GDP and GDP per capita growth data for 2002 and 2003, we observe negative rates for Brazil. This is indeed a source of concern for this nation. However the other three BRIC nations had impressive figures compared to those of the G6 countries.

For the 2003–2007 projected period, we see a fall in the figures of GDP and GDP per capita for the BRIC nations as compared to their figures for 2003. This is a challenge for Russia, India and China to ensure that a

Table 2.2   Average annual growth of GDP and GDP per capita

	1993–2003 GDP	1993–2003 GDP-pc	2002 GDP	2002 GDP-pc	2003 GDP	2003 GDP-pc	2003–07 GDP	2003–07 GDP-pc
Brazil	2.3	1.0	1.9	0.7	−0.2	−1.4	3.9	3.2
Russia	1.4	1.8	4.7	5.2	7.3	7.8	5.0	5.4
India	5.9	4.1	4.1	2.5	8.6	7.0	6.2	4.9
China	8.6	7.6	8.3	7.6	9.1	8.4	7.7	7.0
France	2.3	1.9	1.2	0.7	0.1	−0.3	2.1	−
Italy	1.8	1.7	0.4	0.4	0.3	0.4	1.3	−
USA	3.4	2.1	2.4	1.4	2.9	2.0	4.4	−
UK	2.8	2.5	1.8	1.5	2.2	2.1	3.2	−
Germany	1.5	1.3	0.2	0.0	0.0	−0.1	1.7	−
Japan	1.2	1.0	0.3	0.2	2.7	2.7	2.9	−

Source: World Bank (Country at a Glance) and CIA World Fact Book.

diminishing growth rate does not result in the near future. For Brazil, there is a silver lining. In 2003–2007, it seems that it will have positive and high growth rates as compared to its negative figures of 2003. Note that in the same time period the GDP growth rates of the G6 nations show substantial increments, with the USA projected to more than double (4.4 percent) its 2003 figure (2 percent).

Overall the BRIC nations have not fared too badly in terms of growth of their GDP and GDP per capita, when compared to the G6 nations. However, in terms of absolute dollar values, these nations lag far behind the G6 nations. This is revealed in Table 2.3, where GNI per capita means gross national income per capita, that is, gross national income divided by mid-year population. The World Bank favors this measure instead of GNP per capita or GDP per capita. The BRIC nations have a long way to go in order to surpass the GDP value, and especially the per capita measure, of the six developed nations. Figure 2.2 shows the relative positions of the ten nations in terms of their GDP values for the year 2003.

A revealing feature of Table 2.1 is that although the BRIC nations have impressive GDP growth rates, they rank relatively low with respect to G6 nations in the terms of GDP per capita. How can this be? Surely, this can only result if the populations of these nations are relatively larger or exhibit higher growth rates over the years. Let us now look at Table 2.4. The table shows that by 2015, the BRIC nations will have the largest populations of the ten nations. China will emerge as the most populous nation, followed by India, the USA, Brazil and Russia. This portion of our discussion on population should have ideally come in the next (that is, social challenges)

Table 2.3   Economic data, 2003

Country	GDP (US$ bn)	GNI per capita (US$) Atlas method
Brazil	492.3	2 720
Russia	432.9	2 610
India	600.6	540
China	1 412.3	1 100
France	1 748	24 770
Italy	1 465.9	21 560
USA	10 881.6	37 610
UK	1 794.9	28 350
Germany	2 400.7	25 250
Japan	4 326.4	34 510

Source: The World Bank Group (Country at a Glance Tables)

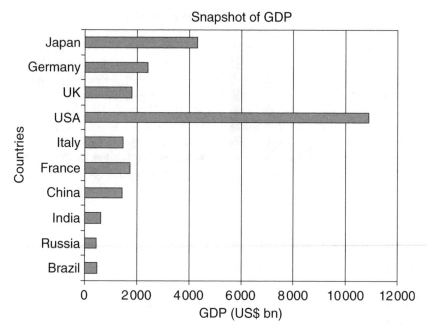

Source: Table 2.3 of this chapter.

Figure 2.2   Snapshot of 2003 GDP

Table 2.4   Population dynamics

Country	1990 (millions)	2003 (millions)	2015 (millions)	Average growth rate (%) 2003–15
Brazil	148.0	176.60	201.0	1.1
Russia	148.3	143.4	134.5	−0.5
India	849.5	1064.4	1231.60	1.2
China	1135.2	1288.4	1389.5	0.6
France	56.7	59.8	61.8	0.3
Italy	56.7	57.6	55.1	−0.4
USA	249.6	290.8	318.0	0.7
UK	57.6	59.3	60.0	0.1
Germany	79.4	82.5	80.6	−0.2
Japan	123.5	127.6	124.7	−0.2

Source: World Bank.

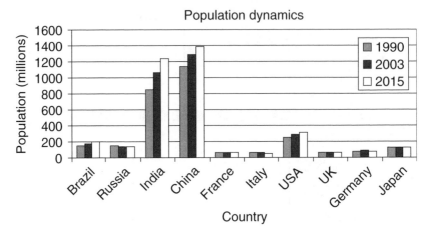

Source: Table 2.4 of this chapter.

Figure 2.3   Population dynamics

section, but we take it up here as it has relevance for the GDP per capita measure.

Interestingly a few nations – Russia, Italy, Germany and Japan – will exhibit negative growth rates of population between 2003 and 2015. This means that these nations will substantially decrease their population growth rate as of the current period. India will have the maximum growth rate of an average 1.2 percent, followed by Brazil's 1.1 percent. Thus a very important challenge for the BRIC nations, especially India, will be to contain their respective population growths. In sum, to have relatively higher GDP per capita beyond 2015 (that is, around 2040 or 2050), the BRICs must devise policies and practices that will tend to restrict population growth. The population dynamics of the ten nations of our interest is shown in Figure 2.3.

Foreign direct investment (FDI) constitutes a very important factor in a nation's development and economic growth. FDI is considered the best complement to domestic investment to bridge the gap between the investment needs of a nation and its savings. Thus for BRIC nations, inflow of FDI from foreign nations and outflow of FDI to other countries will determine how these economies will fare towards becoming dominant economic forces in the future.

We show Table 2.5 to indicate the pattern of FDI inflow between 1985 and 2003 to the ten nations of our focus. Although at a first glance it seems that the BRIC nations have attracted much lesser inflow as compared to the developed nations such as USA and UK, a closer look reveals that growth of FDI inflow has been appreciable in the BRIC nations. For example, in

Table 2.5   FDI inflow (millions of dollars)

Country	1985–95	1999	2000	2001	2002	2003
Brazil	1 713	28 578	32 779	22 457	16 590	10 144
Russia	424	3 309	2 714	2 469	3 461	1 144
India	455	2 168	2 319	3 403	3 449	4 269
China	11 887	40 319	40 715	46 878	52 743	53 505
France	11 913	46 545	43 250	50 476	48 906	46 981
Italy	3 341	6 911	13 375	14 871	14 545	16 421
USA	44 434	283 376	314 007	159 461	62 870	29 772
UK	16 589	87 979	118 764	52 623	27 776	14 515
Germany	3 331	56 077	198 276	21 138	36 014	12 866
Japan	675	12 741	8 323	6 241	9 239	6 324

Source: World Investment Report 2004 (online).

2003, China attracted the maximum inflow amongst the ten nations, surpassing the USA and the UK who were the leading FDI attractors between 1985 and 1995. Between 1985 and 1995 and in 2003, the overall growth rate for India was the maximum, followed by Japan, Brazil, Italy, China, France, Germany and Russia. In fact for the USA and the UK, there was a decline in FDI inflow between 2001 and 2003. Of the four BRIC nations, China and India have witnessed steady growth in inflow. However, Brazil and Russia exhibit a changing growth–fall pattern. Thus although India and China need to continue to enhance their growth rates in the years to come, the challenge for Russia and Brazil is to ensure a relatively steady growth rate of FDI inflow.

Figure 2.4 indicates how these ten countries fare in terms of inward FDI performance and potential. UNCTAD uses the Inward FDI Performance Index to rank countries by the FDI they receive relative to their economic size. The matrix shown in Figure 2.4 compares the two indices. Any country will prefer to be figured in the top right quadrant (High–High), as Brazil, China, Germany, France and UK have been. The least attractive location is the bottom left quadrant (Low–Low) where India is located. In short we may infer that Brazil and China are on the right track but Russia needs to enhance its performance. The challenge for India is twofold: it must devise policies to enhance both its FDI attractiveness and performance.

Let us now look at Table 2.6. At the first glance, it is seen that the FDI outflow data for the BRICs are much lower compared to similar data for nations as the USA, the UK and France. And that is true. The four major nations that had highest outflow both during 1985–1995 and in 2003 were the USA, the UK, Japan and France; the BRIC nations ranked in the

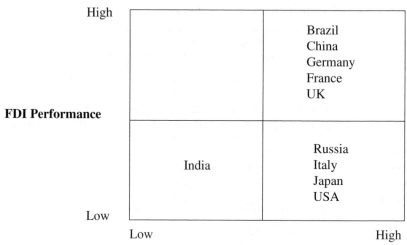

Source: UNCTAD.

Figure 2.4   Matrix of inward FDI performance and potential, 2000–2002

Table 2.6   FDI outflow (millions of dollars)

Country	1985–95	1999	2000	2001	2002	2003
Brazil	465	1 690	2 282	−2 258	2 482	249
Russia	94	2 208	3 177	2 533	3 533	4 133
India	23	80	509	1 397	1 107	913
China	1 591	1 775	916	6 884	2 518	1 800
France	18 057	126 856	177 449	86 767	49 434	57 279
Italy	4 710	6 722	12 316	21 472	17 123	9 121
USA	42 571	209 391	142 626	124 873	115 340	151 884
UK	25 994	201 451	233 371	58 855	35 180	55 093
Germany	17 607	108 692	56 557	36 855	8 622	2 560
Japan	24 584	22 743	31 558	38 333	32 281	28 800

Source: *World Investment Report,* 2004 (online).

lowest bracket during the two time periods. Notice that the outflow pattern for all the nations has been non-uniform over the years, meaning there have been upswings and downswings in the outflow pattern. However, in 1985–95 and 2003, the average growth rate was the maximum for Russia, followed by India, the USA and France. But in dollar values, the amounts

Table 2.7   FDI Confidence Index 2004

Country	Score	Status
Brazil	0.91	Moved down
Russia	0.97	Moved down
India	1.40	Moved up
China	2.03	Maintained ranking
France	1.03	Moved up
Italy	0.98	Moved up
USA	1.45	Maintained ranking
UK	1.25	Moved up
Germany	1.17	Maintained ranking
Japan	0.97	Moved up

Source: A.T. Kearney

for BRIC nations have been much lower than for the G6 nations. A major challenge for the BRICs is ensuring a steadily growing pattern of FDI outflow. Although FDI flows depend on world economic trends and strategies of global investors, the BRIC nations need to devise and employ a number of FDI promotion initiatives.

Overall, it emerges from the previous discussion that the performance of BRIC nations in terms of FDI potential is much lower than those of the other six nations that we are comparing them with. Unless the BRIC nations manage to improve considerably their FDI-attracting potential, it will remain a real challenge for them to rank closer to the G6 nations (Mello, 2005; Weidenbaum, 2004).

BRIC: Social Challenges

So far we have discussed how the BRIC nations fare economically as compared to six other developed nations of the world. Let us examine how the BRICs rank in terms of how they are perceived by others. A good perception is necessary for any nation as it has long-term implications for current and future trade, investments from multinational corporations, tourism and so on. Table 2.7 shows the FDI Confidence Index prepared by global management consulting firm A.T. Kearney, and provides a score for each of the ten countries (for details see http://www.atkearney.com). This index is based on an annual survey of executives from the world's largest companies.

As seen in the table, China has the highest score of 2.03 followed by the USA (1.45), India (1.40), and the UK (1.25). But although China maintained its ranking and India's ranking moved up, the rankings for Brazil and Russia have moved down. However, ranking has not gone down for a single G6 nation. A major challenge for BRIC nations is to enhance their respective Confidence Index score and status.

A major issue for many a nation's lack of growth and well-being is the presence of corruption in various forms. Corruption fosters self-interest through abuse of power and resources, and makes a nation's exchange process opaque and inefficient (Akhter, 2004). When a nation is perceived as being high in corruption, it does not auger well for its trade, commerce, investment or even tourism. Let us look now at Table 2.8.

The Corruption Perception Index (CPI) lists countries with respect to the degree in which corruption is noticed among office-holders and politicians. Note that the BRIC nations have consistently had the lowest scores (and the highest rankings) compared to the G6 nations. In fact, in 2004, the BRIC economies exhibited a drastic fall in CPI rankings as compared to their 2000 and 2002 figures. The UK and USA consistently had the best ranks in this regard over the years. A big challenge for the BRIC nations is to develop national policies that will strive to reduce corruption as it exists in various forms.

Just as a business needs to possess, acquire and develop valuable resources and capabilities, so a nation needs to generate and acquire valuable inputs for its growth and sustenance. These resources include various investments, domestic products and services, and of course the invaluable human capital. However, business resources need to be suitably deployed in the market. So nations also need to utilize their resources in order to become efficient

Table 2.8   Corruption Perception Index

Country	2000 score	2000 rank	2002 score	2002 rank	2004 score	2004 rank
Brazil	3.9	49	4.0	45	3.9	59
Russia	2.1	82	2.7	71	2.8	90
India	2.8	69	2.7	71	2.8	90
China	3.1	63	3.5	59	3.4	67
France	6.7	21	6.3	25	7.1	22
Italy	4.6	39	5.2	31	4.8	42
USA	7.8	14	7.7	16	7.5	17
UK	8.7	10	8.7	10	8.6	11
Germany	7.6	17	7.3	18	8.2	15
Japan	6.4	23	7.1	20	6.9	24

Source: Transparency International.

players in the global market. But several factors need to be taken care of in order to ensure that valuable national resources are suitably utilized. These factors are collectively termed as governance (for a discussion on governance infrastructure, readers may refer to the work of Globerman and Shapiro, 2003).

The World Bank has delineated six major components of governance. These are (1) voice and accountability; (2) political stability; (3) government effectiveness; (4) regulatory quality; (5) rule of law; and (6) control of corruption. These six indicators are based on several hundred individual variables measuring perceptions of governance, drawn from 37 separate data sources constructed by 31 different organizations (see http://info. worldbank.org/governance for details).

Table 2.9 ranks the ten nations according to these six components of governance. We see that the BRIC nations have lower percentile ranks compared to G6 nations in the first component. Notice that the ranks of China and Russia are indeed very low. The ranks of Brazil and India are barely above the world average of 49.9 (in 2004) in this regard. Germany has the highest ranking, followed by the UK and France. This means that the extent to which the citizens of BRIC nations are able to participate in the selection of governments is much lower than in the G6 nations. In political stability, the second governance indicator, Japan is the best followed by Germany and the UK. Here again the ranks of BRICs are lower than those of the G6 nations. Of particular concern is the fact that the ranks of all BRIC nations are below the world average of 49.9 for 2004.

Table 2.9   Components of governance (2004) (figures indicate percentile rank, 0–100)

Country	Voice and accountability	Political stability	Government effectiveness	Regulatory quality	Rule of law	Control of corruption
Brazil	55.8	43.7	58.2	58.1	46.9	53.2
Russia	25.7	21.8	48.1	30.5	29.5	29.1
India	53.9	24.3	55.8	26.6	50.7	47.3
China	7.3	46.6	60.1	35.0	40.6	39.9
France	90.8	63.1	90.4	77.3	88.9	88.7
Italy	82.0	56.3	70.2	81.8	71.0	74.9
USA	89.3	60.7	93.8	86.7	92.3	92.6
UK	94.2	71.4	94.2	94.1	93.7	94.6
Germany	94.7	79.1	88.5	88.7	93.2	93.1
Japan	78.2	83.5	86.5	83.7	89.9	86.2

Source: World Bank.

Likewise the ranks of BRIC nations in the components of government effectiveness, regulatory quality, rule of law and control of corruption are lower than those of the other six nations. Particularly noticeable are the low ranks of Russia in these four components, and the rank of India in the area of regulatory quality. Overall the BRIC economies have a long way to go in setting their governance parameters close enough to the G6 nations. Unless this can be achieved, there will always remain a huge challenge for the BRICs to become dominant global forces, despite having huge investment inflows or domestic production of goods and services. Inefficient governance will render the utilization of resources to be far from efficient.

BRIC: Individual Challenges

What does a nation mean without its people being considered? After all, the economic and non-economic growth indicators will not mean a lot if the individuals residing in a nation do not prosper or if they do not happen to possess a decent quality of life. Just as any organization's competitive advantage is indicative of the quality of the human resources it possesses (see Bartlett and Ghoshal, 2002), so a nation's well-being is reflected in terms of its various social indicators. Better indicators reflect better standards of living which in turn will signify a more effective national workforce and proficient human capital. Let us look at some these indictors.

The World Bank defines poverty as the percentage of population living below the national poverty line. Their national estimates are based on population-weighted subgroup estimates from household surveys. 'Life expectancy' at birth means the number of years a newborn infant would live if prevailing patterns of mortality at the time of its birth were to stay the same throughout its life. 'Infant mortality' refers to the number of deaths of infants under one year of age per 1000 live births in a given year. 'Illiteracy' refers to the proportion of the population 15 years of age and older who cannot, with understanding, both read and write a short simple statement on everyday life. The 'Human Development Index' (HDI), published by the United Nations, is an objective measure of human condition and can be considered to be reflective of an environment which helps people develop their full potential and productive lives.

When we consider poverty data in Table 2.10, it is seen that India has 29 percent of its population living below the poverty line. China has the least value of 5 percent. The data for Russia and Brazil are very close. However, since 1996, China's figure has come down from 6 percent to 5 percent, and India's figure dropped from 36 percent to 29 percent. Brazil's figure for 1998 was 22 percent and Russia's figure for 1994 was 30.9 percent (Source: World Bank, not shown in table). These values roughly show that BRIC nations

Table 2.10   Most recent social indicators (1997–2003)

Country	Poverty	Life expectancy	Infant mortality	Illiteracy	HDI rank*
Brazil	22	69	33	14	72
Russia	21	65	12	0	57
India	29	63	65	39	127
China	5	71	30	9	94
France	6.5	79	4	1	16
Italy	–	78	4	1	21
USA	12	77	7	3	8
UK	17	77	5	1	12
Germany	–	78	4	1	19
Japan	–	82	3	1	9

Note: *Rank for 2002.

Source: The World Bank Group (Country at a Glance), CIA World Fact Book, and UNDP).

have not been able to bring down their poverty rates at a fast rate. Given their huge populations, it is indeed a stupendous task. However, in percentage terms, China is in a better position than France, the USA or the UK. But in sheer number terms, more people live below the poverty line in China than in France, the USA or the UK.

Except China, the other three BRIC nations have relatively lower life expectancy values than the G6 nations. Japan has the highest value of 82 and India has the lowest value of 63. Thus Brazil, Russia and India need to initiate policy measures that enhance conditions towards increasing life expectancy. It is possible that much of their human capital is lost prematurely in these nations.

The values of infant mortality for BRIC nations are much higher than those of the G6 nations. Consider India's 65 to USA's 7. These two values reflect a simple yet crucial notion – for every 1000 births, India loses 58 more lives than the USA does. Similar values will be reached if one compares Brazil with Japan or Russia with France. A huge challenge for BRIC nations is, therefore, to bring the infant mortality rates down in the years to come. Unless this is done, valuable lives, that is, human resources and the future workforce, will continue to be lost.

A literate workforce is a nation's valuable resource, and illiteracy among members does not augur well for a society's development. The illiteracy values for the BRIC nations show that as of 1997–2003, India had the highest illiteracy rate, followed by Brazil and China. Russia is best in this regard with its population being fully literate. We notice that figures for the

G6 nations are really low, and very similar. When one compares Brazil, India and China with any of the G6 nations, it becomes clear that these three BRIC nations have a long way to go in terms of eradicating illiteracy. The governments of these nations need to implement various education-related measures so that many more people can be made literate in the near future.

The 2002 HDI rankings, shown in the last column of Table 2.10, show that a wide range of rankings exists for the BRIC nations (57–127) and a smaller range for the G6 nations (9–21). These indicate that the G6 nations are more similar to each other in terms of life expectancy, education and income per person, whereas wide differences exist among the BRIC nations. Needless to say, BRIC countries, especially India and China, require a lot of effort in order to improve so that they may achieve higher rankings in the future and come closer to the G6 nations. Overall, the BRIC economies lag far behind the G6 nations with regard to the various social indicators. Our discussion is summarized in Figure 2.5.

CONCLUSION

This chapter has attempted to answer two relevant questions that emanate in the light of current optimism about the BRIC nations and predictions made in the GS research. First, why in the past were these economies not held to be greatly promising? In answering this we have tried to discuss some of the relevant issues and constraining factors that prevented these nations to reach growth stages as they are now in. In addressing the second question, that is, what factors have contributed to the current interest in these four nations, we have highlighted how the BRICs developed and showed gradual emergence over the years, economically and non-economically, and how they overcame much of the negative legacies of their respective pasts. While elaborating on these two queries, we have attempted to show how the BRIC nations have grown over the years and what their current promises are. In short, we helped trace the development of BRICs' dreams.

Additionally, in the last section of this chapter, we have highlighted some of the challenges that face these four nations. As these challenges have wide-ranging implications for realizing the predicted growth of the BRIC nations, we stress that adequate considerations need to be given to these issues so as to enable these nations to emerge better in the future. However, our discussion is not exhaustive. Many more challenges can be pondered over and discussed. These challenges, if not at least minimized, will pose insurmountable obstacles to the realization of the BRICs' dreams.

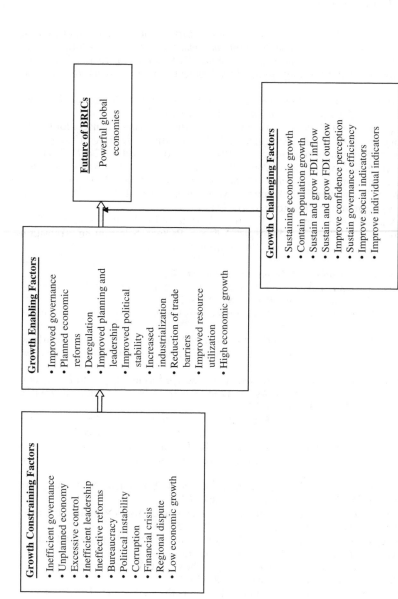

Growth Constraining Factors

- Inefficient governance
- Unplanned economy
- Excessive control
- Inefficient leadership
- Ineffective reforms
- Bureaucracy
- Political instability
- Corruption
- Financial crisis
- Regional dispute
- Low economic growth

Growth Enabling Factors

- Improved governance
- Planned economic reforms
- Deregulation
- Improved planning and leadership
- Improved political stability
- Increased industrialization
- Reduction of trade barriers
- Improved resource utilization
- High economic growth

Future of BRICs

Powerful global economies

Growth Challenging Factors

- Sustaining economic growth
- Contain population growth
- Sustain and grow FDI inflow
- Sustain and grow FDI outflow
- Improve confidence perception
- Sustain governance efficiency
- Improve social indicators
- Improve individual indicators

Figure 2.5   Factors impacting growth of BRICs

REFERENCES

Akbar, Y.H. and M. Samii (2005), 'Emerging Markets and International Business: A Research Agenda', *Thunderbird International Business Review*, **47**(4), 389–96.

Akhter, S.H. (2004), 'Is Globalization What it's Cracked Up to Be? Economic Freedom, Corruption, and Human Development', *Journal of World Business*, **39**, 283–95.

Bartlett, C.A. and S. Ghoshal (2002), 'Building Competitive Advantage Through People', *MIT Sloan Management Review*, **43**(2), 34–41.

Dasgupta, D. (2004), 'Glory or Gloom? The Growth Rate is not a Panacea for India's Economic Woes', *Telegraph* (Calcutta, India), 11 March. Retrieved 18 July 2005, from http://www.telegraphindia.com/1040311/asp/opinion/story_2757222.asp.

Globerman, S. and D. Shapiro (2003), 'Governance Infrastructure and US Foreign Direct Investment', *Journal of International Business Studies*, **34**(1), 19–39.

Goldman Sachs (2003), 'Dreaming with BRICs: The Path to 2050', from www.gs.com/insight/research/reports/99.pdf.

Hitt, M.A., D. Ahlstrom, M.T. Dacin, E. Levitas and L. Svobodina (2004), 'The Institutional Effects on Strategic Alliance Partner Selection in Transition Economies: China vs. Russia', *Organization Science*, **15**(2), 173–85.

Hoskisson, R.E., L. Eden, C.M. Lau and M. Wright (2000), 'Strategy in Emerging Economies', *Academy of Management Journal*, **43**(3), 249–67.

Khanna, T., K.G. Palepu and J. Sinha (2005), 'Strategies that Fit Emerging Markets', *Harvard Business Review*, **83**(6), 63–76.

Klein, L.R. (2004), 'New Growth Centers in this Globalized Economy', *Journal of Policy Modeling*, **26**, 499–505.

London, T. and S.L. Hart (2004), 'Reinventing Strategies for Emerging Markets: Beyond the Transnational Model', *Journal of International Business Studies*, **35**(5), 350–70.

Mazumder, S.K. (2004), 'The Hidden Hand and the License Raj to an Evaluation of the Relationship between Age and the Growth of Firms in India', *Journal of Business Venturing*, **19**(1), 107–25.

Mello, L.D. (2005), 'Brazil's Economy – Showing Strength', *Organization for Economic Cooperation and Development, The OECD Observer*, **248**, 30–31.

Metzger, B., R.N. Dean, D. Bloom and K. Ratnikov (2002), 'A New Russian Revolution: Corporate Governance Reform', *International Financial Law Review*, 21–7.

Mistry, D. (2004), 'A Theoretical and Empirical Assessment of India as an Emerging World Power', *India Review*, **3**(1), 64–87.

Rao, V.V.B. (1996), 'Indian Economic Reforms and ASEAN-India Economic Relations', *Journal of Asian Economics*, **7**(4), 759–68.

Rezende, F. (1998), 'The Brazilian Economy: Recent Developments and Future Prospects', *International Affairs*, **74**(3), 563–75.

Saran, A. and C. Guo (2005), 'Competing in the Global Marketplace: The Case of India and China', *Business Horizons*, **48**, 135–42.

Sheth, J. (2004), 'Making India Globally Competitive', *Vikalpa: The Journal for Decision Makers*, **29**(4), 1–9.

Shleifer, A. and D. Treisman (2000), *Without a Map. Political Tactics and Economic Reform in Russia*, Cambridge, MA: MIT Press.

Sweetwood, D.M. (2002), 'Is Brazil's Economy Coming Back to Life?', *Multinational Business Review*, **10**(1), 54–9.

Tan, J. and M.W. Peng (2003), 'Organizational Slack and Firm Performance During Economic Transitions: Two Studies from an Emerging Economy', *Strategic Management Journal*, **24**(13), 1249–63.

Venkitaramanan, S. (2003), 'BRIC is the Future – Will Brazil, Russia, India and China Dominate the Global Economy?', *Telegraph* (India), 10 November 2003. Retrieved on 18 July 2005 from http://www.telegraphindia.com/1031110/asp/opinion/story_2530585.asp.

Weidenbaum, M. (2004), 'The Uncertain Prospects for the Russian Economy', *Vital Speeches of the Day*, **70**(22), 681–3.

Wilson, D. (2005), 'The BRICs Have Arrived: A Growing New Force in Global Market', *Institutional Investor*, **39**(3), 4–6.

Witzel, M. (2005), 'What We Owe to Chinese Classical Economics', *European Business Forum*, **20**, 89–91.

World Bank Report (2005), *Total GDP 2004*, retrieved on 4 May 2006 from http://siteresources.worldbank.org/DATASTATISTICS/Resources/GDP.pdf.

APPENDIX

*Table 2A.1   BRIC economies: A snapshot of growth constraints,
transformations, and challenges*

Country	Earlier growth constraints	Contemporary transformations and future potential	Key challenges
Brazil	• Slow industrialization • Military intervention • Recession • Inflation • Inconsistent GDP growth • Inefficient public administration	• Developing manufacturing base • Developing services • Tight fiscal policy • Improving investments • Improving exports • Reducing trade barriers	• GDP growth • GDP/capita growth • FDI inflow • FDI outflow • Confidence index • Governance • Corruption • Poverty • Crime rate • Life expectancy
Russia	• Weak manufacturing base • Weak banking system • Poor business climate • Excessive government control • High inflation • Corruption • Communist dictatorship • Political instability	• Market economy • Political reforms • Democracy • Growing economy • Growing foreign reserves • Natural resources	• GDP growth • GDP/capita growth • Population • FDI inflow • FDI outflow • Confidence index • Governance • Corruption • Life expectancy
India	• Overpopulation • Ineffective public policies • Bureaucracy • Inefficient control • Corruption	• Economic liberalization • Industry growth • Services growth • Privatization • Removal of trade barriers • Policy reforms • Contributions from non-residents	• GDP growth • GDP/capita growth • Population • FDI inflow • FDI outflow • Confidence index • Governance • Corruption • Poverty
China	• Centralized economy • Overpopulation • Centralized administration • Corruption	• Market economy • FDI inflow • Growing exports • Accession to WTO • Manufacturing base • Growing services • Large consumer base	• GDP growth • GDP/capita growth • Population • FDI inflow • FDI outflow • Confidence index • Governance • Life expectancy

PART II

Market opportunity

3. Economic growth with the advent of international economic law: implications for emerging economies

Linda Yueh

INTRODUCTION

One of the most intriguing issues accompanying the emergence of major developing economies is how they will cope with the vast changes in international economic law that have occurred in the past decade. This is particularly the case with the establishment of the international system of the World Trade Organization (WTO) and the invocation of a rules-based system that will affect trade, financial flows, investment, technology transfers, intellectual property rights, the movement of people, and even the resolution of cross-border disputes. This chapter will address the various ways in which the economic growth prospects of emerging economies will be affected by the confines of international economic law, and in places enhanced by the system. This will be of importance to the prospects of growth of these economies and to the vision of business that will take place in these economies. Given their growing incremental contribution to global growth, their prospects are also of wider concern to the global economy.

This chapter analyses the effects of international economic law on models of long-run economic growth. In particular, we will focus on the implications for countries which are undergoing development as well as transition, as their progress will now be linked to the development of the international legal system. The chapter will first briefly introduce the advent of international economic law in the past decade. The next part will present a law and economics view of economic growth. This will be followed by an analysis of the implications for the growth prospects of emerging economies with some brief illustration from China, the largest emerging economy in recent times. The chapter will conclude with a look ahead at the evolution of reforms and growth in the global economy.

INTERNATIONAL ECONOMIC LAW

The establishment of the World Trade Organization (WTO), which succeeded the General Agreement on Tariffs and Trade (GATT), by the Marrakech articles, adopted in 1994 with effect from 1995, transformed global cross-border economic transactions. The various annexes further extended the reach of this rules-based system to cover matters ranging from the global trade system to the protection of intellectual property rights, and perhaps eventually government procurement, competition policy and investment. This system of international economic law even offers a dispute settlement mechanism that resolves disagreements among member nations in a type of arbitration proceeding. As the 148 members of the WTO account for approximately 95 percent of world trade, with another 30 countries applying for membership as of 2005, the coverage is substantial. Moreover, the growth in international trade and falling costs of transport have heralded a period of globalization. Growth in worldwide trade is 22 times what it was in 1950 and world trade has averaged over 9 percent per annum, well exceeding the average rate of global economic growth per annum of 3.8 percent in the post-World War II period.

Part of what is extraordinary about this period of globalization is the change in the rules of operating in the global economy. Whereas cross-border economic transactions had been premised on notions of sovereignty, the framework governing the international flow of goods, services, factors such as people and capital, and technology is now subject to an international regime. The 'law of the jungle' has been replaced by a set of international economic laws, norms, rules and institutions (Lowenfeld, 2002). This legal and institutional framework will exert an influence on the nature of economic growth in this era of international economic law. The implications for emerging economies will certainly be significant as many of them are also developing domestic laws and institutions which must now adhere to the strictures of international law. Also, how they proceed with their approach to growth will be influenced by the requirements of the international system.

A LAW AND ECONOMICS VIEW OF ECONOMIC GROWTH

Neoclassical models of long-run growth are premised on a number of assumptions, which essentially presume that there are no frictions or institutional impediments in markets. The Solow model, for instance, considers economic growth where there are no barriers to the movement of capital, no impediments in capital markets so that interest rates reflect the internal rate of return to capital, technology is costlessly shared, and there is no movement of people or natural resources, the latter of which is not typically modelled. Of course, it is well known that the Solow model does not explain growth well since one of the main predictions of the model has not held up when viewed in the growth experience of countries in the post-World War II period. Namely, this refers to the lack of convergence in growth rates of per capita GDP around the world (Baumol, 1986; DeLong, 1988). Figure 3.1 gives a picture of the growth rate of the world's economies plotted against their initial levels of income. If there is evidence of convergence, then there should be an inverse correlation between the rate of growth and the initial level of income. This is not seen in the figure.

However, the neoclassical framework remains useful, particularly the variants in which technology is modeled and human capital is introduced. New growth theory, especially endogenous growth theory, provides a more complex view of growth, which is richer but also seems not to explain well the main drivers of economic growth (Temple, 1999).

Starting with the neoclassical view, economies will reach a steady state level of growth (Jones, 2002). The two functions which drive this result are the production function and the investment function of the economy. Cross-border aspects are introduced in the Solow model as an extension of the concept of diminishing returns to capital. In a Cobb-Douglas production function, $Y = F(K, L) = K^{\alpha}L^{1-\alpha}$, where Y is output, K is capital, L is labour and A is technology, there are constant returns to scale but diminishing returns to capital. Economies with high levels of capital stock will encounter fewer and fewer returns to capital investment. In contrast, developing countries which have lower levels of capital stock will allow capital to reap a higher return. This well-known mechanism will generate convergence in growth rates as capital moves from countries with lower to ones with higher returns. This theory of 'catch-up' growth, however, has not been borne out completely. For example, if capital can move freely, then there should be no correlation between national savings and national investment. The Feldstein-Horioka paradox shows a positive correlation (Feldstein and Horioka, 1980). The movement of capital is apparently driven by a range of factors not just related to a simple view of returns, but is also dependent on risk and domestic infrastructure, among many others (Navaretti and Venables, 2004).

In fact, in this sense, the neoclassical models suffer from some of the same failings as microeconomic views of market failure. The high transaction costs in capital markets in developing countries and the lack of well-defined property rights because institutional foundations are not established will reduce the flow of capital that is critical in generating growth. In other

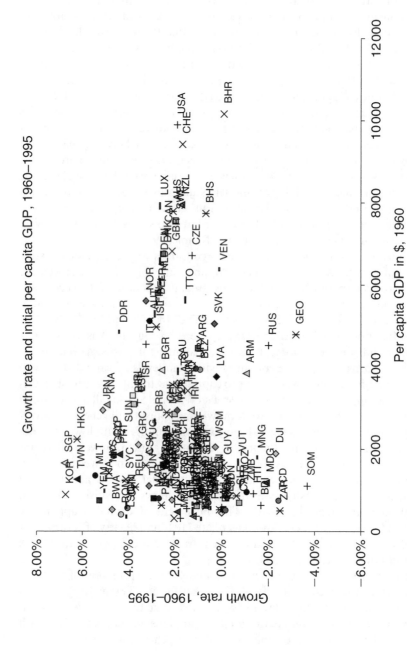

Figure 3.1   Growth rate and initial income, 1960–95

words, developing countries are poorer than developed ones, which imply a lower level of national savings. This is due to the poor having a lower marginal propensity to save because more of their income is consumed, as well as having to cope with imperfect credit markets which often exist in developing countries that make it more difficult to channel what savings there is into funds for investment.

The level of growth in the Solow model is dependent on an investment function that reflects the amount of savings in the economy. The lower marginal propensity to save of poorer and primarily agricultural households in developing countries will lead these economies to have a lower steady state. This can be seen in Figure 3.2. The figure depicts two countries, A and B, with different rates of saving and therefore different steady state levels of output.

To see this, we take the production function and the capital accumulation equation together. The production function is given in terms of output per worker or $\tilde{y}$, and the capital accumulation function is also given in terms of capital per worker or $\tilde{k}$. In addition to the production function, there are two further curves in Figure 3.2, which are both functions of k, capital per person or the capital–labour ratio. To derive output per person, we first assume that the labor force participation rate is 100 percent. Then,

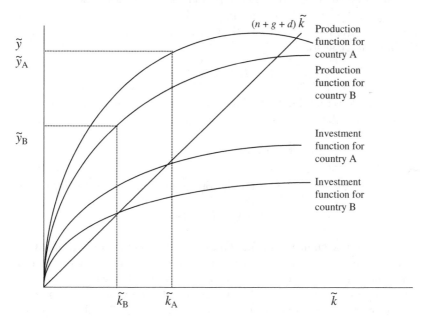

Figure 3.2   Steady state levels of growth for two countries with a high and a low saving rate

we rewrite the capital accumulation equation in terms of capital per person, which will then give us the amount of output per person for the given level of capital stock per person in the economy.

First, we take the logarithms as follows:

$$k \equiv \frac{K}{L},$$

$$\log k = \log K - \log L.$$

Then, we take the derivatives: $\frac{\dot{k}}{K} = \frac{\dot{K}}{K} - \frac{\dot{L}}{L}.$

Similarly, we rewrite the production function by first taking logs:

$$y = k^\alpha,$$

$$\log y = \alpha \log k.$$

And then, taking the derivatives: $\frac{\dot{y}}{y} = \alpha \frac{\dot{k}}{k}.$

Then, let us consider the growth rate of the labor force, $\frac{\dot{L}}{L}$. The Solow model assumes that the labor force participation rate is constant and that population growth is given by n. This implies that the labor force participation rate is also given by n. Alternatively, we can infer the exponential growth of the labor force as follows:

$$L(t) = L_0 e^{nt}.$$

Taking the logs and differentiating once again gives n as the growth rate.

Combining the capital accumulation equation with the above gives:

$$\frac{\dot{k}}{k} = \frac{sY}{K} - n - d \Rightarrow \frac{sy}{k} - n - d.$$

This now gives the capital accumulation equation in per worker terms:

$$\dot{k} = sy - (n+d)k.$$

This can be seen in Figure 3.2. One curve depicts the amount of investment per person, $sy = sk^\alpha$. The curve has the same shape as the production function, but is translated in terms of the function s. There is another curve which represents the amount of new investment per person required to keep the amount of capital per worker constant, $(n+d)k$. Population growth (n) and depreciation (d) will both reduce the amount of capital per person, which is captured here.

Therefore, country A with a higher level of savings and investment will have a higher steady state level of output than country B. This will mean a lower level of per capita GDP for country B unless it has access to foreign capital, which can bolster the level of domestic savings and therefore raise the level of economic growth.

This computation will give the steady state of growth. But, to generate sustained growth in per capita income, we have to introduce technological progress. Thus, we include a technology variable, A, in the production function: $Y = F(K, AL) = K^\alpha (AL)^{1-\alpha}$, where Y is output, K is capital, L is labour and A is technology. So, where technology is 'labor-augmenting', this means that a unit of labour is more productive when the level of technology is higher. It could instead be 'capital-augmenting'.

As seen in Figure 3.3, where there is technological progress, there is a positive rate of growth. The economy grows and reaches a new steady state denoted by $\tilde{y}^{**}$ from $\tilde{y}^*$. However, technology in this model is exogenous.

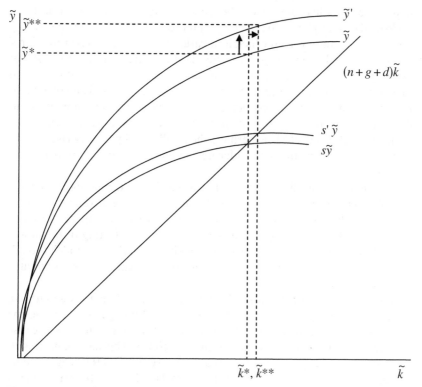

Figure 3.3   Technological progress in the Solow model

It is an important assumption of the model, but one that has been viewed as akin to 'manna from heaven'. Somehow technology comes into the economy regardless of what is happening within the economy.

Endogenous growth models modify the neoclassical framework by introducing a production function for ideas. The reason is because one of the exogenous components in the neoclassical models is the driver of the rate of economic growth, that is, technological progress. The Romer model, which introduces the production of ideas, attempts to explain differential growth rates among countries by exploring the differences among countries in the amount of skilled workers who can innovate and create technological progress. Therefore, technological progress is determined within the model.

This raises further questions in terms of laws and institutions. One of the main impediments to innovation is the nature of ideas (Arrow, 1962). Because ideas are essentially like public goods where many can benefit from one idea, there is a risk of expropriation. Since the protection of ideas is incomplete, this can deter investment in innovation. On the other hand, because ideas have wider benefits than just to the innovator, there is a social cost to restricting the dissemination of ideas or imposing a cost on them. The main way in which innovation is encouraged is through protection of intellectual property rights (IPRs), which reduces the risks of expropriation but creates an artificial monopoly for a time which increases the cost of using that technology. Other methods involve fiscal incentives and public investment. For instance, the government could offer tax credits to entrepreneurs or give concessions to businesses as well as invest in R&D itself. It is perhaps the intellectual property rights issue which is most relevant to considering the law and economics aspects of growth.

One of the assumptions of the Solow model is that technology was freely available. Developing countries could imitate the more advanced technology of developed countries and 'catch up' in their growth rates by not having to duplicate existing technology. As they are starting from a lower level, they would be expected to grow quickly. In the Romer model, though it endogenizes technological progress, it does not explain how a country accumulates innovators.

Both the neoclassical and the Romer model of endogenous growth are affected by the legal framework (Lucas, 1988; Romer, 1986). The norms surrounding IPRs internationally had differed among countries because the overriding principle was respect for sovereignty. This has changed with the trade-related aspects of intellectual property rights (TRIPS agreement) which is Annex C to the WTO articles (WTO, 1999). This harmonized the different IPR regimes into a system of global recognition of IPRs.

By protecting the innovation globally, it may increase the number of researchers who innovate, as in the Romer model. By doing so, it also increases the cost of acquiring technology relevant to the Solow model, as developing countries cannot simply imitate existing technology in order to catch up in terms of their growth rate. Even before the TRIPS agreement, multinational corporations often received value for any technology transfers that accompanied foreign direct investment (FDI). This could provide a further explanation for the lack of convergence among growth rates since costly transfer would hamper the catching up process as envisioned by the Solow model and in addition to the explanations posited by those seeking to explain the Feldstein-Horioka paradox.

Moreover, a law and economics framework for long-run economic growth would consider the legal rules that govern property rights, the factors that influence the movement of broad concepts of capital (human, physical and social), and the rate of technological progress, which is the key component in differential rates of growth. In fact, where evidence of convergence has been found, countries are found to converge to their own steady states. The legal and institutional considerations of each country, therefore, can influence the steady state level of growth through its shaping of the factors relevant to growth. And, importantly, the formal institutions have and will certainly continue to affect the rate of technological progress that drives differential growth rates.

IMPLICATIONS FOR EMERGING ECONOMIES

Once legal and institutional considerations are introduced into the growth models, there is another dimension to understanding the global growth experience of the past 50 years. Even before the establishment of the WTO, the lack of capital mobility and imperfect capital markets would have hampered the catch-up process of growth. Table 3.1 shows the divergent growth rates among developed and developing countries.

The implications for the growth of developing countries extend to the factors that will influence the steady state as well as growth rates. Trade in goods and services has undoubtedly expanded world markets and offered some countries the opportunity to experience economies of scale, which would not have been possible or more difficult in a less globalized economy. The controlled way in which global markets were used by countries such as Brazil and India, and China later in its development path, however, reflects the need for developing countries to control the pace of liberalization. WTO liberalization requirements, though, ask countries to open their markets and frown upon restrictive practices such as import substitution or

Market opportunity

Table 3.1   GDP of country groups

	GDP (in US$ billions)	GDP in US$ billions (PPP adjusted)	GDP per capita (in US$)	GDP per capita in US$ (PPP adjusted)	Annual GDP average growth rate, 1972–2002 %
Developing countries	6 189.30	19 848.50	1 264	4 054	2.3
Least developed countries	204.70	897.70	298	1 307	0.5
Arab States	712.30	1 466.30	2 462	5 069	0.1
East Asia and the Pacific	2 562.60	9 046.90	1 351	4 768	5.9
Latin America and the Caribbean	1 676.10	3 796.10	3 189	7 223	0.7
South Asia	757.10	3 898.70	516	2 658	2.4
Sub-Saharan Africa	303.50	1 157.40	469	1 790	−0.8
Central and Eastern Europe and the CIS	971.10	2 914.70	2 396	7 192	−1.5
OECD	26 298.90	28 491.50	22 987	24 904	2

Source: World Bank, *World Development Indicators* (2004).

restrictions on traded goods and services. These are considered to be anti-thetical to the norm of free multilateral trade. The countries which had adopted rapid liberalization have not seemingly benefited as much from the globalization trend, while countries with some controlled liberalization (China, East Asia) and inward orientation (Brazil, India) have seemingly been more successful at least for a time. The choice, though, is not a clearly acceptable one to be made under international economic law. Although there are exceptions and safeguards to help developing countries in the WTO rules, the general trend of liberalization even without firmly estab-lished legal and institutional rules is already evident. In some ways, the third-generation financial crises which hit emerging markets around the world in the mid- to late 1990s was linked to the rapid liberalization agenda. Their 'thin' financial markets and lack of credit assessment tools held the ingredients for a crisis.

These concerns would extend to the flow of capital, short and long term. Short-term portfolio flows can be useful in providing liquidity in markets, but have had destabilizing effects. Long-term inward foreign direct investment is less fickle and can bolster national savings in devel-oping countries, but the free market principles of international law would reduce the control over such investments that some countries have utilized to maximize their benefits. For instance, the restrictions on FDI that China imposed at the start of its reform period with the Special Economic Zones may be more difficult to achieve with financial liberalization.

In fact, China since WTO accession in 2001 is confronted with the challenge of liberalizing its financial and banking sector despite apparent weaknesses and opening its domestic market to entry by foreign multi-national corporations.

Factors such as labour and their human capital will also be subject to international economic law. In particular, the researchers and entrepreneurs who can generate innovation are more likely to move across borders than before, raising questions about the implications for the growth models which assume a stock of domestic researchers or labourers who complement capital.

Finally, one of the most influential aspects of international economic law in terms of affecting growth will be the limitations, restrictions and costs of technology transfers and creation. TRIPS has transformed over 100 years of legal norms, governed by the Paris and Berne Conventions. Imitation with cost and paying monopoly rents for technology transfers could reduce the benefits of a technological breakthrough or 'shock' that drives catch-up growth in a neoclassical model. On the other hand, the protection of innovation and the incentives offered to labor to acquire skills to become innovators could increase the domestic stock of researchers in the endogenous growth theories that will increase growth. The evidence is not yet clear, though the answer will greatly affect the prospects of emerging economies.

An example from China provides an illustration. Technology transfers can be direct or indirect, that is, explicit contracted technology transfers or 'learning by doing'. In 2000, before WTO accession, about three-quarters of FDI went into China as joint ventures (JVs), partnered with Chinese enterprises. In 2003, two years after WTO accession, about 71 percent were wholly foreign-owned enterprises. Though there are many reasons for this shift, including a change in the type of FDI that is invested in China, there is less scope for both types of technology transfers when investment comes in this form.

Perhaps more crucially, it was not just that joint ventures were the required form of FDI, but that China required potential JV partners to meet two criteria. The first is to possess advanced technology and the second is that this technology will produce goods that will be demanded in global markets. Moreover, these agreements were frequently accompanied by technology transfer agreements, usually included as an annex to the joint venture contract. With a decline in the number of JVs, companies will need to licence technology and may not be able to develop absorptive capacity as readily when operating on their own. The 'learning by doing' element is less viable. More costly transfer of technology will reduce the gains of the developing country, which will affect the rate of economic growth, as seen in Figure 3.4.

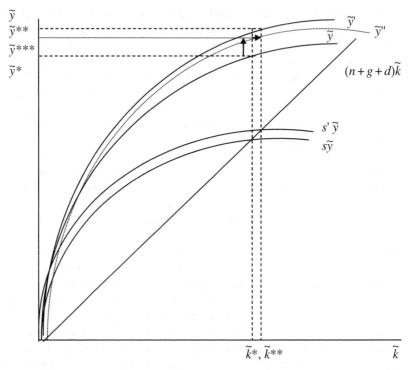

Figure 3.4   Costly technology transfers in the Solow model

In Figure 3.4, the increased cost of technology transfer flattens the gradient of the production function, $\tilde{y}''$, as output is more costly for a given level of technology and inputs, than if the technology were imitated at low or no cost, $\tilde{y}'$. This results in a level of per capita output, $\tilde{y}^{***}$, which is lower than $\tilde{y}^{**}$, though still higher than if there had been no technology transfer, $\tilde{y}^{*}$.

However, if the increased protection of intellectual property rights due to the TRIPS agreement results in more advanced technology being transferred because innovators feel more secure from the risk of expropriation and are willing to introduce this knowledge into China, then it is possible that technological progress will be as seen in Figure 3.3, and perhaps even progress faster, resulting in a higher level of output for the economy. This will also differ considerably among countries. China has controlled its opening to the global economy and the form of FDI allowed into its borders to a considerable extent. For countries which have not had such a history, the predictions are likely to be rather different.

Nevertheless, technology transfers have not been costless across borders even when capital has flowed from developed to developing countries. This implies that the predictions of convergence in the growth rates of the world's economies are unlikely to hold. When there is explicit protection and therefore positive costs of sharing technology, the outcome will be that developing countries may well gain the use of advanced technologies that make their production more efficient but they will pay a cost for the use. Therefore, convergence in growth rates will be slower than the predictions of economic models.

CONCLUSION

We have outlined the implications for economic growth with the advent of international economic law and drawn out several implications for emerging economies. This a step toward developing a law and economics view of growth, which is an understandably new area given the vast changes in the international economic sphere in the past few years. The prospects of continuing growth and reform in emerging economies, however, will be intricately tied to the international economic and financial systems.

In particular, the harmonizing effects of international economic law, the push for international financial architecture, international standards for the governance of financial markets, along with the Singapore issues will affect development. In terms of growth models, both new endogenous growth theories and the neoclassical framework identify two key drivers of long-run growth that will be affected by factors intrinsic to a law and economics outlook which hold consequences for the 'catch-up' growth of emerging economies. The convergence hypothesis has not been borne out due not only to investment flows as argued by Feldstein and Horioka, but also to costly technology transfers as argued in this chapter. In terms of long-run growth, investment is important in influencing the steady state, but technology will be the crucial factor in determining sustained long-run growth rates. Thus, this may be the more important of the two, but both will be affected by international economic law in the coming years.

For emerging economies like the BRICs (Brazil, Russia, India and China), their growth strategies will fall increasingly within the limits of international economic law, unlike the current developed economies which were much more autonomous in the early stages of their development. The continued growth prospects of emerging economies will indeed hinge on their interactions with the evolving international system.

REFERENCES

Arrow, K. (1962), 'Economic Welfare and the Allocation of Resources for Invention', in R. Nelson (ed.), *The Rate of Inventive Activity: Economic and Social Factors*, Princeton, NJ: Princeton University Press.

Baumol, William J. (1986), 'Productivity Growth, Convergence, and Welfare: What the Long-run Data Show', *American Economic Review*, **76**, 1072–85.

DeLong, J. Bradford (1988), 'Productivity Growth, Convergence, and Welfare: Comment', *American Economic Review*, **78**, 1138–54.

Feldstein, Martin and Charles Horioka (1980), 'National Saving and International Capital Flows', *Economic Journal*, **90**, 314–29.

Jones, Charles I. (2002), *Introduction to Economic Growth*, New York: W.W. Norton.

Lowenfeld, Andreas (2002), *International Economic Law*, Oxford: Oxford University Press.

Lucas, Robert E., Jr. (1988), 'On the Mechanics of Economic Development', *Journal of Monetary Economics*, **22**, 3–42.

Navaretti, Giorgio Barba and Anthony J. Venables (2004), *Multinational Firms in the World Economy*, Princeton: Princeton University Press.

Romer, Paul (1986), 'Increasing Returns and Long Run Growth', *Journal of Political Economy*, **94**, 1002–37.

Temple, Jonathan (1999), 'The New Growth Evidence', *Journal of Economic Literature*, **37**, 112–56.

World Trade Organization (1999), *The Legal Texts: The Results of the Uruguay Round of Multilateral Trade Negotiations*, Cambridge: Cambridge University Press.

4. Global strategies of Brazilian firms in an era of economic liberalization

Preet S. Aulakh

Economic liberalization around the world and the general phenomenon of globalization has provided tremendous market access, investment and sourcing opportunities for large multinational corporations in emerging economies. A simultaneous consequence of this process, which has received limited research attention, is the growing presence of firms from developing economies in an integrated global economy. Some of the major objectives of liberalization policies are to: (1) move away from inward-oriented import substitution policies towards outward-oriented export-led growth (Kotler et al., 1997); (2) access foreign technology and capital in order to make domestic firms competitive in the global economy; and (3) enhance capabilities in value-added manufacturing industries rather than relying on traditional commodity goods (Aulakh et al., 2000; Thomas et al., 2000). These objectives have been reinforced by the success of many companies from the newly industrialized countries, such as South Korea, Taiwan and Singapore, which have achieved a significant competitive position in the manufacturing sector in foreign markets. Accordingly, individual governments have initiated programs that provide incentives for local firms to actively internationalize and compete in foreign markets (Seringhaus and Rosson, 1990).

Although the presence of private enterprises from emerging economies is increasing in the global competitive landscape, there has been a lack of systematic analysis of international strategies followed by these firms (Dominguez and Sequeira, 1993; Vernon-Wortzel and Wortzel, 1988). Existing literature has examined the internationalization process of emerging-economy firms (Wortzel and Vernon-Wortzel, 1981), the relationship between organizational characteristics and export performance (Christensen et al., 1987) and the links between macro-policy initiatives, trade liberalization and economic development at the country level (Otani and Villanueva, 1990; Singer and Gray, 1988). Furthermore, as suggested by Dominguez and Brenes (1997), 'much of what has been written dates back to the 1970s and early 1980s, and may no longer be applicable, as many of these firms were state-owned then. Reportedly, the key to success then lay in close government ties, preferential access to financing, protection from imports, dominant share of domestic markets, subsidized inputs, and kinship-based management organizations'. In the contemporary global environment of market and trade liberalization, the importance of private enterprises in emerging economies as engines of outward-oriented growth necessitates an examination of their strategies to build competitive advantages in foreign markets (Aulakh et al., 2000; Aulakh and Kotabe, 2001).

The purpose of this chapter is to examine the international strategies of Brazilian firms. Brazil, part of the BRIC group, is considered one of the important emerging economies not only as an attractive FDI and market opportunity site for foreign multinationals, but also as a powerhouse trying to compete with established multinationals for global markets. Brazilian companies' attempts to compete in global markets are taking place within a global environment of economic liberalization as well as the new policy directions pursued by the Brazilian government. Thus an important research issue that emanates from this is whether the internationalization of Brazilian firms and their focus on specific value chain activities and geographical markets is fulfilling the macro-objectives of policy-makers. In this chapter, I first briefly describe the evolution of Brazil's macro-environment to highlight the changes in policy directions and objectives. Next I describe the data collection and the nature of the sample. This is followed by a discussion of the findings related to the cross-border alliance strategies of Brazilian firms, their diversification and competitive strategies in global markets and the associated performance implications. The final section discusses the implications of these findings.

ECONOMIC POLICIES IN BRAZIL: IMPORT SUBSTITUTION INDUSTRIALIZATION TO EXPORT-LED GROWTH

After World War II, Brazil was a producer of primary goods with 66 percent of its labour force employed in the agriculture sector (Gauvea, 2004). However, with increasing rates of population growth (the population tripling in 40 years), the country needed economic growth to provide employment for its population through industrial development (Abreu et al., 1996). Thus Brazil initiated the policy of import substitution industrialization in the 1950s to build internal capabilities and move towards greater industrialization. This push towards industrial development was made through the establishment of national ownership of public services including telecommunications, utilities and transportation; nationalization of key strategic industries such as oil and iron; and the establishment of national industries such as steel, petrochemicals, and aeronautics and electronics (Goldstein, 1999). These programs were successful in creating the foundations for national industries and making the country less dependent on agriculture. The government also created various incentives for companies that exported non-traditional products as well as provided incentives for firms for technological innovations. For instance, the government developed the FUNTEC (Program for Technological Development) in 1964 to enhance R&D efforts in Brazil (Amman and Baer, 2002). A number of state organizations such as Petrobras (petroleum), Copel (electricity) and Telebras (telecommunications) started their own research institutes as a result of these government initiatives. The overall results of these policies initiated after World War II and running into the mid-1980s were mixed. On the one hand, there was a development of indigenous industries and increase in exports of Brazilian industrial goods to other South American countries, as well as the emergence of key players who were becoming internationally competitive, such as Embraer in the aviation industry. However, the technology acquired in Brazil was imported from foreign firms, leading to a lack of indigenous technological innovations.

In 1985, after 21 years of military rule, a democratically elected civilian government took charge in Brazil. It was faced with a general economic decline owing to the oil shocks of the previous decade, and high inflation rates ranging from 40.8 percent in 1978 to 1240 percent in the early 1990s (Abreu et al., 1996). Owing to both domestic pressures and IMF concerns, the government pursued numerous macroeconomic initiatives which form the bases for the economic objectives in the era of globalization. First, to remedy the inflationary pressure, the Brazilian government launched the Real plan whereby the new currency was fixed with respect to the US dollar. Second, the government tried to improve international competitiveness by internationalizing the economy. The formation of MERCOSUR was one attempt to intensify trade and financial relationships between countries in South America. Furthermore, the Brazilian government tried to stimulate trade by reducing tariffs which fell from an average of 51 percent to 14 percent. The prices of imported technology goods such as computers and machinery declined, leading to lower investment costs and increased access to foreign technology (Abreu et al., 1996). A favorable investment climate also saw a surge in inward FDI, and between 1996 and 1998 Brazil received $53 billion through FDI. Third, the government began to privatize industry through its 1990 National Plan for Privatization (Procianoy and Sabrino, 2001). Fourth, the government attempted to stimulate domestic technological innovations through three programs: the Technology Capacity Program which aimed to improve technological capability through new incentives for R&D; the Quality and Productivity Program aimed at improving efficiency in manufacturing; and Law 8661 which decentralized control over the creation and diffusion of technological capabilities. It aimed to develop linkages between R&D institutions, universities and the private sector through financial incentives for technological development.

Thus, similar to some other countries in Latin America as well as BRIC compatriots such as India, Brazil instituted drastic reforms in the 1980s and 1990s, including: privatization of state-owned companies and the increased role of private enterprises in fostering economic growth; opening of domestic markets to foreign competition in order to infuse capital, new technologies and to instill high powered incentives for efficient enterprises in the economy; policy initiatives to invigorate non-commodity and higher value-added industries; and emphasis on export-led growth. The results of these policies have generally been positive for Brazil. Total exports increased from $27 billion in 1984 to $81 billion in 2004, with the share of manufactured exports increasing from 50 percent in 1984 to 65 percent in 2004, (World Bank Group, 2005). Despite these positive gains in the internationalization of the economy through inward FDI and the increase in exports of manufactured goods, the share of high value-added exports has been relatively stagnant (for example in 2000 they represented 18.6 percent of total manufactured exports and in 2003 only 12 percent of total manufactured exports) (World Bank Group, 2005).

These raise some interesting issues regarding the competitiveness of Brazil as a country and, more specifically, the international competitiveness of Brazilian firms as they compete in a globally liberalized environment where they face competition from both established developed-country multinationals but also emerging multinationals from developing economies. In the rest of the chapter, I examine three specific issues related to strategies followed by Brazilian firms and subsequently link them to the macro-country objectives. In particular, I report findings from a study of 80 mid-sized Brazilian companies related to their international alliances, their diversification efforts into various geographical markets, and the bases of their competition in export markets.

Research Context

Through various chambers of commerce, published directories and business school contacts, 357 firms were selected as the target sample. These firms were first contacted via a phone call (a total of 1200 calls were made) during which the caller explained the nature of the study and asked the name(s) of the persons that would be in charge of the company's export operations. Subsequently, 294 of the 357 firms were effectively contacted. In the second stage, 294 questionnaires were mailed out to these firms. However, soon after the mailing, there was a nationwide postal strike and sabotage. Due to the nature of the strike, numerous firms did not receive the questionnaire. Hence, some surveys had to be hand-delivered or faxed to respondents. A total of 93 surveys were returned, out of which 80 were complete, for an effective response rate of 27.2 percent. The sample consisted of firms from the following industries: manufactured durables 20.5 percent, manufactured non-durables 65.8 percent, services 5.5 percent, and food/agricultural manufactured products 8.2 percent. Average sales of the firms in the sample was US$250 million and the firms on average employed 3347 people.[1]

Cross-border Alliance Strategies of Brazilian Firms

As mentioned earlier, one of the important features of Brazilian economic reforms is the different levels of collaboration (trade agreements, private–public sector cooperation, and business–business alliances) to achieve objectives of international growth and enhancing indigenous innovation capabilities. Thus, of particular interest in this aspect is whether the motivations and success of collaborations permeates commercial collaborations between Brazilian and foreign firms. Firms in the sample responded to various questions related to different aspects of their collaboration experiences and those results are discussed below.

Motivations for cross-border alliances
There exists a rich literature on why firms seek collaboration in their competitive efforts (Hamel, 1991; Hagedoorn, 1993). Firms seek partners when they face resource deficiencies to meet competitive challenges. Where firms are resource capable, they make strategic choices regarding the deployment of these scarce resources, recognizing the opportunity costs of their utilization (Kotabe et al., 2000). As in the case of gains from trade between nations based on comparative advantage, firms can gain through alliances with others who have complementary resources. Additionally, firms may be motivated by competitive forces to seek collaboration. By allying with a potential competitor, this firm may be co-opted to reduce competitive intensity and/or raise barriers to entry in both geographic and product markets. Third, by sharing resources, collaborating firms can reduce costs and risks associated with participating in particular ventures. In light of this literature, responding firms in this sample were asked to identify their motivations for allying with foreign firms and the results are summarized in Figure 4.1.

The most important motivation relates to access to foreign partners' technical expertise, with 29 percent of the firms in the sample stating this

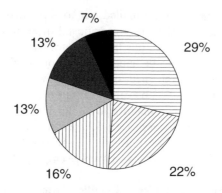

Figure 4.1   Motivation for cross-border alliance

as the most important factor. This is tied closely with a strategic concern for Brazilian firms that they lack innovative capabilities and, given a paucity of an innovative domestic environment, access to foreign technological know-how becomes imperative in the global competitive environment. About 22 percent of firms identified access to marketing expertise as the motivating factor in strategic alliances. This includes marketing infrastructure, and relationships with important customers and recognized brand names. Here the underlying rationale for this motivating factor is increased access to global markets as well as learning opportunities that could be transferred into the domestic market. For another 16 percent of the firms in the sample, accessing foreign financial resources through their alliances was the motivating factor. This is not surprising given the prevalence of domestic capital constraints. Domestic credit is scarce and that which is available tends to be prohibitively expensive for these firms. Nascent stock markets in the countries have eased capital access pressure for only the larger firms, but the Brazilian austerity program shows how these events affect portfolio investment stability. Direct investment in firms tends to be more stable, but implies a lot of control, which many firms are not willing to cede. By joining forces with capital-rich partners, Brazilian firms can access funds while simultaneously maintaining their legal independence. Thus, from the above discussion, we can conclude that about two-thirds of the firms in the sample highlighted the seeking of resources to improve their internal capabilities as the primary motivating factor in cross-border alliances.

Besides the resource-seeking motivations, we also find that about a third of the firms were motivated to form alliances in order to seek foreign markets (13 percent), minimize costs and risks (13 percent) and as a competitive move (7 percent). Direct access to foreign markets is sought by many Brazilian firms via their alliances in order to overcome trade barriers and other restrictions, obtain regulatory permission from host countries, and in some cases also to access specialized labor pools in foreign markets. Even where Brazilian firms face less regulatory pressures, lack of knowledge about the market itself poses a significant barrier to entry (in the case of Brazilian firms, it may be due to the double effect of the liability of newness in foreign markets and the liability of foreignness, especially in developed countries). This need to access foreign market knowledge is likely to be the most pressing in culturally distant markets (Kotabe et al., 2000). Risk and cost reduction and competitive motivations relate to sharing limited resources and the co-optation of potential competitors, respectively.

Types of cross-border alliances
Besides the motivations for seeing cross-border alliances, I also examined the transformation of motivations to actual alliance formation. As shown in Figure 4.2, the alliances that Brazilian firms did initiate with foreign partners reflected their motivations: 74 percent of the alliances formed were related to resource seeking in upstream activities (technology and know-how transfer alliances representing 45 percent and production alliances 29 percent). Only 26 percent of the alliances were marketing alliances which probably represents more of market-seeking motivations and if there is any resource seeking, it is more at the downstream value chain activities.

Success of alliances
I examined the success of the three types of alliances. Each respondent was asked to rate the performance of a specific alliance on a number of standard economic indicators. The results are summarized in Figure 4.3. The average performance of these alliances falls in the range of 2.4 to 3.3 on a scale of 5. However, the interesting aspect is that technology and know-how alliances are seen as less successful (mean rating of 2.43) than marketing

Market opportunity

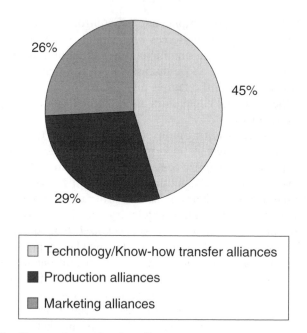

Figure 4.2   Types of cross-border alliances

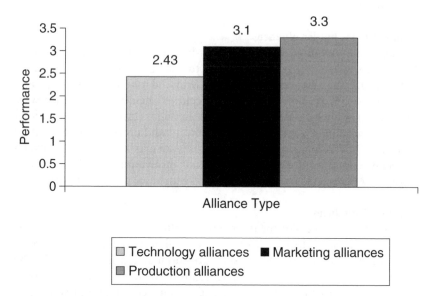

Figure 4.3   Success of cross-border alliances

(mean of 3.1) and production (mean of 3.3) alliances. Thus the more common alliances (45 percent of the alliances were technology transfer alliances) were achieving lower objectives from the perspective of Brazilian firms than the production and marketing alliances. What explains this? One possible factor could be the reluctance of foreign firms to part with their proprietary know-how to Brazilian partners. Given that the latter are aggressively seeking know-how and the knowledge flows are more one way from foreign firms to Brazilian firms, the reluctance of the former to share the latest know-how may be leading to suboptimal performance from the perspective of the foreign firms. Production and marketing alliances in the sample may be more symmetrical in terms of the complementarity of the resources that the Brazilian and foreign firms bring into the relationship, thus leading to better perceived performance.

To examine the performance of Brazilian alliances further I also examined the factors that impact performance. Existing literature on interorganizational relationships identifies various possible determinants of performance. Based on this literature stream, I examined three types of possible determinants: relational, structural and cultural. The results summarized in Figure 4.4 suggest that the most important indicators of alliance success between Brazilian firms and foreign partners are the relational

Factors	Importance
Relational Aspects • Trust • Contract flexibility	HIGH
Structural Aspects • Equity sharing • Decision-making sharing	MEDIUM
Cultural Factors • National cultural distance • Organizational cultural distance	LOW

Figure 4.4   Determinants of alliance success

factors such as trust and flexibility. The next most important determinants of alliance success were the structural aspects of the relationship, including the nature of symmetry between partners on both the equity side, and in the sharing of decision-making. Surprisingly, the cultural factors (both in terms of differences between the national cultures of the Brazilian firms and the home countries of partner firms, as well as between the organizational norms and values of partner firms) did not play a major role in determining alliance performance. This finding is important from the point of view that cultural differences are in a sense exogenous to the partnering firms, with each organization having very little control over these. However, past research has demonstrated that both relational aspects as well as shared decision-making can be either incorporated in the terms of the contract or developed over time with repeated interactions. In other words, the more important factors impacting alliance success are at the discretion of managers and thus more amenable to managerial actions.

GEOGRAPHICAL DIVERSIFICATION OF BRAZILIAN FIRMS

One of the strong pillars of Brazil's economic growth model in recent years has been the internationalization of the economy. In order to examine this issue at the level of individual firms, I examined the geographical diversification of exports of Brazilian manufacturers. The distribution of export markets of the sample firms is provided in Figure 4.5. As shown in the figure, it seems that geographical proximity plays an important role in

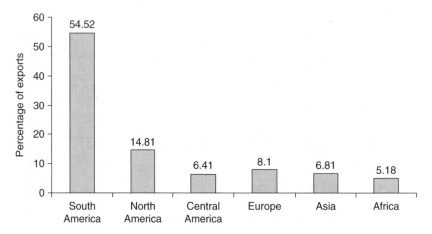

Figure 4.5   Export diversification of Brazilian firms

the extent of exports to various regions. More than half of the exports go to other South American markets (54.52 percent), which is followed by North America (14.81 percent), Europe (8.1 percent), Asia (6.81 percent), Central America (6.41 percent) and Africa (5.18 percent), in order of importance. Besides the geographical proximity, membership in regional trading blocs also plays a factor in terms of specific countries where exports are targeted. A broader implication is that Brazilian firms are probably still in the early stages of internationalization whereby firms target geographically and/or culturally similar countries.

A body of literature in strategic management and international business has examined the impact of international diversification strategy on firm performance (for example Hitt et al., 1997; Tallman and Li, 1996; Geringer et al., 1989; Kim et al., 1989). These studies argue that diversification into a foreign market from its home base or across multiple markets allows the firm to build and sustain competitive advantage by attaining economies of scale and scope, achieving synergies across geographically dispersed locations, arbitraging across individual country markets, and leveraging ownership, internalization and location advantages, among others (Hitt et al., 1997). Empirical studies support the performance implications of international diversification. For instance, Kim et al. (1989) found a linear effect of international diversification on performance while Hitt et al. (1997) found an inverted U-shaped relationship, that is, very low levels of international diversification are insufficient to allow for any synergy gains, moderate levels of international diversification enhance performance, while very high levels of diversification are detrimental to performance as the costs of geographical diversification start outweighing the potential benefits. Similarly, Kim et al. (1989), Hitt et al. (1997) and Tallman and Li (1996) found interactive effects between international and product diversification on firm performance. While these studies use different diversification and performance measures, the theoretical rationale and empirical findings point toward international diversification as an important strategic variable to build and sustain competitive advantage.

However, most of the literature on international diversification has focused on large multinational corporations and has examined diversification in terms of dispersion of value-chain operations across multiple markets, accomplished through foreign direct investment. Existing studies do not provide insights into whether diversification advantages will accrue to firms that are not involved in foreign direct investment. This is a crucial issue for a large number of emerging-economy firms whose primary mode of foreign market participation is through exports. Furthermore, internationalization models (Johanson and Vahlne, 1977) suggest that firms follow a sequential path of international involvement, that is, when

expanding abroad firms, because of limited managerial and financial
resources and high risk aversion, choose low-risk entry modes such as
exporting. Since firms from emerging economies are still in the early stages
of internationalization (Vernon-Wortzel and Wortzel, 1988; Dominguez
and Sequeira, 1993), they are likely to export products from their home
base rather than engage in foreign direct investment. The primary issue for
these firms is to determine the number of countries they will export their
products and services to (that is, export diversification) and the impact
diversification will have on export performance.

For exporting firms, the main benefits of export diversification arise from
four sources (Aulakh et al., 2000). First, exporters face much higher exchange
rate exposure than multinational corporations, since their costs are in one
currency and revenues from product sales come from the foreign market currency. Thus, a major benefit of export diversification is to minimize the transaction risks as the exporting firm can lower exposure by trading in multiple
currencies (Dominguez and Sequeira, 1993). Second, there are economies-
of-scale advantages of export diversification. Government export promotion
programs in a number of emerging economies are targeted to increase export
sales, and thus firms develop products especially for export markets. Here the
only way to achieve scale advantages is to increase foreign sales, which is
accomplished by simultaneously targeting a number of foreign markets.
Third, from an organizational learning perspective expounded by Kogut and
Zander (1993) and internationalization theory (Johanson and Vahlne, 1977),
exporting firms can leverage their accumulated knowledge of one country to
target other economically and culturally similar foreign markets. The factors
described above suggest that exporting firms can achieve and leverage their
competitive advantage by targeting multiple foreign markets for their products and services.

Exporting firms also face challenges of diversification similar to those
faced by multinational corporations (Hitt et al., 1997). First, increased
geographical diversification increases the coordination costs of managing
exports operations. Cavusgil and Zou (1994) and Madsen (1987) suggest
that important determinants of export performance are the amount of
support provided to foreign distributors and the commitment shown to an
individual export market. Thus, increased geographical diversification has
the potential to spread managerial resources thinly across markets, reducing the ability to support marketing programs of foreign distributors.
Second, as described by Hitt et al. (1997), geographical diversification
increases managerial information processing needs because of dealing
with culturally diverse markets and the enhanced transaction costs
which arise due to different tariff and non-tariff barriers faced in different
countries.

Given the above discussion related to the advantages and disadvantages of geographical diversification, and the public policy initiatives in Brazil to diversify the market base for Brazilian exporters, which is also evidenced in Figure 4.5, I examined the performance implications of the geographical diversification of Brazilian firms. I measured performance in terms of profitability and related factors of the firms' export activities and calculated an entropy measure of their geographical diversification (Aulakh et al., 2000). First I examined the direct relationship between diversification and performance, which was not statistically significant. This may be due to the canceling out of benefits and managerial costs of diversification identified in the literature discussed above. To get around this, I focused on the moderating role of two variables: the number of cross-border alliances and the product innovation levels of the Brazilian firms. The results of this analysis are summarized in Figure 4.6.

The top chart in Figure 4.6 shows the impact of cross-border alliances on the diversification–performance linkage of Brazilian firms. In particular, it shows that diversification leads to greater performance for firms that have more foreign alliances while firms that internationalize on their own do not reap the benefits of geographical diversity of their markets. Foreign alliances help the Brazilian firms get easier access to markets, overcome some liability of foreignness aspects, and help in minimizing the risks and coordination costs of going into unfamiliar markets. The lower half of the figure provides the impact of product innovation on the diversification– performance linkage. Here the results show that innovation positively moderates the relationship, that is, innovative firms reap the benefits of diversification. This can probably be explained from the revenue point of view. More innovative firms can charge premium prices that overcome the coordination and other costs of entering diverse markets. These results, taken together, point towards the need for both external acquisition of capabilities (through alliances) as well as internal development of innovation as important considerations for Brazilian firms' successful diversification strategies.

COMPETITIVE STRATEGIES AND EXPORT PERFORMANCE

Various typologies dealing with organizational-level competitive strategies have been advanced in the management literature. In this study, I examine the performance implications of cost-based and differentiation-based strategies. One of the objectives of firms from emerging economies is to move away from cost-based expansion and offer differentiated products.

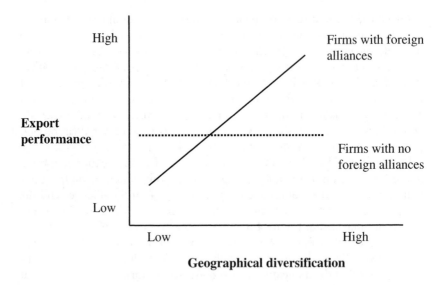

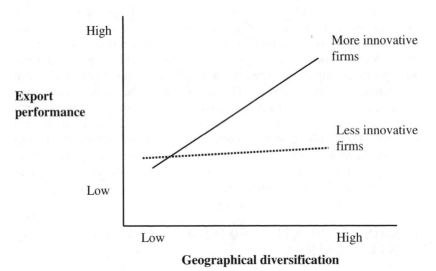

Figure 4.6   Diversification, alliance strategy, innovation and performance

These are based on the assumptions that differentiation allows firms a more enduring advantage, and as firms move up the value chain in terms of manufacturing maturity, they start competing based on superior products rather than just on their cost advantages. In order to evaluate how the move up the value chain for Brazilian firms impacts international competitiveness, I focus on these two generic strategies.

Firms following a differentiation strategy aim at creating a product or service that customers see as unique. This is usually accomplished through a superior brand image, technology, and/or customer service. The objective of firms pursuing a differentiation strategy is to build customer loyalty and thus create barriers to entry for new entrants. Because of the loyalty created for the brand, the demand is price-inelastic, leading to higher profit margins for the manufacturer. While firms following a differentiation strategy hope to achieve competitive advantage by providing more value for products and services to customers, a cost leadership strategy involves giving consumers comparable value at lower costs. According to Porter (1980, 1986), cost leadership requires 'aggressive construction of efficient-scale facilities, vigorous pursuit of cost reductions from experience, tight cost and overhead control, . . . and cost minimization in areas like R&D, service, sales force, and advertising'. This strategy can provide above-average returns because firms following cost leadership can lower their prices to match those of their competitors, and still earn profits.

Recent research points to the need to examine the links between cost and differentiation strategies and performance within a contingency framework, especially of the external environment. Based on this, I examine the strategy–performance relationships of Brazilian firms within the contingency framework based on the foreign market environments in which these firms compete. As mentioned earlier, the important environmental factors relevant here, which have found some support in the context of developed markets, are the degree of competition and environmental uncertainty (with its underlying dimensions of dynamism and instability). Given that the firms in the sample are competing in numerous countries each with different levels of competition and uncertainty, and that our focus is to examine the strategy and performance links at the corporate rather than the individual market level, we feel that a surrogate measure of the environment will be more appropriate. Accordingly, I use a categorical variable, 'foreign market focus' dichotomized into developed countries and developing countries. The rationale here is that developed countries represent markets that are more competitive (that is, large numbers of resource-endowed competitors and demanding consumers) and dynamic (that is, frequent changes in consumer tastes and the introduction of innovative products and services) than those of developing economies. These differences in environmental conditions may have differential impacts on emerging economies' firms that compete primarily in developed countries versus those whose primary foreign market focus is developing countries.

The results are summarized in Figure 4.7. The relationship between cost leadership and export performance is shown in the top part of the figure. I find that as firms from Brazil increase their cost leadership strategy (that is, compete on the basis of costs), their performance in foreign markets increases. This is consistent both for firms with a developed-country focus as well as for those with a developing-country focus. However, the relationship also suggests that the impact of cost leadership on export performance is stronger for firms with a developed-country focus than for those with a developing-country focus. In essence, what this finding points towards is that Brazilian firms need to compete on the basis of cost leadership when they export their products to developed countries.

The relationship between differentiation strategy and export performance is shown in the bottom part of Figure 4.7. The results show that differentiation strategy has a much stronger positive impact on export performance for firms who export primarily to other developing economies. That is, firms having highly differentiated products will have higher performance in developing countries than those with low differentiation. On the other hand, we do not find a significant increase in performance for firms implementing a differentiation strategy in developed-country markets. Why haven't Brazilian firms built a competitive advantage through product and market differentiation when they export to developed countries? In general, developed-country markets are characterized by competitive and dynamic environments. Firms exporting to these markets are at a relative disadvantage with respect to local firms because the latter have more financial, managerial and technological resources, established brands and innovative products. Furthermore, past research has shown that consumers in developed markets perceive products and brands from emerging economies negatively, and generally equate them with low price and low quality. Thus a combination of a poor-quality image and the presence of resource-rich competitors makes it very difficult for emerging-economy firms to build advantage by differentiating their products and services from local competitors. A differentiation strategy, on the other hand, works in other developing economies for a number of reasons. First, research suggests that consumers in developing countries perceive foreign-made products (from both industrialized and emerging economies) to be of superior quality and are willing to pay a price premium over domestically made products. This suggests that exporters can leverage positive consumer perceptions by differentiating their products on the country-of-origin dimension

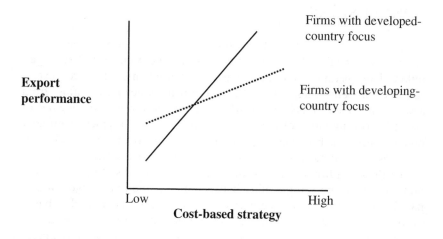

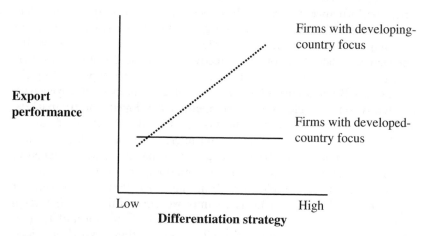

Figure 4.7   *Competitive strategies and performance*

and over time build enduring brand reputations. Second, the cost of implementing a differentiation strategy will be lower in emerging economies than in developed countries, since the former are less competitive markets with fewer entrenched local competitors having established brands or other reputations.

CONCLUSIONS

In this chapter, I have tried to establish linkages between the macro-objectives of the Brazilian government and the micro-analysis of strategies followed by medium-sized Brazilian firms within the overall context of country competitiveness. Since the government policy moved away from a state-controlled model to one where private enterprises are engines of growth, an examination of the role played by the latter in achieving broader policy objectives becomes important. From the data on cross-border alliances, geographical diversification and competitive strategies followed by the Brazilian firms discussed in the previous sections, it becomes clear that there is strong compatibility between macro and micro objectives. In particular, the government's objectives of moving from commodity-based exports to value-added production and internationalization as an engine of growth permeates firm-level actions in terms of Brazilian firms looking for resource-seeking partnerships, diversifying into distant geographical markets beyond those of South America, and attempting to initiate differentiation-based strategies in foreign markets.

However, if one examines whether these firm actions have resulted in better performance, the results have been mixed. In particular, the data show that although access to technology and know-how from foreign firms is a major motivation for cross-border alliances of Brazilian firms, the knowledge transfer has not been effective, as evidenced from the low performance evaluation of such alliances. This is further supported by the finding that Brazilian firms have not been able to compete effectively with differentiation strategies in more competitive developed-country markets. Thus, there seems to be a disconnection between the objectives of moving up the value chain at both macro and micro levels, and achieving these objectives. Similarly, the results suggest a disparity between aggressive internationalization to diverse markets, and doing so effectively.

One can infer some implications from the above. Part of the reason for the inability of Brazilian firms to improve competitiveness in foreign markets is their lack of resources. These could be in the form of technological assets, brand strength and equity, or international experience vis-à-vis more entrenched multinational competitors. The implication of this is that besides providing incentives to their respective firms to internationalize, policy initiatives in Brazil also need to facilitate the acquisition of necessary resources for domestic firms in order for the latter to compete effectively in foreign markets. This could be accomplished by providing the necessary environment that makes it easier for domestic firms to acquire and internalize new technologies as well as facilitate cross-border alliances and partnerships that allow such transfers of know-how.

NOTE

1. In the following paragraphs, I provide descriptive results and charts without mentioning the statistical techniques used. This is done primarily due to the nature of the targeted audience of this volume. Detailed statistical tests were performed in terms of measurement as well as in testing trends and differences across various categories.

REFERENCES

Abreau, M., D. Carneiro and R. Werneck (1996), 'Brazil: Widening the Scope for Balanced Growth', *World Development*, **24**(2), 241.

Amman, E. and W. Baer (2002), 'The Development of Brazil's Technology Capabilities in the Post War Period', *Latin American Business Review*, **3**(1), 1–29.

Aulakh, P.S. and M. Kotabe (2001), 'Building Competitive Advantage in World Markets: Lessons from Latin American Companies', *Global Focus*, **13**(2), 83–94.

Aulakh, P.S., M. Kotabe and H. Teegen (2000), 'Export Strategies and Performance of Firms from Emerging Economies: Evidence from Brazil, Chile and Mexico', *Academy of Management Journal*, **43**(3), 342–61.

Cavusgil, S.T. and S. Zou (1994), 'Marketing Strategy–Performance Relationship: An Investigation of the Empirical Link in Export Market Ventures', *Journal of Marketing*, **58**(1), 1–21.

Christensen, C.H., A. Rocha and R.K Gertner (1987), 'An Empirical Investigation of the Factors Influencing Exporting Success of Brazilian Firms', *Journal of International Business Studies*, Fall, 61–77.

Dominguez, L.V., P.B. Rose and C.G. Sequeira (1993), 'Environmental and Managerial Factors in Export-led Development: An Exploratory Test of Porter's Competitive Advantage of Nations', *Journal of Macromarketing*, **13**(2), 5–22.

Dominguez, L.V. and C.G. Sequeira (1993), 'Determinants of LDC Exporters' Performance: A Cross-national Study', *Journal of International Business Studies*, **24**(1), 19–40.

Garten, J.E. (1997), *The Big Ten: The Big Emerging Markets and how They Will Change our Lives*, New York: Basic Books.

Gauvea, R. (2004), 'Brazil: A Strategic Approach', *Thunderbird International Business Review*, **46**(2), 165–74.

Geringer, J.M., P.W. Beamish and R.C. daCosta (1989), 'Diversification Strategy and Internationalization: Implications for MNE Performance', *Strategic Management Journal*, **10**, 109–19.

Goldstein, A. (1999), 'Brazilian Privatization in International Perspective', *Industrial and Corporate Change*, **8**(4), 673–711.

Gomez, H. (1997), 'The Globalization of Business in Latin America', *International Executive*, March–April, 225–54.

Hagedoorn, J. (1993), 'Understanding the Rationale of Strategic Technology Partnering: Interorganizational Modes of Cooperation and Sectoral Differences', *Strategic Management Journal*, **14**(5), 371–86.

Hamel, G. (1991), 'Competition for Competence and Inter-Partner Learning within International Strategic Alliances', *Strategic Management Journal*, Summer, 83–104.

Hitt, M.A., R.E. Hoskisson and H. Kim (1997), 'International Diversification: Effects on Innovation and Firm Performance in Product-diversified Firms', *Academy of Management Journal*, **40**(4), 767–98.

Hitt, M.A., R.D. Ireland and R.E. Hoskisson (1997), *Strategic Management: Competitiveness and Globalization*. St Paul: South-Western College Publication.

Johanson, J. and J.E. Vahlne (1977), 'The Internationalization Process of the Firm: Managerial Behavior, Agency Costs, and Ownership Structure', *Journal of International Business Studies*, **8**, 23–32.

Kim, L. and Y. Lim (1988), 'Environment, Generic Strategies, and Performance in a Rapidly Developing Country: A Taxonomic Approach', *Academy of Management Journal*, **31**(4), 802–27.

Kim, W.C., P. Hwang and W.P. Burgers (1989), 'Global Diversification Strategy and Corporate Profit Performance', *Strategic Management Journal*, **10**, 45–57.

Kogut, B. and U. Zander (1993), 'Knowledge of the Firm and the Evolutionary Theory of the Multinational Corporation', *Journal of International Business Studies*, **24**, 625–45.

Kotabe, M., H. Teegen, P.S. Aulakh, M. Arruda, R.J. Santillan-Salgado and W. Greene (2000), 'Strategic Alliances in Emerging Latin America: A View from Brazilian, Chilean, and Mexican Companies', *Journal of World Business*, **35**(2), 114–32.

Kotler, P., S. Jatusripitak and S. Maesincee (1997), *The Marketing of Nations: A Strategic Approach to Building National Wealth*. New York: Free Press.

Madsen, T.K. (1987), 'Successful Export Marketing Management. Some Empirical Evidence', *International Marketing Review*, **6**(4), 41–57.

Otani, I. and D. Villanueva, (1990), 'Long-term Growth in Developing Countries and its Determinants: An Empirical Analysis', *World Development*, **18**(6), 769–83.

Porter, M.E. (1980), *Competitive Strategy: Techniques for Analyzing Industries and Competitors*, New York: Free Press.

Porter, M.E. (1986), *Competition in global industries*. Boston, MA: Harvard Business School Press.

Porter, M.E. (1990), *The Competitive Advantage of Nations*. New York: Free Press.

Procianoy, J.L. and J. Sabrino, (2001), 'Does Privatization of State Companies Improve their Performance', *Latin American Business Review*, **2**, 5–36.

Singer, H.W. and P. Gray (1988), 'Trade Policy and Growth in Developing Countries: Some New Data', *World Development*, **16**(2), 1271–94.

Tallman, S. and J. Li (1996), 'Effects of International Diversity and Product Diversity on the Performance of Multinational Firms', *Academy of Management Journal*, **39**, 179–96.

Thomas, V., A. Dhareshwar, R.E. Lopez, Y. Wang, N. Kishor, M. Dailimi and D. Kaufmann (2000), *The Quality of Growth*, Washington, DC: World Bank.

Vernon-Wortzel, H. and L.H. Wortzel (1988), 'Globalizing Strategies for Multinationals from Developing Countries', *Columbia Journal of World Business*, Spring, 27–35.

World Bank Group (2005), 'Country Reports: Brazil', www.worldbank.org.

Wortzel, L.H. and H. Vernon-Wortzel (1981), 'Export Marketing Strategies for NIC and LDC-based Firms', *Columbia Journal of World Business*, **16**(Spring), 51–9.

5. Corporate governance and business strategies in Russia

Igor Filatotchev

INTRODUCTION

Russia stands at an important crossroads in its path of economic and institutional transformation, and the transition from central planning to a market economy is proving to be a long and difficult process. Although the Russian economy has emerged from the unprecedented economic collapse and social distress of the early transition years with rapid growth,[1] progress with changes in institutional and business environments continues to be slow (Peng et al., 2003). For example, while appropriate legislation has been enacted, national and international government agencies continue to debate the implementation of effective corporate governance mechanisms that will deliver managerial accountability and accompanying increases in enterprise efficiency. A key aspect of these deliberations for private and privatized enterprises concerns the reconciliation of the need to enhance efficiency with the interests of enterprise stakeholders, including foreign investors, in an environment where legal enforcement is problematical (Aukutsionek et al., 1998).

Open capital markets based on the Anglo-American model, nominally at least, formed a major plank of the government's market reform programs designed to increase enterprise efficiency. However, a rather different outcome has evolved. Mass voucher privatization in the manufacturing sector during 1991–94 resulted in widespread equity ownership by management and employees as two of the main groups of stakeholders in enterprises. Subsequently, however, the 'loans-for-shares' scheme resulted in the transfer of ownership of some of the largest, most important companies to a few well-placed Russian financial institutions and individuals, promoting the development of integrated financial-industrial groups (FIGs) comprising large diversified holding companies focused on banks (Filatotchev et al., 2000).

Some FIGs disappeared after 1998, however, and the most recent trends in the Russian economy are associated with the rapid development of non-bank holding companies and the role of the state. In the natural resources sector in particular, holding companies such as Sibneft, Tyumen Oil Company (TNK) and Alfa Group are fixing the borders of their empires through intra-holding consolidations, mergers and share swaps. These holding companies have two common features: ownership is concentrated, and outside shareholders – at different stages and to various degrees – have suffered equity dilution. In addition, many industries in Russia have also experienced rapid development of holdings by trading companies and so on. Some authors argue that these variations on the theme of the holding company provide a form of industrial organization that may create a private, internal capital market through developing long-term relations between other members of the group in which banks play an important role (Perotti and Gelfer, 2001). The ability of the holding company to capture the benefits from control ensures a steady supply of financing (Modigliani and Perotti, 1997). However, this ownership redistribution has not been accompanied by the expected firm-level restructuring and performance improvement. A growing number of studies based on detailed surveys of large numbers of enterprises and outside investors in Russia have indicated that the process of post-privatization restructuring is not speedy, and nor is there strong evidence of improving enterprise performance (see, for example, Filatotchev et al., 1996, 2000, 2001a, for a discussion).

In this environment, although privatization was initially aimed at removing its influence, the state as stakeholder increasingly plays a role as a counterbalance to dominant insider shareholders. Recent legal challenges and tax claims against the largest businesses in Russia, such as Yukos and TNK-BP, indicate that the Russian government has toughened its stance on private and, more specifically, foreign ownership of companies, in particular in the natural resources sector. It has also placed a cap on overseas participation in some strategic projects due to be auctioned in 2005–2006 (*Financial Times*, 13 April 2005). The involvement of the state in business activities in Russia implies the creation of some form of relational network governance in contrast to pure US- or UK-style market (or 'shareholder') governance, where share price and the threat of hostile takeovers represent the main channels of managerial discipline by shareholders (Noteboom, 1999).

While there has been examination of the role of managers and outsider institutional investors in corporate governance (Earle et al., 1996; Rapaczynski, 1996) and strategic aspects of business groups (Perotti and Gelfer, 2001; Pappe and Galukhina, 2005), an integrated analysis of governance and strategy trends in different sectors of the Russian economy has been less extensive. This chapter, therefore, aims to address these conceptual and empirical gaps by focusing on corporate governance characteristics and business strategies in three main segments of the Russian corporate sector: enterprises that have emerged from the mass privatization of 1992–6, business groups and state-controlled conglomerates. The first section concentrates on a background of the post-privatization evolution of Russian companies. The second section analyses emerging governance patterns and restructuring strategies of firms that have been divested by the state through insider buy-outs and 'voucher' privatization. The third section considers the governance and strategy aspects of integrated FIGs, followed by a fourth section that is focused on the role of the state in running some of the largest businesses in Russia. Finally, some conclusions are drawn regarding the scope and implications of the government's development of the corporate governance regime.

POST-PRIVATIZATION DEVELOPMENT OF THE RUSSIAN INDUSTRY 1992–2000

An important feature of the Russian program of economic reforms, especially in its earlier stages, was the aim of rapid transfer of public sector assets to private ownership. Privatization of state assets by management and workers was a major aspect of this program (Boycko et al., 1995). This process helped to achieve the crucial political aim of securing the move away from central planning. It was anticipated that governance mechanisms would evolve over time to resemble those observed in developed market systems, especially Anglo-American economies.

In Russia, management and workers could obtain equity stakes in the businesses in which they were employed in a number of ways. The leasing legislation of 1989 enabled enterprise assets to be leased by insiders, with or without the option to buy (Filatotchev et al., 1996). The privatization program of 1992 issued vouchers to all Russian adults, who could then exchange them for enterprise stock. Under this 'give-away' approach, insiders could acquire enterprises in one of three ways. Under variant 1, employees obtained 25 percent of the stock in an enterprise using their vouchers, plus a further 10 percent purchased at a discount. The second privatization variant enabled employees to obtain 51 percent ownership using their vouchers. The third variant provided for insiders to acquire 20 percent of the equity at face value if they agreed to maintain output and a further 20 percent stake at a discount. Finally, insiders could make direct purchases of enterprises outside the formal voucher privatization program. In addition, buy-outs have also been widely used for the privatization of large numbers of small and medium-sized enterprises including shops (Barberis et al., 1996).

Voucher privatization was followed by the 'loans-for-shares' scheme that allowed a number of well-connected businessmen and politicians to acquire valuable assets of formerly state-owned enterprises at a substantial discount to their economic value (see Filatotchev et al. 2001a, for an extensive discussion). This redistribution and divestment of state assets gave impetus to the rapid development of holding companies controlled by powerful oligarchs. A particularly characteristic example of this trend is the oil and gas industry in Russia, which is dominated by holding companies such as Sibneft, Tyumen Oil Company (TNK) and LUKOil. These companies are fixing the borders of their empires through intra-holding consolidations, mergers and single-share swaps. They are also characterized by concentrated ownership. In addition, many economic sectors in Russia have also experienced a rapid development of integrated financial-industrial groups (FIGs) such as Severstal Group, Alfa Group and Interros. These groups represent large diversified holding companies owned by banks and trading companies, and sometimes they become simply a vehicle for creating pyramidal ownership structures. La Porta et al. (2000) suggest that these structures can be used by controlling shareholders to make existing shareholders pay the costs, but not share all the benefits, of restructuring of existing assets as well as the development of new ventures.

A more recent trend in the Russian corporate sector is associated with the consolidation of state control over the largest firms in Russia, and increasing involvement of state bureaucracy in firm-level governance and business strategy. The traditional roles of the state in the stakeholder model are external to the firm's governance system (Wright et al., 2003). The state usually 'voices' its governance functions indirectly, by setting the 'rules of the game'. These rules include the protection of minority shareholders, approval of regulatory and self-regulatory standards, and defining principles of corporate social responsibility. However, the state in Russia may also be a primary stakeholder and a direct shareholder in an enterprise. This is most clearly seen in the case of state-owned conglomerates such as Gazprom, the world's largest producer of natural gas, and the oil company Rosneft.

As a result of these economic and political trends, the Russian corporate sector today exhibits a high degree of heterogeneity in terms of organizational structures, business strategies and corporate governance. Bearing in mind these general observations, it may be suggested that actual corporate governance and strategy in Russia may have a dual nature depending on the sector, with some overlaps between shareholder- and stakeholder-based models.

On the one hand, the 200-plus natural resource-based companies (for example firms in metals, timber, oil and gas) quoted on the Russian Trading System (RTS) come closest to shareholder-based governance in that there is a market in their shares so that shareholders can exert exit-based governance. These quoted companies are relatively resource-rich and do not face immediate high investment demands that they cannot finance from plow-back or borrowing. Similarly, most of these firms were not subject to mass privatization, so employee influence on strategic decisions is also low (Wright et al., 2003). This sector is expanding, but investment finance is relatively easy to obtain, since natural resources can themselves be used as collateral. Trading volumes in these shares are low, and outside shareholders' rights are seriously under-protected. Yet, there is at least some prospect that managers' decisions will be ultimately influenced by share price movements. However, in Russia the weak enforcement of laws and taxes threatens this governance regime.

Elsewhere, however, most 'non-strategic' manufacturing firms privatized through the mass voucher program do not have share quotations and are characterized by insider ownership (Filatotchev et al., 2000). Shareholder influence here is mainly felt from managers and other employees, though major exceptions are provided by high-tech companies previously part of the Military Industrial Complex (MIC), where the state (another relational stakeholder) still retains a large degree of control in firms that in many cases still have not been privatized. The majority of manufacturing firms in Russia are in desperate need of long-term investment. These mass-privatized enterprises are generally complex in organizational terms, comprising enormous vertical hierarchies, and, in the case of certain 'strategic' former MIC-sector firms, can also be described as technologically complex. Since most of the firms privatized through voucher schemes are not quoted, there is no reliable market information on the potential value of their assets, performance and so on. Therefore their operations are opaque and costly to monitor for unrelated outside investors. These firms also rely on outdated technology designed for mass production within the realms of a centrally planned economy, and their restructuring and modernization requires both process and product innovation. Finally, although most of these firms are in a contraction phase of their life cycle, their rapid turnaround requires large new investments (see above).

With this background of corporate developments in Russia, we turn now to the evidence on actual corporate governance configurations and business strategies in the major parts of the Russian corporate landscape.

MASS PRIVATIZATION IN RUSSIAN INDUSTRY: GOVERNANCE AND STRATEGY OUTCOMES

This section provides empirical evidence on the corporate governance and business strategies of privatized, unquoted Russian industrial firms. These firms were privatized at the early stages of economic reforms, and their assets have been divested using various forms of employee and management buy-outs and voucher schemes.

Governance

Using a number of firm-level surveys, Table 5.1 shows the extent, and evolution, of stakeholders' share ownership in these firms. Despite some methodological differences between studies (Estrin and Wright, 1999), it is clear that typically, insiders are majority owners in Russian privatized enterprises, with managers owning around a fifth of shares. Comparing our evidence relating to ownership in 1997 with earlier studies, indications are that insider ownership in Russia is falling over time, albeit slowly. Among insiders there is a marked shift in equity-holding from employees to managers. This decline seems to have continued subsequently (Table 5.1).

In discussing trends in employee ownership it is important to recognize the difference between ownership and control. Evidence from the early stages of the privatization program suggests that although employees may have significant equity stakes, their involvement in boards of directors and other control mechanisms is generally very low (Filatotchev et al., 1996).

However, a few longitudinal firm-level studies of firms in Russia indicate that there have been substantial changes in their ownership structure after privatization. Table 5.2 provides evidence on the governance dynamics of unquoted industrial firms assembled by Russian Economic Barometer, a research center conducting business surveys since 1991 using a network of respondents from different industries and regions. As Table 5.2 clearly indicates, in 2003 insiders remained the largest group of shareholders with a combined stake of 46.6 percent of the total stock. However, as a result of post-privatization redistribution of ownership titles, managers have emerged as the largest shareholders. At the same time, outside shareholdings have increased as well, and in 2003 the equity stake held by outside owners was approximately equal to that of insiders (44%).

Dolgopyatova (2005) provides survey evidence indicating that insiders retain their control over the firm's board (Table 5.3). Firms with employee board representatives were significantly more likely to be larger and to be employee-owned. Managers represent the second-largest group of board members. Employee representation on boards seems to have increased over

Table 5.1 *Equity ownership by stakeholders in privatized unquoted Russian firms, 1993–99: a comparison of empirical studies (% share of ownership)*

Owners	Earle et al.[1] (1994)	Buck et al.[2] (1994)	Blasi et al.[3] (1996)	Jones[4] (1996)	Wright et al.[5] (1996)	Aukutsionek et al.[6] (1997)	Filatotchev et al.[7] (1999)	Dolgopyatova[8] (1999)
Insiders	69	66	58	59	59	52	46	42
Managers	21	19	18	13	12	15	14	11
Employees	48	47	40	46	47	37	32	31
Outsiders	20	14	32	27	31	39	47	50
Large	–	11	26	15	23	25	28	30
Small	–	3	6	12	8	14	19	20
State	11	20	9	14	10	7	7	8
Sample (no. of firms)	214	171	357	111	314	139	150	200

Notes: Years in brackets refer to date of survey, share ownership represented as percentage held by each group of shareholders. Large outside shareholders refer to institutional and corporate investors, small outside shareholders are individuals.

Sources:
1. Earle et al. (1996).
2. Buck et al. (1996). Includes enterprises privatized through State Privatization Program and lease buy-outs.
3. Blasi et al. (1997). Figures do not sum to 100 in original due to rounding errors and missing data. Includes enterprises privatized through State Privatization Program.
4. Jones (1998).
5. Wright et al. (2003). Includes enterprises privatized through State Privatization Program and lease buy-outs.
6. Aukutsionek et al. (1998).
7. Filatotchev et al. (2001b).
8. Dolgopyatova (2000).

Market opportunity

*Table 5.2   Ownership structure of enterprises in REB Annual Surveys,
1995–2003 (average shareholdings, %)*

Categories of shareholders	1995	1997	1999	2001	2003
Insiders, total	54.8	52.1	46.2	48.2	46.6
Managers	11.2	15.1	14.7	21.0	25.6
Workers	43.6	37.0	31.5	27.2	21.0
Outsiders, total	35.2	38.8	42.4	39.7	44.0
Non-financial outsiders	25.9	28.5	32.0	32.4	34.4
Private individuals	10.9	13.9	18.5	21.1	20.1
Other enterprises	15.0	14.6	13.5	11.3	14.3
Financial outsiders, (banks, investment funds, holding companies etc)	9.3	10.3	10.4	7.3	9.5
State	9.1	7.4	7.1	7.9	4.5
Other and non-identified shareholders	0.9	1.7	4.3	4.2	5.0
Grand total	100	100	100	100	100
Number of enterprises	136	135	156	154	102

Source: Aukutsionek et al. (2004).

the 1998–2001 period (Table 5.3). Corresponding increases in representation were most notable in respect of outside private individuals. The proportion of board seats held by management and Russian corporations is similar across the surveys. Board representation by the state, banks and foreign investors remained unchanged at a low level.

The survey findings provided by Wright et al. (2003) indicate that banks were members of executive boards in 5.4 percent of cases and members of a supervisory board in 7.1 percent of cases. Investment funds, private individuals from outside the company, industrial organizations and the state all had greater degrees of involvement on supervisory and executive boards than did the banks.

Banks were found to have very low influence on the appointment of directors, on restricting operational and strategic decisions of managers, and on the setting of directors' remuneration. Their main channels of influence were reported to be, in declining order of importance, telephone contacts, the review of accounts of the enterprise on a regular basis, the monitoring of debt covenants, visits to the company and supervisory board representation (Table 5.4). Enterprises report apparently active monitoring by banks of situations where interest and capital repayments have not been

Table 5.3   *Board representation in unquoted manufacturing firms in Russia (various enterprise surveys)*

	% of board seats		
	HSE-1 (1998)	BEA (1999)	HSE-2 (2001)
Insiders, including:	57.4	68.8	56.2
Managers	38.0	39.2	35.2
Employees	19.4	29.7	20.9
State, including:	8.9	5.4	6.6
Federal level	3.2	2.7	2.5
Regional and local level	5.7	2.7	4.1
Outside shareholders, including:	33.7	25.8	37.2
Russian non-financial enterprises	15.0	10.8	13.0
Russian banks, investment companies, funds	11.2	4.1	1.2
Foreign shareholders	2.1	1.4	–
Others (mainly individuals)	5.4	9.5	23.0
Average number of board seats	*7.9*	*7.4*	*6.8*

Notes:
HSE-1 (1998) – Higher School of Economics survey of 267 privatized firms in 1998
HSE-2 (2001) – Higher School of Economics survey of 307 privatized firms in 2001
BEA (1999) – Bureau of Economic Analysis survey of 275 privatized firms in 1999

Source: Dolgopyatova (2005).

Table 5.4   *Channels of bank influence in unquoted manufacturing firms*

Channel of influence	Mean score (standard deviation)
Representation on supervisory board	1.6 (1.7)
Review of accounts on a regular basis	3.6 (2.6)
Regular visits to the company	2.3 (2.1)
Telephone contacts	4.4 (2.5)
Monitoring of debt covenants	3.0 (2.4)

Source: Wright et al. (2003). Scores based on scale 1 through 7 where 1 = low importance to 7 = high importance. Responses based on 105 privatized enterprises surveyed in 1997 and 1998.

met. The most common form of action is to engage in personal discussion to resolve the problem. However, in a significant percentage of cases banks have either rescheduled loans or refused to grant new loans.

Between the two years covered by the survey there is some indication of a hardening of the approach adopted by the banks in terms of a shift from discussions or ignoring the problem towards refusing to give new loans and the taking of legal action. These findings are consistent with evidence from detailed interviews with banks reported in Wright et al. (1998). Banks used relationships to support formal monitoring mechanisms, because of the difficulties in obtaining reliable information in accounting reports even where this was specified in loan agreements. Whether or not there was a representative on the board of the company, good contacts with the company through visits and telephone calls were important in verifying information and the use of credits. Despite these relationships, some of the banks reported using firms' financial difficulties as a means of putting pressure on companies to sell shares to them, in order that the banks can obtain controlling interests. Bank ownership remains generally low but there are indications that in a minority of cases banks have become the largest single shareholder in the firm (Filatotchev et al., 2001a).

Although banks were making some progress in Russia in monitoring of clients, the turmoil of late 1998 undermined their ability to intervene. Many banks became technically insolvent and some lost their licenses, including banks such as Inkombank that were actively involved in monitoring enterprises (Wright et al., 1998). However, in the post-1998 period other banks are trying to impose more stringent control over managerial discretion. The hardening of budget constraints on enterprises may, in principle, both help the banks' financial position as well as place pressure on enterprises, but the feasibility of this option in the current environment is unclear.

Business Strategy

Survey evidence indicates that, contrary to expectations, employee ownership is not significantly related to a reduction in strategic restructuring actions (Buck et al., 1999). This may be either because the reduction in levels of employee ownership in the enterprises (see above) did not afford a significant degree of decision control in the face of acute business crisis, or because the effect of their control is neutral in retrenchment terms. Alternatively, Russian employees may fear that enterprise survival is threatened and that all jobs are threatened if no retrenchment occurs. The unresponsiveness of restructuring to employee ownership may also have been because of employees' apathy and social immobility (Bim, 1996), the give-away nature of the share distribution process (that is, low stakeholder legitimacy), restrictions on share sales that gave employees little incentive to act as shareholders, or because of the generally low level of employee representation on boards or strategic decision-making bodies (Filatotchev et al., 1996).

Productivity performance data suggest that no one ownership form has been consistently associated with higher productivity in Russia

(Wright et al., 2003), although in a study covering Russian firms over the period 1992 to 1997, Yudaeva et al. (2003) found that after controlling for selection bias, foreign-owned firms were approximately 2.7 times more productive in terms of total factor productivity than domestic ones. However, they noted that the productivity of foreign-owned firms was negatively affected by the slow progress of reforms in the regions where they operated. They failed to find evidence that either the size of the foreign ownership stake or the size of the foreign-owned firm was associated with performance differences. There was support for the importance of human capital as foreign firms working in regions with better-educated labor were more productive.

In terms of HRM strategies, Earle et al. (1996) found in Russia that wages were lowest in worker-owned enterprises. A survey of Russian enterprises by the International Labor Organization (ILO), conducted in 2000 and analysed by the present author and his colleagues shows that there is no significant association between employee ownership and wages for managers, skilled and unskilled workers. Bonuses for managers and skilled workers were, however, found to be significantly higher when employee ownership was high, and similarly for two categories of workers' benefits. Buck et al. (2003) also showed that higher spending on social benefits for employees (either on the old Soviet model of welfare provision or on patterns proposed by new, high-commitment human resource management) was associated with improved firm performance. Cost-cutting HRM strategies were found to have a consistently negative influence on performance in the context of the former Soviet Union (FSU).

In terms of strategic restructuring, Filatotchev et al. (2000) in a study of manufacturing firms found that managerial ownership was associated with a reluctance to take necessary (employment and capital) downsizing actions. Employee-dominated firms were significantly less likely to involve managerial turnover than outsider-dominated firms, but significantly more likely to do so than manager-dominated firms (Filatotchev et al., 1999). Although most of these firms are in a contraction phase of their life cycle, their rapid turnaround requires large new investments (see above). However, Dolgopyatova (2005) provides the enterprise-level survey evidence indicating that internally generated resources remain the main source of investment funding amounting to over 80 percent of total investment expenditures. The second-largest source of investment funds is the state budget (see Table 5.5).

On one hand, a stakeholder-based industrial system combined with conflict between firms and a distant state bureaucracy does not augur well for corporate restructuring. On the other hand, evidence from recent joint venture discussions, between General Motors and AvtoVAZ near Tolyatti

Table 5.5 Sources of investment funds in privatized companies

Investment sources	% of total investments		
	HSE-1 1998	BEA 1999	HSE-2 2001
Own sources of investment	86.8	88.9	80.5
Bank credits	2.6	5.8	10.9
Federal budget	4.6	0.2	0.3
Regional and local budgets		0.7	1.4
Russian trade partners	3.6	3.5	3.6
Other Russian external investors	1.4		2.2
Direct foreign investments	1.0	0.0	0.8
Securities market (shares, bonds)	...	0.004	0.3
Other sources	–	0.9	–

Notes:
HSE-1 (1998) – Higher School of Economics survey of 267 privatized firms in 1998
HSE-2 (2001) – Higher School of Economics survey of 307 privatized firms in 2001
BEA (1999) – Bureau of Economic Analysis survey of 275 privatized firms in 1999

Source: Dolgopyatova (2005).

and between Fiat and GAZ in Nizhny Novgorod (now abandoned), for example, suggests that conditions in large privatized manufacturing firms have now become so bad, despite the prosperity of the primary sector, that managers and employees are discarding some of their uncertainty avoidance in favor of a positive attitude towards outside (and foreign) strategic investors.

Finally, in terms of internationalization strategies, Filatotchev et al. (2001b) extended Earle et al.'s (1996) finding that outsider-owned firms in Russia export significantly more than firms with other forms of ownership. They focused on exporting as a percentage of total sales as a key strategic outcome, since this exposes firms to the need for improved quality control. They showed that while ownership structure had an insignificant direct association with performance, governance did affect mediating strategies, and different strategies were in turn related to performance. For example, managerial ownership was positively related to a product strategy that focused on domestic rather than export markets, and to a strategy of product diversification through firm acquisition. In turn, these strategies were negatively associated with export performance. In each of these studies, between-country variations were insignificant. If confirmed elsewhere, these findings of managerial ownership apparently holding back necessary downsizing strategies and export-oriented strategies may have serious implications for conventional measures of performance.

Interestingly, the influence of outsiders through board representation may have as important impact as equity ownership on some aspects of restructuring in Russia (Buck et al., 2000). Despite majority managerial control, outside board representation in enterprises tended to be positively associated with presence of a foreign partner and export-oriented product development (Filatotchev et al., 2001b). Increases in outside control were negatively associated with external acquisitions and positively associated with managerial turnover.

LISTED ENTERPRISES AND BUSINESS GROUPS

At the other end of the Russian corporate spectrum are large industrial conglomerates whose shares are often listed on the Russian stock exchanges and abroad. Most of them have developed operations in the key sectors of the Russian economy, such as energy, natural resources and telecommunications. For example, shares in oil and gas companies account for 63 percent of the Russian Trading System (RTS) capitalization (of which 21 percent is accounted for by Gazprom alone), followed by power (14 percent), telecoms (12 percent) and metals (7 percent) conglomerates. Only three manufacturing stocks are traded beyond an insignificant level (GAZ, KamAZ and Red October Confectionery).

Another very important characteristic of this corporate sector is the rapid development of integrated financial-industrial groups that are consolidating their position in different sectors of the Russian economy. Table 5.6 provides information on sector activities and companies under the control of the largest business groups in Russia. As this table clearly indicates, these groups are characterized by a high degree of horizontal and vertical integration and diversification. As a rule, there is a bank or financial corporation at the centre of these holding structures.

Studies on emerging economies have uncovered important contextual factors that may contribute to the formation of diversified business groups, such as the development of market institutions, (high) levels of government involvement, industry structures, ownership patterns and enforcement of business laws (La Porta et al., 1998). For instance, business groups have become intermediaries and organizational arrangements that fill 'institutional voids' in some emerging economies. These groups have also been found to play an important role in firm restructuring in some developing countries (Kim and Hoskisson, 1996). It may be expected that in combination with the prominent role for networks that is encouraged by cultural

Table 5.6　Leading financial industrial groups in Russia

FIG	Divisions/members	Economic sectors
Gazprom	• JSC Gazprom • Sibur • Salavatnefteorgsintez • Gazprombank	• Gas and oil • Refining and petrochemicals • Finance and banking
LUKOil	• LUKOil Corporation • LUKOil Neftekhim • Investment finance house, Kapital • Finance corporation, Uralsib	• Oil • Refining and petrochemicals • Finance and banking
Alfa	• TNK-BP • Vympelcom • Megaphon • Golden Telecom • Trade house, Perekrestok • STS-Media • Alfa Bank	• Telecoms • Gas and oil • Media • Retailing • Finance and banking
Interros	• Norilsk Nikel • Agros • Siloviye Mashiny • Prof-Media • RosBank	• Metals • Food and agriculture • Heavy engineering • Media • Finance and banking
Base Element	• Russian Aluminium • RusPromAvto • Continental Management • Soyuz Bank • Ingosstrakh	• Metals • Transport • Car manufacturing • Banking and insurance

Source:　Pappe and Galukhina (2005).

aspects associated with local collectivism in Russia, these institutions will have governance and strategic characteristics similar to industrial groups elsewhere.

Corporate Governance

A study of the 21 largest listed Russian firms by Black (2001), using 1999 data, identifies a highly significant correlation between an index of corporate governance risk factors and market value. The index of corporate governance used included the provision of pre-emptive rights in corporate charters, representation of minority shareholders on boards of directors, and presence of a controlling shareholder. He notes large variations in the quality of corporate governance indices between companies.

Table 5.7 provides ownership and board structure data for the 12 largest quoted firms in the oil, gas and metallurgy sectors. In terms of ownership structure, the state retains a stake in only five companies, but it is relatively large (31.4 percent per company on average). On the other hand, insider ownership is on average relatively small, accounting for only 8.9 percent of total equity on average. Half the 12 firms in the sample are free of insider ownership completely. However, a number of firms such as Gazprom, Magnitogorsk Metal and Severstal have a substantial shareholding by managers and employees.

These firms are differentiated from the majority of Russian companies by a substantial amount of shares that are in free float (26.2 percent on average), which brings them closer to the UK or US type of corporate governance. However, as Table 5.7 clearly shows, private large-block holders, such as outside wealthy individuals, industrial partners and holding companies, retain a considerable amount of shares, 51.8 percent on average. Therefore, the largest Russian firms have a mixed ownership structure, with minority shareholders co-existing with extremely concentrated private owners who retain their shares away from the stock market.

In terms of board characteristics, the largest Russian firms are moving closer to a conventional UK/US system of corporate governance. As Table 5.7 shows, the average board size is close to 11 members, with 65 percent of the directors being non-executives. However, as the last two columns clearly show, the majority of non-executive directors were appointed by the controlling shareholders, in particular large-block private owners, which makes the extent of their independence questionable.

These findings are supported by a recent survey of boards in the largest quoted Russian firms conducted under the auspices of the Russian Federal Securities Commission (RFSC, 2002). The RFSC sample included 56 companies with an average of 11 000 employees and an average number of shareholders of 16 000. In terms of industrial breakdown, 33 percent of the firms were from oil, gas and energy sectors, 30 percent from transport and telecommunications, and 10 percent from the metallurgy and mineral extraction sectors. These enterprises were located in 34 regions of Russia, and represented flagships of the regional and national economy. Average board size was nine, very close to the results reported in Table 5.6. According to this survey, the majority of firms were complying with 'good corporate governance' principles, with 70 percent of board members being

Table 5.7   Ownership structure and board characteristics of the largest listed enterprises in resource sectors in Russia, 2002

Company	Sector	Share ownership by type of investors				Board characteristics			
		State	Managers and employees	Large-block private investors	Minority shareholders	Total number of board directors	Number of non-executives	Number of directors appointed by large-block shareholders	Number of directors appointed by the State
Yukos	Oil	0.0	0.0	79.0	21.0	15	13	13	0
Udmurtneft	Oil	0.0	0.0	79.2	20.8	7	6	5	0
Tatneft	Oil	34.2	5.0	19.1	41.7	15	9	5	4
Surgutneftegaz	Oil & gas	0.0	0.0	67.0	33.0	9	1	1	0
Sibneft	Oil	0.0	0.5	87.5	12.0	9	4	2	0
Gazprom	Gas	38.4	31.0[a]	5.0	25.6	11	9	2	6
LUKOil	Oil	15.6	8.1	24.3	52.0	11	7	5	2
Sakhalineftegaz	Oil & gas	51.0	0.0	28.0	27.0	10	8	4	4
Purneftegas	Oil & gas	0.0	0.0	64.7	35.3	9	8	8	0
Norilsk Nickel	Metals	0.0	3.7	81.1	15.2	9	8	8	0
Magnitogorsk Steel	Metals	18.0	42.8	21.8	19.0	10	4	2	2
Severstal	Metals	0.0	16.6	64.4	18.8	15	7	7	0
Sample average		13.1	8.9	51.8	26.2	10.8	7.0	5.2	1.5

Note: a Including share ownership of companies that are controlled by Gazprom management.

Source: Troika Dialog Research (2002) Corporate Governance: Risk Profiles of Russia's Largest Companies. Moscow, March 2002; the author's calculations.

non-executive directors. However, only 20 percent of directors were truly independent from the company according to Western governance criteria. Almost 70 percent of surveyed board directors considered their participation in the strategy development process as their main duty on behalf of shareholders. However, 62 percent of board members admitted that they do not use any formal procedures for evaluating the performance of top executives. Approximately 40 percent of directors are also board members in other companies, which indicates a relatively high density of board 'interlocks' in Russia.

To summarize, these findings indicate that the largest Russian firms are gradually moving towards a conventional US/UK model of governance. Important differences still remain, notably disproportionately large ownership by concentrated (dominant) shareholders and a relatively small number of truly independent directors. In this governance system, there is typically relatively low protection of minority investors and extensive expropriation of minority outside shareholders by controlling shareholders (La Porta et al., 2000). Hence, the primary agency problem is not the failure of professional managers to satisfy the objectives of diffuse shareholders, but the expropriation of minority shareholders by powerful stakeholders such as banks and insiders (Filatotchev et al., 2001a). In environments with weak legal protections it may be optimal to have more than one large blockholder. When control is dissipated among several large investors, a decision to expropriate minority shareholders requires the consent of a coalition of investors. This coalition might hold enough cash flow rights to choose to limit the expropriation of remaining shareholders and pay the profits as efficient dividends (Bennedsen and Wolfenzon, 2000). There is case study evidence that suggests coalitions of controlling shareholders in Russia may be an equilibrium response to a firm's operating characteristics and its legal and competitive environments (Filatotchev et al., 2001a).

Business Strategy

Case study evidence (for example Pappe and Galukhina, 2005) suggests that, to consolidate their competitive position on domestic and global markets, business groups in Russia are relying heavily on two major corporate strategies: horizontal diversification and vertical integration. As Table 5.6 clearly shows, groups in traditional, resource-based sectors are successfully diversifying into other fast-growing segments of the Russian economy, such as telecommunications, media and finance. This allows them to generate a stable cash flow that may compensate for a potential long-term deterioration of their traditional resource base. Another important strategic trend is rapid vertical integration accompanied by increasing concentration of capital. For example, most of the metallurgical industry in Russia is controlled by six large business groups, such as Evraz Holding, Severstal and Mechel. In addition to their steel-making capacity, these holding companies also include extracting divisions, transport and distribution systems. Similarly, FIG Base Element, in addition to its controlling stake in Russian Aluminum, has secured control over RusPromAvto which, in turn, controls car-maker GAZ and a number of bus manufacturers, large consumers of aluminum (Pappe and Galukhina, 2005).

These development and diversification strategies require financial resources that are beyond the internal capacities of FIGs. In terms of financing strategy, they are increasingly relying on external sources of funding. We indicated above that business groups account for the lion's share of capitalization of the Russian capital markets, such as RTS. In addition, beyond the RTS, 57 Russian firms had American Depository Receipts (ADRs) in February 2003, and this suggests more share liquidity and openness via the NYSE (New York Stock Exchange). Foreign strategic partners represent another important source of investment finance. For example, Conoco Phillips has acquired 10 percent equity stake in LUKOil, and both companies reached an investment agreement to develop the vast Timano-Pechorsky oil field. EADS has obtained the Russian government's permission to acquire 10 percent of shares of aviation corporation Irkut. Both partners intend to develop a number of joint investment projects, including the production of components for Airbus planes (Pappe and Galukhina, 2005).

In terms of internationalization strategies, Russian FIGs are actively looking outside Russia in search of investment opportunities. More specifically, large companies in the metallurgical sector have made a number of upstream and downstream strategic acquisitions abroad, including Norilsk Nickel's acquisitions of Gold Fields (South Africa) and Stillwater (USA). Russian Aluminium has purchased 20 percent of shares in Queensland Alumina (Australia) which should make up for its shrinking access to raw materials in Russia. Finally, Russian business groups have started expansion in the 'near abroad', for example in the former Soviet Republics. For example, Russian telecoms giants have acquired controlling stakes in KaR-Tel (Kazakhstan) and UzdunOrbita (Uzbekistan).

STATE-CONTROLLED CONGLOMERATES

A more recent trend in the Russian corporate sector is associated with the consolidation of state control over the largest firms in Russia and an increasing involvement of state bureaucracy in firm-level governance and business strategy. This is most clearly seen in the case of a state-owned enterprise, but it needs to be recognized that even in privatized enterprises the state may have a significant residual stake.

Corporate Governance

Besides its role in setting the framework within which enterprises operate, the state may have an important role as a significant shareholder in ensuring enhanced outsider involvement in preventing entrenchment behaviors by management. This may be especially important in the context of the prevailing corporate governance 'vacuum' in Russia.

So far, the state has not played a widespread active role in constraining managerial discretion in privatized Russian firms. For example, there is no evidence that conditions attached to the 'loans-for-shares' deals have ever been enforced. However, there are the first signs that the state is trying to get involved more proactively in Russian firms. Despite the fall in state ownership and board representation noted above, the state authorities remain one of the most important stakeholders in Russian privatized companies. The state still holds substantial proportions of company equity in the MIC and primary and telecommunications sectors. For example, in the largest firm in Russia, Gazprom, the state still owns 38.4 percent of total voting shares, whereas foreign investors own 5.5 percent of shares (Wright et al., 2003). It is clear that the state remains the largest single shareholder in the firm. Direct state interference in the corporate governance of Gazprom enhanced shareholder salience by bringing more effective shareholder power. At Gazprom's 2001 AGM, the state representatives obtained 6 of the 11 seats on the company's board of directors, allowing a simple board majority to replace top managers at any time rather than the previous requirements for unanimity. Prior to this at the 2000 AGM, Dmitri Medvedev, a senior government adviser, had been appointed company president, while a month before the 2001 AGM, the CEO was replaced by Alexei Miller, a personal aide of Russian President Putin.

In addition, enterprise survey data show that enterprise liabilities to the state in terms of deferred payments of taxes, national insurance contributions and so on were constantly increasing during the 1995–2005 period (Dolgopyatova, 2005). At the same time, firms were heavily reliant on the state for financial support, as clearly indicated by survey results in Table 5.5.

However, familiar questions arise concerning the role of state bureaucrats and their potential for collusion with management. A more pessimistic view would suggest that the wheel of reform is coming full circle back to unwelcome state interference. On the other hand, a more optimistic interpretation is that state involvement may be a transitory mechanism for counterbalancing undesirable behavior by managers in an environment where enforcement of governance legislation is presently problematic.

As a direct shareholder, the state may have a dual role in the enterprise (Pedersen and Thomsen, 1997). While the state has to ensure that the firm fulfils its financial obligations to society in terms of corporate taxation and other payments from its profits (Rapaczynski, 1996), the Russian state's direct (and sometimes considerable) ownership stakes in firms may provide an opportunity to exercise 'voice' directly through involvement in the firm's corporate governance mechanism. In its role as a shareholder, the state may seek to maximize its income as the sum of dividends and capital gains, expressed as a rate of return on the funds invested, and to invest funds according to prospects for rates of return, not soft loans with poor prospects. However, the objectives of the state as shareholder may be compromised by the other roles of politicians and the state (Shleifer and Vishny, 1997). First, the state may seek to collect high levels of corporate taxation from the firm (Rapaczynski, 1996). In this case, the state could opt for strategies that raise profits and hence tax payments. Second, and perhaps more importantly in a transition context, the state and politicians may wish to promote the utility of their various groups of supporters. These could include employees of the firm, who seek job preservation and creation within the firm, friends and cronies, who have similar objectives to employees but for themselves, and customers of the firm, who may benefit, for example, as low-income families enjoying subsidized product prices. In the short run, state preference to maintain employment may mean that profits are diverted to low-return projects, grants or soft loans (Shleifer and Vishny, 1997). The promotion of the interests of each of these groups may involve reduced long-run performance as the firm must cope with higher manning levels, managers placed by the state who may not be the best for the job, and lower revenues. Of course, these actions may threaten the state's objectives as shareholder through, for example, soft loans or grants to the firm. From this perspective, the gains from economies in information collection by the state as shareholder must be balanced against the potential costs for other state roles. The state may want to impede takeover in a firm where it has some voice, either through a golden share or through direct board representation. Unless the objective is to protect an infant industry to enable it to achieve economies of scale, impeding takeovers is likely to delay restructuring and lower long-run profitability.

Business Strategy

So far, evidence of strategic outcomes of state involvement in corporate governance of the largest Russian firms is rather controversial. The largest state-controlled holding, Gazprom, is rapidly consolidating its position as one of the world's leading companies in natural resources and energy sectors. However, this process is underpinned not only by market-based strategies but also by direct state interference in the energy sector. For example, the Russian government decided in 2004 to merge Gazprom with Rosneft, another state-controlled holding, to create the largest integrated oil and gas company in the country. Gazprom has also acquired assets of Sibur that was effectively re-nationalized under pressure from the Russian authorities (Pappe and Galukhina, 2005). In addition, Gazprom has obtained control over 10.6 percent of shares in the largest power generator in Russia, United Electricity Systems, becoming as a result its second-largest shareholder after the state.

Gazprom is pursuing its acquisitive strategy against the backdrop of the authorities' continuous dismantling of the Yukos oil group and the sale of Yukos's main subsidiary, Yuganskneftegas. Despite President Putin's recent attempts to persuade businesses that the administrative assault on Yukos would not be repeated, Russia's bureaucrats have delivered another blow in form of a $1 billion extra tax demand for TNK-BP, the joint venture oil company (*Financial Times*, 13 April 2005).

In the financial sector, state-owned banks are also consolidating their positions through acquisitions and subsequent turnaround of distressed private banks and financial companies. For example, in July 2004 Vneshtorg Bank acquired private Guta Bank and Guta Insurance. However, Vneshtorg Bank also purchased a substantial shareholding in the financially sound Industrial-Construction Bank of St Petersburg.

These trends indicate not only that the state refuses to withdraw from Russian companies as a major shareholder, but that it is trying to consolidate its position in various sectors of the Russian economy. State holdings are pursuing rapid expansion through mergers and acquisitions, and this strategic development is supported by administrative attacks on major competitors. From the corporate governance perspective, state holdings have developed a unique governance mechanism that combines administrative control with the Western-style channels of shareholder influence.

DISCUSSION AND CONCLUSIONS

This chapter has focused on corporate governance and business strategies of Russian companies that represent various parts of the Russian corporate landscape. In terms of corporate governance, it focused on the role of employees, banks and the state as three main groups of stakeholders in Russia. Using secondary and survey data, each group was found to have various degrees of influence, even though employees have significant ownership stakes, especially in the unquoted sector.

With respect to employee stakeholders, it is evident that employee ownership in the US and UK and employee participation in Germany have offered significant efficiency gains as employees identify with their firms, offering internal flexibility and cooperation in return (Berndt, 1998; Blair et al., 2000). In Russia, any impact of employee share ownership has not been to reduce necessary employment downsizing, and in this sense some of the usual criticisms of industrial democracy are unfounded in this context, for example the suggestion that employee involvement leads to entrenchment. It must be remembered, however, that employees' board representation is weak and employee share ownership may overstate their influence.

Banks are another group of important stakeholders in Russian companies in general, and in FIGs in particular. Previous research (Baetege and Thiele, 1998; Baums, 1993; Franks and Mayer, 1997; Kim and Hoskisson, 1996; Prowse, 1990) indicates that bank ownership and control in Germany and Japan resulted in accelerated economic development but, after long periods of national crisis and weak governance, the contingency of economic recession has more recently highlighted the potential weaknesses of bank governance in disciplining managers and achieving necessary downsizing. These exigencies have become so severe that delayed restructuring is now taking place with rationalization of the six *keiretsu* groups in Japan into four new configurations, the emergence of leveraged buy-outs of parts of *keiretsu*, the acquisition of controlling stakes in major Japanese corporations by Western companies and pending sell-offs of industrial shares by banks in Germany.

If banks are to contribute to filling the governance void in Russian manufacturing firms, however, the state has a role to play in achieving improved governance of the banks themselves and in designing rules to compartmentalize and make transparent banking and investment operations within bank-led industrial groups (Abarbanell and Meyendorff, 1997; Meyendorff and Snyder, 1997).

Emerging as a potentially important, but so far neglected, stakeholder in Russia is the state. Some authors suggest that the state could provide an example of a 'model owner' and make sure that the firm complies with its own regulations and directives in a situation in Russia where, although appropriate legislation has been enacted, there are only weak enforcement mechanisms (Wright et al., 2003). As a significant shareholder, the state may be able to act as an insider to put pressure on management to undertake needed reforms. However, there are questions about the capacity of state bureaucrats to act as a model shareholder in terms of both their skills and the extent to which they are open to pressure to collude with management (and other stakeholders) and be passive regarding pressure to reform.

Further policy and research attention clearly needs to be focused on the role of the state following privatization in Russia. More generally, our analysis points to the need to recognize that it may be naive to take the view that the role of the state ends when enterprises are privatized. Further analysis is required concerning the extent to which the role of the state needs to be transitory or whether it has a more permanent function.

Finally, our arguments are consistent with those advanced in Western developed market economies that suggest a need for different governance systems in different sectoral environments (for example Mayer, 1994; Roe, 1997). This again emphasizes a role for the state, at least in the short term, to bolster the institutional framework to permit various forms of governance to function effectively. Hence, following La Porta et al. (1997) there is a need for the state to enforce shareholder protection for listed Russian firms mainly in the resource sector to bolster shareholder-based governance. The state also needs to enforce the protection of non-managerial stakeholders to enable stakeholder-based governance across the bulk of the privatized unquoted manufacturing sector. However, our evidence also suggests that there may be negative effects of direct state involvement in management of enterprises in terms of corporate governance and competition, and further analysis of the strategic aspect of state-controlled holdings in Russia is urgently needed.

In this chapter we used secondary data on listed companies and evidence from surveys of unquoted enterprises in Russia to provide preliminary insights into the extent of involvement of different stakeholders in the governance of firms in Russia. Our evidence from the unquoted industrial sector has used the existence of certain governance arrangements as a minimal level proxy for their viability. Further research might usefully develop more detailed analysis in a number of directions. First, there is a need to provide more direct and systematic comparisons of the governance arrangements in the quoted natural resource sector and the unquoted industrial sector. Second, there is a need to examine the determinants of different corporate governance mechanisms in Russian firms, as well as their links with performance and efficiency; this research may need to await further developments with transition that will bring about more reliable performance information. Third, given that transition is by definition a dynamic phenomenon, subsequent research might also examine the changing role of different stakeholders.

NOTE

1. According to the World Bank estimates, the growth rebound since the 1998 financial crisis has resulted in an average annual GDP growth over 1999–2002 of 6.4 percent. This has led to a significant reduction in poverty levels, from their peak of about 40 percent in 1999 to 27 percent in 2002 (World Bank, 2004).

REFERENCES

Abarbanell, Jeffrey and Anna Meyendorff (1997), 'Bank Privatization in Post-Communist Russia: The Case of Zhilsotsbank', *Journal of Comparative Economics*, **25**(1), 62–96.

Aukutsionek, Sergei, Igor Filatotchev, Rostislav Kapelushnikov and Vladimir Zhukov (1998), 'Dominant Shareholders, Restructuring and Performance of Privatized Companies in Russia: An Analysis and Some Policy Implications', *Communist Economies and Economic Transformation*, **10**(4), 495–518.

Aukutsionek, Sergei, Kapelushnikov Rostislav and Natalya Dyomina (2004), *Ownership Concentration and Corporate Performance: A Case of Russia*, Moscow: Russian Economic Barometer.

Baetge, Jörg and Stefan Thiele (1998), 'Disclosure and Auditing as Affecting Corporate Governance', in Klaus J. Hopt, Hideki Kanda, Mark J. Roe, Eddy Wymeersch and Stefan Prigge (eds), *Comparative Corporate Governance: the State of the Art and Emerging Research*, Oxford: Clarendon Press, pp. 719–41.

Barberis, Nicholas, Maxim Boycko, Andrei Shleifer and Natalia Tsukanova (1996), 'How Does Privatization Work? Evidence from the Russian Shops', *Journal of Political Economy*, **104**, 764–90.

Baums, Theodor (1993), 'Takeovers Versus Institutions in Corporate Governance in Germany', in Dan D. Prentice and Peter, R.J. Holland (eds), *Contemporary Issues in Corporate Governance*, Oxford: Clarendon Press, pp. 151–83.

Bennedsen, Morten and Daniel Wolfenzon (2000), 'The Balance of Power in Closely Held Corporations', *Journal of Financial Economics*, **58**(1/2), 113–39.

Berndt, Christian (1998), 'Corporate Germany at the Crossroads? Americanization, Competitiveness and Place Dependence', Working Paper #98, ESRC Centre for Business Research, Cambridge: University of Cambridge.

Black, Bernard (2001), 'The Corporate Governance Behavior and Market Value of Russian Firms', Working Paper 212, John M. Olin Research Program in Law and Economics, Stanford Law School.

Blair, Margaret, Douglas Kruse and Joseph Blasi (2000), 'Is Employee Ownership an Unstable Form? Or is it a Stabilizing Force?', in Margaret Blair and Thomas A. Kochan (eds), *The New Relationship: Human Capital in the American Corporation*, Washington, DC: Brookings Institution.

Blasi, Joseph R., Maya Kroumova and Douglas Kruse (1997), *Kremlin Capitalism: Privatizing the Russian Economy*, Ithaca, NY: Cornell University Press.

Boycko, M., A. Shleifer and R. Vishny (1995), *Privatising Russia*, Cambridge, MA: MIT Press.

Buck, Trevor, Igor Filatotchev, Natalia Demina and Mike Wright (2000), 'Exporting Activity in Transitional Economies: An Enterprise-Level Study', *Journal of Development Studies*, **37**(2), 44–66.

Buck, Trevor, Igor Filatotchev, Natalia Demina and Mike Wright (2003), 'Insider Ownership, Human Resource Strategies and Performance in a Transition Economy', *Journal of International Business Studies*, **34**, 530–49.

Buck, Trevor, Igor Filatotchev, Mike Wright and Yves van Frausum (1996), 'The Process and Impact of Privatization in Russia and Ukraine', *Comparative Economic Studies*, **38**(2–3), 45–69.

Buck, Trevor, Igor Filatotchev, Mike Wright and Vladimir Zhukov (1999), 'Corporate Governance and Employee Ownership in an Economic Crisis: Entrepreneurial Strategies in the Former USSR', *Journal of Comparative Economics*, **27**(3), 459–74.

Dolgopyatova, Tatiana (2000), 'Ownership Relationships and Models of Corporate Control in Russian Industry', Discussion Paper 3, Higher School of Economics, Moscow (in Russian).

Dolgopyatova, Tatiana (2005), 'Corporate Ownership and Control in Russian Companies after the Decade of Reforms', Discussion Paper, Higher School of Economics, Moscow.

Earle, John, Saul Estrin and Larisa Leshchenko (1996), 'Ownership Structures, Patterns of Control and Enterprise Behavior in Russia', in Simon Commander, Qimiao Fan and Mark Schaeffer (eds), *Enterprise Restructuring and Economic Policy in Russia*, Economic Development Institute, EDI Development Studies, Washington, DC: World Bank, pp. 205–52.

Estrin, Saul and Mike Wright (1999), 'Corporate Governance in the Former Soviet Union: An Overview', *Journal of Comparative Economics*, **27**, 398–421.

Filatotchev, Igor, Sergei Aukutsionek, Rostislav Kapelushnikov and Natalya Dyomina (2001a), 'The Effects of Ownership Concentration on Investment and Performance in Privatized Firms in Russia', *Managerial and Decision Economics*, **22**, 299–313.

Filatotchev, Igor, Trevor Buck, Irena Grosfeld, Judit Karsai and Mike Wright (1996), 'Buy-Outs in Hungary, Poland and Russia: Governance and Finance Issues', *Economics of Transition*, **4**(1), 67–88.

Filatotchev, Igor, Trevor Buck, Robert Hoskisson and Mike Wright (1996), 'Corporate Restructuring in Russian Privatizations: Implications for US Investors', *California Management Review*, **38**(2), 87–105.

Filatotchev, Igor, Trevor Buck and Vladimir Zhukov (2000), 'Downsizing in Privatized Firms in Russia, Ukraine and Belarus: Theory and Empirical Evidence', *Academy of Management Journal*, **43**(3), 286–304.

Filatotchev, Igor, Natalya Dyomina, Mike Wright and Trevor Buck (2001b), 'Effects of Post-Privatization Governance and Strategies on Export Intensity in the Former Soviet Union', *Journal of International Business Studies*, **32**(4), 853–71.

Filatotchev, Igor, Mike Wright and Mike Bleaney (1999), 'Privatization, Insider Control and Managerial Entrenchment in Russia', *Economics of Transition*, **7**(2), 481–504.

Franks, Julian and Colin Mayer (1997), 'Corporate Ownership and Control in the UK, Germany and France', *Journal of Applied Corporate Finance*, **9**(4), 30–45.

Frydman, Roman, Katharina Pistor and Andrzej Rapaczynski (1996a), 'Investing in Insider-Dominated Firms: A Study of Russian Voucher Privatization Funds', in Roman Frydman, Cheryl Gray, and Andrzej Rapaczynski (eds), *Corporate Governance in Central Europe and Russia: Vol. 1. Banks, Funds, and Foreign Investors*, Budapest: Central European University Press, pp. 187–241.

Frydman, Roman, Katharina Pistor and Andrzej Rapaczynski (1996b), 'Exit and Voice after Mass Privatization: The Case of Russia', *European Economic Review*, **40**(3–5), 581–8.

Gilson, Ronald, J. and Mark Roe (1993), 'Understanding the Japanese Keiretsu: Overlaps Between Corporate Governance and Industrial Organization', *Yale Law Journal*, **102**(4), 871–906.

Hillman, Amy J. and Gerald D. Keim (2001), 'Shareholder Value, Stakeholder Management, and Social Issues: What's the Bottom Line?', *Academy of Management Journal*, **22**(1), 125–139.

Hopt, Klaus J (1998), 'The German Two-Tier Board: Experience, Theories and Reform', in Klaus J. Hopt, Hideki Kanda, Mark J. Roe, Eddy Wymeersch & Stefan Prigge (eds), *Comparative Corporate Governance: the State of the Art and Emerging Research*, Clarendon Press: Oxford, pp. 227–258.

Hoskisson, Robert E. Cannella, Albert A.Jr., Tihanyi, Laszlo and Rosario Faraci (2001), '*The Effects of Group Affiliation on Asset Restructuring*', Paper at the 2001 Annual Academy of Management Meeting, Washington, DC.

Jack, Andrew (2001), 'Moscow Tightens Grip on Gazprom', *Financial Times*, 1 July, 8.

Johnson Juliet (1997), 'Understanding Russia's Emerging Financial-Industrial Groups', *Post-Soviet Affairs*, **13**(4), 333–365.

Jones, Derek C. (1998), 'The Economic Effects of Privatization: Evidence from a Russian Panel', *Comparative Economic Studies*, **40**(2), 75–102.

Khanna, Tarun and Krishna Palepu (2000), 'The Future of Business Groups in Emerging Markets: Long-run Evidence from Chile', *Academy of Management Journal*, **43**, 268–285.

Kim, Hicheon and Robert E. Hoskisson (1996), 'Japanese Governance Systems: A Critical Review', in Benjamim Prasad (ed.), *Advances in International Comparative Management*, Greenwich, CT: JAI, pp. 165–89.

La Porta, Rafael, Florencio Lopez-De-Silanes, Andrei Shleifer and Robert Vishny (1997), 'Legal Determinants of External Finance', *Journal of Finance*, **52**(3), 1131–50.

La Porta, Rafael, Florencio Lopez-De-Silanes, Andrei Shleifer and Robert Vishny (1998), 'Law and Finance', *Journal of Political Economy*, **106**, 1113–55.

La Porta, Rafael, Florencio Lopez-de-Silanes, Andrei Shleifer and Robert Vishny (2000), 'Investor Protection and Corporate Governance', *Journal of Financial Economics*, **58**(1/2), 3–27.

Mayer, Colin (1994), 'Stock Markets, Financial Institutions and Corporate Performance', in Nicholas Dinsdale and Martha Prevezer (eds), *Capital Markets and Corporate Governance*, Oxford: Clarendon Press, pp. 179–94.

Meyendorff, Anna and Edward Snyder (1997), 'Transactional Structures of Bank Privatizations in Central Europe and Russia', *Journal of Comparative Economics*, **25**(1), 5–30.

Modigliani, Franco and Enrico Perotti (1997), 'Protection of Minority Interest and the Development of Security Markets', *Managerial and Decision Economics*, **18**(7/8), 519–28.

Noteboom, Bart (1999), 'Voice- and Exit-Forms of Corporate Control: Anglo-American, European, and Japanese', *Journal of Economic Issues*, **33**(4), 845–60.

Pappe, Yakov and Y. Galukhina (2005), *Russian Big Business: Events and Trends in 2004*, Moscow: Centre for Macroeconomic Analysis and Short-term Forecasting (in Russian).

Pedersen, Torben and Steen Thomsen (1997), 'European Patterns of Corporate Ownership: a Twelve-Country Study', *Journal of International Business Studies*, **28**(4), 759–78.

Peng, Mike, Trevor Buck and Igor Filatotchev (2003), 'Do Outside Directors and New Managers Help Improve Firm Performance? An Exploratory Study of Russian Privatization', *Journal of World Business*, **38**, 348–60.

Perotti, Enrico and S. Gelfer (2001), 'Investment Financing in Russian Financial-Industrial Groups', *European Economic Review*, **45**(9), 1601–17.

Prowse, Steven D. (1990), 'Institutional Investment Patterns and Corporate Financial Behavior in the United States and Japan', *Journal of Financial Economics*, **27**, 43–66.

Rapaczynski, Andrzej (1996), 'The Roles of the State and the Market in Establishing Property Rights', *Journal of Economic Perspectives*, **10**(2), 87–103.

RFSC (2002), *Structure and Organisation of Boards of Directors in Russian Joint Stock Companies*, Capital Markets Investment Advisory Services, INVAS Centre, Moscow (in Russian).

Roe, Mark J. (1997), 'The Political Roots of American Corporate Governance', *Journal of Applied Corporate Finance*, **9**(4), 8–22.

Shleifer, A. and R. Vishny (1997), 'A Survey of Corporate Governance', *Journal of Finance*, **52**, 737–83.

World Bank (2004), 'Russian Economic Report', June 2004, Washington DC: The World Bank.

Wright, Mike, Igor Filatotchev, Trevor Buck and Kate Bishop (2003), 'Is Stakeholder Governance Appropriate in Russia?', *Journal of Management and Governance*, **7**(3), 263–90.

Yudaeva, Ksenia, Konstantin Kozlov, Natalia Melentieva and Natalia Ponomareva (2003), 'Does Foreign Ownership Matter?', *Economics of Transition*, **11**(3), 383–409.

6. Acquisitions in BRIC economies: the case of India

Prashant Kale

INTRODUCTION

In the last few years emerging economies such as China, India, Eastern and Central Europe, and Latin America have become an increasingly important part of the global business landscape. This has been especially true after the recent regulatory liberalization of the business environment in many of these countries. These countries not only present a huge potential market for products and services for companies around the world, but also provide companies an opportunity to leverage their low-cost, but high-quality, production and development capabilities. A recent influential report that suggests that the BRIC economies (Brazil, Russia, India and China) will emerge among the top economies of the world by 2030 has increased the interest of managers and academics in these economies even further.

The growing interest in emerging and BRIC economies has led management scholars to study many different issues in the context of the evolving business environment in these countries. For instance, scholars have begun studying the evolution of the institutional environment in these economies (Kogut and Spicer, 2002), the role of diversification and business groups (Khanna and Palepu, 1997) and the dynamics of joint ventures and alliances (Luo et al., 2001; Kale and Anand, 2001). The examination of these phenomena and topics is not surprising since all of them have become relevant to managers of both multinational (MNC) and local companies operating in these economies, after the recent and ongoing liberalization of their business environment. This chapter examines one such phenomenon that has become very important in this context, namely the use of mergers and acquisitions (M&A) by companies to enter or expand their presence in these markets. We undertake this study for two reasons. First, from a practical standpoint, we see that there has been a marked increase in M&A activity in emerging economies in recent years – and yet, there are hardly any studies that investigate whether the companies involved in these transactions have actually benefited from them. Second, from an academic standpoint, we believe that the patterns of acquisition benefits or value creation that we might see in emerging or BRIC economies are likely to be somewhat different to those traditionally observed in such transactions in developed markets of the world.

In the rest of the chapter, we discuss the general M&A patterns observed in emerging economies and we provide arguments about the kind of value-creation patterns we are likely to see, and why. We conceptualize value creation in acquisitions in terms of value that is created for shareholders of acquirer companies based on abnormal stock returns following the announcement of any given acquisition – this approach is consistent with that of the vast finance and strategy literature studying this aspect in developed-country settings. We use India, which is one of the most important BRIC economies, as the primary context of our study. We also present some preliminary evidence to support some of our arguments. We believe that the arguments and observations provide a foundation for more detailed future research into the various issues that we highlight – they also provide managers currently involved in M&A in emerging economies like India with some useful pointers about factors they might like to consider in understanding the key value drivers in such transactions.

THEORY AND HYPOTHESES

Emerging Economy Acquisitions: An Opportunity for Acquirers to Create Value

Prior research suggests that companies can potentially create value through acquisitions in several different ways. First, they can use acquisitions to exploit synergy benefits that might exist between the acquiring and the target company (Seth et al., 2000; Bradley et al., 1988). The synergistic gain usually arises either due to cost reduction on account of scale or scope economies and elimination of duplication between the combining companies (Capron, 1999), or due to revenue enhancement (Singh and Montgomery, 1987; Seth, 1990) on account of greater market power or cross-selling opportunities for the combined firm. Second, acquirers can benefit by accessing new and valuable resources or capabilities from the target firm so as to enhance their competitive position in the market. Third, accordingly to the 'market for corporate control' argument (Jensen and Ruback, 1983), an acquiring firm can create value by taking over a poorly managed firm and improving its performance, by replacing the target's management team with its own team (that presumably has superior skills and practices).

But extant research has also observed the 'acquisition paradox' widely cited in the literature. Although acquirers can potentially create value in acquisitions in several different ways, identified above, in reality data show that acquirers typically fail in their acquisitions. As a result, when they announce or make acquisitions, on average they experience negative abnormal returns to their stock price – in other words they destroy, rather than create, value for their shareholders. This pattern has been consistently observed in acquisition studies mostly conducted in developed-market settings such as the US or Europe. The main reasons for acquirers' failure to create positive value in their transactions are as follows. First, acquirers often face myriad post-acquisition integration obstacles such that the administrative costs of integrating the acquired company exceed the synergy benefits they hope to earn by acquiring it (Haspeslagh and Jemison, 1991; Datta, 1991). Second, negative returns to acquisitions arise due to bidding or auction situations observed in most acquisition situations in well-developed acquisition markets in developed countries (Barney, 1988). Consequently acquirers eventually pay a price for the target that is well over the additional synergy value they hope to gain in the first place. Third, according to the hubris hypothesis (Hayward and Hambrick, 1997), managers of acquiring companies systematically overestimate their ability to exploit synergy or other gains from their acquisition and subsequently they end up overpaying for the target company – which once again destroys value for their own shareholders.

Effectively, research in most developed-country settings suggests that all of the above factors collectively have a negative impact on value creation for acquiring companies' shareholders. In other words, when companies make acquisitions stock markets on average react negatively to such moves, as they do not expect the acquiring firm actually to realize the benefits or value that might potentially exist, on account of the several reasons cited above. Consequently, the acquisition and the market's reaction to it destroy value for the acquiring company's shareholders. A large number of studies, most of which have examined acquisitions in developed-market settings, show that acquirers' shareholders earn generally zero or negative abnormal stock market returns following the announcement or consummation of such transactions (Bradley et al., 1988; Singh and Montgomery, 1987)

But we feel that in emerging-economy settings there might be some important differences in terms of the factors that potentially create value-creation opportunities for acquirers, as well as in the factors that traditionally prevent companies from actually realizing that potential. Most emerging economies, including the BRIC economies, had very restricted and regulated business environments until recently (that is, until the late 1980s or early 1990s) which created many growth and value-creation obstacles for companies operating in these economies. For instance, there were severe licensing and capacity expansion restrictions that prevented companies in these economies from organically increasing their scale of business to generate greater efficiencies. There were also regulatory restrictions that prevented companies from consolidating and increasing the scale of their operations through inorganic means such as acquisitions. As a result, industries remained fragmented and companies lacked efficiency or market power advantages to create sufficient value for their shareholders. The existence of both tariff and non-tariff barriers also protected companies in these economies from international competition, thus reducing their incentive to become more competitive either through generating more efficiencies or by acquiring or building new capabilities.

But since the late 1980s and early 1990s many emerging economies, including the BRIC countries, have begun liberalizing their business environment and removing or relaxing many of the restrictions mentioned earlier. This was particularly true for India, which has been rapidly liberalizing its business environment since mid-1991 (Ahluwalia and Little, 1998; Ghemawat and Khanna, 1998). Following liberalization, companies had the need, as well as the ability or freedom, to exploit many growth and value-creation opportunities they lacked earlier. Liberalization reduced or removed the licensing and capacity expansion restrictions in the country, as well as led to an increase in foreign and local competition in the country. This meant that companies could enhance their efficiencies and/or market power by increasing their scale of operations through organic growth or through consolidation. Companies were also driven by the need to improve their resources or capabilities in the face of rising competition. With the removal of restrictions on acquisitions, companies could now make such transactions in order to address many of these issues (Anandan et al., 1998). Hence liberalization in emerging economies like India made acquisitions, which provided many potential benefits, a reality and necessity for companies in these economies. And theoretically speaking, if companies made such transactions they were likely to enjoy the potential benefits they provided.

On the other hand, if liberalization created an opportunity for companies to make acquisitions in emerging economies and enjoy the benefits they potentially created, what about the risks and costs associated with such transactions? We feel that in emerging-economy settings at least some of the risks and costs that are typically associated with acquisitions in developed-market settings might not exist – at least, not to the same extent! We present a couple of arguments to explain this. First, it is important to note that until liberalization, acquisitions were generally not allowed. This implies that several companies that were perhaps 'attractive' acquisition targets, and could or should have been otherwise acquired, were perhaps simply not acquired. But once liberalization was initiated and acquisitions became possible, acquirers were able to take them over. In the case of such 'low-hanging fruit' (Zollo, 1998), post-acquisition integration challenges might be limited. And even if they did exist, the benefits of acquisition perhaps outweighed the challenges and costs involved. As a consequence, when acquirers in emerging economies begin making acquisitions in the post-liberalization period, investors and stock markets react positively to them since they expect acquirers to benefit from these transactions. As a consequence, these transactions created value, in terms of abnormal stock returns, for acquiring companies' shareholders. From a supply side too, given the dearth of acquisitions in emerging economies for such a long time, there should be a huge availability of such 'low-hanging fruit' (Zollo, 1998) in these economies – and to the extent that is true, acquirers in these countries should stand to benefit.

Second, acquirers destroy value by overpaying for acquisitions due to very competitive bidding situations. But in emerging-market settings, we feel that the 'market for acquisitions' will not be as competitive as typically seen in developed-market settings. This might be true for two reasons. From a supply-side or seller standpoint, the traditional restrictions on acquisitions mean that once acquisitions become possible there is probably sufficient initial availability of such potential targets. From a demand-side or acquirer standpoint too, the situation may be slightly different, especially in the first few years of the liberalization period. Although post-liberalization acquisitions become feasible, many companies may have hesitated to jump immediately into the fray. This might be because companies lacked the necessary experience to get into the acquisitions game, or the lack of well-developed regulatory frameworks and institutions that facilitate acquisitions prevented them from doing so. In either case, the supply- and demand-side factors might imply that in emerging economies, acquirers are less likely to face very competitive bidding or auction situations. To the extent that is true, they are generally less likely to overpay for their acquisitions and thus stock markets will react less adversely to their share prices when they make such transactions. This, in turn, means that there will be a less adverse impact on the value creation to acquirers' shareholders.

To summarize, if firms in emerging acquisitions are free and able to make such transactions to exploit the opportunity to enjoy the many benefits they potentially provide, and if some of the factors that typically have an adverse impact on acquirers' value creation are less relevant in these economies, then it is possible that acquisitions in emerging economies will create positive value for acquiring company shareholders.

Hypothesis 1: Acquisitions in emerging economies will create, on average, positive value for acquiring-company shareholders.

Emerging-Economy Acquisitions: The Relevance of Business Relatedness

Existing research has distinguished between related and unrelated acquisitions and investigated value-creation differences across these two types of transactions (Singh and Montgomery, 1987; Healy et al., 1997). Acquisitions are related when the combining firms share a common skill, resource, market or purpose; that is, they employ similar production techniques, use similar distribution channels, and so on (Rumelt, 1974). Researchers have observed that, in general, related acquisitions create positive value for their shareholders, while unrelated acquisitions do not. This is because related acquisitions provide a greater opportunity to exploit many of the operational synergies between combining companies, as described earlier (Singh and Montgomery, 1987; Healy et al., 1997; O'Shaughnessy and Flanagan, 1998; Capron, 1999). Due to the relatedness of their resources, firms in such acquisitions can add value by creating either greater market power or greater efficiencies through the elimination of duplication, and through the exploitation of scale and scope economies. Unrelated acquisitions, on the other hand, have limited value-creation potential due to lack of business synergies between the combining firms. At best, they provide some business risk diversification to firms (Seth, 1990).

We feel that the value-creation difference between related and unrelated acquisitions is more relevant in developed-market settings, but perhaps not so much in emerging economies. To understand why this might be true, we briefly examine the literature on business diversification and relatedness in the context of both developed and emerging economies. In developed markets such as the US, since the 1980s academics, investors and managers have emphasized that companies remain focused on either a single line of business, or at best on a set of 'related' businesses (Rumelt, 1974; Prahalad and Hamel, 1990). This was true regardless of whether a company grows organically or through acquisition. Relatedness was preferred, obviously due to the greater synergy possibilities that might exist in such instances. In contrast, stock markets did not prefer unrelated diversification, organically or through acquisitions, because investors felt that in the absence of any obvious synergies between combining businesses, such moves merely lead to managerial empire building and the creation of inefficient management structures to coordinate widely dispersed business portfolios (Rumelt, 1974). The bust-up takeovers of unrelated business conglomerates in the 1980s were partly a response to such value-destroying, unrelated diversification. It was felt that given the well-developed nature of the capital markets in developed countries, instead of engaging in rampant, unrelated diversification, managers were better off returning any excess cash from their existing business to investors so that the investors, in turn, could diversify their risk in any form or manner they desired.

In emerging economies, however, unrelated diversification has been widespread and popular, even more so before the extensive liberalization of the business environment in these economies, or even in the immediate few years thereafter. Two factors possibly explain this situation. First, many of these economies placed strong restrictions on firms' capacity expansion and growth in their existing business, to prevent the growth of monopolies in these markets. Therefore, if a company had to grow, it could do that mainly by diversifying into other new businesses. But in that case too, companies required a license from the government to enter any new business. Consequently, companies in many of these economies expanded or entered into any industry for which licenses were available, regardless of its fit or synergy with their existing business mix. Second, and more importantly, Khanna and Palepu (1997) have suggested that the relatively underdeveloped state of these economies' capital, labor and product markets also encouraged the growth of unrelated, conglomerate diversification. In the absence of well-developed external markets, large, unrelated conglomerates created internal capital and labor markets to attract and allocate resources more effectively. Due to a combination of these factors, unrelated expansion and diversification has been widely observed and valued in most emerging economies.

It is possible that as emerging economies begin to liberalize and ease restrictions on business entry and expansion, one might expect companies in these economies to adapt their strategies to these changes. Consequently, the pattern of diversification (both through internal development or through acquisitions) might begin converging with that in the developed markets; that is, related diversification and growth might be pursued, given the greater value creation opportunities that it provides. The need for unrelated diversification would reduce since regulatory restrictions that previously forced companies in this direction are discarded (Anandan et al., 1998). Secondly, as these economies begin to liberalize, there will be a gradual improvement in their external labor and product markets that enables single-business companies to attract and retain employees or capital from the market as well as, or even better, than large unrelated conglomerates. To the extent this happens, related diversification would become more attractive given its obvious potential for greater synergy benefits. We believe, however, that this adaptation may not occur instantly in most emerging economies; instead, it may occur more gradually over time. Even if these economies liberalize, it may be a while before capital and labor markets in these economies grow and fully develop the necessary infrastructure and norms necessary for small or single-business companies to grow without having the benefits of conglomerate parentage.

These arguments become relevant in the context of acquisitions, since companies can acquire either related or unrelated companies. Given the prevalence and partial relevance of unrelated diversification in emerging economies, it is likely that even when companies engage in such acquisition transactions they are not adversely penalized as they might be in developed economies. Thus while related acquisition may still be valued more by investors and markets, we feel that in emerging-economy settings we might see relatively smaller differences in acquisition value creation between related and unrelated transactions. It is possible however, that this difference increases over time as conditions in emerging economies converge with those in developed markets and the relevance of unrelated diversifications (through acquisitions) begins to decrease. Therefore:

Hypothesis 2: Acquisitions in emerging economies will not exhibit significant differences in the value creation to acquirers involved in related and unrelated transactions respectively.

Emerging-Economy Acquisitions: The Relevance of Acquirer Identity

Prior research has observed significant differences in acquisition success and acquisition value creation, based on who the acquirer is. More specifically, most of these differences have been linked to differences in companies' acquisition capabilities (Zollo, 1998; Zollo and Singh, 1997). Scholars have observed that firms with greater acquisition capabilities create positive and greater value for their shareholders when they announce or make such transactions, than firms that lack such capabilities. Based on case-based work, we know that firms like Cisco, GE, Symantec, etc. fall within this category.

Scholars have built on work in evolutionary economics and organizational learning to suggest that firms build their acquisition capabilities through two sets of mechanisms. First, they develop this capability through repeated acquisition experience, i.e. through 'learning-by-doing' (Ghemawat and Spence, 1985) and second, they build it through proactive investments in understanding and capturing 'lessons learnt' from either their own acquisition experience or that of others, and then leveraging that learning to manage future acquisitions. This involves activities such as articulating their acquisition experience, creating codified tools to help managers make acquisition related decisions, training their managers through formal and informal means to build their personal acquisition skills, and so on (Zollo, 1998; Zollo and Winter, 2001). Firms with acquisition capabilities are expected to be more likely to succeed with their acquisitions because their well-developed skills ensure that they identify appropriate/better acquisition opportunities or targets, generally do not overpay for them, or even manage the post-acquisition integration successfully to realize the value potential that an acquisition offers. Therefore, when such firms make or announce acquisitions, they create positive value for their shareholders because stock markets react favorably to them – markets feel that given their acquisition experience and capability, these firms will realize the benefits that potentially exist.

We believe that in emerging-economy settings, acquisition capability is strongly linked to acquirers' origin, especially whether they are local acquirers or multinational corporations (MNCs). This would be especially true when acquisition activity first picks up in emerging economies following the liberalization of their business environment. Globally, MNCs have been involved in acquisitions for many years as part of their expansion and growth strategies. Therefore, by virtue of their substantial acquisition experience MNCs should generally have well-developed acquisition capabilities. Since acquisitions have been traditionally important to them, many MNCs have also undertaken explicit efforts to institutionalize and build their acquisition capabilities by investing in processes and infrastructure to learn key skills from prior experience and codify and reuse that learning. Consequently when MNCs make acquisitions in emerging economies, investors might expect them to have a greater chance of succeeding in those transactions. Hence markets react favorably to MNC acquirers and create value for their shareholders, in terms of abnormal returns, when they announce or make acquisitions.

This would be also true for MNCs' local subsidiaries in emerging economies, even though they may not have made acquisitions in a particular emerging country till the liberalization of the environment in that economy permitted such transactions. This is because, even though the local subsidiary may be new to acquisitions, it can more readily access and acquire these skills from its MNC parent or from its sister companies in the MNC network. Subsidiaries often do so by sending local managers to the parent or sister companies to get trained or exposed to acquisition skills; conversely, the parent may also send some expatriate managers from the headquarters that are experienced or skilled at acquisitions by having undertaken them in the MNC's operations in other parts of the world.

On the other hand, local companies in emerging economies are relatively new to making acquisitions. Hence they hardly have any exposure or experience in such transactions, especially when acquisition activity initially begins in their economies following liberalization; unlike MNCs, they also lack the ability to access or acquire such a capability from any other part of their business. Given their newness to acquisitions, they are also not sufficiently savvy, at least initially, to make proactive investments in learning processes to build their acquisition capability. As a result, these companies lack sufficiently strong acquisition capabilities (or markets at least perceive them to lack them), and hence when they announce or make acquisitions markets may react unfavorably to them. Consequently local companies will create less value, or even negative value, for their shareholders as compared to their MNC counterparts. Their lack of acquisition capability would increase concerns about their ability to identify the best acquisition opportunities, minimize the risk of overestimating the target value or overpaying for it, successfully manage post-acquisition integration, and so on. Therefore:

Hypothesis 3: In emerging-economy acquisitions, MNC acquirers will create, on average, greater value for their shareholders, than local acquirers do.

In the next section, we provide some preliminary analysis in support of our hypotheses.

DATA AND METHODS

India provides an excellent context to examine acquisition value-creation trends and drivers in emerging economies, including the BRIC countries. India experienced a significant liberalization of its business environment in 1991 (Anand and Delios, 1995; Ghemawat and Khanna, 1998) that was largely influenced by the foreign exchange crises confronting the country. The changes in 1991 were sufficiently large and sudden that they effectively created a distinct business environment, generally referred to as the post-liberalization environment, following this year (Ghemawat and Khanna, 1998). Liberalization included many economy-wide reforms such removal of restrictions on entry into various industries, discontinuation of licensing restrictions on capacity expansion, removal of restrictions on foreign direct investments, relaxation of limits on foreign entry and ownership, and permission of growth through acquisitions (Thomas, 1994). While some of the specifics might vary across sectors, the general trend of liberalization in terms of the above aspects was seen across the economy as a whole.

There was also a huge burst in acquisition activity following liberalization. Companies made hardly any acquisitions up to 1991, but by 1995–96 the number of transactions had reached almost 250 in terms of volume, and Rs 30 billion in value terms; by 2002, these numbers exceeded 600 in volume terms and Rs 360 billion in value terms. This preliminary study is based on a sample of 498 acquisitions made in India between 1992 and 2002. The data come from various sources such as CMIE, SDC and so on.

VARIABLES

Acquisition Value Creation

The measure of acquisition value creation is based on incremental value creation for acquiring companies' shareholders, measured in terms of abnormal stock market gains, following acquisition announcements. Prior acquisition research has relied quite widely on this methodology (Singh and Montgomery, 1987; Bradley et al., 1988; Anand and Singh, 1997; Capron and Pistre, 2002). To estimate incremental value creation for each firm, we use residuals from a standard asset-pricing model to predict acquiring firms' returns following acquisition announcements. We used daily data on stock markets returns for each firm (local and MNC) listed on the Indian stock exchange in the sample over a 180-day period prior to the event day to estimate the market model (Fama, 1976):

$$r_{it} = \alpha_i + \beta_i r_{mt} + \varepsilon_{it}$$

Here r_{it} represents the daily returns to firm i on day t, r_{mt} denotes the corresponding daily returns on the value-weighted on the BSE sensex (index of the Bombay Stock Exchange), α_i and β_i are firm-specific parameters and ε_{it} is distributed i.i.d normal. The estimates obtained from this model are then used to predict returns for each firm over a 14-day period surrounding the event day, that is, event days -10 to $+3$, as:

$$R_{it} = \alpha_i + \beta_i r_{mt}$$

where R_{it} are the predicted daily returns, and α_i and $\beta_i r_{mt}$ are the model estimates. Thus the daily firm-specific excess returns can be calculated as:

$$\varepsilon_{it} = r_{it} - R_{it}$$

where ε_{it} are the daily firm-specific excess returns.

The excess returns reflect the daily, unanticipated movements in the stock price for each firm over the event period. We calculated these returns for all acquiring companies in the sample.

Acquisition relatedness

For each transaction, we had detailed information about the acquiring company's primary motives for undertaking that transaction, and how it planned to create value. We also had information on the primary business of the acquiring and target companies and their four-digit SIC codes. Three investment bankers, who were involved in acquisition transactions in India, used this information to categorize each transaction as 'related' or 'unrelated' based on relatedness in terms of customers, product markets or the resources and capabilities of the acquirer and target companies. We then used a simple dummy variable to code each transaction as related or unrelated.

Acquirer identity

We used a dummy variable to identity each acquiring company. As we mentioned earlier, we are using this as proxy for the acquiring firm's acquisition capability. All foreign acquirers were coded as 1, whereas all local Indian acquirers were coded as 0.

Control variables

We included variables to control for other factors in our analyses such as the industry in which the acquiring company is present (using industry dummies), the size of the acquiring company (in terms of annual revenue), and the relative size of the acquiring and target companies (by taking a ratio of their respective size in terms of annual revenues). We also controlled for acquisition time or period as described below.

'Acquisition period' refers to the time at which the acquisition was undertaken. Although liberalization in India was initiated in 1991, the liberalization process has continued since then. Some scholars (Ahluwalia and Little, 1998) have viewed the post-liberalization period as comprising two distinct periods – the first 5–6 years (1992–97) and the next five years (1997–2002). The first five years represent the initial burst of liberalization during which restrictions, in general, were eased for both capacity expansion in existing businesses and for entry or expansion into other industries for both Indian and foreign firms. Acquisition activity in India was initiated during this period as a result. But there were some important changes in later years, especially related to the capital markets and the market for corporate control. Foreign institutional investors became important players in the Indian stock market after 1996–97, as the government permitted them to hold more than 20 percent of the capital of publicly listed companies – this led to a gradual convergence of business and investment norms in India to those of more developed countries. Similarly, the Securities and Exchange Board of India (SEBI) passed a regulation in 1997 on the Substantial Acquisition of Shares and Takeovers (often referred to as the Takeover Code) to formally facilitate and regulate acquisition activity in India. In light of the above, we divide India's post-liberalization period into two distinct periods (1992–96 and 1997–2002) and use a dummy variable to distinguish them.

ANALYSES AND RESULTS

We observe that the mean acquisition value creation for acquiring companies during the entire study period is 1.63 percent which is not only positive, but also significantly different than 0. It provides support for hypothesis 1 that argues that acquisitions, on average, create positive value for the acquiring firms in emerging economies like India.[1]

We conducted Factorial ANOVA analysis (Kleinbaum et al., 1998) to test the remaining hypotheses since most of our main independent variables were categorical variables. A summary of the results for the main variables is presented in Table 6.1.

The results in Table 6.1 show that related acquisitions do create greater value than unrelated acquisitions, but the difference is only marginally significant ($p < 0.10$) – this provides partial support for hypothesis 2. In terms of absolute values, the average abnormal returns for related acquisitions were 2.13 percent, while those for unrelated acquisitions were 1.23 percent. When we compared the returns for MNCs and local acquirers we see that, as hypothesized, MNC acquirers create significantly greater value in their acquisitions than local acquirers do ($p < 0.05$). In absolute terms, the average abnormal returns for MNC acquirers were 3.39 percent while those for local acquirers were only 1.31 percent.

Amongst the control variables, we found that acquisition value creation also varies significantly across the two different phases of India's post-liberalization period (as seen in the results in Table 6.1). The value creation, in terms of abnormal returns, is significantly higher in the first five-year period than in the latter period. We discuss some interesting implications of this in the next section. Acquisition returns also varied across different industries, which was not surprising.

Table 6.1   Summary of the ANOVA results

Effect	Parameter value	t-value	p-value
Intercept	0.0169	2.0496	0.043
Acquirer identity	0.2377	2.037	0.0494
Acquisition relatedness	0.2136	1.872	0.0649
Acquisition period	0.2813	1.986	0.0562

DISCUSSION AND CONCLUSION

Emerging economies have increasingly become an important part of global business. This is particularly the case for BRIC economies, including India. Further, in these economies acquisitions have become a very important part of most firms' strategies after the liberalization of the business environments in these countries. This study sought to examine whether such transactions created value for the shareholders of acquiring firms involved in them, and to understand some of the main factors that might impact this aspect. In doing so, it was also possible to observe whether the acquisition value creation patterns and the factors that affected them, in emerging economies like India, were similar or different to those traditionally observed in developed-economy settings.

On average, acquisitions have failed to create positive value for acquiring companies' shareholders in most developed-economy settings. But in emerging economies like India that is clearly not the case. Here, acquisitions seem to create significant positive value for acquiring companies' shareholders – which implies that in these economies, markets and investors expect acquirers actually to realize the benefits that acquisitions potentially offer. Since this result is quite contrary to that observed in developed-country settings, it calls for more research into the likely causes that might explain this. We also see that in emerging economies like India, both related and unrelated acquisitions create positive value for their shareholders, even though the value creation for unrelated acquisitions is lesser than that of related transactions. While the result of related acquisitions creating positive value for acquirers is somewhat similar to that in developed-country settings (which have been widely studied in extant acquisition research), in emerging economies like India the difference between the value creation in related and unrelated acquisitions is quite marginal.

Finally, there is a stark difference in the value creation and returns to MNC and local Indian acquirers. In our view, this signals some opportunity for MNCs to use acquisitions to enter and expand in emerging economies. On the other hand, it acts as a wake-up call to local companies, which need to investigate more closely what explains this difference. If the difference is explained by differences in these companies' respective acquisition capabilities, as we hypothesize, then clearly local Indian companies need to make greater effort in improving their acquisition capability.

The difference in acquisition value creation across two different periods of India's post-liberalization period is very intriguing, and hence worthy of more investigation in future. The fact that acquisitions returns, although positive, are much smaller in the second period implies that some of the adverse factors that typically impact value creation are perhaps becoming more relevant only as the Indian economy continues to liberalize further. Are the returns to acquisitions reducing over time because the market for acquisitions is becoming more competitive (leading companies to overpay), or it that the supply of 'low-hanging fruit' in terms of acquisition targets is drying up? This finding clearly highlights that the changes in the macro-environment in emerging economies will possibly have a huge possible impact on whether, and how, acquirers benefit from acquisitions to create value for their shareholders when they announce or make such transactions. Given this result, it would be equally interesting in future research to study whether the influence of the factors that we have studied here (that is, acquisition relatedness and acquirer identity or capabilities) also varies according to changes in the regulatory liberalization of emerging economies over time.

In this chapter, we have used India as the context to collect and analyze data to provide preliminary support for some of our arguments. To the extent that other emerging economies, including the other BRIC countries, are similar to India in terms of its evolution from a protected regulated environment (where company growth in general, and through acquisitions, was hampered) to a liberalized business environment (that also allowed and encouraged acquisitions), we might expect to see similar patterns and drivers of value creation in acquisitions. But there are also some differences across these countries in terms of the timing and extent of their liberalization, the nature of the local companies that exist there, and so on. To the extent that such differences exist, we have to factor them in too, in the arguments that we generally make and find support for.

To conclude, this chapter takes an initial step to examine an important but less investigated question in the context of emerging economies, as they become a more integral part of global business. Do acquisitions create value for acquiring companies involved in these transactions, and what are some of the factors linked to the nature of value creation? This chapter, which is perhaps among the first few of its kind, provides an initial insight into this critical question and it creates a foundation for more investigation of these questions in future.

NOTE

1. We also estimated the abnormal returns for those target companies in our sample that were publicly listed. We observed that, on average, target-company shareholders earned positive abnormal returns in these acquisitions and their returns were also much greater than that of acquiring companies – this latter result is quite consistent with that typically observed in acquisitions in developed-economy settings too.

REFERENCES

Anand J. and A. Delios (1995), 'India: A Dream Deferred or a Dream Shattered', *Business Quarterly*, **60**(2), 22–7.

Anand, J. and H. Singh (1997), 'Asset Redeployment, Acquisitions and Corporate Strategy in Declining Industries', *Strategic Management Journal*, **18**, 99–118.

Anandan R., A. Kumar, G. Kumra and A. Padhi (1998), 'M&A in Asia', *McKinsey Quarterly*, **2**, 193–201.

Ahluwalia, I.J. and I.M.D. Little (1998), *India's Economic Reforms and Development: Essays for Manmohan Singh*, Delhi: Oxford University Press.

Barney, J. (1988), 'Returns to Bidding Firms in Mergers and Acquisitions: Reconsidering the Relatedness Hypothesis', *Strategic Management Journal*, **9**, 71–8.

Bradley, M., A. Desai and E. Kim (1988), 'Synergistic Gains from Corporate Acquisitions and Their Division Between the Stockholders of Target and Acquiring Firms', *Journal of Financial Economics*, **21**(1), 3–40.

Capron, L. (1999), 'The Long-term Performance of Horizontal Acquisitions', *Strategic Management Journal*, **20**(11), 987–99.

Capron, L. and N. Pistre (2002), 'When do Acquirers earn Abnormal Return', *Strategic Management Journal*, **23**(9), 781–94.

Datta, D. (1991), 'Organizational Fit and Acquisition Performance: Effects of Post-Acquisition Integration', *Strategic Management Journal*, **12**, 281–97.

Ghemawat, P. and T. Khanna (1998), 'The Nature of Diversified Business Groups: A Research Design and Two Case Studies', *Journal of Industrial Economics*, **44**(1), 35–61.

Ghemawat, P. and A. Spence (1985), 'Learning Curve Spillovers and Market Performance', *Quarterly Journal of Economics*, **100**(5), 839–52.

Haspeslagh, P. and D. Jemison (1991), *Managing Acquisitions*, New York: Free Press.

Hayward, M. and D. Hambrick (1997), 'Explaining the Premium Paid for Large Acquisitions: Evidence of CEO Hubris', *Administrative Science Quarterly*, **42**, 103–27.

Healy, P.M., K. Palepu and R. Ruback (1992), 'Does Corporate Performance Improve After Mergers', *Journal of Financial Economics*, **31**, 135–76.

Healy, P., K. Palepu and R. Ruback (1997), 'Which Takeovers are Profitable? Strategic or Financial?', *MIT Sloan Management Review*, **38**(4), 45–57.

Jensen, M. and R. Ruback (1983), 'The Market for Corporate Control: The Scientific Evidence, *Journal of Financial Economics*, **1**, 5–50.

Kale, P. and J. Anand (2001), *Effects of Market Liberalization of Joint Venture Contributions, Control, Stability and Performance*, Academy of Management Best Paper Proceedings: Washington, DC.

Khanna, T. and K. Palepu (1997), 'Why Focused Strategies May be Wrong for Emerging Markets', *Harvard Business Review*, **75**(4), 41–8.

Kleinbaum, D., L. Kupper, K. Muller and A. Nizam (1998), *Applied Regression Analysis and other Multivariate Techniques*, Duxbury Press: Pacific Grove, CA.

Kogut, B. and A. Spicer (2002), 'Capital Market Development and Mass Privatization are Logical Contradictions: Lessons from the Czech Republic and Russia', *Industrial and Corporate Change*, **11**(1), 1–137.

Landis, J. and G. Koch (1977), 'The Measurement of Observer Agreement for Categorical Data', *Biometrics*, **33**, 159–74.

Lubatkin, M. (1987), 'Merger Strategies and Stockholder Value', *Strategic Management Journal*, **8**(1), 39–53.

Luo, Y., O. Shenkar and M.K. Nyaw (2001), 'A Dual Parent Perspective on Control and Performance in International Joint Ventures: Lessons from a Developing Economy', *Journal of International Studies*, **32**(1), 41–58.

O'Shaughnessy, K.C. and D. Flanagan (1998), 'Determinants of layoff announcements following M&A', *Strategic Management Journal*, **19**(10), 989–99.

Prahalad, C.K. and G. Hamel (1990), 'The Core Competence of the Corporation', *Harvard Business Review*, **68**(3), 79–91.

Rumelt, R. (1974), *Strategy, Structure and Economic Performance*, Boston, MA: Division of Research, Harvard University.

Seth, A. (1990), 'Sources of Value Creation in Acquisitions', *Strategic Management Journal*, **11**(6), 431–46.

Seth, A., K. Song and P. Richardson (2000), 'Synergy, Managerialism or Hubris? An Empirical Examination of Motives for Foreign Acquisitions of US Firms', *Journal of International Business Studies*, **31**(3), 387–405.

Singh, H. and C. Montgomery (1987), 'Corporate Acquisition Strategies and Economic Performance', *Strategic Management Journal*, **8**, 377–86.

Zollo, M. (1998), *Knowledge Codification, Process Routinization and the Creation of Organizational Capabilities: Post-Acquisition Management in the US Banking Industry*, UMI Dissertation Services: Ann Arbor, Michigan.

Zollo, M. and H. Singh (1997), *Knowledge Accumulation and the Evolution of Post-acquisition Management Practices*, Academy of Management Conference Proceedings: Boston, MA.

Zollo, M. and S. Winter (2001), 'Deliberate Learning and the Evolution of Dynamic Capabilities', *Organization Science*, **13**(3), 339–53.

7. Development prospects of China's industries

Zhiwu Chen[1]

> It is often said that the peril of to-day is not the Chinese behind the gun, but the Chinese as the manufacturers of guns and of many other things, equally calling for the highest technical skill. It has been the fashion of newspaper writers dealing with the development of China to state that the danger to the West lies in the industrial expansion of China, and it is averred that the Chinese, with their cheap labour and keen aptitude for imitation, competing with the dear labour and the heavy cost of transportation of the West, would certainly be able to beat the latter.

The above quote resembles what one would read in newspapers and books of today, but in fact it is from page 291 of the book by S.R. Wagel (1980), *Finance in China*, originally published in 1914 and reprinted in 1980. Though it is a description of the China debate back then, it sounds so familiar even today. Like more than 90 years ago, the growth story of China has occupied much media headline space in recent years. According to many measures, China's development over the past two decades has been remarkable. Since its economic reform started in 1978, GDP growth has averaged more than 9 percent, raising purchasing power parity adjusted per capita GDP from $338 in 1978 to about $5000 in 2003 (see Figure 7.1), and more than 200 million people have been lifted out of poverty. China's urbanization ratio (as measured by the percentage of urban population) was 16 percent in 1978 and increased to 41.8 percent by 2004.[2] After engineering a soft landing from an overheated state in the mid-1990s, the Chinese economy managed to come out of the Asian financial crisis virtually unscratched. During the global economic slowdown since the bursting of the high-tech bubble in 2000, China's economy has not only maintained its momentum, but has also provided a strong source of growth energy for many countries in Asia, Latin America, the Middle East and other continents, especially resource-rich countries.

Is today's China really different from the China of 90 years ago? In terms of population size (and hence labor force size and labor costs) and natural resources, China today is almost no different from 90 years ago. China's

Source: United Nations Statistics Division Common Database.

Figure 7.1   Per capita GDP of China

population in 2006 is over 1.3 billion (about 22 percent of the world's population), while it had 437 million people in 1914 (about 25 percent of the
world's population then; Maddison, 2001). Therefore, if the vast and cheap
labor force has been the driving factor behind the recent growth, this same
factor should have driven China towards prosperity back then, as the relative population size of China was even larger. But that did not happen.
Instead, after 1913, China went through periods of turmoil, stopping its
growth back then. While the China growth story today is still going strong,
we are thus led to ask the natural question: what makes the present experience different?

   With that in mind, in this chapter I will first review how the two periods
differ, why the recent growth had its roots in the late Qing Dynasty, where
the recent growth has come from, and what China's current industrial
structure is. Then I will attempt to address a frequently-asked question:
which industries present realistic and promising growth opportunities in
China going forward? This broad question is clearly important, but difficult
to answer. For this reason, I will mostly follow an institutional economics
approach to look for an answer. Of course, upon seeing this statement,
readers may immediately ask: hasn't China's growth experience invalidated
the central proposition of institutional economics, that institutions matter?
It has been observed by commentators that China's legal and informational
institutions are not market-friendly and have much to be desired, yet its
GDP has grown at an average rate of more than 9 percent, which seems to
suggest that institutions do not matter for growth.[3] There appears to be a
contradiction. I will argue that China's growth has mostly come from
manufacturing industries that are less dependent on institutions. Indeed,

unless China takes more aggressive steps to reform its legal and informational institutions, manufacturing industries will still be where growth opportunities lie in the near future.

GENERAL OVERVIEW

China's population was 1.28 billion at the end of 2002, with 753 million 'working-age' citizens, which the 2003 *China Statistical Yearbook* defines as those between the ages of 15 and 65. Such a large employable population ranks China #1 in the world. Although services and industry are responsible for an increasingly large number of jobs in the economy, agriculture still accounts for some 50 percent of employment in China.[4] However, the agriculture sector contributes only 15.4 percent to the country's GDP. Women typically work outside the home, with 72 percent of them having outside jobs, which ranks China 18th in the world in terms of the fraction of women employed, ahead of the US, the UK and Japan.[5]

The average working-age person has 6.4 years of schooling, which ranks China 45th in the world. This level of education is a serious impediment that the government is trying to remedy through training programs and schools. China's goal is to achieve 'nine years of basic universal education' by 2010. While the average education level may be low, it is important to keep in mind that the absolute number of people with a college or higher degree is more than 60 million. This supply of educated and skilled labor is enough to support any large-scale development in high-tech industries.

Up until recently, the government had tightly restricted the legal movement of workers both from the countryside to urban areas and between urban areas, through a strict residence registration system. Out of social instability concerns, this was done to stem the potential population flows into urban centers where jobs have been increasing at an estimated 3 percent per annum over the past 12 years.[6] However, except for a few large cities such as Beijing and Shanghai, population mobility today is much higher than before and depends on employment qualifications. In principle, a person can leave the countryside to find a cleaning job in Beijing and stay there for years, even though they may not have a legal residence permit for Beijing. In such a case, they would not have access to any benefits provided by the local government; neither can their children go to the local public schools.

Before the mid-1990s, while working for companies and organizations, employees would have had housing, health care, education and pensions provided by the government. Costs of these benefits were large burdens on state-owned enterprises (SOEs) and government agencies. However, in 1994, the government loosened restrictions on laying off employees, and as a result the SOE sector laid off 25 million employees.[7] Today, employment benefits have been reduced, with workers paying for their own health insurance and housing. Some companies offer pensions and other retirement benefits, but many do not. Retirement has become a major problem financially for many workers.

Labor unions have also flourished during this transformation period of great turmoil, and the government appears to have supported their efforts by enacting a labor union law in October 2001. Additional reforms include allowing workers to form unions for better representation.[8] In theory, these new rules and laws should protect union representation. However, the concerns and legal rights of union workers are often ignored because of the often significant influence that the factory managers wield with the local government, or out of 'social stability' concerns. Therefore, in practice labor unions do not have much influence and cannot organize activities independent of the government or the Communist Party.

To summarize, in addition to low worker wages in Chinese factories, employee benefits are also exceptionally minimal and the workers cannot really organize themselves to seek higher wages or benefits. This picture of labor supply and labor costs is at the heart of China's recent growth story, underscoring its global competitive advantage. It also directly determines China's industrial structure. Based on 2003 data, China's economy is 15.4 percent in agriculture (as measured by its contribution to GDP), 51.1 percent in industry and 33.5 percent in the service sector.[9] This industrial structure of today is a result of the reform-plus-open door policies that started in 1978. Back then, China's economy was 28.1 percent agriculture, 48.2 percent industry and 23.7 percent in the service sector.

INDUSTRY PERSPECTIVE ON CHINA'S GROWTH

There are many ways to review what has contributed to China's growth over the past 27 years. I will do this from both the macro policy and the industry perspective.

Market-Oriented Transformation and Open-Door Policy

At the macro policy level, growth has come mainly from two drivers: 'Open-Door' policy and market-oriented transformation. First, right after the death of Chairman Mao China ended the disastrous Cultural Revolution in 1976. By 1978, Deng Xiaoping succeeded in taking over the government from Mao's hand-picked successor and started the transformation from a planned to a market-oriented economy in that year. This reform immediately unleashed the traditional entrepreneurial spirit in the Chinese culture and redirected people's energy from ideology to productive purposes, resulting in a dramatic improvement in economic efficiency. The market-oriented transformation has been so significant that now the non-state sector (comprising of the private sector, urban collectives and township and village enterprises) makes up nearly two-thirds of GDP. Between 1999 and 2002, while the state sector lost 14.09 million jobs, the non-state sector added nearly 37 million jobs.[10] According to Tseng and Rodlauer (2003), after 1978 market-oriented structural reforms made a direct contribution of 2–4 percent a year to total factor productivity growth.

Second, the Open-Door policy reopened China for foreign capital and for international trade. This policy has created two results: China is now the largest destination for foreign direct investment (FDI) and it has become an export-oriented manufacturing powerhouse, taking advantage of its vast labor supply and its trade-oriented infrastructure. When the Open-Door policy started in 1978, FDI inflow was almost zero; by 1992, it exceeded \$10 billion for the first time. In 2004, the FDI inflow was \$60.6 billion.[11] According to Tseng and Zebregs (2003), this policy's contribution to China's GDP growth was estimated to be nearly 3 percent a year.

Of course, Open-Door as a policy *per se* is not just a recent phenomenon in China. Starting from the late thirteenth century (Yuan Dynasty) and except for such brief periods as around 1400 in the early Ming Dynasty, China was closed to the outside world, with sea-going Chinese traders punishable by death. This Closed-Door policy continued until the 1839–42 Opium War with Britain. China lost the war and signed the Nanjing Treaty in 1842, which forced China to open five port cities (Xiamen, Guangzhou, Fuzhou, Ningbo and Shanghai) for foreign investments and international trade. From 1842 to 1949 when the People's Republic of China (henceforth, PRC) was founded, China was increasingly more open to the outside world and its economy was becoming more export-oriented.

As Table 7.1 shows, by 1870 (28 years after the Nanjing Treaty), China's export dependence (as measured by the merchandise export: GDP ratio) was 0.7 percent, higher than Japan's 0.2 percent but much lower than India's 2.6 percent (perhaps because India was part of the British Empire). In 1913, China's export dependence increased to 1.74 percent, contemporaneously below those of both Japan and India. Note that relative to Japan, China has had a lower export dependence since probably the 1880s to the present, except during the immediate years after World War II (for example in 1950 Japan had an export dependence of 2.2 percent, lower than China's 2.64 percent). Also, even after the reform and Open-Door period started in 1978, China has always had a lower export dependence than the average of Asian countries (see Table 7.1). For this reason, it is more appropriate to

Table 7.1   Export dependence across countries

	1870	1913	1950	1973	1998
China	0.74%	1.74%	2.64%	1.58%	4.91%
India	2.6%	4.6%	2.9%	2.0%	2.4%
Japan	0.2%	2.4%	2.2%	7.7%	13.4%
Asia	1.7%	3.4%	4.2%	9.6%	12.6%
World	4.6%	7.9%	5.5%	10.5%	17.2%

Note: Export dependence is measured by total merchandise export as a percentage of GDP.

Source: Maddison (2001), Table F-5.

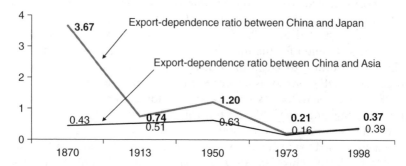

Note: The ratio in export dependence between China and Japan is used to reflect how open the Chinese economy is relative to the Japanese economy at the same time. The same interpretation for the ratio between China and all of Asian countries.

Source: Maddison (2001), Table F-5.

Figure 7.2   China's export dependence relative to Japan and Asia

use the ratio in export dependence between China and a benchmark country (or countries) to compare the three different periods: (1) the late Qing (1870–1911); (2) the Republic of China (henceforth, ROC) period from 1911 to 1949; and (3) the PRC period (since 1949).

As shown in Figure 7.2, in 1913 China's export dependence was 0.51 times Asia's average. In 1950 (at the end of the ROC period), this ratio was 0.65. In 1973 (during the Cultural Revolution), China's export dependence came down to 0.16 times Asia's average. Even after 20 years of reform and Open-Door, in 1998 this ratio was at 0.39, implying a much larger gap with Asia's average export dependence than during both the late Qing and the ROC years. Thus, while the Open-Door policy has been viewed as a

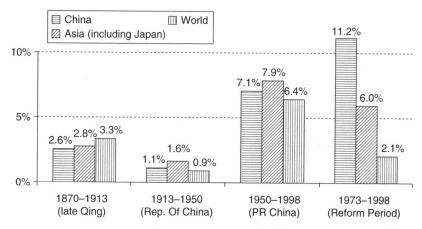

shown in the chart are annual export growth rates during different periods.

Source: data are adapted from Tables F-2, F-3 and F-4 in Maddison (2001).

Figure 7.3   Export growth rates in China vs other countries

fundamental cause of the recent China growth story, its economic openness relative to Asia as a whole is still lower than during the earlier periods under different governments. In this sense, Open-Door is necessary to achieve growth, but by itself this policy cannot be the only direct cause of growth for China in the recent reform years. In other words, from a pure policy perspective, the late Qing and the ROC period were similarly open for international trade as the China of today, but the earlier two governments were not able to reap as much economic results as the current one. Therefore, while Open-Door facilitates growth, it must be coupled with something else to produce the China growth story as we know it today.

Figure 7.3 shows the merchandise export growth rates for China, Asia and the world during the different time periods. Based on the displayed growth rates, China performed similarly to an average Asian country during both the late Qing and the PRC years. The post-reform period is when China's export grew at 11.2 percent a year, much faster than both the Asia average and the world's average. Therefore, unlike during the late Qing and the ROC years when their Open-Door policies did not create as much of an economic miracle, the post-1978 Open-Door policy has provided an opportunity for China to take full advantage of what today's world can offer because of matured manufacturing technologies, lower transportation costs, much higher transportation capacities, faster and easier communication, and, equally importantly, a much more trade-friendly international order that has been made possible after the end of the Cold War.

Industry Composition and its Development

In the preceding subsection, we have seen that Open-Door alone may not
have been enough for China to grow at such a fast pace in the recent period.
It must be that unlike previous periods, the post-1978 period happened to
be the right time for the Open-Door policy to yield exceptional results. We
can now turn to explaining why the recent period has been the 'right time'
by examining the development history of the textile industry, as this industry has been the main driver of China's export growth. As is known, during
the first half of the 1980s much of China's economic growth came from
agriculture, specifically due to the replacement of the collective commune
system by the market incentive-oriented family-responsibility system in the
countryside. In this chapter, let us focus on the textile industry, through
which we can see why the Open-Door policy has worked this time but not
in the late Qing or the ROC periods.

Since 1978, China has followed a manufacture export-oriented growth
model, much like Japan and the Asian tiger economies in the 1950s through
the 1980s. The main difference is that China started later and it has done so
on a larger scale and with much cheaper labor costs.

China's international trade (imports plus exports) was $20.6 billion ($9.75
billion in exports) in 1978 and had grown to $1154 billion ($593 billion in
exports) in 2004.[12] See Figure 7.4 for the annual export values since 1978.
After explosive growth of 35 percent in 2004, China surpassed Japan as the
third-largest exporter, behind Germany and the US. Manufactured goods
comprised 92 percent of China's exports in 2004. The composition of those
manufactured exports has shifted from low-tech basic goods (for example
toys and textiles) to high-tech electronics and machineries. Until 1996,

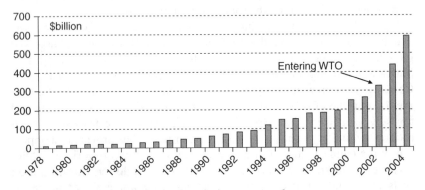

Source: Ministry of Commerce statistics database at gcs.mofcom.gov.cn

Figure 7.4   Export values of China

textiles and clothing was the largest export category, taking a 23 percent share in 1980, 30 percent in 1994 and 16.1 percent in 2004 of all exports from China. However, in 1996 machinery and electronics took the lead and achieved a 20.6 percent share of all exports. In 2004, the export share of machinery and electronics sky-rocketed to 54.5 percent, with a total export value of $323.4 billion. In the same year, textile exports totaled $95.1 billion. Therefore, the composition of China's exports today is of a different nature to 20 years ago, reflecting the increasing sophistication of engineering and technical expertise.

Indeed, over the past decade, a nation known primarily for its low-end goods ranging from cheap garments to toys has stepped up its ambitions to trade up the value chain and join the leading ranks of world-class manufacturers. Recent years have seen China shipping increasing volumes of more higher-end products to the United States and other countries, including computers, DVD players and ships.

An illustrative example is China's semiconductor industry, which two years ago accounted for 9 percent of the world's semiconductor production capacity and is projected to grow to over 20 percent in 2005.[13] This emphasis on capacity is symptomatic of Chinese industry in general – China now ranks third in capacity for primary petroleum processing, fourth in synthetic rubber production and fifth in synthetic resin.

Export-oriented manufacturing growth served to boost not only industrial and agricultural output, but also the service sector. The spillover effect is typically what an export-oriented growth model depends on. For example, while the manufacturing exports went from $2.2 billion in 1978 to $47.5 billion in 2004, manufacturing jobs went from 53.3 million to 83.1 million, with a net gain of 30 million jobs during the whole reform period (see Figure 7.5). However, the number of manufacturing jobs peaked at 98 million in 1995. Since then, the state-owned enterprises (SOEs) have been cutting jobs and going through privatization, resulting in a net loss of 15 million jobs over the last ten years. Given manufacturing overcapacity and increasing difficulty in expanding the export markets for Chinese manufactures, the Chinese government does not expect the manufacturing sector to create many more jobs. Instead, the realistic goal is to maintain the current employment in manufacturing while letting the increasing industrial output generate more spillover effects into the service sector.

As Figure 7.5 shows, while the manufacturing sector has not created new jobs since 1989, the retail, wholesale and restaurant service industries have added 24 million jobs during the period. The spillover effect of manufacturing into other sectors is quite apparent.

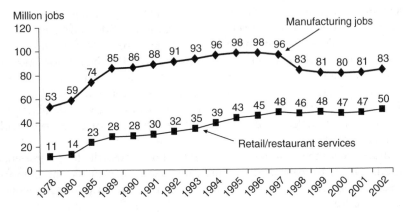

Source: *China Statistical Yearbook*, (2003).

Figure 7.5 *Employment in manufacturing and retail restaurant industries*

History of China's Textile Industry

It is well known now that China's approach has been to take full advantage of its cheap and vast labor force, focus on manufacturing, and make China the world's factory. Besides the labor supply factor, next we want to understand what has made this approach successful in the past 27 years. As discussed earlier, the late Qing China and the Republic of China before 1949 also had a vast labor force. So, why didn't the previous two governments succeed economically?

Let us start with a brief review of the development history of China's textile industry. This industry is a good example to illustrate why China's industrialization efforts have succeeded since the 1980s, while they failed in the late Qing and the Republic of China. This industry had been the largest driver of export growth from 1978 until 1995. A natural question is: Could the late Qing government have done this too to lead China into an economic boom back in the late nineteenth century?

Before the 1850s, China's textile industry was one of handicrafts and manual manufacture. After the Treaty of Nanking signed between Britain and China in 1842, China's market opened five port cities for international trade and removed many trade barriers. The cheap, high-quality textile products from Britain and the United States soon flooded into China, while India and Japan followed suit later on. With the import of large quantities of foreign machine-manufactured cotton products into China, native cotton handicraft production could not beat the competition.[14]

China's initial response to foreign manufacturers' competition was slow and sporadic, which delayed the development of China's modern mechanized textile industry. Many factors contributed to this slow reaction. First, science and hence modern technology were totally foreign to the Chinese population. Worse still, right after the Opium Wars, the emotional resistance to anything Western was running high, which presented a formidable challenge to anyone who wanted to adopt modern technologies and promote science education in Chinese schools. Second, it took until the late 1860s and early 1870s when the first batch of machinery was imported into China from the US and Britain. Third, with the lack of scientifically and technically trained personnel in China at the time, it took many years before the first batch of imported machines would be put to use effectively. The key point here is that while China was forced to be open for international trade after the Opium Wars, there was no industrial technology knowledge or a manufacturing industrial base to allow China then to take advantage of its labor force.

Like its mechanized manufacturing industries, China's modern textile industry developed much later than its Asian neighbors, in particular Japan and India. Only in 1890 did the first modern cotton factory make its appearance in China. After a long period of preparation, a public–private joint enterprise, Shanghai Machine Weaving Mill, was finally established in that year, with its stated goal being 'to prevent benefits from flowing to foreign countries'. The mill was equipped with 35000 spindles and 530 power looms, which was considerable during that period of time.

However, when the first cotton mill began operating in China, the Japanese cotton textile industry had reached so high a development level that it was able not only to drive foreign yarns out of the Japanese market, but also to start exporting textile products to China.[15] In the following decades, the infant Chinese textile industry had to confront massive competition from abroad.

From 1895 to 1903, new private cotton textile mills were established. After the signing of the Shimonoseki treaty in 1895, foreign investors started to set up textile factories in China. From 1896 to 1899, a total of eight Chinese-owned cotton mills were added, which, together with the factories established previously, raised the industry's capacity to 336 722 spindles and 2016 looms. After 1899, however, the construction of new mills came to a halt, partly because of the inadequate supply of raw materials and skilled labor, and partly because of the lack of credit and transport facilities. The development activities were not resumed until 1905 when the Russo-Japanese War presented a good opportunity for domestic cotton goods. By 1913, 11 more Chinese-owned mills had been added, increasing the number of spindles to 484 192 and the number of looms to

2016, which represented 58.8 percent of the total spindles and 54.5 percent of the total looms operating in China at the time.[16] However, initial technological and organizational difficulties caused some factories to drop out of the market.[17] All the mills that managed to survive reported profits in the period of 1890–1901.

It is clear that during the late Qing years the infant textile industry was being jump-started while the country was gradually exposed to science and industrial technology. The cultural barrier and resistance to Western ideas (including technologies) were formidable. Against this background, while China's share of the world population was even bigger back then than now, and hence labor supply was at least equally abundant, China could not have succeeded in making itself the 'world's factory' back then. It was just starting to catch up with modern technology and science.

The outbreak of World War I in 1914 marked the beginning of a massive expansion period for China's cotton textile industry, as the competing pressure from abroad came to a stop. The lack of transportation caused manufacturers in Britain and other European countries to give up their Far Eastern markets. The withdrawal of British textiles from the Far East also forced Japanese companies to readjust their export structure, creating an opportunity for Chinese textile mills. The sharp reduction of imports led to a dramatic price increase for cotton textile products in China, making Chinese textile mills highly profitable during this period from 1914 to 1922. The high profitability in turn attracted many new players into the industry. Total production capacity went from 865 777 spindles in 1914 to 3 010 720 spindles by 1922, while the number of looms increased from 4798 to 19 228 during the same period.[18]

The post-World War I period also experienced a large increase in foreign-invested textile ventures, especially from Japan. For example, the number of Japanese-owned spindles went from about 100 000 in 1914 to more than 1.4 million by 1928, with a similar increase in the number of Japanese-owned looms. That period was comparable to the recent period in terms of FDI attracted to China.

Another distinct feature about that period is that unlike in the preceding years in which new industrial ventures were often required to have the government's involvement (that is, partial state ownership), private ventures were the main driver of industrial development, making it the only period of true free-market capitalism in modern Chinese history. The private efforts and FDI ventures greatly accelerated the industrialization process in China, especially in the textile industry. The 1914–28 period was one in which Chinese technical sophistication in manufacturing reached a new and mature level, preparing China for a more dominant role in the global textile markets 50 years later.

From about 1928 to the founding of the PRC in 1949, however, the Chinese textile industry went through much turbulence and significant downsizing. First of all, by that time most European textile players had recovered from World War I and increased their capacities as well. With the overexpansion of the textile industry in China, the world's demand for cotton reached an unprecedented high level while the supply of yarn was also the highest, driving up cotton prices and depressing yarn prices. This led to large losses for many textile firms in China and elsewhere. Secondly, the Great Depression in the US and other Western countries following the 1929 stock market crash created a context in the 1930s for all countries to put up high import tariffs and restrict the importing of numerous products. That was another fatal blow to China's textile industry, as it had become China's major exporting industry by that time. These two factors caused many Chinese textile companies to go out of business.

From the late 1930s to 1949, the period was first marked by the Japanese occupation of much of China, especially the lower Yangtze River region surrounding Shanghai where China's textile industry was located. Right after the end of the eight years of the Anti-Japanese War in 1945, the civil war broke out again between the ROC government and the Communist Party. The civil war continued until 1949 when the PRC was founded on the mainland by the Communist Party and the ROC government was forced to retreat to Taiwan. These war periods slowed down China's industrialization process, during which its export growth stagnated (see Table 7.1 and Figure 7.3).

A theme common to both the late Qing and the ROC periods is that foreign-owned textile firms in China owned more than half of the country's spindle and power loom capacities. During the late Qing and the early ROC years, British capital was the main FDI source, which was gradually replaced by Japanese capital. While this fact has been used to inflame the nationalistic sentiment over the past century, it does show that the Open-Door policy is not something new in China. If anything, China was probably far more open during the late Qing and the ROC period than in the recent reform period.

The founding of the PRC in 1949 was followed by a massive nationalization movement of private and foreign businesses. By 1956, the entire textile industry was state-owned. From the 1950s to the end of the Cultural Revolution in 1976, the Chinese government focused most of its industrial development resources on heavy industries, with the textile industry occupying a secondary place in importance. In addition, these early decades of the PRC were marked by Communist ideological zest and political power struggles, with economic development dramatically de-emphasized. In fact, it is during this period that many factories along the coast were dissembled and transported to such mountainous 'third-line' provinces as Ningxia and Guizhou.[19] This massive relocation movement of China's industrial base from the coastal to inner provinces was intended to make China's industries foreign invasion-proof. The real result of that relocation program was a reduction in China's industrial capacity.

When the current Open-Door and reform policies started in 1978, more than 90 percent of textile firms were state-owned. But the share of state-owned enterprises (SOEs) in the textile industry went down to about 52 percent by 1991 and 29 percent by 1995. Both the privatization of former textile SOEs and the formation of new private businesses have contributed to China's emergence as the world's textile power.

Today, the textile industry is unique among Chinese industries because SOEs do not comprise a significant portion, only 21 percent. Instead, free market forces have shaped the competitive landscape, with private enterprises accounting for 16 percent, foreign companies 30 percent, and collective ownership entities the remainder.

The expiration of the WTO Agreement on Textiles and Clothing on, 31 December 2004, lifting worldwide textile and garment quotas, has given Chinese producers a boost in the $500 billion worldwide industry. The agreement had imposed a quota system in 1974 on many Asian countries, which added 10 to 50 percent to the average price an American company paid for an import. China's accession to the WTO was contingent upon the removal of these quotas.

The brief development history review of China's textile industry has indicated that at the policy level there has not been much new in the recent reform period, when compared to the late Qing and the ROC periods. The late Qing was the initial learning period about industrial technology and about science. At that time, even though China had the largest population in the world, the Qing government could not have taken advantage of the vast and cheap labor force to make China the world's factory. In addition, the international order of the late nineteenth century would not have made it possible for China to become the world's factory, because China did not have a large and powerful military force when a large navy was necessary for engaging in international trade of significant scale. The ROC government followed an Open-Door policy for most of the years when it was ruling the mainland. In fact, technical knowledge and industrialization had reached a decent level, which made it more possible than before to engage in export-oriented manufacturing. But, the two World Wars and China's own civil wars did not allow the ROC government's policies to yield much in the way of significant results. Thus, the ROC government was unlucky, to state the obvious.

The PRC has been the most fortunate of all. First, by 1978, China had had more than a century to acquire scientific knowledge and mechanized manufacturing technology. The century-long accumulation of modern textile, shipbuilding, machine building and other mass production technologies had created a large technical workforce, which would of course have been impossible without the foundational efforts started in the late Qing years. Second, soon after China started its reform and Open-Door policy in 1978, the Cold War came to an end and such international organizations as the World Bank, the IMF, the WTO and the United Nations turned to facilitating global trade, jump-starting the second globalization wave. This unprecedented trade-friendly international order has made it possible for China's new Open-Door policy finally to work its magic, enabling China to become the world's factory, something that was not possible in the late Qing and ROC decades.

FDI and Its Geographical Distribution

Much of China's manufacturing base and hence China's economy today is located in the coastal provinces. First, as in other countries, coastal locations offer easy access to waterways, making the transport of raw materials and manufactured goods less costly than from any inland place. Second, because of this natural transportation advantage in terms of both costs and capacity, China's coastal provinces have for hundreds of years enjoyed international and regional trade, nurturing a more business-friendly culture in these regions than elsewhere in China. Informal financial markets and lineage structures are far better developed, and entrepreneurship is much encouraged, in these provinces. Third, at least since the Song dynasty in the tenth century, people from these provinces have emigrated into Singapore, the Philippines, Thailand and other Asian countries. Most overseas Chinese before the 1950s had been immigrants or their descendents from Guangdong, Fujian and Zhejiang provinces. These overseas Chinese have played a crucial role in bringing FDI and building the export-oriented factories along the coast. They have also played a pivotal role in facilitating international trade linkages for Chinese and joint venture firms. Consequently, both FDI flow and manufacturing in China have concentrated in the coastal provinces. Figure 7.6 depicts both utilized and contracted foreign investment (direct and indirect) by province as of 2000.

Partly because of the above reasons, China's population and economic activity are concentrated along the coast (including Shanghai, Guangdong, Fujian, Zhejiang and Jiangsu), with the eastern third of the country making up much of China's economy. As shown in Figure 7.7, the top nine provinces in terms of per capita GDP are all in the coastal region, whereas seven of the bottom ten are in the western region. The richer provinces on the coast boast active manufacturing centers and export markets. As a

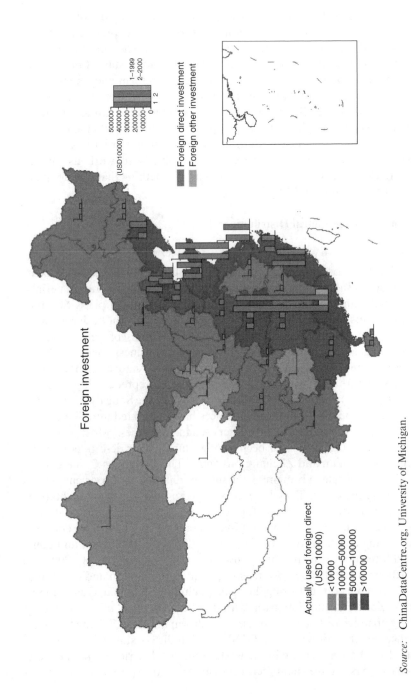

Foreign investment

(USD10000)
500000
400000   1–1999
300000
200000   2–2000
100000
0   1   2

Foreign direct investment
Foreign other investment

Actually used foreign direct
(USD 10000)

<10000
10000–50000
50000–100000
>100000

Source: ChinaDataCentre.org, University of Michigan.

Figure 7.6   FDI and hence manufacturing distribution in China

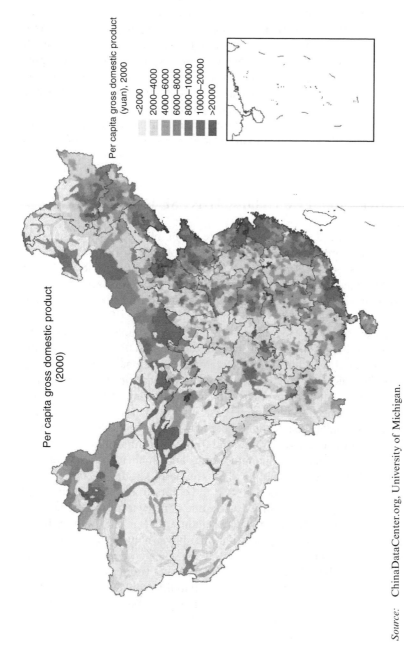

Per capita gross domestic product
(2000)

Per capita gross domestic product
(yuan), 2000

<2000
2000–4000
4000–6000
6000–8000
8000–10000
10000–20000
>20000

Source: ChinaDataCenter.org, University of Michigan.

Figure 7.7 Per capita GDP by region

result, they are much more pro-trade than their poorer agrarian counter-parts. This per capita GDP map illustrates the dramatic wealth disparity between the coastal and the interior provinces. There are pockets of economic activity in mineral-rich areas such as Inner Mongolia and Xinjiang.

FDI has played a central role in China's export-oriented growth approach, as much of the FDI has gone into export manufacturing projects. China's accession to the World Trade Organization in December 2001 contributed to a 12.5 percent increase in utilized FDI in 2002. FDI came primarily in the form of wholly foreign-owned ventures, which have supplanted equity joint ventures and contractual joint ventures as the investment vehicle of choice. Manufacturing accounted for 70 percent of utilized FDI as well as contracted FDI.[20]

FUTURE PROSPECTS OF CHINESE INDUSTRIES

Over the past two decades, China has relied on manufacturing, especially export-oriented manufacturing, to generate growth in not only the industry sector, but also in the service sector and agriculture. Going forward, can China's growth originate from non-manufacturing sectors, say, the service sector? After all, China's service sector made up only 33.5 percent of its total GDP in 2004, which ranks China among the lowest (if not the lowest) among countries with a population of at least 5 million. In contrast, the service sector had a 72.5 percent share in total US GDP in 2003. Thus, the growth potential for China's service sector is exceptionally high. However, why has China not developed its service sector or made its service sector take full advantage of the spillover effect of manufacturing growth? To answer this question, we need to address one basic institutional economics question: What institutional infrastructure is necessary for the service sector to grow?

The answer lies in the rule of law and freedom of information. To understand this, let us compare manufacturing and financial transactions. In auto manufacturing, for example, what is made and traded is a tangible car. A car buyer can look at the design style and colors, open the trunk and even the engine to inspect the quality, and do one or more test-drives. The informational asymmetry between the manufacturer (or the seller) and the buyer is limited, though it always exists. And the buyer may never need to open the informational brochures provided by the seller, because inspecting and test-driving may be sufficient for the buyer: 'What you see is what you get'. Of course, legal enforcement of product liability would be desirable. But, in the absence of reliable legal recourse, many car buyers may be able to overcome legal deficiencies by inspecting and testing the cars 'harder'. Besides, even if the buyer finds product deficiencies later on, he may be able to live with it as long as the car still runs, which offers a good cushion and reduces the importance of legal enforcement of product liability remedies.

The tangibility of a physical product affords the informationally disadvantaged side in such a trade a decent ability to mitigate or hedge transactional risks, so that the buyers and sellers can still engage in transactions and such markets can still develop. In other words, the Akerlof (1970) 'market for lemons' problem exists in physical goods markets, but not to the extent that these markets eventually have to shut down. The buyers' ability to take advantage of the tangibility of physical goods to mitigate transactional risks means that manufactured goods markets can develop even without a decent institutional infrastructure.

This may explain why used car markets still exist and function in many countries, even after the classic Akerlof (1970) paper has become well known. It also explains why countries without an acceptable degree of rule of law or free press can grow their economies by engaging in manufacturing tangible goods. The Asian Tigers (except Hong Kong) in the 1960s through the 1980s and China in the last two decades are outstanding examples. To put it differently, it is not that market-friendly institutions are not necessary for economic growth; rather, it is that for some industries their dependence on legal and informational institutions is weak. Therefore, as long as a country focuses its development on agriculture, mining and manufacturing industries, its economy can go a long way and for a long period of time without the familiar institutions that are taken for granted in developed countries.

In contrast, what is traded in a securities transaction (say, a corporate stock) is a financial contract written on a piece of paper or recorded electronically. What is sold in a stock trade is a claim on a future cashflow stream. This claim will be worth nothing if it is not backed by investor-friendly securities law and supportive legal procedural rules and by an independent, effective judiciary. A title to a future cashflow is worth something only if the buyer is confident that there are acceptable legal rules on the books and that throughout the lifetime of the claim, reliable and independent legal recourse is available whenever needed. Precisely because of the intangible nature of a financial security, a stock buyer is at a severe informational disadvantage: the financial contract being traded has no color, no style, no weight and no flavor; neither can the buyer test-drive it. The buyer has to rely on the information disclosed by the seller, in order to value the security. If he is lucky and the transaction takes place in a market economy where the flow of information is free and uninhibited, he can also rely on the independent and possibly unbiased information provided by the press and other third-party sources.

Given the intangible nature of a financial security, the buyers have only two ways to mitigate or reduce their transactional risks: (1) stay out of the securities market; and (2) rely on the informational institutions to ensure the quantity and quality of information for valuation and on the legal institutions to enforce contractual rights. Therefore, securities markets are far more dependent on institutions than manufactured goods markets, and they are more subject to the Akerlof (1970) 'market for lemons' problem. This is why many countries can develop manufacturing industries but few can achieve well-developed financial markets.

For similar reasons, health care and educational services depend more on the institutional infrastructure than manufacturing. In health care, what a patient is paying for is a service provided by a doctor or nurse, where the patient usually has no expertise to evaluate the quantity or quality of the service he is getting. In education, the quality of the service is even more difficult for the paying customer (and his parents) to determine. All of these markets represent situations where the transacting parties face severe informational asymmetry. The free and uninhibited flow of information is one crucial way to reduce the level of informational disadvantage faced by the customers.

Therefore, unlike mining and manufacturing, growth of the service sector depends critically on the free flow of information and the rule of law. To examine whether this statement is empirically supportable, we can look at cross-country data. Since the rule of law and press freedom are highly correlated for each country, I will focus on the relationship between press freedom and service-sector development. In particular, I use the 1990 press freedom ratings of 106 countries by Freedom House as a proxy for the uninhibitedness of information flow in a country (http://www.freedomhouse. org/ratings/). Then, if I use the service sector's share in GDP to measure the degree of development of a country's service sector, I find a country's press freedom and its service sector's development to be highly correlated: the correlation between press freedom rating in 1990 and the service sector's share in GDP in 2002 is 61.5 percent.[21]

In Figure 7.8, I divide the 106 countries into three equal-sized groups according to their 1990 press freedom ratings: free-press countries, countries with middle press freedom ratings, and countries with the lowest press freedom ratings. Then, the average service sector's share in GDP in 2002 is 62.4 percent for free-press countries, 57.1 percent for countries with average press freedom and 48.5 percent for countries with the least free press. Freedom of the press indeed facilitates the service sector's development.

To make more sense of the statistics, note that the press freedom rating in 1990 is 12 for the US (the ratings are on a 1–100 scale, with 1 representing the most free press and 100 the most restrictive informational environment), 30 for Hong Kong (ranked 47th most free out of 106 countries), 60 for Singapore, and 89 for China (ranked 105th). On the other hand, the service sector's share in GDP is 70.7 percent for the US, 86.5 percent for

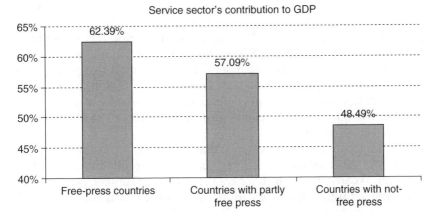

Service sector's contribution to GDP

Notes: Based on 1990 press freedom ratings from Freedom House (http://www. freedomhouse.org/ratings/), 106 countries are divided into three equal groups. The average service sector's share in a country's 2002 GDP is reported for each country group.

Source: United Nations Development Database (for service sector data).

Figure 7.8 *Service sector development and press freedom*

Table 7.2 *Press freedom and service sector development: examples*

Country	1990 press freedom rating	Service sector's contribution to GDP in 2002
USA	12	70.70%
Hong Kong	30	86.50%
Singapore	60	64.10%
China	89	27.50%

Note: Press freedom rating is on a 1–100 scale, with 1 representing the freest press.

Source: United Nations Development Database (for service sector data).

Hong Kong, 64.1 percent for Singapore and 27.5 percent for China. Table 7.2 lists these statistics.

What is surprising out of Table 7.2 may not be the strong correlation between press freedom and service sector development, but rather the fact that the service sector's share in Singapore is actually lower than in the US. Singapore has long followed this known policy of 'free economic press but restricted political press', based on the assumption that economics and politics can be separated. Given the overall economic progress in Singapore, one would expect this 'selectively free press' policy to have worked well. Given the lack of natural resources and land space in Singapore, one would also expect Singapore's dependence on the service sector to be higher than that of the US (after all, the US is endowed with rich natural resources and has built a vast manufacturing base). But, the reality is that Singapore's service sector weight is not as high as in the US. This means that the Singapore service sector's growth potential is still high (especially compared to Hong Kong). Perhaps Singapore first needs to relax its press and informational environment.

The Singapore experience suggests that it is hard to separate the political press from the economic press. First, economic corruption is often linked to political corruption, which makes the borderline between political and economic information difficult to define. Second, if and when a pivotal bank, for example, is about to collapse and its collapsing will take the country's economy with it, will the information concerning the financial health of the bank be considered 'state secrets'? As another example, an investigative story may concern the financial conditions of a corporation of national strategic importance. Thus, when the political press is restricted, even economic information cannot flow freely. Third, the issue of critical importance may not be whether you allow the economic press to be free and the political press to be restricted, but the overall informational environment that such a selectively free press will create. It ruins the confidence that market participants will have in the quality and reliability of information.

I can also look at the cross-country experience in financial market development to confirm the importance of free information flow. For this purpose, according to their 1972 press-freedom ratings, I divide 57 countries with stock markets into three equal groups. Then, for each group of countries, I compute the median ratio between a country's stock market capitalization and its GDP as of 1995. The market capitalization to GDP ratio serves to measure the developedness of a country's stock market. Figure 7.9 plots the result, showing that the free-press countries have the most developed stock markets (with a median ratio of 35.25 percent), while the not-free-press countries have the least developed markets (16.55 percent).

Given the strong correlation between press freedom and service sector development (and capital market development), one is bound to ask the causality question: does the free flow of information cause the service sector to develop better, or does the service sector's development lead to a more free press? In a separate paper, I will specifically address this question.[22] But rigorous econometric tests demonstrate strong evidence supporting our claim here that the free flow of information is one necessary institution to facilitate service sector development in general and financial services in particular.

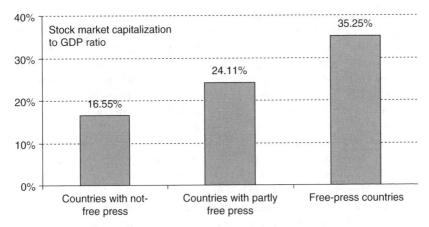

Notes: Based on 1972 press freedom ratings from Freedom House (http//www. freedom.org/ratings/), 57 countries are divided into three equal group. The median ratio between stock market capitalization and GDP is reported for each country group.

Source: The stock market capitalization data is from La Porta, Lopez-de-Silanes, Shleifer and Vishny (1998).

Figure 7.9   Press freedom and stock market development

CONCLUSIONS

For more than two decades, China has taken advantage of its vast and cheap labor force and its industrial base developed since the late Qing Dynasty, to focus its efforts on the hardware manufacturing sector. Even though the legal and informational institutions in the country still leave much to be desired and are far away from being market-friendly, the manufacturing sector has only a relatively weak dependence on such institutions. Consequently, China has been able to grow. The China story does not reject the central proposition of institutional economics. Rather, the existing literature on institutional economics has not made a distinction between different sectors and industries in their degrees of institutional dependence.

If there has been any 'China miracle', then that miracle must have been in the making since the late Qing when the 'Westernization Movement' started in the 1860s. The Open-Door policy during the late Qing period only served to expose the country to science and industrial technology, changing the educational content and training technical workers. The gunboat-based international order of the nineteenth century also did not make it possible for the late Qing's Open-Door policy to yield any 'China miracle'. Since the 1980s, the PRC's Open-Door policy has succeeded because: (1) industrial technologies had matured sufficiently to be easily transferable across borders; (2) China's technical knowledge had reached a high enough level of sophistication, thanks to the Westernization Movement started in the late Qing dynasty; and (3) the rules-based international order coupled with the UN, the IMF and the World Bank has provided an efficient framework for China to conduct cross-border trade at low costs. Therefore, the 'China miracle' is a result of globalization and technological advances.

Based on the analysis in the previous section, it is clear that China today is at a crossroad. Unless the media are free, and legal institutions (especially judicial independence) are better developed, manufacturing may continue to be the main sector for China to rely on in the future. The service sector will have some room for growth because of the natural spillover effect from the manufacturing sector. But the potential for the service sector as generated by the manufacturing sector cannot be fully realized unless the press is free and further legal development takes place in China.

NOTES

1. Zhiwu Chen would like to thank the BRIC Conference participants at the University of Connecticut for their comments, and Junlin Du for his able research assistance. Any errors remain the author's responsibility.
2. China National Bureau of Statistics (2004).
3. See Kristof (2003) and Thakur (2003).
4. China National Bureau of Statistics, *China Statistical Yearbook 2003*.
5. International Labor Organization Report, 2002.
6. Brooks and Ran (2003), p. 3.
7. Brooks and Ran (2003), p. 17.
8. Brooks and Ran (2003).
9. China National Bureau of Statistics, *China Statistical Yearbook 2003*, available at www.stats.gov.cn.
10. China National Bureau of Statistics, *China Statistical Yearbook 2003*.
11. China National Bureau of Statistics, *China Statistical Yearbook*, various issues.
12. *China Customs Statistical Yearbook*, various issues.
13. See Keliher (2004).
14. Koo (1982), p. 128.
15. Ko (1966), pp. 194–5.
16. Koo (1982), p. 143.
17. Ko (1966), p. 114.
18. Ko (1966), p. 119.
19. In the 1960s and the first half of the 1970s, there were frequent political movements to prepare China for a defensive war with the West. It was thought that attacks on China would likely come from the sea. Thus, the coastal provinces were often referred to as the 'front line', the immediate adjacent interior provinces the 'second line', and the next ring of provinces the 'third line'. Third-line provinces such as Hubei, Guizhou and Ningxia are usually mountainous and lack reliable transportation (rail or road), which was thought to be a strategic advantage as the enemy would not be able to reach there. After factories were relocated there, it was later realized that it was extremely difficult and expensive to transport raw materials into, and manufactured products from, the factory sites.

20. Data source: The Economist Intelligence Unit.
21. Data source for service sector GDP shares: United Nations Development Database.
22. See Chen (2005).

REFERENCES

Akerlof, George A. (1970), 'The Market for "Lemons": Quality Uncertainty and the Market Mechanism', *Quarterly Journal of Economics*, **84**(3), 488–500.

Brooks, Ray and Tao Ran (2003), 'China's Labor Market Performance and Challenges', IMF Working Paper No. 03/210.

Chen, Zhiwu (2005), 'Press Freedom and Economic Development', Working Paper, Yale School of Management.

China National Bureau of Statistics (2004), *China Economic and Social Development Yearbook 2004*, available at www.stats.gov.cn.

China National Bureau of Statistics, *China Statistical Yearbook*, various issues.

Keliher, Macabe (2004), 'China Set to Flood the World with Chips', *Asia Times*, retrieved 3 February 2004 from http://www.atimes.com/atimes/China/FB03Ad01.html.

Ko, Sŭng-je (1966), *Stages of Industrial Development in Asia: A Comparative History of the Cotton Industry in Japan, India, China, and Korea*, Philadelphia, PA: University of Pennsylvania Press.

Koo, Shou-eng (1982), *Tariff and the development of the cotton industry in China: 1842–1937*, Garland Publishing: New York, NY.

Kristof, Nicholas (2003), 'Freedom's in 2nd place?', *New York Times*, 29 August.

La Porta, Rafael, Florence Lopez-de-Silanes, Andrei Shleifer and Robert Vishny (1998), 'Law and Finance', *Journal of Political Economy*, **106**, 1113–55.

Maddison, Angus (2001), *The World Economy: A Millennial Perspective*, Organisation for Economic Co-operation and Development: Washington, DC.

Moore, Thomas (2002), *China in the World Market: Chinese Industries and International Sources of Reform in the Post-Mao Era*, Cambridge University Press: Cambridge.

Thakur, Ramesh (2003), 'China is Outperforming India', *International Herald Tribune*, 7 January.

Tseng, Wanda and Markus Rodlauer (eds) (2003), *China Competing in the Global Economy*, International Monetary Fund: Washington, DC.

Tseng, Wanda and Harm Zebregs (2003), 'Foreign Direct Investment in China: Some Lessons for Other Countries', in Wanda Tseng and Markus Rodlauer (eds), *China Competing in the Global Economy*, International Monetary Fund: Washington, DC.

Wagel, Srinivas R. (1980), *Finance in China*, New York and London: Garland Publishing. Originally published in 1914 by North-China Daily News and Herald, Shanghai.

PART III

Strategic direction

8.   International business strategies in Brazil*

Robert Grosse

INTRODUCTION

Brazil is the country of the future – and it always will be.[1] This statement has been voiced for at least half a century, and today it seems only slightly more likely to be rebutted than Moore's Law on semiconductors.[2] That is, Brazil seems to have enormous natural resource wealth and competitive capacity, but some problem always seems to arise to defeat an emergence of the country into the group of global industrial leaders. A strictly inward-looking growth path in the 1970s and 1980s led to relative economic stagnation (compared to much of the rest of Latin America). A boom in the 1990s was cut short by an economic crisis in 1998–99, when the currency devalued by over 50 percent in January 1999, and GDP grew at a rate of about –1 percent per year for the two years. Election of a leftist president, Luiz Inacio Lula da Silva, in 2002 has produced a stable growth path in the early 2000s – so perhaps there is a possibility that the old saying may be contradicted in the new century.

Foreign company presence in Brazil has been large and sustained over the last half-century, befitting the traditionally largest market in Latin America (recently replaced by Mexico in that measure of economic size). For most of the period, foreign companies have been significantly restricted in their local business activities, through pressures to take on partial local ownership, through pressures to include significant local content in products sold in Brazil, and through market reservation policies such as in the computer industry during the 1980s. Beginning at the end of the Latin American debt crisis, in the early 1990s, Brazil's governments have relaxed some of their restrictive policies toward foreign business, so it is likely that a greater amount of FDI and importing will characterize the Brazil of the early twenty-first century. By 2003, the large corporate sector in Brazil included many foreign as well as domestic firms, as shown in Table 8.1.

Business strategies to operate successfully in Brazil require a company to possess capabilities to compete against major local and multinational rival

Table 8.1 The Largest Firms in Brazil, 2003

Company	City/state	Business field	Sales ($US mil)	Country of origin
1 Petrobras	Rio de Janeiro, RJ	Petroleum and Energy	38 441	
2 BR Distribuidora	Rio de Janeiro, RJ	Wholesale (fuel)	10 567	
3 Telemar	Rio de Janeiro, RJ	Telecommunications	6 311	
4 Telefonica	São Paulo, SP	Telecommunications	5 699	Spain
5 Ambev	São Paulo, SP	Beer and drinks	5 344	
6 Ipiranga	Rio de Janeiro, RJ	Wholesale (Fuel)	5 060	
7 Volkswagen	São Bernardo, SP	Automobiles	4 791	Germany
8 Shell	Rio de Janeiro, RJ	Wholesale (Fuel)	4 382	UK/Neth
9 General Motors	São Caetano, SP	Automobiles	4 131	USA
10 Brasil Telecom	Brasilia, DF	Telecommunications	3 913	
11 Bunge Food	Gaspar, SC	Food and Drink	3 866	Argentina
12 Pão de Açucar	São Paulo, SP	Retailer	3 858	
13 Vale do Rio Doce	Rio de Janeiro, RJ	Mining	3 628	
14 Carrefour	São Paulo, SP	Retailer	3 628	France
15 Braskem	Camaçari, BA	Petrochemical	3 345	
16 Esso	Rio de Janeiro, RJ	Wholesale (Fuel)	3 192	USA
17 Texaco	Rio de Janeiro, RJ	Wholesale (Fuel)	3 175	USA
18 Embratel	Rio de Janeiro, RJ	Telecommunication	3 167	Mexico
19 Cargill	São Paulo, SP	Food and Drink	3 163	USA
20 Eletropaulo	São Paulo, SP	Utilities (Electricity)	3 056	
21 Nestle	São Paulo, SP	Food and Drink	2 916	Switzerland
22 FIAT	Betim, MG	Automobiles	2 813	Italy
23 CEMIG	Belo Horizonte	Utilities (Electricity)	2 649	
24 CSN	Rio de Janeiro, RJ	Iron and Steel	2 573	

Firm	City	Industry	Revenue	Country
25 VARIG	Porto Alegre, RS	Transportation (air carrier)	2 375	
26 Unilever	São Paulo, SP	Pharmacy and Hygiene	2 319	UK/Neth
27 Souza Cruz	Rio de Janeiro, RJ	Tobacco	2 284	UK
28 Embraer	São José Campos, SP	Airplanes	2 243	
29 Gerdau	Porto Alegre, RS	Iron and Steel	2 206	
30 Usiminas	Belo Horizonte, MG	Iron and Steel	2 200	Brazil/Japan
31 Itaipu	Brasília, DF	Utilities (Electricity)	2 184	Brazil/Paraguay
32 REFAP	Canoas, RS	Petrochemical	2 131	
33 Casas Bahia	São Caetano do Sul, SP	Retailer	2 112	
34 AGIP	São Paulo, SP	Utilities	2 108	Italy
35 Correios	Brasília, DF	Postal Service	2 074	
36 DaimlerChrysler	São Bernardo, SP	Automobiles	2 022	Germany
37 Sadia	Concórdia, SC	Food	1 966	
38 Light	Rio de Janeiro, RJ	Utilities (Electricity)	1 891	France
39 Copesul	Triunfo, RS	Petrochemical	1 891	
40 Ford	São Bernardo, SP	Automobiles	1 890	USA
41 Vivo	São Paulo, SP	Telecommunications	1 870	Portugal/Spain
42 Furnas	Rio de Janeiro, RJ	Utilities (Electricity)	1 757	
43 Bunge Fertilizers	São Paulo, SP	Fertilizers	1 725	Bermuda
44 CPFL	Campinas, SP	Utilities (Electricity)	1 576	
45 Cosipa	São Paulo, SP	Iron and Steel	1 573	
46 Nokia	Manaus, AM	Electronics	1 550	Finland
47 Sabesp	São Paulo, SP	Utilities (Water & Sewage)	1 515	
48 Perdigão	São Paulo, SP	Food	1 483	
49 BASF	São Bernardo, SP	Chemicals	1 461	Germany
50 Copersucar	São Paulo, SP	Wholesale (sugar & alcohol)	1 448	

Source: Exame 500 Largest Firms in Brazil (2004), http://www.v-brazil.com/business/largest-corporations.html.

firms. The US$500 billion local market attracts Fortune 500 firms as well as many local ones into most sectors of the economy. Brazil's geographic distance from industrial-country markets in the US and Europe has made it less attractive as a base for offshore assembly, in contrast to Mexico and even relative to Asian countries such as China and ASEAN members. Thus, most FDI into the country is either market-serving or natural resource-exporting. Strategies for foreign firms operating in Brazil thus tend to divide into these two categories.

This chapter is divided into background sections on the Brazilian economy and business and on government policies toward business, followed by discussion of the characteristics of foreign business in Brazil, and then of Brazilian business that has succeeded in competing internationally. Individual company experiences are used to exemplify these situations and the strategies that have been used by foreign and domestic firms. Lessons are drawn about the capabilities or competitive advantages that have enabled each type of firm to succeed in Brazil and in international competition.

BRIEF COUNTRY BACKGROUND: RECENT ECONOMIC HISTORY

Brazil's population of approximately 180 million people constitutes about one-third of the Latin America and Caribbean total, and its GDP at US$498 billion for 2003 accounted for about 29 percent of Latin America's GDP. These percentages have declined over the past two decades, as Mexico in particular has grown much faster than Brazil (and Mexico's GDP is now larger than Brazil's). Some measures of Brazil's relative economic size appear in the Appendix to this chapter.

With its extensive natural resource endowments and still relatively low wage costs, Brazil has comparative advantages relative to the US, Japan and European countries in many areas, including agricultural products (coffee, soybeans, sugar, oranges, tobacco and cocoa); livestock products (meat, poultry and leather footwear); wood products (pulp, paper, veneer and plywood); and mineral and metal products (iron, steel and aluminum). As a result, Brazil is a world leader in production and export of these commodities.

After World War II the country's economic development was based on a policy framework of import-substituting industrialization (ISI), which was facilitated by the huge domestic market. For 35 years the economy expanded relatively rapidly, and a large and diversified industrial sector was developed, mainly in the states of São Paulo, Rio de Janeiro and Minas Gerais. This success story had its share of weaknesses (perhaps most importantly, the dependence on natural resources), but growth was note-worthy in the largest Latin American economy.

The Latin American debt crisis, which hit in 1982, set off a decade of economic stagnation and external financial problems, which were only resolved in Brazil in the early 1990s, with the launching of the Real Plan in 1992 and the election of the plan's architect, Fernando Cardoso, as president in 1994. Cardoso's plan produced a much more stable and growing economy than Brazil had accomplished in more than a decade, and his endorsement of the global trend toward economic opening encouraged foreign multinational firms to enter Brazil and to bring in massive amounts of foreign direct investment. FDI into Brazil went from slightly over US$1 billion in 1993 to over US$10 billion in 1996.

Economic growth was rapid for several years in the mid-1990s, until the shock of the financial crisis in January of 1999. The average annual GDP growth rate in 1994–2002 was 2.7 percent, higher than the Latin American average of 2.1 percent. During the 1990s, the share of the population in extreme poverty declined from 19 to 14.5 percent in the country as a whole. The bright prospects were set back dramatically with the financial crisis that hit in January of 1999, producing more than a year of deep recession. By the time that Lula was elected president in 2002, Brazil had regained a positive though unimpressive economic growth path. The economy under Lula's leadership has grown a bit more rapidly during 2002–2004, averaging about 3 percent per year.

BRIEF COUNTRY BACKGROUND: GOVERNMENT POLICY REGIME

The Cardoso administration secured congressional approval in August 1995 for key amendments to the 1988 constitution that eliminated legal distinctions between majority foreign-owned and majority domestic-owned companies operating in Brazil. Legally registered companies – foreign or domestic – now enjoy the same rights and privileges, and compete on an equal footing when bidding on contracts or seeking government financing. Foreign-owned Brazilian companies may also explore for and extract mineral resources (EIU Country Report, Brazil, 2005 http://db.eiu.com/site _info.asp?info_name=ps_country_reports&entry1=psNav&page=noads).

The Lula government (2002–2006) has not changed the previous direction of policy toward business, despite the President's populist rhetoric and trade union background. The federal government continues to encourage foreign business in areas deemed important to Brazil's development, and largely treats foreign firms similarly to domestic firms. Subsidy policies to attract business activity, foreign and domestic, may be seen as the general strategy of the government to pull business into the activities and locations desired.

These most recent governments have not been typical of Brazilian policy-makers in the past half-century. Much more intervention in business has been the rule. Perhaps the example of the computer industry provides the best illustration of this (earlier) approach.

One Example of Brazil Federal Government Policy: The Computer Law

Brazil's protectionist computer policy (1985–92) is an outstanding example of an attempt to keep foreign multinationals at bay and to stimulate local firms' activities in this sector. The policy required local ownership and production of PCs and minicomputers (while allowing mainframes to be imported). The intent was to foster local technology development and creation of competitive firms in this sector. The result of the policy was a period of stifled development of computers and software, as other countries around the world moved ahead, benefiting from the technological advances of companies such as IBM, Microsoft, Toshiba, Apple and Dell. By requiring that PCs and mini-computers be made in Brazil by Brazilian firms, the government essentially cut off access to the rapidly developing technology of personal computers. No competitive Brazilian firm grew out of the protectionist regime, and Brazil faced continuing criticism by industrial-country governments for its antagonistic stance against the international computer companies. For these reasons, the policy failed completely, and was dropped after seven years of frustrating and acrimonious relations between the Brazilian government and foreign MNEs, as well as between the Brazilian government and foreign governments, local users of computers, and other groups hurt by the policy (Schoonmaker, 2002).[3]

The bargaining model of Behrman and Grosse serves well here to demonstrate that the dissimilarity of interests between foreign multinational firms and the national government is what drove the Brazilian government to push for localization of the computer industry, despite the large resource advantage of the foreign computer producers and their relatively low stakes in Brazil (see Figure 8.1). Over the course of half a decade the Brazilian government recognized the futility of the protectionist policy (given the local companies' initial and continuing inability to develop leading-edge, competitive computer technology). And under very weak macroeconomic conditions, with pressure from the US government to eliminate the anti-competitive barriers, the government ultimately dropped its inward-looking policy and joined the rest of the emerging markets and

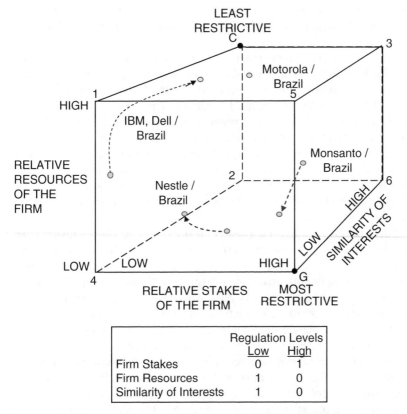

Figure 8.1   The bargaining relation between MNEs and the Brazilian government

industrial countries in promoting an open market for computer development and production.[4]

In 1992, the market reserve ended and was replaced by a new Informatics Law, which focused on local production instead of ownership. Under this law, companies that produce PCs locally avoid the national value-added tax (known as the IPI), which runs as high as 15 percent on computers. In order to qualify, PC makers must assemble the motherboard in Brazil as a minimum standard of value added. They must also commit 5 percent of their revenues to R&D, either through their own R&D spending or through contributions to Brazilian universities and other research institutions. Some parts of the Informatics Law expired in 1997, and the rest ended in 1999.

Local production incentives in the Informatics Law have encouraged companies such as IBM, Compaq and Hewlett-Packard to produce PCs and peripherals in Brazil, and the government hopes to attract suppliers of components such as motherboards, disk drives, CD-ROMs and semiconductors.[5]

Under the market reserve regime, a number of Brazilian companies were producing computers and peripherals for the domestic market. After 1992 when the restrictions were eliminated, most of these companies disappeared, or moved into other markets such as services and distribution. The only major remaining local company is Itautec, a subsidiary of the large Itau bank. Itautec is the third leading PC vendor in Brazil, and also produces TV sets, monitors, memory chips and consumer electronics. Local companies have been replaced by multinationals such as Compaq, IBM and HP, who produce all of their PCs for sale in Brazil locally. Compaq uses Brazil as a production base for much of Latin America, and exported $170 million worth of PCs in 1997.

An important center for computer production is the Campinas area, near Sao Paulo, which is a production site for Compaq and IBM, as well as other electronics companies such as Lucent, Philips and Motorola. Campinas offers an adequate infrastructure, proximity to the largest market in Brazil, a good supplier base, and has good universities that supply people and conduct some R&D in conjunction with leading companies. Other production centers include the Rio de Janeiro area, Minas Gerais, Bahia and the Manaus Free Trade Zone in the Amazon region.

The end of the market reserve brought about a drastic drop in prices for computers. One analyst estimates that prices dropped 50 percent the first year after the policy ended, although others point out that prices were declining even in the last years of the reserve. The real boom in IT spending happened three years later, however, after inflation was brought under control and companies could better calculate the costs and benefits of such investments. According to government data, spending on hardware, software and services grew from $7.7 billion in 1993 to $13.8 billion in 1997 (Figure 8.2). IDC data, which does not include industrial automation and microelectronics, put Brazil's IT market at just over $10 billion in 1997.

The largest supplier in Brazil was IBM, whose sales were $1.7 billion in 1997. Following IBM were Itautec, Unisys, HP and Compaq. The PC market has likewise grown rapidly, with unit sales growing from 650 000 in 1994 to 1.3 million in 1997. IDC's reported market shares for desktop PCs, based on revenue volume, are shown in Table 8.2.

Compaq also led in notebook sales, with a market share of 24 percent, followed by IBM, Toshiba, Texas Instruments and Hitachi. Estimating PC sales is complicated by the fact that about half the market consists of sales by small local assemblers, some of whom skirt the law to avoid import tariffs on components. The government is now trying to crack down on this

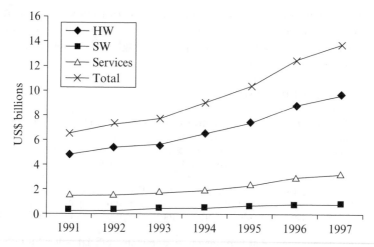

Source: Ministry of Science and Technology.

Figure 8.2   Brazil's IT market, 1991–97

Table 8.2   Top 5 PC vendors and market share (%)

1. Compaq	16.6
2. IBM	13.6
3. Itautec	12.2
4. Tropcom	5.4
5. UIS	4.0

Source: IDG Brazil website: http://www.idgnowbrazil.com.br

'grey' market, with the help of the big PC vendors. The situation is even worse in notebooks, where it is estimated that 65 percent of the market consists of smuggled goods.

By the year 2000, most PCs in Brazil were locally manufactured by global players including IBM, Compaq, ABC Bull and Hewlett-Packard, and Brazilian manufacturers such as Itautec, Microtec, UIS and Tropcom.[6] Companies manufacturing PCs locally receive fiscal benefits through the Basic Productive Process (PPB) which assures more competitive prices to PC local manufacturers as long as they invest 5 percent of their gross revenues in research and development in the sector. In these cases, Brazilian-made PCs retail at a price up to 35 percent less than imported ones. Personal computers, video monitors, printers and digital switchboards are currently subject to a 30 percent import tariff, which makes competition with local manufacturers stiff. In fact, this fiscal incentive may be more indicative of Brazilian policy toward business in the twenty-first century than the protectionist policies of the past – though it also encourages local investment and production.

Brazil's Industrial Incentive Policy

Brazil offers an interesting incentive to encourage R&D in the IT industry (manufacture of semiconductors and related electronics and components, digital equipment and software). To be eligible, an investor must expend at least 4% of its domestic sales revenue on R&D in Brazil (of which about ½ must be invested in an official research institution). The investor is entitled to 95% reduction in federal excise (IPI) in 2001, tapering down to 70% reduction from 2006 to 2019.

Several major foreign investors participate in this scheme, which has generated R&D expenditure of about $2.5 billion since it was first introduced in 1991. The scheme began as an alternative to the 'go-it-alone' model of information technology development that had previously dominated official policy on technology development. The earlier approach clearly entailed risks to Brazil's competitiveness. However, there appears to be no sustained assessment as to whether the incentive has led to cost-effective outcomes. This could be done before the scheme is extended to other activities, as seems to be foreshadowed in the Industrial, Technology and Trade Policy. (UNCTAD, 2005, p. 53)

In summary of the discussion of Brazil's policy regime toward foreign business, it appears that the lesson of the computer policy of reserving the market to local firms was learned very well by subsequent governments. The policy regime has moved to channel MNE activities into desired areas through incentives rather than penalties. This one line of reasoning should not be overstated, however, since the global move away from government intervention in business toward greater reliance on the private sector after the fall of the Soviet Union has also undoubtedly played a key role in guiding the Brazilian government's decisions. Next, the discussion turns to the approaches taken by foreign firms toward doing business in Brazil.

STRATEGIES OF FOREIGN MNEs IN BRAZIL: AUTOS

Although the experience of foreign computer companies was severely negative during the 1985–92 period, this was certainly not the outcome in all sectors in Brazil, even during the period of inward-looking growth. Companies such as Continental Grain and Cargill, Nestlé, and other food-related firms have long histories of success in the Brazilian market. And in the capital-intensive sector of auto manufacture, the Brazilian rules demanding greater local participation did not force out the international firms, which now have a long history of operating in the country with significant success.

General Motors has operated in Brazil since 1925. Despite its early-mover advantage, GM has been behind Volkswagen and Ford in vehicle sales in Brazil for more than two decades. In 2004 for the first time in recent history, GM sold more cars in Brazil than any other manufacturer, but that exception was followed by a return to third place for the first quarter of 2005. Regardless of GM's ranking among the auto makers, it has still pursued a reasonably successful strategy in Brazil over the years. That strategy has involved local assembly of some vehicles, importing others when the regulations permitted, and generally operating the Brazilian affiliate as a local company with external technology and financial help.

As with the other auto firms, GM has its manufacturing facilities in São Paulo state (in São Caetano do Sul). This is Brazil's industrial heartland, similar to Detroit or the US Midwest in general. GM has a major product development facility in São Caetano as well, and has used it to develop two vehicles (the Celta sedan and the Meriva minivan) for sale outside of Brazil as well as in the local market. Interestingly, the auto firms all carry out some degree of R&D in Brazil, due significantly to the government policy of subsidizing local production of vehicles if R&D (5 percent of the subsidy value) is carried out in Brazil.

Since there are no local competitors in this highly capital-intensive sector, it is not possible to demonstrate GM's competitive advantages relative to local rivals – though in principle it could be argued that the huge capital costs and need for extensive R&D to develop new vehicles is itself the competitive advantage that enables GM to avoid facing the creation of local rivals. The other foreign auto companies provide plenty of competition, and in fact GM has not led the sector in sales for more than one of the past 20 years.

A particular feature of GM's manufacturing in Brazil that differs from its operations elsewhere in the world is that GM Brazil has suppliers co-located with the plant in São Caetano, and the suppliers produce numerous assemblies that are then incorporated into the final vehicles at the same location by GM. So, the assembly line process actually includes third parties along with GM's own workers and inputs, to produce the vehicles in a manufacturing alliance. This degree of cooperation has not been possible for GM elsewhere in the world to date.

Ford has also been in Brazil for almost a century, establishing its first facilities in 1919 for importing kits and assembling Model T cars from the US. Ford then built a plant in São Paulo, producing 40 cars and tractors per day in 1923. Over time, Ford established assembly facilities for Ford,

Lincoln and Mercury cars and Ford trucks. Due to the government programs of import-substituting industrialization pursued by consecutive Brazilian governments after World War II, Ford incorporated more and more local content into vehicles, achieving 40 percent local content in 1953.

In 1979 Ford launched its first alcohol-powered vehicles in Brazil, responding to the government's program to subsidize alcohol-driven cars and thus to reduce oil imports. In 1983 Ford launched production in Brazil of the Escort model, a 'world car' that was exported to other markets from Brazil. In 1986 Ford and Volkswagen formed the joint venture, Auto Latina, to reduce costs by sharing production facilities in Argentina and Brazil. This venture was dismantled in 1995 after ten reasonably successful years.

In a step toward integrating suppliers more closely into the actual production of a vehicle, Ford Motor Co.'s assembly plant near Porto Alegre uses extensive supplier-built modules for assembling vehicles. One supplier delivers a 'rolling chassis', much like Dana Corp. is doing at Daimler Chrysler's pickup truck plant in Brazil. Other suppliers are responsible for powertrain, steering, braking and suspension modules. Ford provides the body and much of the interior. Some suppliers actually build up their products within the walls of the assembly plant, just as in the GM facility described above (Ward's Auto World, http://www.wardsauto.com/ar/auto_ fords_new_brazil/).

STRATEGIES OF FOREIGN MNEs IN BRAZIL: TELECOMMUNICATIONS

The telephone sector in Brazil was opened to foreign telecom service providers in 1997, when cellular phone licenses were granted to domestic and foreign investors. Then in 1998 the fixed-line telephone system of government-owned Telebras was divided into 12 separate companies, which were then sold off to the highest bidder for each. The privatization and licensing process generated about US$30 billion dollars for Brazil's government, two-thirds of which came from the purchase of the fixed-line companies.

Embratel (long-distance call carrier) was purchased by MCI for US$2.3 billion; Bell South, Sprint, Air Touch, and Southwestern Bell participated unsuccessfully in the bidding. In 1996, still under government ownership, Embratel's net profits reached US$405 million, a record in its 32 years of operation, and net revenues totaled US$1.7 billion.

Telesp (Sao Paulo fixed-line company) was purchased by Telefonica de España, Iberdrola, Banco Bilbao Vizcaya, RBS (one of the largest media and telecommunications companies in Brazil) and Portugal Telecom for US$5 billion. Telefonica de España and various partners also purchased

Tele Sudeste Celular (including cellular companies of Rio de Janeiro and Espirito Santo) for US$1.2 billion, and Tele Leste Celular (Bahia and Sergipe cellular companies) for US$370 million.

Tele Norte Leste includes the fixed-line Telecommunication Company of the state of Rio de Janeiro, Telerj, plus the state companies of Minas Gerais, Espirito Santo, Bahia, Amazonas, Para, Roraima and Amapa. Tele Norte Leste was purchased by Andrade Gutierrez (one of the largest civil construction companies in Brazil), La Fonte Alianca do Brasil, Inepar (an important business group from southern Brazil, Brazilian partners of Motorola's Iridium project), Brasil Veiculos and Macal. The purchase price was US$3 billion. This is an all-Brazilian consortium.

According to Anatel, in November 2002 Brazil had over 81 million telephones. Of this total, approximately 49 million were fixed lines (39 million effectively in service), and 32.6 million wireless. These figures demonstrate extraordinary growth compared to the mere 13.3 million fixed lines existing in 1994. Telephone density (the number of lines installed compared to the country's population) has also increased significantly. For each group of 100 inhabitants, the number of telephone terminals installed went from 8.6 in 1994 to 29.3 in December 2002. Many multinational players established domestic manufacturing plants to provide products and services to major new operators, increasing jobs in the sector by over 40 percent.

The main competitive advantages that appear to have favored the foreign telecom companies were: (1) available funding; and (2) the capability to successfully operate a telephone service company (that is, knowledge of the business). Brand names, access to foreign markets, and other advantages did not appear to play a major role in the process through which the foreign telecom firms took control of most of Brazil's market for telecom services.

STRATEGIES OF FOREIGN MNEs IN BRAZIL: BANKS

As in the case of telecom service, commercial banking was opened to foreign (private sector) banks in the 1990s, also as part of the privatization and economic opening process. Different from the telephone service, Brazil's government retained ownership and control of the two largest financial institutions: Banco do Brasil[7] and CEF. Banco do Brasil is a full-service commercial bank, competing both in Brazil and internationally. The Caixa Economica Federal (national savings bank) is oriented to the domestic market and serves households as in the case of US savings and loan associations. CEF and Banco do Brasil together control about one-third of total Brazilian banking assets and liabilities.

The remaining two-thirds of the country's banking business has switched greatly into the hands of foreign-owned banks, led by Banco Santander and BBVA from Spain, HSBC from the UK, and Citibank and Bank of America from the US.[8] These banks entered or grew extensively in the 1990s, due primarily to their financial resources, their access to foreign financial markets and instruments, and their ability to manage large-scale financial operations. This process was pushed extensively at the end of the decade, with Brazil's financial crisis and maxi-devaluation of 1999 making it 50 percent less expensive for the foreign banks (and other foreign firms) to buy Brazilian assets. (See the Brazilian real/US dollar exchange rate history in Figure 8.3.) As shown in Grosse (2004), banks tend to be able to compete overseas through competitive advantages such as proprietary skills and distribution networks – but again in the Brazilian context, sheer financial size has played a very important role in these banks' ability to acquire existing Brazilian institutions and to expand in Brazil.

PACIFIC exchange rate service

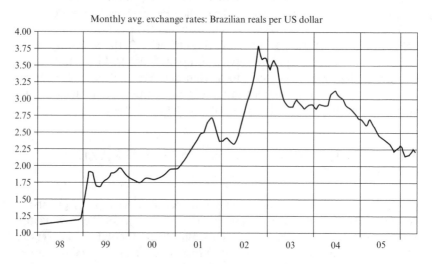

Monthly avg. exchange rates: Brazilian reals per US dollar

Note: Time period shown in diagram: 1 January 1998 to 25 April 2005.

Figure 8.3   The Brazilian real against the US dollar

Table 8.3   The largest banks in Brazil, 2004

Rank	Bank	Number of employees	TC	Balance Sheet Date	Headquarter City	Total Assets
1	Banco do Brasil	83.751	1	Dec-04	BRASILIA	90.044.508
2	CEF (Caixa Econ Federal)	106.061	1	Dec-04	BRASILIA	55.676.069
3	BRADESCO	100.164	3	Dec-04	OSASCO	55.834.704
4	ITAU	68.155	3	Dec-04	SAO PAULO	46.505.187
5	UNIBANCO	48.532	5	Dec-04	SAO PAULO	27.474.690
6	SANTANDER BANESPA	23.488	4	Dec-04	SAO PAULO	25.070.862
7	ABN AMRO	21.540	4	Dec-04	SAO PAULO	22.283.973
8	SAFRA	28.229	3	Dec-04	SAO PAULO	15.386.478
9	HSBC	4.721	4	Dec-04	CURITIBA, PR	12.950.120
10	NOSSA CAIXA	25.968	2	Dec-04	SAO PAULO	11.773.608
11	VOTORANTIM	14.125	3	Dec-04	SAO PAULO	13.783.407
12	CITIBANK	360	4	Dec-04	SAO PAULO	8.271.965
13	BANKBOSTON	2.505	4	Dec-04	SAO PAULO	8.067.572
14	BNB	3.700	1	Dec-04	FORTALEZA, CE	4.960.599
15	BANRISUL	8.725	2	Dec-04	PORTO ALEGRE, RS	4.597.159
16	CREDIT SUISSE	10.978	4	Dec-04	SAO PAULO	5.112.549
17	ALFA	10	3	Dec-04	SAO PAULO	2.930.398
18	JP MORGAN CHASE	849	4	Dec-04	SAO PAULO	2.480.793
19	PACTUAL	305	5	Dec-04	RIO DE JANEIRO	3.191.269
20	SANTOS	417	3	Oct-04	SAO PAULO	2.399.679
21	BNP PARIBAS	256	4	Dec-04	SAO PAULO	2.550.841
22	BBM	254	3	Dec-04	SALVADOR, BA	2.068.882
23	RURAL	207	3	Dec-04	RIO DE JANEIRO	2.009.960
24	DEUTSCHE	2.214	4	Dec-04	SAO PAULO	2.086.886
25	BIC	195	3	Dec-04	SAO PAULO	1.688.915

Notes: TC (Control Type): 1 – Federal Government Owned, 2 – State Government Owned, 3 – Domestic Private, 4 – Foreign Controlled Private, 5 – Foreign Participation Private

Source: Central Bank of Brazil.

COMPETITIVE ADVANTAGES OF THE FOREIGN FIRMS

Based on the examples given above, and on other foreign company histories in Brazil, it is clear that a number of common competitive advantages characterize these firms, in sectors from autos to telecoms. The common

Table 8.4   Competitive advantages of foreign MNEs in Brazil

Advantage	Examples	Companies/sectors
Proprietary technology	Computer software; product designs	IBM; Autos; Siemens
Financial resources	Available funds; ability to borrow	Fortune 500 companies; Telefónica
Access to foreign markets	Global distribution network; existing dist. in US or EU	Autos; Nestlé
Brand name and image	High-quality image; superior advertising	Branded consumer goods; Microsoft; HSBC
Management skills	Know-how for managing production, managing people	MNEs generally relative to Brazilian firms

competitive advantages include those set out in Table 8.4. These advantages are quite similar to those characterizing leading firms' capabilities for competing in Triad countries around the world. That is, they constitute almost a set of benefits of being foreign in Brazil, as opposed to the often-studied 'liability of foreignness' that must be overcome by MNEs in the high-income, industrialized countries.[9]

STRATEGIES OF BRAZILIAN FIRMS

The number of large Brazilian firms that are competitive at an international level is quite limited. Firms such as Petrobras (the national oil company) and Embraer (a privatized aircraft manufacturer) are regularly cited as success stories, but the number of large Brazilian firms competing internationally is far smaller than the number from Mexico. This section describes some of the international reach of four of the leading Brazilian firms that do compete internationally on a large scale.

Embraer

Empresa Brasileira de Aeronautica grew from investments of successive government administrations in the Aeronautics Technological Institute (ITA) and the Aeronautics Technology Center (CTA), aimed at training Brazilian engineers and pilots. Both organizations were located in San Jose dos Campos, in the São Paulo state. In 1969 the government decided to enter into production of military and commercial aircraft, and formed Embraer for that purpose. The turbo-prop Bandeirante, Embraer's first passenger airplane, was launched in 1973.

Embraer entered international business with export sales in Uruguay and Chile in the mid-1970s. In 1978 the firm sold its first Bandeirante in the United States, to a regional airline in Florida. By 1981, 39 planes were sold in the US market, which then became Embraer's most important outside of Brazil. By the end of 1984, 22 US commuter airlines were flying 130 Bandeirantes in the United States.

The process of internationalization was not as smooth as may appear from the above, and Embraer entered into difficulties with slow growth and high costs in the late 1980s. The company made losses for several years, and in 1994 was privatized. It was only in 1998 that the firm re-established a solid financial position and began a fresh start with new management, and a new (jet) airplane, the ERJ 145. Even this success has been tempered by an ongoing battle over subsidies with the Canadian firm Bombardier. Just as with Boeing and Airbus in larger planes, Embraer and Bombardier have regularly battled through the World Trade Organization and other fora to try to force each government to reduce subsidies to the planemaker.

In 2004 Embraer was the world's largest producer of regional jet aircraft, with Bombardier close behind. Embraer is owned by investment conglomerate Cia. Bozano and pension funds Previ and Sistel, which control 60 percent of the voting shares, and by a consortium of European aerospace companies – Dassault Aviation, EADS, Snecma, and Thales – which jointly own another 20 percent. The remaining shares are traded on the São Paulo stock exchange.

Petrobras

The Brazilian national oil company, was founded in 1953. It was the largest company in Latin America in 2004, with annual revenues of US$37 billion. As with most major multinationals in this industry, Petrobras has its greatest investment in the exploration and production of oil (the upstream business), most of which it obtains in Brazil. In addition, Petrobras has major divisions in refining and distribution of oil and derivative products, especially gasoline (the downstream business), and in natural gas production and distribution.

The company was partially privatized in 1997, with a sale of shares to the national development bank, BNDES, and to investors on the São Paulo stock exchange. The privatization law of 1997 allowed sale of up to 49.9 percent of Petrobras voting shares, with control required to remain with the Brazilian government. Further share sale took place in 2000 through a primary issue of American Depositary Receipts (ADRs) on the New York Stock Exchange. Today about one-fourth of the total voting shares are traded as ADRs. In 2005 Petrobras was owned 56 percent by the Brazilian government, 27.5 percent by holders of ADRs, 1.9 percent by BNDES, and in small portions by three additional investor groups.

The company traditionally was operated as a domestic firm, with export sales and some foreign activities, but fundamentally focused on the Brazilian market. In 2002 Petrobras embarked on a new strategy, buying the Argentine oil company Perez Companq for US$700 million. Petrobras also began to establish gasoline stations in Argentina under its own name, thus becoming a major retail participant in the Argentine domestic market today. This new direction may easily be extended to other South American countries, as Petrobras aims to be a leader in the energy business in South America. In 2004 Petrobras had operations in ten countries outside of Brazil, and it was the eighth-largest publicly-traded international oil company. The company's stated intent was to 'lead the Latin American oil, oil products, and natural gas market, and work as an integrated energy company, with selective expansion in petrochemical and international activities' (Petrobras Strategic Plan 2015, presented 20 May 2004 to institutional investors in New York).

CVRD

Companhia Vale do Rio Doce is the largest diversified mining company in the Americas. It is the largest global producer of iron ore, and has developed additional businesses in manganese, aluminum, potash, copper and nickel. The company was formed as a state-owned iron ore producer in 1942, and was privatized in 1997. The largest share of the privatized company was purchased by the national steel company CSN, which owned 42 percent of outstanding shares in 2004. Another 40 percent of total shares were traded on stock exchanges, and the government retained one 'golden' share, which provides veto rights over any major change in ownership or activities of the company.

In the early 2000s, CVRD has moved extensively into transportation services, operating the largest freight transport business in Brazil. CVRD owns the largest railroad business in Brazil, and operates several port facilities. This diversification is largely limited to transporting the minerals and metals that CVRD mines, but of course the transport network is used by additional clients, and has proven to be a very successful new line of business.

As far as internationalization is concerned, CVRD has for many years been the largest exporter of iron ore in the world. The firm has further expanded its portfolio of export products to include manganese, copper, potassium, kaolin (used for coating paper) and nickel. As of 2004, CVRD was not involved in any production activities outside of Brazil, but was selling a majority of its products outside of Brazil. The firm has invested in exploration for coal deposits in Mozambique and Australia, for potash in Argentina, and is pursuing other metals and minerals production ventures outside of Brazil, such that CVRD will have a global production presence in the near future.

Ambev

At the time of the 2004 merger with Interbrew, this was the largest beverage company in Latin America and the sixth-largest globally. Ambev itself was formed only in 1999, following the merger between Brazil's two largest brewing companies, Brahma and Antarctica. In addition to beer, Ambev was and continues to be a major competitor in other beverages, particularly soft drinks. It got the Pepsi franchise for Latin America in the early 2000s, and also produces soft drinks such as Guarana, Soda Limonada and Sukita.

In 2004 Ambev agreed to a merger with the Belgian brewer Interbrew, and the now-combined company (InBrew) has headquarters in Leuven and São Paulo. The company is the number one brewer in the world by volume, selling 202 million hectoliters (hl) of beer and 31.5 million hl of soft drinks in 2004. As well as size, the combined firm had industry-leading financial performance in recent years. AmBev was viewed as one of the best-managed, most profitable brewers in the world with industry-leading margins and a return on equity of over 30 percent. Interbrew was delivering industry-best compounded annual growth in earnings per share of 24.6 percent during 1994–2003 through developing new positions and building leadership brands in key markets worldwide.

Thus, Ambev today is a global organization, but only partly based in Brazil. The group's competitive strengths include global brands (Stella Artois, Brahma and Beck's), more extensive distribution than competitors, and cost leadership relative to the major multinational competitors.

IDENTIFYING COMPETITIVE ADVANTAGES IN BRAZILIAN FIRMS

The key competitive strengths of Brazilian firms in competing with foreign multinationals both at home and abroad tend to arise from local market and regulatory features. That is, the Brazilian firms tend to dominate sectors that are or have been protected by the government (historically, public services and natural resources), and sectors that can be managed by dominating local distribution channels (see Table 8.5).

The problem with utilizing these competitive strengths is that the firms tend not to have the financial ability or the knowledge to build international networks of affiliates. So they tend to end up competing defensively against foreign entrants into Brazil, rather than attacking foreign competitors on their own turf. This limitation is not unusual for emerging market firms, but given Brazil's large domestic market size, it is perhaps surprising that more domestic firms have not made the jump to international competitiveness.

Table 8.5   Competitive advantages of Brazilian firms

Competitive advantage	Description	Examples
Key advantages in domestic competition		
Government protection	tariffs against imports; subsidies; 'buy local' policies; local ownership rules	electric power; Embraer
Access to local distribution channels	Preferential access to local physical distribution or promotional vehicles	Local food processors; Globo; Ambev
Membership in an economic group	Conglomerate spread of activities; ability to realize economies of scope	Grupo Itausa; CVRD; Odebrecht; Votorantim; Globo
Internal capital market	internal financing availability	Bradesco; Itausa
Key advantages in overseas competition		
Low-cost production	Based on small-scale manufacturing or low wages	CVRD; Odebrecht; Votorantim
Access to raw materials	Based on natural resource wealth	Petrobras; CVRD;
Ethnic connections		Brazilian banks in USA
Technology		Unclear if this is more than infrequent

The first three of our four examples of large Brazilian multinationals may indeed end up competing against the world-leading firms in many countries, as shown by their expansion activities in recent years.

CONCLUSIONS

This discussion of international business strategies of Brazilian firms and foreign firms in Brazil leads to a number of interesting conclusions. First and foremost, it is not at all clear what competitive advantages will enable Brazilian firms to compete internationally against foreign rivals. In the domestic market they can (to some extent) rely on knowledge of the local conditions, domination of distribution channels, ability to share risks across several business lines in economic groups, and sometimes government support – but these elements are missing when such firms look overseas. The search for sustainable competitive advantages in Brazilian firms is still under way.

For foreign companies coming into Brazil, the competitive strengths that allow them to compete in industrial countries serve just as well in Brazil. These typically include proprietary technology, marketing skills, access to foreign markets, and financial resources. And in this market, which is much smaller than the US or EU or Japan, the bargaining capabilities of the firms relative to local government are much greater, leading to potentially better ability to obtain favorable treatment from regulators. Given the global acceptance of market capitalism in one form or another, it appears very likely that foreign firms will be welcome in Brazil for many years to come.

While the problems of being an emerging market continue to plague Brazil, there may be a leap to successful internationalization and competitiveness under way in this new century. The market continues to become more open to competition, foreign and domestic firms are competing strongly against each other, and the growth of the economy appears sufficient to allow the government to maintain its relatively free-market policy regime. These are very positive signs indeed.

NOTES

*   I would like to thank Gnel Khaohatryan, Tania Marcinkowski, and Nitin Chauhan for their excellent research assistance on this project.
1. See, for example: http://www.stonebridge-international.com/News/lula-oped.html; http://www.brookings.edu/press/books/brazil.htm?String=newsrel; http://www.aei.org/publications/pubID.11894/pub_detail.asp; http://www.columbia.edu/cu/bw/b_and_w/nov04/columns/verily/verily.html.
2. Moore's Law states that computer memory chips will double in capacity every 18–24 months, and it has been correct for more than 25 years.
3. Also see: http://www.floridabrasil.com/brazil/about-brazil-science-technology-computer-industry-policy.htm, and http://www.country-data.com/cgi-bin/query/r-1817.html.
4. This episode may have been one key factor in Intel's decision to choose Costa Rica, rather than its other site alternatives of Chile and Brazil, to set up a multi-billion dollar chip manufacturing plant in 1998.
5. This period is discussed in Sa et al. (2003).
6. By 2003 PC market share had evolved to include a local manufacturer, Metron, with a slightly higher market share than Hewlett-Packard (6 percent to 5 percent), but most of the market was still supplied by unbranded PCs (Kepp, 2003).
7. For example, shareholding in Banco do Brasil in 2005 was distributed as follows:

Shareholders	% ON
National Treasury	72.1
Previ	13.9
BNDESpar	5.8
Free Float	**6.8**
Individuals	2.9

8. Despite the extensive entry of foreign banks, there remain three private-sector Brazilian banks that make up a major portion of the total financial market: Bradesco, Itau and Unibanco.
9. The 'liability of foreignness' has been studied extensively in the international business literature over the past few years. See, for example, Lou and Menzias (2002).

REFERENCES

Banco Central do Brasil (2004), 'Capitais Brasileiros No Exterior – Resultados 2001, 2002, 2003', retrieved from http://www.bcb.gov.br/?CBE, mimeo.

Beausang, Francesca (2003), *Third-World Multinationals*, New York: Palgrave Macmillan.

Carvalho, F.C. (2000), 'New Competitive Strategies of Foreign Banks in Large Emerging Economies: The Case of Brazil', *Banca Nazionale del Lavoro Quarterly Review*, **213**(June), 135–69.

Economist Intelligence Unit (EIU) (2004), 'Brazil', *Country Profile, Country Finance, Country Commerce*, London, www.eiu.com.

EIU (2005), *Country Report*, Brazil, retrieved from http://db.eiu.com/site_info. asp?info_name=ps_country_reports&entry1=psNav&page=noads.

EXAME (2004), '500 Largest Firms in Brazil', retrieved from http://www.v-brazil. com/business/largest-corporations.html.

Goldstein, Andrea (2002), 'Embraer: From National Champion to Global Player', *CEPAL Review*, **77**, 97–115.

Grosse, Robert (2004), *The Future of Global Financial Services*, London: Blackwell.

Kepp, Mike (2003), 'Pushing Silicon: Metron romps in Brazil's consumer computer market, but that's not nearly enough', *Latin Trade*, May.

Lou, Y. and J.M. Mezias (eds) (2002), 'The liability of foreignness', *Journal of International Management*, Special issue, **8**.

Sá, Luciana, Sabrina Marczak, Jorge Audy, and Jairo Avritchir (2003), 'Effectiveness Of Fiscal Incentives To Attract IT Investments: A Brazilian Case', *EJISDC*, **15** (2), 1–10, retrieved from http://www.is.cityu.edu.hk/research/ejisdc/vol15/v15r2.pdf.

Schoonmaker, Sara (2002), *High-Tech Trade Wars*, Pittsburgh, PA: University of Pittsburgh Press.

Szapiro, Maria, Jose Eduardo Cassiolato, Helena Lastres, and Marro Antonio Vorgas (2001), 'Local Systems of Innovation in Brazil, Development and Transnational Corporations: A Preliminary Assessment Based on Empirical Results of a Research Project', Nelson and Winter Conference, Dinamarca, **237**, Maio.

UNCTAD (2004), 'OCCASIONAL NOTE: Outward FDI from Brazil: poised to take off?', Geneva: UNCTAD, UNCTAD/WEB/ITE/IIA/2004/16.

UNCTAD (2005), *Investment Policy Review – Brazil*, Geneva: UNCTAD, January 24, [UNCTAD/ITE/IPC/MISC/2005/1] http://www.unctad.org/en/docs/iteipc misc20051_en.pdf.

APPENDIX: ECONOMIC COMPARISON OF BRAZIL WITH SELECTED COUNTRIES

Table 8A.1   Comparative economic indicators, 2002

	Brazil	US	Mexico	Russia	Argentina	China	India
GDP (US$ bn)	440.0	10457.1	632.1	347.3	107.4	5208.3	562.5
GDP per head (US$)	2500	36440	6210	2420	2840	4072	1786
Consumer price inflation (av; %)	8.5	1.6	5.0	15.8	25.9	−1.2	4.4
Current-account balance (US$ bn)	−8.7	−483.4	−17.0	29.7	7.1	13.1	−1.4
Current-account balance (% of GDP)	−2.0	−4.6	−2.7	8.6	6.6	1.0	−0.3
Exports of goods fob (US$ bn)	60.3	684.8	155.7	105.6	25.3	238.8	68.2
Imports of goods fob (US$ bn)	−47.1	−1156.8	−166.9	−61.2	−9.4	209.4	71.9
External debt (US$ bn)	220.4	n/a	157.4	148.4	135.7	107.1	97.3
Debt-service ratio, paid (%)	48.9	n/a	39.8	15.2	23.7	10.8	13.4

Source: *Country Watch* figures from year 2002.

9. The tortuous trail toward corporate governance in Russia

Daniel J. McCarthy and Sheila M. Puffer

TWO RUSSIAS

To put corporate governance in Russia in context, it should be helpful to start by considering the views of a founder and vice-chairman of Ilim Pulp, a company that was engaged in a long struggle against a hostile takeover in the early 2000s. He summarized the dilemma faced by his and other companies as he described two Russias in a speech to the US–Russia Business Council in October 2002. One Russia he saw as a modern, civilized, dynamic country. The other was an isolated country where market principles are unknown, and which is plagued by pervasive corruption and illegal takeovers of independent enterprises. He summarized the dilemma, stating: 'You may go to bed in one Russia and wake up in the other . . . To prevent the recurrence of these incidents we must build one Russia, where written and unwritten laws are the same and where property rights and universal principles of basic business ethics are respected' (Zingarevich, 2002, p. 11). He added that, when Ilim executives realized that the laws did not seem to be protecting the company's rights, they went directly to President Putin and also publicized their situation in the Russian and international press. They thought that by going to the President, the company might benefit from Putin and the government's work toward improving the overall investment climate that was needed to gain entrance to the World Trade Organization (Keaton, 2002a).

Ilim's case against the hostile takeover was pursued over some years in court battles. At the same time, Ilim's owners and managers attempted to steer the company on a course of becoming a legitimate member of the international business community. Ilim's chairman affirmed the company's position on corporate governance: 'We are committed to leading the way in Russia toward responsible business practices, including greater transparency and improved corporate governance. It is critical that we stay committed to Russian business reform as well as the growth and vitality of our company and industry' (Ilim Pulp, 2002a). As noted in the same release, the president of the US–Russia Business Council, which Ilim had recently joined, recognized Ilim's progress: 'We are pleased by Ilim Pulp's commitment to transparency, effective resource management, free market approach and commitment to fair and legal resolution of property disputes.' Such a seemingly enlightened approach, however, would not ensure victory in the Russian courts nor in any other way a successful defense against a powerful and aggressive oligarch's attempts to take over Ilim Pulp.

BEGINNINGS OF THE TORTUOUS TRAIL TOWARD CORPORATE GOVERNANCE

In the spring of 2002, Ilim Pulp, Russia's largest forest products company, became the target of a hostile takeover by one of Russia's powerful oligarchs, Oleg Deripaska, and the saga continued well into 2004. The battle over Russia's forest products industry is understandable, given the country's still incomplete corporate governance structure, its nascent legal system, and the extraordinary attractiveness of the industry itself. And Ilim, with 65 percent of its production going to export, is the most attractive takeover target in an industry that is one of the last to be consolidated. The battle 'is also a sign that doing business in post-Soviet Russia – for Russian and Western investors – is still a tangled and complicated affair, with much of the battles taking place behind the scenes, in the media and on the streets' (Bellaby, 2002).

IMPROVING CORPORATE GOVERNANCE: A TWO-EDGED SWORD

Founded in 1992 as a small trading company during the government's privatization program, Ilim Pulp became the largest forest products company in Russia, producing over 60 percent of the country's output. The company ranked among the world's ten largest in terms of timber reserves and logging volumes, and among the top 70 in sales volume. Headquartered in St Petersburg, it has operations throughout Russia, including three of the country's four largest pulp and paper mills as well as other mills, logging companies, a trading company, and a mill in the Czech Republic. The largest mill, the Kotlas plant in the far-northern Arkhangelsk region, was acquired in 1995, while the Bratsk mill was acquired in 1999 and the Ust-Ilimsk mill in 2000. The company's revenues were estimated to be approaching $900 million in 2002. Nearly two-thirds of the company's products are exported to more than 90 countries, particularly to Eastern

Europe, China and the Middle East. The company employed nearly 50 000 people in 2004. Ilim is a privately held company controlled by four major shareholders with backgrounds in the forestry industry. Two were research analysts while two were engineers, and all had mill experience in Soviet times. The holding company is 100 percent owned by these four individuals, giving them control over 90 percent of Ilim's four major operations. One major subsidiary is 53 percent controlled by the four owners, while a German company, a strategic investor, owns 40 percent. 'That's the structure right now [late 2002], and the job of combining everything under a unified share on our way to the capital markets is basically about consolidating the company so that it has a unified share structure owned by the holding company which would have some minority investors', explained then senior managing director Mikhail Moshiashvili in a November 2002 interview with the authors.

Zakhar Smushkin, one of the founders, was appointed chairman of the board at the general shareholders' meeting on 25 December 2000, having been chief executive officer since the company's start in 1992. He was succeeded as CEO by Sergey Kostylev, who had been CFO since 1993. These appointments were dictated by changes in the company's corporate governance requiring that major shareholders serve on the board of directors rather than on the executive board. Ilim's actions preceded the announcement in early 2002 of the Code of Corporate Conduct, which required the separation of CEO and chairman of the board. And in June 2001, the company announced that it had engaged PricewaterhouseCoopers (PWC) as its auditor, that its last three years would be restated, and that those and subsequent years would be reported according to IAS and GAAP standards. Its plans called for entering international financial markets in 2003, seeking listing on domestic and international stock exchanges. Recognizing the progressive steps in Ilim's corporate strategy as well as the company's increasing value, an industry source reported: 'A few years ago, IPE [Ilim Pulp Enterprises] adopted the corporate strategy of operating its mills on a Western standard. This meant the company had to present a transparent financial history in order to obtain financing from the international markets ... PWC valued the Kotlas unit at around $600 million ... Kotlas's value had risen to $1 billion one year later, following a series of investments' (www.paperloop.com, 2002a).

But Ilim's efforts at improving corporate governance through transparency and proper organizational structures, in an attempt to attract international investors, also drew the unwelcome attention of a powerful corporate raider. 'Ilim's current plight is a stark warning to all those Russian companies seeking to make a break with a sometimes murky past. In order to gain international respectability and attract foreign capital, they have become more transparent. But that merely advertises their attractiveness to the kind of financier whose grasp they are trying to escape' (Smith, 2002). That report went on to note the dangers of transparency in Russia, and explained why many companies were unwilling to move toward more openness: ' "The company's attempts to address the concerns some people may have had about its structure prompted the attack by exposing the value of the company," says Derek Bloom, a partner with Coudert Brothers in St Petersburg. The previous lack of transparency, he says, "reflected what had been a common and prudent response to problems faced by many Russian companies" ' (Smith, 2002).

FOREST PRODUCTS: A HUGELY ATTRACTIVE INDUSTRY

The forest products industry is clearly one of Russia's most attractive industries, a fact not lost on oligarchs like Oleg Deripaska who is on record as wanting to consolidate the industry under his Continental Management holding company. The industry is known for exporting the majority of its base products, which over time should lead to excellent profitability. 'The forest products sector ranks fifth in Russia's gross domestic product in terms of output volume . . . Most of the rest of Russia's natural resources sector has been taken over and the only industry in Russia that is not wholly consolidated is the pulp and paper industry' (Keaton, 2002a).

'Forestry is particularly attractive, as it has several of the features which made oil so tempting – a working industrial structure, large reserves and an orientation to exports that earn hard currency. Forestry registered export sales of US$4.2 bn last year, making Russia the world's fifth largest exporter of timber products' (Economist Intelligence Unit, 2002). With its incredible reserves, the industry is poised for expansion on the world markets, except that plants are operating at close to their present capacity, and will require substantial investment to realize their growth potential.

Forest products is the latest industry in a series of many that have been targeted by powerful oligarchs:

> In the last two years, a relatively small number of financial-industrial groups has asserted control over the oil, metals and automotive sectors. According to a study by Brunswick Warburg, eight major shareholder groups control 85 percent of Russia's 64 top privatized firms. These groups had revenues in 2000 of US$62 bn, 50 percent larger than the federal budget that year and well above the US$47 bn amassed by gas giant Gazprom, electricity monopoly UES, the state bank Sberbank, and telcom's monopoly Svyazinvest. (Economist Intelligence Unit, 2002)

Industry experts as well as potential investors agree that the industry has the potential to bring riches to some, and possibly contribute to the country's economic prosperity. The actual result will depend largely upon the way the ownership of the industry materializes:

> To many observers, pulp and paper is the next natural resource-based industry that will make fortunes for Russian tycoons and cause nightmares for Western European competitors. The natural resource is plentiful, the equipment is heavily depreciated, and energy, the only other major operating cost, is cheap. Under competent management, it adds up to a license to print money. Take ZAO Ilim Pulp Enterprises, the country's largest pulp and paper group. It is forecasting an operating profit of $282 million this year [2002] on sales of only $868 million despite a heavy capital expenditure program. Unfortunately for Ilim, such conspicuous success makes it an obvious target for corporate raiders. (Smith, 2002)

The industry, and especially Ilim Pulp, have attracted the attention of Oleg Deripaska for many reasons, one of which is the extraordinary degree of concentration with around ten plants producing nearly 90 percent of industry output. Ilim Pulp itself owns the largest mill, Kotlas, and the company produces over 60 percent of industry output in its four mills. The company has clearly shown that it will not easily give up such a valuable business, even to a powerful oligarch. As one commentator noted: 'The stakes are high – the Kotlas paper mill is one of the biggest in a country that boasts nearly a quarter of the world's forests. It is the centerpiece of current management Ilim Pulp Enterprise's forestry operations, which expects sales to top dlrs [dollars] one billion this year' (Bellaby, 2002).

THE BATTLE FOR ILIM PULP

The attack by a powerful corporate raider was to play out over the next couple of years in a drama involving big business, an aggressive oligarch, numerous court cases, and even President Putin himself. Ilim owned a number of mills, each of which was a separate stock company with its own shares, the great majority of which Ilim owned as a holding company. The initial battle occurred in December 2001 when oligarch Oleg Deripaska's armed private security force occupied Ilim Pulp's Bratsk pulp mill as the culmination of a Bratsk minority-shareholder challenge. Deripaska also laid claim to Ilim's Ust-Ilimsk plant using the same technique.

This approach had all the earmarks of Deripaska's many strong-arm takeovers during the 1990s that consolidated his control of over 70 percent of the country's aluminum industry in his company, Sibirsky Aluminium or Sibal, which was subsequently named Basovyi Element. 'The two enterprises were ultimately recovered by Ilim, but only after its owners had secured financial backing from a rival magnate, oil baron Mikhail Khodorkovsky' (Economist Intelligence Unit, 2002). Also in 2001, a group of former competitors filed charges in a US district court seeking damages of $3 billion against Deripaska's company for alleged murder, bribery, fraud and money laundering. These charges were rejected by the company as untrue (Chazan, 2002).

The Next Salvo

The next salvo was fired on 25 April 2002, five time zones away from Ilim's Kotlas mill located in the far-northern Arkhangelsk region. A minority Kotlas shareholder who owned a mere 20 shares filed a suit at a local court in Siberia's Kemerovo region, alleging that Ilim had not complied with all the conditions of its 1994 privatization (Tavernise, 2002). Other charges alleged that the Kotlas mill had been unlawfully privatized, and also that investment obligations by the holding company, Ilim, had not been fulfilled. An earlier suit had alleged the same thing about Ilim's Bratsk mill. The judge declared in favor of this Kotlas minority shareholder, awarding $113 million in damages against Ilim, and sequestering Ilim's Kotlas stock as collateral. These shares were then confiscated by the State Property Commission and resold to Deripaska and his partner, Vladimir Kogan, for around $100 million. Ilim claimed that all this occurred before it was informed that anything was happening. 'But what is certain, is that the Property Fund took possession of Kotlas' shares and resold them before Ilim Pulp had any time to exercise any right of appeal and, it seems, without conducting even the most cursory check into the legality of the Kemerovo court's judgment' (Smith, 2002).

In early August 2002, as Ilim was developing its legal defenses against the bizarre suit, Deripaska's private security forces prepared to take over the Kotlas mill. Ilim, however, had fortified the mill, which was defended by Ilim managers, the company's own security forces, and local law enforcement officers. The entrance to the plant was barricaded with buses, cars and other such defenses. 'At this time, Ilim said, "Armed Sibal's troops are camped outside the Kotlas pulp and paper/fiberboard complex pushing for the chance for Sibal to install its own board of directors"' (Keaton, 2002a). Ilim's forces refused to turn the mill over to Deripaska's men, and Ilim filed countersuits in the Russian courts. According to Ilim's chairman Zakhar Smushkin 'They've probably gone for our assets because they're the best in the sector' (*Moscow Times*, 2002).

An Oligarch's Ambitions

Deripaska's apparent plan was to combine the Kotlas Mill with others owned by Sibirsky Aluminium and its allies, and to attempt to dominate the country's forest products industry. In July, Deripaska had announced plans to create a huge forest products company, and he and his partners had already acquired a 61 percent stake, disputed by Ilim, in the Kotlas mill (Chazan, 2002). His company sought to take over not only the Kotlas mill but also two other Ilim mills. It appeared that a new power grab at the Bratsk mill had begun in early August 2002. COO Frank Graves said, 'the front entrance to the Bratsk mill is now protected by concrete barricades "like the White House" . . . you can't drive a car or a tank up to it' (Keaton, 2002b). Sibal had apparently also attempted a takeover of another company's very large plant, the Arkhangelsk pulp and paper mill (Keaton, 2002a). According to Ilim's COO, 'It's not that the bully wants to take our ball, but that the bully wants to take the whole bloody playground' (Chazan, 2002).

> A Russian pulp and paper source familiar with the case said that Ilim, which started as an export trading company, had acquired its shares legally with money that it had earned . . . Illegitimate owners have used various pretexts to oust earlier owners, he noted, adding 'minority shareholders can do a lot with just one share.' The report noted, 'Ilim is hardly the first Russian forest products company in a decade to find itself in a battle to retain control'. (Keaton, 2002a)

In an apparent attempt to diffuse any violence, the company announced in July that it had signed an agreement with Deripaska brokered by Arkhangelsk's governor pledging to refrain from using force. The involvement of local officials should not be surprising, given the importance of the Kotlas plant to the town of Koryazhma and to the region. It employed 7000 people, 3000 of whom owned stock in the plant, and equally important, the plant paid 80–82 percent of Koryazhma's town budget and 10–12 percent of the Arkhangelsk regional budget (Romriell, 2002).

Keeping the Business Running

While the battle for Ilim Pulp continued in the courts, the company was still attempting to improve its operations to become a more efficient global competitor. In the summer of 2002, the company's chairman noted that operations were running smoothly: 'In spite of this difficult situation, all of our manufacturing sites are running according to the budget that was approved at the beginning of this year' (Keaton, 2002b). For instance, the Kotlas mill announced plans for a $267 million modernization effort to meet its growth needs and improve environmental safety (Romriell, 2002). The plant had acquired new machinery from major European companies like Voith Siemens Hydro, as well as control systems from IBM and Honeywell. According to the Kotlas head of production, Ilim had invested more than $100 million in new machinery over the past six years (Smith, 2002).

Referring to the hostile takeover, Coudert Brothers partner Richard Dean noted that in his many years in Russia he had never seen such a level of abuse of the judicial system: 'Ilim's circumstances are pretty extraordinary . . . This is a real case for the Russian government to prove it is serious about reform' (Keaton, 2002a). And it was becoming ever clearer that Ilim's situation could become a landmark case in determining the future of Russian business and corporate governance, and seeing whether the legal system would support legitimate interests including private property.

Positive Signs

Some positive signs were developing. As an Ilim spokesman noted: 'The dispute has dragged on since last fall in what could be a sign that Russia's rough and tumble days of carving up property are coming to an end. They could have swallowed us up two years ago and nobody would have noticed . . . Now it's much harder for them to work, but they don't want to believe that times have changed' (*Moscow Times*, 2002). An Ilim release stated that 'various decisions in four different courts all ruled in favor of Ilim in its quest to fend off the hostile takeover. The suits established the legitimacy of Ilim's ownership of the Kotlas Mill, ruling against Sibirsky' (Ilim Pulp, 2002b). And Russian law was changing in the direction of protecting ownership rights. Changes in the law that became effective in August 2002 required shareholders involved in commercial disputes to bring proceedings to a court of arbitration in the region where the company was based. The changes meant 'there'll be fewer opportunities for people in ski masks to seize control of a company', said Veniamin Yakovlev, chairman of Russia's Supreme Court of Arbitration (Chazan, 2002). Had the law been on the books earlier, the entire Ilim affair might not have occurred.

But progress would not develop without setbacks. Energoregistrator, the company that had become the new registrar of the Kotlas shares, had its license revoked by the Federal Commission for the Securities Market (FCSM). The chairman stated: 'We see that the registrar violated shareholder rights, violated the law' (Clark, 2002a). The legitimacy of a registrar is often the issue at the center of ownership battles in Russia, and thus the FCSM's decision appeared to be a major setback for Ilim. The commission's decision, however, was later overthrown by a court decision.

UNFOLDING EVENTS

Events from November 2002, when it appeared that Ilim might have won its court cases, and continuing well into 2004 indicated that the legal system had not yet definitively settled Ilim's ongoing ownership disputes, and that both sides continued to battle in the courts and in the press. Meanwhile, Ilim continued to operate as a progressive independent entity, strengthening its presence in global forest products markets, while preparing to obtain financing on global capital markets.

In early January 2003, Ilim's chairman Zakhar Smushkin, in a speech at Russia's Adam Smith conference on corporate takeovers in Russia, said: 'Corporate takeovers in Russia occur when one of the parties wants to swallow the assets of another or obtain them significantly below the market price.' He explained that two basic reasons why this practice of hostile takeovers is widely found in Russia are the poorly developed legislative framework and its associated corruption, as well as the mentality of Russian business people. He concluded: 'Such a practice in the market must be viewed as unacceptable, and if we have the task of doubling the GDP, then the mentality must be changed fivefold. Making changes in the hostile takeover situation must be viewed as one of the basic tasks of the business community' (www.lenta.tu, 2003).

Little Victories

Ilim's New York public relations firm, Fleishman-Hillard, continued presenting Ilim's story, noting in a March 2003 press release:

> Publicizing the opponent's [Deripaska's] unsavory tactics deprived him of the secrecy he required for success. Already concerned about his international reputation because of a need for Western business partners and investors, this fresh scrutiny forced him to back off and pursue other means to achieve his goals. The opponent clearly underestimated the resources – including Fleishman-Hillard – that his much smaller adversary had amassed.

The report noted that Ilim's case had been widely publicized, with a front-page story in the *New York Times*, as well as features in the *Boston Globe*, *Wall Street Journal Europe*, major Russian newspapers such as the *Moscow Times*, and leading Russian and Frankfurt newspapers, as well as German trade websites and publications (Fleishman-Hillard, 2003).

In the spring of 2003, Ilim achieved a key strategic objective by changing its organizational structure to a single or unified share structure with a central holding company. This required the approval of shareholders, as well as providing an opportunity for minority shareholders to cash out rather than continue as minority shareholders under the new structure. At the April 2003 annual shareholders' meeting, minority shareholders of Ilim's three companies, Kotlas, Pulp-Cardboard and Bratskomplexholding, overwhelmingly approved conversion of their shares to unified shares of the newly created open stock company, Ilim Forest Industries Enterprises (Ilim Pulp, 2003a).

On 15 July 2003, Ilim won another major court victory in its ongoing ownership battle. The High Arbitration Court of the Russian Federation sustained the rights of Ilim Pulp versus Sibirsky Aluminium (later renamed Bazovyi Element) by upholding the legitimacy of both the Kotlas and Energoregistrator positions. In doing so, the court denied the petition of Sibirsky's partners, one of which was the original registrar of the Kotlas shares from which Ilim switched when it engaged Energoregistrator as the registrar of its shares. This had been the trigger event for the FCSM to step in and declare that transfer invalid (Ilim Pulp, 2003b).

Despite this impressive court victory, it was clear that the dispute was still not settled. In early January 2004, Ilim announced that it had made a proposal to Continental Management, Deripaska's forest products group, to resolve the dispute between the two parties. The proposal was reviewed by Continental's shareholders, and subsequently lawyers for both parties began drafting a mutually acceptable agreement. The proposal called for settling the dispute amicably in a Russian court of arbitration (Ilim Pulp, 2004a).

Ilim Prevails?

In November 2002, it appeared that Ilim would win its battle with Deripaska. Despite a number of delays before the case was reheard in Kemerovo, fortunately for Ilim the court was changed to the regional commercial court from the original court of general jurisdiction. The change of venue was the result of a new Code of Commercial Court Procedure that had become effective in July. The commercial courts had a growing reputation for fairness and deeper knowledge of commercial law (Mason, 2002). The regional court dismissed the allegations against Ilim, and Derek Bloom expressed confidence that the ruling would end the dispute, with a subsequent hearing, likely in Kemerovo where the Kotlas mill was located. Bloom noted that the dispute was a benchmark case for the Russian legal system: 'Firstly, this strategy could be used to attack any Russian company that was privatized, and secondly, it represents a very aggressive abuse of Russia's courts. It is crucial that this decision be undone' (www.paperloop.com, 2002b).

On 4 November 2002, the Kemerovo court presidium overturned the $95 million decision against Ilim Pulp Enterprises. At the same time, the presidium overturned a 5 billion ruble decision in a case brought by another super-minority shareholder against a different Ilim subsidiary (Clark, 2002b). An Ilim Pulp press release noted at the time that the lower courts had violated Russian law by neglecting to notify Ilim Pulp about the trial and lawsuits, and that they had failed to validate the plaintiffs' claims before ruling against Ilim. It was also stated that the presidium's chairman had disclosed that the judge who had heard the original Kotlas lawsuit had been suspended for disciplinary reasons (Ilim Pulp, 2002c). The situation in late 2002 was put in perspective by Derek Bloom: 'The story has broad importance. This really could cause chaos in that all major Russian companies could have questions raised about their privatization. The legal theory here would destabilize many leading Russian companies' (Clark, 2002b).

Ilim Looks Ahead

In spite of the enormous distraction of the ownership dispute, Ilim continued to invest in modernizing its operations. The general director of the Kotlas mill stated in January 2004:

> We have had smooth operations at the Kotlas mill for several years. We work evenly, consistently, and as an entire system. Last year we broke the Russian record by producing 912,000 tons of pulp . . . This is due to investments in technological equipment made by Ilim Pulp . . . We have everything to grow the business: infrastructure, energy resources, and people. I think that in April we will begin building a new Ilim Pulp wood processing plant. (Sukhoparova, 2004)

And as further evidence of its commitment to the future, Ilim announced it would invest more than 27 million euros in 2004 in the latest imported technology for its forest products operations. This was part of a five-year plan to invest 170 million euros from 2003 to 2007 in upgrading and improving Ilim's technology, plant, equipment, safety and working conditions (Ilim Pulp, 2004b and c). Ilim's investment plans can be interpreted as providing the resources necessary to implement the company's strategies of improving operational efficiency and providing the ability to move into new product lines, all in fulfillment of the company's corporate strategy to compete effectively in world markets.

While Ilim continued to build a global business, the opposition reignited the controversy in the press. In early February 2004, in what was reported as a surprising and unclear prediction, Oleg Deripaska was quoted as saying: 'Kotlas needs a good owner, and I think he will soon appear.' He also inferred that there were no ongoing negotiations with Ilim. An Ilim spokesperson was then quoted as being bewildered by Deripaska's statements. Additionally, an expert from the Bumprom forestry products association stated: 'I don't understand how Deripaska can become the new owner of Kotlas without being in talks with Ilim. These are not the times for a powerful grab of enterprises' (Khrennikov, 2004). It became clear that the forestry wars were still not over.

CORPORATE GOVERNANCE: KEY TO RUSSIA'S ECONOMIC FUTURE

All of these issues led to what many observers saw as a bizarre but dangerous situation in a country that was attempting to become a member of the world economic community. A hostile takeover of Ilim Pulp by a powerful oligarch exposed the fragility of Russia's transition to a market economy supported by the rule of law. It also threatened the progress made thus far, and questioned the role the government would play in supporting progress toward a civilized business climate. In the words of one analyst: 'It [the struggle for the Kotlas mill] has also shown the limits of Mr. Putin's "civilizing effect" on Russia's financial-industrial groupings, and it underlines that the battle for control of Russia's forestry is reaching a potentially decisive stage' (Economist Intelligence Unit, 2002).

Ilim Pulp is all about the progress and problems of corporate governance in Russia, which in turn affects the ability of companies to develop into effective global competitors, and to access global capital markets. Transforming itself and embracing corporate governance and transparency allowed Ilim to become a far more competitive and more highly valued company, but at the same time invited the attention of one of Russia's most aggressive oligarchs. The company's situation underscores the need for strong corporate governance in large Russian companies, as well as the vital support of an effective judicial system. The presence of both would almost certainly prevent the type of hostile takeover exhibited in this situation.

A crucial result of such improvements would be increased confidence on the part of the global investment community to provide the funds so badly needed to modernize Russian industries. Such progress would facilitate not only the development of strong Russian global competitors, but also contribute to the country's economic and social progress as a civil society.

ILIM'S SITUATION REFLECTS THE TORTUOUS TRAIL

Although Ilim Pulp's situation might strike some observers as bizarre, in the context of 2002, it is reflective of the ever-changing conditions for corporate governance in Russia. The Code of Corporate Conduct promulgated in that year by the Federal Commission for the Securities Market seemed to signal that the country and its major companies were ready to subscribe to substantial requirements for transparency, responsible reporting and protection for various shareholder groups. The code could be considered as the culmination of a number of years of progress toward more responsible corporate governance. However, the turbulent history of corporate governance during the 1990s had provided a platform for continuing problems and setbacks. We summarize the business environment of those years in four stages, as well as the difficulties that began in the late 1980s and prevailed into the mid-2000s (Table 9.1). The table shows the government's objectives and the accompanying foundations for building corporate governance as well as inhibitors toward achieving that goal.

The first stage, which we call commercialization, ran from the mid-1980s through 1992, a period in which the government began to stimulate the economy by allowing managers of then state-owned enterprises some freedom in decision-making. The seeds of both entrepreneurship and abuses of power were sown at that time.

The second period, voucher privatization, began in 1993 and continued through 1994, with the government's objective of distributing ownership of state enterprises to managers, workers, and other citizens. The idea of private property took hold, accompanied by abuses on the part of many managers who saw an opportunity for self-enrichment. Examples of such abuses are presented in Box 9.1.

The third, which we call the *nomenklatura* stage, lasted from mid-1994 through 1997. The government sought to stimulate investment in enterprises, but exercised little control over methods and processes for doing so. One result was the rise of the oligarchs who gained control of the country's most valuable natural resources and industrial assets. They did so by using methods like the nefarious loans-for-shares scheme in which oligarchs colluded with high government officials in rigged auctions.

The fourth period, which we call statization, began after the country's financial crash in 1998 with attempts by the government to stabilize the economy and the country's financial situation by increasing government involvement. Starting during President Yeltsin's last months in office, the process accelerated under President Putin and has appeared not to have abated. Some positive foundations for corporate governance developed such as the 2002 Code of Corporate Conduct, which was based upon widely accepted Western corporate governance principles. Examples of other improvements in corporate governance that occurred in the late 1990s are described in Box 9.2. However, abuse of shareholder rights continued, particularly those of minority and foreign shareholders.

Table 9.1 Stages of the tortuous trail of corporate governance (1980s–2006)

Stage of business environment	Government's objectives	Foundations for development of corporate governance	Inhibitors to development of corporate governance
Commercialization (mid-1980s through 1992)	• To stimulate the economy and introduce competition by granting enterprise managers more autonomy and responsibility	• Enterprise managers began to view themselves as 'owners,' with more responsibilities and decision-making discretion	• Unclear legislation and poor enforcement sowed seeds for managers' abuse and self-enrichment at the expense of the state and its citizens
Privatization (1993 through mid-1994)	• To distribute ownership of state enterprises through voucher privatization to managers, workers, and the public	• Government launched privatization of formerly state-owned property, including many enterprises, and created private shareholders	• Many enterprise managers instantly became real owners, accumulated shares at nominal cost, enriched their own positions and diluted ownership rights of employees and others
Nomenklatura (mid-1994 through 1997)	• To stimulate investment into newly privatized enterprises, the State Property Committee sold shares in enterprises at auctions	• Continued the process of creating private shareholders in place of the state by putting more shares in the hands of individuals	• Little new investment for privatized enterprises due to risks regarding ownership rights and other uncertainties
	• Government policies seemed aimed at laissez-faire capitalism, and were implemented inconsistently	• The market economy continued to develop in ostensibly positive directions, attracting additional foreign direct investment and joint ventures	• Managers continued accumulating shares
			• High point of the abuse of power and denial of minority shareholder rights

Table 9.1 (continued)

Stage of business environment	Government's objectives	Foundations for development of corporate governance	Inhibitors to development of corporate governance
		• Foreign investors discovered the Russian stock market, increasing the number of shareholders in some enterprises	• Economic and political power were consolidated in the hands of a limited number of insiders known as the nomenklatura
Statization (1998–2006)	• To stabilize the economy and the country's financial situation by increasing government involvement and regulation, especially after August 1998	• Government and business groups began developing positive measures and influenced laws aimed at increasing enterprise transparency and disclosure	• Little progress until Putin's election in 2000
	• Putin signaled the need for more state involvement in the economy and business, with the objective of joining the WTO	• Some additional protection of minority shareholder rights through measures like the 2002 Code of Corporate Conduct	• Abuse of rights of minority shareholders, including foreign investors, continued but through more sophisticated methods

---

BOX 9.1 EXAMPLES OF CORPORATE GOVERNANCE ABUSES (EARLY THROUGH MID-1990S)

Powerful financial industrial groups, or FIGs, were created, including Menatep, Onexim, Inkombank and Alfa. This concentration of power led to numerous abuses of minority shareholder rights.

- In 1994, MMM-Invest created a voucher investment fund, essentially a Ponzi-type pyramid scheme that promised unrealistically high returns. Inevitably, the scheme collapsed, enriching the fund's creator and friends, while other shareholders and thousands of citizens lost their money.
- Rising oligarch Boris Berezovsky convinced managers at AvtoVAZ, the major state-owned automobile manufacturer, to produce a large volume of cars for him. He sold them on consignment and paid for the vehicles after two years with dramatically devalued rubles, realizing a personal financial windfall. He later gained control of AvtoVAZ, and in late 2002, the prosecutor general accused him of stealing over 2000 cars from the company through a dealer he controlled.
- In late 1995, the leading oligarchs, in exchange for supporting Yeltsin's re-election and offering low-interest loans to the government, were allowed to make essentially unchallenged bids for controlling shares in some of the country's major enterprises. They not only ran the auctions but also bid on the companies, with predictably successful results for themselves.

Referring back to Ilim Pulp, the oligarch Oleg Deripaska amassed most of his power and wealth by consolidating the aluminum industry during the privatization and *nomenklatura* periods. He had obviously changed neither his objectives nor his tactics by 2002 when he attempted his hostile takeover of Ilim.

AN OVERVIEW OF CORPORATE GOVERNANCE IN RUSSIA

To help understand the developments in corporate governance during the four periods mentioned above, as well as more recent events, we refer to a

BOX 9.2   EXAMPLES OF CORPORATE
GOVERNANCE IMPROVEMENTS
(MID-1990S THROUGH 2003)

- Yukos Oil became known as a leader in corporate governance reform. Chairman and CEO Mikhail Khodorkovsky, earlier recognized as a nefarious oligarch heading Menatep, led the reforms at Yukos. He apparently saw the benefits to increasing the company's valuation through transparency, disclosure and dividends to minority shareholders.
- Wimm-Bill-Dann, a major food-processing firm, also listed on the NYSE after engaging in serious corporate governance reforms. In the process, it was necessary to disclose that the company's major shareholder had a criminal past. Yet, the stock offering was very successful, apparently validating the importance of transparency and disclosure, even of negative information.
- Leaders at Hermitage Capital Management and Renaissance Capital Management pressured companies for transparency and disclosure, and sought seats as independent directors on company boards of directors. Pressure also came from other sources, including Troika Dialog's annual evaluation of corporate governance practices of major companies.
- President Putin replaced the corrupt CEO and CFO of Gazprom, who had led the numerous abuses of corporate governance in that leading energy giant. The magnitude of the company's scandals was often compared to those at Enron Corporation, and also led to the replacement of the company's auditors, PricewaterhouseCoopers. Putin also appointed a distinguished economist to the company's board to help protect the government's substantial investment as the company's major shareholder.
- After improvements in the corporate governance of Sidanco, Russia's seventh-largest oil producer, British oil giant BP increased its ownership position from 10 to 25 percent.

framework we developed. That model incorporates stakeholder relationships, as well as the influences of environmental forces on corporate governance in the country and its major companies (Figure 9.1). We also provide a summary of the way the major environmental forces affected

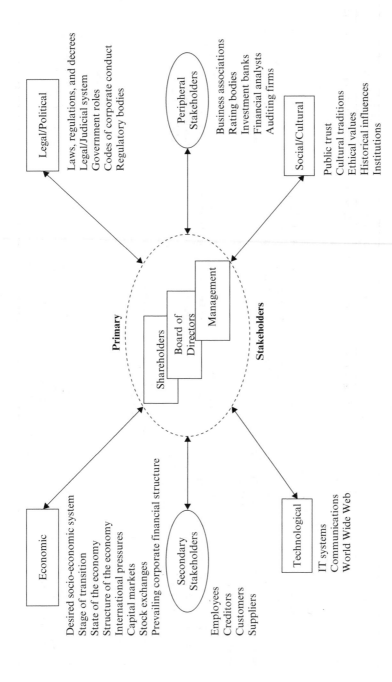

Figure 9.1   Influence of environmental forces on Russia's corporate governance and major companies

Table 9.2   Effects of environmental variables on three stakeholder groups (before Khodorkovsky trial and verdict in 2003–2005)

Environmental variables	Primary stakeholders	Secondary stakeholders	Peripheral stakeholders
Economic: Positive directions but most economic elements still in early stages.	Basically positive for shareholders, boards, management.	Basically positive for all parties.	Basically positive for all parties.
Legal/political: Laws, codes, etc., being developed but as yet ineffective enforcement. Government's major role breeds uncertainty.	Direction is positive for shareholders and boards, but some managements might see government involvement and weak enforcement as helpful to their own objectives.	Direction is positive for all parties, but weak enforcement and government policies could hurt all.	Direction is positive for all parties, but weak enforcement and government policies could hurt all.
Social/cultural: Traditional values may inhibit the development of open and transparent corporate governance.	All parties could be negatively affected, but management might prefer traditional ways to maintain control.	Most, except creditors, might also be satisfied with traditional ways that are familiar to them.	Some traditional values negatively affect all parties, by making it difficult for them to fulfill their functions.
Technological: Improvements, especially in IT, can help implement good corporate governance through increased accuracy, quantity, and speed of information.	Shareholders and boards benefit; management can also realize benefits, but might resist to maintain more control.	All parties benefit.	All parties benefit.
Cumulative effect of environment on stakeholders at current stage of economic transition.	Many problems remain, but directions are beneficial to shareholders and boards, and potentially for management.	Many problems remain, but directions are beneficial to all parties.	Many problems remain, but directions are beneficial to all parties.

224

corporate governance up to the fall of 2003 (Table 9.2). The overall conclusion we draw from Figure 9.1 and Table 9.2 is that progress was being made in corporate governance, particularly during the early 2000s. Numerous events in the economic, legal-political, socio-cultural and technological environments signaled positive influences for improving corporate governance, as well as relationships among the various stakeholders. This improving situation, however, came to a sudden halt in October 2003.

Chilling Effects of the Khodorkhovsky Trial and Verdict

The arrest and jailing of Mikhail Khodorkhovsky, chairman of Yukos Oil as well as the richest man in Russia, seemed to signal a major change in the role of the government and the legal establishment, two of the main influences in the environment for corporate governance. The resulting uncertainty over whether other companies and executives would be targeted for tax evasion, fraud or other illegal acts committed during the privatization period produced a chilling effect on openness and transparency. Yukos under Khodorkovsky had been considered during the early 2000s as a model of responsible corporate governance, and the company in disclosing the names of its major shareholders went as far as would ever be expected for any Russian company. Although only a part of the picture, the company's openness and transparency seemed to have produced the second side of corporate governance's two-edged sword when Khodorkovsky and his senior partner, Platon Lebedev, were both jailed in late 2003 and convicted in mid-2005.

So even though situations like the attempt of a hostile takeover of Ilim Pulp by a powerful oligarch continued through the early 2000s, progress had been made toward responsible corporate governance through 2003. The Yukos trial, however, derailed all such progress at least through mid-2005. President Putin seemed to recognize the damage done by the Yukos trial, not only to corporate governance but to prospects for attracting foreign investment. His response was to reduce the statute of limitations on contesting privatization abuses to three years, effectively closing the door on such charges. Many observers, however, including some of the country's most prominent executives, were sceptical that any such order or law would be implemented.

By this action, Putin seemed to be trying to add more certainty to the government's role in dealing with business, which if implemented, should produce a more stable environment for business, including corporate governance. In mid-2005, however, uncertainty still prevailed, and it was clear that the progress of corporate governance, already derailed for two years, would not regain momentum for at least another year.

IMPLICATIONS AND CONCLUSIONS

Companies like Ilim Pulp that are attempting to improve their corporate governance through increased openness and transparency will continue to face the threat of a double-edged sword that could strip ownership rights by actions of powerful oligarchs, corrupt courts, changing laws or even actions of the government itself. Progress in corporate governance will be made slowly, if at all, until more certainty is introduced into the various aspects of the environment for business and corporate governance.

Corporate governance will likely remain in transition for some time in Russia since there is so much to be done internally among the three primary stakeholder groups, as well as within all of the external factors of the framework affecting the primary and secondary stakeholders. The Khodorkovsky trial and guilty verdict set the progress of corporate governance back by at least several years.

Corporate governance will continue to vary greatly among Russian companies of all sizes, even among the very large companies that have led the move toward more responsible corporate governance.

The government is in a position to play a key role in influencing the external environment for corporate governance since it works with a top-down approach, and the Federal Commission for the Securities Market has so far borrowed mostly from Western agency theory.

Over time, changes in relationships among the board of directors, managers and shareholders will depend heavily on socio-cultural influences, but institutional changes can have major effects in the shorter run. For the time being, institutions will be likely to continue to reflect heavily influences from the past. This situation will occur as the legal and governmental influences reflect traditions and values from the past rather than embracing changes necessary for enlightened corporate governance.

The future of corporate governance in Russia remains uncertain, but positive, major changes will likely develop slowly. The evolving system will likely reflect a Russian character rather than a continuation of the Western influence of agency theory. However, the need for foreign investment could stimulate activities by the government and major companies that produce positive changes in a shorter time frame.

REFERENCES

Bellaby, M.D. (2002), 'Paper Mill Managers Battle Over Ownership Rights with one of Russia's Most Powerful Businessmen', *Associated Press*, 9 August.

Chazan, G. (2002), 'Competition, Russian-style: At Disputed Kotlas Mill, Corporate Fighting is Bare-knuckle', *Wall Street Journal Europe*, 12 August.

Clark, T. (2002a), 'FSC Accuses Ilim of Black PR Campaign', *Moscow Times*, 15 August.

Clark, T. (2002b), 'Ilim Pulp: Court Overturns $95m Decision', *Moscow Times*, 5 November.

Economist Intelligence Unit (2002), 'Russia Industry – Oligarchs Target Timber', EIU ViewsWire, 12 August.

Fleishman-Hillard (2003), 'Pulp Non-fiction: Outmaneuvering an Oligarch in a Russia-style Hostile Takeover', New York, March.

Ilim Pulp (2002a), 'Ilim Pulp is First Russian Forestry Company to Join US–Russia Business Council', press release, 25 September.

Ilim Pulp (2002b), 'Ilim Pulp Reports Four Favorable Court Decisions, Expresses Confidence of Another Case at Heart of Attempted Hostile Takeover', press release, 20 August.

Ilim Pulp (2002c), 'Ilim Pulp, Russia's Biggest Pulp and Paper Company, Wins Major Court Rulings in Fight Against Hostile Takeover', press release, 4 November.

Ilim Pulp (2003a), 'Minoritarnye Aktsionery Predpriiatii Korporatsiia "Ilim Palp" Podderzhivaiiut Perekhod na Edinuiu Aktsiiu' [Minority Shareholders of Ilim Pulp Support Transfer to Unified Share], press release, 17 June.

Ilim Pulp (2003b), 'Vysshii Arbitrazhnyi Sud RF Otkazal "Bazovomu Elementu"' [High Arbitration Court of the RF Dismissed 'Bazovyi Element'], press release, 23 July.

Ilim Pulp (2004a), ' "Ilim Palp" Predlozhil Mekhanizm Uregulirovaniia Konflikta' [Ilim Pulp Proposes a Mechanism to Resolve the Conflict], press release, 8 January.

Ilim Pulp (2004b), ' "Ilim Palp" v 2004 Godu Investiruet Bolee 27 Millionov Evro na Tekhnicheskoe Perebooruzhenie Lesnogo Kompleksa' [Ilim Pulp Will Invest More than 27 Million Euros in 2004 in Technical Upgrading of its Operations], press release, 29 January.

Ilim Pulp (2004c), 'Ust'-Ilimskii LPK (Korporatsiia "Ilim Palp") Vydelil 14,9 Millionov Rublei Dlia Vypolneniia Tselovoi Programmy po Okhrane Truda i Uluchsheniiu Uslovii Truda' [Ust'-Ilimskii LPK (Ilim Pulp Corporation) Spent 14.9 Million Rubles to Fulfill its Program to Improve Safety and Working Conditions], press release, 22 January.

Keaton, D. (2002a), 'Ilim Pulp Enterprise Fighting Hostile Takeover Attempt', *Forestweb*, 2 August, www.info@forestweb.com

Keaton, D. (2002b), 'Ilim Pulp Enterprise's Bratsk Mill Under Threat Again', *Forestweb*, 6 August, www.info@forestweb.com

Khrennikov, I. (2004), 'Orakul Deripaska' [Deripaska the Oracle], *Vedomosti*, 2 February, posted on www.ilimpulp.ru.

Mason, V. (2002), 'Court Orders Retrial of Ilim Pulp Takeover Case', *World Markets Analysis*, 5 November.

Moscow Times (2002), 'Chips Fly in Fight Over Paper Mill', 8 June.

Romriell, L. (2002), 'The Kotlas Paper Wars of Koryazhma', *Russia Journal*, 29 July.

Smith, G. (2002), 'Pulp Mill Fight Shows the Danger of Success in Russia', *Dow Jones News Service*, 12 August.

Sukhoparova, N. (2004), 'My Rabotaem ne Tol'ko na Segodnia, no i na Dalekoe' [We are Working Not Only for Today, But Also for the Long Term], *Pravda Severa*, 21 January posted on www.ilimpulp.ru.

Tavernise, S. (2002), 'Handful of Corporate Raiders Transform Russia's Economy', *New York Times*, 13 August, A1.

www.lenta.ru (2003), 'V Moskve Otkrylac' Konferentsiia "Korporativnye pogloshcheniia v Rossii"' [Corporate Takeover Conference Opens in Moscow], 1 July, posted on www.ilimpulp.ru.

www.paperloop.com (2002a), 'Battle for Kotlas Hots [sic] Up'.

www.paperloop.com (2002b), 'Russia's Ilim Pulp Enterprise Wins Key Court Cases in Mill Ownership Dispute', 4 November.

Zingarevich, B.G. (2002), 'The Russia We Choose', *Russia Business Report*, US–Russia Business Council, Washington, DC. Speech delivered to the US–Russia Business Council, 4 October.

Sources of Materials for This Chapter

The material on Ilim Pulp was taken primarily from 'Ilim Pulp Battles a Hostile Takeover', in Daniel J. McCarthy, Sheila M. Puffer and Stanislav V. Shekshnia (eds) (2004), *Corporate Governance in Russia*, Cheltenham, UK and Northampton, MA, USA: Edward Elgar, Chapter 16, pp. 300–23.

Some other materials, particularly the tables, boxes and the figure, were originally published in the following articles, which were also reprinted in our book, *Corporate Governance in Russia*, noted above:

McCarthy, Daniel J. and Sheila M. Puffer (2003), 'Corporate Governance in Russia: A Framework for Analysis', *Journal of World Business*, **38**(4), 397–415.

Puffer, Sheila M. and Daniel J. McCarthy (2003), 'The Emergence of Corporate Governance in Russia', *Journal of World Business*, **38**(4), 284–98.

10. Strategic evolution and partnering in the Indian pharmaceutical industry

Ravi Sarathy

In 2005 India recognized product patents, as a condition of joining the WTO, which required that India's IP laws be TRIPS compliant. Previously, India had recognized only process patents. The process patent regime allowed Indian pharmaceutical companies to reverse-engineer molecules, develop non-infringing processes, and develop 'generic' versions of best-selling drugs, selling them cheaply within India, and exporting them to countries such as Russia, China, Brazil and African countries. Indian companies gained considerable skill at developing generic versions of drugs.

The patent law change forced Indian companies to reconsider their product development policies, and to begin spending more on R&D. The change in law also led pharmaceutical and biotech multinationals (MNCs) to consider whether it was the right time to begin expanding their R&D in the Indian market, as well as other activities such as contract research, contract manufacturing and marketing activities in India. One consequence is that India received 1312 patent applications for pharmaceutical products by September 2005, second only to the US, which had received 2111 over the same period. (However, it is likely that much of the patent filing activity was of a catch-up nature, seeking to obtain patents in India for existing molecules under the new product patent regime).

This chapter considers the strategies of Indian pharmaceutical companies and evaluates how their strategies might evolve in response to the changed patent law and other global pharmaceutical industry changes. It also reviews the capabilities that Indian pharmaceutical firms possess and will need in the future to compete successfully in the evolving Indian and global pharmaceutical market. In addition, the chapter reviews how foreign pharmaceutical multinationals might respond to the changes in the Indian market and increase their presence in India, at several levels of the value chain.

MARKET SIZE

In 2003, Indian pharmaceutical sales were around $5.25 billion, of which $3.28 billion was export sales. Imports were $930 million. The bulk of exports were low-priced generic drugs; hence, while the Indian industry global market share was 8 percent by volume, and No. 4 in the world, it was only 1 percent of world revenues, and No. 13 by value. The industry spent relatively little on R&D, at an average of 2 percent of sales, far below the average R&D spending of US big pharmaceutical companies, which typically exceeded 10 percent of sales. While the Indian industry is currently heavily dependent on export sales (and hard currency revenues and earnings), the future potential of domestic consumption within India is large. Current per capita consumption is approximately $5 per person per year, a figure which is only likely to increase significantly as per capita incomes rise and the Indian government spends more of its budget on national health care for the poorest portions of the population. Thus, the McKinsey consulting firm projects the Indian pharmaceutical market to reach $25 billion in size by the year 2010. Future growth in market size will also be influenced by the emergence of drugs targeted to diseases with high local incidence and to local therapeutic area opportunities, the development of the local health care system and how health care is paid for. Furthermore, drug affordability, accessibility, drug pricing controls and new drug approval process; all these will be influential, in addition to the implementation of the new patent laws.

INDIAN PHARMACEUTICAL FIRMS: HISTORIC STRATEGIES AND CAPABILITIES

Indian drug firms had long reverse-engineered popular drugs, developed a non-infringing manufacturing process, and then sold the resulting formulations at low cost domestically and in other developing countries, such as Brazil, China and Russia, and in Africa. With the change in the law, such a strategy is no longer viable. Future competitive success will depend on innovative ability, not on who can copy the fastest.

Khanna and Palepu (2005) consider how companies from emerging markets can compete effectively with global MNCs (become 'emerging giants' themselves) by exploiting their knowledge of their domestic markets, use unique knowledge of domestic factor markets effectively, and cite Ranbaxy and Dr. Reddy's Labs as two Indian pharmaceutical company examples. Madhok and Osegowitsch (2000) specifically investigate international transactions in the biotechnology industry, looking at licensing agreements, R&D contracts, joint ventures, acquisitions, equity investments, and, the formation of international subsidiaries, and found that the search for dynamic capabilities underpinned the number, direction and flow of such transactions. Griffith and Harvey (2001) have suggested that it is the speed of change that requires firms to develop global dynamic capabilities, and that asset specificity, predictability and market knowledge all increase a partner's power in the international arena, that is, in this instance, between Indian and global pharmaceutical firms. This suggests that Indian pharmaceutical firms need to develop assets specifically tied to the partnering relationship they might form with a global partner, such as developing R&D skills focused on a specific project of interest to the partner; that Indian pharma firms will benefit from a partnership arrangement where they have a degree of predictability regarding their foreign partner's needs and goals; and, Indian partners will gain greater power when they can demonstrate significant market knowledge about the domestic Indian market as well as key foreign markets they are active in, that is, in principal markets such as those of China, Russia and Brazil. The role of asset specificity in encouraging partnerships runs counter to traditional transaction cost analysis, which typically suggests that asset specificity should lead to internalization of operations. Murray (2001) suggests that trust between partners is paramount, and additional variables that influence partnership seeking include partner commitment, technological uncertainty, transaction frequency, the similarity of long-term objectives, resource constraints, uncertainty avoidance, government regulations, and, local knowledge.

Katila and Yang (2003) have focused on the decision to collaborate as a means of gaining capabilities, and have shown that collaboration is more likely when both partners enjoy patent protection, are highly committed to R&D – high R&D intensity – have significant experience from prior collaborations, and, there exist external factors that are supportive of collaboration, such as legal structures, and state and industry associations – what they describe as support infrastructures. This suggests that as Indian support infrastructures develop, as Indian firms commit greater funds to R&D, as they develop additional collaborative experience, and, as the patent protection regime becomes clarified, the overall pace of partnering between Indian and global pharmaceutical firms is likely to increase.

However, not all Indian firms will develop such capabilities at an equal rate. Knight and Cavusgil (2004) suggest that early internationalization is more likely when firms have a managerial vision wedded to internationalization, and, when they have gained international experience and knowledge ahead of the rest of their competitors. Thus, Indian firms that are already active in export markets, gain a significant share of their sales from exports and have top management committed to globalization, are more likely to gain the needed dynamic capabilities to compete in the changed Indian environment.

India has also been a prime location for low-cost contract manufacturing of drugs, as it has the largest number of FDA certified manufacturing facilities conforming to Good Manufacturing Practices (GMP), outside of the US – over 80 in 2004. Other resources that the Indian pharmaceutical industry environment offers include low-cost human capital, particularly scientists, chemists and chemical engineers, who can be deployed in the investigation and development of new molecules, and new drugs, as well as work on new drug delivery systems. India can also be inviting as a location to conduct clinical trials at low cost and in a speedy manner, and India's proven software and information technology skills could be extended to related fields such as bio-informatics, data analysis and post-launch support.

Some of India's attraction flows from the serious concerns that large pharmaceuticals have over the cost, pace and effectiveness of their global drug discovery programs. Large pharmaceutical companies face difficulties in three areas:

- efficient and effective drug discovery;
- moving quickly from discovery to development;
- conducting clinical trials in a timely fashion.

Drug discovery programs are getting more expensive, with the average cost of a successful drug bordering on $1 billion and taking as long as ten years from discovery to successful FDA approval (Ernst & Young 2004). This leaves little time for the drug companies to earn sales and profits and recoup their R&D investments, as patent filing takes place early in the discovery cycle, and the lengthy development and approval process reduces the period of patent validity within which exclusivity and high margins can be exercised. Hence, drug companies face a pressing need to lower the cost of drug discovery, improve its effectiveness (the rate at which new drugs are discovered) and reduce the time it takes to discover new drugs (Linder et al. 2004). Countries such as India, which can offer a pool of qualified but lower-cost scientists, chemists and lab technicians, are attractive because they provide an avenue for the global drug industry to meet their drug discovery goals of cost reduction, speed and greater effectiveness.

At the same time as the number of patented high-priced blockbuster drugs go off-patent, large pharmaceutical companies have begun strengthening their own generic drug operations, and India is also attractive as a source of generic drug manufacture, be it in wholly-owned facilities or through subcontracting with efficient and low-cost Indian drug firms.

Information analysis is also becoming important, as drug companies move to automated methods of high-throughput screening of large numbers of molecules, in an effort to isolate the few that would be worthy of further intensive investigation. Such methods throw off large amounts of data which require considerable manpower to develop software analytical programs and statistical data analysis. Both of these operations can also be done effectively in India, given its recent successes with software and business process outsourcing. Indeed, the very companies that have dominated the Indian IT industry, such as TCS, Wipro and Infosys, have set up divisions devoted to bio-informatics and software development for the drug discovery and clinical test phases of the industry.

PHARMACEUTICAL VALUE CHAIN AND INDIA'S ATTRACTIVENESS

The Indian market may be attractive both as a market and as a resource base. It has potential as a market, given the large population, growing incomes and prospects for increased health care spending. India also offers promise for conducting drug research, clinical testing and information analysis. Resource availability and costs are critical to choosing India as a source of supply and location for upstream value chain activities. Resources from the Indian context that can be brought to bear on the drug industry value chain can be summarized as follows:

- drug discovery: availability of research professionals, managers; costs, and productivity;
- clinical testing; Contract Research Organizations (CROs); the ease of attracting patients for new drug testing, the attraction of a drug-naive population, ethical issues, quality of testing procedures and reliability of information;
- the availability and reliability of low-cost manufacturing, FDA certified GMP plants;
- experience and productivity in generic drugs manufacturing;
- supplying APIs and bulk drugs;
- India as an export platform
- packaging, multiple drug delivery forms;
- bio-informatics, data analysis, data management and marketing support.

An interesting question concerns India's biotech capabilities: whether India has sufficient abilities to be attractive as a location for biotech research and bioprocess-based manufacturing. Are Indian pharmaceutical companies building up biotech capability? Indian companies are active in vaccines, biogenerics and in genomics research, drawing on the biodiversity of India. There are also industry activities focusing on agriculture and on developing enzymes for industrial users. Biocon, discussed later, is an example of the rapid development of biotech capabilities in India. Biotech in India is clustered primarily in Bangalore and Hyderabad, and in Pune, near Bombay (Mumbai). Figure 10.1 summarizes the links between Indian pharmaceutical firm capabilities and the global pharmaceutical value chain.

Complementing the value chain fit, there are broad economic advantages flowing from lower labor cost, more industry-friendly government policies than in the past, increased availability of venture capital, the widespread use of English as a business language, and the changed patent laws. However, since the patent law change has been in effect for just a few months as of December 2005, MNCs are concerned about how the new IP regime will be enforced. For example, how will challenges to patents be considered, and what are the time limits within which such challenges will be judged? Otherwise, challenges can become a tactic for indefinitely postponing patent issuance. Other implementation conditions include the existence of compulsory licensing regulations and the conditions under which such compulsory licensing would be required; and controls that would prevent 'evergreening' of patents, that is, the attempt by patent holders to extend patent life based on minor improvements.

Some of the disadvantages of India as a location include limited biotech skills (though these are rapidly improving), social issues centered around affordability that seek to control drug pricing and profits, poor infrastructure, cultural gaps, political attitudes towards MNCs, possible political risk stemming from left-wing and Congress Party electoral alliances, and macroeconomic risks such as foreign exchange rate fluctuations, inflation and economic growth rate reductions (from the levels of around 8 percent that India has averaged over the past several years).

Alternative locations, specially China, would be considered by the pharmaceutical MNCs. China's advantages include a government that has been relatively friendly towards inward foreign investment, an equally large population with per capita incomes about twice that of India, and low labor costs. China and India each present somewhat different advantages and disadvantages as alternative locations for overseas activities for global pharmaceutical MNCs.

The environment surrounding the Indian pharmaceutical industry is also relevant. Key environmental actors include government regulators, both in the central government, and at the state level; funding sources, including venture capital investments; and the Indian social and political

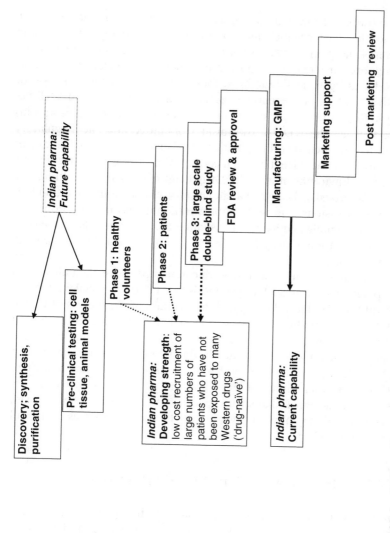

Figure 10.1   Indian pharma and the global pharma industry value chain

Discovery; synthesis, purification

Pre-clinical testing: cell tissue, animal models

Phase 1: healthy volunteers

Phase 2: patients

Phase 3: large scale double-blind study

FDA review & approval

Manufacturing: GMP

Marketing support

Post marketing review

Indian pharma: Future capability

Indian pharma: Developing strength: low cost recruitment of large numbers of patients who have not been exposed to many Western drugs ('drug-naïve')

Indian pharma: Current capability

environment, which encompasses concerns over accessibility and affordability of drugs in a low-income country, and left-wing political parties with generalized suspicion of multinationals.

GOVERNMENT REGULATION AND INFLUENCE

The central government in Delhi, as well as various state governments, influence the pharmaceutical industry through laws and regulations, vision statements and plans for the industry, funding for R&D and other industry programs, the creation of government policy in critical areas such as stem cells and genetically modified foods, and through the provision of incentives such as tax reductions, accelerated depreciation and VAT tax changes. Regulatory actions and controls are spread across several ministries, such as the RDNA Appraisal Committee and the Regulatory Committee on Genetic Manipulation, both within the Department of Biotechnology, the Genetic Engineering Approval Committee in the Ministry of Environment, and the Drug Controller-General of India (for new drug approvals). The new patent law is of critical importance, both in its central provisions, and in its implementation, with modifications and rules being promulgated as the law is enforced. There are also price controls, with a National Drug Price Index, and a National Pharmaceutical Pricing Authority.

The central government also has educational plans for the industry, to develop human capital, such as proposals to establish national postgraduate institutions for biotechnology, along the lines of the successful Indian Institutes of Technology. There also exist national academic centers of excellence such as the Nehru Centre for Advanced Scientific Research, focusing on human genetics, located in Bangalore. Major regional centers for the industry include Hyderabad, Bangalore, Pune and Chennai. Another interesting source of expertise and entrepreneurial energy are overseas non-resident Indians with specializations in biotechnology, who are actively seeking Indian opportunities to start companies and fund entrepreneurial efforts.

INDIAN PHARMACEUTICAL COMPANIES

There are about 80 medium-sized and large Indian pharmaceutical and biotech companies currently active in India, and in export markets. Some of the largest Indian pharmaceutical companies include Ranbaxy, Dr Reddy's Labs, Nicholas Piramal, Wockhardt and Biocon. Table 10.1

Table 10.1 Major Indian pharmaceutical companies

Indian Pharma co.	2004 Sales $M	Net income $M	Stockholders equity $M	Total assets $M	ROE %
Dr Reddy's	463	57	485	613	12
Ranbaxy	1178	164	600	946	27
Nicholas Piramal	348	50	114	214	44
Wockhardt	346	62	144	346	43
Biocon	137	34	135	156	25

summarizes key sales and profit figures for these leading Indian pharmaceutical firms.

The broad industry strategy and business models, in recent years, has consisted of:

- Manufacture Western drugs with non-infringing manufacturing process.
- Sell such generic equivalents at low price in India and in export markets – Latin America, Africa, China, Russia; in conjunction with these export efforts, Indian companies have started developing marketing organizations in their key overseas markets.
- Target US and European generic market, attempt to be first to file and get ANDA approval, challenge existing patents, and if successful, take advantage of 180-day (Hatch-Waxman Act) exclusivity period.
- Partnering and subcontracting with overseas pharmaceutical MNCs in activities such as contract manufacturing, contract research, clinical testing and information analysis.
- Export of bulk intermediates and APIs (active pharmaceutical ingredients).
- Some companies have also initiated R&D to develop drugs for diseases with high incidence in India, that is, malaria, TB.

The 2005 patent law changes had been discussed for several years, and the larger Indian companies therefore had time to prepare for these changes. They have increased spending on R&D, increased partnering with foreign pharmaceutical companies, and have attempted to balance their focus on the US market by increasing their attention on European markets, and have begun consolidating, through M&A, to increase scale and be able to compete in the new environment.

A central concern is the long-term goals of the major Indian pharmaceutical companies. Are they interested in developing an independent global presence over time? Or, are they content to seek a partnership with major pharmaceutical MNCs, providing complementary resources and sharing in the results, including markets and profits? This fundamental long-term strategic choice will influence the nature of partnering that emerges over time between Indian and foreign pharmaceutical companies.

We now briefly review strategies at specific major Indian pharmaceutical companies, focusing on their research activities, generic drug manufacture, M&A activity and overseas marketing.

RANBAXY

Ranbaxy is India's largest drug company, with a strong emphasis on the manufacture and export of generic drugs. In generics, it had over 40 Abbreviated New Drug Application (ANDA) projects in its pipeline, and was engaged in litigation with Pfizer over Lipitor, a major cholesterol reducing blockbuster drug. Its exports were about 65 percent of sales, with an emphasis on the US and European markets. In its research activities, it has multiple therapeutic foci for drug discovery. It has formed a number of research alliances; for example, a drug discovery and clinical development alliance with GSK (a five-year partnership). It also initiated an anti-malarial drug development program with the Medicines for Malaria Venture. It also out-licensed the RBx 2258 molecule (a possible application for benign prostatic hyperplasmia and urological disorders) to Schwarz Pharmaceutical, and has allocated internal funds for research on new drug delivery systems, and on developing herbal medicines for the Indian market. As it has grown in size over the years, it has developed both manufacturing and marketing activities, dispersed across Brazil, China and Russia, in addition to its US and Europe focus.

Ranbaxy and the Generic Drugs Segment

Table 10.2 summarizes the financial profiles of some leading generic drug manufacturers. Major US generic drug firms are able to obtain (reasonable) rates of return on equity, between 13 and 14 percent, on sales exceeding $1 billion. Such profits can be attractive to Indian pharmaceutical companies seeking to develop scale and obtain dollar-based earnings with which to fund significantly larger R&D programs on new drug development. It is estimated that over $37 billion worth of branded patented drugs will be exposed to generic competition in 2005. Amid growing concerns over the high cost of health care, nearly half of all prescriptions filled in the US were filled with generic drugs.

Table 10.2   The attraction of generic drugs: major generic drug Firms

Generic drug company	Sales 2004 $ billions	Net Inc before special charges	Stockholders equity	Total assets	ROE
Teva pharma	$4.8b	$958.4m	$5.4b	$9.6b	14.3%
Mylan Labs 80% generics	$1.4b	$300m	$1.66b	$1.9b	13.2%
Barr Labs	$1.3b	$123m	$1.04b	$1.33b	14.9%
Ivax	$1.8b	$199m	$1.49b	$3.21b	13.3%

Table 10.3   Range of profit from generics: the Provigil example

	Ranbaxy and original patent holder (AG*)	Ranbaxy/Barr and AG	Ranbaxy, Barr, Teva and Mylan and AG
Price discount to branded drug	50%	65%	80%
Ranbaxy sales, first 180 days	$63m	$26m	$10m
Ranbaxy profits	$34m	$14m	$5m

Note: AG – Authorized Generic.

Source: Morgan Stanley Equity research, April 2005.

While mature and competitive generic drugs offer low margins and yield profits from high-volume sales, generic drug profitability can be higher if a firm is one of the first to challenge the existing patents on a drug by filing an ANDA (Abbreviated New Drug Application). While the legal discovery process can take three to four years, if such a challenge is successful, and the challenged patent is held invalid, under the Hatch-Waxman Act the filing firm can obtain a 180-day period of marketing exclusivity for its generic version. This exclusive period can help it recoup its legal and marketing costs while enabling to charge a higher price, and first entry can also help it obtain and maintain market share once the period of exclusivity ends. Of course, more than one generic drug company can simultaneously file a challenge to an existing patent, in which case, if the challenge is successful, the exclusivity period is shared, reducing prices and profits. Table 10.3 summarizes such a scenario for a patent challenge to Provigil (generic modafinil) filed by Ranbaxy, as did Barr, Teva and Mylan.

As Table 10.3 shows, being the first and only filer is a profitable strategy, one that Indian firms such as Ranbaxy have begun to gain capabilities in, thus potentially enhancing their hard currency cash flows and profits, and thus being able to finance internally a strategy that focuses on greater participation in new drug discovery.

DR REDDY

Dr Reddy, another major Indian drug company had 2003–2004 sales of $463 million, of which branded formulations accounted for 37 percent of sales; active pharmaceutical ingredients (APIs) 38 percent and generics, 22 percent. Nearly 50 percent of its sales were derived from the US, Europe and Russia, with the domestic Indian market providing 36 percent of sales. Dr Reddy has estimated that it has a comparative advantage in R&D costs, at about one-quarter of US cost levels. Hence, its goal is to develop promising molecules, shepherd them through the crucial Phase I trials, and if successful, seek partnerships after Phase 2, and out-license new drugs developed in-house to major pharmaceutical multinationals. For example, it has licensed new diabetes compounds to Novartis and Novo Nordisk for further clinical trials. Its research focus has been on selected therapeutic areas: that is, diabetes, and anti-infectives. Like most Indian drug firms, it faces a capital constraint; Dr Reddy's total R&D expenditures in 2003–2004 were $46 million, of which $17 million was targeted to drug discovery of new chemical entities (NCEs). This is miniscule compared to the multi-billion dollar R&D budgets of major Western pharmaceutical companies. It derived significant export revenues from its earlier emphasis on developing branded formulations, for the markets of India, Russia, Brazil and other countries (these being compounds developed while the process patent regime was prevalent in India).

Strategic M&A

Dr Reddy has been active in moving into the US market, through small acquisitions in niche therapeutic segments. As an example, it acquired the US firm Trigenesis for $11 million in May 2004. This gave Dr Reddy access to the dermatology prescription market segment, a small market with an estimated total size of $5.3 billion. This market was seen as having a low entry threshold, with the need to reach relatively few physicians, ~ 10 000, therefore easy to reach; this meant that the firm would need a relatively small detailing sales-force; and the relatively small market would make it less competitive, because it would be unattractive to large pharmaceutical companies, and thus below the radar of large pharmaceuticals. With the acquisition, Dr

Reddy's long-term goal is to launch a NCE in the US by 2009, if Phase III is successful. The goal is to establish a US specialty company to serve as the base for becoming a globally integrated mid-sized pharmaceutical company.

LUPIN LABS

Lupin Labs is a medium-sized Indian pharmaceutical company, with a plan to develop a significant generic drug position so as to fund R&D on drugs to treat TB, a disease with high incidence in India. The Indian government currently funds about 40 percent of TB research. Lupin plans to generate additional funding with its generic bet on ceftriaxone, a drug sold by Hoffman-LaRoche and expected to go off-patent in July 2005. Given the drug's total market of $600 million worldwide, Lupin plans to obtain market share with its generic version and use profits to fund relatively low-cost R&D on TB therapeutics. Its R&D cost advantage stems from the fact that its 74 PhD scientists earn between $12 000 and $30 000, depending on experience; significantly below Western levels. Lupin plans to partner with Baxter Healthcare to market its generic versions to hospitals. Lupin faces competition from a foreign drug MNC, AstraZeneca, which has established a center of excellence for TB research in Bangalore. Such foreign MNC presence is likely to increase as the new patent regime makes the Indian location more attractive for drug discovery activities.

BIOCON

Figure 10.2 summarizes Biocon's strategic approach to biotechnology, as one of India's successful pioneers in the nascent biotech sector. As India's leading biotech company, it initially developed strength with its fermentation capabilities, gradually moving to focus on partnering and independent operations along the entire drug value chain. As Figure 10.2 indicates, it has organized itself into separate subsidiaries for early stage drug discovery, in both synthetic chemistry and molecular biology; for clinical trials, focusing on diabetes, oncology, lipidemia and cardiovascular diseases; and for commercialization, of over 25 enzymes and biopharmaceuticals. It is the only Indian company to manufacture FDA approved lovastatin, and it has submitted a Drug Master File (DMF) to the FDA for human insulin (a step in gaining approval to manufacture and sell a drug).

Biocon has specialized in the cholesterol-lowering drugs segment, a $20 billion global market. Several effective blockbuster drugs to treat high cholesterol, such as Pravastatin and Simvastatin, are expected to be going

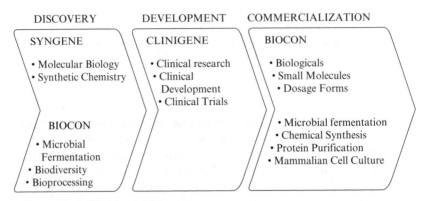

Source: Biocon 2004 Annual Report.

Figure 10.2   Biocon's biotech-focused strategy

off-patent in 2005 and 2006, providing huge generic drug opportunities. Biocon has also developed competitive capability in recombinant biotherapeutics, focused on the global insulin market with a market size of about $7 billion, 70 percent recombinant human insulin. Biocon has developed capabilities to produce recombinant human insulin, GCSF (granulocyte colony stimulating factor), and monoclonal antibodies, all biotech-based processes. Looking to the future, Biocon has focused its R&D efforts on drugs for diabetes and cardiovascular diseases. It has also focused on developing unique biotech processes for manufacturing a variety of biotherapeutics. It classifies such efforts as R&D to fund long-term platform technologies to develop NCEs, while focusing on generics in the medium term. It also expects that it will partner with other companies to manufacture their NCEs, using its bioprocess capabilities.

NICHOLS PIRAMAL (NPIL)

NPIL, another innovative leading Indian drug firm, has as its core strategy the goal of partnering with innovator companies across the drug life cycle, even after patent expiry. Currently, formulations are about 75 percent of business. In this formulations segment, its strategy is to build marketing-led international formulations business, focused on attractive niche markets. It plans to exploit opportunities globally, across multiple geographic markets, with a clear focus on custom manufacturing and branded formulations.

Figure 10.3 displays Nicholas Piramal's strategy of positioning itself to be the preferred partner for 'innovator companies' – global pharmaceutical companies. It does not plan to participate in marketing activities with

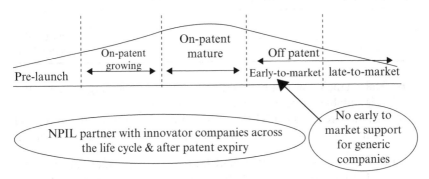

NPIL'S Strategy is to be the partner
of choice for international pharmacos

Source: Nicholas Piramal Annual report.

Figure 10.3   Nicholas Piramal's Partnering Biased Strategy

generic drug companies, thus avoiding being seen as a competitor by the global pharmaceutical companies it hopes to partner with, and thus clarifying its intended strategy of strategic partnering with global pharmaceutical companies.

Nicholas Piramal has also been active in acquiring specialist small international pharmaceutical companies that can help it achieve its strategic goals of niche dominance. For example, it has acquired two international manufacturers of inhaled anesthetics (IA) products. Key aspects of the acquisition include:

- Acquired Rhodia's inhaled anesthetics business; to add to an existing internal IA business, itself acquired earlier from ICI in 2002. The two acquisitions helped NPIL gain significant domestic Indian market presence.
- The IA line had accumulated 40 years of brand equity (with the Halothane and Isoflurane products).
- The overall anesthetics global market was estimated at $675 million, with Halothane and Isoflurane together obtaining 20 percent of market revenues, and 41 percent by volume.
- Thus, the leading IA is Servoflurane, with a 68 percent market share (though only 43 percent by volume); as is to be expected, it is the most expensive anesthetic on the market, requiring a special vaporizer. Hence, it has low use in emerging markets which are price conscious.

Table 10.4   Market share for Inhaled Anesthetics (IA)

Anesthetic type	Rhodia	NPIL	Other
Halo	48%	25%	
Iso	15%	0.8%	Abbott 41%; Baxter 21%

- Halothane's low cost makes it widely used in emerging markets, and it is suitable for pediatric and veterinary use.
- All these reasons led NPIL to concentrate its focus on the lower end of the anesthetic market, using acquisitions to build such a position.

Table 10.4 outlines the market share for the two major anesthetic product lines and Nicholas Piramal (NPIL) and acquired company Rhodia's market share in these two distinct market segments. Thus, the acquisitions helped NPIL obtain a dominant (73 percent) market share at the lowest end of the market, with Halothane, while beginning to build a reasonable starting position in the Isoflurane segment.

Other benefits to NPIL included:

- getting access to IA's global distributors in 90 countries;
- obtaining a platform for developing a global hospital and critical care business, positioning it to bolster plans to launch Sevo, the latest generation IA, in 2006–2007;
- complementing NPIL geographic market presence: NPIL was strong in Latin America, Africa, the Middle East and Asia, while Rhodia, the acquired business, was strong in the EU, the US and Japan.

INDIAN PHARMACEUTICAL FIRMS: CAPABILITIES

Based on a review of these strategic thrusts by some of India's key pharmaceutical companies, we can assay an initial summary of current Indian pharmaceutical firm capabilities. These are summarized in Table 10.5.

These capabilities or the lack thereof will affect how Indian pharmaceutical firms make strategic choices between:

- generic drugs or discovery: new molecules;
- offer bulk intermediates and APIs;
- contract manufacturing and contract services;
- focus on new elements of the value chain, that is, clinical trials;
- focus on new drug discovery.

Table 10.5   *Indian pharmaceutical firms: current and future (needed)*
capabilities

Strengths/capabilities	Weaknesses/future capabilities required
Manufacturing strength: from developing non-infringing processes for local versions of drugs to developing generics for US/Europe markets	Biotechnology knowledge and experience
Human capital, expertise in chemistry, growing pool of graduates, labor cost advantage	Financial Capital for investments in drug discovery and development
Market share and market presence in developing countries-BRICs	Risk Management to move to upstream value chain activities – drug discovery, clinical testing
Regulatory and Legal knowledge – to enter US and European generic markets	FDA Approval process for New Drugs, shepherding through Phases 1, 2 and 3.
	Global Marketing, across countries and segments

The same analysis of capabilities will drive their choice of foreign partners, seeking partners with complementary capabilities and partners that offer knowledge transfer and learning opportunities in areas including:

- knowledge based: biotech capability;
- market oriented: to penetrate specific markets;
- value chain based: license drug for marketing into specific markets and segments;
- finance oriented: source of risk capital.

Based on the foregoing, we can suggest the following hypotheses, which can be investigated through field study. Indian pharmaceutical firms are likely to:

Hypothesis 1a: Increase their investments in drug discovery and development.
Hypothesis 1b: Increase their investments in biotechnology-based drug discovery and development.
Hypothesis 1c: Increase their partnering with foreign pharmaceutical MNCs in drug discovery and development.
Hypothesis 1d: Will increase projects focused on therapeutic treatments for diseases with high local incidence.

Hypothesis 2: Increase their strategic focus on conducting clinical trials in India for foreign pharmaceutical MNCs.

Hypothesis 3: Maintain or increase their strategic focus on developing generics for global markets.

Hypothesis 4: Maintain or increase their strategic focus on marketing branded formulations in India.

Hypothesis 5a: Maintain or increase their strategic focus on US and European markets.

Hypothesis 5b: Maintain or increase their strategic focus on international markets.

Hypothesis 5c: Increase their partnering with foreign pharmaceutical MNCs in international marketing.

Hypothesis 6: Increase their partnering with venture capital.

Hypothesis 7a: Will increase acquisition activity of Indian pharmaceutical companies.

Hypothesis 7b: Will increase acquisition activity of foreign pharmaceutical companies.

THE VIEWPOINT OF FOREIGN PHARMACEUTICAL FIRMS

Outsourcing and strategic partnering can be critical to the global competitiveness of major pharmaceutical firms. A T Kearney has estimated that around $50 billion in pharmaceutical spending can be outsourced, with savings of $5–8 billion over a five- to ten-year horizon (Paddison et al. 2004). Such outsourcing has been constrained by several pharmaceutical industry fears, some of which are legitimate. The industry has concerns in several areas, including:

- poor intellectual property protection;
- partner's goals, ability, knowledge base (quality of partner selection);
- quality of drugs manufactured, reliability of supply;
- trust;
- impact on reputation (of partnering and its outcomes);
- ethical issues (criticism of conducting clinical trails in poor countries, backlash from outsourcing);
- fear of lawsuits stemming from poor outsourcing performance;
- fears of local (host country) government regulation and interference;
- cultural and managerial difficulties of distant operations in unfamiliar locations;
- FDA acceptance.

In some ways, these are concerns that many other global industries have undergone and resolved as they become global industries. The pharmaceutical industry has been somewhat late to the game and its globalization difficulties might be seen as teething troubles that will be resolved over time, as the gains justify the effort necessary to find reliable and effective outsourcing partners, in India and elsewhere.

FOREIGN PHARMACEUTICAL MNCs IN INDIA

There are several foreign pharmaceutical and biotech MNCs active in India, such as Glaxo SmithKline India, Abbott India, Pfizer India, Aventis Pharma India, AstraZeneca India, NovoNordisk India and Merck. Companies in related fields include Quintiles CRO in India, and Covance. Others include Monsanto, Alfa-Laval, Millipore and Affymetrix, active in fields such as plant genetics, bioprocessing and instrumentation. The new patent laws have increased attention to India, and foreign pharmaceutical and biotech companies in India have to reconsider the range of activities that they will perform in India as well as key areas of future focus.

Foreign pharmaceutical MNCs' activities in India include:

- Contract manufacturing and sourcing of intermediates, APIs.
- Clinical trials; GSK conducted four clinical trials in India in 2004. Its goal is to have 30 percent of clinical trials conducted offshore in 2005; with estimated savings of $10 000 per patient.
- The incentive is that it is quicker to recruit patients (half the time relative to the US) and quicker to analyze and interpret results: hence cost savings of 50–60 percent.
- Establish captive R&D facilities; for example, AstraZeneca's TB research facility in Bangalore. Also, Pfizer doubled its clinical research investment in India to $13 million over the 2004–2005 period.
- Establish R&D partnerships. Examples include Novartis, with its drug discovery alliances with Dr Reddy's and Torrent. Similarly, GSK signed a five-year R&D partnership with Ranbaxy.
- Bring local marketing in-house: Roche Diagnostics took back marketing activities which had been conducted by NPIL.

As the range of activities outlined above suggest, a particularly important choice is between increasing in-house activities in areas such as R&D and marketing, versus choosing to partner with Indian companies. What are the desired Indian partner characteristics for activities including clinical research, marketing, manufacturing and clinical testing? What might foreign

MNCs plan with respect to partnering activities, introducing new drugs to the Indian market, expanding manufacturing and other activities in India, and M&A activity, that is, buying control of Indian pharmaceutical and biotech companies (Ruckman 2005)? Thus, foreign pharmaceutical MNCs in India would need to consider, with regard to their future directions:

- Will foreign pharmaceutical companies increase in-house R&D in India or expand partnering?
- Will India be a favored location for pharmaceutical activities? Alternatives include China and Eastern Europe.
- For each stage of the value chain, whether to perform in-house, partner or outsource offshore (in India); criteria for decision-making.
- How to select partners? India or elsewhere?
- Medium-term and long-term goals; greater independence or greater partnering?

Thus, we can suggest some useful hypotheses concerning foreign pharmaceutical MNCs in India's pharmaceutical sector. It is likely that foreign pharmaceutical MNCs in India will:

Hypothesis 1: Increase overall investment in India's pharmaceutical industry.
Hypothesis 2: Increase in-house captive drug discovery and development investments relative to other modes of entry.
Hypothesis 3: Increase partnering in contract manufacturing investments.
Hypothesis 4: Increase partnering in contract research investments.
Hypothesis 5: Increase projects focused on therapeutic treatments for diseases with high local incidence.
Hypothesis 6a: Increase sourcing of generics.
Hypothesis 6b: Increase sourcing of intermediates and active pharmaceutical ingredients (APIs).
Hypothesis 7: Increase acquisition activity of Indian pharmaceutical companies.

CONCLUSION

The Indian pharmaceutical industry is at the cusp of major strategic evolution, as the domestic market is expected to grow rapidly and as Indian pharmaceutical firm capabilities evolve and improve. In this context both Indian pharmaceutical firms and foreign pharmaceutical MNCs in India will evolve strategies to take best advantage of these new and promising developments. This chapter has reviewed likely developments and suggested hypotheses that could be explored through field research in the Indian pharmaceutical market place.

REFERENCES

Ernst & Young (2004), *Progressions – Global Pharmaceutical Report*.

Griffith, David and Michael G. Harvey (2001), 'A Resource Perspective of Global Dynamic Capabilities', *Journal of International Business Studies*, **32**, 597–606.

Katila, Riitta and Paul Yang (2003), 'Exploiting Technological Opportunities: the Timing of Collaborations', *Research Policy*, **32**, 317–32.

Khanna, Tarun and Krishna Palepu (2005), 'Emerging Giants: Building World Class Companies in Emerging Markets', HBS Case Services 9-703-431.

Knight, Gary A. and S. Tamar Cavusgil (2004), 'Innovation, Organizational Capabilities, and the Born-Global Firm', *Journal of International Business Studies*, **35**, 124–41.

Linder, Jane C., Samuel Perkins, U. Srinivasa Rangan and Philip Dover (2004), 'The Drug Industry's Alliance Archipelago', Babson Executive Education.

Madhok, Anoop and Thomas Osegowitsch (2000), 'The International Biotechnology Industry: A Dynamic Capabilities Perspective', *Journal of International Business Studies*, **31**, 325–35.

Murray, Janet Y. (2001), 'Strategic Alliance Based Global Sourcing Strategy for Competitive Advantage', *Journal of International Marketing*, **9**(4), 30–58.

Paddison, Chris, Chris White and Carol Cruickshank (2004), 'Pharma Explores Uncharted Territory', *A T Kearney, Executive Agenda*, **7**(4).

Ruckman, Karen (2005), 'Technology Sourcing through Acquisitions: Evidence from the US Drug Industry', *Journal of International Business Studies*, **36**, 89–103.

Uhlenbruck, Klaus (2004), 'Developing Acquired Foreign Subsidiaries: The Experience of MNES in Transition Economies', *Journal of International Business Studies*, **35**, 109–23.

Recent Newspaper Articles on Indian Pharmaceutical

Aggarwal Yogi, (2005), 'Is it the End of Cheap Drugs from India?', *Business Times Singapore*, 12 April.

Economic Times (2005), 'Drug Companies Hone Strategy for New Patent Regime', 12 April.

Naik, S.D. (2005), 'New Patent Regime', *The Hindu*, 12 April.

Sridharan, R. (2005), 'Indian Pharma's Mid-Life Crisis', *Asia Africa Intelligence Wire*, 27 February.

Tannan, S.K. and P. Tannan (2004), 'Impact of the WTO on the Indian Pharmaceutical Industry', *Chemical Business*, April–June.

Unni Krishnan, C.H. (2005), 'India Enters a New Era', *Manufacturing Chemist*, **76**(2), 27–30.

'India Senses Patent Appeal' (2005), *Wall Street Journal*, 11 April.

11. Transitions in innovation: musings on the propensity and factors towards proactive innovation in China

William H.A. Johnson

This chapter is the result of musings over China's present and future innovation efforts in light of the incredible economic growth seen there at the beginning of the twenty-first century. Recently, I had the opportunity to travel to Southern China on a trip organized by the Center for International Business Education and Research (CIBER). The group I traveled with consisted of business professors from American universities and a few affiliated consultants. We visited a number of companies and educational institutions including Baoshan Steel Company, Yanfeng Visteon Automotive Trim Systems Co. Ltd and Fujikon Industrial Co. Ltd as well as Jiaotong and Sun Yat-Sen universities.

Being a student of innovation management, I found myself asking questions about R&D expenditures and innovation efforts of the company representatives we met while on the China trip. Not surprisingly, given that the majority of China's international trade is in the manufacturing of goods and driven at least somewhat by the country's low labor costs, the typical response was characterized by a propensity towards imitation or mimetic behaviors in innovation efforts. This was probably not to be unexpected given the trajectory of Chinese technological innovation in its modern history. In fact, since that trip, a paper has been published in the *Academy of Management Review* that suggests imitation might be the preferred or expected path of innovation for firms within countries that are far from the global technological state-of-the-art frontier (Mahmood and Rufin, 2005). However, while the theory presented in that paper is persuasive, there are other factors such as political and cultural elements that affect the propensity towards innovation. In particular, perhaps at the risk of debasing towards a stereotype, I was struck with the cultural attitudes towards imitation and mimetic behaviors found within China. These leanings are old and can be found in the quote from a source circa 1914 cited in Professor

Zhiwu Chen's Chapter 7 within this volume regarding China's 'cheap labour and keen aptitude for imitation'. I believe that this prejudicial bias towards imitation at least partially helps to explain the lack of proactive innovation on the part of the Chinese themselves, despite the paradoxical reverence for learning and knowledge held by the Chinese people. China's political environment also seems to undermine the drive towards fruitful innovation efforts. While an analysis is beyond the scope of this chapter, a comparison between the Chinese and the Taiwanese may be in order, in terms of proactive innovation propensity. While both of these countries have Asian cultures, Taiwan has been exemplary with regard to proactive innovation (for example Henderson, 2003), particularly in terms of technological innovation in business.

The chapter starts by briefly mentioning some innovations of China's glorious past as one of the first civilizations of the world. It then leads into a discussion of the present situation of Chinese innovation efforts. This discussion concludes that China's focus has been on mimetic innovation efforts as opposed to proactive innovation. The next section discusses reasons for this lack of proactive innovation from various economic, political and cultural perspectives. Within the cultural subsection interview data from Chinese students is used to examine the effect of education on the propensity towards mimetic behavior. Finally, the chapter ends with a discussion of the implications of this propensity and the Chinese innovation milieu in general for the future of Chinese innovation within the context of the world stage.

PAST INNOVATION IN CHINESE HISTORY

China has a great history of invention. Paper, the compass, gunpowder and printing have all been attributed to Chinese civilization. In fact, in some Chinese classrooms portraits of the four bearded Chinese sages responsible for these 'Four Great Inventions' have replaced the four bearded Westerners of Marx, Engels, Lenin and Stalin (Becker, 2000, p. 202). However, as lamented by some, Chinese innovation on the grand scale of its previous offerings did not persist over the centuries. The pinnacle of Chinese innovation took place in the fifteenth century. Within the last 200 years, some claim that China has lacked a system and a spirit of innovation (Zhan and Renwei, 2003).

Chinese intellectuals have always supported the bureaucracies of Chinese government. At the time, this was by rule of the Emperor, and all four major examples of innovation given above can be seen to be based in the support of bureaucracy. That is, the characteristics of the four great inventions all seemed to fit well with the needs of the bureaucratic state. None of these inventions appear to be commercially based and the lack of innovative behavior has been cited as a consequence of the absence of a free market, the values of Chinese society and its totalitarian nature (Landes, 1998, pp. 55–7).

In the twentieth century, China had moderate success in reinventing such innovations as nuclear weapons, satellites, synthetic human insulin and others driven by government-initiated, Soviet-type innovative programs.

INNOVATION EFFORTS TAKING PLACE TODAY IN CHINA

China is once again a place where innovation efforts are embarked upon, largely due to the introduction of Western technology via foreign direct investment (Buckley et al., 2002; Liu and Wang, 2003). Much of this innovative effort is mimetic in nature (something which leads to the main thesis of this chapter that Chinese culture is, by nature, supportive of mimetic innovation behavior rather than of radical innovation). Considering that China is still regarded as a developing country, its expenditures on innovation activities are admirable. Indicators of science and technology from OECD sources are depicted in Table 11.1 and show that compared to non-OECD countries, China has room for improvement but nevertheless is doing well. Table 11.2 depicts data from UNESCO on R&D factors and education in China compared to other Western countries and India. In comparison to the West, China's expenditure is low, but in comparison to India, another emerging country widely cited as attracting foreign ventures (Farrell, 2004), it is spending more. The question is whether such funds have been well spent. Illiteracy is still quite high at 153 million people over 15 years of age, especially among women, with 71 percent unable to read in 1997 (Becker, 2000, p. 411). Other sources suggest that illiteracy is only at 9 percent (*Economist*, 2004) but it is unclear how this number was calculated. One issue is the notoriously poor nature of information validity, with government sources being considered highly unreliable.

At least since 1953, when the Chinese Communist Party embarked on its first Five-Year Plan, the transfer of technology from foreign sources has been a major focus in Chinese innovation efforts. This first started with the efforts to import Soviet technology and the use of turnkey plants built by Soviet expertise. When the relationship between Russia and China cooled in the late 1950s other sources of foreign technological innovation became important. Japan was previously and continues to be a source of technology transfer (Howe, 1997).

Table 11.1 Science and technology indicators for OECD and non-OECD countries

	China	Israel	Russian federation	Singapore	EU 15	OECD Total	Italy	Japan	Poland	Sweden	US
Gross domestic expenditure on R&D GERD (million current PPP$)[1]	72 076.80	6 359.70	14 190.40	2 129.70	162 813.30	578 749.40	13 556.50	96 532.30	2 367.70	9 232.70	252 938.50
GERD as a percentage of GDP[1]	1.29	4.73	1.24	2.19	1.93	2.33	1.07[2]	3.09	0.67	4.27	2.82
Total researchers per thousand total employment[1]	1.10	N/A	7.50	9.00	5.80[2]	6.50[2]	2.90[2]	10.20	3.80	10.60	8.60[3]
Percentage of GERD financed by industry[1]	57.60[2]	69.60[2]	32.90[2]	55.00[2]	56.20	63.60	43.00[4]	73.00	30.80	71.90	68.30
Percentage of GERD financed by government[1]	33.40[2]	24.70[2]	54.80[2]	40.30[2]	34.50	28.90	50.80[4]	18.50	64.80	21.00	26.90
Business enterprise expenditure on R&D BERD (million current PPP$)[1]	44 099.20	4 643.50	9 915.70	1 308.20	105 121.20	403 243.60	7 275.20	71 119	848.40	7 166.80	188 122.80
BERD as a percentage of GDP[1]	0.79	3.46	0.87	1.34	1.06[2]	1.48	0.43[4]	2.25	0.21	3.07	1.92
Number of 'triadic' patent families per million population[5]	0.055	54.167	0.490	19.118	35.897	37.417	12.103	89.400	0.233	94.216	52.712

Table 11.1 (continued)

	China	Israel	Russian federation	Singapore	EU 15	OECD Total	Italy	Japan	Poland	Sweden	US
Number of patents in the ICT sector applications to the EPO per million population[5]	0.031	61.714	0.320	22.177	35.313	30.754	9.360	60.810	0.129	88.793	40.337
Number of patents in the biotechnology sector applications to the EPO per million population[5]	0.008	11.739	0.095	2.294	5.341	5.153	1.042	4.691	0.052	7.456	9.634

Source: Huang et al. (2004) (original source OECD 2003c).

Notes:
1. Non-OECD countries data without the superscript are the year of 2002. The OECD countries' data without superscript are the year of 2001.
2. The data are the year of 2000.
3. The data are the year of 1999.
4. The data are the year of 1997.
5. The data were calculated by Huang et al. (2004), from which the table is adapted. The patent data are from the year of 1998. Source of Data of Population (1998) except for EU 15 and OECD Average: World Bank World Development Indicators (WDI) database Data Query. The data of EU 15 and OECD Average are from World Urbanization Prospectus, the 2001 Revision, United Nations Population Divisions.

Table 11.2   Country statistics on R&D and education

	China	USA	India	UK	Russia
Pop. (millions)	1 285	288	1 033	59	145
Per capita GDP	4 240	34 740	2 560	25 550	7 720
Researchers (per million)	584	4 099	99	2 667	3 494
R&D (%GDP)	1.1	2.8	0.8	1.9	1
Education spending (%GDP)	2.1	5.7	4.1	4.8	3

Source: UNESCO (2001).

Recent examples of innovation efforts and R&D focus continue to show a propensity towards technology transfer models rather than full-fledged internal R&D efforts. This is exacerbated by the continual presence of foreign direct investment coupled with the influx of new technologies as multinational companies from the US, Europe and Japan, for example, have built manufacturing plants within the country. This has produced a momentum towards commercial-based R&D efforts away from the historic focus on government-sponsored non-commercial R&D efforts. UNESCO data (shown in Figure 11.1) suggest that China's expenditures on R&D are closer in nature to the US than to Russia. Both the US and China have greater than 55 percent of R&D expenditures coming from business sources compared with Russia's 34 percent and its major focus on government R&D sources.

In a recent edition of *R&D Management* devoted to Chinese R&D efforts, Gassman and Han (2004) discussed R&D frameworks based on input-performance motivations and business-ecological motivations for the propensity towards establishing R&D programs within China. In their paper they suggested that input-performance motives for China included the 'availability of highly qualified personnel, tapping informal networks and knowledge sources, customer and market specific development, adaptation to local production processes and cost advantages' (p. 428). Business-ecological motivations included 'government policy, continuing economic growth in the market size and peer pressure'.

Intellectual property infringement is still a major concern, particularly for foreign entrants into the Chinese market. Examples of knock-off products are well known and until recently nothing has been done about such matters. Even today, there remain questions as to whether the Chinese legal system can support a modern, high-technology economy in which property rights exist and are enforced. Recently the Chinese

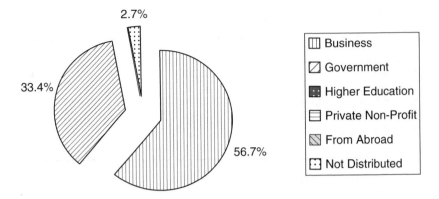

Source: UNESCO website.

Figure 11.1a   Sources of R&D expenditure: China

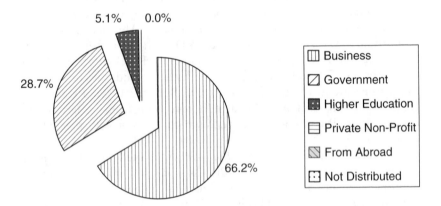

Source: UNESCO website.

Figure 11.1b   Sources of R&D Expenditure: USA

automaker Chery was accused of stealing and completely copying the design of a new GM Daewoo model (*Ward's Auto World*, 2005). It still remains to be seen whether GM will have any legal recourse. Similar accusations by foreign automakers have had little impact. Toyota lost its recent lawsuit alleging IP infringement of its trademark logo by Chinese automakers Geeley (*Wall Street Journal*, 2004). Table 11.3 depicts the estimated trade losses due to patent infringement in China. (Adapted from Huang et al., 2004, p. 382). The effects of poor patent laws can be seen in

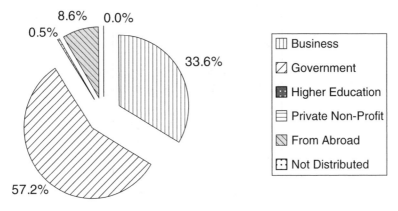

Source: UNESCO website.

Figure 11.1c   Sources of R&D Expenditure: Russia

Table 11.1, which shows a very low number of patents being issued. Intellectual property protection is essential to improving international innovation in general (Chin and Grossman, 1990). Yang and Maskus (2003) have shown how stronger intellectual property protection could increase the rate of innovation in a developing country like China, and I will address this later.

REASONS FOR THE LACK OF PROACTIVE INNOVATION

While the preceding discussion has clearly shown that China is engaged in many innovation efforts, I have been increasingly interested in the reasons for the lack of proactive and/or radical innovation efforts after my inquiries to some Chinese executives. There has been some suggestion that this lack may be the result of a culture specific to China (Becker, 2000; Landes, 1998). The obstacles to growth that China faces – 'its fragile banking system, the lack of a transparent legal system, corruption, the risk of social political unrest caused by widening income inequalities or the abuse of human rights' (*Economist*, 2004) – may also be seen as obstacles to efficient and effective innovation efforts. And while some may argue that this technological development is based on generic economic and political bases (Mahmood and Rufin, 2005), from a general perspective in my research on China, at least three major areas of influence can be identified. The roots

Table 11.3   Intellectual property losses in China

Industry	1999		2000		2001		2002		2003	
	Loss	Piracy rate	Loss	Piracy rate	Loss	Piracy rate	Loss	Piracy rate	Loss	Piracy rate
Motion pictures	120.0	90%	120.0	90%	160.0	88%	168.0	91%	178.0	95%
Records and music	70.0	90%	70.0	93%	47.02	90%	48.0	90%	286.0	90%
Business software applications[1]	437.2	91%	765.1	94%	1140.2	92%	1637.3	92%	N/A	N/A
Entertainment software	1382.5	95%	N/A	99%	455.0	92%	N/A	96%	568.2	96%
Books	128.0	N/A	130.0	N/A	130.0	N/A	40.0	N/A	40.0	N/A
Total	2137.7	–	1085.1	–	1932.5	–	1893.3	–	–	–

Source: Huang et al. (2004) (original source: International Intellectual Property Alliance).

of these areas are economic, political and, just as important within the Chinese context, the cultural or social.

Economic Factors

According to a Schumpeterian perspective, economic factors will both impact, and be impacted by, the technological innovation frontier (for example David, 1975; Fagerberg, 1994; Grossman and Helpman, 1991; Malecki, 1997; Teece, 1986). China's case is no different. As Fischer and von Zedwitz (2004) point out, demand for products has never outstripped supply in China and therefore the pressure to innovate from a market perspective has not existed.

The economic impact of the low labor costs and introduction of foreign direct investment into China has also had a negative effect on Chinese innovation. There are simply very few reasons for Chinese companies to innovate, particularly in light of the poor history to date of IP protection discussed above. As such, industrial product innovation has been incremental and mimetic in nature. Process-related innovation has also not been visible due to low labor costs. Process innovations meant to lower production costs through automation are not necessary when labor is so cheap. The introduction of automation in production plants such as the Volkswagen plant outside of Shanghai, toured during my Chinese trip, has been by foreign manufacturers and driven mainly by objectives regarding quality rather than cost issues. Patenting behavior geared more towards external design (that is, incremental innovations towards new designs for shape, design or color of a product) is driven by industry with the geographic distribution of these types of patents primarily in southern China. Sun (2000), from which the geographic distribution data come, argues that this may be due to the higher percentage of foreign ownership in the south than in the north where state-owned enterprises are predominant. Interestingly, he states, with regard to these data, that: 'It is common in China that non-state-owned domestic enterprises are more sensitive to exterior designs than state-owned ones, which are used to operating in a planned economy . . . this may also be because of the cultural differences between southern and northern China, where the southern Chinese are more outward looking than those in the north' (Sun, 2000, p. 444).

Political Factors

Of course, the socialist policies of the Chinese Communist government have emphasized innovation that is focused on the betterment of the state in general rather than the on the betterment of the individual's consumer

welfare and industry in general. As stated above regarding Chinese innovation of the mid-twentieth century, this resulted in an initial emphasis
on Soviet-style national science and technology (S&T) programs, which
have been somewhat important to national security. The political milieu
and the predisposition towards imitation stemming from these S&T
efforts also has given rise to the open policy of espionage as evident in the
availability of a 'spy guide' to stealing Western technology in the National
Library of Beijing (Gilley, 1999).

The political environment towards innovation has been uncertain and
fluctuating, resulting in a cyclical response of the Communist Party to S&T
efforts. Paranoia brought on by government actions underlies much of the
behavior of another underlying theme of Chinese politics: the lack of
reliable information available to the public. An example of both themes was
seen in the introduction of the one-child program that was ruth-
lessly enforced for some without much forethought by party leaders. Later
it was found that local officials had taken bribes and much of the rural
population consisted of families with three or more children (Becker,
2000, p. 372).

A sad example of the cyclical response of politics in Chinese was seen in
the aftermath of the 'Cultural Revolution'. The political effects of the
Cultural Revolution have had a devastating impact on the factors of
education needed to support high-end technological innovation. A report
by Fang Yi quoted in Becker (2000, p. 210) showed that over 13 years
during the uprising of the Cultural Revolution, China had not awarded a
single degree.

The so-called 'Cultural Revolution', of course, was a backlash by the
Communist government against all things perceived to be intellectual
within the People's Republic, which took placing during the 1970s. During
the political persecutions, teachers, doctors and others of high education
and positions were intimidated into obscurity, imprisoned or killed.
Needless to say, the result was a huge set-back for China in terms of innovation. It reinforced the cyclical response to 'progress' mentioned above
and may have had a negative and reverberant effect on the desire of Chinese
individuals to participate in intellectual endeavors, which may go in and out
of fashion depending upon the whim of those in power and the political
situation.

Cultural and Social Factors

The propensity towards mimicking Western technology is even more interesting in light of the traditional negative attitude towards the importation
of Western ideas and goods. Gerth (2003) states that:

Attempts to nationalize consumer culture usually insisted that the provenance of a style was not the issue. Any style (Chinese or Western) was acceptable as long as the producers themselves were Chinese. At the same time, the movement sought to counter the perception that spread during the nineteenth century that everything foreign was superior to anything Chinese, an equation that heightened demand for imports.

As mentioned already, some researchers suggest that mimetic behavior is the result of the trajectory of technological development, with firms in countries far from the world technological frontier being more likely to enact mimetic or imitative behaviors (Mahmood and Rufin, 2005). There seems to be some validity to this theory, though the cultural basis towards mimicry and the bias towards assimilation and against innovation inherent within Chinese culture still remains. Here much could be made of Hofstede's classification of the Chinese as a group-oriented culture (Hofstede 1980). It could also be said that the prevailing governments of China have always been totalitarian in nature, depending strongly on the national propensity towards group association. There is little to distinguish the senior party members of today's Communist Party from the aristocrats of earlier empires.

The Chinese national anthem found in MacNair (1951, p. xxxv) is a testament to the collective psyche of Chinese culture. It reads as such: 'San Min Chu I, our aim shall be, to found a free land; world peace be our stand. Lead on, comrades; Vanguards ye are! Hold fast your aim, by sun and star! The earnest and brave your country to save. One heart, one soul; one mind, one goal!'

Educational experience of Chinese students
One important cultural factor strongly related to innovation propensity is education. The importance of education to the Chinese is well recognized, and indeed one of the ironies of studying Chinese innovation and education is the treatment of intellectuals and educators in the recent century within China, in spite of the obvious reverence towards knowledge held by the Chinese in general. The 'Cultural Revolution' is a bizarre indictment to this perplexing conundrum. Education, however, is often seen as a way out of poverty. *The Diary of Ma Yan* is one recent account of a 13-year-old Chinese girl from Zhangjiashu and her peasant family's struggles to keep her in school in hopes that education might provide her a better life (Haski, 2004).

In order to get a better account of what it is like to be educated within the Chinese system and what emerged from their experiences, I interviewed a few students who grew up in China. Two students actually grew up in Hong Kong but one came from northern China and went to Beijing for one year for college education before being selected to go to Hong Kong University. A couple of themes, not quite unexpected, seemed to emerge from the interviews. The first was discipline and unity, echoing the emphasis of the Chinese anthem above. As the north Chinese student stated:

> As far as I remember – the early education – the emphasis relied on discipline and uniform . . . in the very beginning, I remember, we had a strict rule on the way we sit, we have to sit straight, with our hands like this, putting back and then you really pay attention – you really look at the teacher . . . Basically it is like, everything is connected in a uniform way, and you have to be – to do whatever other students do. It's not like you do whatever you want – that would be out of the discipline – most likely, you would not be considered a very good student.

Another was the predisposition towards an emphasis on rote memorization:

> Memorizing is a very important part of language learning no matter if it is in Chinese or English, it is pretty much emphasized in Chinese education and I think there is a reason behind it. For example, for classical Chinese reading, that is exactly the way all the scholars, all the Asian Chinese people, are taught that way . . . Probably you could say that our education is pretty much exam oriented so a lot of times if it is tested on the exams, it is emphasized.

Another concept related to rote memorization that emerged from the interviews was the emphasis on copying as a behavior utilized for learning. Of course, basic learning practices often utilize mimetic behavior that could be characterized as 'imprinting' the knowledge of the person or thing being copied. One hypothesis I had already generated after visiting a school in the outskirts of Shanghai was the effect of learning the Chinese *kanji* on the cultural predisposition towards mimetic learning behaviors. Children, of course, begin to learn the *kanji*, words which are ideological or pictorial representations of ideas (as opposed to Western words which represent sounds that when combined create ideas), by using stencils to practice creating them (see Figure 11.2). Thus, at an early age, Chinese students focus on mimetic behaviors for learning basic literacy. The very structure of the language requires this type of learning.

> Copying, at the very beginning, especially for Chinese study because for Chinese we have special characters, it is not like English where you only learn 26 letters and you have different combinations, but for Chinese, we have each characters so you have to repeat a lot, copy a lot, like for one character you copy like 10 times in order to remember. But later, I don't think so, but it could be in a different form, like for example, if you are doing math problems, and it is not every time that the teacher gives you a new type of exercise, so it would probably be like the same type of thing with different numbers and then you practice a lot and then in the exams, it could be that same type of question repeated.

Source: Trip to Southern China-Shanghai suburbs taken January, 2005

Figure 11.2   Chinese students learning the calligraphy of kanji using stencils

The memorization of Chinese characters did not always require comprehension as one student suggested:

> I mean, for science and math, if you memorize the equations at least you have to understand how to use it before you memorize it. But for those Chinese things, you just have to memorize it even if you understand it or not, if you memorize them, you'll be fine, but you don't really need to know what they mean – if that makes sense.

Of course, the interview data here is only indicative of the cultural influence of education on the basic attitudes towards learning that will have an impact on innovation efforts. The influence of education is only one factor, and the foundation of most Chinese education programs is strong, as evident in the quality of foreign Chinese students. While the learning of an ideologically-based alphabet like the Chinese *kanji* may be less efficient than a phonetically-based one like English, and may be creating an obstacle to universal literacy due to the devotion needed to learn it (Becker, 2000, p. 216), it alone provides only the basic underlying approach to learning. The success of Hong Kong and the Taiwanese, which have similar educational and cultural institutions but different historical and political influences, attests to the possibility that such 'learning biases' are not necessarily detrimental to innovative thinking. However, the basic learning approaches of the Chinese do seem to emphasize the knowing of what is (that is, the status quo) and de-emphasize the creating of what might be (which is a basic notion of innovative thought). Coupled with other cultural and political factors of socialism and the economic factors of a developing nation, the effect on proactive innovation does not bode well for the immediate future of Chinese technological innovation. But all may not be lost.

FUTURE OF INNOVATION IN CHINA

At this point in time the future of innovation in China is at a crossroads. While there has been much in terms of foreign direct investment leading to R&D and innovative activities within its borders (as seen in the November 2004 issue of *R&D Management* devoted to the topic of R&D in China), the political and cultural aspects of China, as we have seen here, still negatively affect the propensity towards proactive innovation necessary to compete in the global technology market. Will China follow the path of Japan to become a potential threat to Western technological innovation? That is also an open question. History suggests that the two countries are very different. The Japanese had extensive American help after WWII and no Communist government environment affecting the innovation milieu. The devastation and destruction of Japanese industry during WWII also helped, if I may use that term, to provide a clean slate towards development. Also, the influence of government through the auspices of organizations like the Ministry of International Trade and Industry helped to focus efforts, which changed the traditional perspective of many Japanese goods from a perception of shoddy quality to that of world-class quality.

It is quite clear that in order to move towards the global frontier and proactive innovation, the Chinese system will need to prove its stability in terms of protection against IP infringement and capitalist-driven innovation efforts. During my recent trip to the country, a businessman was quoted as stating:

> There have been lots of great innovations in the history of China but in the last 100 years or so, these institutions that protect intellectual property just crumbled and I think China is beginning to realize that, so it wouldn't be for long that they would attempt to clean up the IP violation problems. And it is very difficult to enforce IP protection when they don't have much IP to protect and they can benefit from pirating foreign IP. But I think they have crossed that threshold and once they need to protect their own creations, then they would create laws to protect those creations. So I think the future is getting much brighter than when you look at the last century or so.

To speed up the trajectory towards proactive innovation, foreigners and expatriates returning to the country need to feel that there is a measure of security in the socio-economic and political environment in order to introduce innovations. Recent political cycles suggest that that (perception of) security does not yet exist. A sad story is that of expatriate Professor Dong Jiebao, who returned to China with a sense of patriotism during the 'Great Leap Forward' under Mao to help build the country's resources, and later committed suicide after being persecuted by his fellow citizens (Becker, 2000, p. 178). Chinese individuals have proven to be creative, intelligent and innovative – when allowed to develop outside the system of China itself. The question is whether expatriate Chinese will want to return and, if so, whether they will be allowed to flourish. As another businessman during the trip said when asked if China could become another Japan technologically:

> Yes, they could become another Japan if you look at the rash of Nobel laureates who are Chinese, at least the nominees – look at some of the newest discoveries in medicine. I think in the *Herald Tribune* today they had this advance in DNA technology, one of the co-inventors is Chinese – he is based in Houston. Will he go back to China and take the knowledge, maybe, maybe not, but there are so

many being employed by Universities now, I believe that even if a small percentage goes back, it will give the institutional support for that to happen.

   The cultural and education section of this chapter would suggest that the
Chinese are not creative, but the fact that many emigrant Chinese are entrepreneurial and creative suggests that the lack of creativity is not an innate
Chinese characteristic, but rather one that is driven (or supported) by the
socio-eco-political structure of the country itself. In conversation with a
food scientist who had worked with many Asian scientists over the years,
a comment was made that 'although they were good at understanding a
problem and methodology, they never seemed to be good at coming up with
creative solutions to the problems we were looking at'. This suggests a
propensity to analysis thinking (breaking down problems into constituent
parts and solving the methodological issues of studying the parts) versus
synthesis thinking (developing creative, novel approaches to solving
complex problems). Much of this may be due to the educational process
most Chinese are required to go through during their formative years.
   Finally, it may be instructive to recognize the old adage that 'Necessity
is the mother of invention'. Given the wisdom of that proclamation it seems
natural that the Chinese, like anyone else, should start with innovation
efforts directed at problems that exist internally for them. In the recent past
of China, innovation necessity was nationalistic, especially given the views
and needs for power of the Communist Party. From a national perspective
atomic weapons were developed, based on Soviet technology, because the
Chinese government needed to feel protected in the age of atomic
weaponry. Innovation in the commercial setting requires a driving economic need. Companies innovate only when the cost of not doing so outweighs the investment in innovative efforts. In a setting where labor costs
are extremely low, foreign direct investment is high and IP protection is
non-existent, the cost to innovate will far outstrip the cost of not innovating. Thus, until the Chinese socio-economic and political environment
improves in terms of lowering the costs of innovation (by improving IP protection) coupled with the increased costs of not innovating (improving
standards of living), innovation will stagnate. Of course, China does
show signs of moving in this direction and unless there is a significant
change in the attitude towards economic growth, innovation efforts will
continue to grow towards more internally-driven, proactive efforts.
Whether a less-developed country like China can leapfrog the US in technological innovation is unlikely but debatable, and something for which
more specific, focused research is warranted. Looking at the factors of economic, political and, particularly, cultural aspects of innovation will help
develop a better understanding of the ongoing processes of technological

innovation that China (and the rest of the world) will face in the coming years.

REFERENCES

Becker, J. (2000), *The Chinese*, New York, Free Press.

Buckley, P.J. and J. Clegg and C. Wang (2002), 'The Impact of Inward FDI on the Performance of Chinese Manufacturing Firms', *Journal of International Business Studies*, **33**(4), 637–55.

Chin, J.C. and G.M. Grossman (1990), 'Intellectual Property Rights and North–South Trade', *The Political Economy of International Trade*, R.W. Jones and A.O. Krueger (eds), Oxford, Basil Blackwell.

David, P.A. (1975), *Technical Choice, Innovation and Economic Growth*, New York: Cambridge University Press.

The Economist (2004), A Survey of the World Economy, Special Feature, 'The Dragon and the Eagle', 2 October.

Fagerberg, J. (1994), 'Technology and International Differences in Growth Rates', *Journal of Economic Literature*, **32**(3), 1147–75.

Farrell, D. (2004), 'The Case for Globalization', *International Economy*, **18**(1), 52–5.

Fischer, W.A. and M. v. Zedtwitz (2004), 'Chinese R&D: Naissance, Renaissance or Mirage?', *R & D Management*, **34**(4), 349–65.

Gassmann, O. and Z. Han (2004), 'Motivations and Barriers of Foreign R&D Activities in China', *R&D Management*, **34**(4), 423–37.

Gerth, K. (2003), *China Made: Consumer Culture and the Creation of the Nation*, Cambridge and London, Harvard University Asia Center: Harvard University Press.

Gilley, B. (1999), 'China's Spy Guide', *Far Eastern Economic Review*, **162**(51), 14–16.

Grossman, G.M. and E. Helpman (1991), *Innovation and growth in the global economy*, Cambridge, MA: MIT Press.

Haski, P. (ed.) (2004), *The Diary of Ma Yan*, London: Virago Press.

Henderson, S. (2003), ' "Designed" in Taiwan', *Design Management Journal*, **14**(2), 36–44.

Hofstede, G. (1980), *Culture's Consequences: International Differences in Work-Related Values*, Sage.

Howe, C. (1997), 'Technology and Competitiveness in Asia: Case Studies in Japanese Technology Transfer with Implications for the People's Republic of China', *Chinese technology transfer in the 1990s: current experience, historical problems, and international perspectives*, C. Feinstein and C. Howe (eds), Cheltenham, UK and Lyme, USA: Edward Elgar publishing, pp. 38–61.

Huang, C., C. Amorim, M. Spinoglio, B. Gouveia and A. Medina (2004), 'Organization, Programme and Structure: An Analysis of the Chinese Innovation Policy Framework', *R&D Management*, **34**(4), 367–87.

Landes, D.S. (1998), *The Wealth and Poverty of Nations: Why Some are so Rich and Some so Poor*, New York: Norton.

Liu, X. and C. Wang (2003), 'Does Foreign Direct Investment Facilitate Technological Progress? Evidence from Chinese Industries', *Research Policy*, **32**(6), 945–53.

MacNair, H.F., (ed.) (1951), *China*, United Nations series, Berkeley, CA: University of California Press.

Mahmood, I.P. and C. Rufin (2005), 'Government's Dilemma: the Role of Government in Imitation and Innovation', *Academy of Management*, **30**(2), 338–60.

Malecki, E.J. (1997), *Technology and Economic Development*, London: Longman.

Sun, Y. (2000), 'Spatial Distribution of Patents in China', *Regional Studies*, **34**(5), 441–55.

Teece, D.J. (1986), 'Profiting from Technological Innovation: Implications for Integration, Collaboration, Licensing and Public Policy', *Research Policy*, **15**(6), 285–305.

UNESCO Institute for Statistics (UIS) website http://www.uis.unesco.org/countryprofiles/html/EN/countryProfile, accessed 4 October 2005.

Wall Street Journal (Eastern Edition) (2004), 'World Watch-Suit May Test China's Intellectual-Property Laws', New York, 1.

Ward's Auto World (2005), 'GMDAT Sues Chery Over QQ', **41**, 10.

Yang, G. and K. Maskus (2003), 'Intellectual Property Rights, Licensing and Innovation', World Bank Policy Research Working Paper 2937, February, available at http://econ.worldbank.org/ files/24162_wps 2973.pdf, accessed on 20 April 2005.

Zhan, W. and H. Renwei (2003), 'What Will the World Gain from China in Twenty Years?', *China Business Review*, **30**(2), 36–40.

PART IV

Entry alternatives

PART II

Entrepreneurs

12. The future shape of world exports to the BRIC countries

Stephen Coelen

Dominic Wilson and Roopa Purushothaman of Goldman Sachs absorbed much of the world's attention focused on international growth in 2003 with the release of their projection of likely future development in Brazil, Russia, India and China. They project in their work, 'Dreaming with BRICs: The Path to 2050',[1] that in less than 40 years, the four countries referred to as BRIC could be larger than the G6 countries of France, Germany, Italy, Japan, the United Kingdom and the United States. Such growth seems plausible given the human and natural resources controlled by the four BRIC countries, their emphasis on development, and the level of foreign direct investment likely to emanate from Europe, Japan and the US. Growth, as or if it occurs, is likely to have a sizable effect on the volumes of international trade emanating from or terminating in the BRICs. We[2] have just recently calculated from the most comprehensive, if slightly dated, source on international trade – the UNCTAD Comtrade database on international trade and the comparable World Bank GNP data – that 40.3 percent of the total world production (some \$36.416 trillion) is included in the international stream of imports and exports (some \$14.686 trillion) transmitted around the world. Increases of the size projected by Goldman Sachs in the BRIC countries' GNP, accumulating at a 7.12 percent annual average compound rate compared to the G6 accumulating at a 2.03 percent rate, are not only likely to lead G6 capital to chase the higher growth rates in the BRIC countries but also significantly to increase the world's stream of traded goods. From a purely national perspective, with new-found income and trade growth, this gives residual hope for many that the increase in imports of BRIC countries will have effects on those not yet engaged and on the rest of the world.

This chapter considers what kinds of trade are likely to accompany income growth in the BRIC countries and, because of the findings that trade patterns of the BRIC are quite disparate among the individual countries, the plausibility of the uniform growth projected by Wilson and Purushothaman. Without producing an alternative forecast, we nonetheless conclude that development in the BRIC may occur in ways and rates contrary to the Goldman Sachs paper, depending simultaneously on the distribution of income (not considered by Wilson and Purushothaman) as well as prior levels and factor changes. The chapter starts by considering several aspects of the international trade of the BRIC countries. It evaluates current imports and the change in imports of the BRIC to determine whether there is a consistency among the BRIC countries. One would expect that such consistency would exist if indeed the BRIC are growing similarly with regard to income. However, we find that there is no consistency and further, with regard to import patterns, it is likely that the BRIC will not continue to depend as heavily on the G6, as previously – with G6 penetration rates into BRIC import markets falling in the future.

Since imports of the BRIC are not consistent among the individual countries, we look more closely at changes in incomes, evaluating the logic presented by Wilson and Purushothaman in their growth model. We conclude that an appropriately specified model must consider an endogenous component explaining the distribution of income which is likely to differentiate future growth among the BRIC.

THE BRIC COUNTRIES: A COMMON FONT OF NEW DEMAND FOR G6 EXPORTS? OR FOUR DISTINCT SETS OF DEMANDS?

Analysis of international trade can be done at many levels of detail: aggregated to include only totals of all trade, everywhere; or disaggregated to evaluate specific trade emanating from specific industrial or commodity groupings. Knowing little initially about the trade flows and the similarities and differences that may exist in the flows of the individual BRIC, we begin by looking at the flows at the commodity level, allowing us to identify what specific commodities are important to the BRIC. But even here, there is the possibility of evaluating trade at different levels of detail: 2-, 4-, 6-, or higher levels of detail, referring to the international harmonization of the nomenclature that defines each commodity grouping agreed upon by the WTO and its member nations to the six-digit level of detail.[3]

In this section, we present data on the current and changing patterns of the import trade of the BRIC countries. Such presentations can be more comprehensible at more aggregate, less data-laden levels,[4] but the underlying differences in trade activity can be badly blurred with the aggregation. Focus on detail is necessary if one wants to look at the similarities or differences among countries in trading patterns. We have taken data on imports from the United Nations Comtrade Database,[5] whereas comparable data on income and population are taken from the World Bank's World Development Indicators database.[6] Our conclusions derive from several figures and tables which are best discussed simultaneously. Therefore, we start with simple descriptions of Figures 12.1 and 12.2 and Tables 12.1 and 12.2, leaving conclusions until after presentation of the data.

Figure 12.1 shows a simple pie chart of the most current import data on the BRIC countries at the two-digit level of commodity classification. The figure presents the composition of the import stream for the ten largest commodity groupings, hiding all other commodity groupings in the aggregate 'Other' category.

Figure 12.2 shows a bar chart for the ten two-digit commodity groupings registering the highest gains, and the ten two-digit groupings registering the greatest losses in imports (from anywhere). Data on individual bars represent the change in imports over the period, 1998 to 2003 – a period showing, as much as possible, long-term change.[7] Separate bar graphs in Figure 12.2 show data for each of the individual BRIC countries. One simple way of evaluating homogeneity is to look at how many times the commodities listed in any of the panels of Figure 12.2 repeat across the BRICs. Three commodity groupings (electrical machinery and sound and TV equipment; nuclear reactors, boilers and non-electrical machinery; and mineral fuel, oils etc. and bituminous substitutes) registered as among the top ten 'up' or 'down' commodities simultaneously for all four BRIC countries. These three commodity groupings, however, were mixed in terms of change across the BRIC – imports up in some of the BRIC, down in others. Commodity Changes on the left of the axis imply a decrease in imports; commodity changes on the right side of the axis imply an increase in imports.

Commodity groupings among the top or bottom ten in import changes for at least three BRICs simultaneously, noting groupings that had a homogeneity of change with regard to imports – were always down for cereals but always up for iron and steel, regardless which BRIC country reported the change. These were additionally six commodities common among at least three of the four BRIC countries, but mixed as to whether these were increases or decreases in commodity flows: aircraft, fertilizer, ships, vehicles, organic chemicals and special classifications of commodities. All other commodities with big increases or decreases applied to only one or two of the BRICs.

Table 12.1 applies to each of the individual BRIC countries. It shows data on the correlations of the changes in imports (from 1998 to 2003) across the BRIC for the two-digit commodity classifications. It also shows annual compound growth rates for imports, gross national product and population in the four BRIC countries.

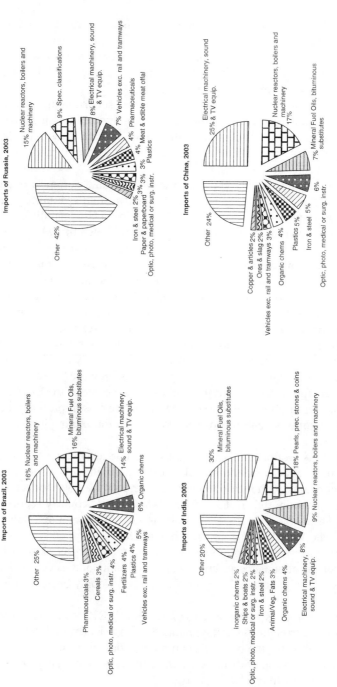

Imports of Russia, 2003

Nuclear reactors, boilers and machinery 15%
Spec. classifications 9%
Electrical machinery, sound & TV equip. 8%
Vehicles exc. rail and tramways 7%
Pharmaceuticals 4%
Meat & edible meat offal 4%
Plastics 3%
Paper & paperboard 3%
Iron & steel 2%
Optic, photo, medical or surg. instr. 3%
Other 42%

Imports of China, 2003

Electrical machinery, sound & TV equip. 25%
Nuclear reactors, boilers and machinery 17%
Mineral Fuel Oils, bituminous substitutes 7%
Optic, photo, medical or surg. instr. 6%
Iron & steel 5%
Plastics 5%
Organic chems 4%
Vehicles exc. rail and tramways 3%
Ores & slag 2%
Copper & articles 2%
Other 24%

Imports of Brazil, 2003

Nuclear reactors, boilers and machinery 16%
Mineral Fuel Oils, bituminous substitutes 16%
Electrical machinery, sound & TV equip. 14%
Organic chems 6%
Vehicles exc. rail and tramways 5%
Plastics 5%
Fertilizers 4%
Optic, photo, medical or surg. instr. 4%
Cereals 3%
Pharmaceuticals 3%
Other 25%

Imports of India, 2003

Mineral Fuel Oils, bituminous substitutes 30%
Pearls, prec. stones & coins 18%
Nuclear reactors, boilers and machinery 9%
Electrical machinery, sound & TV equip. 8%
Organic chems 4%
Animal/Veg. Fats 3%
Iron & steel 2%
Ships & boats 2%
Optic, photo, medical or surg. instr. 2%
Inorganic chems 2%
Other 20%

Figure 12.1   Composition of imports of the BRIC countries, 2003

Because much is lost by looking only at aggregate descriptions of commodities, Table 12.2, like Figure 12.2, steps the analysis of import flows up to six-digit commodity classifications. This table reports for each of the BRICs the country's top five imports, giving for each the value of the import, the rank of the commodity among all commodities imported, and the percentage each commodity represents of the country's GNP. In the last three panels of the table we present, for the other three BRICs, the ranking the commodity had among flows observed in those BRICs and the percentage it represents of the other BRIC's GNP.

It is important to emphasize that a country's imports and predictions of how imports are likely to grow with increases in income are greatly clouded by the variety of purposes to which imports are put. In the newly globalized economy, we can no longer assume (if we ever could) that a country's imports add to its accumulation designed for final consumption – such would be a great oversimplification. If imports were primarily chosen to satisfy consumer demand, then increases in imports would be linked primarily to income, income growth, changes in tastes and preferences, prices and quality differences among the different commodities. These are all things that shift demand for imports within a country. One country's import activities would play only a small role in other countries' demands. But goods are often imported as intermediate products, used in producing final goods for eventual consumption, but not themselves being the commodity of final consumption. Consumption of such goods is significantly influenced by the movements of productive capacities around the world as producers seek the lowest possible input costs. In this way, one country's import activities do very significantly influence a second country's activity, especially if the multinational companies most associated with such activity withdraw from one country to begin production in new countries.

Against such a warning note, Figures 12.1 and 12.2 and Tables 12.1 and 12.2 allow us to reach three independent, strong conclusions about trade among the BRIC, primarily focusing on how BRIC growth will affect import absorption from the G6.

Russia, among the BRICs, is different, focusing more on final-consumption good imports

Figure 12.1 shows that only in Russia do the top ten imported commodities represent significantly less than 75 percent of imports. In all of the other three countries, the top ten imported commodities represent 75 percent or more of all imported commodities by value. This suggests a high degree of concentration of import activity in just a few commodity groups for most

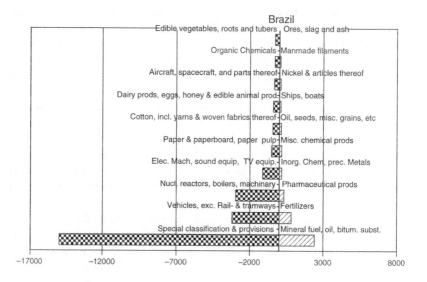

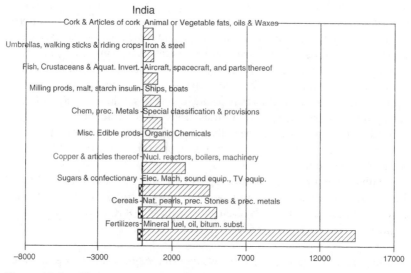

Figure 12.2   Changes in imports for largest gaining and losing 2-digit commodities in the BRIC

Russia

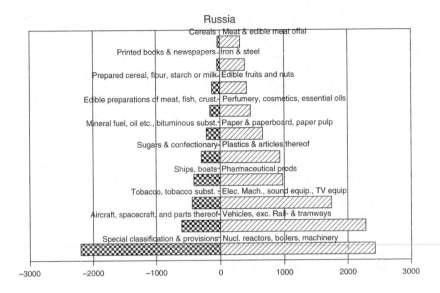

China

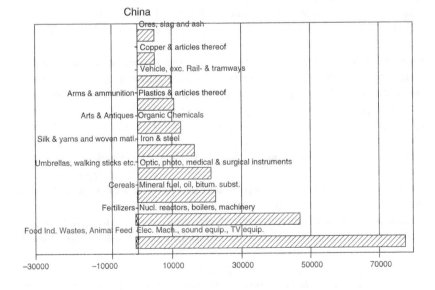

Entry alternatives

Table 12.1   Correlations among imports/growth rates in imports, GNP and population for BRIC

	Correlations among changes in imports for BRIC countries				Annual compound growth rates		
	Brazil	*Russia*	*India*	*China*	Imports[1]	GNP[2]	Population[2]
Brazil	1				−3.5%	−1.8%	1.3%
Russia	−0.216371589	1			−0.5%	21.9%	−0.5%
India	0.25780301	0.184838174	1		12.7%	7.7%	1.6%
China	−0.381964119	0.186794391	0.499368542	1	24.1%	9.3%	0.7%

Notes:
[1] Imports are from the UNCTAD Files, for 1998–2003
[2] GNP and Population are from World Bank Files, for 1999–2003

of the BRIC countries. The top ten imports at the two-digit level in Russia, by contrast, include only 58 percent of all Russian imports, implying a much wider dispersion of import activity. One suspects that the greater diversity of imports in Russia may stem from its history, beginning from a more developed stage than the other BRICs, Brazil, India and China. Figure 12.1 indicates that Russia's import absorption is more oriented toward final consumer products than those in the other BRICs. This is difficult to tell from a two-digit commodity description, but Russia, for example, absorbs more in the two-digit pharmaceutical category (clearly not a category of commodities shipped in partially manufactured or completed stages, as for example, shirts and other products often are) than the other BRICs do.

There is a Critical Dependence of the BRIC Upon One Another

This conclusion builds from the perspective either that sharing great growth and still at a state of relative underdevelopment BRIC imports focus on a common set of commodities or that the competition among the BRICs make their focus on commodities overlap. This conclusion develops from the following observations:

1. Across all of the BRIC countries (including Russia), only a quarter of the 40 commodities represented in Figure 12.1 stand alone as uniquely important imports of just one of the individual BRICs. This 'non-uniqueness' of commodities important to the BRIC shows up both with regard to levels of imports in Figure 12.1 at a two-digit level and with regard to changes in imports in Figure 12.2 at a six-digit level. In

Table 12.2 Differences in major current imports of BRIC countries for 6-digit HS commodities

		Top Brazilian imports from the rest of the world							
		Brazil			China		India		Russia	

HS6 Code	Commodity	Rank	Trade Value/current GDP in million	Percentage	Rank	Trade Value/current GDP in percent	Rank	Trade Value/current GDP in percent	Rank	Trade Value/current GDP in percent
270900	Petroleum oils, oils from bituminous minerals, crude	1	7883.80	7.64%	2	4.79%	1	24.09%		0.00%
271000	Oils petroleum bituminous distillates, except crude	2	3918.57	3.80%	8	1.42%	6	2.23%	48	0.28%
100190	Wheat except durum wheat and meslin	3	2256.72	2.19%	1	0.00%		0.00%	174	0.10%
854211	Monolithic integrated circuits digital	4	2054.90	1.99%	1	5.26%	62	0.15%	98	0.16%
852990	Parts for radio/TV transmit/receive equipment	5	1486.22	1.44%	6	1.70%	33	0.36%	57	0.26%
	Total imports, all commodities		103 238.41	17.05%						

Table 12.2 (continued)

Top Russian imports from the rest of the world

HS6 Code	Commodity	Russia			Brazil		China		India	
		Rank	Trade Value/current GDP in million	Percentage	Rank	Trade Value/current GDP in percent	Rank	Trade Value/current GDP in percent	Rank	Trade Value/current GDP in percent
9999AA	Commodities not specified according to kind	1	12258.07	9.26%		0.00%	49	0.31%	15	0.72%
870323	Automobile spark ignition engine of 1500–3000 cc	2	3423.17	2.58%	14	0.82%	17	0.68%	166	0.06%
300490	Medicaments nes in dosage	3	2990.85	2.26%	9	1.20%	113	0.16%	90	0.11%
170111	Raw sugar cane	4	1970.44	1.49%		0.00%	470	0.03%	506	0.02%
281820	Aluminium oxide, except artificial corundum	5	1656.82	1.25%	735	0.02%	39	0.33%	466	0.02%
	Total imports, all commodities		132 445.56	16.84%						

Table 12.2 (continued)

		India			Brazil		China		Russia	
					Top Indian imports from the rest of the world					
HS6 Code	Commodity	Rank	Trade Value/current GDP in million	Percentage	Rank	Trade Value/current GDP in percent	Rank	Trade Value/current GDP in percent	Rank	Trade Value/current GDP in percent
270900	Petroleum oils from bituminous minerals crude	1	31 052.90	24.09%	1	7.64%	2	4.79%	9	0.85%
710231	Diamonds (jewellery) unworked of simply sawn, cleaved	2	9834.84	7.63%		0.00%	90	0.19%		0.00%
710812	Gold in Unwrought forms non-monetary	3	7695.07	5.97%		0.00%		0.00%		0.00%
852520	Transmit-receive apparatus for radio, TV etc.	4	3076.65	2.39%	30	0.39%	12	1.01%	6	0.98%
710813	Gold, semi-manufactured forms, non-monetary	5	3053.90	2.37%		0.00%		0.00%		0.00%
	Total imports, all commodities		128 883.55	42.45%						

Table 12.2 (continued)

Top Chinese imports the rest of the world

HS6 Code	Commodity	China			Brazil		India		Russia	
		Rank	Trade Value/current GDP in million	Percentage	Rank	Trade Value/current GDP in percent	Rank	Trade Value/current GDP in percent	Rank	Trade Value/current GDP in percent
854211	Monolithic integrated circuits, digital	1	15 500.33	5.26%	4	1.99%	62	0.15%	98	0.16%
270900	Petroleum oils, oils from bituminous minerals, crude	2	14 130.29	4.79%	1	7.64%	1	24.09%	9	0.85%
854219	Monolithic integrated circuits except digital	3	10 063.15	3.41%	15	0.80%	38	0.29%	665	0.03%
847330	Parts and accessories of data processing equipment	4	8198.86	2.78%	8	1.21%	10	1.05%	82	0.18%
901380	Optical devices, appliances and instruments nes	5	8127.36	2.76%	31	0.39%	785	0.01%		0.00%
	Total imports, all commodities		294 828.39	19.00%						

Figure 12.2 there are only 23 of the 77 (less than 30 percent) listed important commodity groups with large changes in imports that are unique to a single BRIC. This seems to imply that most of the important (among the top ten) imports of the BRIC, whether talking about levels or changes in imports, are 'common' imports, absorbed simultaneously by more than one of the BRICs.

2. We see evidence in Figure 12.2 that some of the commonality in changes in top products across the BRIC is caused by substitution among countries receiving imports of intermediate goods as, in all likelihood, certain operations of international corporations left Brazil and/or Russia, moving into India and China. This is most clear in electrical machinery and sound and TV equipment, and in the broad composite category, nuclear reactors, boilers and non-electrical machinery. Imports of these commodities declined for Brazil but increased for the other three BRICs. It is also clear that the negative change in imports of organic chemicals in Brazil, and in aircraft and spacecraft in both Brazil and Russia, was offset by increased absorption in both China and India (organic chemicals) and in India (aircraft and spacecraft). Therefore, we must expect that the BRICs, as they grow, will remain competitors among themselves, often one BRIC growing at the expense of the others. This is also substantiated by the low, even negative, correlations of the change in imports in the BRIC shown in Table 12.1 and the flipping of commodities in Figure 12.2, up in one or more of the BRICs while down in the rest.

3. This same point is substantiated in Table 12.1 which shows that the highest correlation in changes for imports of the BRIC countries occurs between India and China. This is nearly 0.5, but in Brazil and Russia, both subject to declines in total imports, there are negative correlations among imports. This might be caused by the disparate income and product (GNP) growth between the two countries (Brazil's GNP down by 1.8 percent per annum, compounded, and Russia's up by 21.9 percent per annum, compounded). But we see much contradictory evidence between the correlation of changes of imports and GNP growth. Consider, for example, the larger income growth differential between Brazil and China than between Brazil and India. If larger levels of income growth were to lead to lower, or more negative, correlations between import changes, as in the Brazil–Russia case, we see Brazil and India with a much more positive correlation between their import changes than Brazil and China which have the most negative correlation in import changes. This leads us to believe that it is not only GNP growth that will affect future shifts in import demand among the BRIC; this growth will be affected by relations among

the BRIC themselves, a consideration not made by Wilson and Purushothaman.

Growth and Decline of Individual Commodity Imports Depend on the Macro Economy

Figure 12.2 shows that in comparison to Brazil and Russia, India and China have fewer commodities with declining levels of imports (and smaller losses per commodity). Undoubtedly, this is consistent with the overall declining imports of Brazil and Russia (shown in Table 12.1) that has been quite well documented (beginning with financial journalists like Thomas Friedman,[8] and Paul Blustein,[9] and ending with academic authors like Padma Desai),[10] as being spawned by the financial crisis in Southeast Asia that spread to Russia, Brazil and Argentina. Undoubtedly, a macroeconomic model is necessary to explain overall tendencies in import and export data.

Finally then, Figure 12.3 evaluates both the top 20 commodity imports measured as flows from the G6 and, as an alternative, the top 20 commodity imports as flows from the rest of the world (ROW). Because nine commodities overlap (and are among the top 20 for both the G6 and the ROW simultaneously), only 31 circles show in Figure 12.3. The figure is a bubble chart simultaneously representing the size of the market (by the bubble's size), the growth of the market over the last five years, 1998–2003 (the bubble's position on the y-axis), the change in the penetration rate of G6 countries into the market between 1998 and 2003 (the bubble's position on the x-axis) and whether the commodity was in the top 20 of the G6, the ROW, or simultaneously both G6 and ROW (the shading of the bubbles, respectively: no shading or white – important primarily to the G6 only; dotted – more important to the ROW; or solid black – important to both G6 and ROW). Finally, Figure 12.3 presents, in the downward-sloping red line, a regression indicating the general orientation between commodity market growth (totaling across the four BRICs) and the G6's penetration into the commodity market in the BRIC.

The most important conclusion about trade with the BRICs from the perspective of the G6 derives from Figure 12.3. This figure shows imports by commodity type (of which, to not clutter the figure, only a few are identified), the size of the market, the market's importance to the G6 versus the rest of the world, and the change in the G6's penetration into the BRIC. By putting the overall growth of the market on the ordinate axis and the change in G6's penetration rate on the abscissa, we find (by the downward-sloping regression line through these data, representing the central tendency inherent in the relationship between market growth and penetration) that market growth is highest in those markets in which the G6 are losing

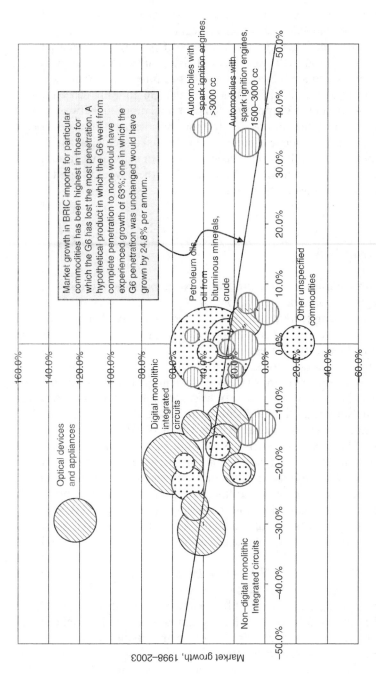

Figure 12.3   *World market growth in BRIC imports vs. change in G6 penetration: 31 commodities representing BRIC's top 20 imports from either the G6 or the Rest of the World (or both)*

285

penetration to the rest of the world. For markets in which the G6 have neither lost nor gained penetration, growth from 1998 to 2003 was approximately 24.8 percent per annum. The G6 lost penetration in markets, on average, in which growth was higher. This occurred in commodities like optical devices and appliances and monolithic integrated circuits.

Conversely, there was a tendency for the G6 to gain penetration in markets that declined. We posit no behavioral relationship between growth and the loss in penetration – only that this describes the historically observed, central tendency, but our conclusion nonetheless is that the import pattern of the BRIC has been that growth of imports from the G6 has not matched overall BRIC market growth; there would seem to be no likely reason why this might change.

GROWTH OF THE BRIC: THE PROJECTION OF GOLDMAN SACHS

The above section has shown that shifts in imports of the BRIC do not move regularly with changes across BRIC income or growth. Table 12.1 showed, for example, that Brazil's GNP declined in the five-year window through which we see consistent import declines. However, the opposite rise in GNP in Russia, the largest in all the BRIC countries, is inconsistently linked also to import declines. Even for India and China, increases in GNP and imports seem less than perfectly consistent: China's GNP grew a little more than 20 percent faster than India's, yet China's imports grew nearly 90 percent more than India's. Inconsistencies like these compel us to look closely at the growth in product expected in the BRIC.

The Goldman Sachs model (GS), giving rise to all the recent focus on growth of the BRIC countries, is quite simple – perhaps too simple. It is based on a Cobb-Douglas production function with: constant returns to scale to increases in capital and labor; exogenous changes in both input factors; and a multiplier for technological progress (Wilson and Purushothaman's total factor productivity).

Mathematically, the model is specified as:

$$Y_t = AK^\alpha L^{(1-\alpha)}. \tag{12.1}$$

The term A is described as total factor productivity (or alternatively, the level of technological progress); K is the capital stock; and L is labour. This model, however, in the absence of other modifying equations and/or assumptions about resources, treats capital and labor as always fully utilized resources. There is neither unemployment, nor idle capital. This means that there are no imperfections allowed in the market and that labor and capital are imbued with the ultimate flexibility to move among industrial sectors as the BRIC economies grow across the stages of economic development predicted to occur in the BRIC. Such conditions hardly describe the current case for the BRIC countries. Typically, they are not the case across the development cycle of any of the developing country economies. We shall see that in the context of long-run change from less-developed to fully-developed country, these assumptions are significant weaknesses in describing rapid development.

A by-product of using this type of model (because of its multiplicative form) is also that it gives a tautological result in which the percentage change in national income, Y_t, over time is approximately[11] proportional to:

- the percentage change in A over time;
- α times the percentage change in capital, Kt over time; and
- $(1 - \alpha)$ times the percentage change in labor over time.

Specifically, the calculus implies that $\%\Delta Y \approx \%\Delta A + \alpha \%\Delta K + (1 - \alpha)\%\Delta L$, for small changes in the variables A, L and K. With the return to capital, α, postulated by GS at 0.33, then one might think much of the growth differential between BRIC and G6 countries comes from the labor advantage of the BRIC over the G6 since a α of 0.33 gives a much larger weight, $(1 - \alpha) = 0.67$, to labor in the model. Furthermore, because labor derives from its implicit underlying base of the country's population, greater population bases and higher growth rates in the BRIC countries (than the G6) would make much of the greater prospective income growth seem likely to come from this source. The BRIC countries in 2000 represented a population 3.9 times the population of the G6; but because of the way that the model works, the size of the population has nothing to do with the projected growth rates. All income convergence between BRIC and G6 from labor comes out of the fact that the BRIC population is assumed fully employed across time from 2000 to 2050 and the BRIC population growth rate is 0.52 percent per annum compared to only 0.28 percent per annum for the G6. (There are, of course, major differences forecast by the US Bureau of the Census[12] in population for individual G6 and BRIC countries.)

Income in the BRIC countries, however, is projected to grow much, much faster than that in the G6 – by a factor of more than 17 times over the 50-year period considered by Wilson and Purushothaman. BRIC GDP is projected to grow from 2000 to 2050 in the GS model from 2700 to 84 201 in US dollars, or by 3018.5 percent over the 50 years and by 7.12 percent per annum, compounded. G6 GDP in contrast is projected to grow, over the same time period, from 19 702 to 54 433 in US dollars, or by 176.3 percent over the 50 years and by 2.05 percent per annum, compounded. These changes are big enough that population changes are not enough to account fully for the full size of this differential between BRIC and G6.

Some of the convergence in the GS model derives from the capital accumulation expected in the BRIC countries. This is because GS assume investment rates (out of income) to hold constant throughout the forecast period at recent historical rates, 19 percent for Brazil, 22 percent for India, 25 percent for Russia and 36 percent[13] for China. With an assumption common throughout the BRIC of a low, 4 percent, depreciation rate, BRIC capital growth is then quite likely to be brisk, although its precise rate of growth cannot be specified without knowing the capital output ratio used in the GS model. Much of such investment, however, must come as foreign direct investment, and whether this can be held at as high a rate of growth as income of the BRIC is certainly questionable. Without having data on the series of capital used in building the GS model, it is not possible to be more specific.

However, we can be more specific with regard to the third factor, A, which accounts for the remainder of the difference in the model's income growth between BRIC and G6. GS hypothesizes that $A_t = (0.013-0.015\ln((Y_{BRIC}/P_{BRIC})/(Y_{US}/P_{US}))A_{t-1}$.[14] The 0.013 (1.3 percent) is taken as the long-term total factor productivity growth rate for the US, and the –0.015 is the convergence factor between growth rates between the BRIC and G6 over time as per capita incomes converge. In 2000, when the BRIC countries had a per capita income less than one thirty-third of that of the US, we calculate according to the GS formula that technological growth in the BRIC is 6.56 percent, more than fivefold larger than the presumed 1.3 percent growth in the US. By 2050 the model shows the BRIC countries with a technological growth rate slowing (Goldman Sachs convergence) to 3.11 percent, but still more than twice the growth in technological progress of the US. Over the 50-year forecast period, we calculate the average technology growth in the BRIC to be 4.8 percent. With such shifts in the technological progress multiplier, it is easy to say that this factor, Wilson and Purushothaman's total factor productivity, produces much if not most of the relative growth between the BRIC and G6 over time.

The significance of total factor productivity as a critical component in developing-country catch-up has been persistent in the literature evaluating growth differences across countries. Códoba and Ripoll (2005)[15] explain:

[Hall and Jones, (1999)] . . . conclude that most of the differences in the productivity of labor across countries is explained by TFP differences. A similar conclusion is obtained by Klenow and Rodriguez-Clare (1997), and Parente and Prescott (2000), among others, using a similar technology.

The use of per capita income to drive the convergence of technological progress in the two countries is but a simple measure of the distribution of income, here more between countries than within. In fact, however, the internal distribution of income is more likely to influence the outcomes than is the macro, first moment, per capita income average number. This is the topic in the following section.

GROWTH: A FUNCTION OF BOTH INCOME AND ITS DISTRIBUTION

The use of production functions to explain long-term growth is not new in development economics. Many, including those referenced above in note 15, the World Bank,[16] the US Government Accounting Office (GAO)[17] have used such functions in very much the same way as Wilson and Purushothaman, comparing growth among countries and focusing on the critical role played by the total factor productivity (TFP) term.

The TFP term, wherever used, seems to play the role of 'grand equalizer': whatever growth is not explained by changes in factor inputs is explained by this ubiquitous shift in total factor productivity. And we ourselves have found that this term explains the majority of the differential shift in output between the BRIC and G6 countries projected by Wilson and Purushothaman. Of course, use of a total factor productivity term makes explanation much simpler, the model not having to assign separate productivity growth terms to the individual factors. But because of the importance of the term, questions have been raised about links between growth occurring through TFP and income inequality, either forward (inequality, either slowing or hastening growth), or backward (growth, producing or eliminating inequality).

A wonderful review of literature on inequality and growth appeared in the *Journal of Economic Literature*, 'Inequality and Economic Growth: The Perspective of the New Growth Theories', by Aghion et al.[18] The review noted that recent literature has produced overwhelmingly strong empirical findings of the relationship between growth and inequality:

> Within this vast literature, several studies have examined the impact of inequality upon economic growth. The picture they draw is impressively unambiguous, since they all suggest that greater inequality reduces the rate of growth.

Consistent with this strong relationship, Códoba and Ripoll propose that the total factor productivity term be made endogenous to the whole model of growth.

The now longstanding belief is that growth occurs initially in a period when the distributional variance of income is increasing, and then in later stages when the distributional variance is declining. This has come to be known as the 'Kuznets hypothesis'. Recent literature has tried to move beyond the inverted U-shaped relationship between inequality and growth, seemingly consistent with the proposition that incentives derived from the desire to escape the poverty associated with inequality would provide the drive necessary for economies and players therein to move toward greater efficiency and further growth. But recently, others have raised the possibility of feedback linkages: reductions in inequality influence growth, and growth, in turn, reinforces further movement toward either lessened inequality (the virtuous cycle) or increased inequality (the vicious cycle).

In the course of applying a model driven by the growth of population, capital and total factor productivity, much is left unstated. The primary issues are:

1. The degree of un- and underemployment of labor, significantly associated with rural environments, but throughout the BRIC, is not taken into account in making calculations of production. If there is un- or underemployment, then only a portion of the existing population should be used as an input to the production function. The paper by Wilson and Purushothaman appears to use the full value of population throughout its forecast. The utilization of greater 'paper' amounts of population over the course of development is a rationale for why the model must have a free factor built off of TFP explaining extraordinary growth when the shifts in 'paper amounts' of labor do not shift by much. Wilson and Purushothaman set growth in this to equal 1.3 percent taken to be the developed-country steady state growth rate minus a convergence speed between developed and developing countries of 1.5 percent times the relative per capita incomes in developing and developed countries. It is unlikely that all of the individual BRICs would move at this single pace, especially if they are initially faced with differential amounts of unemployment. However, growth in total factor productivity must be facilitated by access to education, and that depends on the distribution of income.

2. Separate from the above issue of how much population is entered into the model production function, the degree of cross-training of labor as it moves with development from states either of un- or underemployment or of relative unskilled jobs to more skilled jobs requires an educationally mobile population which is not considered in the model. But access to education is clearly related to income, and economies with great levels of inequality may be less likely to educate their populations

appropriately. If unemployment results because the population is unable to make the switches, the problem recurs as above, and the unemployed population should not be included in calculations, but the probability of successful shifts of labor must depend on the distribution of income, and differential movements of various economies must be associated with the internal distribution of income, and access to education.

3. The extent of withdrawal of income from the BRIC, as development occurs (such withdrawal facilitating payment of returns to foreign direct investment used in production), is not considered as a potential influence on further capital accumulation in the BRICs. The Wilson and Purushothaman model assumes that the investment rates are constants for each of the BRIC countries, changing only in China (declining, from one constant to another) in 2010 and beyond. This has two effects. First, it does not leave an endogenous source for renewing investments in the BRIC – these depend on the investments from the rest of the world and many conditions seem required for these to hold steady, including that foreign sources must offset accumulating depreciation on prior investment and then build on it at an assumed constant future rate. Such foreign investment is from country sources whose levels of income and growth are unknown to the Wilson-Purushothaman model. Second, there seems likely to be a far different level of growth in income retained by the BRIC than income produced by them. As stated much earlier, this will certainly drive a wedge between future import growth and GNP growth.

In this context, there are two dominant ways in which distribution affects future growth. A model built without consideration of these cannot show differentials in the degree to which countries, here the BRIC countries, are prepared to facilitate continuing growth. Hence, it is impossible to determine which of the BRICs are more likely to surge ahead of the others. Wilson and Purushothaman's model, indeed, does not consider the issue of distribution.

The first difficulty inherent in the GS model is not just that the model confuses factor inputs and productivity (the primary focus of point 1 above) but that there is no way inherent in equation (12.1), above, to show differences in patterns of countries capable of sustaining the growth referred to in point 2 above. One would think that the degree of un- or underemployment should relate directly to the extent that portions of the population are uneducated. This is determined from the within-country distribution of education: At what point does the population have the minimum required education and skills to be currently employable?

In the same vein, the ability of the BRIC countries to retain significant portions of the foreign direct investment they currently attract, point 3 above, may very well depend on future growth in educational attainment in the BRIC. There is little doubt that the BRIC have attracted significant foreign direct investment already, leading to total investment rates in the BRIC of 19 percent in Brazil, 22 percent in India, 25 percent in Russia and 36 percent in China. This has been fueled by existing high levels of educational attainment. But in order to continue to attract more FDI, as GS believes the BRIC will, the BRIC must continually improve broader access and attainment for its population. Wider and wider portions of populations need to be well educated compared to competitor nations' populations for the BRIC at the margin to be more attractive to further FDI than those countries which they have previously beaten in the race to attract such FDI. This is determined from the extra-country distribution of education: at what point do the BRICs start to lose FDI to other countries?

All of the above requires some focus on the distribution of education among a nation's population. This must become a part of the inherent growth model. But there is a wide literature describing how access to education depends on income. The more widely the distribution of income is spread among a population, the more widely spread will be the educational outcomes for that population. This is a primary reason why a model (projecting as far into the future as the Goldman Sachs model does) must consider the distribution of income.

The second difficulty inherent in the GS model is more direct. The distribution of income affects both returns to capital and labor on the one hand, and individuals, rich and poor on the other hand. The former will affect how much income growth will be retained in the BRICs, and likely the future rate of investment either directly from within the countries or indirectly as FDI from outside. The latter should impact on differing marginal propensities to consume out of income, versus saving and investing. In both cases, the distribution will have very direct effects on developing-country investment rates, considered perhaps inappropriately by GS as constants.

For the reasons laid out in this section, without the additional data on how growth and distribution associate, it is impossible to associate future import activity with income growth.

NOTES AND REFERENCES

1. This chapter has been the subject of much interest, including in newspapers, academic courses, and academic journals. It is available at http://www.goldmansachs.com/insight/research/reports/report6.htmls. See chapter 1 of this volume.

2. Here, we represent WISER, the World Institute for Strategic Economic Research, located at www.WISERTrade.org.
3. This means that specific commodities of individual countries described by the most detailed commodity code of the individual countries, must share the same first six digits as commodities produced and classified elsewhere. Beyond six digits, the complete coding of the same product produced and classified in different countries may be different.
4. To give an indication of volume of detail at the six-digit level, for 2003, there were actually 4544 different individual six-digit commodity classifications reported for Brazil and 4649 for Russia, 4583 for India, and 4748 for China.
5. This is available by subscription at http://unstats.un.org/unsd/comtrade/.
6. This is available by subscription or in limited format at http://web.worldbank.org/WBSITE/EXTERNAL/DATASTATISTICS/0,,contentMDK:20394802~menuPK:1192714~pagePK:64133150~piPK:64133175~theSitePK:239419.00.html.
7. The harmonized system was implemented in 1998 and comparable data is not available for earlier periods.
8. Friedman, Thomas (2000), *The Lexus and the Olive Tree*, New York: Anchor Books.
9. Blustein, Paul, (2001), *The Chastening*, New York, NY: Public Affairs Press.
10. Desai, Padma, (2003), *Financial Crisis, Contagion, and Containment From Asia to Argentina*, Princeton, NJ: Princeton University Press.
11. The approximation stands for the representation that the conditions of calculus hold, their being small changes in the exogenous factors so that the calculus indeed holds as changes approximate zero. In the ebb and flow of development, of course, the changes that transpire are not small. Hence the results of this statement are only approximate, not to apply to the full shifts likely to occur. It is instructive, nonetheless, to evaluate what happens with changes in each of the exogenous variables in the model.
12. US Census forecasts were used by GS, as the future trend of population for the various countries, BRIC and G6 alike. Brazil, Germany, Italy and Japan are projected to have a declining population, the rest increasing. The US, alone, is projected to increase by more than any other country under consideration other than India, 0.79 percent to 0.91 percent.
13. The investment rate for China is assumed to fall from 36 percent to 30 percent in 2010.
14. Wilson, Dominic and Roopa Purushothaman (2003), 'Dreaming with BRICs: The Path to 2050', Global Economics Paper No. 99. New York: Goldman Sachs, p. 18. See chapter 1 of this volume.
15. Códoba, Juan Carlos and Marla Ripoll (2005), 'Endogeneous TFP and Cross-Country Income Differences', working paper, p. 2. Paper available from Research Papers in Economics, RePEc, http://repec.org/
16. See 'Measuring Growth in Total Factor Prodcutivity', PREMnotes, No. 42, September 2000, Development Conomics Vice-Presidency and Poverty Reduction and Economic Management Network, World Bank.
17. See the description of the model used in providing the Analysis of Long-Term Fiscal Outlook, July 2000, available at http://www.gao.gov/special.pubs/longterm/ technical. pdf.
18. Aghion, Phillippe, Eve Caroli and Cecilia Garcia-Peñalosa (1999), 'Inequality and Economic Growth: The Perspective of the New Growth Theories', *Journal of Economic Literature*, **37**, 1617.

13. The international joint venture performance of American firms: a comparative analysis of emerging markets and non-emerging markets

Hemant Merchant

Emerging markets have witnessed a phenomenal level of in-bound direct investment, much of it through international joint ventures (*World Investment Report*, 1997). Corporate attention to these markets not only reflects their strategic importance to firms but also indicates these markets' potential for augmenting firms' economic performance (Garten, 1996). However, business press accounts of firms operating in some of the prominent emerging markets (Brazil, Russia, India and China) furnish mixed evidence in support of these markets' economic promise. It appears that the lack of performance of firms – especially American firms – operating in these markets arises, fundamentally, from an inability to fully comprehend the distinct nature of emerging markets vis-à-vis that of markets in which American firms have previously conducted their international joint ventures (IJVs). Thus, it is likely that the configuration of American firms' IJVs may be less than optimal for the context in which these ventures are formed. Implicitly, there is a need to understand better the drivers of these firms' joint venture performance across distinct environments – each of which requires a unique blend of variables to create shareholder value for American parents (Merchant, 2004). This chapter attempts to fill the gap.

The study compares various influences on shareholder value created when IJVs involving American firms and their non-American partners are first publicly announced. This chapter groups IJVs based on their (announced) location: (1) emerging-market countries of Brazil, Russia, India and China (henceforth, BRIC); (2) newly industrialized countries; (3) developed countries; and (4) developing countries, including other emerging markets. Given the economic imperative for firms seriously to include the emerging markets of BRIC in their strategic growth plans, and high expected failure rates in emerging markets (Merchant, 2005), this study asks the following research question: Which variables differentially influence – and how – shareholder value creation in American firms whose IJVs are located in the above-mentioned environments?

To fulfill its objective of comparing the drivers of IJV-based shareholder value creation in emerging markets of BRIC versus other types of markets, this chapter offers a theoretical rationale that highlights the role of, and interrelationships between, salient organizational and locational influences on firm performance. This discussion provides a basis for generating three propositions. Next, the study describes its research protocol and methodologies that are used to test the theoretically derived propositions. A brief overview of the study's empirical results is presented thereafter. The concluding section discusses these findings and outlines three areas for future research.

DEVELOPMENT OF RESEARCH PROPOSITIONS

Drawing upon the OLI paradigm (Dunning, 1980), previous work has recognized the interconnectedness between organizational and locational influences (O-factors and L-factors respectively) and its performance implications for IJVs (for example see Dussauge and Garrette, 1995). However, most researchers have neglected an explicit discussion of this jointness (Dunning, 1998) although there are exceptions (for example Merchant, 2004). A discussion of how the O-factors and L-factors co-mingle is therefore useful given the heterogeneous institutional environments in which American firms operate their IJVs. Indeed, Garten (1996) and others have argued that the context of emerging markets is markedly different from those of markets not deemed to be so. Thus, a discussion of how O-factors and L-factors interact is necessary. Although, in principle, there are numerous influences on IJV performance, a recent survey of influences on shareholder value creation in American firms has identified a limited number of O-factors and L-factors across studies (see Merchant, 2000b). These factors as well as the theoretical rationale underlying their impact are available upon request. The information is not presented here under the assumption that it is common knowledge to IJV researchers (and so does not merit repetition) as well as to conserve space.

The Role of Locational Factors vis-à-vis Firm Performance

Researchers have argued that L-factors, such as small economic and/or cultural distance and market potential, represent opportunities for a more efficient deployment of O-factors (Dunning, 1998, p. 51). Their interaction can offset certain O-factors which otherwise might constrain shareholder value creation. Stated differently, some L-factors better leverage O-factors by enabling firms to deploy their firm-specific advantages without compromising their value-in-use (Dunning and Rugman, 1985). This facilitates economic value creation to the extent that firms can concentrate more on achieving resource-based synergies, and relatively less on navigating institutional hazards (Merchant, 2000c).

In general, previous work has often suggested that developing countries – many of them emerging markets – have 'unfavorable' L-factors; in contrast, developed countries and NICs are usually associated with 'favorable' L-factors such as economic and/or cultural similarity. Needless to say, the implied differential performance effect of O-factors and L-factors across the above-mentioned location clusters needs to be unpacked carefully.

To illustrate, economic and/or cultural similarity between the homes of firms and the host countries of their ventures can compensate for certain O-factors, say small firm size and limited international experience. Although all firms can benefit from their O-factors, economic similarity especially benefits small, usually resource-constrained, firms because it facilitates scale economies and enhances firms' ability to serve foreign markets (Davidson, 1980). Likewise, cultural similarity permits information about a new product to be disseminated 'more efficiently and effectively' (Davidson, 1980, p. 10), and lowers managerial uncertainty or ignorance of local conditions. Thus, cultural similarity can make up for firms' limited international experience and reduce their costs of managing activity in foreign markets.

As Benito and Gripsrud noted, such economies are 'of particular importance in early stages of internationalization when firms often are small and face severe resource constraints. Countries close to home country in geographical, economic, and/or cultural terms may be the preferred choices for first investments because the knowledge needed does not differ substantially from the knowledge *already* acquired' (1995, pp. 46–7; emphasis added). Clearly, some L-factors negate at least some impositions arising from restrictive O-factors. Thus, for example, small firms would be expected to undertake joint ventures in activities close to the their core business and to do so in nearby markets (Agarwal and Ramaswami, 1992) – both of which enable these firms to optimize their finite resources (Davidson, 1980). Clearly, it is possible that greater shareholder value will be created for these firms due to the low marginal costs of such resource deployments.

Some L-factors can offset other O-factors as well. For example, large and/or growing markets may permit firms without any clear dominant market position to avail themselves, at least in the short run, of scale economies embedded in host-country market potential (Kravis and Lipsey,

1982). Likewise, host countries can offer fiscal incentives to increase their attractiveness to (say) technologically sophisticated, but small and internationally inexperienced, firms. Indeed, evidence suggests these incentives may still be important to small firms (Meyer and Qu, 1995), allowing them to circumvent impositions arising from the possession of certain limiting O-factors.

The Role of Organizational Factors vis-à-vis Firm Performance

Conversely, some O-factors may be able to minimize the downside effects of punitive L-factors such as high levels of political risk and substantial cultural dissimilarity. Researchers typically associate such L-factors with developing countries and emerging markets. The riskiness of operating in such locations requires a different set of O-factors which enable firms to explore the efficiency frontiers of their own firm-specific advantages (Merchant, 2000b). These firms would augment their shareholder value by availing themselves of options on economic rents which might not accrue to firms that do not possess such O-factors.

To illustrate, possibly lucrative options could arise from advantages such as possession of slack resources which usually manifest in firm size. To the extent that large firms possess more resources than do small firms, the abundant resources held by large firms indicates their propensity for greater risk-taking (Reuer and Miller, 1997) and higher risk-tolerance (Benito and Gripsrud, 1995, p. 49). In general, such a propensity could be interpreted as large firms' greater capacity to absorb 'spatial transaction costs' (Dunning, 1998). There is some support for this view. For example, Merchant (2000a) hinted at a positive association between the size of American firms and the diversity of their IJV host-country portfolios. Firms can offset the risks associated with locational diversity by entering into partnerships with locally knowledgeable firms (Makino and Delios, 1996), but incur the risk of opportunistic exploitation by host-country partners. In principle, although all firms invoke this hazard, large firms may be 'less concerned' (Agarwal and Ramaswami, 1992, p. 4) with such a possibility. Stated differently, given their cost-absorbing capacity, large firms can better withstand the effects of limiting L-factors.

Regardless of their size, firms may compensate for L-factors in other, but conceptually distinct, ways. For example, firms can rely on O-factors such as past experience (Davidson, 1980) to reduce the impositions of locating their IJVs in, say, more culturally distant countries. As Park and Ungson concluded, prior relationships offer firms 'a powerful *counterbalance* to cross-cultural differences' (1997, p. 301; emphasis added) since experience-based learning is able to negate conflict and misunderstanding caused by cultural distance between cross-border partners. Likewise, greater experience would permit firms to undertake IJVs in more economically and/or geographically distant markets. To illustrate, Davidson (1980) found that more experienced firms exhibited less affinity for near and similar markets: these firms gave higher FDI priority to markets that were initially perceived as being less attractive because of high uncertainty. However, the uncertainty-reducing efficacy of greater experience depends upon the institutional context (that is, developed or developing country) in which the experience was derived (Barkema et al., 1997).

Although the preceding discussion focused primarily on complementarities across O-factors and L-factors, such complementarities also exist within each set of factors. For example, Barkema et al. (1997, p. 437) suggested that higher levels of partner-venture business relatedness can offset firms' low experience and still have positive implications for joint venture success. Likewise, firms' strong competitive position accommodate small firm size as well as limited IJV experience (Merchant, 2000a), and largeness of firms may allow for low levels of partner-venture business relatedness (Meyer and Qu, 1995). A high level of locationally embedded risks is offset by large markets that may also compensate for slow-growing markets (Culem, 1988), to the extent that market size and potential denote interchangeable paths to achieving economies of scale (Davidson, 1980). For developing countries, economic policy variables can make up for weak property rights regimes (Seyoum, 1996), and economic infrastructures and expanding domestic markets counteract the need for host-country 'location tournaments' involving fiscal and other short-term incentives (Wheeler and Mody, 1992, p. 72). Clearly, the above exposition could be extended to other O-factors and L-factors. However, an exhaustive treatment of the suggested complementarities would be difficult given the multidimensionality of firms' internal (that is, firm-specific) and external (that is, location-specific) contexts.

RESEARCH PROPOSITIONS

The preceding discussion underscores systematic differences in configurations of O-factors and L-factors vis-à-vis their impact on firm performance, including shareholder value creation in American firms who enter into IJVs. This expectation agrees with Dunning's (1980) OLI paradigm as well as numerous empirical studies of IJV performance (for example, see Dussauge and Garrette, 1995; Merchant, 2000a; Sim and Ali, 1998). In formal terms, the distinctive nature of various environments and their implications for the role of O-factors can be summarized in terms of three interrelated propositions:

Proposition 1: The configuration of O-factors and L-factors for IJVs located in emerging markets of BRIC (Brazil, Russia, India and China) will differ significantly from configurations involving IJVs located in newly industrialized countries, developed countries and developing countries.

Proposition 2: Distinct configurations of O-factors and L-factors will manifest in significant differences vis-à-vis shareholder value creation for American firms whose IJVs are located in the above-mentioned groups.

Proposition 3: Both O-factors and L-factors will vary in terms of their influence on shareholder value creation for American firms whose IJVs are located in the above-mentioned groups.

METHODOLOGY

Sample

This study searched the Dow Jones News Retrieval Service for announcements of two-party equity joint ventures formed between American firms and non-American partners during the mid-1980s through the early 1990s. To be included in the sample, a venture's American parent had to be a publicly traded firm listed on the New York, American or NASDAQ stock exchange. The 'publicly traded' requirement was needed to develop a popular capital market-based measure, abnormal returns (see below). The study constructed this measure only for the sample's American parents because most non-American partners were not traded on the above-mentioned stock exchanges. Concerns about the access to and reliability of non-American stock exchange data was another reason why the study restricted its capital market-based measure to American parents. The study deleted JV formation announcements that did not meet the above sampling criteria.

The abnormal returns measure is sensitive to announcements of other firm-specific events of economic relevance (for example dividend payout). In other words, its use could distort findings – if these extraneous events are not controlled for. To circumvent their confounding effects, this study further deleted announcements containing such non-joint venture formation events during the 'announcement period'. Following convention, this study defined its announcement period as the two-day window surrounding the day when firms publicly announced their IJV formation. This protocol for controlling the confounding effects of multiple announcements during a given period follows McWilliams and Siegel's (1997) recommendations for the use of the abnormal returns measure. Moreover, the adopted protocol is fully consistent with those adopted in earlier studies employing this measure.

Entry alternatives

The use of a capital market-based measure is justified empirically as well as theoretically. There is considerable precedent supporting the use of these measures in empirical joint venture literature (Gulati, 1998, p. 309). Relying on analyst judgements is also supported on theoretical grounds. One key advantage of employing a capital markets perspective to evaluate joint venture performance is that market judgements are believed (for example Allen, 1993) and empirically validated (Chen et al., 1993) to be least biased vis-à-vis those of corporate managers and academics. Moreover, market-based measures of firm performance do not suffer from measurement problems caused by firms' multi-industry participation (Nayyar, 1992). Such measures also reflect the risk-adjusted performance of firms (Jensen, 1969).

The sampling criteria yielded a cross-sectional sample of almost 950 IJV formation announcements involving American firms and their non-American partners, after a handful of IJVs without local partners were deleted. The sample's non-American partners were domiciled in more than 50 countries worldwide. Given its objectives, this study did not restrict IJVs in terms of their host-country locations. Thus, IJVs in the sample were also located in more than 50 countries worldwide. As mentioned previously, these countries were classified into four groups: (1) emerging markets of Brazil, Russia, India and China; (2) newly industrialized countries; (3) developed countries; and (4) developing countries (including emerging markets other than Brazil, Russia, India and China). The above groups comprised 14 percent, 4 percent, 67 percent and 15 percent of the final sample respectively. The sample included manufacturing as well as non-manufacturing American firms, approximately 70 percent and 30 percent respectively.

IDENTIFICATION OF LOCATIONS

This study classified IJV locations into four groups based on the IMF's *World Economic Outlook* (1993): (1) emerging markets of Brazil, Russia, India and China (BRIC group); (2) newly industrialized countries (NIC group); (3) developed countries (DC); and (4) developing countries including non-BRIC emerging markets (DG group). To verify the accuracy of the IMF's classification, member countries in each group were cross-referenced with other data sources. As expected, there were very few discrepancies – most of them of a minor nature; these were easily resolved. Analysis of MANOVA results indicated significant differences ($p < 0.0001$) across the four groups in terms of their institutional profiles; all individual ANOVAs were also highly significant (all $p < 0.0001$).

The BRIC group consisted of the four leading emerging markets noted previously, whereas the DC group consisted of industrialized countries. The NIC group included only the four 'Asian tigers' (Hong Kong, Singapore, South Korea and Taiwan), and the DG group consisted of developing countries as well as transition and non-BRIC emerging markets. This aggregation derived from an imperative to obtain groupings with generally similar locational characteristics (Hoskisson et al., 2000). A list of countries in each group and the number of IJVs located in a specific country is available upon request.

VARIABLE OPERATIONALIZATION

Consistent with its research objectives, this study included several O-factors and L-factors in its research protocol. As noted previously, these factors were selected based on their theoretical influence on joint venture-based shareholder value creation (see Merchant, 2000b).

Task-Related O-factors

Per Koh and Venkatraman (1991) and many others, this study defined 'business scope' in terms of relatedness between the American partner and its IJV along four dimensions: product, market, technology and science-based research. The study measured each dimension on a five-point scale (1 = Low to 5 = High) and added these individual scores to generate an overall measure of business relatedness. This variable's construction relied on descriptive information about firms' business scope reported in *Value Line Investment Surveys*, *Directory of Corporate Affiliations* and company-specific 10-K reports. Relying collectively on these sources permitted this study to triangulate data, and so to minimize the varying (but not internally inconsistent) emphasis and intensity of each source's reporting practice. Moreover, this study ascertained the validity of this subjectively coded variable; the test results confirmed the variable's validity. These results are available upon request, but are not reported due to space constraints.

This study measured 'IJV functional role(s)' in terms of three non-mutually exclusive dichotomous variables: R&D, manufacturing and marketing. Each variable assumed a value of 1 if a IJV involved that particular function, otherwise the variable assumed a value of 0. Data required to code this variable were obtained from the text of the joint formation announcement which explicitly – and consistently – reported the ventures' functional roles. In rare cases where data were ambiguous or unavailable, the study coded functional role(s) as missing values. One limitation of this data source was that it did not allow the study to detect whether partners shared a specific functional activity.

Partner-Related O-factors

Following Das et al. (1998) and numerous others, this study measured firm size in terms of logarithm of American firms' market value over the two-day announcement period. A firm's market value was defined as the product of its stock price and the number of outstanding shares (in million US dollars). Data needed to construct this variable were obtained from CRSP (Center for Research on Security Prices) tapes compiled by the University of Chicago.

This study operationalized American firms' relative competitive position in terms of their 'financial strength' index reported in *Value Line* ($1 = $ Low to $9 = $ High). This measure was based on Strebel's (1983) thesis that 'financial market's assessment of [a firm's relative competitive position] is implicit in the proportion of the firm's value which it associates with *future growth*' (p. 280, emphasis added). More recently, Gulati (1998) observed that researchers had treated firms' financial attributes as 'proxies for [firms'] *strategic imperatives*' (p. 300; emphasis added). This study assessed the validity of financial strength proxy by correlating it with three additional measures not included here: (1) earnings predictability index; (2) stock price growth persistence index; and (3) index of competitive pressures on the firms. The first two indices are published in *Value Line* whereas the third index was subjectively coded on the basis of firm-specific information in each IJV case file. All three indexes were coded on a five-point scale ($1 = $ Low; $5 = $ High). The sample-wide correlations between financial strength and each of the above-mentioned indices were significant below $p < 0.0001$. The statistics ought to alleviate concerns about the financial strength proxy.

Following Weber's (1990) guidelines for 'content analysis', this study coded American and non-American partners' motives for JV formation in terms of four non-mutually exclusive dichotomous variables (see Dunning, 1998). Efficiency-seeking motives denoted issues such as a firm's need to gain scale or scope economies or attain cost reductions. Market-seeking motives denoted issues such as a firm's need to sell its products in 'new' markets. Resource-seeking motives denoted issues such as a firm's imperative to access the resources of its JV partner or resources located in a host country (for example skilled labor).

Each variable assumed a value of 1 if the joint venture involved that particular motive, otherwise the variable assumed a value of 0. Data required to code this variable were obtained from the text of IJV formation announcement which often revealed partners' stated motivations for forming a joint venture. Examples of these revelations are available upon request. Where an explicit identification was lacking for American partners, this study relied on the *Value Line* description of these partners' business context to assess more accurately the firm's probable motive(s) for joint venture formation. Such additional information was unavailable for non-American partners. When a firm's particular joint venture motivation could not be coded unambiguously, a missing value was entered for that variable. Despite precautions to increase the variables' reliable coding, it should be recognized that IJV motives may lack coding precision.

Per Harrigan (1988) and others, this study measured 'previous IJV experience' as the frequency of American parents' IJV participation over a two-year period immediately preceding the year in which firms announced their respective ventures; higher frequencies denoted greater experience, and vice versa. This period was selected on the basis of available Dow Jones data and resource constraints. The data source explicitly identified American firms which had entered into IJVs. A list of these ventures was generated for 1983 through 1993 along with the firms' names. All American firms in this study's sample were looked up in the above list. Prior IJV experience equaled the number of times an American firm's name appeared on that list during a given two-year period.

Following Lummer and McConnell (1990), this study defined 'partner type' as a dummy variable with a value equal to 1 if the non-American partner was a firm; the variable assumed a value of 0 if the non-American partner was a state-owned enterprise. Data needed to categorize the type of non-American partner were obtained from the Dow Jones text which contained information about the firms' IJV formations. Usually half a page or more, this text almost always explicitly noted if the non-American partner was a government-owned entity. When an explicit identification was lacking or ambiguous, the study checked the status of non-American partner in company directories such as the *International Directory of Corporate Affiliations*. If the partner's name was included in such directories, the study coded this variable to signify the non-American partner was a firm – and not a state-owned enterprise. If the name did not appear in such directories, it was highly likely the non-American partner was a state-owned enterprise. The variable was coded as having a missing value if investigation into the status of non-American partner drew a blank, which was rarely the case.

Joint Venture-Related O-factors

This study measured 'equity ownership' as the percentage of an IJV's total equity held by the American parent. Data needed to code this variable were obtained from the Dow Jones text which contained information about equity distribution between partners. This data was reported very frequently. The study assumed a 50:50 equity ownership between partners when the ownership percentages were not reported. This protocol agrees with reports that a 50:50 ownership position is the most dominant form of equity ownership in joint ventures (for example Blodgett, 1991 and citations therein). Needless to say, this coding protocol introduces a bias. Although the bias is present in this study, various dispersion statistics indicate it does not seem to be significant; these statistics are not reported due to space constraints, but are available upon request.

Per Saxton (1997) and others, this study defined a IJV's decision-making structure as a dichotomous variable. The variable assumed a value of 1 if both partners shared the decision-making process; otherwise the variable assumed a value equal to 0. Information needed to code this variable was reported in the text of JV formation announcement in Dow Jones. In most cases, the text explicitly noted if only one partner was responsible for decision-making; this reporting practice was observed to be consistent across the sampled years. This study discarded observations with ambiguous information pertaining to the above variable.

Institutional L-factors

This study operationalized 'cultural distance' between JV parents in terms of Kogut and Singh's (1988) index which is extensively used to proxy cultural distance between two countries. This index represents the cumulated deviation between the variance-adjusted culture score(s) of partner countries. The culture scores were obtained from Hofstede (1980) which first published these numerical scores.

This study operationalized 'political risk' in JV host countries along three dimensions: FDI risk, transfer risk and export risk. The required data were obtained from Political Risk Services, a reputed international agency providing political risk assessments. For each dimension, the agency assigned categorical ratings which the study recoded as numerical scores (1 = Low to 10 = High). The individual scores were added to generate an overall measure of political risk.

The above-mentioned data source also reported information about an IJV host country's estimated future GDP growth rate (in percentage terms). This study defined 'industry growth' in terms of percentage change in industry shipments in American parents' principal four-digit SIC industry over the year immediately prior to that in which firms announced their IJVs. Data pertaining to industry shipments were obtained from the *Annual Survey of Manufactures*.

Methods

Event study technique

This study generated abnormal returns from CRSP tapes using the event study method (Fama et al., 1969). An abnormal return refers to the difference between the firm's historical return and the stock market return associated with a given event involving that firm (for example the event of JV formation). Following convention, this study computed the abnormal return on day t for each firm i as $AR_{it} = R_{it} - (a_i + b_i*R_{mt})$, where R_{it} denotes the actual rate of return for firm i on day t; a_i and b_i respectively denote the estimated intercept and slope parameters for firm i; and R_{mt} denotes the rate of return on value-weighted market portfolio on day t.[1] For each firm i, the study cumulated abnormal returns over the two-day announcement period consisting of the day when the firm's participation in JV was first publicly announced and the following day. This aggregation is routine to event studies, and is undertaken to account for stock markets' reaction to announcements that may have been made after trading hours. Consequently, this study continues the tradition of using cumulated abnormal returns.

Other techniques

To test its first two propositions – identifying differences in O-factors and L-factors and differences in shareholder value creation across the four groups – this study conducted ANOVA analysis. The analysis took the general form, $Y_i = f_n (Group)$, where Y_i denoted a specific variable(s) of interest and *Group* denoted the four location clusters identified previously. The ANOVA analyses were conducted only on continuous variables and invoked the 'least squares means' option for making pairwise comparisons across the groups. The study did not require Bonferroni adjustments because the three pairwise comparisons of interest were pre-planned in accordance with the research propositions. The study performed Chi-square analysis to identify differences in the distribution of categorical variables. It performed three separate Chi-square analyses – one for each paired comparison of interest – to examine differences in the distribution between O-factors and L-factors in the BRIC group and those in the remaining three groups.

To test its third proposition – uncovering influences on shareholder value creation for American firms in each location cluster – this study conducted regression analysis, details of which are available upon request. This method for analyzing data has been adopted previously by those who conducted a similar inquiry (for example Sim and Ali, 1998). One unavoidable drawback of using regression pertained to the decrease in sample size for each group. This decrease arises because regression analysis discards the entire observation even if only one variable (associated with that observation) has a missing value.

EMPIRICAL RESULTS

The results in Table 13.1 support the study's first proposition that configurations of O-factors will vary significantly across American firms' IJVs located in the BRIC, NIC, developed and developing countries. An examination of these results indicates significant differences for a majority of variables in each O-factor category. Indeed, all statistically

Table 13.1   ANOVA results and pairwise comparisons

	p-value	BRIC-NIC	BRIC-DC	BRIC-LDC
Task-related O-factors				
Business relatedness	n.s.	n.s.	n.s.	n.s.
IJV function: RND	0.0089	n.s.	0.0123	n.s.
IJV function: MFG	0.0001	0.0384	0.0001	0.0001
IJV function: MKTG	0.0027	n.s.	0.0021	n.s.
Partner-related O-factors (American partner)				
Firm size	0.0073	n.s.	n.s.	0.0981
Rel. competitive position	0.0001	n.s.	0.0018	n.s.
Previous IJV experience	n.s.	n.s.	n.s.	n.s.
IJV motive: Efficiency	0.0476	n.s.	0.0612	n.s.
IJV motive: Markets	0.1011	n.s.	0.0235	n.s.
IJV motive: Resources	n.s.	n.s.	0.0372	n.s.
Partner-related O-factors (Non-American Partner)				
Type of partner	0.0001	0.0005	0.0001	0.0439
IJV motive: Efficiency	0.0043	0.0097	n.s.	0.0025
IJV motive: Markets	0.0001	n.s.	0.0001	n.s.
IJV motive: Resources	0.0001	n.s.	0.0001	0.0042
Joint venture-related O-factors				
Equity ownership	0.0038	0.0051	0.0061	n.s.
Decision-making structure	n.s.	n.s.	n.s.	n.s.
Institutional L-factors				
Cultural distance	0.0001	0.0001	0.0001	0.0001
Political risk	0.0001	0.0001	0.0001	0.0001
Future GDP growth rate	0.0001	0.0001	0.0001	0.0001
Industry growth rate	n.s.	n.s.	n.s.	n.s.

Table 13.2   ANOVA results and pairwise comparisons

	p-value	BRIC-NIC	BRIC-DC	BRIC-LDC
Performance variable Abnormal returns	n.s.	n.s.	n.s.	n.s.

significant ANOVAs (except one) are significant below the 5 percent level; the remaining ANOVA approaches significance at the 10 percent level. Turning to pairwise comparisons of average differences for these O-factors, there is robust support for the view that the configuration of O-factors in BRIC economies most systematically differs from that in the developed economies. Although the configuration of O-factors in BRIC economies also differs from those in NIC economies and developing economies, the overall nature of these (latter) differences is less pronounced than for the BRIC–developed economies comparisons. The results in Table 13.1 moreover support (intuitive) expectations that L-factors also vary across the four location-based groups. Indeed, three of the four ANOVAs are highly significant (all $p < 0.0001$). All pairwise comparisons for these three L-factors are also highly significant (all $p < 0.0001$).

Interestingly, the distinct configurations reported above do not manifest themselves differentially in Table 13.2. The results in Table 13.2 do not indicate differential shareholder value creation in American firms in each of the four groups. Thus, the results do not support this study's second proposition.

In contrast, the study's findings support its third proposition that both O-factors and L-factors will vary in terms of their influence on shareholder value creation in American firms. The results presented in Table 13.3 validate this point. At least three points are worth a mention. Firstly, despite a decrease in sample size (for reasons noted previously), all four regression models are statistically significant below the 5 percent level. Secondly, the list of significant O-factors and L-factors varies across the four groups. Thirdly, the directionality of influence of both O-factors and L-factors often varies across these groups. Thus, this study's findings support propositions 1 and 3, but not proposition 2. A brief discussion of this non-finding would therefore be necessary.

DISCUSSION AND CONCLUSIONS

According to at least one recent study involving manufacturing firms' IJVs located in emerging markets, firms can traverse multiple paths to approach

Entry alternatives

Table 13.3   Regression results

	BRIC	NIC	DC	LDC
O-factors				
Business relatedness	–	−0.55/0.0719	0.17/0.0075	0.29/0.0503
IJV function: MFG	–	0.60/0.0356	–	–
Firm size	–	–	–	0.24/0.0992
IJV motive: Efficiency (US)	0.26/0.0345	1.48/0.0039	–	–
IJV motive: Markets (US)	–	–	−0.13/0.0615	0.39/0.0100
Type of partner	–	−0.76/0.0293	0.11/0.0490	–
L-factors				
Cultural distance	−0.24/0.0668	−1.37/0.0370	0.15/0.0161	–
Political risk	0.44/0.0031	2.71/0.0042	–	–
Future GDP growth rate	0.32/0.0269	−0.69/0.0350	–	0.27/0.0949
Industry growth rate	–	–	–	−0.27/0.0948
Sample size	66	23	303	45
Model p-value	0.0107	0.0374	0.0130	0.0342
R-square	19.87%	92.21%	10.08%	25.76%
Adjusted R-square	13.76%	71.45%	5.05%	16.24%

Notes:
1. Only significant variables are reported for each regression model.
2. Number before the slash is standardized parameter estimate.
3. Number after the slash is the estimate's p-value.

similar levels of economic performance (Merchant, 2000c). Merchant's study found that American joint venture parents achieved (statistically) identical levels of shareholder value creation by being selective about the locational context in which they operated their ventures. Based on a unique research protocol, Merchant concluded that 'strong' firms can alleviate possible impositions of 'weak' L-factors by offsetting these factors against their own O-advantages. Moreover, 'weak' firms can offset their O-disadvantages by positioning themselves in contexts characterized by 'strong' L-factors. In other words, this study's finding regarding homogeneous shareholder value creation across the four groups may be due to unique interactions between O-factors and L-factors in each group (for example see Miller and Friesen, 1984). Thus, instead of viewing lack of support for proposition 2 in a negative light, the finding ought to be construed favorably. Implicitly, treating O-factors *per se* as primary drivers of firm performance may, at best, be an incomplete depiction of the reality vis-à-vis shareholder value creation in IJVs. Academics (and practitioners) therefore must explicitly recognize the context in which they study the phenomenon of IJV performance.

The above caveat derives further support from the results presented in Table 13.3. The table reveals that some O-factors have a differential impact across location-based groups. In other words, it would be a big mistake for researchers to assume the universality of an O-factor's or an L-factor's impact on shareholder value creation in firms. The performance effect of O-factor(s) must not be viewed independently of their L-factor(s) counterpart, and vice versa. Rather, researchers need to consider explicitly the manner in which O-factors co-mingle with L-factors.

In conclusion, this chapter has contributed to the literature on IJVs as well as emerging markets. With respect to the former literature, this study provided a comparative analysis of influences on shareholder value creation in American firms whose IJVs are located in four distinct market groups, most notably the emerging markets group of Brazil, Russia, India and China. Further, it explicitly rejected the popular view that O-factors have a homogeneous effect across distinct locational contexts. The study attempted to contribute to the emerging markets literature by focusing on four leading emerging markets and offering a snapshot of O-factors and L-factors driving American firms' shareholder value in these markets. Unlike many singular studies on emerging markets (for example Merchant, 2000b), this work benchmarked the BRIC economies against non-BRIC economies. In a small way, this study has broadened the parochial focus of emerging-markets literature.

Future work can continue this inquiry along several dimensions. Principal among these dimensions is a focus on individual emerging-market economies (for example drivers of shareholder value creation in India and China) given the strong possibility that individual emerging markets are different from one another (see Merchant, 2005).[2] Another dimension would be to compare the drivers of positive performance (however defined) and those of negative performance in a single emerging-market economy. Yet another extension would be to undertake a more detailed analysis of positive and negative drivers of shareholder value creation across a range of individual emerging markets. Improving upon this study's limitations would present additional research opportunities in this emerging area of study.

NOTES

1. It is useful to state that equation $(a_i + b_i{}^{*}R_{mt})$ represents a firm's historical returns. These historical returns are commonly described by the market model: $R_{it} = A_i + B_i{}^{*}R_{mt} + E_i$

where R_{it} is the actual rate of return for firm i on day t, R_{mt} is rate of return on the value-weighted market portfolio on day t, A_i and B_i are intercept and slope parameters (respectively) for firm i, and E_i is the firm-specific disturbance term. To obtain estimates of A_i and B_i, a_i and b_i, this study appraised the above market model over a 200-day period beginning 51 days before the day a JV's formation was first publicly announced.

2. I am thankful to Bob Grosse for suggesting this extension.

REFERENCES

Agarwal, S. and S. Ramaswami (1992), 'Choice of Foreign Market Entry Mode: Impact of Ownership, Location, and Internalization Factors', *Journal of International Business Studies*, **23** (1), 1–27.

Allen, F. (1993), 'Strategic Management and Financial Markets', *Strategic Management Journal*, **14**(Special Issue), 11–22.

Barkema, H., O. Shenkar, F. Vermeulen and J. Bell (1997), 'Working Abroad, Working with Others: How Firms Learn to Operate International Joint Ventures', *Academy of Management Journal*, **40**(2), 426–42.

Benito, G. and G. Gripsrud (1995), 'The Internationalization Approach to the Location of Foreign Direct Investments: An Empirical Analysis', in M. Green and R. McNaughton (eds), *The Location of Foreign Direct Investment: Geographic and Business Approaches*, Aldershot: Avebury, pp. 43–58.

Blodgett, L. (1991), 'Partner Contributions as Predictors of Equity Share in International Joint Ventures', *Journal of International Business Studies*, **22**(1), 63–78.

Chen, M-J., J-L. Farh and I.C. MacMillan (1993), 'An Exploration of the Expertness of Outside Informants', *Academy of Management Journal*, **36**(6), 1614–32.

Culem, C.G. (1988), 'The Locational Determinants of Direct Investments Among Industrialized Countries', *European Economic Review*, **32**, 885–904.

Das, S., P.K. Sen and S. Sengupta (1998), 'Impact of Strategic Alliances on Firm Valuation', *Academy of Management Journal*, **41**(1), 27–41.

Davidson, W.H. (1980), 'The Location of Foreign Direct Investment Activity: Country Characteristics and Experience Effects', *Journal of International Business Studies*, Fall, 9–22.

Dunning, J.H. (1980), 'Toward an Eclectic Theory of International Production: Some Empirical Tests', *Journal of International Business Studies*, Summer, 9–30.

Dunning, J.H. (1998), 'Location and the Multinational Enterprise: A Neglected Factor?', *Journal of International Business Studies*, **29**(1), 45–66.

Dunning, J.H. and A. Rugman (1985), 'The Influence of Hymer's Dissertation on the Theory of Foreign Direct Investment', *American Economic Review*, **75**(2), 228–32.

Dussauge, P. and B. Garrette (1995), 'Determinants of Success in International Strategic Alliances: Evidence from the Global Aerospace Industry', *Journal of International Business Studies*, **26**(3), 505–30.

Fama, E.F., L. Fisher, M.C. Jensen and R. Roll (1969), 'The Adjustment of Stock Prices to New Information', *International Economic Review*, **10**, 1–21.

Garten, J.E. (1996), 'The Big Emerging Markets', *Columbia Journal of World Business*, Summer, 7–31.

Gulati, R. (1998), 'Alliances and Networks', *Strategic Management Journal*, **19** (Special Issue), 293–317.

Harrigan, K.R. (1988), 'Strategic Alliances and Partner Asymmetries', in F.J. Contractor and P. Lorange (eds), *Cooperative Strategies in International Business*, Lexington, KY: Lexington Books, pp. 205–26.

Hofstede, G. (1980), *Culture's Consequences: International Differences in Work-Related Values*. Newbury Park, CA: Sage.

Hoskisson, R.E., L. Eden, C.M. Lau and M. Wright (2000), 'Strategy in Emerging Economies', *Academy of Management Journal*, **43**(3), 249–67.

International Monetary Fund (IMF) (1993), *World Economic Outlook*, Washington, DC.

Jensen, M.C. (1969), 'Risk, the Pricing of Capital Assets, and the Evaluation of Investment Portfolios', *Journal of Business*, **29**, 167–247.

Kogut, B. and H. Singh (1988), 'The Effect of National Culture on the Choice of Entry Mode', *Journal of International Business Studies*, **19**(3), 411–32.

Koh, J. and N. Venkatraman (1991), 'Joint Venture Formations and Stock Market Reactions: An Assessment in the Information Technology Sector', *Academy of Management Journal*, **34**, 869–92.

Kravis, I.B. and R.E. Lipsey (1982), 'The Location of Overseas Production and Production for Export by US Multinational Firms', *Journal of International Economics*, **12**, 201–23.

Lummer, S.L. and J.J. McConnell (1990), 'Stock Valuation Effects of International Joint Ventures', in S.G. Rhee and R.P. Chang (eds), *Pacific-Basin Capital Markets Research*. North-Holland: Elsevier Science.

Makino, S. and A. Delios (1996), 'Local Knowledge Transfer and Performance: Implications for Alliance Formation in Asia', *Journal of International Business Studies*, **27**(5), 905–28.

McWilliams, A. and D. Siegel (1997), 'Event Studies in Management Research: Theoretical and Empirical Issues', *Academy of Management Journal*, **40**(3), 626–57.

Merchant, H. (2000a), 'Configurations of International Joint Ventures', *Management International Review*, **40**(2), 107–40.

Merchant, H. (2000b), 'Event Studies of Joint Venture Formation Announcements: A Synthesis and Some Possible Extensions', in S.B. Dahiya (ed.), *The Current State of Business Disciplines*, Rohtak, India: Spellbound Publications, pp. 1837–61.

Merchant, H. (2000c), 'How Do Firm-Specific and Location-Specific Factors Complement One Another?: The Case of Joint Venture Configurations in Big Emerging Markets', paper presented at the Academy of Management meeting, Toronto, Canada.

Merchant, H. (2003), 'Joint Venture Characteristics and Shareholder Value: The Pervasive Role of Partner Nationality', *Management International Review*, **43**(1), 21–40.

Merchant, H. (2004), 'Revisiting Shareholder Value Creation via International Joint Ventures: Exploring Interactions among Firm- and Context-Specific Variables', *Canadian Journal of Administrative Sciences*, **21**(2), 129–45.

Merchant, H. (2005), 'Joint Venture Characteristics: 20 Years Later', working paper, Simon Fraser University, Vancouver, Canada.

Meyer, S. and T. Qu (1995), 'Place-Specific Determinants of FDI: The Geographical Perspective', in Milford B. Green and Rod B. McNaughton (eds), *The Location of Foreign Direct Investment: Geographic and Business Approaches*, Aldershot: Avebury.

Miller, D. and P. Friesen (1984), *Organizations: A Quantum View*, Englewood Cliffs, NJ: Prentice-Hall.

Nayyar, P.R. (1992), 'Performance Effects of Three Foci in Service Firms', *Academy of Management Journal*, **35**(5), 985–1009.

Park, S.H. and G.R. Ungson (1997), 'The Effect of National Culture, Organizational Complementarity, and Economic Motivation on Joint Venture Dissolution', *Academy of Management Journal*, **40**(2), 279–307.

Reuer, J.J. and K.D. Miller (1997), 'Agency Costs and the Performance Implications of International Joint Venture Internalization', *Strategic Management Journal*, **18**(6), 425–38.

Saxton, T. (1997), 'The Effects of Partner and Relationship Characteristics on Alliance Outcomes', *Academy of Management Journal*, **40**(2), 443–61.

Seyoum, B. (1996), 'The Impact of Intellectual Property Rights on Foreign Direct Investment', *Columbia Journal of World Business*, Spring, 51–9.

Sim, A. and Y. Ali (1998), 'Performance of International Joint Ventures from Developing and Developed Countries: An Empirical Study in a Developing Country Context', *Journal of World Business*, **33**(4), 357–76.

Strebel, P. (1983), 'The Stock Market and Competitive Analysis', *Strategic Management Journal*, **4**(3), 279–91.

Weber, R.P. (1990), *Basic Content Analysis*, Newburry Park, CA: Sage.

Wheeler, D. and A. Mody (1992), 'International Investment Location Decisions', *Journal of International Economics*, **33**, 57–76.

World Investment Report (1997), 'Transnational Corporations, Market Structure, and Competition Policy', New York: United Nations.

14. Inward and outward FDI and the BRICs

Karl P. Sauvant[1]

INTRODUCTION

Foreign direct investment (FDI) has become more important than trade for delivering goods and services to foreign markets: in 2003, the sales of foreign affiliates ($18 trillion) were twice as large as exports ($9 trillion). In addition to integrating markets, FDI also integrates production activities internationally through the corporate production systems established by transnational corporations (TNCs). Such 'deep integration' constitutes, in many ways, the productive core of the globalizing world economy.

All countries are, to a higher or lower degree, involved in this integration process. This chapter focuses on Brazil, the Russian Federation, India and China (the BRICs), four economies that are particularly important[2] and promising and whose rise will transform the world economy (Wilson et al., 2004). They have participated in this integration so far primarily through inward FDI, that is, foreign firms undertaking direct investment in their territories. The next section documents briefly the extent to which this has occurred. In brief, while all four countries have attracted substantial amounts of FDI, this performance has been highly uneven, whatever measure is used. In particular, while China has made great strides to become the workshop of the world, India is at the commencement of becoming its office.

More interesting is the fact that all four economies are becoming sources of outward FDI; that is, firms from BRICs undertake direct investment abroad, in developed countries as well as in other emerging markets (that is, developing economies and economies in transition).[3] Again, the performance of these 'emerging outward-investor countries' is uneven – but what matters more perhaps is that each of these countries may be taking off in this respect. This is indicated, for example, by a number of recent high-profile acquisitions by TNCs from BRICs in a number of developed countries – some of which (like the attempted acquisition of Unocal by

CNOOC) encountered fierce resistance. Outward FDI (OFDI) from the BRICs, in turn, is part of the rise of such investment from emerging markets and the desire of their firms to increase their competitiveness by acquiring portfolios of locational assets. This newer and less well-known aspect of deep integration is the focus of this chapter. The questions it seeks to answer are: in the framework of the rise of OFDI from emerging markets in general, how far have the BRICs come with their OFDI? Who are the main actors? What is driving them? What role has policy played? And what are the prospects for further growth?

INWARD FDI

Global FDI inflows have risen spectacularly during the past two decades, from $60 billion in 1984 to an estimated $612 billion in 2004 (Figure 14.1),[4] accumulating to a stock of some $8 trillion in 2003. Developing economies participated in this trend, with an increase from $18 billion to some $256 billion between 1984 and 2004; for the economies in transition, inflows grew from $1.7 billion to $22 billion between 1992 and 2004. The BRICs, too, saw their FDI inflows grow, from $3 billion in 1984 to $98 billion in 2004 (Figure 14.2), representing, respectively, 15 percent and 35 percent of all inflows to emerging markets; this compares to their share of 25 percent and 38 percent, respectively, in the GDP of all emerging markets. This aggregate figure disguises, however, vastly different performances (Table 14.1).

In the 1980s, Brazil was one of the most attractive host countries, ranking among the top five developing economies in terms of FDI inflows and stock (Tables 14.2, 14.3). The country did not, however, participate fully in the FDI boom of the 1990s – other locations became more attractive. However, FDI inflows peaked in the early 2000s (driven by privatizations), and the country ranked again among the top five developing host economies. The importance of FDI in the economy as measured by FDI inflows as a percentage of gross domestic capital formation and FDI inflows per capita is higher than the average for all developing economies as well as the other three BRIC countries (Table 14.1).

Brazil's position on UNCTAD's Inward FDI Performance Index (which measures the success of a country in attracting FDI in relation to its GDP) in 2000–2002, where it ranked 37th, as compared with that on UNCTAD's Inward FDI Potential Index (which captures the potential of a country to attract FDI, based on a combination of variables), where it ranked 68th, suggests that it actually performs above its potential (Table 14.4). This performance is however due largely to a privatization programme open to

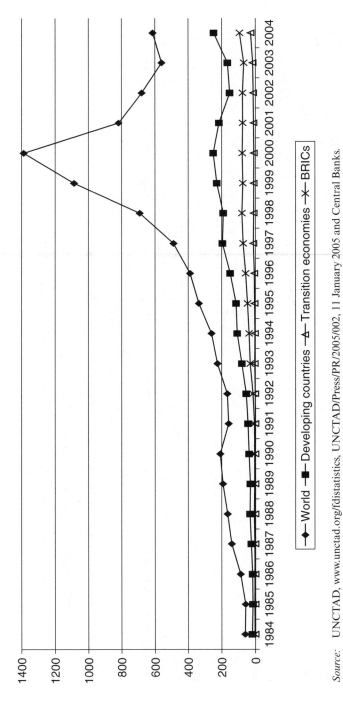

Source: UNCTAD, www.unctad.org/fdistatistics, UNCTAD/Press/PR/2005/002, 11 January 2005 and Central Banks.

Figure 14.1 FDI inflows, by group of countries, 1984–2004 (billions of dollars)

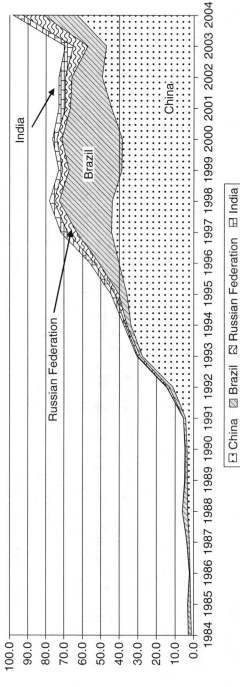

Note: ^a Data prior to 1992 are not available for the Russian Federation, but they were negligible.

Source: *UNCTAD, www.unctad.org/fdistatistics, and Central Banks.*

Figure 14.2   FDI flows into the BRICs, by country, 1984–2004^a *(billions of dollars)*

316

Table 14.1 Importance of FDI in the BRICs, 1984–2004

Item	Brazil			Russian federation			India			China		
	1984	1994	2004	1984[a]	1994	2004	1984	1994	2004	1984	1994	2004
FDI inflows ($mil)	1 415[b]	2 615[c]	14 966[d]	–	1 322[c]	7 697[d]	44[b]	1 219[c]	4 351[d]	1 184[b]	32 384[c]	53 126[d]
FDI inward stock ($mil)	22 844	56 549	132 799[e]	–	3 230	86 772[e]	641	3 490	30 827[e]	3 663	96 408	478 202[e]
FDI inflows as a percentage of GFCF	3.9[b]	2.3[c]	18.1[f]	–	1.9[c]	7.1[f]	0.1[b]	1.7[c]	3.4[f]	1.3[b]	14.6[c]	10.5[f]
FDI inflows per capita	10.7[b]	16.6[c]	93.9[d]	–	8.9[c]	32.9[d]	0.1[b]	1.3[c]	3.6[d]	1.1[b]	26.8[c]	36.2[d]
FDI inflows per $1000 GDP	6.7[b]	4.6[c]	33.7[d]	–	3.8[c]	13.0[d]	0.2[b]	3.9[c]	7.2[d]	4.5[b]	58.0[c]	36.5[d]
Foreign affiliates exports	–	–	–	–	–	–	361[g]	979	1 421[h]	–	34 709	169 990
Foreign affiliates exports as a percentage of total exports of goods and services	–	–	–	–	–	–	3.0[g]	3.0	2.7[h]	–	29.1	46.5[i]

Notes:
[a] Data prior to 1992 are not available for the Russian Federation, but they were negligible.
[b] Averaged over 1983–85 to even out lumpiness.
[c] Averaged over 1993–95 to even out lumpiness.
[d] Averaged over 2002–2004 to even out lumpiness.
[e] 2003.
[f] Averaged over 2001–2003 to even out lumpiness.
[g] 1985.
[h] 1999.

Source: UNCTAD, www.unctad.org/fdistatistics, UNCTAD estimates and Central Banks.

Table 14.2   The top 15 emerging markets in terms of FDI inflows, average 1983–85, 1993–95 and 2002–2004[a]
(billions of dollars)

	1983–85			1993–95			2002–2004	
Rank	Economy	Value	Rank	Economy	Value	Rank	Economy	Value
1	Saudi Arabia	3.4	1	**China**	**32.4**	1	**China**	**53.1**
2	Mexico	1.9	2	Mexico	9.7	2	Hong Kong, China	18.8
3	**Brazil**	**1.4**	3	Singapore	8.3	3	**Brazil**	**15.0**
4	**China**	**1.2**	4	Hong Kong, China	7.0	4	Mexico	14.6
5	Singapore	1.2	5	Malaysia	5.4	5	Singapore	12.7
6	Malaysia	0.9	6	Argentina	4.0	6	**Russian Federation**	**7.7**
7	Egypt	0.8	7	Indonesia	2.8	7	Bermuda	6.6
8	Bermuda	0.8	8	**Brazil**	**2.6**	8	Korea, Republic of	5.2
9	Colombia	0.7	9	Peru	2.2	9	**India**	**4.4**
10	Hong Kong, China	0.7	10	Chile	2.2	10	Cayman Islands	3.9
11	Argentina	0.5	11	Thailand	1.7	11	Chile	3.7
12	Cayman Islands	0.4	12	Viet Nam	1.6	12	Malaysia	3.5
13	Nigeria	0.3	13	Bermuda	1.5	13	Kazakhstan	2.7
14	Thailand	0.3	14	Philippines	1.5	14	Azerbaijan	2.7
15	Indonesia	0.3	15	Nigeria	1.5	15	Colombia	2.3
36	**India**	**0.04**	16	**Russian Federation**	**1.3**			
—	**Russian Federation**	—	18	**India**	**1.2**			

Note: [a] Flows have been averaged over three years to even out lumpiness.

Source: UNCTAD, www.unctad.org/fdistatistics, and UNCTAD estimates.

Table 14.3 The top 15 emerging markets in terms of FDI inward stock, 1984, 1994 and 2003 (billions of dollars)

Year	Brazil		Russian Federation		India		China	
	Performance index	Potential index	Performance index	Potential index	Performance index	Potential index	Performance index	Potential index
1988–90	77	47	–	–	98	74	46	45
1989–91	90	48	–	–	103	72	50	43
1990–92	95	69	108	35	118	99	43	55
1991–93	95	70	107	40	113	94	19	61
1992–94	104	72	110	40	112	97	9	60
1993–95	103	74	109	37	108	93	11	57
1994–96	91	71	106	27	104	92	15	47
1995–97	81	75	101	39	103	98	20	41
1996–98	65	76	107	39	111	96	31	43
1997–99	52	77	104	39	116	94	42	41
1998–2000	45	70	104	36	118	97	51	43
1999–2001	37	73	107	36	121	91	56	44
2000–2002	37	68	111	33	121	89	50	39
2001–2003	46	–	119	–	114	–	37	–

Source: UNCTAD, www.unctad.org/fdistatistics, and UNCTAD estimates.

Table 14.4   BRICs: Ranking by FDI performance and potential indices, 1988–2003ᵃ (ranking)

	1984			1994			2003	
Rank	Economy	Value	Rank	Economy	Value	Rank	Economy	Value
1	Hong Kong, China	183.5	1	Hong Kong, China	221.3	1	China	**478.2**
2	**Brazil**	**22.8**	2	**China**	**96.4**	2	Hong Kong, China	375.0
3	Indonesia	21.6	3	**Brazil**	**56.5**	3	Mexico	165.9
4	Saudi Arabia	21.3	4	Singapore	54.9	4	Singapore	147.3
5	Mexico	16.8	5	Indonesia	46.3	5	**Brazil**	**132.8**
6	Singapore	11.5	6	Mexico	33.2	6	**Russian federation**	**86.8**
7	South Africa	11.4	7	Saudi Arabia	24.3	7	Bermuda	80.9
8	Turkey	9.2	8	Bermuda	23.4	8	Malaysia	59.0
9	Bermuda	7.0	9	Malaysia	22.9	9	Indonesia	57.2
10	Malaysia	6.5	10	Argentina	22.4	10	Korea, Republic of	47.5
11	Argentina	6.4	11	Thailand	15.7	11	Chile	46.8
12	Egypt	4.5	12	Taiwan Province of China	14.2	12	Thailand	36.9
13	Nigeria	3.9	13	Egypt	14.1	13	Cayman Islands	36.4
14	**China**	**3.7**	14	Turkey	14.1	14	Argentina	35.1
15	Tunisia	3.6	15	Chile	13.9	15	Venezuela	34.2
26	**India**	**0.6**	26	**India**	**3.5**	17	**India**	**30.8**
28	**Russian federation**	–	28	**Russian federation**	3.2			

Notes:
ᵃ The UNCTAD Inward FDI Performance Index is a measure of the extent to which a country receives inward FDI in relation to its economic size. It is calculated as the ratio of a country's share in global FDI inflows to its share in global GDP. The Index ranks countries by the amount of FDI they receive relative to their economic size. The Inward FDI Potential Index is a measure based on 12 economic and policy variables, factors that are likely to affect FDI and thus measure a country's potential to attract FDI. Rankings are based on data covering 140 economies.
ᵇ Three-year average.

Source: UNCTAD, *World Investment Report*, various years, www.unctad.org/WIR.

*Table 14.5   BRICs: FDI policy changes related to FDI, 1992–2003
(number)*

Country	More favourable to FDI	Less favourable to FDI	Total
Brazil	13	3	16
Russian Federation	37	5	42
India	45	–	45
China	131	7	138

Source: UNCTAD.

Table 14.6   BITs and DTTs, end-2003 (cumulative number)

Country	BITs	DTTs[a]
Brazil	14	26
Russian Federation	52	52
India	55	62
China	107	64
World	2 320	2 476

Note: [a] DTTs covering income and capital only.

Source: UNCTAD database on BITs and DTTs, www.unctad.org/iia.

FDI. More recently, the government is making an effort to attract FDI into a wide range of industries. Indicative is an event organized by UNCTAD and the government of Brazil in January 2004, during which President Luiz Inacio Lula da Silva and five of his ministers met with a large number of investors in Geneva to send one message: 'Brazil is open for business'.[5] The government followed up with an Investment Policy Review with UNCTAD, to help formulate a strategy to attract more FDI to the country. Whether this will lead to concrete changes in policy remains to be seen; so far, Brazil has been the BRIC with the lowest number of policy changes made between 1992 and 2003 (Table 14.5). Although Brazil has signed 14 bilateral investment treaties (BITs) (Table 14.6), these have not been ratified because of opposition in Congress; no new BIT has been negotiated since 2000 (Figure 14.3). Brazil has, however, a programme to conclude double taxation treaties (DTTs – Figure 14.4 and Table 14.6).

There was little FDI in the Russian Federation in the 1980s, apart from a few joint ventures. With the transition to a market economy, policy changes favourable to FDI were made and investment began to flow in,

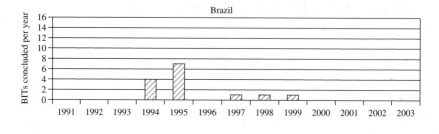

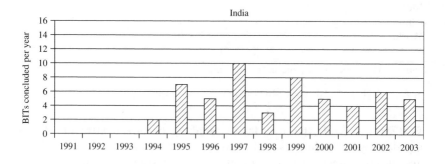

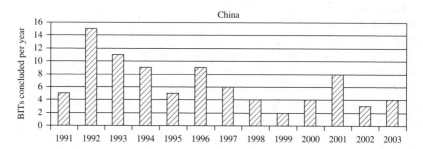

Source: UNCTAD, www.unctad.org/iia.

Figure 14.3   BITs concluded by BRICs, per year, 1991–2003 (number)

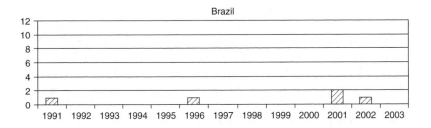

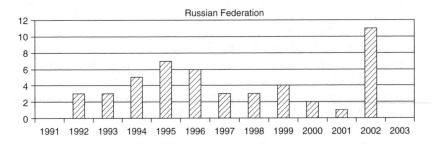

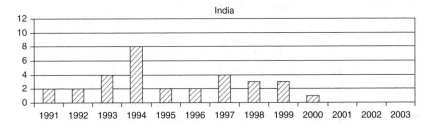

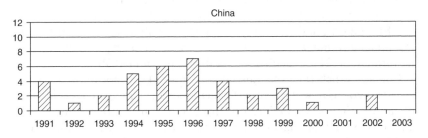

Note: a DTTs covering income and capital only.

Source: UNCTAD, www.unctad.org/iia.

*Figure 14.4   DTTs concluded by BRICs, per year, 1991–2003*a *(number)*

particularly in natural resources. The level of flows at the beginning of the 2000s was still relatively low, which is reflected in the country's low rankings by FDI inflows among host countries and on the Inward FDI Performance Index. The Russian Federation has concluded a fairly large number of BITs and DTTs (Table 14.6) between 1994 and 2004 particularly in the mid 1990s (Figures 14.3, 14.4). Over the past decade, the relative importance of FDI for this country was quite similar to that for India, except for FDI per capita which was higher in the case of the Russian Federation (Table 14.1). But as the ranking on the Inward FDI Potential Index compared with that on the Inward FDI Performance Index suggests (33 vs 111, in 2000–2002), there is considerable room for higher flows. Given the recent decisions that appear to limit FDI in natural resources, such flows would however have to take place in manufacturing and services – sectors that, so far, have not received much attention.

Among the emerging markets, India is a country with high potential to attract FDI – given its large market and abundant labour resources – if it makes the transition from 'red tape' to 'red carpet'. Since the mid 1980s, the country has received low FDI inflows, a fact reflected in the relevant absolute and relative figures and rankings. Its inflows in 2002–2004 were below those of Singapore and were one-twelfth of those of China. But India began to liberalize its FDI regime in the 1990s and is now undertaking a review of its FDI policy. For that purpose, the government established a national Investment Commission (headed by Ratan Tata) in December 2004 to formulate recommendations with the goal of attracting $150 billion in FDI over the next ten years. It has already concluded a fairly large number of BITs (all since 1994), it has the third highest number of DTTs among emerging markets (Table 14.7) and it is negotiating a number of free trade agreements with investment components. Reflecting its large size and low FDI inflows, and relatively weak position with respect to some of the locational advantages sought by TNCs, India ranks low in terms of FDI performance (121st in 2002–2002) and FDI potential (89th).

China – which (like the Russian Federation) did not allow FDI two decades ago – is now the star performer among emerging markets in terms of inward FDI: since 1992 (except for 2000), it has attracted the highest amounts of FDI among all emerging markets, and the relative importance of FDI for the country's economy is considerable. (Most FDI, however, is located in the coastal provinces.) In fact, given the size of its economy, one would expect even higher inflows, as suggested by its relatively low ranking on the Performance Index (50th in 2000–2002). Not surprisingly, the country has made by far the highest number of policy changes favourable to FDI since 1992 among all emerging markets. China has also the highest number of BITs and DTTs among emerging markets (Tables 14.7, 14.8).

Table 14.7   The top ten emerging markets in terms of the number of DTTs, end 2000

Economy	Number of DTTs
China	64
Romania	63
India	62
Russian Federation	52
Republic of Korea	51
Malaysia	48
Thailand	44
Indonesia	41
Pakistan	41
South Africa	41

Note: ᵃ DTTs covering income and capital only.

Source: UNCTAD, www.unctad.org/iia.

Table 14.8   The top ten emerging markets in terms of the number of BITs, end 2003

Economy	Number of BITs
China	107
Egypt	88
Romania	81
Republic of Korea	73
Malaysia	66
Turkey	65
Bulgaria	62
Indonesia	58
Argentina	57
Cuba	57

Source: UNCTAD, www.unctad.org/iia.

The country's success in attracting investment (combined with its high savings rate, foreign exchange reserves and the domination of a number of industries by foreign investors) has even triggered a debate over whether continued high FDI inflows are desirable. Perhaps this will lead to a more pronounced switch from a second-generation FDI attraction strategy (the liberalization of FDI regimes plus active efforts to attract such investment across the board) to a third-generation FDI strategy in which China makes extra efforts to target types of investment of particular interest to its development objectives and focuses more on obtaining greater benefits from FDI, especially as far as the creation of innovatory capacity is concerned (UNCTAD, 2001, pp. 123–124).[6]

In sum, the BRICs have not exhausted their potential to attract FDI – but all of them are pursuing policies to change that. If they do indeed reform their regulatory frameworks accordingly (and assuming the economic FDI determinants are right), they should be able to absorb more foreign investment, both domestic-market oriented and export-oriented FDI, and in all sectors. Moreover, the tradability revolution (Sauvant, 1990), as expressed in the offshoring of services (UNCTAD, 2004a), opens new possibilities, given the relative abundance in the BRICs of the skills needed for the provision of information technology and related services. Similarly, the possibilities offered by the Clean Development Mechanism of the Kyoto Protocol (which entered into force in February 2005) hold promise for more FDI in BRIC economies (Niederberger and Saner, 2005). Finally, the sectoral distribution of FDI in all BRICs shows that manufacturing and primary products are still important (Table 14.9) – while, worldwide, services account for some 70 percent of FDI inflows and 60 percent of the inward stock; this suggests room for expansion in the services sector as well. Higher FDI flows to the BRICs do not, however, necessarily come at the expense of other developing countries,[7] as the pool of such investment is not fixed.

OUTWARD FDI

Outward foreign direct investment (OFDI) from emerging markets – although not new[8] – is the neglected twin of their inward FDI. On the surface, the reason for this neglect, especially from a policy perspective, is clear: emerging markets typically face a foreign exchange shortage and are capital constrained; hence they should import, not export capital. But this view neglects at least two considerations:

- individual companies may well have the capital to expand abroad;
- companies increasingly need a portfolio of locational assets to remain competitive.

The second point is particularly important. The globalizing world economy is characterized by the liberalization of trade and investment regimes. Companies can no longer withdraw into the safe havens of their

Table 14.9   BRICs: the sectoral composition of inward FDI, 2003

Country	Flows (%)	Stock (%)
Brazil[a]		
Primary	11	2
Secondary	35	34
Tertiary	54	64
Russian Federation[b]		
Primary	20	18
Secondary	31	31
Tertiary	49	50
India		
Primary	–	–
Secondary	25	–
Tertiary	75	–
China		
Primary	2	2
Secondry	70	63
Tertiary	28	31
World[c]	100	100
Primary	9	6
Secondary	24	34
Tertiary	67	60

Notes: Data exclude 'private buying and selling of property' and 'unspecified' items that cannot be classified under any of the three economic sectors.
[a] Stock data refer to the year 2000.
[b] 2002.
[c] Data for flows refer to the period average 2001–2002, while those for stock refer to 2002.

Source: UNCTAD (2004a).

home markets as a relatively secure source of profits. Rather, competition from foreign firms is everywhere – through imports, inward FDI, non-equity forms of participation, and so on. These conditions make it all the more important for firms to pay attention to their competitiveness (their ability to survive and grow while maximizing profits) vis-à-vis their competitors.

How is OFDI relevant here? Take a firm in a developing country. It competes with its local rivals. It also competes with foreign firms to the extent that they export to the developing country in question and/or invest in it to produce for the local and/or world markets. In this scenario, the foreign firms that are TNCs have a number of advantages that bolster their competitiveness (UNCTAD, 1995, p. 131):

- Cost savings are achieved through the internationalization of activities within a TNC system where this allows members of the system *privileged access* to the firm's proprietary resources; the benefits of reduced transaction costs as compared with those of arm's length international transactions; better resource allocation and specialization; an intra-firm international division of labour; and economies of scale and scope.
- *Advantageous access* of foreign affiliates, through backward linkages to a wider pool of assets and experience.
- A larger financial resource base due to access to larger markets.
- Resilience to shocks – for example, changes in exchange rates or cyclical conditions – is increased by the cross-border diversification of locational assets and the advantages of being active internationally through more than one modality.

In short, foreign firms with FDI have access to factors of production in host economies and can organize their production internationally, thus reaping the benefits of an international (intra-firm) division of labour, in the framework of which discrete parts of the value-added chain (or the production of entire products) are located where they can be produced best. They have the strategic option to acquire a 'portfolio of locational assets' (UNCTAD, 1995) that becomes a source of their efficiency and hence competitiveness.[9]

Conversely, firms – whether big or small, from developed countries or emerging markets – that are not allowed to invest abroad to establish a portfolio of locational assets, are deprived of one source of efficiency, even though they may have the ownership-specific advantages to do so.[10] To put it differently, they are handicapped: they face competition from their foreign rivals in their own markets, but they can compete in their rivals' markets only through exports, not FDI. By liberalizing OFDI, governments can eliminate this handicap and allow their firms to exploit their ownership advantages abroad, thereby helping them to remain competitive and, in the process, improve access to markets, technology and resources and foster economic restructuring.[11]

Developed countries have long recognized the importance of OFDI for the competitiveness of their firms and the performance of their economies. They have not only liberalized their OFDI policies virtually completely,[12] but actually put in place a whole set of policy tools to assist their firms in investing abroad. OFDI promotion programs include the provision of information and technical assistance (information about investment opportunities, matchmaking, support of missions, feasibility studies), equity and loan financing; and investment insurance (UNCTAD, 1995, ch. VII). Developed countries have also led the process of concluding BITs and DTTs. No wonder, then, that the number of TNCs – firms that control assets abroad – has increased rapidly over the past three decades: for 15 developed countries for which data are available, the number of TNCs headquartered in these countries rose from 7000 in 1968–69 to at least 35 000 at the beginning of the twenty-first century (UNCTAD, 2004a, p. 273);[13] worldwide, there are now at least 60 000 TNCs. Among the world's top 100 TNCs (measured in terms of the size of their assets abroad), 96 were headquartered in developed countries in 2002 (UNCTAD, 2004a, pp. 277–8).

Emerging markets are, however, beginning to recognize the importance of OFDI for their firms' competitiveness and their economies' performance. The number of such countries that reported OFDI flows rose from 70 in 1985 to 122 in 2003 (Appendix Table 14A.1). OFDI flows from emerging economies rose from a negligible amount at the beginning of the 1980s to $46 billion in 2003 (Figure 14.5),[14] accounting now for 8 percent of world FDI outflows. (For economies in transition alone, OFDI flows grew from virtually zero to $10 billion over the same time period.) The OFDI stock of developing countries alone reached $853 billion in 2003, with a world share of 10 percent. (The OFDI stock of economies in transition alone stood at $75 billion in 2003.) Some two-thirds of the OFDI stock of emerging economies is accounted for by five economies.[15] A substantial share of this investment is in other developing countries, including in the same region. In Asian developing countries, the latter share may be as high as 40 percent; in Latin America and Africa, it may be around 15 percent or less.

The picture regarding the magnitude of OFDI from emerging markets looks different when OFDI flows are considered in relation to total investment in a number of emerging markets (Table 14.10). A few of them invest relatively more abroad than important developed countries; for example, the ratio of OFDI to gross fixed capital of formation was 36 percent for Singapore, compared to 7 percent for the United States in 2001–2003. Some emerging markets are among the top 15 on UNCTAD's Outward FDI Performance Index (Table 14.11).

These data reflect the activities of a cohort of emerging market TNCs that hail from all continents (Appendix Table 14A.2). Most of the developing countries' top 50 TNCs in terms of foreign assets are headquartered in Asia, followed by Latin America (11) and Africa (7 – all from South Africa) (Figure 14.6). The list of the largest non-financial TNCs from Central and Eastern Europe is dominated (with five entries) by TNCs from the Russian Federation, Slovenia and Hungary (Appendix Table 14A.3). But in terms of the absolute size of assets abroad, TNCs from emerging markets are not yet in the same league as their rivals from developed countries – as mentioned before, only four developing-country TNCs are among

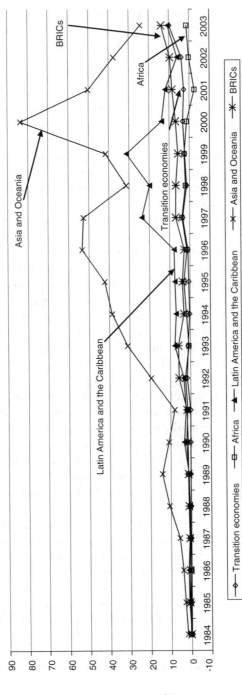

Source: UNCTAD, www.unctad.org/fdistatistics, and UNCTAD estimates.

Figure 14.5   FDI outflows from emerging markets, by group of economies, and BRICs, 1984–2003 (billions of dollars)

Table 14.10   Emerging markets: FDI outflows as percentage of gross fixed capital formation, 1983–2003[a] *(%)*

Economy	1983–85	1993–95	2001–2003
World	2.3	5.2	9.4
Developing economies	0.6	3.5	2.9
Singapore	1.6	15.3	35.6
Hong Kong, China	11.7	55.7	27.9
Taiwan Province of China	0.5	4.5	10.5
Chile	0.2	5.3	7.4
Malaysia	2.2	6.1	5.3
Mexico	0.2	0.2	1.8
Korea, Republic of	1.0	1.5	1.8
Thailand	0.0	0.9	0.9
Egypt	0.1	0.5	0.1
Argentina	0.2	2.3	−0.5
South Africa	0.7	6.0	−6.3
Transition economies	–	0.4	3.9
Croatia	–	0.5	4.6
Romania	–	0.06	0.1
Developed countries	2.8	5.8	11.4
France	1.9	7.6	22.5
United Kingdom	10.0	20.0	19.1
United States	1.8	7.9	6.6
Germany	3.6	4.9	4.2
Japan	1.5	1.3	3.2
BRICs	0.2	0.9	1.5
Russian Federation	–	0.9	7.9
India	0.01	0.1	1.0
China	0.3	1.3	0.9
Brazil	0.3	0.7	0.2

Note: [a] Economies, in each group, are ranked on the basis of their magnitude in 2001–2003.

Source: UNCTAD, www.unctad.org/fdistatistics, and UNCTAD estimates.

the world's 100 largest TNCs, the biggest of them in place 16. But the degree of transnationalization of the top 50 TNCs from developing countries is now quite high (although not as high as that of the top 100; Figure 14.7), having risen rapidly during the past decade, more so in fact than that of the largest TNCs from developed countries: it rose from 32 percent in 1995 to 49 percent in 2002 (compared with 51 percent and

Table 14.11   *Outward FDI Performance Index[a] of the top 15 economies and BRICs, 2001–2003[b]*

Ranking	Economy	Index
1	Belgium and Luxembourg	22.741
2	Panama	6.548
3	Singapore	5.104
4	Netherlands	4.643
5	Azerbaijan	3.764
6	Hong Kong, China	3.477
7	Sweden	2.329
8	Bahrain	2.309
9	Switzerland	2.303
10	France	2.209
11	Spain	2.178
12	Denmark	1.921
13	Canada	1.869
14	United Kingdom	1.603
15	Portugal	1.487
	BRICs	
38	Russian Federation	0.484
58	China	0.150
61	India	0.114
91	Brazil	0.017

Notes:
[a] The UNCTAD Outward FDI Performance Index is calculated as the ratio of a country's share in global FDI outflows to its share in global GDP.
[b] Based on average flows for the three years.

Source: UNCTAD (2004a), p. 18.

57 percent, respectively, for the top 100) (Table 14.12). The top 50 TNCs span a wide range of activities. The main ones were in electrical and electronic equipment (gradually declining in importance), food and beverages (UNCTAD, 2004, p. 21). The 25 largest TNCs from Central and Eastern Europe were mainly in natural resources.[16]

Within the framework of the need to strengthen corporate competitiveness, the motives for OFDI often begin with the desire to support trade – from warehouses to assembly plants, distribution networks and financial services (banking, insurance). The same type of investment can also be made to break into new markets. In the services sector, in particular, new markets typically can only be opened through investment (given the limited tradability of most services). Access to natural resources and cheap

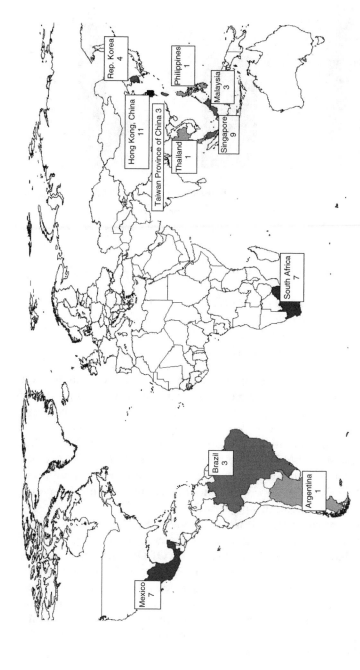

Rep. Korea
4

Philippines
1

Malaysia
3

Hong Kong, China
11

Taiwan Province of China 3

Thailand
1

Singapore
9

South Africa
7

Mexico
7

Brazil
3

Argentina
1

Note: ᵃ Reliable data on Chinese TNCs were not available.

Source: UNCTAD (2004a), pp. 21–3.

*Figure 14.6 The location of the 50 largest TNCs based in developing economies, 2002*ᵃ

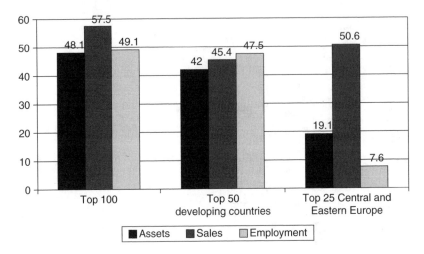

Note: ᵃ Financial TNCs are not included.

Source: UNCTAD (2004a), pp. 11, 21, 317.

Figure 14.7   *Comparison of the foreign share of the top 100 TNCs*
worldwide, the 50 largest TNCs based in developing
economies and the 25 largest TNCs based in Central and
Eastern Europe, 2002ᵃ (%)

labour also plays a role for a number of firms, as does the desire to diversify risk and profits. In all of these cases, furthermore, matching – or pre-
empting – competitors can play a role. Finally, investments are becoming
more important that are meant to strengthen the technological capacity of
firms, traditionally one of the firm-specific advantages that actually lead
firms to invest abroad (as opposed to being the result of it). Cost considerations are also becoming important, but they are by far less important
than for TNCs from developed countries and compared with the motivations mentioned earlier in this paragraph.

What is impressive is that this rise of FDI and TNCs from emerging
markets has taken place largely against the background of government
policies that have not paid much attention to OFDI, have been restrictive
or have not been actively supportive. The BRICs aside (discussed in the
next section), there are, however, notable exceptions. They include a
number of the principal emerging outward investors, for example Chile,
Mexico, the Republic of Korea, Taiwan Province of China and a number
of CEE countries. Singapore has even embarked on building, through FDI,
an 'external wing' of its economy.

Table 14.12   The degree of transnationality[a] *of TNCs, 1995–2002 (%)*

Country	1995	1996	1997	1998	1999	2000	2001	2002
Top 50 TNC from developing countries	32	35	34	37	39	35	45	49
Brazil	7	7	15	17	19	15	8	15
India	–	8	8	8	10	–	–	–
China	–	20	24	28	–	35	39	–
Top 25 TNCs from Central and Eastern								
Europe	–	–	31	32	32	32	30	32
Russian Federation	–	–	–	20	31	36	36	32
World's top 100 TNCs	51	55	55	54	52	56	58	57

Note: [a] The non-weighted average of the ratios of foreign assets, sales and employment to the respective total for each indicator.

Source: UNCTAD, *World Investment Report*, various years, www.unctad.org/wir.

Often, various liberalizing and promotional measures have been put in place by governments of emerging markets in a phased manner, starting with an approval process and ceilings that are progressively set higher until they are abolished. Other policy measures are to allow non-equity forms or to permit (at least initially) OFDI only in the form of equipment and technology exports, through foreign borrowing or the reinvestment of earnings. Going beyond liberalization, some governments also provide information about investment opportunities and frameworks, organize fact-finding business missions and business seminars and forums, and establish databases. They also offer financial and fiscal support. BITs and DTTs, increasingly also between emerging markets, are proliferating, as are other agreements covering investment matters. There are many approaches, but no single model, to move from restrictive to permissive to proactive policies.

All this reflects the recognition of governments that, in the interest of the international competitiveness of their firms and the performance of their economies (for example through increased exports), they need to find a way to balance macroeconomic balance-of-payments considerations with the microeconomic competitiveness requirements of individual firms. But once an enabling framework for OFDI exists and the firms from emerging market economies are unleashed, the growth of OFDI from these economies shows that they can become important players in the world FDI market.

THE BRICS: OVERVIEW – WHAT ABOUT OFDI FROM THE BRICS?

Although comprising some of the largest economies among the emerging markets, the BRICs combined accounted for only 18 percent of the OFDI stock and 30 percent of OFDI outflows of the respective totals of all emerging markets in 2003, compared to 38 percent of GDP. Outflows have, however, risen fairly consistently between 1990 and 2004 for the group as a whole (Figure 14.8), placing all of them (except Brazil) within the group of the 15 top emerging outward investor economies (Table 14.13). The Russian Federation, Brazil and China occupy ranks 3, 5 and 7 in the league table of emerging markets in terms of OFDI stock in 2003, while India ranks 20th (Table 14.14). In relation to gross fixed capital formation, OFDI is around 1 percent or less, except in the case of the Russian Federation (about 8 percent) (Table 14.15); this is half or less of the ratio for the emerging markets as a group. In the Outward FDI Performance Index for all countries (Table 14.11), they rank between the 38th place (Russian Federation) and the 91st place (Brazil) – far behind the leading developing country, Singapore (3rd). The transnationality index of their firms in the top TNCs varies greatly, from very low for Brazilian and Indian firms, to relatively high for Chinese and Russian firms (Table 14.12).[17] Between them, the BRICs have a substantial number of TNCs – including many small and medium-sized firms that control assets abroad – headquartered in their territories (Table 14.16), with a number of the top ones in natural resources.

A good part of the OFDI of all BRICs is located within their respective regions, although firms from China and India also have significant investment elsewhere. There is little bilateral FDI among the four (Table 14.17), although this may change somewhat if various planned projects of Chinese firms in Brazil materialize. The sectoral distribution of OFDI from BRICs is skewed towards services (Table 14.18). The traditional areas of finance and business services account for the lion's share of BRICs' OFDI. However, construction, public utilities, transport and communication services also play a not unimportant role, as does manufacturing. An interesting recent trend is that the past two years have witnessed a notable increase in OFDI from most of the BRICs in natural resources, particularly through cross-border M&As. Government encouragement has played a role in some cases, strengthening firms' efforts to secure supplies. Considerations associated with financial centres play a role in OFDI from some BRICs, although a good part of the funds involved may well be redirected to other locations.

The drivers and motivations for the transnationalizion of firms are similar across the BRICs and do not differ significantly from those of firms in developed countries (and, for that matter, other emerging markets). In particular,

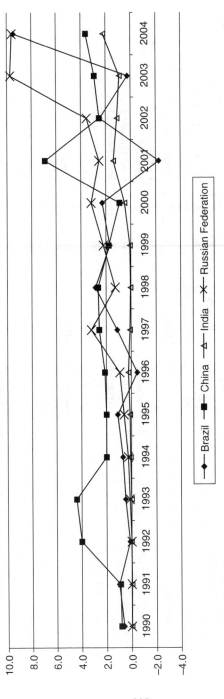

Note: [a] Data prior to 1992 are not available for the Russian Federation, but they are negligible.

Source: UNCTAD, www.unctad.org/fdistatistics, UNCTAD estimates and Central Banks of individual economies.

Figure 14.8 FDI flows from the BRICs, 1990–2004[a] (billions of dollars)

Table 14.13   The top 15 emerging markets in terms of FDI outflows, 1983–89, 1993–95 and 2001–2003[a] (billions of dollars)

1983–89			1993–95			2001–2003		
Rank	Economy	Value	Rank	Economy	Value	Rank	Economy	Value
1	Taiwan Province of China	1.7	1	Hong Kong, China	21.4	1	Hong Kong, China	10.9
2	Hong Kong, China	1.7	2	Singapore	3.7	2	Singapore	8.8
3	Korea, Republic of	0.5	3	Virgin Islands (British)	2.9	3	Taiwan Province of China	5.3
4	**China**	**0.5**	4	**China**	**2.8**	4	**Russian federation**	**5.3**
5	Kuwait	0.4	5	Taiwan Province of China	2.7	5	**China**	**4.1**
6	Saudi Arabia	0.3	6	Korea, Republic of	2.5	6	Virgin Islands (British)	3.7
7	Singapore	0.3	7	Malaysia	2.0	7	Korea, Republic of	2.8
8	Malaysia	0.2	8	Indonesia	1.7	8	Mexico	2.2
9	Panama	0.2	9	South Africa	1.3	9	Cayman Islands	1.9
10	**Brazil**	**0.2**	10	Argentina	1.1	10	Iran, Islamic Republic of	1.9
11	South Africa	0.1	11	**Brazil**	**0.8**	11	Panama	1.6
12	Venezuela	0.1	12	Chile	0.7	12	Malaysia	1.2
13	Nigeria	0.1	13	**Russian federation**	**0.6**	13	**India**	**1.1**
14	Mexico	0.1	14	Thailand	0.5	14	Chile	1.1
15	Liberia	0.05	15	Venezuela	0.4	15	Venezuela	0.8
40	**India**	**0.01**	28	**India**	**0.1**	24	**Brazil**	**0.2**
—	**Russian Federation**	—						

Note: [a] Flows have been averaged over three years to even out lumpiness.

Source: UNCTAD, www.unctad.org/fdistatistics, and UNCTAD estimates.

338

Table 14.14 The top 15 emerging markets in terms of OFDI stock, 1984, 1994, 2003 (billions of dollars)

1984			1994			2003		
Rank	Economy	Value	Rank	Economy	Value	Rank	Economy	Value
1	**Brazil**	**39.4**	1	Hong Kong, China	58.8	1	Hong Kong, China	336.1
2	South Africa	8.6	2	**Brazil**	**43.4**	2	Singapore	90.9
3	Argentina	5.9	3	Singapore	26.3	3	**Russian federation**	**72.3**
4	Singapore	4.1	4	Taiwan Province of China	22.2	4	Taiwan Province of China	65.2
5	Panama	1.9	5	South Africa	19.1	5	**Brazil**	**54.9**
6	Hong Kong, China	1.4	6	**China**	**15.8**	6	Korea, Republic of	34.5
7	Bermuda	1.4	7	Argentina	9.1	7	**China**	**33.0**
8	Kuwait	1.3	8	Malaysia	7.9	8	Malaysia	29.7
9	Malaysia	1.2	9	Korea, Republic of	7.5	9	Virgin Islands (British)	26.8
10	Bahrain	0.6	10	Virgin Islands (British)	6.3	10	South Africa	24.2
11	Saudi Arabia	0.5	11	Panama	4.3	11	Cayman Islands	21.9
12	Botswana	0.4	12	Nigeria	3.9	12	Argentina	21.3
13	Korea, Republic of	0.4	13	Venezuela	3.8	13	Mexico	13.8
14	Morocco	0.3	14	Kuwait	3.8	14	Chile	13.8
15	Colombia	0.3	15	Mexico	2.8	15	Panama	8.7
16	**China**	**0.3**	16	**Russian federation**	**2.5**	20	**India**	**5.1**
30	**India**	**0.1**	35	**India**	**0.4**			
–	**Russian Federation**	–						

Source: UNCTAD, www.unctad.org/fdistatistics, and UNCTAD estimates.

Table 14.15 Importance of FDI from the BRICs, 1984–2004

Item	Brazil			Russian Federation			India			China		
	1984	1994	2004	1984[a]	1994	2004	1984	1994	2004	1984	1994	2004
FDI outflows ($mil)	104[b]	759[c]	158[d]	–	636[c]	5 264[d]	4[b]	67[c]	1 139[d]	285[b]	2 800[c]	4 101[d]
FDI outward stock ($mil)	39 358	43 378	64 363[e]	–	2 547	81 874[e]	90	376	6 592[f]	271	15 768	38 000
FDI outflows as a percentage of GFCF	0.3[b]	0.7[c]	0.2[g]	–	0.9[c]	7.9[g]	0.01[b]	0.1[c]	1.0[g]	0.3[b]	1.3[c]	0.9[g]
FDI outflows per capita	0.8[b]	4.8[c]	0.9[d]	–	4.3[c]	36.6[d]	0.01[b]	0.1[c]	1.1[d]	0.3[b]	2.3[c]	3.2[d]
FDI outflows per $1000 GDP	0.5[b]	1.3[c]	0.3[d]	–	1.8[c]	14.5[d]	0.02[b]	0.2[c]	2.2[d]	1.1[b]	5.0[c]	3.2[d]

Notes:
[a] Data prior to 1992 are not available for the Russian Federation, but they were negligible.
[b] Averaged over 1983–85 to even out lumpiness.
[c] Averaged over 1993–95 to even out lumpiness.
[d] Averaged over 2002–2004 to even out lumpiness.
[e] Estimated by adding 2004 OFDI flows to the 2003 stock.
[f] As of 31 March 2004.
[g] Averaged over 2001–2003 to even out lumpiness.

Source: UNCTAD, www.unctad.org/fdistatistics, and UNCTAD estimates.

Table 14.16 BRICs: number of parent corporations and their foreign affiliates, latest available year

Economy	Year	Parent corporations based in the economy	Foreign affiliates
Brazil	2003	1702[a]	3526
Russian Federation	1994	–.	7793
India	2003	1700[b]	3000[b]
China	2003	2000[c]	4550[c]

Notes:
[a] Includes all types of investors (direct, portfolio, derivatives, etc).
[b] Approval data.
[c] Estimate.

Source: UNCTAD (2004a); Brazil, Central Bank; China, Ministry of Commerce; Liu et al. (2005); Pradhan (2005).

Table 14.17 Intra-BRIC FDI stock, 2003 (%)[a]

Reporter/partner	Brazil	Russian Federation	India	China
Brazil		–	–	–
Russian Federation	–		–	2[b]
India	0.2	16.7		0.9
China	1.1	4.8	–	

Notes:
[a] The percentage shares of each BRIC partner country in the total outward stock of the BRIC (reporter) country. Data for India and China are on an approval basis.
[b] Based on Russian FDI outflows 1995–99.

Source: UNCTAD; Kalotay (2003).

firms have developed various ownership-specific advantages that allow them to be competitive in foreign markets – and increased competition in their own markets (through imports and inward investment) makes it necessary to exploit these advantages to strengthen their international competitiveness. Major specific reasons include access to resources abroad – not only natural resources, but also technology and skills – to acquire brand names (for example the acquisition of IBM's personal computer division by China's Lenovo), to build distribution networks and to diversify the production base. As in the case of their developed country rivals, M&As are being used as a mode of entry: between 2000 and 2003, Indian firms clinched 111 deals,

Table 14.18   BRICs: the sectoral composition of outward FDI, 2003 (%)

Country	Flows	Stock
Brazil[a]		
Primary	10	1
Secondary	−40	3
Tertiary	129	97
Russian Federation[b]		
Primary	−	−
Secondary	−	0.3
Tertiary	−	99.7
India[c]		
Primary	−	10
Secondary	58	87
Tertiary	42	3
China[d]		
Primary	49	20
Secondary	22	6
Tertiary	28	74
World[e]	100	100
Primary	7	4
Secondary	22	29
Tertiary	71	67

Notes:
[a] Flow data were estimated as the difference between stock in 2003 and stock in 2002.
Negative flows were recorded in the secondary sector.
[b] Stock data refer to 2000.
[c] Data for flows are on an approval basis while stock data refer to 1997.
[d] Data for flows are based on MOFCOM's statistics of approved non-financial investment
projects abroad. Stock data are actual data.
[e] Data for flows refer to the period average 2001–2002, while those for stock refer to 2002.

Data may not add to 100% due to rounding. Data exclude private buying and selling of
property and unspecified items that cannot be classified under any of the three economic
sectors.

Source: UNCTAD.

Chinese firms 86 deals, Brazilian firms 32, and Russian firms 86. Some of
these deals are quite large (Appendix Table 14A.4). Many firms still go
through the traditional sequence of first exporting before setting up trade-
supporting facilities and, eventually, production facilities. But this process
seems to take less time than in the past and, in any event, does not apply to
many services investments. As BRIC firms strengthen their ownership-
specific advantages in manufacturing and services, combined with their

financial muscle, they can be expected to expand further abroad. Indian information technology (IT) companies are examples.

Government support for OFDI across the four countries varies. The government of China has an established policy ('Go Global') to encourage OFDI which dates back to 2000. Brazil's leadership wants to create global players, but there is not yet a policy in place to advance this objective. India is liberalizing, but its focus is now on attracting more inward FDI. The Russian Federation does not have a specific policy promoting OFDI, and capital controls exist. But the international side of a policy framework, as provided by the BITs and DTTs concluded by BRICs, is already largely in place for most of them. These are treaties that do not apply, after all, just to inward but also to outward FDI.[18]

What does all of this suggest? One thing that emerges from the data and is common to all four BRICs is that each of them has a substantial potential to become a much more important outward investor. Each BRIC already has a number of firms that are important players, and more are emerging. They need nurturing, and they need an enabling framework that supports their internationalization, to become truly global players – a topic that will be addressed in the conclusions below. At the same time, the picture varies greatly from country to country. Hence the next sections look at each of the BRICs separately.

BRAZIL: TAKING OFF?[19]

Salient Features

With an OFDI stock of $55 billion in 2003 (created by some 1000 Brazilian TNCs), Brazil is the fifth-largest source of FDI from among the emerging markets, after Hong Kong (China), Singapore, the Russian Federation and Taiwan Province of China. Its OFDI stock is 1.4 times that of Portugal, 1.7 times that of China, and three-fifths times that of Singapore. OFDI flows from Brazil have increased significantly recently, rising from $0.2 billion in 2003 to $9.5 billion in 2004 (Figure 14.9). A large increase in overseas M&As in 2004 helped push Brazilian OFDI to this unprecedented level.

The Latin American region is a major destination for Brazil's OFDI, in terms of both M&As and greenfield investment. This suggests that Brazil may play a growing role in the regional integration process through investment and production linkages. Resource-rich neighbouring countries, such as Argentina and Chile, are among the recipients of Brazilian OFDI.

More than two-thirds of the country's OFDI went to such offshore financial centres as the Cayman Islands, Bahamas and British Virgin Islands

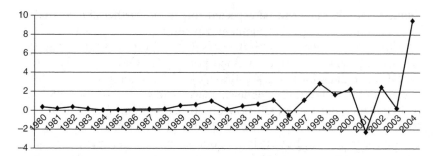

Source: UNCTAD, FDI/TNC database, based on information from the
Central Bank of Brazil.

*Figure 14.9	Brazil: outward FDI stock, by major destination, 2003
			(millions of dollars)*

(Table 14.19). Financial motivations (to park funds there) played a key role,
but often investment was redirected from these centres to other locations.
This has some similarities with OFDI from China and to some extent India
and the Russian Federation. It also explains the significant dominance of services in statistics on OFDI from Brazil: over 95 percent of Brazil's OFDI was
in service industries, particularly finance and business services (Table 14.20).

But Brazilian firms have also been actively investing overseas in primary
industries in recent years. For instance, in 2002–2004, most of Brazil's
greenfield projects were in energy and mining industries (Table 14.21).
Petrobas led in overseas energy investment. Firms such as Ambev have also
invested in other Latin American countries for market-seeking reasons in
the food and drink industries. Brazilian firms in general prefer greenfield
projects as a mode of entry. For instance, during the period 2002 to
February 2005, Brazilian firms invested in 102 greenfield FDI projects as
compared with 24 cross-border M&A deals in 2002–2004 (Table 14.22,
Appendix Table 14A.5). Fifteen countries accounted for more than four-
fifths of Brazilian overseas greenfield investment projects between 2002 and
February 2005. Brazilian companies are also making cross-border M&A
purchases in a number of different industries (Table 14.23).

Drivers and Motivations

The key drivers of Brazil's OFDI include financial motives and the channel-
ing of investment to other locations through offshore financial centres.
Other important reasons include access to raw materials, resources and
markets. Firms such as Petrobas, CVRD, Petroleo Brasiliero SA, and
Companhia Siderurgica Nacional have invested abroad to access resources.

Table 14.19   FDI outflows fromBrazil, 1980–2004ᵃ (billions of dollars)

Economy	Equity	Intra-company loans	Total
World	44 769	10 123	54 892
Cayman Islands	15 097	7 151	22 248
Bahamas	6 565	360	6 925
British Virgin Islands	6 314	396	6 710
Uruguay	2 810	831	3 641
United States	2 100	193	2 293
Luxembourg	2 055	7	2 062
Spain	1 775	19	1 794
Argentina	1 549	100	1 650
Portugal	066	13	1079
Panama	478	301	779
Netherlands	599	143	742
Madeira Island	716	–	716
Bermuda	593	7	600
Netherlands Antilles	294	225	520
Gibraltar	458	–	458
United Kingdom	420	19	439
Austria	324	–	324
Chile	203	12	216
France	85	101	186
Germany	124	8	132
Others	1 143	235	1 378

Note: ᵃ In 2004, Ambev (a Brazilian drinks group) and Interbrew (a Belgium-based brewer) merged and created a new group InBev AS (Interbrew Ambev), based in Belgium. The deal was around $5 billion. The former shareholders of Ambev (former BRACO Control Group) were paid with shares of the new group, now holding 44% of Stichting Interbrew, the holding company of InBev.

Source: UNCTAD, www.unctad.org/fdistatistics, UNCTAD estimates and Central Bank of Brazil, www.bcb.gov.br.

Brazil's manufacturing OFDI has been minimal, dominated by food and beverages and by resource-related products such as coke and petroleum products and metal and metal products. The desire to gain access to markets and distribution networks encouraged Brazilian firms to venture abroad in manufacturing activities, including through M&As (Appendix Table 14A.4). For instance, Ambev acquired John Labatt Ltd (Canada) in the food and drinks business for $7.8 billion in 2004 and Quinsa (Quilmes International-Argentina) for $346 million in 2003, and Petrobas acquired gasoline service stations from Perez Companc SA (Argentina) for $1 billion in 2003.

Table 14.20   Brazil: outward FDI stock,[a] *by sector and industry, 2003 (millions of dollars)*

Sector/industry	Value
Total	**44 769**
Primary	**259**
Agriculture, hunting, forestry and fishing	59
Mining, quarrying and petroleum	200
Secondary	**1 190**
Food, beverages and tobacco	230
Textiles, clothing and leather	41
Wood and wood products	39
Publishing, printing and reproduction of recorded media	0.1
Coke, petroleum products and nuclear fuel	205
Chemicals and chemical products	30
Rubber and plastic products	143
Non-metallic mineral products	23
Metal and metal products	158
Machinery and equipment	104
Electrical and electronic equipment	134
Precision instruments	0.1
Motor vehicles and other transport equipment	83
Other manufacturing	0.3
Tertiary	**43 319**
Electricity, gas and water	20
Construction	695
Trade	1 908
Hotels and restaurants	14
Transport, storage and communications	207
Finance	22 355
Business activities	17 982
Education	1
Community, social and personal service activities	138

Note: [a] Data refer to equity only.

Source: UNCTAD, FDI/TNC database, based on information from the Central Bank of Brazil.

Government's Role and Policy Development

The government is supportive of OFDI. President Luiz Inacio Lula da Silva urged Brazilian businesspersons in 2003 'to abandon their fear of becoming multinational businesspersons',[20] and Minister Luiz Fernando Furlan

Table 14.21   Brazil: the 20 largest greenfield FDI projects by Brazilian firms,[a] *2002–2004*[b] *(millions of dollars)*

Rank	Name of company	Investment value	Year	Destination country	Industry
1	Petrobras	1 300	2003	Venezuela	Energy
2	Sondotecnica	1 000	2003	Portugal	Chemicals
3	Petrobras	600	2002	Bolivia	Energy
4	Petrobras	400	2002	Bolivia	Energy
5	Companhia Siderurgica Nacional	375	2004	Portugal	Metals/mining
6	Sigma Pharma	359	2004	Portugal	Pharma
7	Odebrecht	320	2003	Ecuador	Energy
8	Petrobras	285	2004	Argentina	Energy
9	Petrobras	200	2004	Argentina	Energy
10	Mister Sheik	175	2002	Argentina	Hotels, tourism and leisure
11	Petrobras	60	2004	Peru	Energy
12	Ambev[c]	50	2003	Guatemala	Food and drink
13	Petrobras	50	2002	Bolivia	Energy
14	Rima Industrial	45	2002	Uruguay	Metals/mining
15	Ambev[c]	40	2003	Peru	Food and drink
16	Ambev[c]	40	2004	Peru	Food and drink
17	Maritima	40	2002	Colombia	Energy
18	CVRD	36	2003	Norway	Metals/mining
19	Petrobras	35	2003	Argentina	Energy
20	Petrobras	34	2004	Iran	Energy

Notes:
[a] Based on projects for which the investment value is known.
[b] Until September 2004.

Source: UNCTAD, based on information from OCO Consulting, LOCOmonitor website, www.locomonitor.com.

added that 'the Brazilian Government expects the country to have 10 really transnational companies by the end of President Lula's term of office'.[21] There is growing interest among Brazilian firms to transnationalize their operations, as witnessed by the Global Players project of Fundaçao Dom Cabral, a leading Brazilian business school (Box 14.1). In fact, as of the late 1990s, there were already some 1000 Brazilian firms that had invested abroad (UNCTAD, 2004a, p. 273). In 2003, at least ten Brazilian firms had

Table 14.22   Brazil: geographic distribution of cross-border M&A purchases
by Brazilian companies, 1995–2004 (number of deals)

Economy	1995	1996	1997	1998	1999	2000	2001	2002	2003	2004	1995–2004
Total world	14	6	4	13	11	10	8	6	8	10	90
Developed countries	3	2	1	5	3	3	5	–	4	3	29
United States	–	–	–	2	1	1	2	–	1	1	8
Portugal	–	1	–	–	–	–	1	–	1	1	4
Spain	–	–	–	1	2	1	–	–	–	–	4
Canada	1	–	–	–	–	1	1	–	–	1	4
United Kingdom	–	1	–	2	–	–	–	–	–	–	3
Developing economies	11	4	3	8	8	7	3	6	4	7	61
Argentina	4	1	3	6	3	5	2	5	2	1	32
Colombia	1	–	–	1	–	–	–	–	–	2	4
Peru	2	–	–	–	–	–	–	–	–	2	4
Venezuela	1	2	–	1	–	–	–	–	–	–	4
Bolivia	1	–	–	–	1	1	–	–	–	–	3

Source: UNCTAD, cross-border M&A database.

three or more foreign affiliates with combined total sales of at least $34 billion (Table 14.24).

So far, however, OFDI is encouraged but not actively promoted. But that may be changing as the internationalization of enterprises is increasingly viewed as a means to improve the competitiveness of firms and the performance of the economy. The government has recently made known its intention to support Brazilian firms to become global players; as of March 2005, there are no limitations on OFDI from Brazil. Brazilian businesspersons have accompanied President Lula and ministers on visits to other countries.[22] A seminar involving a substantial number of Brazilian firms took place on 30 May 2005; organized by the Fundacao Dom Cabral, the Ministry of Development, Industry and Foreign Trade and UNCTAD, it deliberated on international experiences, identified obstacles and discussed policy issues to support OFDI.

Unlike in China and India, the government of Brazil has not introduced specific measures to support OFDI. Moreover, firms are investing abroad on their own accord without support of the government – in contrast, for example, to Chinese firms which receive support from their government.

OFDI from Brazil may well take off as firms feel the competition from increased imports and inward investment: the former rose by 41 percent between 1993–94 and 2002–2003, the latter by seven times between 1993–94 and 2003–2004. The benefits of OFDI in helping to build international competitiveness are increasingly being appreciated. This development will

Table 14.23 Brazil: industry distribution of cross-border M&A purchases by Brazilian companies, 1995–2004 (Number of deals)

Industry	1995	1996	1997	1998	1999	2000	2001	2002	2003	2004	1995–2004
Total	14	6	4	13	11	10	8	6	8	10	90
Primary	2	1	–	–	–	–	–	–	–	1	4
Mining	1	1	–	–	–	–	–	–	–	1	3
Agriculture, Forestry, and Fishing	1	–	–	–	–	–	–	–	–	–	1
Secondary	8	1	3	6	6	7	6	3	7	6	53
Food, beverages and tobacco	3	1	1	1	1	–	1	–	–	3	12
Metal and Metal Products	2	–	1	1	1	3	–	–	2	2	12
Oil and Gas; Petroleum Refining	1	–	–	2	1	–	1	1	1	–	7
Chemicals and chemical products	1	–	–	–	–	–	1	2	1	1	6
Services	4	4	1	7	5	3	2	3	1	3	33
Finance	1	3	1	2	–	–	–	2	1	–	10
Trade	–	–	–	3	2	1	–	1	–	–	7
Transport, storage and communications	2	1	–	1	1	–	–	–	–	2	7
Business Services	–	–	–	1	2	1	2	–	–	1	7

Source: UNCTAD, cross-border M&A database.

349

### BOX 14.1	THE GLOBAL PLAYERS PROGRAMME OF FUNDAÇAÕ DOM CABRAL

While Brazilian companies have started the process of transnationalization, there is no place where they could go and simply 'learn' it. Recently, however, Fundaçaõ Dom Cabral, a business school, has established the Global Players Programme to help firms accumulate knowledge about the transnationalization process.

The objectives of this programme are:

● to exchange experiences on the transnationalization of the participating firms;
● to increase the understanding of issues relating to the transnationalization of Brazilian firms;
● to create a network for evaluating the business opportunities and possibilities of partnership; and
● to develop an international mindset among participants in the programme.

The basis for the programme is experience sharing, education and knowledge development. This is done through training, seminars, workshops, case studies and research projects, discussed and defined by a Coordination Committee. The companies in the Committee include Ambev, CVRD, Embraco, Multibras, Natura, Petrobrás, Sadia, Tupy, Votorantim and WEG.

Source:	http://www.domcabral.org.br.

---

encourage Brazilian firms to look outward to access global markets, resources, skills and technologies. A government programme supportive of OFDI would facilitate this process.

THE RUSSIAN FEDERATION: A SIGNIFICANT INVESTOR

Salient Features

OFDI from the Russian Federation has risen rapidly since 1996, with a dip in 1998 – the year of the Russian financial crisis (Figure 14.10).[23] By 2003,

Table 14.24 *The 25 largest Brazilian TNCs in the manufacturing and non-financial services, 2003 (millions of dollars and number)*

TNC	Industry	Sales	Affiliates[a]			
			Total	Number of foreign affiliates	Number of host countries	Host economies
Petroleo Brasileiro-PETROBRAS	Petroleum	24 958	77	14	6	Angola, Argentina, Bolivia, Cayman Islands, Netherlands, United Kingdom
Odebrecht	Engineering and construction	5 634	35	14	14	Angola, Argentina, Bolivia, Chile, Colombia, Dominican Republic, Ecuador. Mexico, Peru, Portugal, United Arab Emirates, United States, Uruguay, Venezuela
Brasken	Petrochemical	3 819	13	5	2	Bahamas, Cayman Island
Companhia Vale Do Rio Doce-CVRD	Mining and quarrying	2 360	36	6	4	Belgium, Bermuda, Netherlands, Portugal

Table 14.24 (continued)

TNC	Industry	Sales	Affiliates[a]			Host economies
			Total	Number of foreign affiliates	Number of host countries	
Empresa Brasilera de Aeronautica-EMBRAER	Transport and storage	2043	4	1	1	United States
Companhia Siderurgica Nacional-CSN	Steel producer	2003	11	2	2	Cayman Island, Panama
Gerdau Acominas S/A	Metals	857	15	2	2	Chile, Uruguay
WEG	Electrical and electronic equipment	484	10	6	5	Belgium, Portugal, Spain, United Kingdom, United States
Tupy Fundicoes Ltda.	Machinery and equipment	354	6	3	3	Argentina, Germany, United States
Marcopolo	Motor vehicles	303	7	1	1	Portugal
Tigre Tubos E Conexoes	Chemicals	257	5	2	2	Argentina, Bolivia
Sao Paulo Alpargatas	Textiles	242	20	2	2	Argentina, United States
Construtora Andrade Gutierrez	Construction	225	16	3	3	Peru, Portugal, United States
Politec Ltda.	Other business services	104	2	1	1	United States

352

Teka Tecelagem Kuehnrich	Other business services	70	2	1	Germany
IBF – Industria Brasileira de Filmes	Precision equipment	61	3	2	United States
Soletur Sol Agencia de Viagens E Turismo	Leisure	53	2	1	United States
Forjas Taurus	Machinery and equipment	38	6	2	United States
Tomra Latasa Reciclagem S/A	Metals	23	15	13	Canada, Denmark, Finland, Germany, Netherlands, Norway, United States
Renner Herrmann	Chemicals	19	3	1	Argentina
Sisalana – Industria E Comercio	Textiles	11	2	1	United States
Seisa Clerman Emprendimentos Imobiliarios	Construction	2	2	1	Uruguay
Embratel Participaçoes	Telecommunications	–	5	1	United States
Companhia de Bebidas Das Americas – Ambev	Beverages	–	12	3	Dominican Republic, Ecuador, Uruguay
Altus Participaçoes	Other business services	–	5	3	Argentina, Germany, United States

Note: [a] Majority-owned affiliates only.

Source: UNCTAD, and company annual reports.

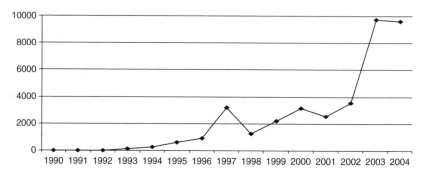

Source: UNCTAD, www.unctad.org/fdistatistics and www.cbr.ru/eng/statistics.

*Figure 14.10   Russian Federation: outward FDI flows, 1990–2004
                  (millions of dollars)*

OFDI flows had exceeded $9 billion, contributing to an accumulated
outward stock of $82 billion in 2004.[24] This suggests that the Russian
Federation may become a major capital exporter (although part of it consists of roundtripping), especially if prices for oil and minerals remain high.
The Russian Federation was the third-largest investor among emerging
markets. Its OFDI stock in 2003 was one-fifth that of Hong Kong (China)
but 1.3 times that of Brazil, 1.7 times that of China and about 11 times that
of India. OFDI from the Russian Federation is expected to increase further
as more Russian firms are likely to invest abroad to position themselves to
benefit from transnationalization, increase control over their value chains
and diversify their operations.

Most Russian OFDI is in energy- and mining-related industries, including in refining and the distribution of petroleum and gas. Significant
outward Russian investors include Lukoil, Novoship, Norilsk Nickel and
Primorsk Shipping Corporation (Table 14.25).[25] But few of them are truly
global players in terms of assets abroad.

Russian TNCs, in particular energy and mining firms, have invested in
many countries, establishing themselves as important actors. The European
Union and the United States lead, but FDI is also important in the neigh-
bouring countries of the Commonwealth of Independent States (CIS).
Fifteen countries accounted for two-thirds of Russian overseas greenfield
FDI projects between 2002 and February 2005 (Appendix Table 14A.5).
Five of them were CIS countries. A TNC such as Lukoil has projects in
numerous countries, including Dubai, Iran, Kazakhstan, Saudi Arabia,
Ukraine, Venezuela and other CEE and CIS countries. Gazprom has pro-
jects in China, Hungary, Macedonia, Poland, Uzbekistan and in the CIS.

Table 14.25 Russian Federation: selected largest TNCs, 2002 (millions of dollars)

Corporation	Industry	Assets		Sales		Employment	
		Foreign	Total	Foreign	Total	Foreign	Total
Lukoil JSC	Petroleum and natural gas	5 354	22 001	10 705[a]	15 334	13 000[b]	180 000
Novoship Co	Transportation	963	1 094	271	351	85	6 291
Norilsk Nokel OJSCMMC	Mining	502	9 739	2 360[a]	3 094	34	96 410
Primorsk Shipping Corporation	Transportation	332	384	96	134	1 305	2 611
Far Eastern Shipping Co[b]	Transport	123	160	101	187	233	5 608

Notes:
[a] Including export sales by parent firm.
[b] 2001 data.

Source: UNCTAD (2004a).

However, non-resource based Russian TNCs have recently made overseas greenfield investments that are concentrated in only a few countries. For instance, Mobile Telesystems has telecommunication infrastructure projects in Belarus and Ukraine, and RusPromAuto has projects in transport equipment in Belarus, Cuba, Ukraine and Viet Nam.

Russian companies are also investing abroad through M&As (Appendix Table 14A.4). This entry strategy has become more important since 2000: in 2002–2004, Russian companies made 77 M&As, as compared with 17 in 1995–97 (Table 14.26). More than half of Russian M&A purchases in 1995–2004 were concentrated in transition economies. In the developed world, Russian companies have bought companies principally in the United Kingdom, the United States and Germany. Most Russian M&A purchases were confined to a few key industries in services and manufacturing (Table 14.27). However, most of the large M&As were in natural resources or heavy industries (Appendix Table 14A.4). A few Russian

Table 14.26   *Russian Federation: geographic distribution of cross-border M&A purchases by Russian companies, 1995–2004 (number of deals)*

Economy	1995	1996	1997	1998	1999	2000	2001	2002	2003	2004	1995–2004
Total world	2	12	3	7	8	12	22	21	31	25	143
Developed countries	1	6	1	3	3	4	12	10	10	13	63
Lithuania	–	–	–	–	–	2	–	3	2	2	9
United Kingdom	–	–	–	–	1	1	1	1	1	1	6
United States	–	–	–	–	–	–	1	1	1	3	6
Czech Republic	–	–	–	1	–	–	–	–	–	4	5
Germany	1	–	–	–	–	–	1	2	1	–	5
Latvia	–	–	–	–	2	–	1	–	1	–	4
Netherlands	–	1	–	–	–	–	2	–	–	1	4
Developing economies	–	–	–	–	–	–	–	2	1	1	4
Mongolia	–	–	–	–	–	–	–	2	–	–	2
Turkey	–	–	–	–	–	–	–	–	–	1	1
China	–	–	–	–	–	–	–	–	1	–	1
Transition economies	1	6	2	4	5	8	10	9	20	11	76
Ukraine	–	1	1	–	1	7	2	6	3	4	25
Armenia	–	–	–	–	–	–	–	–	6	2	8
Belarus	–	1	1	–	–	1	3	–	–	1	7
Uzbekistan	–	–	–	–	–	–	1	1	3	2	7
Bulgaria	1	1	–	–	1	–	1	1	1	–	6
Georgia	–	–	–	3	–	–	1	–	–	–	4
Kazakhstan	–	–	–	–	1	–	1	–	–	2	4

Source: UNCTAD, cross-border M&A database.

Table 14.27   Russian Federation: industry distribution of cross-border M&A purchases by Russian companies, 1995–2004 (number of deals)

Industry	1995	1996	1997	1998	1999	2000	2001	2002	2003	2004	1995–2004
Total industry	2	12	3	7	8	12	22	21	31	25	143
Primary	–	–	–	–	–	–	–	2	1	–	3
Agriculture, forestry, and fishing	–	–	–	–	–	–	–	1	–	–	1
Mining	–	–	–	–	–	–	–	1	1	–	2
Secondary	1	6	1	4	6	4	8	12	15	10	67
Food, beverages and tobacco	–	1	–	–	1	–	1	1	5	–	9
Oil and gas; petroleum refining	–	2	–	1	–	2	1	3	2	3	14
Chemicals and chemical products	1	1	–	–	1	1	3	1	2	–	10
Metal and metal products	–	–	–	1	1	–	2	3	3	5	15
Services	1	6	2	3	2	8	14	7	15	15	73
Electric, gas and water distribution	1	–	–	–	1	–	1	–	3	2	8
Trade	–	–	–	–	1	3	1	–	2	2	9
Transport, storage and communications	–	–	1	–	–	–	–	2	4	4	11
Finance	–	5	1	1	–	4	10	2	4	5	32
Of which Commercial banks, bank holding companies	–	4	1	1	–	3	6	2	1	2	20
Insurance	–	–	–	–	–	1	2	–	2	2	7

Source: UNCTAD, cross-border M&A database.

telecommunication companies have entered the fray: for example, Vimpelcom bought Kar-Tel Ltd. (Kazakhstan) for $425 million in 2004.

Drivers and Motivations

OFDI from the Russian Federation seems to be driven, at least partly, by a set of factors different from those of the other BRIC countries. Avoiding high taxes (Bulatov, 1998), regulatory constraints at home and the business climate (Kalotay, 2002) are relevant here. The exploitation of technological leads in such industries as aerospace had influenced earlier Russian OFDI (Elenkov, 1995). The improved financial position of Russian national resource firms (based on high prices for such resources in export markets) has been a factor since the late 1990s (Liuhto and Jumpponen, 2002). Privatization programmes in neighbouring countries (mainly ex-socialist countries) offer opportunities to acquire strategic assets (Liuhto and Jumpponen, 2003). For resource-based Russian OFDI, the desire to control the value chain and increase global sales by establishing distribution networks abroad have been major determinants.

Government's Role and Policy Development

The government of the Russian Federation does not have a specific policy to promote OFDI by Russian companies. As in other emerging markets (see Part II in this volume), OFDI is sometimes regarded with suspicion, partly because these countries consider themselves as capital-importing countries, partly because OFDI may be suspected to be linked to capital flight. Capital controls exist, and (according to the December 2003 Currency Law) approval from the Central Bank is needed for OFDI above $10 million.

Barring economic crises, the prospects for further growth of OFDI from the Russian Federation are promising. Resource-based, export-oriented Russian TNCs will continue to expand abroad to strengthen the control of their value chains and global market reach. The drive to diversify and spread their operations internationally will add to further growth, as would a stronger national economy. The global competition for access to resources, including distribution facilities, will tempt more Russian firms to go abroad to match their competitors' moves. Competition at home will also increase once the country joins the WTO, forcing domestic firms to increase their competitiveness, including through OFDI. A new phenomenon in the country's OFDI pattern is the growing investment made by non-resource based firms. As the experiences of these companies in terms of the benefits of transnationalization are appreciated by other, non-resource based firms, they are likely to follow suit, seeking to improve their competitiveness by securing markets and technology, as well as building global brands. Diversification will remain a key motivation for future OFDI.

INDIA: A NEW VIGOUR[26]

Salient Features

Indian firms have been investing abroad for a long time (Lall, 1986), but it is only since the economic reforms launched in 1991 that it started to pick up. Still, India is only the 20th-largest investor from the emerging markets in

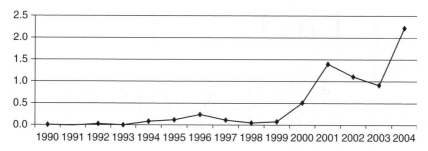

Source: UNCTAD, www.unctad.org/fdistatistics, and Reserve Bank of India, www.rbi.org.in/.

Figure 14.11 India: outward FDI flows, 1990–2004 (billions of dollars)

terms of stock. Its outward FDI flows have risen rapidly, particularly since 1999 (Figure 14.11). The country's OFDI stock – the result of investment by perhaps as many as 1700 Indian firms in some 3000 foreign affiliates (Table 14.16) – rose from less than $0.05 billion in 1990 to $6.6 billion in March 2004. The United States and the Russian Federation were the two main destinations for Indian OFDI flows, driven by different sets of motives that correspond to those two countries' location advantages – the former for technology and markets, the latter for oil and gas.[27] The two countries accounted for more than one-third of Indian OFDI during fiscal years 1996–2005 (Table 14.28). Other important destinations include offshore financial centres such as Mauritius, the British Virgin Islands and Bermuda, suggesting that financial motives, in particular tax privileges, are another driver of Indian OFDI. Asia is the largest region for Indian OFDI, led by significant outflows to Hong Kong (China), Singapore and Viet Nam. Between April 1999 and November 2004, payments by Indian affiliates to their parent firms in India (dividends; payments for technical know-how, royalties, engineering fees and consultancies) amounted to $890 million (Table 14.29).

Reflecting the sectoral composition of India's leading TNCs (Table 14.30), more than half of India's OFDI in fiscal years 1999–2005 was concentrated in manufacturing (especially fertilizers, pesticides and seeds; drugs and pharmaceuticals), followed by non-financial services (37 percent), which include IT, business processing operations and media broadcasting and publishing (Table 14.31). However, in 2004–2005, non-financial services (including software development) overtook manufacturing for the first time since 2001–2002, suggesting that the services sector may take the lead in the transnationalization of Indian firms. This also reflects the structural shift of the Indian economy towards the services sector which, today, accounts for half of the country's GDP.

Table 14.28 India geographic distribution of approved outward FDI flows, top 20 destinations, fiscal years 1996–2005[a] (millions of dollars; per cent)

| Economy | Fiscal year | | | | | | | Total | |
	1996/2000	2000/2001	2001/2002	2002/2003	2003/2004	2004/2005[b]		April 1996–Nov 2004	Share
United States	378.5	734.2	428.1	185.3	207.1	212.2		2 145.4	18.8
Russian Federation	3.3	3.5	1 741.9	0.2	1.4	1.1		1 751.4	15.3
Mauritius	221.6	242.3	154.5	133.4	175.6	78.4		1 005.7	8.8
Sudan	–	–	–	750.0	162.0	–		912.0	8.0
British Virgin Islands	752.1	18.0	6.4	3.3	4.9	18.7		803.4	7.0
Bermuda	156.9	0.7	75.0	29.0	142.5	221.3		625.3	5.5
United Kingdom	269.8	55.3	85.5	34.5	138.5	36.9		615.6	5.4
Hong Kong, China	391.4	37.6	16.1	14.8	16.2	55.0		531.1	4.6
Australia	2.6	2.5	1.9	95.0	92.9	139.4		334.3	2.9
Singapore	88.5	39.4	25.0	46.8	15.9	36.7		251.3	2.2
Viet Nam	0.4	0.2	228.2	0.1	0.0	0.1		228.9	2.0
Netherlands	49.1	65.7	43.1	15.9	30.2	21.3		225.4	2.0
Oman	139.8	64.9	0.2	0.4	1.5	5.0		211.7	1.9
United Arab Emirates	87.2	11.3	11.8	12.6	32.1	18.5		173.4	1.5
Sri Lanka	51.8	8.4	1.4	6.6	44.5	7.7		120.4	1.1
Kazakhstan	3.2	–	1.3	0.1	75.0	39.1		118.6	1.0

Iran	59.2	–	–	43.6	0.5	0.2	103.4	0.9
China	17.1	7.9	13.3	29.6	26.6	8.9	103.4	0.9
France	2.6	1.8	0.7	1.8	84.4	9.7	101.0	0.9
Malta	–	–	21.7	24.4	40.3	0.8	87.1	0.8
Memorandum:								
Brazil	2.5	5.4	5.1	5.2	5.0	8.9	32.0	0.3
Total	3 138.8	1 377.2	3 027.0	1 472.1	1 450.9	986.9	11 434.8	100.0

Notes:
[a] Data cover equity, loans and guarantees.
[b] Covers April–November 2004.

Source: Ministry of Finance, India.

Table 14.29   *India: inflows of dividends and other technical fees from Indian joint ventures and wholly-owned subsidiaries abroad, fiscal years 1999–2004 (millions of dollars)*

Fiscal year	Dividends	Others (tech. know-how, royalty, engineering fees, consultancy, etc.)	Total
1999/2000	17.6	31.6	49.2
2000/2001	12.5	38.9	51.4
2001/2002	36.3	243.0	279.3
2002/2003	33.6	68.7	102.3
2003/2004	19.0	324.5	343.5
2004/2005[a]	12.0	52.0	63.9
Total	131.0	758.6	889.6

Note: [a] Covers April–November 2004.

Source: Ministry of Finance, India.

In particular, a relatively recent phenomenon is the overseas expansion of Indian software and service providers. Since the acquisition of British Telecom's business process operation in Belfast, Northern Ireland, by HCL in 2001, more Indian business process operation firms are seeing the benefits of going abroad to expand markets and their client base, including to secure orders for customized services from firms that are reluctant to outsource business to an offshore location. Companies such as Tata Consultancy, Infosys Technologies, Wipro, Birlasoft, Daksh eServices and Datamatics Technologies have operations in many host countries. Secova eServices, a human resource firm, recently acquired Empact EBS (United States), Office Tiger took over a London-based recruiting and outsourcing firm, and ICICI OneSource acquired a 51 percent stake of Pipal Research (United States) and Account Solutions Group (United States), a consumer collections agency; these are examples of Indian service firms carrying out IT service activities beyond India. By the end of 2004, 480 Indian companies had invested in the United Kingdom, most in the IT business,[28] making India the tenth-largest investor in that country. In fact Indian FDI in the United Kingdom was higher that year than United Kingdom investment to India. Not only are large IT firms such as Infosys and Wipro investing abroad, but mid-sized ones are doing so as well. For instance, Take Solutions acquired 4BSoft (United States) in February 2005 for $1 million with the aim to expand its reach in overseas markets.[29]

Greenfield OFDI remains an important market entry strategy (Appendix Tables 14A.4 and 14A.5). But cross-border M&As (and not

Table 14.30 Selected large TNCs headquartered in India, early 2000 (millions of dollars and number)

Company	Industry	Foreign assets	Total assets	Employees
Industrial				
Reliance Industries Limited	Petroleum refining	278.3	13 493.0	12 915
Tata Tea Company Limited	Food preparations, not elsewhere classified	170.6	804.5	56 099
Aurobindo Pharma	Pharmaceutical preparations	144.1	334.3	2 450
Doctor Reddy's Laboratories Limited	Pharmaceutical preparations	144.0	490.5	5 852
Sterlite Industries Limited	Copper smelting & refining	133.1	1 414.0	–
Larsen & Toubro	Construction machinery	99.8	2 754.7	–
Asian Paints (India) Limited	Paints, varnishes, lacquers, enamels, and allied products	88.9	280.2	–
Orient Paper & Industries Limited	Hydraulic cement	82.9	217.1	4 208
Southern Petrochemicals Industries Limited	Phosphate fertilizers	82.8	906.4	2 591
Wockhardt Limited	Pharmaceutical preparations	67.5	243.9	2 928
Tertiary				
Saty am Computer Services Limited -ADR	Prepackaged software	127.3	596.3	9 759
Tata Infotech Limited	Data processing services	17.8	82.7	2 700
Digital Globalsoft	Computer programming services	16.9	83.2	2 490
Sonata Software Limited	Prepackaged software	15.4	35.8	645
CMC Limited	Computer programming services	12.0	103.8	3 368
Hinduja TMT	Prepackaged software	7.4	124.7	–
Infosys Technologies Limited	Computer programming services	–	823.9	15 356
Indian Hotels Company Limited	Hotels & motels	–	638.4	7 540
Pentamedia Graphics Limited	Prepackaged software	–	320.1	–

Table 14.30 (continued)

Company	Industry	Foreign assets	Total assets	Employees
Finance and insurance				
Bank of India	National Commercial Banks	3 845.4	16 168.2	43 141
Bank of Baroda	National Commercial Banks	2 415.6	16 490.1	40 313
Canara Bank	National Commercial Banks	312.8	17 543.0	47 566

Source: Thomson Analytics, http://analytics.thomsonib.com/; Dun and Bradstreet, 2003.

Table 14.31   India: industry distribution of approved outward FDI flows, fiscal years 1999–2005[a]

Fiscal year	Industry										Total
	Manufacturing		Financial services		Non financial services		Trading		Others		
	Amount	Percentage	Amount	Percentage	Amount	Percentage	Amount	Percentage	Amount	Percentage	
1999/2000	548.8	31.2	4.3	0.2	1 143.5	65.1	58.3	3.3	2.3	0.1	1 757.0
2000/2001	370.7	26.8	16.6	1.2	876.5	63.4	89.2	6.5	29.1	2.1	1 382.2
2001/2002	2 210.9	73.1	48.6	1.6	565.5	18.7	139.2	4.6	61.3	2.0	3 025.5
2002/2003	1 056.7	71.9	1.8	0.1	280.2	19.1	69.9	4.8	61.7	4.2	1 470.3
2003/2004	765.6	52.8	35.1	2.4	438.8	30.2	76.9	5.3	134.1	9.2	1 450.6
2004/2005[b]	432.4	43.8	4.0	0.4	437.4	44.3	40.4	4.1	73.0	7.4	987.2
Total 1999–2005	5 385.2	53.5	110.4	1.1	3 741.9	37.1	473.9	4.7	361.6	3.6	10 072.8

Notes:
[a] Data cover equity, loans and guarantees.
[b] Covers April–November 2004.

Source: India, Ministry of Finance.

only by large firms) have become increasingly popular, particularly for entry into developed countries, facilitated by good corporate profitability and financial reserves. M&As are taking place in all sectors (Appendix Table 14A.4 and Table 14.32), often involving large-value transactions. Most Indian M&As in developing countries were in Asia (Table 14.33). The preferences of Indian TNCs are also shifting from minority-owned foreign affiliates to majority-owned ones. At the same time, reinvested earnings are becoming a major component of OFDI, implying decreasing reliance on the home country as a source of finance for expansion abroad.

Drivers and Motivations

Growing competitiveness based on improved ownership advantages (especially, most recently, in IT industries) and improved profitability and financial strength have been key drivers of the transnationalization of Indian enterprises; these include, increasingly, also small and medium-sized firms. These capabilities combine with the desire to gain access to technology, distribution networks, skills, markets and brand names. Important also is the need for Indian exporters to help them penetrate foreign markets through on-the-spot after-sale services. Moreover, the desire of Indian firms to secure natural resources in such areas as energy and commodities has driven them to invest in such resource-rich countries as Australia, Indonesia, Sudan, the Russian Federation, and West and Central Asia. The increasing shift of the Indian economy towards open markets has also contributed to the drive to expand operations overseas. In this respect, India exemplifies what was discussed earlier in this chapter, namely that, in a globalizing world economy in which imports, inward investment and technology imports are liberalized (and, in the case of India, the industrial licensing system is being dismantled), national firms have to go abroad to establish their own portfolio of locational assets as a source of corporate competitiveness.

Building brand names – or strengthening the use of Indian brand names abroad – has played a role in the acquisition of Daewoo Commercial Vehicle Company (Republic of Korea) by Tata Motors Ltd., Infosys Technologies' acquisition of Expert Information Services Pty. Ltd (Australia), Ranbaxy Technologies' acquisition of RPG Aventis (France) and Tata Tea's acquisition of Tetley Tea (United Kingdom). Similarly, acquiring foreign firms that are technology and knowledge intensive is a strategic move to strengthen a firm's competitiveness. Such moves by Indian firm's include Wipro's acquisition of Nerve Wire Inc (United States), I-Flex's acquisition of Supersolutions Corp (United States) and Reliance Infocomm's acquisition of Flag Telecom (United Kingdom). Setting up R&D facilities abroad provides another channel for accessing

Table 14.32   India: industry distribution of cross-border M&A purchases by Indian companies, 1995–2004 (number of deals)

Industry	1995	1996	1997	1998	1999	2000	2001	2002	2003	2004	1995–2004
Total industry	8	3	9	5	15	32	21	22	36	56	207
Primary	1	–	1	–	1	1	1	1	2	–	8
Agriculture, forestry, and fishing	1	–	–	–	–	–	–	–	–	–	1
Mining	–	–	1	–	1	1	1	1	2	–	7
Secondary	7	1	2	2	7	8	4	9	16	21	77
Chemicals and chemical products	2	1	–	1	1	3	–	4	8	8	28
Metal and metal products	–	–	1	1	–	1	–	–	4	3	10
Oil and gas; Petroleum refining	1	–	1	–	1	1	1	1	–	3	10
Electrical and electronic equipment	–	–	–	–	2	1	1	1	–	1	6
Food, beverages and tobacco	1	–	–	–	–	1	–	2	–	1	5
Machinery	1	–	–	–	2	1	–	–	–	1	5
Services	–	2	6	3	7	23	16	12	18	35	122
Business activities	–	2	6	3	5	21	13	7	14	22	82
Of which: prepackaged software business services	–	–	–	–	2	7	6	3	2	5	25
Finance	–	1	5	2	1	1	–	2	–	1	13
Transport, storage and communications	–	–	1	–	–	1	–	2	1	2	7
Hotels and restaurants	–	1	–	–	–	–	–	–	–	3	4
Trade	–	–	–	–	–	–	1	–	–	3	4

Source: UNCTAD, cross-border M&A database.

Table 14.33   India: geographic distribution of cross-border M&A purchases by Indian companies, 1995–2004 (number of deals)

Economy	1995	1996	1997	1998	1999	2000	2001	2002	2003	2004	1995–2004
Total world	8	3	9	5	15	32	21	22	36	56	207
Developed countries	7	3	7	3	7	25	16	20	22	35	145
United States	2	–	1	1	4	15	11	7	10	15	66
United Kingdom	–	1	3	1	1	4	2	8	7	6	33
Germany	1	–	–	–	–	2	2	2	1	5	13
Australia	–	1	2	–	–	3	1	–	2	3	12
France	1	–	–	–	–	–	–	–	1	2	4
Italy	1	–	–	–	2	–	–	–	1	–	4
Developing economies	1	–	2	2	8	6	4	2	14	20	59
Singapore	–	–	–	–	3	1	1	1	1	4	11
Sri Lanka	1	–	–	–	3	–	–	–	2	–	6
United Arab Emirates	–	–	–	–	–	–	2	–	1	2	5
Malaysia	–	–	–	1	–	–	1	–	1	1	4
Egypt	–	–	–	–	–	–	–	–	–	3	3
Sudan	–	–	–	–	–	–	–	–	1	2	3
Transition economies	–	–	–	–	–	1	1	–	–	1	3
Bosnia and Herzegovina	–	–	–	–	–	–	–	–	–	1	1
Romania	–	–	–	–	–	1	–	–	–	–	1
Russian Federation	–	–	–	–	–	–	1	–	–	–	1

Source: UNCTAD, cross-border M&A database.

technologies and knowledge. For instance, Tata Consultancy has set up development centres in countries such as China and the United States.

Indian firms have also increased their efforts to secure supplies of natural resources to meet growing demand at home. Backed by the government, Indian firms have been actively making acquisitions of oil and gas fields abroad. Hindalco's acquisition of copper mines in Australia, ONGC's acquisition of oil fields in Sudan, ONGC–Videsh's acquisition of a 20 percent stake in the Sakhalin-1 oil and gas field in the Russian Federation, are examples. More recently, ONGC received approval from the government to buy a 15 percent stake of Yuganskneftegas in the Russian Federation for an estimated $2 billion,[30] and Indian Oil Corporation made a $3 billion deal for a gas field in Iran.

Government's Role and Policy Development

Prime Minister Manmohan Singh has encouraged Indian firms to go global, asserting that 'All our firms, be they in the public sector or the private sector, must become more competitive so that they can face increased competition with success from abroad . . . many Indian firms today do have the managerial leadership to go global and compete at the global level . . . we need to understand how we can replicate such success stories so that more and more India firms go global.'[31] This stance reflects a significant policy change on OFDI:

> The government policy with respect to outward FDI (O-FDI) also has been successively liberalized . . . The O-FDI policy that existed during 1974–91 was highly restrictive and intended to discourage outward FDI by Indian enterprises as the country itself was suffering from resource scarcity. Joint ventures with minority Indian equity were permitted. The policy had used O-FDI as a means of export promotion by prohibiting cash remittances towards equity participation and requiring that it should be in the form of exports of Indian made capital goods and know-how. During 1990s government had instituted an automatic approval system for O-FDI and successively had raised the permissible investment limit and reduced other regular constraints in promoting Indian direct investment abroad. (Pradhan, 2003, pp. 23–4)

This change was accompanied by a geographical reorientation, from South–South cooperation towards global competitiveness.

Since 2000, in particular, significant policy changes were introduced (Box 14.2). OFDI procedures have been streamlined and foreign exchange controls have been considerably relaxed to make overseas investment easier. Various restrictions such as investment ceilings under the automatic route and profitability conditions have been lifted. Sectoral restrictions such as those on overseas investment in agricultural activities have been relaxed. Indian companies can make 100 percent wholly-owned overseas acquisitions in unrelated businesses.

In addition to policy liberalization and facilitating OFDI, the Prime Minister and ministers have included Indian firms in their teams for visits to other countries.

The prospects for further growth of Indian OFDI (whose past characteristics are captured in Figure 14.12) are promising. Improved enterprise competitiveness, profitability, strengthened financial resources and the need to be global players will encourage further growth in overseas investment. A further liberalization and streamlining of approval procedures would add to the impetus for Indian firms to transnationalize their activities. So would active backing by the government. In this respect, the government has already taken steps to encourage and support OFDI by Indian firms through the provision of information and increasing the number of BITs signed with numerous countries. Also important are the government's policies to improve the country's locational advantages, especially as regards skill formation, institution building and improvements in the infrastructure.

BOX 14.2   SELECTED SIGNIFICANT INDIAN
             OVERSEAS INVESTMENT POLICY
             CHANGES SINCE 2000

- Indian companies can make overseas investment in joint ventures and wholly-owned subsidiaries by market purchases of foreign exchange without prior approval of the Reserve Bank of India of up to 100 percent of their net worth, up from the previous limit of 50 percent.[a]

- An Indian company with a proven track-record is allowed to invest up to 100 percent of its net worth within the overall limit of $100 million by way of market purchases for investment in a foreign entity engaged in any bona fide business activity starting fiscal year 2003/2004. The provision restricting overseas investment in the same activity as its core activity at home of the Indian company is removed.[b] Listed Indian companies, residents and mutual funds are permitted to invest abroad in companies listed on a recognized stock exchange and in a company that has the shareholding of at least 10 percent in an Indian company listed on a recognized stock exchange in India.

- The annual limit on overseas investment was raised to $100 million (up from $50 million) and the limit for direct investment in South-Asian Association for Regional Cooperation countries (excluding Pakistan) and Myanmar was raised to $150 million (up from $75 million); for Rupee investment in Nepal and Bhutan the limit was raised to Rs. 700 millions (up from Rs. 350 millions) under the automatic route.[c]

- Indian companies in special economic zones can freely make overseas investment up to any amount without the restriction of the $50 million ceiling under the automatic route, provided the funding is done out of the Exchange Earners Foreign Currency Account balances.[d]

- The three years profitability condition has been removed for Indian companies making overseas investment under the automatic route.[e]

- Overseas investment is allowed to be funded up to 100 percent by American Depository Receipt/Global Depository Receipt proceeds, up from the previous ceiling of 50 percent.[f]

- An Indian party that has exhausted the limit of $100 million a year may apply to the Reserve Bank of India for a block allocation of foreign exchange subject to such terms and conditions as may be necessary.[g]
- Overseas investment was opened to registered partnership firms and companies that provide professional services.[h] The minimum net worth of Rs. 150 million for Indian companies engaged in financial activities in India was removed for investment abroad in the financial industry.
- During fiscal year 2003/2004, the policy on Indian OFDI was further streamlined with the following changes:
  (i)   Indian firms are allowed to invest in agricultural activities overseas, which was previously restricted, either directly or through an overseas branch; and
  (ii) Investment in joint ventures or wholly-owned subsidiary abroad by way of share swaps is permitted under the automatic route.
- On 7 July 2004, the Reserve Bank announced that an Indian party may acquire shares of a foreign company engaged in bonafide business activity.[i] Since May 2005, eligible Indian entities are permitted to invest in overseas joint ventures and wholly-owned subsidiaries up to 200 percent of their net worth under the automatic route for overseas investment.[j]

Source: Reserve Bank of India and Ministry of Finance, 'Indian direct investment in JVs/WOS abroad', 27 February 2004, August 2004 and 1 April 2005 http://finmin.nic.in/the_ministry/dept_eco_affairs/investment_div/idi_ December2003.htm,
http://finmin.nic.in/the_ministry/dept_eco_affairs/investment_div/idi_dec 2004.htm,
http://finmin.nic.in/the_ministry/dept_eco_affairs/investment_div/ invest_index.htm

Notes:
a. Reserve Bank of India Notification No. 83/RB 2003; 1 March 2003.
b. Reserve Bank of India Notification No. 83/RB 2003; 1 March 2003.
c. Reserve Bank of India Notification No. FEMA.53/2002-RB; 1 March 2002 and FEMA.79/2002-RB; 10 December 2002.
d. Reserve Bank of India Notification No. FEMA.49/2002-RB; 19 January 2002.
e. Reserve Bank of India Notification No. FEMA.40/2001-RB; 2 March 2001.
f. Reserve Bank of India Notification No. FEMA.40/2001-RB; 2 March 2001.
g. Reserve Bank of India Notification No. FEMA.49/2002-RB; 2 March 2001.
h. Reserve Bank of India Notification No. FEMA.40/2001-RB; 2 March 2001.
i. Reserve Bank of India Notification No. FEMA 120/RB-2004, 7 July 2004.
j. Reserve Bank of India/2005/463 A.P., Circular No. 42, 12 May 2005.

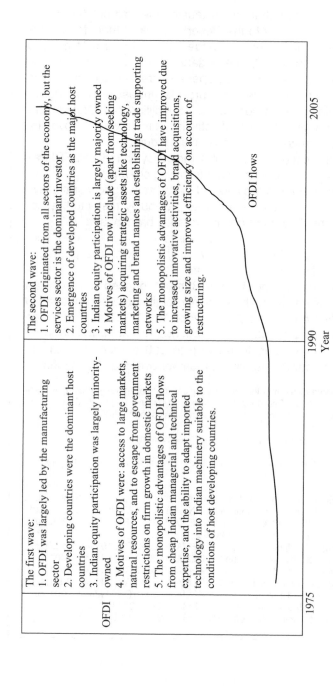

	The first wave:	The second wave:
OFDI	1. OFDI was largely led by the manufacturing sector 2. Developing countries were the dominant host countries 3. Indian equity participation was largely minority-owned 4. Motives of OFDI were: access to large markets, natural resources, and to escape from government restrictions on firm growth in domestic markets 5. The monopolistic advantages of OFDI flows from cheap Indian managerial and technical expertise, and the ability to adapt imported technology into Indian machinery suitable to the conditions of host developing countries.	1. OFDI originated from all sectors of the economy, but the services sector is the dominant investor 2. Emergence of developed countries as the major host countries 3. Indian equity participation is largely majority owned 4. Motives of OFDI now include (apart from/seeking markets) acquiring strategic assets like technology, marketing and brand names and establishing trade supporting networks 5. The monopolistic advantages of OFDI have improved due to increased innovative activities, brand acquisitions, growing size and improved efficiency on account of restructuring.

OFDI flows

1975   1990   2005
Year

Note: This is a free-hand drawn graph.

Source: Pradhan (2005), p. 37.

Figure 14.12   Characteristics of India's OFDI flows, 1975 onwards

More countries are now wooing Indian OFDI, including various South Asian and ASEAN countries, Germany, France and the Russian Federation. For instance, during his visit to India in late 2004, the president of the Russian Federation encouraged Indian high-technology companies to invest in Russia.[32]

CHINA: GOING GLOBAL[33]

Salient Features

China is the seventh-largest investor among emerging markets. The country's OFDI flows rose to $3.6 billion in 2004, from $2.9 billion in 2003 (Figure 14.13). Its OFDI stock increased by 15 times during 1990–2004, from $2.5 billion to $38 billion. The latter is larger than (or comparable to) the OFDI stock of countries such as Ireland, Portugal or Norway. Some 2000 Chinese firms (of which 43 percent are state-owned) have invested in 139 countries, establishing some 4550 foreign affiliates (one-fifth of them in Hong Kong, China). More than 70 percent of the approved non-financial OFDI was accounted for by ten top destinations (Table 14.34). Most Chinese OFDI is located in developing countries. Chinese TNCs can be found in all sectors. In terms of value, two-thirds of the country's OFDI is in the services sector and one-fifth in natural resources (Table 14.35). Recently, OFDI has seen an upsurge in mining- and energy-related industries, which has led to a rapid increase of outflows to resource-rich Latin American countries.

Hong Kong (China) accounted for the lion's share of China's OFDI. Close economic relationships between the two economies have made it easy for Chinese firms to establish holding companies in Hong Kong (China) and to raise finance to fund Chinese TNCs' operations in China or elsewhere. Part of China's FDI in Hong Kong (China) is sent back to the Mainland through the process of roundtripping, or it is redirected to other economies. Financial centres also figure prominently. Among developed countries, the United States and Australia are the major recipients.

Chinese firms are increasingly investing abroad through the acquisition of companies, which allows quick entry as compared with a greenfield strategy. M&As are prominent in oil and mining, but catching up in manufacturing and services (Table 14.36, Appendix Table 14A.4). Most M&A deals were in Asia, contributing to the concentration of China's OFDI in that region (Table 14.37). Chinese companies are also quite active in greenfield FDI activities. Fifteen economies accounted for more than three-fifths of Chinese greenfield FDI projects between 2002 and February 2005 (Appendix Table 14A.5).

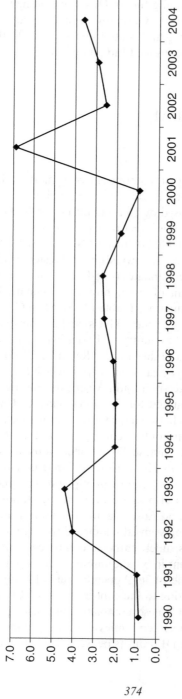

Note: ^a The methodology for reporting data changed in 2003.

Source: UNCTAD, www.unctad.org/fdistatistics, www.safe.gov.cn and MOFCOM, China.

Figure 14.13 China: outward FDI flows, 1990–2004^a (billions of dollars)

Table 14.34 *China: geographic distribution of OFDI stock, top 20*
destinations, 2003 (millions of dollars)

Rank	Economy	Value
1	Hong Kong (China)	24 600
2	Cayman Islands	3 700
3	Virgin Islands	1 500
4	United States	500
5	Macao, China	450
6	Australia	400
7	Republic of Korea	240
8	Singapore	200
9	Thailand	150
10	Zambia	140
11	Peru	130
12	Spain	100
13	Malaysia	100
14	Mexico	100
15	Japan	90
16	Germany	80
17	United Kingdom	80
18	Denmark	70
19	Russian Federation	60
20	Cambodia	60

Notes:
[a] Ranked by cumulative investment value.
[b] The number of projects refers to approved investment involving Chinese companies.

Source: UNCTAD, based on China, Ministry of Commerce (2004).

Drivers and Motivations

The growing competitiveness of Chinese firms and their ownership advantages, including strong financial reserves, are encouraging Chinese firms to transnationalize. Their desire to become global players,[34] build global brands, access technology and distribution channels, secure resources and broaden markets are among the key drivers. For example, TCL is expanding its operations in India to service the market of the SAARC region and Haier is setting up a manufacturing facility in India for market access reasons.[35]

Lenovo's acquisition of IBM's personal computer division for $1.75 billion is the most significant acquisition made to date by a Chinese IT firm to gain an international brand name and access technology and know-how. The merger of the television and DVD operations of TCL with Thomson

Table 14.35   China: OFDI stock, by sector and industry, 2003 (billions of dollars, %)

Sector/industry	Value	%
Primary sector		
Mining	5.9	18
Agriculture, forestry, animal husbandry, fishery	0.5	1
Manufacturing	2.0	6
Services		
Information technology, computer and software	10.9	33
Distribution, wholesale and retail	6.5	20
Communication, transport and storage	2.0	6
Water-conservation, environment and utilities	0.9	3
Electrical power, gas, water	0.7	2
Construction	0.7	2
Other services	2.1	6
Other	1.0	3
Total	33	100

Source: China, Ministry of Commerce (2004).

(France) through the creation of a joint-venture entity, TCL-Thomson Electronics, is another example of the strategy Chinese electronics firms use to build global brand names and access technology and markets. The joint-venture entity has factories in France, Germany, Mexico, Poland, Thailand and Viet Nam.

Chinese firms have also established R&D centres in a number of countries (India, Sweden, Singapore) to strengthen their technological assets. Huawei Technologies, for example, has set up research centres in Dallas and Silicon Valley and Bangalore, and Haier is planning to establish a research centre in India.

The desire to obtain access to natural resources has led Chinese firms (mainly state-owned enterprises) to invest in resource-rich countries in Africa, Asia, Latin America and Australia. Their activities focus on the exploration of oil and gas, the mining of such minerals as bauxite, iron and nickel, and securing other primary commodities. Firms such as COFCO, China National Chemicals Export and Import Corporation, and China Metals and Minerals have invested in Africa, China National Petroleum Company in Sudan, CNOOC in Indonesia, and CNPC in Kazakhstan, Peru and Venezuela. China Minmetals is seeking to buy Noranda Mining (Canada) for about $5.7 billion. Rising demand for resources at home encourages Chinese enterprises to go abroad to secure the supply of natural resources.

Table 14.36   China: industry distribution of cross-border M&A purchases by Chinese companies, 1995–2004 (number of deals)

Industry	1995	1996	1997	1998	1999	2000	2001	2002	2003	2004	1995–2004
Total industry	7	10	25	20	11	20	15	25	26	34	193
Primary	–	–	–	–	1	–	1	1	–	4	7
Agriculture, Forestry, and Fishing	–	–	–	–	–	–	–	1	–	1	2
Mining	–	–	–	–	1	–	1	–	–	3	5
Secondary	6	2	10	6	4	4	6	16	15	13	82
Oil and Gas, Petroleum Refining	1	1	2	1	1	1	1	4	6	4	22
Electrical and electronic equipment	2	–	2	2	1	–	3	3	4	2	19
Metal and Metal Products	–	–	2	1	–	2	–	–	1	1	7
Wood and wood products	–	–	–	2	–	–	1	3	–	–	6
Chemicals and chemical products	1	–	1	–	1	–	–	–	–	3	6
Machinery	–	–	1	–	–	–	–	2	1	1	5
Services	1	8	15	14	6	16	8	8	11	17	104
Finance	–	1	5	4	4	5	3	4	4	9	39
Business activities	1	1	1	4	1	7	2	2	3	4	26
Of which, prepackaged software	–	–	–	1	–	1	–	–	2	2	6
Business Services	–	1	–	1	–	6	2	2	–	1	13
Trade	–	1	3	–	–	2	–	1	2	1	10
Hotels and restaurants	–	1	3	3	–	–	–	–	–	1	8
Telecommunications	–	1	2	1	–	1	–	–	–	–	5

Source: UNCTAD, cross-border M&A database.

Table 14.37   China: geographic distribution of cross-border M&A purchases by Chinese companies, 1995–2004 (number of deals)

Economy	1995	1996	1997	1998	1999	2000	2001	2002	2003	2004	1995–2004
Total world	7	10	25	20	11	20	15	25	26	34	193
Developed countries	6	3	8	6	1	2	5	10	10	12	63
United States	3	–	2	2	–	1	3	4	7	3	25
Australia	1	–	1	2	1	–	–	–	1	3	9
Germany	–	1	2	–	–	–	–	1	–	2	6
Canada	1	1	–	–	–	1	–	1	–	2	6
France	–	–	1	–	–	–	–	2	–	1	4
Japan	–	–	2	–	–	–	–	1	1	–	4
Developing economies	1	7	16	14	10	18	10	14	14	21	125
Hong Kong, China	–	6	12	9	5	14	4	10	8	16	84
Singapore	–	1	–	2	2	–	4	–	–	2	11
Indonesia	–	–	–	–	–	–	–	3	3	–	6
Thailand	–	–	–	1	1	2	–	–	–	–	4
Korea Republic of	–	–	–	–	–	–	–	–	2	1	3
Transition economies	–	–	1	–	–	–	–	1	2	1	5
Azerbaijan	–	–	–	–	–	–	–	1	–	1	2
Kazakhstan	–	–	1	–	–	–	–	–	2	–	3

Source: UNCTAD, cross–border M&A database.

Finally, more intensive competition and sluggish demand at home for certain products encourage Chinese firms to expand their markets abroad. In the electronics industry, Chinese TV producers such as Konka Electronics, Skyworth and Changhong Electronic Groups, and household appliance manufacturers such as Haier and Guangdong Midea Group, are examples. Huaqi Information and Digital Technology Co invested in Singapore to produce and sell MP3 players there.[36] Chinese firms are also transferring their production in mature industries and the simple manufacturing of low-tech and low value-added products to low-cost locations (for example bicycle production in Ghana, DVD production in Indonesia.)

Government's role and policy development

The government began to allow OFDI (albeit initially only on a very selective basis) in 1979. The latest major push began in 2000, with the announcement of the 'Go Global' strategy.[37] In 2003, the State Asset Supervision and Administration Commission announced that it aimed to facilitate the development of 30 to 50 internationally competitive enterprises by 2010.[38] At the 2004 International Forum in Going Global of Chinese Companies, Vice-Commerce Minister Zhang (Zhang, 2004, p. 2) noted: 'The Chinese government will on the one hand strive to improve the quality and level of "bring in", and on the other hand encourage Chinese companies with comparative advantages to go global in a more active manner and enhance their international competitiveness'. The government has a number of objectives in mind (Box 14.3), which it supports with a number of policy measures.

BOX 14.3   CHINA'S 'GO GLOBAL' STRATEGY

In his speech to the 2004 International Forum on Going Global of Chinese Companies, Vice-Commerce Minister Zhang outlined seven aspects of the country's 'Go Global' policy, to quote:

First, gradually increasing outward investment and develop overseas processing trade and overseas assembling trade. While strengthening investment cooperation with the rest of the world, particularly developing countries and regions, we should also try every means to create jobs locally and enhancing the self-development capability of local companies.

Second, intensifying overseas cooperation of resource development. Through cooperating with other countries to prospect, exploit and develop resources such as oil and gas, minerals, forestry, fishing and economic plants, China can transfer its applicable technologies of resource development, create jobs, increase household income and fiscal revenue and strengthen self-development and export capability of local economies so as to help those countries transform their resource advantage to development advantage.

Third, contracting overseas engineering projects. Companies are encouraged to undertake project contracting and design and consulting business by providing financing. Domestic companies are supported to participate in projects in every country and region. It is aimed to form up a number of sizeable and competitive engineering companies.

The fourth aspect is to carry out overseas agricultural cooperation. The advantage of Chinese agricultural technology and equipment should be fully utilized and capable companies are encouraged to carry out projects of comprehensive agricultural development. Multiple means should be taken to establish international agricultural production and processing bases.

The fifth aspect is to facilitate overseas science, technology and talent cooperation. Companies are guided to set up R&D centers in regions endowed with intensive science and technology. They should intensify international technical exchange and cooperation and improve their innovative capability and technology.

The sixth aspect is to elevate the level of foreign-related labour service cooperation. According to the demands of international market, Chinese companies should diversify their approaches and expand the scope of labour service cooperation while progressively perfect management system.

The seventh aspect is to promote cooperation in the field of trade in services. Chinese companies are encouraged to go abroad and engage themselves in trade, distribution, banking, insurance, securities, futures, fund management, telecommunication and information, logistics and shipping, and intermediary services. They are expected to intensify international exchange in service trade in order to facilitate international trade and investment.

Source: Zhang (2004), pp. 4–5.

In particular, the government has taken a series of measures to relax and streamline the approval process and procedures. It has also relaxed foreign exchange controls. The approval ceiling for provincial authorities has been raised to $30 million from $1 million for natural resource-oriented investment and from $1 million to $3 million for non-resource and non-financial investment projects. Since October 2004, OFDI applications to and approval from MOFCOM can be made through a website, and companies do not have to attach feasibility studies to their investment proposals.[39] The number of investment destinations requiring approval from the Ministry of Commerce (as opposed to local authorities) was cut from 30 to 7.[40] The EXIM bank and commercial banks in China have been encouraged to provide preferential interest loans to support Chinese firms going abroad.[41] Fiscal incentives are also provided to qualifying projects, especially for firms that bring machinery, plant and equipment along with them in their overseas ventures. The government especially promotes OFDI in natural resources, R&D activities and projects promoting the export of domestic technologies, products and labor.[42]

Other measures taken by the government include such activities as information gathering, policy discussion and the provision of information. Various seminars on the internationalization of Chinese enterprises have been organized by the government, along with international investment fairs held in different parts of the country. The government has also established an on-line reporting system for firms to report on FDI barriers and discrimination in host countries, with a view towards helping to resolve difficulties through bilateral consultations. Outbound investment missions led by the government have also taken place, with the participation of many firms. The government has supported investment promotion programs for officials in a number of countries, including Bangladesh, India, Pakistan and Sri Lanka, to identify ways to attract Chinese investment to those countries.[43] Finally, investment promotion agencies at all levels now deal not only with inward FDI, but also with OFDI.

With the government's support, more Chinese firms will become significant international players. A testimony to the latter includes the growing number of countries setting up investment promotion offices in various cities in China to attract Chinese FDI. For instance, Denmark, Ireland, Malaysia, Scotland, Singapore, Sweden, Thailand and Wales have each established at least one office in China for that purpose.

The prospects for further growth of OFDI from China are bright. For a number of reasons, Chinese firms need – and want – to become global players. The government is supportive. The BITs and DTTs signed by China with many countries provide a framework and reduce investment risk. The various bilateral free-trade agreements that China has concluded with ASEAN and other countries help. The closer economic relationship that the government is fostering with various countries will also encourage Chinese OFDI. For instance, during his tour of Latin America in November 2004, President Hu Jintao announced that China planned to invest substantial amounts in the region over the next decade.[44] Minmetals had committed $500 million each to mining projects in Cuba and Peru, and is negotiating a $1 billion venture in Brazil. China also plans to invest (including through OFDI) $12 billion in the Russian Federation before 2020 mainly in petroleum.[45] Not surprising, then, that a number of investment promotion agencies around the world consider China among the top five home countries worldwide (UNCTAD, 2004b, pp. 15–16). While this is not the case when the actual data are checked, it nevertheless reflects the expectations investment promotion officials have as regards the transnationalization of Chinese firms.

CONCLUSIONS

The liberalization of international economic transactions and the more intense competition that this entails have changed the framework within which governments of emerging markets operate today. In particular, this makes the international competitiveness of national firms more important for national economic performance. In this context, limitations on OFDI appear in a new light, as they hinder the ability of national firms – and often the most competitive among them – to develop a portfolio of locational assets as a source of corporate competitiveness. Governments are therefore liberalizing their OFDI policies (and a number have moved on to the actual promotion of such investment), seeking to weigh balance-of-payments constraints with the competitiveness requirements of individual firms. More broadly, OFDI adds to and deepens the integration of emerging markets into the world economy.

The BRICs, too, have reconsidered their OFDI policies, or are in the process of doing so. This complements their policies towards inward FDI, although the extent to which individual BRICs attract such investment is quite uneven. Moreover, all four of them have the potential to attract more FDI. Such inflows have helped in their development process, including the rise of competitive indigenous firms.[46]

As a number of indigenous BRIC firms developed ownership-specific advantages, they have begun to invest abroad, for a variety of reasons. Underlying them is the need to complement their existing portfolio of proprietary assets and managerial capabilities with an appropriate portfolio of locational assets as a source of corporate competitiveness. BRIC firms follow in this respect other firms in developing countries that are already quite transnationalized, as they follow their rivals from developed countries. Although there are quite a number of TNCs (including small and medium-sized ones) headquartered in the BRICs, few of them are truly global players compared with those from developed countries, few command world industry leadership, possess global brand names, have world-class management skills and superior business models. Rather, many grapple with the issues that corporate transnationalization entails, ranging from various managerial and organizational matters to issues related to operating in often little-known and risky foreign markets.[47] And many BRIC firms (including small and medium-sized enterprises) that face global competition at home have not yet made the step to transnationalize; however, if the experience of firms from other countries is a guide, they too will need to consider this step. (Most of the world's 60 000 plus TNCs are actually small and medium-sized enterprises.)

What this requires is a two-pronged approach:

1. Governments of emerging outward-investor countries need, first of all, to be aware of the importance of OFDI for the competitiveness of their firms. With that in mind, they need to consider what they can do to create an optimal enabling regulatory framework for their firms that

are transnationalizing or have the potential to be so. They can learn from developed countries, many of which have such a framework in place (see above), as they can learn from a number of developing countries that have already moved in this direction. However, some developing-country governments may face a special dilemma in this respect: as developing countries, they see themselves as capital-importing, not capital-exporting countries; at the same time, they have firms that are already internationally competitive and need to strength their competitiveness further through OFDI. In most cases, the solution to this dilemma may lie in a careful sequencing of policy reforms and the putting into place of various instruments, ranging from the liberalization of OFDI flows to the offering of support to outward investors and the establishment of a dedicated institution to help firms go abroad, in a phased manner. Learning from best practices elsewhere offers a shortcut for emerging outward investors, perhaps facilitated through exchange-of-experiences workshops.

2. Business schools in developing countries and economies in transition in which a number of firms are in the process of transnationalizing (or are at the threshold of doing so) need to offer courses or study groups that cater to the specific problems these firms face when establishing operations abroad. (The Global Players project of the Fundaçao Dom Cabral is an example – Box 14.1.) Such courses could cover subjects such as the development of competitive advantages in a global market, how to identify investment opportunities, assessing the investment environment, strategic options, business plan development, risk management, organizational and human resources issues, governance, training and financing possibilities. Naturally, such courses could also be offered by schools elsewhere. Beyond that, exchanges of experiences among corporate executives from emerging outward-investor countries would be useful.

But the conversation also needs to bring together policy-makers and corporate executives, so that the former understand the needs of business and the latter understand the constraints of governments. This is one of the challenges that an increasing number of emerging markets are facing.

NOTES

1. The author (karlsauvant@earthlink.net) wishes to acknowledge very helpful contributions by Kee Hwee Wee and Masataka Fujita, as well as comments and inputs from Eddie Chen, Veen Jha, Alexandre Sampaio de Arrochela Lobo, Padma Mallampally, Jaya Prakash Pradhan, Fernando Alberto G. Sampaio C. Rocha, Marinus W. Sikkel, James Zhan, Tatiana Krylova, Hamed el Kady, Mohamed Chiraz Baly, Bradley

Boicourt and Lizanne Martinez. Slightly different versions of this chapter were presented at a conference on Meeting the Challenges of the BRICs, University of Connecticut, Storrs, CT, 29–30 April 2005, under the title 'Global Players from the BRICs: The Rise of Outward FDI from Brazil, Russia, India and China', and at the seminar on Global Players from Emerging Markets: Brazil, organized by the Ministry for Development, Industry and Foreign Trade, UNCTAD and Fundaçao Dom Cabral, São Paulo, Brazil, 30 May 2005. A part of this chapter was published in Sauvant (2005).

2. China is the largest emerging-market economy in terms of GDP, followed by the Republic of Korea, Mexico, India, Brazil and the Russian Federation. As the Republic of Korea and Mexico are members of the OECD, the BRICs are the largest non-OECD economies.

3. For the statistical discussion in this chapter, 'developed countries' consist of all members of the OECD, including all members of the European Union, except the Republic of Korea, Mexico and Turkey. 'Emerging markets', for the purpose of this chapter, consist of 'developing economies' and 'economies in transition'. The latter consist of Albania, Bosnia and Herzegovina, Bulgaria, Croatia, TFYR Macedonia, Romania, Serbia and Montenegro and the Commonwealth of Independent States (CIS: Armenia, Azerbaijan, Belarus, Georgia, Kazakhstan, Kyrgystan, Republic of Moldova, Russian Federation, Tajikistan, Turkmenistan, Ukraine and Uzbekistan); all other economies are 'developing economies'.

4. FDI data for 2004 are subject to revision. Revised data are contained in UNCTAD (2005).

5. See http://www.unctad.org/Templates/Search.asp?intItemID=1397&lang=1&frmSearch Str=Lula&frmCategory=all&section=whole#press

6. China has targeted investors before, especially the largest companies in key industries.

7. This has been shown for China; see Lall and Zhou (2005).

8. There was a burst of literature in the 1980s drawing attention to FDI by firms from developing countries – see especially Kumar and McLeod (1981); Lall (1983); Lecraw (1981); Oman (1986); Wells (1983). For a comprehensive recent survey, see Goldstein (2005). In spite of that, data are very patchy and not always reliable, and estimates have to be used often. This needs to be kept in mind for the discussion below.

9. For the results of a survey on the awareness of corporate executives as to the importance of FDI for the competitiveness of their firms, see Dunning (1996).

10. Other important sources of efficiency are a firm's proprietary or firm-specific assets and managerial experience that are in fact generally considered a precondition for engaging successfully in international production activity.

11. This is not to deny that there can also be negative effects on the home country, for example when domestic investment is replaced by foreign investment and output and employment at home are affected adversely.

12. By the end of 2004, only a few OECD countries maintained specific requirements on outward FDI. Portugal required previous authorization for the establishment of branches of credit institutions in a non-European Union member, and for the establishment in a European Union member country of branches of financial companies that are not subsidiaries of credit institutions. Japan restricted outward FDI in fishing. Turkey required prior authorization for outward FDI beyond certain minimum threshold amounts ($5 million). In addition, these and other countries maintained restrictions on the acquisition of real estate abroad by certain financial companies.

13. These countries are Austria, Belgium, Luxembourg, Denmark, France, Germany, Italy, the Netherlands, Norway, Portugal, Spain, Sweden, Switzerland, the United Kingdom, the United States.

14. The data must, however, be interpreted with caution. They are overstated as they include roundtripping (which may be around 25 percent in the case of Hong Kong, China), OFDI by foreign affiliates of (typically) developed countries TNCs in a number of economies such as Hong Kong (China), Singapore, Mauritius, Cyprus and a number of tax havens, and capital flight. On the other hand, OFDI flows from a number of emerging economies are most likely under-reported. Moreover, often firms are not allowed to transfer funds from at home but rather need to raise them locally or in international markets – in which case the extent of their international production activities is not reflected in FDI statistics.

15. Hong Kong (China), Singapore, Russian Federation, Taiwan Province of China and Brazil.
16. 'CEE' refers to the following economies (some of which are now members of the European Union): Albania, Belarus, Bosnia and Herzegovina, Bulgaria, Croatia, Czech Republic, Estonia, Hungary, Latvia, Lithuania, Republic of Moldova, Poland, Romania, Russian Federation, Serbia and Montenegro, Slovakia, Slovenia, TFYR Macedonia and Ukraine.
17. For Chinese and Russian firms, roundtripping may explain part of the relatively high transnationality index.
18. BRIC investors also are beginning to use the political risk insurance facilities of MIGA – but haltingly: between 1990 and 2004, only five guarantees (three to Brazilian firms, two to Indian) were issued (out of a total of 711), for $185 million (out of a total of $13 billion). All cases were between 1998 and 2001 (MIGA).
19. This section builds on UNCTAD's *Occasional Note*, 'Outward FDI from Brazil: poised to take off?', UNCTAD/WEB/ITE/IIA/2004/16, 7 December 2004.
20. President Lula's address at the Portugese Industrial Association, Lisbon, 11 July 2003.
21. Lecture given by the Minister for Development, Industry and Foreign Trade, Luiz Fernando Furlan, at Fundaçao Dom Cabral, 22 March 2003.
22. For instance, President Lula was accompanied by about 500 businesspersons during his visit to China in May 2004 (*International Herald Tribune*, 'China, facing shortages in Asia, aims at South American suppliers', 20 November 2004, http://www.iht.com/articles/2004/11/19/news/china.html).
23. There was little OFDI from the former Soviet Union (Hamilton, 1986). Outward investment started only on a non-negligible scale when the transition to a market economy began in Russia, including the privatizations this involved; for references to the literature, see Vahtra and Liuhto (2004), footnote 1. See also Andreff (2003).
24. As in the case of other BRICs, the data must be interpreted with caution. Roundtripping plays a role and the valuation of assets 'inherited' from the time of the USSR is difficult. At the same time, registration procedures seem to have improved, although it may be difficult to document FDI undertaken by Russian affiliates abroad in third countries. The stock figure is derived by adding 2004 OFDI flows to 2003 OFDI stock.
25. For a description of important Russian TNCs, see Vahtra and Liuhto (2004).
26. This text builds on UNCTAD's *Occasional Note*: 'India's outward FDI: against awakening?', UNCTAD/press/EB/2004/009, 20 October 2004. For a comprehensive discussion, see Pradhan (2005).
27. The acquisition of a 20 percent stake in the Sakhalin-1 petroleum facilities by ONGC-Videsh in 2001 made the Russian Federation the second most popular destination for Indian OFDI in terms of investment value. This deal involved an investment of $1.7 bn, payable over five years (*Hindu Business Line*, 20 February 2002). As of February 2004, ONGC had invested $920 million (*Asian Times*, 4 February 2004).
28. Rediff.com, 'UK to Outsource more High-end Jobs to India', 10 January 2005 (http://www.rediff.com/money/2005/jan/10bpo.htm).
29. Hindustan Times.com, 'Indian Tech Firm buys US Company for $1 million', Indo-Asian News Service, 7 February 2005, (http://www.hindustantimes.com/onlineCDA/PFversion.jsp?article=http://10.81.141.122/news/181_1232...)
30. *Financial Times*, 'India Clears Way for Yugansk Bid', 14 January 2005.
31. Speech given by Prime Minister Manmohan Singh at The Indian CEO: Competencies for Success Summit, 22 January 2005 (http://pmindia.nic.in/speech/content.asp?id=70).
32. See *Channel News Asia International*, 'Russia Wants New Business Partnership with Old Ally India', 6 December 2004, (http://www.channelnewsasia.com/stories/afp_asiapacific/view/120800/1/.html).
33. This text builds on an UNCTAD's *Occasional Note*: 'China: an emerging outward investor', UNCTAD/Press/EB/2003/08, 4 December 2003.
34. Shanghai Automotive Industry Corporation, China's largest automotive manufacturer, aspires to become the sixth largest global automaker by 2010 (BBC News, UK edition, 'Chinese Auto Firm Looks Overseas', 29 November 2004), (http://news.bbc.co.uk/1/hi/business/4050707.stm).

35. *Times of India*, 'Durables Firms from China Follow the Korean Route', 30 November 2004 (http://timesofindia.indiatimes.com/articleshow/940527.cms).
36. *ChinaInvest*, 'Singapore Welcomes Chinese Companies', 18 November 2004, (http://www.chinainvest.com.cn/E/invest/weekly/W20041018–01.html). A total of 1277 Chinese companies had invested in Singapore up to June 2004.
37. The 'Go Global' strategy was formally announced in the 'Suggestion from the Central Commission of the Chinese Communist Party on the Tenth Five-Year Plan on National Economy and Social Development', passed in October 2000, http://www.people.com. cn/GB/paper 464/1711/277326.html.
38. See http://www.china.org.cn/Chinese/EC-c/363743.htm.
39. See MOFCOM, 'Regulations of examination and approval of investing in enterprises aboard', 12 October 2004, (http://english.mofcom.gov.cn/article/200410/20041000289068_1.xml); and *Asian Wall Street Journal*, 'China Cuts Red Tape on Investing Abroad – Simplified Approval Process Paves Way for Expansion, Reducing Pressure on Yuan', 13 October 2004.
40. *China Daily*, 'Rule Simplifies Investment Procedures', 12 October 2004, (http://www.chinadaily.com.cn/english/doc/2004–10/12/content_381576.htm). The 2004 'Interim Administrative Measures on the Approval of Overseas Investment Projects' prescribes that investment projects in Taiwan Province of China and countries without diplomatic relationship need to get approval from the National Development and Reform Commission.
41. China.com, 'Business in China: Overseas Investment Encouraged with Loans', 4 November 2004, (http://english.china.com/zh_cn/business/investment/11021614/20041104/11948630.html).
42. See 2004 'Circular on the Support of Credit Policy on Key Overseas Investment Projects Encouraged by the State' (Chinese), October 2004 (http://fec.mofcom.gov.cn/article/200411/20041100309015_1.xml).
43. See *China Daily*, 'China Eyeing Regional investment', 9 February 2004, http://bizchina.chinadaily.com.cn/openews.shtml?id=358. Such promotion programmes also involve training courses for officials in South and West Asian countries in attracting Chinese investment ('China Eyeing Regional Investment', 9 February 2004, http://ce.cei.gov.cn/enew/new.il/n300ib56.htm).
44. BBC News, UK edition, 'Argentina Gets China Investment', 17 November 2004, http://news.bbc.co.uk/1/hi/world/americas/4018219.stm.
45. *China Daily*, 'China to Invest $12 billion in Russia', 16 October 2004, (http://www.chinadaily.com.cn/English/doc/2004-10/16/content_382940.htm).
46. Countries can use both inward and outward FDI to upgrade the competitiveness of their firms and to facilitate structural change, thereby promoting their dynamic comparative advantage, as in both cases foreign assets are being brought into play. For a discussion of the relationship between inward and outward FDI, see Dunning and Narula (2004).
47. Observed Vice Commerce Minister Zhan Zigang of China in a speech (p. 3) at the International Forum on Going Global of Chinese Companies in April 2004: 'Only a small number of Chinese companies are able to "go global". Many companies lack experiences of international economic cooperation and need to improve relevant management and service systems. So it will not be a plain sailing for Chinese companies to go global. They must be prudent to deal with all kinds of risks and challenges.'

REFERENCES

Andreff, V. (2003), 'The Newly Emerging TNCs from Economies in Transition: A Comparison with Third World Outward FDI', *Transnational Corporations*, **12**, 73–118.
Bulatov, A. (1998), 'Russian Direct Investment Abroad: Main Motivations in the Post-Soviet Period', *Transnational Corporations*, **7**(1), 69–82.

China, Ministry of Commerce (various years), *The Almanac of China's Foreign Trade and Economic Cooperation*, Beijing: Ministry of Commerce.

Dun and Bradstreet (2003), *Who Owns Whom*, London: Dun and Bradstreet.

Dunning, J.H. (1996), 'The Geographical Sources of the Competitiveness of Firms: Some Results of a New Survey', *Transnational Corporations*, **5**(3), December, 1–30.

Dunning, John H. and R. Narula (2004), *Multinational and Industrial Competitiveness: A New Agenda*, Cheltenham, UK and Northampton, MA, USA: Edward Elgar.

Elenkov, Detilin S. (1995), 'Russian Aerospace MNCs in Global Competition: Their Origin, Competitive Strengths and Forms of Multinational Expansion', *Columbia Journal of World Business*, **30**(2), 66–78.

Goldstein, Andrea (2005), *'Emerging Multinationals' in the Global Economy: Data Trends, Policy Issues, and Research Questions*, Paris: OECD Development Centre, mimeo.

Hamilton, Geoffrey (ed.) (1986), *Red Multinationals or Red Herrings: The Activities of Enterprises from Socialist Countries in the West*, London: Pinter.

Kalotay, Kalman (2002), 'Outward Foreign Direct Investment and Governments in Central and Eastern Europe: The Cases of the Russian Federation, Hungary and Slovenia', *Journal of World Investment*, **3**(2), 267–87.

Kalotay, Kalman (2003), 'Outward foreign direct investment from economies in transition in a global context', *Journal of East European Management Studies*, **8**, 6–24.

Kumar, Krishna and M.G. McLeod (eds) (1981), *Multinationals from Developing Countries*, Lexington, MA: Lexington Books.

Lall, R.B. (1986), *Multinationals from the Third World: Indian Firms Investing Abroad*. New Delhi: Oxford University Press.

Lall, Sanjaya (1983), *The New Multinationals: The Spread of Third World Enterprises*, Chichester: Wiley.

Lall, Sanjaya and Yuping Zhou (2005), 'The Impact of China's FDI Surge on FDI in South-East Asia: Panel Data Analysis for 1986–2001', *Transnational Corporations*, **14**(1), 41–6.

Lecraw, Donald J. (1981), 'Internationalisation of Firms from LDCs: Evidence from the ASEAN Region', in K. Kumar and M.G. McLeod (eds), *Multinationals from Developing Countries*, Lexington, MA: Lexington Books.

Liu, Xiaohui, Trevor Buck and Chang Shu (2005), 'Chinese Economic Development, the Next Stage: Outward FDI?', *International Business Review*, **14**, 97–115.

Liuhto, Kari and Jari Jumpponen (2002), 'The Internationalization Boom of Russian Corporations: Studies of Russian Banks, Energy and Metal Companies', Report No. 135, Lappeenranta University of Technology, Department of Industrial Engineering and Management, http://www.compiler.fi/idankaupan/tutkimukset/LTKK12.html.

Liuhto, Kari and Jari Jumpponen (2003), 'Russian Corporations and Banks Abroad', *Journal of East European Management Studies*, **8**, 25–44.

Niederberger, Anne and Richard Saner (2005), 'Exploring the Relationship between FDI Flows and CDM Potential', *Transnational Corporations*, **14**(1), 1–40.

Oman, Charles (ed.) (1986), *New Forms of Overseas Investment by Developing Countries: The Case of India, Korea and Brazil*, Paris: OECD Development Centre.

Pradhan, Jaya Prakash (2003), *Building Indian Multinationals: Can India 'Pick up the Winners'?*, New Delhi: J. Nehru University, mimeo.

Pradhan, Jaya Prakash (2005), 'Outward Foreign Direct Investment from India: Recent Trends and Patterns', Gota, Ahmedabad: Gujarat Institute of Development Research, mimeo.

Sauvant, Karl P. (1990), 'The Tradability of Services', in Patrick A. Messerlin and Karl. P. Sauvant (eds), *The Uruguay Round: Services in the World Economy*, Washington, DC and New York: World Bank and United Nations Centre on Transnational Corporations, pp. 114–22.

Sauvant, Karl P. (2005), 'New Sources of FDI: The BRICs. Outward FDI from Brazil, Russia, India and China', *The Journal of World Investment & Trade*, **6** (October), 639–79.

UNCTAD (1995), *World Investment Report 1995: Transnational Corporations and Competitiveness*, New York and Geneva: United Nations, United Nations publication, Sales No. E.95.II.A.9.

UNCTAD (1999), *World Investment Report 1999: Foreign Direct Investment and the Challenge for Development*, New York and Geneva: United Nations, United Nations publication, Sales No. E.99.II.D.3.

UNCTAD (2001), *World Investment Report 2001: Promoting Linkages*, New York and Geneva: United Nations, United Nations publication, Sales No.E.01.II.D.12.

UNCTAD (2004a), *World Investment Report 2004: The Shift Towards Services*, New York and Geneva: United Nations, United Nations publication, Sales No.E.04.II.D.33.

UNCTAD (2004b), *Prospects for Foreign Direct Investment and the Strategies of Transnational Corporations, 2004–2007*, New York and Geneva: United Nations, United Nations publication, Sales No. E.05.II.D.3.

UNCTAD (2005), *World Investment Report 2005: Transnational Corporations and the Internationalization of R&D*, New York and Geneva: United Nations, United Nations publication, Sales No.E.05.II.D.10.

Vahtra, Peeter and Kari Liuhto (2004), *Expansion or Exodus? Foreign Operations of Russia's Largest Corporations*. Lappeenranta: University of Technology, mimeo.

Wells, Louis T. Jr. (1983), *Third World Multinationals: The Rise of Foreign Direct Investment from Developing Countries*. Cambridge, MA: MIT Press.

Wilson, Dominic, Roopa Purushothaman and Themistokolis Fiotakis (2004), 'The BRICs and Global Markets: Crude, Cars and Capital', Global Economies Paper No. 118, New York: Goldman Sachs.

Zhang, Zigang (2004), Speech at the International Forum on Going Global of Chinese Companies, Beijing, April.

APPENDIX

Table 14A.1   Emerging markets: OFDI flows, by range and economy, 1985 and 2003

	1985		2003	
	Economy[a]	Number of economies	Economy[a]	Number of economies
Above $10 billions	—	—	—	—
$5.0 to 9.9 billions	—	—	Taiwan Province of China; Singapore.	2
$3.0 to 4.9 billions	—	—	Russian Federation: Hong Kong, China; Republic of Korea; British Virgin Islands.	4
$1.0 to 2.9 billions	Hong King, China; China; Republic of Korea; Bermuda; Liberia; Singapore; Mexico; Malaysia;	—	Cayman Islands; China; Islamic Republic of Iran; Chile; Mexico; Malaysia; Venezuela. United Arab Emirates; Panama; Azerbaijan; Colombia; India; Argentina; Bahrain; South Africa; Thailand; Turkey; Brazil; Trinidad and Tobago; Philippines; Liberia; Indonesia; Libyan Arab Jamahiriya; Lebanon; Nigeria; Jamaica; Lao People's Democratic Republic;	7

Table 14.1 (continued)

	1985		2003	
	Economy[a]	Number of economies	Economy[a]	Number of economies
$0.0 to 0.9 billions	Panama; Brazil; Taiwan Province of China; Kuwait; South Africa; Cayman Islands; Argentina; Morocco; Indonesia; Bahamas; Libyan Arab Jamahiriya; Pakistan; Lebanon; Fiji; Venezuela; Seychelles; Cameroon; United Arab Emirates; Trinidad and Tobago; Uruguay; Colombia; Ecuador; Kenya; Costa Rica; Gabon; Belize; Senegal; Egypt; India; Swaziland; Algeria; Paraguay; Barbados; Oman; Niger; Chile; Botswana; Zimbabwe; Sri Lanka; Tunisia; Papua New Guinea; Thailand; Central African Republic; Yemen; Togo; Chad; Mauritius; Peru; Bolivia; Burkina Faso; Rwanda; Sierra Leone; Honduras; Turkey.	62	Qatar; Croatia; Peru; Romania; Ghana; Saudi Arabia; Costa Rica; Mauritius; Botswana; Fiji; Ethiopia; Macao, China; Bulgaria; Egypt; Pakistan; El Salvador; Algeria; Mali; Ukraine; Aruba; Morocco; Senegal; Cambodia; Seychelles; Bangladesh; Guatemala; Gambia; Paraguay; Kyrgyzstan; Zimbabwe; Brunei Darussalam; Sri Lanka; Nicaragua; Georgia; Malawi; Benin; Albania; Uruguay; Papua New Guinea; Cameroon; Bolivia; Jordan; Belize; Kenya; Guinea; Côte d' Ivoire; Belarus; Tunisia; Anguilla; Barbados; Rwanda; Vanuatu; Burkina Faso; Cape Verde; Guyana; Haiti; United Republic of Tanzania; Madagascar; Macedonia, TFYR; Antigua and Barbuda; Republic of Moldova; Ecuador; Bahamas; Burundi; Lesotho; Central African Republic; Chad;	91

| | | Equatorial Guinea; Gabon; Mozambique; Guinea-Bissau. | 18 |

Below $0.0 billions[b] Bangladesh; Jordan; Philippines; Netherlands Antilles; Bahrain; Saudi Arabia; Nigeria; Uganda.   8   Sierra Leone; Saint Lucia; Saint Kitts and Nevis; Honduras; Grenada; Angola; Armenia; Congo; Swaziland; Netherlands Antilles; Oman; Niger; Togo; Namibia; Uganda; Kazakhstan; Bermuda; Kuwait.

Number of economies reporting outward flows   70   122

Notes:
[a] Economies are ordered according to the magnitude of their outflows.
[b] Net negative FDI outflows (i.e. firms from these economies repatriated a higher amount than they invested abroad).

Source: UNCTAD, www.unctad.org/fdistatistics, and UNCTAD estimates.

391

Table 14A.2   The top 50 non-financial TNCs from developing economies, ranked by foreign assets, 2002ᵃ (millions of dollars, number of employees)

Ranking by Foreign assets	Ranking by TNIᵇ	Corporation	Home economy	Industryᶜ	Assets Foreignᶜ	Assets Total	Sales Foreignᵉ	Sales Total	Employment Foreign	Employment Total	TNIᵇ (Percent)
1	10	Hutchison Whampoa Limited	Hong Kong, China	Diversified	48 014	63 284	8 088	14 247	124 942	154 813	71.1
2	14	Singlel Ltd.	Singapore	Telecommunications	15 775ᵈ	19 071	3 247	5 801	9 877	21 716	61.4
3	44	Petronas – Petroliam Nasional Berhad	Malaysia	Petroleum expl./ref./distr.	13 200	46 851	6 600	21 433	4 979	25 940	26.0
4	11	Cemex S.A.	Mexico	Construction Materials	12 193ᵈ	16 044	4 366	7 036	17 568	26 752	67.9
5	33	Samsung Electronics Co., Ltd.	Republic of Korea	Electrical & electronic equipment	11 388	51 964	28 298	47 655	28 300ᶠ	82 400	38.5
6	26	LG Electronics Inc.ᶠ	Republic of Korea	Electrical & electronic equipment	5 845	16 214	11 387	23 553	30 029	55 053	46.3
7	15	Jardine Matheson Holdings Ltd.	Hong Kong, China	Diversified	5 729ᵈ	8 255	4 449ⁱ	7 398	60 000ᶠ	114 000	60.7
8	2	Neptune Orient Lines Ltd.ᶠ	Singapore	Transport and storage	4 580ᵈ	4 771	4 501	4 642	11 187	12 218	94.8

9	17	Citic Pacific Ltd.	Hong Kong, China	Construction	4170	7328	1567	2861	7388	11643	58.4
10	9	Sappi Limited	South Africa	Paper	3733[d]	4641	2941	3729	9807[f]	17572	71.7
11	6	Shangri-La Asia Limited	Hong Kong, China	Hotels and motels	3663[d]	4593	463	601	13000[g]	16300	78.9
12	34	Sasol Limited	South Africa	Industrial chemicals	3623	8960	3687	7114	7107	31150	38.4
13	3	Guangdong Investment Limited	Hong Kong, China	Diversified	3601	3924	815	876	5994	6580	92.0
14	5	Flextronics International Ltd.[k]	Singapore	Electrical & electronic equipment	3488[d]	4897	5903	7812	76187	78000	81.5
15	25	Capitaland Limited	Singapore	Real estate	3165	9403	1114	1823	5111[l]	10333[l]	48.1
16	13	City Developments Limited[m]	Singapore	Hotels	2954[d]	6490	806	1278	11001	13940	62.5
17	50	Petroleo Brasileiro S.A. – Petrobras	Brazil	Petroleum expl./ref./distr.	2863	32018	1085	22612	2200[f]	46723	6.1
18	22	MTN Group Limited	South Africa	Telecommunications	2582	3556	729	1991	1970	4192	52.1
19	21	Anglogold Limited	South Africa	Gold ores	2301	3964	831	1761	30821[g]	53097	54.4

Table 14A.2 (continued)

Ranking by Foreign assets	TNI[b]	Corporation	Home economy	Industry[c]	Assets		Sales		Employment		TNI[b] (Percent)
					Foreign[c]	Total	Foreign[e]	Total	Foreign	Total	
20	12	First Pacific Company Limited	Hong Kong, China	Electrical & electronic equipment	2 276[d]	2 313	1 892	1 892	25[f]	46 422	66.1
21	35	Companhia Vale do Rio Doce	Brazil	Mining & quarrying	2 265[f]	7 955	2 928	4 268	1 493[f]	13 973	35.9
22	31	Metalurgica Gerdau S.A.[f]	Brazil	Metal and metal products	2 089	4 093	1 340	3 136	5 977	18 995	41.7
23	27	Perez Companc	Argentina	Petroleum expl./ref./distr.	2 052	4 090	567	1 484	1 633[g]	3 255	46.2
24	39	America Movil	Mexico	Telecommunications	2 002	10 966	1 664	5 953	6 629	14 572	30.6
25	42	Singapore Airlines Limited	Singapore	Transport and storage	1 969[h]	10 866	2 472	5 260	2 613	14 418	27.7
26	49	CLP Holdings	Hong Kong, China	Electricity, gas and water	1 905[f]	7 793	130	3 350	37[f]	4 303	9.7
27	45	Samsung Corporation	Republic of Korea	Electrical & electronic equipment	1 897[h]	6 370	5 316[i]	29 533	1 223[g]	4 105	25.9
28	29	Kulim (Malaysia) Berhad	Malaysia	Food & beverages	1 729	3 689	166	516	10 800	22 112	42.6

29	40	Keppel Corporation Limited	Singapore	Diversified	1657	6609	604	3087	8722	19947	29.5
30	32	Naspers Limited	South Africa	Media	1655[a]	2498	412	1148	1742[f]	10711[i]	39.5
31	20	Barloworld Ltd.	South Africa	Diversified	1596	2569	1984	3409	9973	23192	54.5
32	41	United Micro-electronics Corporation	Taiwan Province of China	Electrical & electronic equipment	1531	9418	1320	2180	1002[f]	10136	28.9
33	19	Fraser & Neave Limited	Singapore	Food & beverages	1466	4374	1037	1931	9130	11816	54.8
34	46	Hyundai Motor Company	Republic of Korea	Motor vehicles	1461[h]	16694	9746	21070	4379[g]	50038	21.3
35	48	Nan Ya Plastics Corporation	Taiwan Province of China	Rubber and plastics	1403[a]	9743	850	5011	10394[g]	72174	15.3
36	36	Grupo Bimbo SA De Cv	Mexico	Food	1400	3077	1389	4286	16235	72500	33.4
37	16	Orient Overseas International Ltd.[k]	Hong Kong, China	Transport and storage	1148	2189	1012	2458	4039	4743	59.6

Table 14A.2 (continued)

Ranking by Foreign assets	Ranking by TNI[b]	Corporation	Home economy	Industry[c]	Assets Foreign[c]	Assets Total	Sales Foreign[e]	Sales Total	Employment Foreign	Employment Total	TNI[b] (Percent)
38	1	CP Pokphand Company Limited	Thailand	Food	1086	1107	1542	1542	52976[g]	54000	98.7
39	18	Gruma S.A. De C.V.	Mexico	Food & beverages	1084	2148	1301	1986	8314	14887	57.3
40	38	Swire Pacific Limited	Hong Kong, China	Business services	1000[a]	8880	963	1951	17969	55700	31.0
41	7	Savia SA De CV[i]	Mexico	Diversified	941	1362	633	682	5316	7375	78.0
42	37	Grupo Imsa	Mexico	Metal and metal products	831	3037	1182	2827	4149[f]	15800	31.8
43	8	Asia Pacific Breweries Ltd.	Singapore	Food & beverages	814	1056	754	1093	2023[g]	2624	74.4
44	24	Nampak Limited	South Africa	Rubber and plastics	782[a]	1281	328	1317	10962[f]	18062	48.9
45	23	Kumpulan Guthrie Berhad	Malaysia	Rubber and plastics	780	2397	369	811	40199[f]	56143	49.9
46	4	Li & Fung Limited	Hong Kong, China	Wholesale trade	765	781	4642	4779	3466	5313	86.8

47	43	Cintra	Mexico	Air courier services	748[a]	1937	1169	2969	629[f]	19928	27.1
48	30	Advanced Semiconductor Engineering	Taiwan Province of China	Computer and related activities	724[a]	3020	990	1317	5340	20401	41.8
49	28	Hong Kong And Shanghai Hotels Ltd.	Hong Kong, China	Hotels	650	2404	135	332	3653	5953	43.0
50	47	San Miguel Corporation	Philippines	Food & beverages	623[a]	3318	277	2639	5114[g]	27259	16.0

Notes:

[a] All data are based on the companies' annual reports unless otherwise stated.

[b] TNI is the abbreviation for 'Transnationality Index'. The Transnationality Index is calculated as the average of the following three ratios: foreign assets to total assets, foreign sales to total sales and foreign employment to total employment.

[c] Industry classification for companies follows the United States Standard Industrial Classification as used by the United States Securities and Exchange Commission (SEC).

[d] In a number of cases companies reported only partial foreign assets. In these cases, the ratio of the partial foreign assets to the partial (total) assets was applied to total assets to calculate the total foreign assets. In all cases, the resulting figures have been sent for confirmation to the companies.

[e] Foreign sales are based on the origin of the sales. In a number of cases companies reported only sales by destination.

[f] Data were obtained from the company as a response to an UNCTAD survey.

[g] Foreign employment data are calculated by applying the share of foreign assets in total assets to total employment.

[h] Foreign assets are calculated by applying the share of foreign employment in total employment to the balance total assets.

[i] Foreign sales are calculated by applying the share of foreign assets in total assets to total sales.

[j] Data for outside Hong Kong (China) and mainland China.

[k] Data for outside Asia.

[l] Data are for September 2003.

[m] Data for outside East and South-East Asia.

Source: UNCTAD (2004a), pp. 22–3.

Table 14A.3 The top 25 non-financial TNCs from Central and Eastern Europe[a], ranked by foreign assets, 2002 (millions of dollars and number of employees)

Ranking by Foreign assets	Ranking by TNI[b]	Corporation	Home country	Industry	Assets Foreign	Assets Total	Sales Foreign	Sales Total	Employment Foreign	Employment Total	TNI[b] (%)
1	11	Lukoil JSC	Russian Federation	Petroleum and natural gas	5 354.0	22 001.0	10 705.0[d]	15 334.0	13 000[c]	180 000	33.8
2	4	Novoship Co.	Russian Federation	Transportation	962.9	1 093.9	270.7	351.1	85	6 291	55.5
3	3	Pliva d.d.	Croatia	Pharmaceuticals	689.1	1 382.0	668.1	815.5	3 213	7 326	58.5
4	13	Norilsk Nickel, OJSC MMC	Russian Federation	Mining	502.0	9 739.0	2 360.0[d]	3 094.0	34	96 410	27.2
5	1	Primorsk Shipping Corporation	Russian Federation	Transportation	331.8	384.2	96.0	123.9	1 305	2 611	71.3
6	7	Gorenje Gospodinjski Aparati	Slovenia	Domestic appliances	312.8	632.8	531.6	755.6	731	8 772	42.7
7	24	Hrvatska Elektroprivreda d.d.[c]	Croatia	Energy	272.0	2 357.0	8.0	775.0	-	15 071	6.3
8	20	Mercator d.d., Poslovni sistem	Slovenia	Retail trade	224.6	1 040.0	139.1	1 331.0	1 893	14 331	15.1
9	8	Krka Group	Slovenia	Pharmaceuticals	180.7	577.9	282.6	367.7	817	4 332	42.3
10	18	Far Eastern Shipping Co.[c]	Russian Federation	Transportation	123.0	377.0	101.0	318.0	233	5 608	22.8

		Company	Country	Sector							
11	22	Petrol Group	Slovenia	Petroleum and natural gas	108.5	623.5	67.0	1 154.6	25	1632	8.2
12	16	Richter Gedeon Ltd.	Hungary	Pharmaceuticals	105.6	742.7	70.3	388.1	1996	5 124	23.8
13	9	Malév Hungarian Airlines	Hungary	Transportation	105.0	280.0	291.0	392.0	28	2851	37.6
14	12	Podravka Group	Croatia	Food and beverages/pharmaceuticals	102.4	485.8	171.6	384.4	1191	7488	27.2
15	21	MOL Hungarian Oil and Gas Plc.[c]	Hungary	Petroleum and natural gas	95.9	3 243.2	819.2	3 850.0	776	15 218	9.8
16	6	BLRT Grupp AS	Estonia	Shipbuilding	66.2	116.0	53.7	111.3	1778	3 642	51.4
17	2	Zalakerámia Rt.[c]	Hungary	Clay product and refractory	65.0	120.0	39.0	64.0	1889	2 921	59.9
18	17	Intereuropa d.d.	Slovenia	Trade	45.0	216.0	36.0	182.0	701	2 422	23.2
19	23	Merkur d.d.	Slovenia	Trade	43.3	500.5	55.1	517.8	143	2 988	8.0
20	25	Petrom S.A., SNP	Romania	Petroleum and natural gas	31.5	4 558.0	4.9	2 318.0	12	60 459	0.3
21	10	Budimex Capital Group[c]	Poland	Construction	23.8	372.6	50.4	610.0	1076	1 189	35.0
22	15	Croatia Airlines	Croatia	Transportation	23.4	316.1	101.7	164.5	59	992	25.1
23	14	Finvest Corp d.d.	Croatia	Forestry	22.2	71.9	6.6	31.3	–	547	26.1

Table 14A.3 (continued)

Ranking by		Corporation	Home country	Industry	Assets		Sales		Employment		TNI[b] (%)
Foreign assets	TNI[b]				Foreign	Total	Foreign	Total	Foreign	Total	
24	19	Iskraemeco d.d.	Slovenia	Electrical machinery	20.7	85.2	33.1	100.2	201	2 100	22.3
25	5	Policolor S.A.	Romania	Chemicals	17.2	31.0	25.5	47.1	457	933	52.9
Averages					393.1	2 053.9	679.5	1 343.2	1 376	18 050	31.5
Change from 2001 (in %)					5.4	52.1	29.4	11.1	9.9	34.6	1.2

Notes:
[a] Based on survey responses.
[b] The transnationality index (TNI) is calculated as the average of the following three ratios: foreign assets to total assets, foreign sales to total sales and foreign employment to total employment.
[c] 2001 data.
[d] Including export sales by the parent firm.

Source: UNCTAD (2004a), p. 317.

Table 14A.4   BRICs: top 20 M&A purchases, 1996–2004 (millions of dollars)

Rank	Acquiring company	Industry of the acquiring company	Years	Acquired company	Host economy	Industry of the acquired company	Value
Brazil							
1	Ambev	Malt beverages	2004	John Labatt Ltd	Canada	Malt beverages	7758
2	Petrobras	Crude petroleum and natural gas	2003	Perez Companc SA	Argentina	Crude petroleum and natural gas	1028
3	Grupo Votorantim	Cement, hydraulic	2001	Blue Circle Industries PLC-US	Canada	Adhesives and sealants	722
4	Petroleo Brasileiro SA	Crude petroleum and natural gas	2001	EG3(Astra Cia Argentina)	Argentina	Crude petroleum and natural gas	500
5	Bombril SA (Cragnotti)	Abrasive products	1997	Cino-Polenghi-De Rica	Italy	Canned fruits, vegetables, jams, and jellies	386
6	Sinergy	Investors, nec	2004	Avianca SA	Colombia	Air transportation, scheduled	364
7	Ambev	Malt beverages	2003	Quinsa(Quilmes International)	Argentina	Malt beverages	346
8	Banco Citibank SA (Citibank NA)	Banks, non-US chartered	1997	Siembra(Banco Rio de la Plata)	Argentina	Life insurance	250
9	Banco Itau SA	Banks, non-US chartered	1998	Banco del Buen Ayre SA	Argentina	National commercial banks	225
10	Votorantim Metals	Rolling, drawing, & extruding of nonferrous metals	2004	Refineria de Cajamarquilla SA	Peru	Lead and zinc ores	210
11	Braspetro(Petroleo Brasileiro)	Crude petroleum and natural gas	1998	LASMO Oil (Colombia) Ltd (LASMO)	Colombia	Crude petroleum and natural gas	151

Table 14A.4 (continued)

Rank	Acquiring company	Industry of the acquiring company	Years	Acquired company	Host economy	Industry of the acquired company	Value
12	Investor Group	Investors, nec	2001	Portucel Empresa de Celulose	Portugal	Pulp mills	120
13	Cia Vale do Rio Doce (Brazil)	Iron ores	1999	Ferrovia Centro Atlantica SA	Argentina	Railroads, line-haul operating	111
14	Grupo Gerdau	Steel works, blast furnaces, and rolling mills	1995	MRM Steel Ltd (Canam Manac Grp)	Canada	Steel works, blast furnaces, and rolling mills	111
15	Investor Group	Investors, nec	1999	Santa Cruz Refinery, Cochabamba	Bolivia	Petroleum refining	102
16	Petrobras	Crude petroleum and natural gas	2002	Petrolera Santa Fe	Argentina	Petroleum refining	90
17	Paulista de Trens Metro	Railroad equipment	1998	RENFE-Trains(48)	Spain	Railroad equipment	83
18	Petrobras (Brasil)	Crude petroleum and natural gas	1998	Santos Europe	United Kingdom	Crude petroleum and natural gas	80
19	Cia Siderurgica Nacional (CSN)	Steel works, blast furnaces, and rolling mills	2001	Heartland Steel-Machinery, IN	United States	Steel works, blast furnaces, and rolling mills	69
20	Fortilit Sistemas em Plastico	Plastics plumbing fixtures	1998	PVC Tecnocom SA	Argentina	Plastics products, nec	60
Russia							
1	Vimpelcom OJSC	Radiotelephone communications	2004	Kar-Tel Ltd	Kazakhstan	Radiotelephone communications	425
2	MMC Norilsk Nickel Group	Ferroalloy ores, except vanadium	2003	Stillwater Mining Co	United States	Miscellaneous metal ores, nec	341

402

	Acquirer	Industry	Year	Target	Country	Industry	Value
3	LUKoil Europe Ltd (LUKoil)	Crude petroleum and natural gas	1998	Petrotel SA(Romania)	Romania	Crude petroleum and natural gas	300
4	SeverStal JSC	Cold-rolled steel sheet, strip and bars	2004	Rouge Industries Inc	United States	Cold-rolled sleel sheet, strip and bars	286
5	Investor Group	Investors, nec	1996	Fokker Aircraft BV	Netherlands	Aircraft	242
6	Investor Group	Investors, nec	2002	Sibir Energy PLC	United Kingdom	Crude petroleum and natural gas	238
7	OAO LUKoil Holdings	Crude petroleum and natural gas	2003	Beopetrol Beograd	Yugoslavia (former)	Crude petroleum and natural gas	225
8	OAO Mobile Telesystems	Radiotelephone communications	2003	Ukrainian Mobile Commun Ent	Ukraine	Radiotelephone communications	194
9	Norilsk Nickel	Fabricated metal products, nec	2000	Norimet Ltd	United Kingdom	Metals service centers and offices	183
10	OAO LUKoil Holdings	Crude petroleum and natural gas	2003	MV Properties SRL	Romania	Petroleum and petroleum products wholesalers, nec	121
11	OAO Mobile Telesystems	Radiotelephone communications	2004	Uzdunrobita	Uzbekistan	Telephone communications, except radiotelephone	121
12	Yukosneftegaz (Laguna)	Crude petroleum and natural gas	2001	Kvaerner Process Tech.Hydrotec	Norway	Residential construction, nec	100
13	Yukosneftegaz (Laguna)	Crude petroleum and natural gas	2001	Kvaerner ASA-Hydrocarbons	United Kingdom	Industrial organic chemicals, nec	100
14	Yukosneftegaz	Crude petroleum and natural gas	2002	Mazheikiu Nafta	Lithuania	Petroleum refining	85
15	Yukosneftegaz	Crude petroleum and natural gas	2002	Mazheikiu Nalta	Lithuania	Petroleum refining	76

Table 14A.4 (continued)

Rank	Acquiring company	Industry of the acquiring company	Years	Acquired company	Host economy	Industry of the acquired company	Value
16	Yukosneftegaz	Crude petroleum and natural gas	2002	Transpetrol (Slovakia)	Slovakia	Pipelines, nec	72
17	LUKoil Holdings	Crude petroleum and natural gas	2001	Getty Petroleum Marketing Inc	United States	Petroleum refining	71
18	Yukosneftegaz (Laguna)	Crude petroleum and natural gas	1999	Petrol Bulgaria	Bulgaria	Petroleum and petroleum products wholesalers, nec	51
19	OAO Mobile Telesystems	Radiotelephone communications	2004	MCT Sibi Corp	United States	Telephone communications, except radiotelephone	37
20	Gazprom	Crude petroleum and natural gas	2004	AB Lietuvos Dujos	Lithuania	Natural gas transmission	35
India							
1	ONGC	Crude petroleum and natural gas	2003	Greater Nile Petroleum	Sudan	Crude petroleum and natural gas	768
2	Tata Tea Ltd (Tata Group)	Food preparations, nec	2000	Tetley Group Ltd	United Kingdom	Food preparations, nec	431
3	BFL Software Ltd	Prepackaged Software	2000	MphasiS Corp	United States	Prepackaged Software	200
4	Reliance Gateway Net Pvt Ltd	Telephone communications, except radiotelephone	2004	FLAG Telecom Group Ltd	Bermuda	Telephone communications, except radiotelephone	195
5	ONGC Videsh Ltd	Crude petroleum and natural gas	2004	Block 5A	Sudan	Crude petroleum and natural gas	102
6	Tata Motors Ltd	Motor vehicles and passenger car bodies	2004	Daewoo Commercial Vehicle Co	Korea, Republic of	Motor vehicles and passenger car bodies	101

	Company	Industry	Year	Target	Country	Industry	Value
7	Reliance Industries Ltd	Plastics materials and synthetic resins	2004	Trevira GmbH	Germany	Manmade organic fibers, except cellulosic	100
8	Hindalco Industries Ltd	Aluminum extruded products	2003	Straits(Nifty)Pty Ltd	Australia	Copper ores	86
9	Indian Oil Corp Ltd	Petroleum refining	2003	Ceylon Petroleum-Stations (100)	Sri Lanka	Petroleum refining	75
10	Patni Computer Systems Ltd	Computer related services, nec	2004	Cymbal Corp	United States	Computer related services, nec	68
11	SSI Ltd	Prepackaged Software	2000	Albion Orion	United States	Prepackaged Software	63
12	HCL Technologies Ltd	Computer related services, nec	1997	CareAmenca Compensation &	United States	Life insurance	59
13	Wockhardt Ltd	Pharmaceutical preparations	2003	CP Pharmaceuticals Ltd	United Kingdom	Pharmaceutical preparations	39
14	Satyam Infoway Ltd	Information retrieval services	2000	Cricinfo Ltd	United Kingdom	Computer related services, nec	36
15	Orient Information Technology	Prepackaged Software	2001	Hisham & Co-Software Business	United Arab Emirates	Prepackaged Software	35
16	ONGC Videsh Ltd	Crude petroleum and natural gas	2004	Block 5B	Sudan	Crude petroleum and natural gas	34
17	Jindal Stainless Ltd	Steel works, blast furnaces, and rolling mills	2004	Maspion Stainless Steel	Indonesia	Fabricated metal products, nec	32
18	CDC Capital Partners	Investors, nec	2000	Astratel Nusantara PT	Indonesia	Radiotelephone communications	30
19	ICICI Infotech Services Ltd	Security and commodity services, nec	2001	Insyst Technologies (MEA)Ltd	United Arab Emirates	Prepackaged Software	30

Table 14A.4 (continued)

Rank	Acquiring company	Industry of the acquiring company	Years	Acquired company	Host economy	Industry of the acquired company	Value
20	Wipro Ltd	Computer programming services	2002	American Management-Energy	United States	Computer related services, nec	26
China							
1	Goldman Sachs (Asia) Ltd	Security brokers, dealers, and flotation companies	1998	Finl Sector Restructuring-BL	Thailand	Personal credit institutions	645
2	CNOOC Ltd	Crude petroleum and natural gas	2002	Repsol YPF SA	Indonesia	Crude petroleum and natural gas	592
3	BOE	Electronic capacitors	2003	Hydis	Korea, Republic of	Electronic components, nec	380
4	ICBC (China)	Banks, non-US chartered	2001	Industrial & Coml Bk CH-HK	Hong Kong, China	Banks, non-US chartered	365
5	China National Petroleum Corp	Crude petroleum and natural gas	1997	Aktyubinskmunaygaz (Kazakhstan)	Kazakhstan	Crude petroleum and natural gas	325
6	Investor Group	Investors, nec	1998	Aluminium Smelters of Victoria	Australia	Primary production of aluminum	292
7	CNOOC Ltd	Crude petroleum and natural gas	2003	Tangguh LNG Project, Indonesia	Indonesia	Crude petroleum and natural gas	275
8	PetroChina Co Ltd	Crude petroleum and natural gas	2002	Devon Energy-Indonesian Oil	Indonesia	Crude petroleum and natural gas	262
9	CNAC (Civil Aviation Admin/CH)	Air transportation, scheduled	1996	Dragonair	Hong Kong, China	Air transportation, scheduled	255
10	China National Petroleum Corp	Crude petroleum and natural gas	1998	Venezuela-Caracoles Oil Field	Venezuela	Crude petroleum and natural gas	241

	Acquirer	Industry	Year	Target	Economy	Industry	Value
11	ICBC	Banks, non-US chartered	2000	Union Bank of Hong Kong Ltd	Hong Kong, China	Banks, non-US chartered	231
12	Huaneng Power Intl Inc	Electric services	2004	OzGen	Australia	Electric services	227
13	CNPC	Crude petroleum and natural gas	2003	N Buzachi Oilfield, Kazakhstan	Kazakhstan	Crude petroleum and natural gas	200
14	CNPC	Crude petroleum and natural gas	2004	PlusPetrol Norte	Peru	Crude petroleum and natural gas	200
15	Investors	Investors, nec	1996	Asia Satellite Telecommun Hldg	Hong Kong, China	Communications services, nec	181
16	Investor	Investors, nec	1997	Nam Pei Hong (Holdings)Ltd	Hong Kong, China	Pharmaceutical preparations	166
17	Investor Group	Investors, nec	2003	Amerada Hess Indonesia Hldg	Indonesia	Crude petroleum and natural gas	164
18	BOE	Electronic capacitors	2003	TPV Technology Ltd	Hong Kong, China	Computer terminals	135
19	Sinochem	Plastics materials and basic forms and shapes	2003	Atlanlis(Petroleum Geo-Svc)	Norway	Oil and gas field exploration services	104
20	CITIC (China)	National government agency	1997	Asia Satellite Telecommun Hldg	Hong Kong, China	Communications services, nec	102

Source: UNCTAD, cross-border M&A database.

Table 14A.5   *BRICs: greenfield FDI projects to top 15 destinations,*
                2002–February 2005

Rank	Destination	No of projects[a]
Brazil		
1	China	14
2	Argentina	13
3	Portugal	10
4	United States	9
5	Mexico	8
6	Colombia	5
7	Peru	4
8	Bolivia	4
9	Uruguay	4
10	Venezuela	4
11	Angola	2
12	United Kingdom	2
13	Russia	2
14	Japan	2
15	Spain	2
	Total	**102**
Russia		
1	Ukraine	18
2	Kazakhstan	9
3	Uzbekistan	6
4	Romania	5
5	Bulgaria	4
6	Estonia	4
7	Guinea	3
8	Viet Nam	3
9	Tajikistan	3
10	India	3
11	Armenia	3
12	Czech Republic	3
13	Georgia	3
14	China	2
15	Germany	2
	Total	**107**
India		
1	United States	61
2	China	57
3	United Arab Emirates	45
4	United Kingdom	36

Table 14A.5   (continued)

Rank	Destination	No of projects[a]
5	Singapore	24
6	Russia	19
7	Germany	16
8	Brazil	14
9	South Africa	13
10	Australia	13
11	Sri Lanka	12
12	Bangladesh	11
13	Thailand	10
14	Canada	10
15	Oman	10
	Total	**456**
China		
1	Brazil	10
2	Viet Nam	8
3	India	7
4	Russia	6
5	Germany	4
6	Pakistan	3
7	Australia	3
8	Azerbaijan	3
9	Malaysia	3
10	Thailand	3
11	Nigeria	2
12	Kazakhstan	2
13	Mongolia	2
14	Uzbekistan	2
15	Kyrgyzstan	2
	Total	**96**

Note: [a] Includes expansion projects in the host economies.

Source: UNCTAD, FDI/TNC database, and OCO Consulting. LOCOmonitor.

15. Negotiating in BRICs: business as usual isn't

Camille P. Schuster

Companies have long seen the People's Republic of China and India as tantalizing markets because of the size of the population. However, the very small middle class in these countries meant that purchasing power was so low that many products from Western countries were too expensive. With a growing middle class, these markets, in addition to Russia and Brazil, are beckoning.

A challenge is that the marketplace in each of the BRIC countries is not static, just waiting for multinational or global companies to enter. A number of local companies have been doing business with, manufacturing for, and distributing for multinational companies, thereby gaining valuable business expertise. In addition, many young people who have received business degrees from Western countries have returned to find opportunities to use that knowledge while working for local businesses. Each of these countries has companies that are or will emerge as multinational companies. Each of these countries has a growing GDP creating stronger local competitors and a larger middle class.

In the BRIC marketplace, business as usual as practiced in North America or Europe does not guarantee success. The cultural traditions, philosophies and religions result in a different value system and set of business practices. For instance, Dell computer found that the Chinese typically want to touch computers before buying them, making it difficult for a direct selling model to be successful (Hamm, 2004). Hewlett-Packard installed a new computer system for the driver's license system in Poland in exchange for a cut of the fees drivers pay each time they get a new or renew a license (Hamm, 2004). Innovative solutions are necessary for creating products and services that are attractive and affordable for BRIC consumers.

Rethinking assumptions regarding consumer needs, disposable income and marketplace constraints is challenging. Creating these products and services is not sufficient for success in these markets if company representatives do not know how or take the time to adapt to the process of doing business in BRIC countries. For example, Microsoft has refused to sell a cheaper Windows in China to combat the open-source threat and has had four general managers in six years. Jack Gao, who ran Microsoft China from 1999 to 2003, insists that Microsoft has to find new ways of doing things (Hamm, 2004). He now heads Autodesk's China operations. So what does it take to do business in BRIC countries? If business as usual doesn't work, what does work? How do you find a way to adapt successfully?

Negotiations take place between individuals, each with a different personality, cultural background and set of objectives. Therefore, it is impossible to predict precisely how one individual will perform in any given negotiation. However, cultures tend to exhibit specific values, behaviors and beliefs, all of which impact business processes and decision-making. The first step in learning how to negotiate successfully in the BRICS is to identify their cultural characteristics. The second step is to identify similarities and differences in the negotiation process between and among the BRICS and developed countries. The third step is to learn how to adapt your behavior for successful negotiations in the BRICs. This chapter will examine each of those steps.

CULTURAL CHARACTERISTICS

The Culture Classification Model (Schuster and Copeland, 1996) has been reconfigured to reflect the areas of the world being discussed in this chapter: G7 countries (the United States, Canada, Germany, the United Kingdom, France, Italy, Japan) and the BRICS (Brazil, Russia, India and China) (see Figure 15.1). Assumptions regarding the use of time, the approach to the task at hand, and the role of relationships in making business decisions vary throughout the world and have significant implications for how people negotiate in business situations (Ghauri, 1986; Joy, 1989; Lee, 1966; Mortenson, 1992; Perkins, 1993; Salacuse, 1991; Schuster and Keith, 1993; Wasnak, 1986).

Time is a constant, with 24 hours in each day the world over, and is an underlying dimension across all cultures. Depending upon the importance of task and relationship issues in each country, time is used differently. Those cultures depicted on the left-hand side of the continuum generally emphasize the importance of tasks and allocate their time accordingly. Changes in emphasis, with more time being spent building, nurturing and maintaining relationships, occur as groups are placed closer to the right-hand side of the continuum.

Adaptation within the individual negotiation does occur and might even deviate significantly from this model, depending upon how much that person adheres to the norms of the major cultural group in that country, or the degree of biculturalism the individual exhibits in the negotiation.

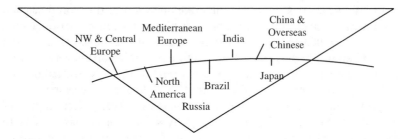

Source: Modified from the Culture Classification Model Schuster and Copeland (1996).

Figure 15.1   BRIC Culture Classification Model

North American (United States and Canada) and Northwestern or Central European (United Kingdom and German) cultural groups are deceptively similar in their orientation toward time, task and relationships. The primary focus of these interactions is on getting to the task at hand and accomplishing it as efficiently and quickly as possible. Typically, the relationship between the buyer and seller on both sides in a negotiation situation is less important than task completion. Time is an important component in these cultures, and using it efficiently is a critical goal and an admired measure of skill. Getting the job done, as efficiently and effectively as possible, is critical and always a key success measure. In a negotiation situation this translates into getting to the job at hand quickly and eliminating time spent on irrelevant non-task matters.

Businesspeople in Mediterranean European (France with the exception of Paris, and Italy) countries are entirely able to do business with representatives from North America and Northwest and Central Europe, using the task orientation with facility and skill. The concept of 'extended tribe' begins here. If an individual is considered to be part of the same clan, tribe, country or cultural group, some effort during the negotiation will need to focus on developing a connection between relatives by establishing a common bond, personally. Another difference is the polychronic attitude toward time. Important tasks come first, even if that requires attending to an important personal or business problem until it can be resolved at the expense of being late for another meeting, not completing another job on time, or delaying delivery of a product. Each important task, in its time, will be given the same focus and attention. Completed tasks remain the measure of success and are viewed in a sequential pattern; time is viewed as the flexible variable.

In Russia there are few, if any, well-established legal, governmental or financial procedures that are generally accepted and followed. The structure for a 'rule of law', contractual obligations and generally accepted business processes are being created, tested and modified. The amount of individual responsibility taken for initiating and implementing new tasks varies among individuals. In addition, the political and economic agenda has been inseparable. The country is now in a transition to a free market economy and a democratic form of government. As with any transition, the changes proceed in fits and starts. Without an ability to rely upon systems, procedures and laws, people still rely upon their personal network. The circle of trusted family members and friends is a source of funds, expertise, employees, introductions and privileges.

As in Mediterranean European countries, businesspeople in Brazil are quite capable of doing business using the North American and Northwestern and Central European process of negotiation, but this clearly is not their preferred method and represents a bicultural understanding on their part that will affect the negotiation process. Identifying a personal link is important; persuasion is often linked to the quality of the relationship between the two parties. Addressing the task is important; however, the importance of relationship changes the role of persuasion. Developing the relationship requires that meetings with the Brazilian representatives occur more than once, include meals with the local people, or involve time spent discussing general business conditions, during which participants begin to know and appreciate each other as individuals. As a result, participants begin to know one another, not as business associates but on a deeper, personal level. This provides a richer and more meaningful context for the relationship to develop, with multiple dimensions from which to draw as the business dynamics of the relationships develop.

As a former British colony, Indian government, financial and legal systems have all developed from and are closely linked with the British systems. Many Indian businesspeople have been educated in, worked in or for North American or British companies and are adept at working within that structure. However, again that is not the preferred style of doing business. As the largest democracy accommodating many different languages, cultures, religious beliefs and philosophies, the ability to work with, around and within different systems is an acquired skill. Well-established and trusted networks are essential for support. Entry into the group provides identity, protection and conscious as well as unconscious preference while, at the same time, requiring adherence to emerging group norms. Negotiating or selling to members of this group is extremely difficult for someone who is not part of the group or does not have a product or service that is in great demand but unavailable elsewhere.

As Asian countries, China and Japan share many cultural, philosophical and religious concepts that are distinctly different from Western countries.

Not only are networks a fundamental element of doing business but also one's position within that network constrains and structures the type of relationships that exist and can be developed with other individuals. The process of establishing networks can be time-consuming and requires a great deal of patience but must be established before it is possible to do business.

Maintaining harmony within a group is important in both China and Japan. Within groups, members do not speak critically of each other. Working together to complete the task is important and competition within the group can bring the project to a standstill. However, competition with other groups can be very effective in spurring the group to work harder to accomplish its goal. Maintaining face is a fundamental concept in these countries, involving the ability to keep and enhance one's dignity, self-respect and prestige. The ability to behave in ways appropriate to one's status and to preserve harmony, even at an individual's expense, is a basic virtue and essential for preserving and enhancing one's status and power in society. As a result, giving and saving face are critical factors in relationships, conversations and business behavior.

While accomplishing tasks is important in all of these countries, that may be done at the expense of personal relationships in some cases, only with well-established relationships in other cases, or in conjunction with creating relationships. Time must be devoted to relationships or divided between relationships and tasks or devoted to tasks in different countries. Knowing where and when to engage in specific business behaviors and how to form persuasive strategies to influence a negotiation are skills that are critical for success in negotiations. The negotiation process differs significantly across these countries and will, therefore, require different behaviors and strategies for success.

INTERNATIONAL NEGOTIATION MATRIX

While the negotiating process itself is fairly standard, research in the area of international negotiation suggests that existing theories and techniques might be culture-bound and not translate well to other cultural groups (Catoline, 1982; Ghauri, 1986; Graham, 1981, 1983, 1984, 1987; Graham and Andrews, 1987; Graham and Sano, 1984). Schuster and Copeland (1996) created a Global Sales and Negotiation Matrix identifying the parts of the negotiation process: Network Entry, Business Relationships, Personal Relationships, Orientation, Interests, Influence and Persuasion, Concessions and Compromise, Agreements, and Maintaining Relationships.

While the elements of the process are standard, the importance of each element differs across countries. The Global Sales and Negotiation Matrix

(Schuster and Copeland, 1996) has been modified to compare the G7 countries with the BRICS (see Figure 15.2). This section of the chapter will briefly highlight the negotiation process in each area, beginning with the G7 countries followed by a discussion of each of the BRICs.

G7 Countries

North America includes the United States and Canada. Western and Central Europe includes Germany and the UK. Three of these countries are Anglophone, with Germany having some similarity to the British and US cultures.

All four of these countries have a strong emphasis on task accomplishment, so obtaining the signed contract is the primary goal of negotiations. Influence and persuasion strategies relying on objective data are used to present strong arguments in support of goals, interests and positions. Giving in or losing is not desirable, can lead to great conflict, and is avoided if possible. Both sides will present their arguments, proceeding through the list of issues in a sequential manner, either compromising to find agreement or developing solutions that allow both sides to satisfy their individual interests.

Negotiating the terms of the contract is often a negotiation in and of itself because these four countries all have low context (Hall, 1981) languages in which communication depends on explicit and verbally expressed terms. Identifying the precise words to convey the intentions of either side is critical to the signing and execution of the contract. Therefore, all the executives and lawyers on either side need to agree to the wording of the contract explicitly. Once the contract is signed, the assumption is that both sides will follow the terms of the contract. The expectation is that, as professionals, the individuals and their company have a responsibility to deliver what they promised on time.

Proposals as well as people are to be evaluated on their merits using objective criteria. Favoritism is frowned upon so connections between companies normally do not rest upon individual friendships. Over time friendships may develop but business decisions are supposed to be objective and not influenced by personal relationships.

These four countries, however, are not identical in their approach to negotiations. Formality ranges from being very high in Germany, to somewhat less in the UK, about the same in Canada, and much less in the US. For example, while colleagues in Germany may not call one another by their first names even after working together for three years, salespeople in the US are normally taught to switch to the other person's first name as soon as possible during a sales call. In Europe, there is still a strong

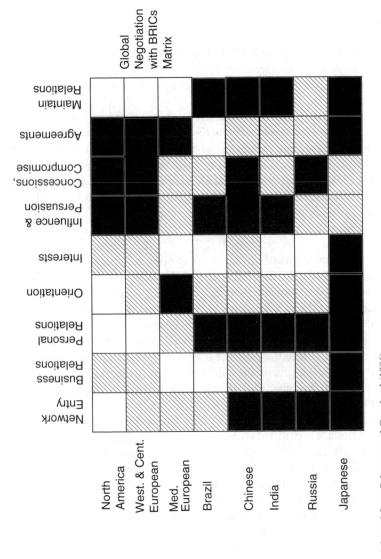

Source: Adapted from Schuster and Copeland (1996).

Figure 15.2   Global sales and negotiation matrix

hierarchical structure based upon school, family and money, and the use of formality is part of that culture. So negotiations take on a more formal, regulated, controlled atmosphere using agendas for structure and to assist in preparation. Businesspeople in the US tend to be less formal; cold calls can be an effective method of generating business contacts, and problem-solving among relative equals is a more common negotiation style. Getting access to the decision-maker is more of a challenge in the other three countries than in the US.

The Mediterranean European countries of France and Italy have a more balanced approach to tasks and relationships. Their legal system is based upon Roman law and/or Napoleonic law that does not rely upon precedent. Rather, it specifies what can and must be done in specific circumstances. As a result, regulations and procedures set the pace of business. A character-istic of the increased importance of the relationship orientation is that pre-senting one's point of view and engaging in conversation is desirable. Having lively conversations is enjoyable and a goal in and of itself, so nego-tiations are likely to be more argumentative and lively.

Deductive forms of argument are common, meaning that the US habit of quickly agreeing to premises and assuming that details can be worked out later or that specific circumstances can be discussed as exceptions creates major problems. Initial premises are accepted as immutable – until the next meeting when a new set of premises may be presented and the dis-cussion will then follow new guidelines.

Changing one's mind during a discussion or agreeing to concessions is considered to be a sign of an ineffective negotiator. New ideas can be pre-sented and argued; however an agreement will probably not occur during that meeting. Rather, both sides need to step back, re-evaluate their posi-tions, rethink the arguments, modify initial premises, if necessary, and begin again.

The influence of royalty and nobility means that network entry, intro-ductions, formality and etiquette are even more important in these coun-tries. *Etiquette* means 'ticket' in French – polite, correct behavior is your ticket to being accepted in society. Family and school connections are important in terms of jobs, introductions and acceptance into certain circles of influence. Obtaining introductions to the right people in the right circles is an important beginning. Demonstrating your understanding and using polite behavior is critical for acceptance and the opportunity to be introduced to people at the next level.

The romance languages of French and Italian have a style that is not quite as low context as the Germanic and Anglophone languages. However, there is more emphasis on how things are said. As a result, there will be lengthy negotiation about the wording of the agreement. The negotiation process itself requires skill in argumentation and is not over until the wording of what was agreed upon in principle is agreed upon by both sides.

The Japanese approach to negotiation is significantly different from the style used in the other G7 countries. Since personal relationships are more important, the emphasis in the process tilts away from the emphasis on persuasion and getting a signed contract. All the initial (time-intensive) phases are very important: getting to know people as individuals not just as representatives of a company or someone filling a specific job function is the first step. Nothing happens until this is established. In the other G7 countries this is perceived as unnecessary and even as a waste of time because procedures and agreements supercede the people who make the agreement.

The contractual agreement is still important in Japan but has a different connotation. Honor and face are extremely important; agreeing to do something is giving your word to work as hard as possible to accomplish the agreed-upon goals. However, the world is an uncertain place. Another layer of ambiguity in this uncertain world is the Japanese language which is high context (Hall, 1981) so the situation, people and relationship change the meaning of words, making it difficult to agree upon what the contract means. As an honorable business person, it is necessary to adhere to the intent of the contract and uphold the relationship. However, that is not identical to the expectation of adhering to the details of a contract.

Words may not be linchpin of the agreement, but honoring the agreement is important. Honoring the agreement is about doing what can be done to move toward the goal, or doing whatever is necessary to honor the intent of the agreement, thereby honoring the relationship. The result may not be exactly what was written, but to the Japanese the words do not convey one specific meaning as they do in American English, British English or German. The words are ambiguous but the relationship is not.

Taking time to establish strong personal relationships is not perceived as a good use of time by the Anglophone and Germanic G7 countries, nor do they view the meanings of words as ambiguous. As a result, creating and abiding by agreements can create a great deal of tension during and after negotiations. In many respects the Japanese approach to negotiation is much closer to that of the BRICs.

BRICs

While Brazil, Russia, India and China have significantly different histories, traditions, languages and culture, they do have something in common that impacts business negotiation. In each of these countries there is not a well-established legal, financial **AND** government system. Creation, development and refinement of these systems is in process. Enforcement of regulations and laws is improving, but not equally applied in all circumstances. Without well-established systems, enforceable regulations and trust of the citizens, reliance on the rule of law or any set of processes is not an accepted method of doing business.

With standard financial practices, executives can compare their company with the average economic indicators in their country, determine the value of their company, and calculate profits based upon standard rates of taxation. With an established legal system, companies can determine ownership of properties or ideas, enter into binding contracts, and expect that contract terms will be upheld or enforced in the courts. With a stable government system, managers know what regulations apply where and when, depend upon impartial evaluation of opportunities, and expect an ethical approach to decision-making. In the BRICs, this set of assumptions does not apply.

Money, status, and/or family connections equal power in the BRICs. This power can be used to influence politicians, judges, court administrators and the police. Often, but not always, the influence is monetary; graft and bribery are issues in all these countries. Financial, government and business processes do not all conform to a transparent rule of law. Without systems, processes or contracts that can be trusted, the negotiation process works differently in these countries.

Brazil

Brazil obviously has strong ties to Mediterranean Europe in terms of language, religion and culture. However, the process of evolving from colony to independent country with a stable legal, government and financial system is taking place with the typical fits and starts of any transition process. On the one hand, there are very close ties with Portugal, Italy and Spain. On the other hand, the interdependency of diverse groups of people created Brazil's distinctive culture.

The importance of formality, manners and appearance is as strong in Brazil as in the Mediterranean countries. Systems and processes are accepted as part of the normal business process. Adhering to them is desirable. Brazil is closer to Italy, Spain and Portugal in following the tradition that 'one works to live'. Living means spending time with friends having fun, participating in or watching sports, and engaging in conversation. Everyone's opinion is important and everyone needs to voice his or her opinion. Conversations are lively, with much interruption, and often loud. Interrupting business meetings for family matters or a discussion of social events is not considered an interruption, because family and social activities are equally, if not more, important than business activities.

Making special concessions or displaying favoritism for family members or close friends is not viewed negatively, but is expected. Loyalty to family and friends is critical to long-term survival. If an individual cannot rely upon systems, processes or the enforcement of laws, then reliance on family and close, trusted friends becomes the norm. When negotiating business deals, it is important to remember that you are making deals with individuals, first, and companies, second. If you take care of individuals who are important to you, they take care of you. That reciprocity or obligation has nothing to do with companies, policies or procedures. As a result, there is no separation between business and personal life.

While negotiations proceed with the expectation that the agreed-upon terms of the contract are desirable and should be upheld, business people in Brazil know that daily life is unpredictable. Governments can be overthrown, currencies can be devalued, inflation can run rampant, and nature is in control of the elements. Roads can be wiped out by a flood, electricity may be erratic or disconnected, and the planned outcome is never certain. Therefore, the terms of a contract are agreed to, valued and met (as is possible). The goal of negotiation is to agree to the terms of a project or deal. However, the signed contract is not viewed as something final or a directive as to what will happen when. Every reasonable person knows that daily circumstances and nature can alter the best-laid plans.

Successful negotiators realize that maintaining close personal contact and closely monitoring daily activities are the best ways of working through issues and accomplishing goals as close to those laid out in the contract as possible.

Russia
Russia is also a country in transition. However, it does not share the language, religion, or culture of Mediterranean Europe. Rather, Russia includes its own unique blend of languages, religions, secularity, economics and cultures. The country is partly in Europe and partly in Asia with some sections bordering on the Middle East. While sharing the tradition of royal families and the social classes of nobility, merchant and peasant with European countries, Russia moved from a system of nobility to a socialist system and is now transitioning to a free market economy.

Given the nature of transition and the uncertainty surrounding the legal, government and financial systems, there is a lack of confidence in contracts by the local population. The Soviet system was characterized as reliable in terms of honoring business contracts, but the Soviet system is no longer in control. Citizens are learning how to do business in a free market economy for the first time. A great deal of distrust and uncertainty remains.

In any transition country and, certainly, in a country with a history of not knowing whom to trust, there is a great deal of suspicion, and reliance on friends and family. As a result, there is generally an 'official' and 'unofficial' method of doing things. Having friends who are well placed makes it possible to bypass some of the official procedures. Laws regarding property, possession and contracts are being passed. A rule of law is being created. Enforcement is increasing. However, the system is not yet transparent and running smoothly.

Until such time as the rule of law becomes the accepted norm for doing business, there will continue to be a great deal of suspicion toward outsiders, and favoritism among friends. Negotiating in this situation is challenging. The other side does not completely necessarily trust you and you are not sure if you can believe the other side. Establishing trust takes time; something business people from North America or Northwestern and Central Europe do not want to give. Trusting the wrong people can be a disaster; many business people can attest to failed business deals. Not only does someone from outside Russia need to be cautious about trusting a new Russian business partner, but also you need to realize that the potential business partner has no reason to trust you either. Only time and continued, close contact can resolve that issue.

Because businesspeople from Russia lack trust and have a 'fixed pie' mentality, they often view negotiation as a 'win–lose' activity. As a result, they do not give concessions easily, continue to badger the other side for concessions, argue their positions strongly, and need to 'win'. Remembering that contracts are viewed as a desirable but not always attainable goal, signing the contract is not the end of doing business together. Again, maintaining those personal relationships means that close contact is necessary throughout the whole business process so that both sides are kept abreast of the current state of affairs, have early warning of any changes, and can be prepared with contingency plans.

India

On the one hand, the culture of India has a long, rich tradition. On the other hand, there are many cultures and traditions within one country. For instance, there are as many as 350 dialects spoken in India. The most common language among the educated and business people across India is English – and most often British English. In many ways the country is bicultural.

India has a strong Hindu and Buddhist (with very many sects) caste system tradition overlaid with the teachings of Christian missionaries. The Hindu and Buddhist traditions of hierarchy, taking care of or being responsible for one's extended family and close friends, and valuing education continue to be strong.

The British system of laws, government and finance form the basis of Indian systems and procedures. India is the largest democracy in the world.

However, the British system was imposed and as Indian natives took control of the country, many of the systems and procedures took on a form that is slightly different from the British model.

Discovery of a large, well-educated, English-speaking, computer-literate population by the multinationals, especially when combined with the attraction of low wages, has resulted in a great deal of outsourced business activity. With modern means of communication and use of technology, this potential for business activity in India provided a boost to businesses in North America, Northwestern and Central Europe, Australia and New Zealand.

However, the use of English and the adoption of British legal, government and financial ideas does not mean that business is conducted in India as it is in the other Anglophone countries. While much of the native population in India learned English and British business procedures, they were not 'conquered' or 'overrun' as the native populations in many other Anglophone cultures were. The native Indians have a bicultural business system in that many people can and do proceed with business in the Western tradition when the need arises; however, they do not necessarily value this process or use it when doing business among themselves. Therefore, it is important to evaluate potential business partners carefully.

Personal and family relationships are important in India, as in the other BRICs. Each family has a set of norms, values and traditions that are important. Any family member who does not uphold them is ostracized and not supported by the family. Therefore, remaining an honored and valued member of the family is critical and always a consideration in any business decision. That is where loyalty lies, and is even more important than any written contract. Creating and maintaining face and honor within the family group is always a foremost consideration.

With a population of almost a billion, a low level of literacy, and no common language for the whole country, a great of paperwork resulting from required processes and systems does accumulate. Not everyone is well educated. Not everyone speaks English. Finding some way to get through the bureaucratic morass becomes a challenge. Dealing with friends and relatives who are part of the system or can make their way through the system is a common choice. Providing some kindness for those who help you through the system is normal. Graft and bribery are common in those countries in which it is more common to rely on other people to help you through the system than it is to rely upon systems that work fairly and independently.

The orientation and influence phases of negotiation in India are particularly important because of the desire of Indians to engage in philosophical and theoretical discussions. Using words and language to investigate and explore ideas, possibilities and alternatives has high priority. Another priority is preserving your own honor and face while building honor and face of your partners. Being polite, tactful and facile with words is a well-developed skill. Being able to notice, identify, appreciate and use subtle nuances of language is a mark of a well-educated, polished business person. Concessions are not easily given, however. It is always important to maintain face.

The process of discussing issues, persuading the other side, and coming to an agreement is often long, involved, and may emphasize the wording of the contract. However, implementation of the contract depends more on personal relationships than the wording of the contract. Depending upon people is often more reliable than the legal, government and financial systems.

China

Important elements of Chinese culture are Buddhism, Zen, Confucianism and Taoism rather than the logic of Aristotle and Plato or the values of Christianity. With a history of dynasties controlling the country followed by socialism, the tradition appears similar to that of Russia. Like Russia, China also spans a great deal of geography encompassing many regional differences. However, the Chinese traditions are based more strongly in the Eastern philosophies and values. In addition, the People's Republic of China is in the process of creating a socialist free market economy rather than transitioning to a democratic free market economy. This unique combination creates a different approach to the process of negotiation.

Personal relationships are important, as they are in all transition countries. Loyalties are personal, based upon networks of family and/or close friends. Business relationships are often described as being like a spider's web – there is a strong central core but the web is often recreated, can grow disproportionately in specific directions, and is loosely connected. While *kerietsus* in Japan and *chaebols* in Korea are formal organizations of businesses with financial ties, groups of Chinese businesses working together on a specific project are loosely aligned and can easily realign for new projects. This flexibility allows companies to respond rapidly to changes and new opportunities in the marketplace.

The strong core of the spider's web is, of course, the patriarch of the family. Decisions, control and responsibility rest there. Developing trust throughout the family network even to be allowed to discuss business opportunities with the patriarch and/or his representative takes time. Serious business is conducted only with honorable business associates. Without a reliable credit agency, business rating or public company records, determining whether a business associate or company is honorable, pays bills and can be respected happens by talking with other business associates or partners of the person or people who know the person and doing business together over time.

Once you are determined to be reliable and trustworthy it does not mean you automatically get the business. Another Chinese tradition is always to check the numbers to make sure a profit will be made on the transaction. Concessions and compromises may be made, if necessary, but the deal needs to accomplish the goal – of gaining technology, making a profit, securing training, obtaining knowledge.

Because the country is in transition, the laws, regulations and procedures are in flux. The relationship between centralized and decentralized decision-making means that the ultimate authority can and does change. In this ambiguous environment, contracts do not specify exactly what will happen, when, with what consequence if not fulfilled. Rather, a signed contract often means that your partner has decided to do business with your company and that the process of negotiation begins. Therefore, maintaining communication between and among business associates at various levels of the hierarchy is critical for success. While some of that communication can be electronic, the electronic forms only supplement face-to-face communication in the country at the factory or service center.

The style of communication is indirect and always mindful of creating and maintaining harmony in the relationship. As a result, direct, straightforward questions are not responded to in like form and direct, straightforward information will not be forthcoming. Commonly given advice is to 'listen to what is not said'. Business executives from the Anglophone and Germanic cultures need to work at developing the skill of indirect communication. Indirect communication takes a good deal of time and the most important information is often not revealed directly, creating a challenge. Concessions are not given easily and usually require a way to save face.

Given the different interpretation of elements of negotiation, traditions and communication styles, some adaptation is required. The next section briefly describes some techniques of adaptation.

ADAPTATION

With differences in the negotiation process, using one style of negotiation is not likely to result in success. Having a plan, goal and strategy is essential. However, there is not one style of negotiation that works well in both G7 countries and BRICs. Obviously, it is not possible to act as a native in all these cultures. That level of adaptation is not necessary or desirable.

However, you do want to know enough about each cultural group and their negotiation process so that you can adapt successfully and achieve your goals. This section will identify some techniques that will assist in the adaptation process:

1. Learn enough about the culture to understand the predominant world-view, values and process of decision-making. Knowing how business-people in that culture think, perceive problems, and what they value as desirable solutions is invaluable information for creating persuasive arguments.

2. Know the status of the legal, financial and political systems and be prepared to spend time getting to know people personally, if necessary. The investment of time may not be comfortable for those in Anglophone or Germanic cultures; however, it may be critical for success.

3. Demonstrate respect for the other culture by asking questions, expressing appreciation, participating in events, and being willing to learn. Taking the time will earn respect. The knowledge will be useful as the negotiation progresses.

4. Develop the ability to switch between a direct and an indirect style of communication. Developing facility with indirect communication takes time, can be uncomfortable, but will be an very important tool.

5. Accept the need for regular face-to-face communication. Travel expenses will be high. However, the investment is small compared to the cost of products that don't meet quality standards or are not delivered on time. Technology provides tools for keeping in contact, but are only effective as supplementary forms of communication.

6. Have a variety of persuasive tools at your disposal. Sometimes objective data is necessary for persuasion; sometimes testimonials from unbiased sources work better; sometimes the testimonials need to be from respected individuals; sometimes an introduction from a respected network member is critical. Knowing which tool is preferable in which circumstances is essential for success.

7. Know and follow your company's and country's regulations on graft and bribery. Different standards apply. Using appropriate behavior is essential for a long-term career.

8. Realize that negotiation takes place between individuals. Country culture is one layer of an individual's worldview. Educational background, company training, cultural competence, travel experience and individual personality all influence an individual's negotiating style. Using assumptions about the other person's style is normal and acceptable as a starting point. Testing the accuracy of those assumptions is critical for success.

Mastering these eight guidelines enables an individual to develop a repertoire of skills and techniques. Developing the capability of using a variety of tools successfully is an important foundation. Determining when to use which tools is the next step for success in negotiations. With the appropriate knowledge and tools, adaptation is possible.

CONCLUSION

The economic power of the BRICs has been and will continue to increase. Businesspeople from these countries are becoming more important as potential business partners every day. To recognize the potential of doing business in the BRICs, businesspeople from the G7 countries need to develop the ability to adapt to different styles of negotiation.

Understanding similarities and differences, learning alternative influence strategies, using different styles of communication, and devoting time to the appropriate parts of the negotiation process makes adaptation possible. Economic activity in the BRICs is increasing. Business activity in these countries will continue to grow. Profitable business ventures belong to those who can adapt their negotiating style.

REFERENCES

Catoline, James E. (1982), 'Bridging Cultures: Strategies for Managing Cultural Transitions', *Digital Equipment Corporation* (June), 25–42.

Ghauri, Pervez N. (1986), 'Guidelines for International Business Negotiations', *International Marketing Review*, 3(6), 72–82.

Graham, John L. (1981), 'A Hidden Cause of America's Trade Deficit with Japan', *Columbia Journal of World Business*, Fall, 5–15.

Graham, John L. (1983), 'Brazilian, Japanese, and American Business Negotiations', *Journal of International Business Studies*, Spring–Summer, 47–61.

Graham, John L. (1984), 'A Comparison of Japanese and American Business Negotiations', *International Journal of Research in Marketing*, 1, 51–68.

Graham, John L. (1987), 'Deference Given the Buyer: Variations Across Twelve Cultures', in P. Lorange and F. Contractor (eds), *Cooperative Strategies in International Business*, Lexington, MA: Lexington Books, pp. 473–84.

Graham, John L. and J. Douglas Andrews (1987), 'A Holistic Analysis of Cross-Cultural Business Negotiations', *Journal of Business Communications*, 23, 63–77.

Graham, John L. and Yoshihiro Sano (1984), *Smart Bargaining: Doing Business with the Japanese*, Cambridge, MA: Ballinger.

Hall, Edward T. (1981), *Beyond Culture*, New York: Doubleday.

Hamm, Steve (2004), 'Tech's Future', *BusinessWeek*, 27 September, 82–9.

Joy, Robert O. (1989), 'Cultural and Procedural Differences That Influence Business Strategies and Operations in the People's Republic of China', *SAM Advanced Management Journal*, Summer, 29–33.

Lee, James A. (1966), 'Cultural Analysis in Overseas Operations', *Harvard Business Review*, May–April, 106–12.

Mortenson, Eileen A. (1992), 'Business Opportunities in the Pacific Rim for Americans in Small Business: The Importance of Cultural Differences in Doing Business', in David O. Braaten and Gary Anders (eds), *1992 Conference on US Competitiveness in the Global Marketplace*. Phoenix, AZ: Thunderbird Publishing Group.

Perkins, Anne G. (1993), 'Diversity', *Harvard Business Review*, September–October, 14.

Salacuse, Jewald (1991), *Making Global Deals*, Boston, MA: Houghton Mifflin Company.

Schuster, Camille P. and Michael J. Copeland (1996), *Global Business: Planning for Sales and Negotiations*. New York: Dryden Press.

Schuster, Camille P. and Janet Keith (1993), 'Factors That Affect the Sale Force Choice Decision in International Market Entry Strategies', *Journal of Global Marketing*, 7(2), 27–49.

Wasnak, Lynn (1986), 'Knowing When To Bow', *Ohio Business*, March, 31–8.

PART V

Challenges and obstacles

16. The impact of coercion on protecting US intellectual property rights in the BRIC economies

Robert C. Bird[1]

INTRODUCTION

The United States economy may lose its competitive edge (Wagman and Scofield, 1999). Brazil, Russia, India and China, collectively known as the BRIC economies, are increasingly influencing the global marketplace. BRIC populations are increasing their standards of living, disposable income, and demand for foreign goods and services. These economies and their markets may potentially surpass the size of the six current largest economies by 2050, which includes the United States (Wilson and Purushothaman, 2003).

American firms must be able to compete in the BRIC markets to remain competitive in the twenty-first century. While significant US penetration in these markets is likely to continue, the likelihood of market leadership in the future is far from certain. One of the most dangerous threats to American business achievements is the uncertain protection of American intellectual property rights in BRIC economies. Intellectual property protection, the notion that an inventor of almost any creation of the human mind should be entitled to a limited monopoly to reap the benefits of that creation, is a well-entrenched value in the United States. The BRIC nations, like many other emerging economies, lack well-established intellectual property laws. As a result, intellectual property violations are the single most significant threat to the competitiveness of many firms doing business on a global scale (Ronkainen and Guerrero-Cusumano, 2001).

A belief in strong intellectual property rights in developing countries is far from established. Cultural traditions, local political interests, economic need, and mistrust of the West all limit the willingness of the non-Western markets to adopt strong protections. The BRIC nations force American firms into a difficult choice. An aggressive entry into the BRIC markets risks triggering a flood of pirated American products that siphon away revenue and damage brand image. An overly cautious approach that waits until the BRICs establish ironclad legislation and enforcement tools could cost American firms significant market share and the all-important 'first-mover' dominance (Rahman and Bhattacharyya, 2003).

The objective of this chapter is to examine the impact of coercion on US firms' efforts to remain competitive in the BRIC markets while maintaining intellectual property integrity in those markets. This chapter will review the largely successful coercive efforts of the United States government to strengthen intellectual property laws in BRIC legal codes. It will also examine the limits of US coercion by showing how threats of sanctions produce limited long-term impact on intellectual property piracy and fraud. The final section of this chapter will discuss the future of coercion as an American trade policy.

THE DEVELOPMENT OF THE MODERN GLOBAL INTELLECTUAL PROPERTY SYSTEM: AMERICAN BUSINESS COERCES THE DEVELOPING WORLD

Intellectual property rights fall within three broad categories – patents, copyrights and trademarks. Patents allow an inventor to prevent the unauthorized making, selling or using of a product, process or technology that is recognized as patentable for a fixed period of time. Trademarks protect the right to use identifiable names, symbols and designs that companies use to represent their goods and services. Copyrights provide exclusive rights to copy and sell creative endeavors such as books, songs, photographs and other media (Maskus, 2000).

For centuries, nations granted intellectual property rights that did not extend beyond national borders. An owner of intellectual property was forced to file for protection in several countries and conform to each nation's laws. Even if the rights holder filed successfully, nations commonly did not grant foreign rights holders the same protections as their own citizens. The result was a limited and cumbersome intellectual property system that persisted for much of the nineteenth century (Emmert, 1990).

In 1873, a patent congress convened in Vienna with the ambitious goal of unifying intellectual property law for all states. After national representatives expressed reluctance toward the idea, the congress narrowed their focus to providing equal national treatment to all rights holders in signatory states. As a result, the Paris Convention of 1883 required national treatment of patents and the Berne Convention of 1886 soon followed, imposing the same requirements for copyrights. Revised and amended extensively over time, these agreements remained the dominant principles of international intellectual property law for nearly a century (Taketa, 2002; Emmert, 1990).

National treatment, however, accomplished little in preventing piracy. Foreigners benefited minimally from national treatment in a foreign state if that state did not provide sufficient protection for its own citizens. Nations could exclude broad classes of intellectual property protection or offer strong protection only in areas where their domestic industries had a technological advantage over foreign competitors. Furthermore, nations could still indirectly prevent equal treatment by requiring that all intellectual property rights be in active use within a short period of time after issuance of the right. For example, US rights holders who may not enter a national market until years after receiving intellectual property rights protection might easily find their intellectual property nullified in a foreign state. Procedural requirements for filing and issuance of rights were sometimes so burdensome and slow that by the time an American patented product entered the marketplace the value of the protection might be nullified. New American industries involving biotechnology, semiconductor chips and software were wholly unprotected by domestic law (Emmert, 1990). By the 1980s, American executives became concerned with the value of intellectual property as a source of wealth as American firms lost their traditional global dominance in manufacturing and other industries (Gerhart, 2000; Dam, 1987). The time had come for American business to use its economic and political muscle to force other nations to respect their intellectual property rights.

These efforts began in earnest during the Uruguay Round of the General Agreement on Tariffs and Trade (GATT), negotiated between 1986 and 1994. Initially, trade topics such as textiles, apparel, agriculture, services and government procurement were the focus on the GATT agenda, and not intellectual property (Mossinghoff, 2000). Even Europe and Japan did not initially consider intellectual property a debatable issue (Drahos, 1999). American business interests reshaped the GATT agenda to their own ends. The Pharmaceutical Manufacturers' Association (PMA), a trade group representing the interest of drug companies, lobbied the US Congress to reframe intellectual property as a trade issue (Gad, 2003). The PMA specifically cited developing countries as having significant deficiencies in intellectual property protection that negatively impacted US market share abroad. A vice-president of IBM argued before Congress that intellectual property issues should be linked with international trade rules (Senate Committee on Finance, 1986). The resulting effect was that the United States government called for linking intellectual property to trade at the GATT negotiations.

Developing countries, led by India and Brazil, resisted American efforts to link trade and intellectual property at GATT (Gerhart, 2000). They preferred the World Intellectual Property Organization (WIPO) as the appropriate forum because it provided one-nation, one-vote decision-making. Developing countries, which made up more than half of WIPO members, could then effectively block any changes to intellectual property standards (Petherbridge, 2004). The United States, supported by the PMA and others, responded by threatening the use of special trade sanction powers delegated by Congress to the executive branch pursuant to the US Trade Act of 1974. This trade sanction power, widely known as a 'Special 301 sanction', authorized a US president to impose sanctions on countries engaging in what he perceived to be unfair trade practices that threatened US economic interests (Yu, 2002). Using Special 301 powers, the United States government through its executive branch threatened that it would limit or close its markets to products of developing countries that did not support the linkage of intellectual property and trade at GATT. This threat of significant economic losses forced developing nations to compromise. Ultimately, nations agreed that intellectual property was a proper agenda for the GATT negotiations in exchange for liberalization of apparel and agriculture trade (Ryan, 1998). The trade–intellectual property link forged at the Uruguay round of GATT would be the precedent for more aggressive action to come.

After its victory at GATT, the United States did not hesitate to wield this Special 301 power. In 1989, American business executives urged the United States Trade Representative (USTR), an agency of the US executive branch that negotiates with foreign representatives on trade matters, to place China on the Priority Watch List for failure to provide sufficient copyright protection for US works (Yu, 2000; Newby, 1995). China attempted to accommodate the United States by passing a copyright law and enacting implementing regulations. The United States found these efforts unsatisfactory and threatened to impose retaliatory tariffs against Chinese shoes, textiles, electronic instruments and pharmaceuticals. China responded with its own threatened counter-tariffs against American aircraft, chemicals, corn and steel. Just hours before sanctions were to be implemented both countries signed a Memorandum of Understanding (MOU) on 17 January 1992. The MOU forced China to make extensive changes to its intellectual property laws by extending the time of patent protection, expanding patent protection to all chemical inventions, acceding to the Berne Convention for the Protection of Literary and Artistic Works, extending copyright protection to 50 years, and including criminal penalties in its trademark statute (Yu, 2000).

American business believed the 1992 MOU to be a major victory toward protecting its interests. However, even after the 1992 MOU intellectual property piracy in China remained rampant. One study reported $850 million in losses for copyright theft alone (USTR, 1995). Entertainment industry representatives were especially concerned because Chinese citizens exported these pirated products to other countries. The US government was forced to again pressure China to control piracy by threatening one hundred percent tariffs on over $1 billion worth of goods (Yu, 2000). China again responded with potential retaliatory trade measures of its own, 'to protect its sovereignty and national dignity' (Yu, 2000, p. 144). Again, an eleventh-hour agreement which included the closure of 29 pirated compact disc factories averted a trade war between the two nations.

Meanwhile, pharmaceutical interests lobbied for Special 301 sanctions to be used to force change in Brazilian patent laws. The PMA filed a petition against Brazil in 1987 alleging that Brazilian patent laws weakened US patent rights, reduced American firms' market share, and prevented further opportunities for trade and investment with Brazil (Gad, 2003). The petition sought not only to curb Brazilian behavior but also to send a signal that nations opposed to the new rise in intellectual property protections would face the PMA's stiff resolve. The PMA characterized Brazil as a leader of those developing countries whose purpose it was to dilute even the most basic minimum standards provided by the Paris Convention (Gad, 2003). As a result, Brazil was the first nation to suffer direct sanctions from Special 301. On 20 October 1988, President Reagan issued Proclamation 5885, increasing US import duties on certain Brazilian products by 100 percent (Federal Register, 1988). Only the Brazilian government's announcement one year later that it would seek improved patent protection legislation for pharmaceutical products and processes caused the US government to lift the sanctions. The cost of the sanctions was estimated at $40 million (Gad, 2003).

India faced similar tactics. With a strong local manufacturing industry of generic drugs and other products, India did not even recognize GATT as an appropriate forum for intellectual property during the first three years of negotiations (Foster, 1998). The United States threatened the imposition of Special 301 sanctions against India in 1991 because of its limit on foreign equity investment, weak national intellectual property laws, unwillingness to sign the Paris convention, and high tariffs (Bershok, 1992).

India continued to resist American pressure through the 1990s. In 1994, GATT members forged a major accord on intellectual property, known as the Trade Related Aspects of Intellectual Property Rights agreement, commonly known as TRIPS. TRIPS made sweeping changes by requiring its signatories to provide broad minimum protections for intellectual property rights, offer favored nation treatment for all signatories, grant minimum terms of protection, and impose significant local enforcement and dispute settlement procedures (Foster, 1998; Sell, 1999). TRIPS also authorized signatory states to impose trade sanctions against nations who failed to comply with TRIPS provisions. According to one author, this agreement would have been 'unthinkable without the concerted efforts of US-based corporate executives' (Sell, 1999, p. 170).

By 1989, most of India's allies (including Brazil, which had succumbed to US Special 301 threats) had grudgingly embraced a TRIPS draft. The Indian government could not resist the United States on its own, even though it was subjected to enormous lobbying from Indian farmers and drug manufacturers. In that same year India suffered an economic crisis which required the government to ask for International Monetary Fund (IMF) assistance. The United States has significant influence over IMF policies. Furthermore, the United States had been providing India with needed direct grants and served as India's largest trading partner. The United States had already fired a warning shot by revoking duty-free treatment of India pharmaceutical exports, costing Indian exports $60 million. India had no choice but to relent on its opposition to TRIPS in order to maintain badly needed US funding and trade access (Foster, 1998).

Finally, Russia was also pressured by the United States to improve its intellectual property regime, albeit on a limited scale. Russia has been the target of Special 301 scrutiny sought by American business interests. Russia has been placed on the USTR's Watch List and Priority Watch List, signifying non-compliance with key intellectual property standards (Neigel, 2000; Kuik, 1999). The US government influenced the Soviet Union to join the Berne Convention in exchange for preferential trade status. The motion picture industry, led by its then president Jack Valenti, successfully lobbied for Congress to withhold ratification of the agreement until the Soviets improved their copyright laws to illegalize piracy of US films (Fleishman, 1993). After the collapse of the Soviet Union, the Russian government assumed the responsibilities of the agreement.

In addition to joining the Berne Convention, Russia enacted protections of computer databases, programs and circuit topologies. Russia also passed a new comprehensive copyright Act in 1993. When private and governmental entities remained active in unauthorized copying, industry groups lobbied for Special 301 findings and sanctions (Neigel, 2000).

Although Russia and its Soviet predecessor have been influenced by American pressure, only Russia out of the four BRICs has been spared the full force of US business-backed American coercion. Most significantly, America has not pursued trade sanctions against the former Soviet state even though piracy was rampant throughout the republic (Neigel, 2000). Russia likely received separate treatment because of non-trade related geopolitical factors that benefited American interests. First, America wanted to support a nascent post-Communist Russian government led by Boris Yeltsin. Second, Russia was a minor trading power compared to China, Brazil and India, and thus much less trade was at stake. Russian piracy was also designed primarily for domestic consumption, rather than the much more harmful export industry like Chinese production. Third, soft treatment of Russian piracy allowed the United States to maintain influence over Russia's nuclear disarmament and non-proliferation policies (Neigel, 2000; Miller, 2000).

RESULTS OF AMERICAN COERCION: AN UNCERTAIN SOLUTION

All four BRIC economies have endured pressure from American-supported business interests and the American government to strengthen domestic intellectual property protections. Brazil faced overwhelming pharmaceutical industry pressure and governmental threats of sanctions from the United States to improve its patent protection for drug products and processes. Brazil gave up its resistance to discussing intellectual property rights at GATT, joined the TRIPS agreement, and now possesses a functioning patent approval system and legislation that is at least fairly consistent with the minimum standards protection required by TRIPS (Schulz, 2004).

Russia endured motion picture industry-backed lobbying by the United States to join the Berne Convention and improve its intellectual property laws or else potentially lose Most Favored Nation trade status with the United States. Although America did not directly target Russia with trade sanctions, the former Soviet republic has enacted a new customs code targeting counterfeit trade, adopted copyright amendments protecting works existing before Russia's modern intellectual copyright regime, and increased applicable fines for administrative misdemeanors (IIPA, 2005a).

India, by contrast, faced the prospect of overwhelming trade penalties and aid losses directly from the United States or being influenced by United States policy, if India did not improve its intellectual property protections. Even in spite of enormous political pressure from farmers and domestic generic drug producers (Foster, 1998), India acceded to sweeping changes of TRIPS and has passed legislation establishing a mailbox system to receive patent applications, protecting geographic indication trademarks, and strengthening copyright law (Embassy of India, 2000).

Finally, China stood toe to toe with the United States regarding its domestic piracy practices, even threatening retaliations in what could have been a devastating trade war for both countries. Just hours before a trade war would have commenced, China agreed to US demands and halted some of its most egregious domestic acts of piracy. Today, Chinese intellectual property law resembles developed nations' legal codes. Since China's accession to TRIPS, it has extended patent protection from 15 to 20 years, protected geographic indication trademarks, and offered the right of judicial review to administrative decisions of the Trademark Review and Adjudication Board (Weinstein and Fernandez, 2004).

There is little doubt that aggressive action by the United States government and American business interests brought about many of the changes in intellectual property rights that the BRIC economies retain today. It is far from certain, however, that American coercion has brought about long-lasting changes in intellectual property protection for American businesses. It is also uncertain whether former strategies for realigning interests with that of the US are sustainable.

The 2005 Special 301 Report published by the International Intellectual Property Alliance, located at http://www.iipa.com, reports damning evidence of insufficient intellectual property protection in all four BRIC nations discussed below.[2] Brazil is plagued with ineffective, non-deterrent criminal enforcement mechanisms for intellectual property. Police interest in piracy varies widely among Brazil's sub-national states. Most investigations into piracy are commenced by private industry and not the government. When police do decide to actually make arrests, criminal copyright cases can take two or three years to reach the trial stage. Even if a case manages to wind its way through trial, less than 1 percent of piracy raids result in criminal convictions. When a rare conviction does occur, sentences usually do not extend beyond fines, community service and probation.

As a result, Brazilian piracy remains rampant. Pirated entertainment represents over half of all music sales and over two-thirds of video game sales. Over one-third of the VHS market is with pirated goods. Pirated DVDs represent 15 percent of the optical disk market. Weak border controls between Brazil and Paraguay allow infringing imports to escape scrutiny. Total trade losses due to Brazilian copyright piracy amounted to $931.9 million in 2004 (IIPA, 2005b).

In Russia, the piracy industry has become one of the largest producers of illegal optical media. Russian pirates now export illegal material throughout the world. Production capacity has nearly tripled in four years. CD and DVD manufacturing plants have grown from two plants in 1996 to 34 plants in 2004 producing 390 million discs per year. Russian authorities withdraw licenses to produce optical media, but do not confiscate equipment when piracy is discovered and do not conduct surprise inspections of factors suspected of piracy. As a result, the International Intellectual Property Alliance recommended that Russia be elevated to Priority Foreign Country status in 2005, a designation reserved for the most blatant national violators. Russian copyright piracy is nothing short of epidemic, resulting in $1.7 billion in losses in 2004 for legitimate producers (IIPA, 2005a).

Piracy in India, like its Russian counterpart, is widespread and well entrenched. Storefronts selling pirated books operate with no resistance from law enforcement and export globally. As a result, 50 to 60 percent of all books sold in India are pirated copies, despite the fact that Indian books are some of the cheapest worldwide. American films appear in pirated markets even before the official release date. A legal rental market for films simply does not exist. Corporate piracy of software exists at companies of all sizes. Total copyright piracy alone has risen from $270 million in 2000 to $464.8 million in 2004. There are no signs of the piracy industry slowing anytime soon in India (IIPA, 2005c).

Finally, losses from piracy in China are some of the largest in the world. Piracy levels remain at or near 90 percent in all sectors. Recent judicial interpretations on piracy show limited enthusiasm for raising penalties imposed upon convicted pirates. Administrative penalties remain so low that they are not a sufficient deterrent. Criminal prosecutions are almost non-existent relative to the rampant nature of pirated activities. Industry is significantly hampered in its efforts to pursue self-help. Industry investigation is simply banned. The investigation and enforcement system in China is completely non-transparent. Total copyright piracy in China cost legitimate producers $2.4 billion in 2004 (IIPA, 2005d).

Considering the extent to which these intellectual property violations are harming American business, it clearly necessitates further attention. Should American interests continue to apply direct pressure to protect intellectual property abroad? The next section of this chapter examines this question.

The Retaliation Cycle: The Chinese Reaction to US Coercion

One of the most prominent examples of the limitations of coercive trade policies involves China's relationship with the United States. Yu (2002) and Feder (2003) examined this relationship and concluded that trade relations between the two powerful states followed a disturbing cycle of US coercion, Chinese concession, and further American coercion over intellectual property rights without significant results. The first step inevitably begins with American business interests complaining to the US government that China is not sufficiently honoring American intellectual property rights. For example, in 1989 American industry lobbied the USTR to place China on its Priority Watch List. A country placed on this list receives active monitoring by the USTR to determine whether further action is necessary against that nation (Liu, 1994). After minor Chinese legislative changes proved unsatisfactory, the United States launched a Special 301 investigation into Chinese intellectual property practices and threatened $1.5 billion in tariffs against Chinese commodities such as pharmaceuticals, shoes and textiles. China responded with threatened counter-sanctions of its own against American commodities such as corn, steel and chemicals. Just hours before the imposition of sanctions, China and the United States averted a trade war by signing a Memorandum of Understanding regarding intellectual property in 1992. China agreed to join major global intellectual property treaties and expand intellectual property protections under its domestic law. The MOU appeared successful in strengthening China's intellectual property policies (Yu, 2000).

In 1994, however, the cycle began all over again as American executives once more complained about the lack of intellectual property protection in China and demanded new sanctions (Yu, 2000). The United States again placed China on its Priority Foreign Country list and launched a Special 301 investigation. The American administration threatened $1 billion in tariffs against Chinese imports. The Chinese responded with 100 percent tariffs against numerous American goods. Just as in 1992, the two countries reached a compromise hours before the deadline in which the sanctions were to take effect. In 1995, China and America agreed upon a highly elaborate action plan that created Chinese enforcement task forces, established a new copyright verification system, and promised that China would aggressively crack down on major infringers. Commentators hailed the agreement as the 'single most comprehensive and detailed [intellectual property] enforcement agreement the United States had ever concluded' (Yu, 2000, p. 148). Large-scale raids of large Chinese factories that were producing pirated goods convinced US officials that the agreement would be successfully implemented (Feder, 2003). Only months later, the USTR concluded that the action plan was not producing its expected results and that Chinese exportation of pirated and counterfeited goods continued at an equal or even greater level than that present at the conclusion of the 1995 agreement (USTR, 1996). In April 1996, US government once again designated China a Priority Foreign Country for its failure to protect intellectual property and announced its intention to impose $2 billion worth of trade sanctions against imported Chinese products (Yu, 2000).

Delay: The Indian Reaction to US Coercion

Not all nations have the economic muscle to resist American pressure directly in this fashion. Nevertheless, nations with less economic leverage have followed their own coercion compliance cycle. Instead of threatening counter-sanctions, these nations simply delay changes as long as possible.

India, for example, has fallen behind China for the claim of leading Asian economic power. While China has embraced globalization and trade with some enthusiasm, Indian economic reforms have been slower to take hold. While citizens of both nations possessed similar per capita incomes 25 years ago, the income of Chinese citizens today is nearly double that of their Indian counterparts (Rajwade, 2005). Furthermore, India has attracted far less foreign direct investment than China, largely because of international skepticism toward India's free-market reforms. While China's free economic zones have begun to merge with the larger economy, India's equivalent free economic areas remain isolated from the rest of the Indian economy. India does not have the Chinese equivalent of a Hong Kong that can finance commercial activity within the broader nation (Parker, 2002). Although India may overtake China in the long term (Huang and Khanna, 2003), today India retains a much weaker economic position in dealing with the United States than its Chinese counterpart. As a result, India has less bargaining power than China with which to resist US coercion because it has little ability to withstand American sanctions and to threaten counter-sanctions in response.

This weakness, however, does not mean that India and nations like it are powerless to thwart US coercive tactics. India, like China, has a history of resisting US intellectual property coercion. India and nations like it (Brazil and Russia for instance) simply use different techniques. For example, India aggressively resisted the GATT efforts to forge the TRIPS accord. Once TRIPS entered into force on 1 January 1995, India pursued the goals of satisfying TRIPS with almost agonizing slowness. For example, one of India's tasks was to establish a system for receiving and processing a broad array of patent submissions. On 31 December 1994, the President of India promulgated an amendment designed to accept submissions for pharmaceutical and agricultural product inventions.[3] The ordinance also stated that processing of these patents would not occur until 1 January 2005, the exact day when India as a developing country was finally forced to comply with TRIPS provisions. Although the amendment became effective on 1 January 1995, it lapsed only three months later on 26 March 1995, when the Indian Parliament failed to address the legislation within the requisite time (Ragavan, 2003). The lower house of Parliament passed a bill that would give effect to the President's patent-strengthening amendment. The upper house of Parliament then took the bill and referred it to a committee, which failed to act on it before the dissolution of the lower Parliament that year, causing the bill to lapse altogether. A ten-member panel established by the Indian government to review TRIPS provisions disbanded before it ever met. This procedural mishandling of the TRIPS-enabling legislation was particularly problematic because India was already receiving numerous pharmaceutical and agricultural product patent applications from foreign interests (Ragavan, 2003; Tomar, 1999).

American impatience with India's slowness resulted in the USTR filing a complaint against India with the World Trade Organization (WTO). The USTR claimed that India had violated TRIPS Articles 70(8), which required signatories like India to accept and retain post-1995 patent applications until full mandatory TRIPS compliance began in 2005 (Baker, 2004). The US charged that India had not established a sufficient 'mailbox' system for receiving and processing patent applications for pharmaceutical products as TRIPS Article 70(8) requires. The US also charged that India had not implemented provisions giving patent filers exclusive marketing rights of their products as Article 70(9) required. These rules required that while the patent application sits in India's 'mailbox', the patent holder must be given five years of exclusive marketing of the product assuming it has been properly patented and registered by another WTO member (Baker, 2004).

In September 1997, A WTO panel found that India failed to comply with both articles. India appealed the finding and lost that appeal in December. After more procedural wrangling,[4] the decision was formally adopted by the dispute settlement body of the WTO in January 1998 and it issued specific recommendations for India to follow (Sherman and Oakley, 2004). Only then did India agree to follow the body's recommendations and pass amendments to its patent law at some point in the future.

American's frustration with India's glacial pace toward reform did not end here. A March 1998 deadline for negotiating a compliance timetable passed without incident. The United States agreed to extend this deadline three times in order to work out a compromise on how to implement Indian patent legislation. In April 1998 the two parties informed the dispute settlement body that they had finally agreed upon a timetable for compliance giving India until 19 April 1999 to implement legislation (Tomar, 1999). In December 1998, India announced that it intended to enter a bill into Parliament to amend its patent law. While the upper house of Parliament passed the legislation, the lower house failed to do so. After an amendment was reintroduced both houses passed the amendments and they were ultimately approved by India's President. The announcement of the amendment on 26 March 1999 finally brought India in compliance with the WTO dispute settlement body (Tomar, 1999).

Even after this tortuously lengthy dispute, Indian law was far from compliant with the TRIPS agreement. In February 2000, the US pharmaceutical industry demanded that the USTR place India on its Priority Watch List for refusing to adopt sufficient pharmaceutical patent protection and for denying equitable market access to US companies. Under threat from

USTR action, the Indian government again introduced legislation to amend its patent law in December 2000 which was finally adopted in May 2002. Current plans were to incorporate a product patent regime through a third amendment before 1 January 2005 (Ragavan, 2003). India did issue a presidential decree on patents in December 2004, but has not passed legislation unambiguously backing up the ordinance. Legislation supporting the decree is currently working its way through lower and upper houses of parliament.

COERCION AS A TRADE POLICY: A RECORD OF LIMITED LONG-TERM SUCCESS

An underlying commonality amongst the above-described efforts by US business during the 1980s and 1990s is the use of coercive tactics as a policy-making tool. Coercion, in the context of international relations, occurs when a stronger nation (S) forces a weaker nation (W) to perform actions that serve the dominant power.[5] Under coercion, S states that it will punish W if it fails to take a certain action. S maximizes its pay-off when W takes the demanded action. Given S's statements, W also maximizes its pay-off if it takes the demanded action and is not punished. The optimal conditions for both W and S are that W complies with S's demands and S does not punish the small state (Goldsmith and Posner, 1999; Swaine, 2002). Coercive behavior in effect alters W's behavior not by raising the equilibrium benefit of W to follow S, but by making the alternative of not performing S's demanded action even less desirable (Gerhart, 2000).

A prominent example of US coercion is its use of Special 301 powers. Special 301 has repeatedly been used to threaten the imposition of punitive measures of countries that do not sufficiently protect the intellectual property rights of American products and processes. Most developing countries, including the BRICs, have been forced to relent at one time or another as the alternative punishment established by the United States was too burdensome to bear.

Coercion can be successful under certain conditions. Threats of trade sanctions by the US government largely demanded by American business interests resulted in major changes to domestic and international intellectual property regimes. Coercion placed intellectual property on the GATT agenda. Coercion forced China to adopt more stringent copyright laws and close major pirating factories. Coercion compelled India to give up its opposition to TRIPS and the radical changes to global intellectual property law contained therein. India relented even in spite of frenetic domestic protests from powerful local industries. Coercion induced Brazil to protect

US pharmaceutical products and processes at the expense of local produc-ers. American coercive threats, backed by economic power and access to its market, have shaped modern intellectual property law in its own image.

Yet, coercive practices have not produced the results that American busi-nesses most need – long-term, stable protection of their intellectual rights abroad. As noted earlier in this chapter, piracy in all four BRIC economies remains rampant. Although some laws are in place, development of these laws occurs at a slow pace, and enforcement of these laws remains lax. There is scant evidence if any that most unilateral economic sanctions by the United States ever actually achieved their stated long-term policy objec-tives (Stalls, 2003; Yu, 2002; Preeg, 1999).

Not only do interests that use coercion fail to achieve their foreign policy goals, but coercive tactics harm American global competitiveness. First, coercion provokes retaliation by the targeted state. For example, China repeatedly responded to US threats of sanctions with sanctions of its own. During the 1990s only repeated last-minute trade agreements between China and the United States averted devastating China tariffs costing American companies millions of dollars. For any economic power with sufficient strength, a strong incentive exists to make the costs of United States sanctions (usually through counter-sanctions) so undesirable that America's optimal state remains not to impose the sanctions at all.

Second, economic sanctions benefiting one American business interest can cause even greater harm to another American business interest. In the 1980s, pharmaceutical interests lobbied the US government to impose sanctions against Brazil because of its lax intellectual property standards. In 1988, President Reagan responded by imposing economic sanc-tions against numerous Brazilian products, including paper products, phar-maceuticals, chemicals, microwave ovens, television cameras, telephone answering machines, tape recorders, moccasins, pistols and jewelry (Getlan, 1995). Once the government announced trade sanctions, General Electric protested the tariffs against imported electrical breakers, Xerox opposed the inclusion of copy paper, Dow Chemical objected to the tariffs on carbon tetrachloride, Ford Motor called for the removal of amplifiers and windshield wipers, and Carrier sought the removal of air conditioners from the tariffs target list. Each of these companies claimed that the sanc-tions harmed their economic interests because they relied on the importa-tion of the targeted products to satisfy consumer needs (Harrison, 2001).

Third, economic coercion isolates the coercive country from its trading partners. Trading partners who witness American coercion applied against another country naturally will reflect on when such sanctions will be applied against themselves. As a result, non-coerced trading partners will be less likely to trust the United States to maintain a harmonious relationship without relying upon unilateral sanctions the moment a dispute arises. Liberal use of coercive sanctions in the past will make forging trade agreements with future partners all the more difficult.

Fourth, sanctions help mobilize and coalesce resistance to external pressure from a foreign state. For example, a United Nations report concluded that the Helms-Burton Act, US legislation that strengthens already existing sanctions against the Cuban government (Kinzel, 2002), actually weakened opposition to Fidel Castro's regime. Helms-Burton did so because it promoted the appearance that foreign interests, and not Cubans residing in Cuba, were attempting to decide Cuba's future, thus increasing support of the current regime (Shapiro, 1997). When the United States, a strong anti-whaling advocate, successfully suppressed an international scientific report concluding that whale stocks were sufficiently large to permit some commercial whaling, it provoked fierce resistance from whaling nations. Nations who were previously dormant or minimally active in commercial whaling sought to reassert their rights to whaling regardless of international protocols. Ireland withdrew its membership from the major international convention regulating whaling, the International Convention to Regulate Whaling. Norway sent six whaling ships to sea. Russia and Japan indicated that they would consider reintroducing whaling practices in the future. Iceland sought to form a coalition of states opposed to US anti-whaling efforts. There was even a possibility that unregulated whaling might again be performed on the open seas, a practice that has not occurred since 1960. Thus, the result of US suppression of pro-whaling data was a remobilized interest group dedicated to opposing US coercive intervention. US sanctions in this case 'fed the sense of grievance that has led the minority to take drastic action' (Chayes and Chayes, 1995, p. 102).

Fifth, coercive tactics fail to address the underlying problems that make intellectual property so rampant in developing countries (Yu, 2002). For example, coercive sanctions do not address, and in fact they may exacerbate, the poverty and unemployment in developing countries that makes purchasing non-generic Western patented drugs all but impossible for most citizens. No matter how sanctions impact an economy, strong incentives still exist for numerous consumers to purchase pirated goods. Sanctions also do not address the significant ideological and cultural differences between developing and developed countries that underlie copying as an accepted social practice.

Finally, coercive sanctions also indirectly impact US competitiveness by destabilizing the international economic system. In 1930, the US Congress passed the Smoot-Hawley Act, imposing on average 50 percent tariffs on thousands of foreign imports in a misguided attempt to protect domestic industry suffering in a feeble economy, an indirect sanction on foreign imports to the United States. The US passed Smoot-Hawley even after the League of Nations had just adopted a convention calling for a halt to tariff increases and planned to start a new round of tariff negotiations shortly thereafter. Smoot-Hawley devastated the global economic system. One by one other nations responded by raising their own tariffs and forcing themselves into their own isolationism. The tariffs hurt all trading nations, deepened the length and severity of the global Great Depression, and contributed to the rise of hostilities of World War II (Gerhart, 2004; Stein, 1983).

GATT drafters learned from this history that unilateral action based on trade disputes can lead ultimately to the collapse of the international trading system (Chayes and Chayes, 1995). Today, trade sanctions can devastate the economies of developing countries who suffer under them. Furthermore, developing countries may resent any sanctions or even the threat of sanctions by the United States as a new brand of economic colonialism (Leaffer, 1991). This resentment may result in nations refusing to participate in free economic trade. Further, the United States as a leading economic power may serve as a role model for emerging nations (Gray, 1995). If the United States does not hesitate to use coercive pressure, this may send a signal to developing nations that coercive economic power is not only acceptable but a preferred method of international trade policy.

THE FUTURE OF COERCION AS AN AMERICAN TRADE POLICY

There is little doubt that American firms achieved significant gains in protecting their global intellectual property rights. American business interests managed to recast intellectual property as a trade issue even in the face of stiff resistance from developing nations. Intellectual property is now a well-settled aspect of international trade. The United States government has not hesitated to use trade sanctions to bring non-compliant nations into line. The result has been a significant change in intellectual property laws in the BRIC economies.

Coercive tactics may be a necessary tool for protecting intellectual property rights abroad, but coercion is certainly not sufficient. China has the economic strength to resist American sanctions and impose sanctions of its own that will injure American interests. India has almost masterfully perfected the art of postponement, satisfying the requirements of international treaties and the demands of US representatives at a sluggish pace, if at all. US sanctions seem to provide only a temporary respite against this repeated practice of procrastination fueled by Indian political parties and other domestic interests dedicated to resisting the implementation of strong intellectual property laws. Similarly, Brazil lacks the political will at the regional and local level to enforce intellectual property laws. Finally, Russia appears to possess too much political capital such that the US cannot coerce the Russian government into submission without jeopardizing important non-intellectual property related global initiatives. The result is that piracy in the BRIC economies is as rampant as ever.

Coercion cannot succeed alone. American interests must look beyond threats and implement incentives to increase compliance with intellectual property laws. Reversing the coercion framework discussed above, the United States (the stronger nation, signified as S) must incentivize the actions of a developing nation (the weaker nation, signified as W) such that the developing nation will act in the interests of the dominant power. S should state that it will reward W if it opts to take a certain action.

S maximizes its pay-off when W takes the demanded action. Given S's statements, W also maximizes its pay-off if it takes the demanded action and receives S's reward. The optimal conditions for both W and S are that W complies with S's demands. Rewards by S alter W's behavior by raising the equilibrium benefit of W to follow S, thereby making the action of not performing S's action less desirable because of the loss of the reward (see Swaine, 2002; Gerhart, 2000; Goldsmith and Posner, 1999).

Numerous opportunities that merit further exploration exist to establish incentives to protect intellectual property rights. Local industries may be recast as collaborators and not competitors. Participating in a joint venture or a licensing arrangement with a foreign local firm will give that firm the incentive to protect the intellectual property right of the US firm it is participating with because its success is now hinged to sale of the foreign product. Developing countries can be encouraged to promote intellectual property protection in areas where such rights benefit local producers. For example, India possesses a massive movie industry, named Bollywood by some, that exceeds in scale and scope the movie empire in the United States. Bollywood, like its American counterpart, suffers significant losses from copyright piracy (Doshi, 2003). American firms susceptible to copyright infringement may benefit from increased protection that would benefit both Indian and US interests. American governmental and business interests can aid in this effort by providing technical assistance to the Indian government to develop an effective mechanism for regulating and enforcing copyrights in India.

Obviously, these efforts are not without their own problems. Sharing intellectual property with a local firm through a joint venture does not guarantee that the local firm will not commit piracy. New laws implemented by developing countries could only be limited to areas where it benefits local interests. For example, technical assistance in promoting a copyright regime to protect Indian entertainment may merely result in a framework that benefits a selected industry rather than the entire arena of creative work. Finally, any effort to creative incentives requires costs that both government and business can ill afford in a competitive twenty-first century economy.

In spite of these drawbacks, the costs of not establishing incentives for intellectual property enforcement and compliance are too great. All four BRIC economies witness rampant piracy that shows no signs of slowing. As these economies grow in strength, they will become increasingly resistant to American coercive tactics. American interests cannot wed themselves to coercive tactics even if they have brought some success in the past. Future trade policy must incorporate benefits for developing nations to join developed countries in implementing and enforcing strong intellectual property rights protections.

NOTES

1. Financial support from Dr Subhash Jain and the University of Connecticut Center for International Business Education and Research is gratefully appreciated. The author acknowledges Christophe Pane and Anne Taylor for providing helpful research and editing assistance during this project.
2. The IIPA focuses mainly on copyright infringement, although it does comment on trademark and patent infringement.
3. Article 123(1) of the Indian constitution authorizes the President to legislate in this fashion when Parliament is not in session or the President believes that he must take immediate action.
4. For a more detailed review of the WTO review and appeal process see Tomar (1999).
5. This example assumes the cost of punishing the weaker state is negligible.

REFERENCES

Baker, Brook K. (2004), 'Arthritic Flexibilities for Accessing Medicines: Analysis of WTO Action Regarding Paragraph 6 of the Doha Declaration on the TRIPS Agreement and Public Health', *Indiana International and Comparative Law Review*, **14**, 613–715.
Bershok, Rhonda (1992), 'Releasing the Tiger? India Moves into the Global Market', *International Legal Perspectives*, **4**(Fall), 53.
Chayes, Abram and Antonia Handler Chayes (1995), *The New Sovereignty: Compliance with International Regulatory Agreements*, Cambridge, MA: Harvard University Press.
Cptech.org (2005), 'Patent Legislation Passed March, 2005', from http://www.cptech.org/ip/health/c/india/patents-act-amendments.html.
Dam, Kenneth W. (1987), 'The Growing Importance of International Protection of Intellectual Property', *International Lawyer*, **21**(3), 627–38.
Doshi, Priti (2003), 'Copyright Problems in India Affecting Hollywood and "Bollywood"', *Suffolk Transnational Law Review*, **26**(Summer), 295–322.

Drahos, Peter (1999), 'Global Property Rights in Information: The Story of TRIPS at the GATT', in P. Drahos (ed.), *Intellectual Property*. Aldershot: Dartmouth Publishing Company, pp. 319–432.

The Economist (2005), 'Patently Unclear: A Crucial New Intellectual Property Regime Disappoints', *The Economist*, 22 January 63.

Embassy of India (2000), 'Embassy of India Policy Statements, Intellectual Property Rights in India', from http://www.indianembassy.org/policy/ipr/ipr_ 2000.htm.

Emmert, Frank (1990), 'Intellectual Property in the Uruguay Round – Negotiating Strategies of the Western Industrialized Countries', *Michigan Journal of International Law*, **11**(Summer), 1317–99.

Feder, Gregory S. (1996), 'Enforcement of Intellectual Property Rights in China: You Can Lead a Horse to Water, But You can't Make it Drink', *Virginia Journal of International Law*, **37**(Fall), 223–54.

Federal Register (1988), 'Increase in the Rates of Duty for Certain Articles from Brazil', Proclamation 5885, *Federal Register*, **53**, 41551.

Fleishman, Lana C. (1993), 'The Empire Strikes Back: The Influence of the United States Motion Picture Industry on Russian Copyright Law', *Cornell International Law Journal*, **26**(Winter), 189–238.

Foster, George (1998), 'Opposing Forces in a Revolution of Patent Protection: The US and India in the Uruguay Round and its Aftermath', *UCLA Journal of International Law and Foreign Affairs*, **3**(Summer), 283–323.

Gad, Mohamed Omar (2003), 'Impact of Multinational Enterprises on Multilateral Rule Making: The Pharmaceutical Industry and the TRIPS Uruguay Round Negotiations', *Law and Business Review of the Americas*, **9**(Fall), 667–97.

Gerhart, Peter M. (2000), 'Reflections: Beyond Compliance Theory – TRIPS as a Substantive Issue', *Case Western Reserve Journal of International Law*, **32**(3), 357–85.

Gerhart, Peter M. (2004), 'The World Trade Organization and Participatory Democracy: The Historical Evidence', *Vanderbilt Journal of Transnational Law*, **37**(October), 897–934.

Getlan, Myles (1995), 'TRIPS and the Future of Section 301: A Comparative Study in Trade Resolution', *Columbia Journal of Transnational Law*, **34**(1), 173–218.

Goldsmith, Jack L. and Eric A. Posner (1999), 'A Theory of Customary International Law', *University of Chicago Law Review*, **66**(Fall), 1113–77.

Gray, Whitmore (1995), 'The Challenge of Asian Law', *Fordham International Law Journal*, **19**(October), 1–8.

Harrison, Christopher Scott (2001), 'Protection of Pharmaceuticals as Foreign Policy: The Canada–US Trade Agreement and Bill C-22 versus the North American Free Trade Agreement and Bill C-91', *North Carolina Journal of International Law and Commercial Regulation*, **26**(Spring), 457–528.

Huang, Yasheng and Tarun Khanna (2003), 'Can India Overtake China?', *Foreign Policy*, http://www.hvk.org/articles/0703/6.html.

IIPA (International Intellectual Property Alliance) (2005a), 'International Intellectual Property Alliance, 2005 Special 301 Report (Russian Federation)', 13–30, http://www.iipa.com/rbc/2005/2005SPEC301RUSSIA.pdf.

IIPA (International Intellectual Property Alliance) (2005b), 'International Intellectual Property Alliance, 2005 Special 301 Report (Brazil)', 51–68, http://www.iipa.com/rbc/2005/2005SPEC301BRAZIL.pdf.

IIPA (International Intellectual Property Alliance) (2005c), 'International Intellectual Property Alliance, 2005 Special 301 Report (India)', 121–36, http://www.iipa.com/rbc/2005/2005SPEC301INDIA.pdf.

IIPA (International Intellectual Property Alliance) (2005d), 'International Intellectual Property Alliance, 2005 Special 301 Report (People's Republic of China)', 183–215, http://www.iipa.com/rbc/2005/2005SPEC301PRCrev.pdf.

Kinzel, Runa (2002), 'Helms Burton: A View From Abroad', *University of Miami International and Competitive Law Review*, **10**(Fall), 81–95.

Kuik, Tim (1999), 'Piracy in Russia: An Epidemic', *Whittier Law Review*, **20**(Summer), 831–37.

Leaffer, Marshall A. (1991), 'Protecting United States Intellectual Property Abroad: Toward a New Multilateralism', *Iowa Law Review*, **76**(January), 273–308.

Liu, Paul C.B. (1994), 'US Industry's Influence on Intellectual Property Negotiations and Special 301 Actions', *UCLA Pacific Basin Law Journal*, **13**(Fall), 87–117.

Maskus, Keith (2000), 'Intellectual Property Rights and Economic Development', *Case Western Reserve Journal of International Law*, **32**(3), 471–506.

Miller, David E. (2000), 'Combating Copyright Infringement in Russia: A Comprehensive Approach for Western Plaintiffs', *Vanderbilt Journal of Transnational Law*, **33**(November), 1203–1222.

Mossinghoff, Gerald J. (2000), 'National Obligations Under Intellectual Property Treaties: The Beginning of a True International Regime', *Federal Circuit Bar Journal*, **9**(4), 591–603.

Neigel, Connie (2000), 'Piracy in Russia and China: A Different US Reaction', *Law and Contemporary Problems*, **63**(4), 179–99.

Newby, Kim (1995), 'The Effectiveness of Special 301 in Creating Long Term Copyright Protection for US Companies Overseas', *Syracuse Journal of International Law*, **21**, 29–62.

Parker, Jesse (2002), 'The Lotus Files: The Emergence of Technology Entrepreneurship in India and China', *Fletcher Forum of World Affairs*, **26**, 119–34.

Petherbridge, Lee (2004), 'Intelligent TRIPS Implementation: A Strategy for Countries on the Cusp of Development', *University of Pennsylvania Journal of International Economic Law*, **25**(Fall), 1133–69.

Preeg, Ernest H. (1999), *Feeling Good or Doing Good with Sanctions*, Washington, DC: CSIS Press.

Ragavan, Srividhya (2003), 'Can't We All Get Along? The Case for a Workable Patent Model', *Arizona State Law Journal*, **35**, 117–85.

Rahman, Zillur and S.K. Bhattacharyya (2003), 'First Mover Advantages in Emerging Economies: A Discussion', *Management Decision*, **41**(2), 141–47.

Rajwade, A.V. (2005), 'India and China: A Comparison', http://www.rediff.com/money/2005/jan/18guest.htm.

Ronkainen, Ilkka A. and Jose Luis Guerrero-Cusumano (2001), 'Correlates of Intellectual Property Violation', *Multinational Business Review*, **9**(1), 59–65.

Ryan, Michael P. (1998), 'The Function Specific and Linkage-Bargain Diplomacy of International Intellectual Property Lawmaking', *University of Pennsylvania Journal of International Economic Law*, **19**(Summer), 535–86.

Schulz, Claudia (2004), 'The TRIPS Agreement and Intellectual Property in Brazil', *American Society of International Law Proceedings*, **98**(March–April), 100–103.

Sell, Susan K. (1999), 'Multinational Corporations as Agents of Change: The Globalization of Intellectual Property Rights', in A.C. Cutler, V. Haufler and

T. Porter (eds), *Private Authority and International Affairs*, Albany, NY: State University of New York Press, pp. 169–97.

Senate Committee (1986), 'Possible New Round of Trade Negotiations: Hearings Before the Senate Committee on Finance', 99th Cong. 144, 149–52, statement of Kenneth W. Dam, Vice-President, Law and External Relations, IBM Corp., on behalf of the Intellectual Property Committee.

Shapiro, David T. (1997), 'Be Careful What You Wish For: US Politics and the Future of the National Security Exception to GATT', *George Washington Journal of International Law and Economics*, **31**(1), 97–118.

Sherman, Peggy B. and Ellwood F. Oakley III (2004), 'Pandemics and Panaceas: The World Trade Organization's Efforts to Balance Pharmaceutical Patents and Access to AIDS Drugs', *American Business Law Journal*, **41**(2/3), 353–411.

Stalls, Justin D. (2003), 'Economic Sanctions', *University of Miami International and Comparative Law Review*, **11**(Fall), 115–72.

Stein, Arthur A. (1983), 'Coordination and Collaboration: Regimes in an Anarchic World', in S. Krasner (ed.), *International Regimes*, Ithaca, NY: Cornell University Press, pp. 115–40.

Swaine, Edward T. (2002), 'Rational Custom', *Duke Law Journal*, **52**(December), 559–627.

Taketa, Jason (2002), 'The Future of Business Method Software Patents in the International Intellectual Property System', *Southern California Law Review*, **75**(May), 943–82.

Tomar, David K. (1999), 'A Look Into the WTO Patent Dispute Between the United States and India', *Wisconsin International Law Journal*, **17**(Fall), 579–603.

USTR (United States Trade Representative) (1995), Office of the USTR, '1995 National Trade Estimate Report on Foreign Trade Barriers'.

USTR (United States Trade Representative) (1996), Office of the USTR, '1996 National Trade Estimate Report on Foreign Trade Barriers'.

Wagman, George R. and Stephen B. Scofield (1999), 'The Competitive Advantage of Intellectual Property', *SAM Advanced Management Journal*, **64**(3), 4–8, 19.

Weinstein, Veronica and Dennis Fernandez (2004), 'Recent Developments in Chinese Intellectual Property Laws', *Chinese Journal of International Law*, **3**(1), 227–38.

Wilson, Dominic and Roopa Purushothaman (2003), 'Dreaming with BRICs : The Path to 2050', Global Economics Paper No. 99, New York: Goldman Sachs.

Yu, Peter K. (2000), 'From Pirates to Partners: Protecting Intellectual Property in China in the Twenty-First Century', *American University Law Review*, **50**(October), 131–242.

Yu, Peter K. (2002), 'Toward a Non Zero-Sum Approach to Resolving Global Intellectual Property Disputes: What we can Learn from Mediators, Business Strategists, and International Relations Theorists', *University of Cincinnati Law Review*, **70**(Winter), 569–650.

17. Corruption in large developing economies: the case of Brazil, Russia, India and China

Mohsin Habib and Leon Zurawicki

INTRODUCTION: THE IMPORTANCE OF BRICs

Ten years ago the International Trade Administration (US Department of Commerce) published a study on ten big (or relatively big) emerging markets holding the greatest potential for the US business (Garten, 1998). The press inflated that image further, dubbing the ten countries the lions of the future. These days the BRIC are labeled as key emerging markets and include Russia which was not on the Commerce Department's list ten years ago. Independently from each other, BRIC nations have made significant economic progress since the early 1990s. These four countries are considered the locomotives of the global development for the years to come according to a widely publicized forecast by Goldman Sachs (Wilson and Purushothaman, 2003). While it is quite tricky to make projections 40 years ahead, there is no denial that the four heavyweight economic giants have a tremendous and yet unrealized growth potential. In 2002, the four countries signed a trade and cooperation agreement which is yet to be filled with meaningful content, but the energy sector is one of the strategic areas they are interested in.

For researchers, the BRIC cluster is one of the possible groupings of very large nations which can be studied in different conjunctions with each other. For example, although thousands of miles apart, Brazil and Russia have certain things in common. Geographically, they are among the largest in the world. The plentitude of natural resources (not only mineral but also huge stocks of timber) can make them suppliers to the world. While their income per capita is quite modest – in the $6500 range – large population (175 and 150 million, respectively) magnifies that into current GDP of $1 trillion/year. Adding India and China, BRICs represent the four highest GDPs in the developing world and it is their size which is a common denominator of the heterogeneous coalition. Given the characteristics and the stage of development of the BRIC countries, the conclusions and implications drawn here may be appropriate for other large countries (such as Indonesia, Mexico, Nigeria and Pakistan) to chart a course for economic development.

The overall progress in BRIC countries has been accelerated by the need for the developed world to consume large quantities of goods and services manufactured efficiently in the developing countries. In meeting that need, the wealthy countries have historically paid minimal attention to the presence of corruption and other negative elements in emerging countries. Lack of governance and transparency has made the problem of corruption worse in many of these nations. Yet, significant FDI and business from the developed world have flown into these countries. Looking at the growth of the economies in the BRIC countries, it is somewhat difficult to see how corruption can have any substantial impact. But it does, because its effects are mostly evaluated in terms of lost opportunities, the amount of business and investment (local and foreign) these countries could have received at a lower level of corruption.

Whether and when the BRIC countries will meet the full economic growth expectations is an open question. But in looking at the success factors one should not ignore the inhibiting forces, such as corruption. The extant literature (Gupta et al., 1998; Mauro, 1995, 2002) documents the negative impact of corruption on economic growth, investment, productivity and income distribution. The following represents some of the key conclusions in that respect.

CONSEQUENCES OF CORRUPTION

Corruption lowers investment and can hurt economic growth (Mauro, 1995; Tanzi and Davoodi, 1997; Habib and Zurawicki, 2002). It can limit the development of human capital in countries like India if individuals are denied basic access to food, health and education. Corruption adds cost to the economy in general (Rose-Ackerman, 1999; Shleifer and Vishny, 1993; Gupta et al., 1998). Delivery of services becomes more costly to the customers. Protracted corruption can question the legitimacy of the state and destroy any confidence the citizens might have in the government. Corruption also makes the playing field uneven for both businesses and individuals. Companies do not necessarily compete on the basis of market forces if corruption is involved. As for individuals, the poorer segment of the population usually suffers the most. In the presence of corruption, the poor will continue to languish within the society.

To learn specifically how bad the impact of corruption is for individual countries requires much greater research effort. Getulio Vargas Foundation's study in Brazil phrased that relationship in hypothetical terms: a 10 percent reduction of corruption in Brazil would nearly double its per capita income by 2020 (da Silva et al., 2002). Most of the other estimates look rather at the total volume of bribes relative to GDP – the World Bank experts average this ratio globally at 3 percent.

CAUSES OF CORRUPTION

As will be demonstrated in this chapter, all four BRIC countries have rather poor ratings on corruption. The preliminary question is whether it is possible to determine a priori which attributes of their economy and polity make the four countries prone to corruption. While the comprehensive perspective on causes of corruption, many of which are endogenous in nature, still needs to be developed, it appears that some of the characteristics which contribute to BRICs' appeal as the key emerging markets do also encourage corruption.

Size of the Country

The ancient Greeks argued that it is 'difficult, if not impossible, for a populous state to be run by good laws' (Aristotle, 2004) and prescribed that a state should be large enough to be self-sufficient, but small enough to be manageable and easily surveyed. While this statement is certainly not a dogma, the argument is worth pursuing following more modern-day reasoning by Tanzi (1994). In fact, in a cross-country regression analysis of 60 countries, Root (1999) found that higher population is significantly associated with greater corruption when controlled for several other key variables. He explained this pattern by economies of scale in bad governance – the rulers of the large countries can more easily extract significant rents from the nation and compensate the constituencies who support them.

Resources

Ades and Di Tella (1999) suggest that all other things being equal, in countries with large endowments of valuable raw materials such as fuels, minerals and metals, corruption may offer greater potential gain to officials who allocate rights to exploit such resources. This has been also referred to as 'resource curse'.[1]

State Interventionism

Somewhat related to the previous argument, the greater the extent of state intervention in the economy, the greater will be the options available for corruption (Tanzi, 1994). In a broader sense, the theoretical work of Banfield (1975), not to mention the views of Milton Friedman, give such a prediction more weight.

PERCEPTIONS OF CORRUPTION

Keeping in mind the above-mentioned general characteristics for BRIC nations, we now need to analyze more specific information on corruption. When comparing the extent of corruption in individual countries, researchers frequently emphasize overall indices such as Transparency International's Corruption Perception Index (CPI). Such an approach allows for a quick evaluation of corruption risk when it comes to two or more markets with clearly different ratings.

General rankings and classifications are important indicators for local governments and politicians and can mobilize public opinion to press for radical improvements. A case in point is Bangladesh where the media has used Transparency International's (TI) rankings and published reports to question the government's competency in combating corruption, and as a result bringing about a change in power. While this effort is certainly appreciated, how relevant these indicators are to business is another story. Local smaller companies might have little alternative to their home base of operations due to both lack of familiarity with the foreign markets and the scarcity of resources (even creditworthiness) allowing such entry. In contrast, the foreign investors are better equipped for entry or exit. They are typically stronger financially and have footholds in numerous national markets. For large businesses with alternative options, perhaps in contrast to governments and politicians, the whole-country all-industry index is not necessarily indicative of the particular corruption issues faced by them.

Hence, from the standpoint of individual (foreign) investors, more targeted indicators are of greater importance. Fortunately, such data are presently available and in this chapter will draw on various general and particular national corruption statistics in order to reach a greater depth of comparisons between the four very large and potentially quickly expanding markets. To the authors' best knowledge, this research represents the first attempt comprehensively to examine dimensions of corruption on an international basis.

Several institutions have developed measures of corruption as it relates to countries across the world. We collected information from the World Bank, Transparency International and the Global Competitiveness Report. We shall discuss some of the findings for the BRIC countries in the following sections.

Table 17.1   Transparency International CPI Index for BRIC

Year	Brazil	Russia	India	China
1996	2.96	2.58	2.63	2.43
1997	3.56	2.27	2.75	2.88
1998	4	2.4	2.9	3.5
1999	4.1	2.4	2.9	3.1
2000	3.9	2.1	2.8	3.1
2001	4	2.3	2.7	3.5
2002	4 (3.4–4.8)	2.7 (1.5–5.0)	2.7 (2.4–3.6)	3.5 (2.0–5.6)
2003	3.9 (3.3–4.7)	2.7 (1.4–4.9)	2.8 (2.1–3.6)	3.4 (2.0–5.5)
2004	3.9 (3.7–4.1)	2.8 (2.5–3.1)	2.8 (2.6–3.0)	3.4 (3.0–3.8)

Source: TI Corruption Perception Index, 1996–2004, http://www.transparency.org/surveys/index.html#cpi

Table 17.1 provides an overview of the perceived corruption in the BRIC countries from 1996 to 2004. The data used is the Corruption Perception Index (CPI) scale measured and collected by Transparency International.

As can be seen, corruption has been a problem for the whole quartet for quite some time. Russia and India have very similar low levels (that is, high corruption) and China and Brazil scored systematically a little bit better. Remarkably and sadly, hardly any improvement in the CPI ratings took place except for a quick initial jump for China and Brazil in 1996–97. At the same time, it is interesting to note a much wider spread of the respondents' ratings for Russia and China as contrasted with Brazil and India. It depicts stronger differences of opinion on corruption in Russia and China – perhaps a more 'fluid' nature of corruption and an indication of a more chaotic as opposed to a better-organized corruption.

The latter observation is in line with some recent findings in the literature. During the last couple of years, researchers undertook attempts to reach beyond the cumulative indices of corruption and to study its specific operational aspects. According to Rodriguez et al. (2005), compared to the median of their cluster of emerging economies, Russia displays a very high arbitrariness (which measures unpredictability of bribes) index – slightly higher than India. However, Russia is close to the median on pervasiveness of corruption where India scores high. Brazil is low on arbitrariness and somewhat below the median on pervasiveness. The results for China were not reported.

Next, various categories of governance which are either complementary or even overlap with corruption are considered for the BRIC countries. Table 17.2 shows the data from the Global Competitiveness Report 2004.

Table 17.2   Global Competitiveness Report 2004 indices and rankings

	Brazil	Russia	India	China
Govt. waste subindex	3.07 (52)	2.46 (76)	2.56 (72)	3.66 (35)
Public institutions index	4.27 (53)	3.34 (81)	4.26 (55)	4.33 (52)
Contracts & law subindex	3.92 (57)	2.74 (91)	4.65 (35)	3.81 (60)
Corruption index	4.62 (56)	3.94 (75)	3.86 (80)	4.84 (50)

Source: Porter et al. (2004).

Overall, the corruption indices for all of the BRICs are higher (more so as they are computed on a seven-point scale) than what is depicted by the CPI (ten-point scale). Also, the corruption indices look relatively better compared to other governance measures. Still, Russia and India fall behind China and Brazil in all categories listed – in reverse order. If we were to average all the four indices for each country, Russia clearly scores the lowest. This suggests that poor institutions accompany corruption (and vice versa) and actually render the business environment even worse.

The World Bank (2002–2003) data on various aspects of governance are summarized in Table 17.3. In terms of corruption, this again shows Brazil performing better, Russia being the worst and India scoring higher than China.

At the same time, for the period covered Table 17.3 does not show much improvement (except for political stability) in any of the categories listed. One practical interpretation of this trend is that over time the different aspects of government and social governance seem to be related and appear to reinforce each other. Consequently, the evil of corruption should be studied in conjunction with other aspects of governance as individually they form part of a wider phenomenon. This broader category encompasses the tolerance for corruption ('voice and accountability' category). Thus, when we apply the term 'corruption' not just in BRIC but perhaps in other countries as well, this notion can be used as a proxy for the whole complex of improprieties in political and business environment.

A more detailed perspective on corruption and related governance issues in BRIC can be derived from the Global Competitiveness Report data as per Table 17.4. The overall perceived cost of corruption to business (item 7.09 in Table 17.4) in all four countries looks quite similar – the range being 3.5 to 4. What it might suggest when juxtaposed with the CPI is that in individual countries businesses find a way to neutralize the prevalence of unethical behavior. It remains to be explained how it is being done, beyond simply stating that the frequency of corruption does not reflect in

Table 17.3 The world bank governance indices 2002–2003

	BRAZIL				RUSSIA				INDIA				CHINA			
Voice and accountability	2002	2000	1998	1996	2002	2000	1998	1996	2002	2000	1998	1996	2002	2000	1998	1996
Estimate (−2.5 to + 2.5)	0.28	0.53	0.6	0.22	−0.52	−0.44	−0.26	−0.34	0.38	0.45	0.26	0.27	−1.38	−1.37	−1.51	−1.22
Percentile Rank (0–100)	58.1	63.9	64.4	59.7	33.8	35.6	41.4	39.8	60.6	62.8	59.2	60.7	10.1	11.5	7.9	12
Political stability																
Estimate (−2.5 to + 2.5)	0.17	0.27	−0.43	−0.01	−0.4	−0.53	−0.49	−0.76	−0.84	−0.35	−0.34	−0.55	0.22	0.27	0.29	0.23
Percentile Rank (0–100)	48.1	56.4	30.9	48.2	33	28.5	26.7	16.5	22.2	37.6	35.2	23.8	51.4	55.2	58.2	56.7
Govt. effectiveness	2002	2000	1998	1996	2002	2000	1998	1996	2002	2000	1998	1996	2002	2000	1998	1996
Estimate (−2.5 to + 2.5)	−0.22	−0.19	−0.16	−0.19	−0.4	−0.61	−0.59	−0.48	−0.13	−0.05	−0.13	−0.16	0.18	0.24	0.18	0.11
Percentile Rank (0–100)	50	48.4	48.1	52.5	44.3	29.9	26.2	33.5	54.1	56	52.5	56.4	63.4	65.8	66.1	68.2
Regulatory quality	2002	2000	1998	1996	2002	2000	1998	1996	2002	2000	1998	1996	2002	2000	1998	1996
Estimate (−2.5 to + 2.5)	0.26	0.36	0.29	0.13	−0.3	−1.55	−0.37	−0.41	−0.34	−0.16	−0.08	−0.13	−0.41	−0.2	−0.07	−0.1
Percentile Rank (0–100)	63.4	63.8	57.6	60.2	44.3	6.5	31.5	31.5	43.8	38.9	41.8	44.2	40.2	35.7	43.5	48.1

Rule of law	2002	2000	1998	1996	2002	2000	1998	1996	2002	2000	1998	1996	2002	2000	1998	1996
Estimate (−2.5 to +2.5)	−0.3	−0.15	−0.09	−0.24	−0.78	−0.86	−0.78	−0.8	0.07	0.23	0.21	−0.01	−0.22	−0.32	−0.22	−0.43
Percentile Rank (0–100)	50	55.1	56.8	46.4	25.3	17.3	23.2	19.9	57.2	63.2	67	56.6	51.5	47	52.4	37.3
Control of corruption	2002	2000	1998	1996	2002	2000	1998	1996	2002	2000	1998	1996	2002	2000	1998	1996
Estimate (+2.5 to +2.5)	−0.05	0.01	0.11	−0.1	−0.9	−1.05	−0.69	−0.69	−0.25	−0.21	−0.17	−0.29	−0.41	−0.34	−0.2	−0.01
Percentile Rank (0–100)	56.7	59.8	68.9	55.3	21.1	10.3	26.8	27.3	49.5	52.7	60.1	43.3	42.3	46.7	57.9	58.7

Source: Kaufmann et al. (2003).

Table 17.4   Corruption and related categories of business environment (Executive Opinion Survey, GCR 2003)

Item	Category (score and rank)	Brazil	Russia	India	China
2.03	Distortive govt. subsidies	4.0 (25)	2.9 (77)	3.0 (67)	3.8 (29)
5.07	Postal efficiency	5.5 (30)	3.8 (60)	4.3 (51)	4.7 (47)
6.01	Judicial independence	3.9 (52)	2.5 (81)	5.2 (25)	3.4 (62)
6.02	Efficiency of legal framework	3.9 (51)	2.5 (85)	4.4 (35)	3.9 (50)
6.03	Property Rights	4.9 (44)	2.7 (96)	5.1 (43)	4.1 (64)
6.06	Burden of regulation	2.8 (53)	1.9 (100)	2.5 (67)	3.3 (21)
6.07	Transparency of govt. policymaking	3.6 (65)	2.5 (97)	4.1 (41)	4.2 (33)
6.08	Favoritism in govt. decisions	3.5 (39)	2.5 (81)	3.2 (57)	3.5 (43)
6.09	Bureaucratic red tape (1–9) – reversed	2.7 (58)	3.4 (92)	2.8 (64)	3.9 (102)
6.13	Reliability of police services	3.1 (81)	2.8 (88)	4.1 (52)	4.2 (48)
6.14	Cost of crime and violence	2.5 (91)	3.5 (71)	5.5 (25)	4.3 (52)
6.17	Cost of organized crime	3.4 (85)	3.3 (87)	5.1 (44)	4.3 (60)
6.18	Informal sector (1–9) – reversed	4.6 (66)	5.6 (86)	4.6 (65)	3.8 (49)
7.01	Bribery in exports & imports	4.4 (56)	3.5 (87)	3.8 (72)	5.0 (43)
7.02	Bribery in public utilities	5.1 (50)	4.0 (79)	3.9 (83)	4.8 (60)
7.03	Bribery in tax collection	4.4 (60)	4.4 (59)	3.9 (71)	4.8 (52)
7.04	Bribery in public contracts	3.9 (45)	3.4 (64)	2.8 (82)	4.5 (36)
7.05	Bribery in loan applications	4.8 (54)	4.1 (77)	4.3 (69)	4.5 (64)
7.06	Bribery in govt. policymaking	3.8 (59)	3.3 (77)	3.3 (78)	4.5 (40)
7.07	Bribery in judicial decisions	4.1 (61)	3.7 (77)	4.5 (52)	4.5 (50)
7.08	Diversion of public funds	3.1 (63)	2.6 (76)	3.0 (67)	3.4 (51)
7.09	Business costs of corruption	4.0 (39)	3.5 (56)	3.7 (50)	3.9 (43)
7.10	Public trust of politicians	2.1 (62)	1.9 (70)	1.7 (82)	3.8 (20)
7.11	Illegal political donations	2.8 (70)	2.4 (86)	2.2 (94)	5.0 (18)
7.12	Effectiveness of legal political donations	3.5 (68)	3.0 (86)	4.1 (37)	4.6 (17)
7.13	Money laundering through banks	4.3 (64)	3.3 (95)	4.6 (50)	4.3 (61)
7.14	Money laundering (other)	3.5 (66)	3.1 (80)	3.3 (73)	4.1 (48)
10.05	Ethical behavior of firms	4.3 (43)	3.4 (87)	3.7 (74)	4.2 (47)

Source: Porter et al. (2004).

the bribe rates. Alternatively, a more alarming thought would be that in highly corrupt environments we face a 'state capture' rather than 'business capture' (Hellman et al., 2000). In that case, the bribing businesses are capable of extracting additional rents which then reduce the ratio of corruption cost to revenue.

SPECIFICS OF CORRUPTION IN BRIC

In what follows, we shall address various manifestations of corruption in the context of interaction between businesses and government agencies.

Table 17.4 also allows the tracing of the purpose of bribing in individual countries. Also, it helps deduce the nuclei of bribing or extortion activities, be it judiciary, government officials or politicians at large (items 7.01–7.07). Overall, there is a much lesser differentiation in China in terms of bribery by specific purpose, than occurs in the three other countries. Bribery in government policy-making (buying laws) is at the top of the list in Brazil and Russia and ranks second in India, whereas in China it is at par with all other categories. Bribing in public procurement is the second most important area in Brazil and Russia and the top category in India. Note that those two spheres are usually associated with so-called 'grand' corruption – high single bribes proportionate to the underlying stakes. In contrast, bribery in public utilities, tax collection and loan approvals can be viewed as a more common and lower level of corruption (Lambsdorff, 2005). If so, then in both Brazil and Russia, grand corruption is more prevalent and harmful than the petty variety.

Irregular payments with respect to judicial decisions are the third-most troubling item in Brazil, while in Russia and India this position is taken by bribes in connection with foreign trade activity. One can speculate that the greater openness of the Brazilian economy induces a top-down imposed, user-friendly climate for exporters and importers, whereas this is not necessarily the case in Russia and India.

In terms of types of unethical behavior displayed by the officials, acceptance of illegal donations stands out in Brazil, Russia and India, followed by favoritism in government decisions, whereas the embezzlement of public funds occupies an equally high position in all of the BRICs. Interestingly, the effectiveness of legal donations is deemed higher in Brazil and Russia than in India and China. While we mentioned before a possibility of 'business capture', especially in Russia and India (which have the worst corruption perception indices), the ratings on bureaucrats' conduct indicate substantial overall lack of probity of the bribe-takers.

Finally, organized crime inflicts huge cost to businesses in Russia and Brazil (in the latter, an even stronger impact is generated by general crime and violence). Organized crime affects relatively fewer companies in China and India. Add to it the phenomenon of money laundering in Brazil, Russia and India, and the crime, corruption and informal economy triangle emerges as a troubling confluence.

Table 17.4 combined with the data from the Executive Opinion Survey (conducted by the World Economic Forum: see Kaufmann, 2004) offers an

Table 17.5   Illegal versus non-criminal corruption in BRICs in 2004

Percentage of **positive** statements	Brazil	Russia	India	China	US*
Corporate Illegal Corruption	50.9	19.9	39.4	43.6	84.0
Corporate Legal Corruption Component	19.9	21.2	29.8	49.4	30.8
Average (1+2) = Corporate Ethics Index	35.4	20.5	34.6	46.5	57.4
Public Sector Ethics Index	35.2	20.4	31.7	42.1	70.1
Judicial Effectiveness Index	41.5	15.8	59.9	42	83.7
Corporate Governance Index	56.3	28.9	55.4	35.3	89.8

Note: *For better insight, the indices for the US were added as gauges.

Source: Kaufmann (2004).

insight into the prevalence of illegal versus more subtle forms of corruption (Table 17.5).

The results are symptomatic. The total scope of corrupt activities – illegal and non-criminal – is the highest in Russia, with China faring much better. Criminal corruption is a plague in Russia, to a much greater extent than in the other three BRICs. Non-criminal corruption is by far most prevalent in Brazil and Russia, with China displaying a cleaner record. The lowest evaluation of the public sector was earned by Russia and the highest by China with Brazil not far behind. The highest rating on judicial effectiveness was secured by India, followed at a distance by China and Brazil. As for corporate governance, companies from Brazil and India – perhaps more exposed to the outside world than their counterparts from Russia and China – scored significantly higher.

Combining the data from Table 17.5 does not lead to unequivocally consistent conclusions as the indices do not move in tandem. Better corporate governance in Brazil and India relative to Russia seems to be associated with lower illegal corruption and it can be further assumed that the higher effectiveness of the judiciary also plays a positive role. Intuitively, this could be expected but, unfortunately, this conclusion gets somewhat weakened when China is added to this analysis. It is interesting, however, that the relatively better corporate governance index in Brazil does not reduce the non-criminal corruption. Perhaps what cannot be accomplished by punishable means is attempted by morally doubtful but non-illegal methods. Thus, the risk of being caught for direct bribes diverts influence-seeking to contributions to political parties, nepotism and other forms of quid pro quo. This substitution in the case of Brazil is not as evident, though, with respect to the remaining BRICs. While clear-cut correlations do not emerge from the above data, they still allow the proposition that the quality of the judiciary can exert a positive influence on both sides of the bribery equation: the public sector on the one hand and the corporations on the other.

CORRUPTION IN RELATION TO FIRMS' CHARACTERISTICS

Selected findings for the BRIC countries based upon the World Bank survey are presented in Tables 17.6a–6d. The survey looks at firms' perceptions regarding several country factors considered important for business. For each factor, the data show the percentage of firms identifying it as a major or very severe obstacle for business. Table 17.6a exhibits the findings on ten factors considered here. Furthermore, it classifies and presents data based on different firm size (small, medium and large). Note that the magnitude of ratings by Brazilian companies is much higher (meaning a much worse impression) than in the case of Russia. Overall, a higher percentage of firms view Brazil as problematic for business due to such factors as economic and policy uncertainty, corruption, crime, anti-competitive practices, and business licensing or operating permits. Russia is also viewed as troublesome, but less so. China is considered problematic by a high percentage of firms due to lack of consistency or predictability of officials' interpretations of regulations, and the lack of confidence in the judiciary system. Data on India are missing altogether.

With respect to firm size, far more small and medium-sized companies in Brazil, as opposed to large ones, perceive corruption to be a major problem. On the contrary, it is the large companies in both Russia and India who are primarily complaining about corruption. It seems the larger companies have become the primary targets for bribery-seeking individuals and entities in these two countries.

In Table 17.6b, the responding firms are classified on the basis of domestic and foreign ownerships. These data are not available for China. For Brazil, more foreign firms see factors such as economic uncertainty, corruption and anti-competitive practices as serious problems than do domestic firms. Perhaps the local firms are more used to the uncertainty and the corruption problems that plague the country whereas the foreign firms, while aware of the problem, find it difficult to cope with. Foreign and domestic firms are fairly similar in their responses for Russia and India. In Brazil, more domestic firms than foreign firms consider the confidence level in the judiciary system as a problem. In India, it is the opposite. For foreign firms, Indian courts and the judicial system have

Table 17.6a   Firm's size and the burden of poor institutions in 2003

Percentage of companies indicating a serious problem with:	Brazil	S	M	L	Russia	S	M	L
Economic and regulatory policy uncertainty	75.9	77	75	74	32	34	33	18
Corruption	67.2	72	65.9	48.2	13.7	13.1	11.1	19.1
Crime, theft and disorder	32.8	32.7	32.6	34.6	9.5	9.5	7.5	11.1
Anti-competitive or informal practices	56.4	58.0	56.0	50.0	14.8	13.3	19.4	15.9
Business licensing and operating permits	29.8	31	29.5	25.3	14.6	14.8	14.4	14.5
Consistency/predictability of officials' interpretations of regulations	34.0	34.5	34.4	31.5	24.9	23.2	33.3	21.9
Avg. time to claim imports from customs (days)	13.8	14.2	14.2	12.8	6.9	6.6	5.4	8.9
Unofficial payments to get things done (% of sales)	–	–	–	–	1.37	1.38	1.04	1.8
Confidence level in the judiciary system	60.4	57.2	61.5	73.5	34.7	29.5	48.4	41.0
Cost of security and protection (% of sales)	1.48	1.76	1.2	1.04	1.79	1.95	1.3	1.78

Source: The World Bank, Investment Climate Surveys, http://rru.worldbank.org/InvestmentClimate/

historically presented serious problems and the experience continues to persist.

Table 17.6c divides the responding firms between exporters and non-exporters and presents the findings for each group. In Brazil, it is the larger percentage of the non-exporting firms which view corruption and anti-competitive practices as major obstacles. It could be that exporters, because of their importance to the nation's overall trade scenario, are provided with some sort of assurance or protection by the government from corruption and other non-market impediments. The picture, once again, is the opposite for India. More exporters view corruption as a major obstacle in that country. The historically inward-looking policies may have given less importance and, hence, less protection to the exporters of the nation from the unnecessary complexities of doing business. For Russia, the distinction between exporters and non-exporters did not show any major difference in responses.

Table 17.6a   (continued)

Percentage of companies indicating a serious problem with:	India	S	M	L	China	S	M	L
Economic and regulatory policy uncertainty	–	20.5	16.9	26	32.9	–	–	–
Corruption	–	35.5	35.3	53.2	27.3	–	–	–
Crime, theft and disorder	–	–	–	–	–	–	–	–
Anti-competitive or informal practices	–	18.6	16.2	20.8	23.7	–	–	–
Business licensing and operating permits	–	13.7	12.5	19.6	21.3	–	–	–
Consistency/predictability of officials' interpretations of regulations	–	30.7	34.6	49.0	66.3	–	–	–
Avg. time to claim imports from customs (days)	10.5	6.2	7.4	8.2	7.9	10.5	8.3	7.9
Unofficial payments to get things done (% of sales)	–	–	–	–	1.9	–	–	–
Confidence level in the judiciary system	–	74.4	72.1	74.5	82.5	–	–	–
Cost of security and protection (% of sales)	1.3	–	–	–	1.5	–	–	–

Finally, in Table 17.6d, the firms' responses are provided on the basis of key economic sectors (industries) in each country. Note that the data for Russia are more complete than is the case of the other three countries. Again, it is striking how divergent the perceptions are both between and within the countries. In Brazil, more firms from the garments sector and the wood and furniture sector view corruption as a major problem. The least corruption in Brazil occurs in the chemical industry. For Russia, more firms from the garments, wood and furniture, beverage, and hotels and restaurants sectors complain about corruption.

In India, interestingly enough, it is the majority of the firms in the IT services sector which see corruption as a severe obstacle for doing business. The boom in information technology-related business in India has created a very demanding market and unscrupulous individuals may have been targeting it for their pecuniary interests. More firms from the IT services sector than any other sector in India also view the economic and regulatory policy uncertainty, the anti-competitive or informal practices, and the lack of confidence in the judiciary system as major obstacles

Table 17.6b   Burden of Poor Institutions to Domestic and Foreign Companies in 2003

% of companies indicating a serious problem with:	Brazil	Domestic	Foreign	Russia	Domestic	Foreign
Economic and regulatory policy uncertainty	75.9	65.5	76.5	31.5	24.7	32.9
Corruption	67.2	53.5	68	13.7	9	14.7
Crime, theft and disorder	32.8	31.0	32.9	9.52	7.7	9.9
Anti-competitive or informal practices	56.4	40.2	57.3	14.8	11.0	15.6
Business licensing and operating permits	29.8	25.3	30.08	14.6	15.0	14.5
Consistency/predictability of officials' interpretations of regulations	34	32.2	34.1	24.9	23.46	25.2
Average time to claim imports from customs (days)	13.8	10.8	14.7	6.9	6.5	7.1
Unofficial payments to get things done (sales %)	–	–	–	1.37	1.12	1.41
Confidence level in the judiciary system	60.4	75.9	59.5	34.7	33.8	34.9
Cost of security and protection (% of sales)	1.48	1.59	1.47	1.79	1.65	1.82

Source: The World Bank, Investment Climate Surveys, http://rru.worldbank.org/InvestmentClimate/

which need to be overcome. Sector-specific data for China are sketchy. It is difficult to compare, but firms in the leather and textile sectors have shown serious concern over the lack of consistency of officials' interpretation of regulations affecting the firms, and the lack of confidence in the judiciary system.

One thing to note is that throughout the data few firms have complained about the problems of the time spent to claim imports from customs. This is just one indicator but it seems to suggest that such 'petty corruption' issues are not what bother the firms most. Rather, the problems of corruption associated with complex economic policies, bureaucracy and the functioning of the judiciary may be of significant importance.

Table 17.6b (continued)

% of companies indicating a serious problem with:	India	Domestic	Foreign	China	Domestic	Foreign
Economic and regulatory policy uncertainty	–	32.4	20.7	32.9	–	–
Corruption	–	38.2	37.4	27.3	–	–
Crime, theft and disorder	–	–	–	–	–	–
Anti-competitive or informal practices	–	24.2	17.4	23.7	–	–
Business licensing and operating permits	–	14.7	13.4	21.3	–	–
Consistency/predictability of officials' interpretations of regulations	–	55.9	35.6	66.3	–	–
Average time to claim imports from customs (days)	10.5	15.6	6.6	7.9	5.2	9.8
Unofficial payments to get things done (sales %)	–	–	–	1.9	–	–
Confidence level in the judiciary system	–	58.8	70.8	82.5	–	–
Cost of security and protection (% of sales)	1.3	–	–	1.5	–	–

CONCLUSION

This chapter has attempted to compare economically similar non-neighbor countries on various dimensions of corruption and related social and ethical issues. An overall index of corruption or its perception (like Transparency International's CPI) is an average of various components. If these can be gauged explicitly, as it is possible nowadays, the researcher is better equipped to check for consistency between the specific areas of corruption within and between the countries. In the case of the BRICs, differences were observed when indices of bribery with respect to different government agencies were examined. Also, when comparing how corruption affects individual industries, important differences emerge. On the face of the data presented here, it is hard to come up with a simple explanation. In future research, an in-depth structural analysis of the economy, the importance of and the industrial

Table 17.6c   Burden of poor institutions to exporters and non-exporters in 2003

% of companies indicating a serious problem with:	Brazil	Exporters	Non-Exp	Russia	Exporters	Non-Exp
Economic and regulatory policy uncertainty	75.9	75.8	75.9	31.5	26.8	32.3
Corruption	67.2	58.3	69.0	13.7	9.3	14.4
Crime, theft and disorder	32.8	36.2	32.1	9.5	12.7	9.2
Anti-competitive or informal practices	56.4	49.2	57.7	14.8	16.1	14.8
Business licensing and operating permits	29.8	25.5	30.6	14.6	12.5	15
Consistency/predictability of officials' interpretations of regulations	34	32.3	34.3	24.9	24.6	24.9
Average time to claim imports from customs (days)	13.8	13.4	14.03	6.87	10	5.84
Unofficial payments to get things done (% of sales)	–	–	–	1.37	1.74	1.32
Confidence level in the judiciary system	60.4	63.9	59.8	34.7	31.6	34.9
Cost of security and protection (% of sales)	1.48	1.07	1.55	1.79	1.97	1.77

Source: The World Bank, Investment Climate Surveys, http://rru.worldbank.org/InvestmentClimate/

concentration in its various sectors, could offer useful hints. Accounting for priorities in government developmental policy will also enhance our understanding of the differences.

This study also emphasized differences in firm characteristics and how those are linked to corruption. For example, in Brazil, small companies suffer more from corruption whereas in Russia large companies are more vulnerable. For the company operating or contemplating operations in a specific sector in otherwise quite similar economies, the knowledge of particular differences in corrupt regimes is actually more vital than general theoretic observations on how things happen across the board.

One other issue draws attention when studying corruption in large (federal) states like BRIC. It is the regional differences in the level and

Table 17.6c (continued)

% of companies indicating a serious problem with:	India	Exporters	Non-Exp	China	Exporters	Non-Exp
Economic and regulatory policy uncertainty	–	27.4	20.1	32.9	–	–
Corruption	–	44.5	36.2	27.3	–	–
Crime, theft and disorder	–	–	–	–	–	–
Anti-competitive or informal practices	–	18.1	17.5	23.7	–	–
Business licensing and operating permits	–	14.5	13.3	21.3	–	–
Consistency/predictability of officials' interpretations of regulations	–	42.2	34.7	66.3	–	–
Average time to claim imports from customs (days)	10.5	10.1	4.9	7.9	5.0	9.8
Unofficial payments to get things done (% of sales)	–	–	–	1.9	–	–
Confidence level in the judiciary system	–	69.3	70.8	82.5	–	–
Cost of security and protection (% of sales)	–	–	–	1.5	–	–

kind of corruption. For Russia, a recent survey (TI Russia, 2003) unveiled substantial differences between 40 provinces with respect not only to absolute volume of bribes paid but, more importantly, in their average amount and relative share to gross regional product. Moreover, in making the distinction between state capture (businesses initiate the purchase of administrative decisions), and business capture (officials unlawfully seize control over firms) it is possible to map the specific regions where certain types of corruption prevail. Whereas business and state captures do not substitute for each other, it is their relative ratio which somehow reflects the countervailing power: business as prey (business capture) vs. business as predator (state capture). Following Dininio and Orttung (2004), one can point to the rise of corruption when the size of the regional economy in Russia increases, and notice the opposite trend when the level of regional development goes up. No similar data are available for the other countries. However, regional differences in per capita income, gross

Table 17.6d   Corruption in Russia by sector of economy in 2003

% of companies indicating a serious problem with:	Industries									
	1	2	3	4	5	7	8	9	10	11
Economic and regulatory policy uncertainty	40	22.2	100		50	20.6	36.4	35.7			37.5
Corruption	25	12.5			25	11.4	10	16.7			21.4
Crime, theft and disorder	8.7	22.2				5.8	10				7.7
Anti-competitive or informal practices	16.7	12.5			75	20.0	10	15.4	33.3	18.8
Business licensing and permits	18.5	25.0	100		50	9.1	9.1				6.3
Consistency/predictability of officials' interpretations of regulations	26.9	33.3		25	50	31.4	30	14.3	33.3	13.3
Average time to claim imports from customs (days)	5.8	5	–		7	9.8	6.2	6	24	1.5
Unofficial payments for typical firm to get things done (% of sales)	1	1.44		0.5	2.25	1.16	0.4	1.14	2.33	1
Confidence in the judiciary system	38.5	44.4	100	50	50	30.3	55.6	42.9	33.3	26.7
Cost of security & protection (% of sales)	2.18	1.29	–	0.5	3	0.95	1.38	1.27	0.67	0.91

Note: Sector Codes: 1 = Beverages, 2 = Chemicals & Pharmaceuticals, 3 = Electronics, 4 = Food, 5 = Garments, 6 = Leather, 7 = Metals & Machinery, 8 = Non-Metallics & Plastics, 9 = Paper, 10 = Textile, 11 = Wood & Furniture, 12 = Advertising & Marketing, 13 = Hotel & Restaurant, 14 = IT, 15 = Real Estate, 16 = Retail & Wholesale, 17 = Telecoms, 18 = Transportation, 19 = Construction, 20 = Mining & Quarrying, and 21 = Automobiles.

Source: World Bank, Investment Climate Surveys, http://rru.worldbank.org/InvestmentClimate/

regional product, population, distance from the political and economic center, and even in the power of the local media to expose corruption suggest that differences in corruption might exist. Regional perspective on corruption can even be instrumental in uncovering specific problems relevant to local industries. Interestingly, illegal logging and exporting of the Amazonian timber resources (World Bank Workshop, 2003; Bohan, 1996) remarkably resemble corresponding activities in the Siberian taiga (BROC, 2000).

Table 17.6d (continued)

% of companies indicating a serious problem with:	Industries								
	12	13	14	15	16	17	18	19	20
Economic and regulatory policy uncertainty	66.7	36.8	50	34.6	36.6		25	32	
Corruption	16.7	21.1		20	11.8		15.6	15.4	
Crime, theft and disorder	16.7	10.5		12	9.3		15.6	12	
Anti-competitive or informal practices	16.7	5.26	16.7	18.5	14.0		12.5	16.7	28.6
Business licensing and operating permits		10.5	16.7	7.4	12.2		21.9	23.1	
Consistency/predictability of officials' interpretations of regulations affecting the firm		16.7		40.7	21.4	50	12.5	26.6	42.9
Average time to claim imports from customs (days)	10	10.3	–		5	12.5	24.5	4.6	–
Unofficial payments for typical firm to get things done (% of sales)	1.17	0.67	1.5	1.27	1.35	0	2.34	2.25	1.17
Confidence level in the judiciary system	40	11.1		35.7	27.7	80	38.7	40.5	28.6
Costs of security and protection (% of sales)	1.33	2.18	0.67	2.42	1.61	2.4	2.35	1.51	

In this study we tried to develop a comprehensive comparative perspective on corruption and business pathology in the BRIC countries. While corruption is a deterrent to the economic progress, our observations confirm that the nature of the problem varies from country to country beyond the general indices and ratings. Hence, for the individual companies the burden of corruption alters by type of activity, ownership, nature of the administrative hurdles, market covered and a number of other factors. This leads to the conclusion that within a country, corruption in some sectors or operations is significantly more detrimental than the average numbers suggest. Explaining this phenomenon and showing how the level can accordingly be improved is a challenging task for a student and practitioner of international business. Furthermore, it is important to note that specific corruption levels do exhibit substantial variations and there are pockets of lesser and greater corruption in every economy. Thus the overall evaluation of the country on the corruption dimension relative to its peers does not preclude its better or worse position in some fields of

Table 17.6d   Corruption in Brazil by sector of economy in 2003

% of companies indicating a serious problem with:	Industries							
	2	3	4	5	6	7	10	11
Economic and regulatory policy uncertainty	65.5	78.5	67.7	75.7	76.9	75.2	84.9	78.7
Corruption	56.6	64.1	61.4	73.1	63.4	61.6	64.2	73.6
Crime, theft and disorder	31.0	29.4	32	34.2	32.6	31.7	37.5	32.3
Anti-competitive or informal practices	46.4	50	55.6	64.5	55.2	49.0	56.6	57.4
Business licensing and permits	44.0	31.7	29.1	29.1	23.9	29.0	34.9	29.2
Consistency/predictability of officials' interpretations of regulations	34.5	39.2	45.7	31.9	30.0	31.1	37.7	34.6
Average time to claim imports from customs (days)	11.0	13.3	15.7	17.3	13.2	14.3	12.0	15.3
Unofficial payments to get things done (% of sales)	–	–	–	–	–	–	–	–
Confidence level in the judiciary system (%)	59.5	57.0	64.6	54.8	60.7	63.5	66.0	62.5
Cost of security & protection services (% of sales)	1.18	2.9	1.82	1.2	1.12	1.52	1.38	1.63

business activity and attraction of more or less investors than generally expected.

While the authors concentrated on the quantitative data, it should be emphasized that the media in Brazil and India and to a lesser extent in Russia and China (where freedom of the media is more suppressed by the state) are replete with the reports of corruption scandals. These provide important and dramatic signals of the malaise to be cured. In that way, public opinion at large is brought up to date on the excesses in bribery, embezzlement, nepotism and the like. While the pressure to reduce corruption comes from different constituencies – government, society, political parties, trade unions, media and business – it is rather difficult to quantify and compare the sum total of the information provided by the press. Suffice it to say that the news services from Brazil, Russia and India (much less from China) abound in juicy stories of corruption which hopefully can incite public opinion to oppose it more vigorously. This is even more important in view of the fact that following the TI surveys in Brazil

Table 17.6d   Corruption in India by sector of economy in 2003

% of companies indicating a serious problem with:	Industries								
	2	3	4	5	6	7	10	14	21
Economic and regulatory policy uncertainty	19.3	18.8	16.8	28.5	18.8	20	23.7	33.3	19.4
Corruption	39.6	36.4	36.3	35	43.1	38.9	36.6	66.7	36.6
Crime, theft and disorder	–	–	–	–	–	–	–	–	–
Anti-competitive or informal practices	15.5	13.7	16.9	18.9	35.4	18.1	17.6	33.3	18.3
Business licensing and permits	14.6	11.5	15.1	12.3	29.2	14.8	8.8	0	13.0
Consistency/predictability of officials' interpretations of regulations	38.8	39.1	30.7	33.9	37.5	38.0	32.0	33.3	35.8
Average time to claim imports from customs (days)	8.4	6.5	5.9	7.2	7.3	4.9	8	7.3	5.5
Unofficial payments to get things done (% of sales)	–	–	–	–	–	–	–	–	–
Confidence level in the judiciary system (%)	71.2	66.3	71.7	76.5	78.5	62.0	65.4	100	75.6
Cost of security & protection services (% of sales)	–	–	–	–	–	–	–	–	–

and Russia, the perceptions of corruption by the public tend to be more unfavorable than analogous impressions by the business community.

The chapter would not be complete without some discussion of the efforts and plans by the BRIC nations to combat corruption. While a full-blown examination of each country is not possible, some examples are offered to provide a general guideline of what to do. In India, the archaic laws and the resulting bureaucracy actually helps corrupt individuals (Basu, 2003). One way to fight corruption would simply be to eliminate the obsolete laws and unnecessary bureaucracy and then rationalize the remaining ones as much as possible (Transparency International India, 2003). As has been pointed out by many, such an enormous task must be jointly pursued by the people, civil society and the government.

In Russia, streamlining bureaucracy and curtailing discretionary powers of the tax authority and local administration is indicative of this country's approach to defeating everyday corruption. Curbing the power of the

Table 17.6d   Corruption in China by sector of economy in 2003

% of companies indicating a serious problem with:					Industries					
	2	3	4	5	6	7	10	14	17	21
Economic and regulatory policy uncertainty	–	–	–	–	29.0	–	22.9	–	–	–
Corruption	–	–	–	–	22.6	–	20.8	–	–	–
Crime, theft and disorder	–	–	–	–	–	–	–	–	–	–
Anti-competitive or informal practices	–	–	–	–	14.5	–	12.5	–	–	–
Business licensing and permits	–	–	–	–	9.7	–	8.3	–	–	–
Consistency/predictability of officials' interpretations of regulations	–	–	–	–	72.6	–	66.7	–	–	–
Average time to claim imports from customs (days)	13.9	7.5	7.5	6.1	3.1	10.4	6.4	11.0	30	10.2
Unofficial payments to get things done (% of sales)	–	–	–	–	1.8	–	1.2	–	–	–
Confidence level in the judiciary system (%)	–	–	–	–	90.3	–	83.3	–	–	–
Cost of security & protection services (% of sales)	–	–	–	–	1.6	–	2.8	–	–	–

oligarchs on the one hand and the quasi-private state juggernaut enterprises on the other is a far greater challenge to pursue.

As part of the good governance agenda, India formally signed up to the ADB-OECD Anti-Corruption Initiative for Asia-Pacific in November 2001. The initiative will require India to develop an anti-corruption plan to address three main areas: civil service reform, reduction of bribery and the closer involvement of civil society (Singh, 2003). The plan expects to create more transparency in government activities. In addition, donor agencies have made it clear that future funding will be tied more specifically to anti-corruption policies in India.

Generally speaking, cooperative efforts by citizen groups, public service agencies and the media (the 'voice' option) have the potential to improve the quality of life (Paul, 2000). For businesses, such involvement of different constituents in a society can eventually improve the context within which they will operate.

After undergoing a massive privatization process by the end of the last century, Brazil enjoys a stronger competitive environment and earns high ratings on investor-friendliness. However, as in Russia the problems to address emerge at the points of contact between the private sector and public authorities in charge of procurement and taxes (local and federal). A corrupt political class and even concerns about the integrity of the police do not facilitate the task. The populist government of Lula da Silva who won the election in 2002 on the anti-corruption ticket has been striving to gain more control over the process. Establishment of the Commission for Public Transparency and Combating Corruption – an 18-member advisory council operating out of the Comptroller General's Office – is one important step in that direction.

In recent years, changes also have taken place in China to fight corruption (Transparency International, 2004). As public procurement is a major source of corruption, in June 2002 the Standing Committee of China's National People's Congress (NPC) passed the Government Procurement Act. The Act provides detailed guidelines for preventing corruption. Experiments with open bidding began in Shanghai in 1996 and currently such bidding is being introduced into state-funded engineering projects. In May 2004, the Supreme People's Procuratorate and the ministries of construction, communications and water resources decided to introduce a blacklisting system to further combat corruption in the construction sector (Transparency International, 2005).

One must realize though that countries like India, China and Russia still have huge, powerful, multilevel administrative apparatus in place that is largely unchecked. While Brazil's situation is somewhat different, the level of transparency and monitoring in BRICs is still not up to standard. Thus, corruption remains an untamed negative force. One can expect to deal with this scourge effectively only through a serious and long-term commitment of all major actors in the society.

NOTE

1. From a 'watchdog' perspective, this is echoed by the head of Transparency International. P. Eigen at the launch of 2004 CPI, 20 October 2004: 'public contracting in the oil sector is plagued by revenues vanishing into the pockets of western oil executives, middlemen and local officials', http://www.transparency.org/cpi/2004/cpi2004. en.html

REFERENCES

Ades, A. and R. Di Tella (1999), 'Rents, Competition, and Corruption, *American Economic Review*, **89**, 982–93.

Aristotle (2004), *The Politics*, eBooks@Adelaide, retrieved from http://etext. library.adelaide.edu.au/a/aristotle/a8po/.

Banfield, E. (1975), 'Corruption as a Feature of Governmental Organization', *Journal of Law and Economics*, **18**, 587–605.

Basu, I. (2003), 'Bureaucratic Corruption Worries India', *United Press International*, 9 October.

Bohan, V. de (1996). *Corporate Power, Corruption and the Destruction of the World's Forests: The Case for a New Global Forest Agreement*, London: EIA.

BROC (2000). 'Plundering Russia's Far Eastern Taiga: Illegal Logging, Corruption and Trade', *A Report by Bureau for Regional Oriental Campaigns*, Vladivostok, Russia.

da Silva, M., F. Garcia and A. Bandeira (2002), *How Does Corruption Hurt Growth? Evidences about the Effects of Corruption on Factors Productivity and Per Capita Income*. Sao Paolo: Fundacao Getulio Vargas.

Dininio, P. and R.W. Orttung (2004), 'Explaining Patterns of Corruption in the Russian Regions', *William Davidson Institute Working Paper 727*, November.

Garten, J. (1998), *The Big Ten: The Big Emerging Markets and How They Will Change Our Lives*, New York: Basic Books.

Gupta, S., H. Davoodi and R. Alonso-Terme (1998), 'Does Corruption Affect Income Inequality and Poverty?', IMF Working Paper, Washington, DC: International Monetary Fund.

Habib, M. and L. Zurawicki (2002), 'Corruption and Foreign Direct Investment', *Journal of International Business Studies*, **33**(2), 291–307.

Hellman, J., G. Jones and D. Kaufmann (2000), 'Seize the State, Seize the Day: State Capture, Corruption and Influence in Transition', paper presented at the ABCDE 2000 Conference, Washington, DC, 18–20 April.

Kaufmann, D. (2004), 'Corruption, Governance and Security: Challenges for the Rich Countries and the World', in M.E. Porter, K. Schwab, X. Sala-I-Martin and A. Lopes-Claros (eds) *The Global Competitiveness Report 2004–2005*, New York: Palgrave Macmillan, pp. 83–102.

Kaufmann, D., A. Kraay and M. Mastruzzi (2003), 'Governance matters III: Governance Indicators for 1996–2002', World Bank Policy Research Working Paper 3106.

Lambsdorff, J.G. (2005), 'Between Two Evils – Investors Prefer Grand Corruption, *Diskussionsbeitrag Nr. V-31–05*, Universitaet Passau.

Mauro, P. (1995), 'Corruption and Growth', *Quarterly Journal of Economics*, **110**, 681–712.

Mauro, P. (2002), 'The Persistence of Corruption and Slow Economic Growth', Working Paper 02/213, Washington, DC: IMF.

Paul, S. (2000), 'Making Voice Work: The Report Card on Bangalore's Public Services', unpublished documents, Public Affairs Centre, Bangalore, India.

Porter, M.E., K. Schwab, X. Sala-I-Martin and A. Lopes-Claros (eds) (2004), *The Global Competitiveness Report 2003–2004*, New York: Oxford University Press.

Rodriguez, P., K. Uhlenbruck and L. Eden (2005), 'Government Corruption And The Entry Strategies Of Multinationals', *Academy of Management Review*, **30**(2), 14–383.

Root, H. (1999), 'The Importance of Being Small', unpublished manuscript.

Rose-Ackerman, S. (1999), *Corruption and Government*. Cambridge: Cambridge University Press.

Shleifer, A. and R. Vishny (1993), 'Corruption', *Quarterly Journal of Economics*, **108**(3), 599–617.

Singh, G. (2003), 'Corruption, Transparency and the Good Governance Agenda in India', EU–India Conference, Brussels, 4 December.

Tanzi, V. (1994), 'Corruption, Governmental Activities, and Markets', IMF Working Paper 94/99, Washington, DC: IMF

Tanzi, V. and H. Davoodi (1997), 'Corruption, Public Investment and Growth', IMF Working Paper 97/139, Washington, DC: International Monetary Fund.

TI Russia (2003), *Regional corruption indices 2002*, Moscow: Center Transparency International – Russia.

Transparency International (2004), *Global Corruption Report 2004*. Country Reports: China, London: Pluto Press, pp. 177–81.

Transparency International (2005), *Global Corruption Report 2005*. Country Reports: China, London: Pluto Press, pp. 129–33.

Transparency International India (2003), 'Corruption in India: An Empirical Study', retrieved from (www.ti-bangladesh.org\ti-india).

Wilson, Dominic and Roopa Purushothaman (2003), 'Dreaming with BRICs : The Path to 2050', Global Economics Paper No. 99, New York: Goldman Sachs.

World Bank Workshop (2003), Aide Mémoire. 'International Workshop on Reform of Forest Fiscal Systems World Bank'. Washington, DC, 19–21 October retrieved from http://www.profor.info/pdf/FFSWorkshopAideMemoire.pdf.

18. BRICs: geopolitical and economic challenges for the US

Subhash C. Jain

A new megatrend is on the horizon. This concerns the emergence of BRICs, referring to four developing nations with large populations: Brazil, Russia, India and China. Currently, these four nations together account for less than 15 percent of the GDP of the G6, which consists of Britain, Japan, Italy, France, Germany and the US. But by 2050, the GDP of BRICs could be larger than that of the G6 (Wilson and Purushothaman, 2003). If indeed this happens, this global change would be as far-reaching as the Industrial Revolution of the eighteenth century, the emergence of Britain as a modern industrial nation in the nineteenth century, and the information and communication developments of the twentieth century. The rise of BRICs, as the trend shows, would depend on whether these nations adopt sound policies: the right fiscal and monetary policies, free trade with the outside world, and massive investment in education.

On the face of it, each BRIC nation has fundamental problems. In China, capital is pouring in so quickly that a combination of speculative frenzy and a backward banking system might eventually burst the bubble. India's major problem is corruption, as shown by the watchdog group Transparency International's recent ranking on the Corruption Perception Index. In the case of Russia, its commitment to capitalism after the recent crackdown on oil giant Yukos is doubtful, which could derail the markets or the economy. Brazil needs economic discipline to keep her finances intact. If the discipline slips, it may fall into a trap similar to the one that led to Argentina's collapse a few years ago.

On the other hand, if history is any guide, nations do rise and fall. In the years after the civil war, America's industrial output lagged far behind that of Germany, France and Britain. But from 1870 to 1914, America's economy expanded fivefold, and the US became the world's leading industrial power.

The impact of the rise of BRICs on the world's demand for resources, center of economic gravity and balance of power will be enormous. Adjusting to such changes might prove difficult (Khanna et al., 2005). The rise of BRICs, particularly China and India, is likely to pose the biggest challenge of all. The dramatic rise of the BRICs raises a number of questions: What economic clout each of these four nations might have? Will these nations challenge the Western concept of government? Will they disturb the global geo-politics balance? Will their development devastate the environment? This chapter seeks to answer these questions under the headings of the economic and geopolitical challenges that the rise of BRICs throws up. The rise of BRIC societies will be the defining story of the world in the foreseeable future.

BRAZIL

Brazil is a large country, similar to the United States in that each country dominates its half of the Americas. Each nation is amply endowed with people, land and natural resources. Each has remained united after gaining independence from the European colonial powers. Each has a strong sense of nationhood and pride. But the similarities end there. While the United States has prospered, Brazil has not. While the United States has become the world's supreme economic power, Brazil has remained underdeveloped.

In 1998, however, Brazil adopted a new policy. It embraced modern capitalism, breaking ties with the sclerotic old model that dominated the country for over 50 years. Traditionally, it has relied on a form of nationalist mercantilism that required state control of commerce and industry. Public sector companies provided infrastructure and services. Manufacturing, industries and agriculture, though they remained in the private sector, were highly protected and subsidized. Brazilians described this arrangement as capitalistic in principle but with substantial state control. The model fostered industrial development to serve the needs of a large internal market. But that did not provide Brazil with the capability to compete outside the home market.

The new economic model embraced by Brazil in the 1990s features a political economy in which private enterprise is encouraged and foreign investment is welcomed. The role of the state, at the same time, is being redefined. The government's spending has moved away from subsidies toward improving education and health services while alleviating poverty. The state role in the productive sectors of the economy is declining rapidly.

As for the future, the question is whether Brazil will be able to maintain the growth tempo or, alternatively, will it turn into another Argentina? From the viewpoint of the United States, a prosperous Brazil is important not only as a political ally in world affairs, but also as a force to unite Central and South America toward a free market of the Americas.

Geopolitical Considerations

United States political relations with Brazil are fundamentally sound. Brazil willingly cooperates with Washington most of the time and expects it to take the initiative on global political issues including those that are of concern to Latin America. But there are specific issues and initiatives over which Brazil has frequently clashed with the United States. For example, Brazil opposes Washington's expanding intervention in Colombia. Further, the United States' lagging effort to promote market agreement for hemispheric free trade has disappointed Brazil (Hakim, 2001). The geopolitical challenge that the United States faces with reference to Latin America is to maintain the goodwill and cooperation that had occurred in the post-Cold War period.

Brazil's agenda

More than anything else, Brazil wants to be a global economic power. Toward this goal, it wants expanded access to US markets and direct investment. But the United States, while paying lip-service to expanding hemispheric trade, has often dragged its feet in the promotion of regional trade. For example, during the Clinton administration, the US Congress, after six years of deliberations, rejected any special preferences for the Brazilian textile exports to the US market.

What the US needs is a well-defined foreign policy relative to Latin America. Unfortunately, the United States takes Latin America and different nations in the region for granted, never figuring it as a primary area to be concerned with. It is in the mutual interest of both Brazil and the United States that the latter takes the initiative to consult Brazil regularly on matters of interest to different Latin American nations. Further, the United States should help Brazil to emerge as a significant nation globally, through economic and political cooperation.

Brazil's drive for a seat on the Security Council

Brazil would want to be a permanent member of the Security Council, along with Japan, Germany and India. The United States has adopted a neutral position on this matter. Following growing international support for Japan, Brazil has been pursuing a more assertive foreign policy to boost its Security Council candidacy. It expects the United States to back its bid. But it is unlikely that the US will support any other nation besides Japan. Indeed, it is going to be a disappointment for the Brazilians. The United States needs a sound rationale for not backing Brazil while giving support to Japan.

Brazil's geopolitical ambitions

Brazil is becoming very assertive in spreading its influence throughout the region. The country wants to establish a second pole of power in the Western hemisphere. For example, a few years ago, then President Cardoso convened in Brasilia the very first summit meeting of South American heads of state. The Brazilian government opposed US efforts to challenge Peruvian elections in 2001, as well as US interference in Colombia. The United States cannot ignore its broader relationship with Brazil, a nation that can affect the success or failure of US policy in the region on different issues.

Beyond regional politics, Brazil has started adopting an independent posture on other geopolitical issues which differ to the US position. It joined China and India to challenge the developed nations in their agricultural subsidies in the WTO meeting in Cancun, Mexico. The matter of the subsidies eventually led to the collapse of the Cancun talks. Brazil, along with a number of other developing countries, supported the formation of a new world forum to counter the World Economic Forum which developing countries consider elitist.

Gone are the days when Brazil would fall strictly into line as dictated by the United States. It is up to the United States to decide how it wants to handle a growing nation in its own hemisphere: to contain it or to cooperate with it.

Free trade areas of the Americas

Brazilians, like most Latin Americans, have grown skeptical of Washington's support for free trade. In 1994, President Clinton convened in Miami the first hemisphere summit meeting since 1967. At the conference, all the assembled leaders agreed to conclude a Western Hemispheric free-trade agreement by 2005. This did not happen for two reasons. First, the Congress refused to give the 'fast-track' trade authority to Clinton to start negotiating the agreement. Second, the financial crises in 1995 and 1998 in Mexico and Brazil respectively interrupted Latin America's economic progress and revealed its vulnerability regarding global competition. President Bush moved quickly to negotiate the Free Trade Area of the Americas (FTAA) agreement, but September 11 events put the matter on the back burner. It is now doubtful that free trade in the region will become a reality during President Bush's second term. As a matter of fact, inclusion of labor and environmental standards in the FTAA is vehemently rejected by Brazil and several other Latin American governments (Sotero, 2004). This further complicates the formation of the free trade market in the region.

Economic Challenges

Presently, Brazil's economy outweighs that of all the other South American countries combined, and the nation is expanding its presence in world markets. It is capable of attracting foreign direct investment through moves that seek growth in efficient new markets. Brazil's abundance of natural resources is another attraction for the multinational firms. Despite these positive signs, Brazil continues to display economic, political and social weaknesses that prevent the nation from realizing its full potential. Brazil's economic future depends on the success of recent socio-economic measures that the government has introduced. Further, the industrial sector of the country is strong, accounting for 20 percent of the GDP. Agriculture contributes another 20 percent to GDP while the remaining 60 percent constitutes natural resources. Brazil is modernizing its industries to compete with China in the world markets consisting of textiles, shoes, chemicals, cement, lumber, iron ore, tin, steel, aircraft, machinery and equipment (Onis, 2000). If the macroeconomic management is successful, and if the price of Brazil's natural resources does not dip abnormally, the nation has a chance to be a major economic player globally.

Economic reforms
In the 1990s, Brazil did well overall. The 1998 problem was handled with care. The devaluation of the real helped to stabilize the currency, and fiscal discipline and austerity measures targeted inflation while cutting the debt. Still Brazil faces tough economic issues; among them weak finances, poverty and unemployment. Brazil's future depends on the ability of the government to continue the process of economic reforms, which in turn will be dictated by the political climate in the country. So far, the left-wing president is committed to orthodox economic policy. But the political realities may force him to reverse the course. The challenge for the United States is to preach economic prudence so that Brazil does not reverse its course. A strong ally in the Western Hemisphere will help the US to create a benchmark for other nations to follow (Baptista, 2004). On the other hand, if Brazil slips, many other Latin nations may slide down with it, which could be dangerous.

Opposition to FTAA
Interestingly, Brazil shows little interest in the region-wide free trade agreement. Brazil views it as a second-order priority. This position reflects the strong opposition to the FTAA, not only in Brazil's labor movement, but also among many in its powerful business community who doubt whether Brazil can compete with US suppliers. Due to Brazil's growing assertiveness

and influence in regional and global affairs, other Latin American nations would find it convenient not to support the FTAA (*The Economist*, 2003). Thus, Washington cannot avoid taking into account Brazil's position on its policy measures in Latin America. A close relationship with Brazil can affect the success or failure of US policy in this region.

Market access
Brazil is rich both in animal rearing and crop growing. It leads the world in coffee production and is the world's second-largest producer of soybeans. It ranks high in beef herds, oranges, tobacco, cocoa, chicken and cotton. In addition, it is among the top competitors in the world market for steel, aluminum, pulp and paper. These resources provide Brazil with a unique opportunity to grow rich. But that requires free market access to the large US market, especially in agricultural products. However, the United States subsidizes agriculture to enable US farmers to compete against the imports. Resolution of this problem is not easy. Perhaps a free-market agreement of the Americas is the answer. But Brazil, for political reasons, opposes the FTAA. The United States has to find some other way to provide market access to Brazil (*The Economist*, 2004a).

Homegrown problems
Corruption dominates the Brazilian system. Even people in high-ranking positions and political leaders have been accused of tax evasion. Prominent people illegally maintain open accounts in the US; they freely deposit money into these accounts and withdraw huge amounts for luxurious living. A new class of illegal money changing, known in Brazil as *doleiros*, has emerged, keeping the remittances to and receipts from foreign sources a secret, thus helping to evade taxes.

Additionally, poverty is a critical issue in Brazil: a major factor impeding the country's economic advancement. Linked to poverty are hunger, sickness and illiteracy, which are increasingly big problems in Brazil. Almost 50 percent of the nation consists of impoverished communities where hunger is customary due to a variety of reasons, including a lack of resources, difficulty in obtaining jobs, and mental or physical disabilities. Poor people do not have access to health care, and as a result are vulnerable to contagious diseases such as HIV/AIDS, tuberculosis and malaria (Lapper, 2005).

More than any other nation in Latin America, Brazil's sex workers and sex trafficking dominate the informal sector, exposing people to contagious diseases. As a large country, the government does not have the resources to ensure health provisions for all the victims. Illiteracy affects 30 percent of the population who do not recognize the motto 'order and progress' written on the Brazilian flag. For more than a century, Brazil has had adult literacy programs to help the illiterates. But in the absence of an educational policy, the programs are ad hoc and perfunctory in nature (*The Economist*, 2005a). It is an example of social failure in the country.

The problems stated above are local in nature and only Brazilians can devise a suitable way to address them. Unfortunately, Brazilians are daydreamers; they hope that someday something will happen to transform their country into a great power. They may be social and economic underachievers, but they always see themselves as a 'country of the future', whose future never arrives. Some of the country's thinkers blame their compatriots' misplaced faith in Messiah figures that will come and perform miracles. In reality, what is needed is awareness of the problems and a will to resolve them. Mass education can play a significant role in this matter. The United States can only serve to render friendly advice, helping Brazilians to organize themselves and work together to build their nation.

RUSSIA

Current media and academia alike offer a wide array of speculations regarding the future state of Russia's economy. Perhaps it will be the future economic powerhouse, combining its powers with India, China and Brazil to dislodge the Western world from its throne of economic prosperity. On the other hand, the country may simply be experiencing a period of abnormal economic growth, and if modern finance has taught us anything, such growth cannot be sustained for long. Thus the two sides of the debate toggle back and forth, each vying to determine Russia's fate in the world arena, be it in the form of a thriving force or, conversely, the skeletal remains of what was once referred to as a superpower. Our purpose is to take a stand regarding Russia's potential seat in the global economic hierarchy, and examine the geopolitical and economic challenges that Russia's emergence might pose for the US.

Geopolitical Challenges

The collapse of the Soviet Union in 1991 ended nearly 75 years of centralized and totalitarian rule. Following the Soviet Union's downfall, the Russian Federation, simply known as Russia, was established. The transition from the Soviet Union to Russia officially occurred on 25 December 1991 when the treaty that created the Soviet Union was dissolved. Russia has been facing serious obstacles in its efforts to create a democratic political system and market economy to replace the systems put in place during Communist periods. Political leaders have continually demonstrated conflicting views on governmental and political directions.

The constitution of 1993 established Russia as a federation. Russia is democratic with a law-based state and a republican form of government. The state is divided into three branches: the executive, legislative and judicial branches, and there is also a local jurisdiction which shares powers with the state.

The executive branch's power is divided between the President and the Prime Minister, with the President holding more power. The Russian President has the power to determine domestic and foreign policy and represents the country in foreign affairs. The President also has the power to appoint the Prime Minister with the consent of the Parliament and to appoint justices to the Russian Court System. Passing decrees without the consent of Parliament is another power of the President, as well as being head of the armed forces as the commander-in-chief, and head of the National Security Council. The President has the unlimited power of forming an administration and hiring a staff to assist him.

Currently in Russia, there are major political and legal issues that may affect US companies doing business there. First, crime in Russia continues to be a huge problem. Russia's homicide rate is among the worst in the world, and there is massive organized crime contributing to counterfeiting, narcotics and extortion problems. A major governmental problem is that more and more criminals are pursuing political careers and the government is corrupt. This is due to the immunity granted to the Members of Parliament, even if non-political crimes are committed (*Financial Times*, 2005).

Another problem found in Russia is the government's lack of respect for civil rights, despite the establishment of the Civil Code. Serious problems include restrictions on freedom of the press, including governmental pressure on the media to have stories approved before print, or denying access to certain information. Other problems stem from law enforcement agencies. Many prisoners are tortured; prison is often life-threatening. Police beat, harass and extort money from the people. Often there is racial profiling among police officers. Problems continue with the right to due process and the right to a fair and timely trial (*Financial Times*, 2005). The judicial branch has also been manipulated by political authorities and experiences case backlogs and trail delays. Privacy rights continue to be violated, and violence against women and children remains a serious problem. Discrimination against women and religious and ethnic minorities plagues the Russian society.

Breakdown of the system
A problem that has plagued Russia, especially since the collapse of the Soviet Union, has been corruption and the growth of organized crime.

In a way, the corruption has stemmed from the Communist days, when all facets of the economy were controlled and 'paid for' by the state. While doctors' visits were, in theory, free to the public, if one wished to get better service or to see better doctors, a gift was required. Such forms of bribery were both common and expected. Upon the dissolution of the Soviet Union, and the breakdown of the legal, political and economic systems that the Russian citizens knew so well, the perfect opportunity emerged for both organized and unorganized crime to develop (Weidenbaum, 2004). The risks associated with engaging in criminal activities dramatically decreased upon the breakdown of governmental police enforcement systems and the weakening of central oversight systems in general. In addition, the desertion of the central planning system, the advent of privatization, and greater access to retail markets have provided an abundance of opportunities to engage in many forms of criminal activities. However, the environment alone would not necessarily dictate the emergence of such behavior. Instead, the drastic decline of real income due to inflation, delayed wage payments and unemployment served to provide the motivation for many people to get involved mainly in unorganized forms of crime such as prostitution, burglary, theft and drug dealing. Russia is able to flourish where business owners are close to the government. An example is the circumstances surrounding Yukos, a Russian oil company. Russian authorities jailed Mikhail Khodorkovsky, who was the CEO of Yukos, in 2003. They arrested him on fraud and tax evasion charges following a variety of back-tax claims against the company. While the claims have been valid, the government does not have a sufficiently stable legal framework and tax collection system to prosecute one company among the multitude that are guilty of the same charge. In fact, the charge was seen as a politically motivated effort by the Kremlin to rein in the ambitious oil tycoon. This perhaps may be the Kremlin's desperate attempt to control the oil industry and keep it in a firm grasp. Because of such widespread government interference, many foreign investors are kept at bay, declaring the risk too great to get involved with a country that still does not respect the right of private enterprise, despite its claim to support a capitalist system.

The state of Russia's political system has raised a blitzkrieg of condemnatory reaction in the US, questioning whether Russia will be able to survive as a liberal state. The US has a strategic interest in Russia's evolution as a democratic country for a variety of reasons. Russia fully supports America's concerns of fighting terrorism, and preventing nuclear proliferation. Further, Russia is a significant political partner in keeping resurging China at bay. Lastly, Russia's oil reserves provide a viable alternative for reducing America's dependence on the Middle East.

Strategic location

Russia boasts of its prime location, linking Europe and Asia. It plays a central role in the development of transcontinental infrastructure corridors linking Europe and Asia – including the revival of the Trans-Siberian Railroad and its future linking with the Korean peninsula and Japan. Because Russia spans both continents, it is in a position to provide not only a physical bridge between them, but also a political one through its foreign policies. In its prime years, the Soviet Union was a pivotal supplier of skills, information and goods to the developing nations of China and India. In an effort to regain this status, Russia has proposed important foreign policy initiatives aimed at improving relationships with these two upcoming foreign giants in order to develop a 'strategic triangle'. This proposition will ensure Russia an important seat among the prime future economic players. As has been said: 'Russia has become of prime importance to both the EU and China because Russia is now seen as the eastern and western buffers, respectively, of their spheres of influence . . . policy toward Russia [is] part of a larger effort to surround the Union with a "ring of friends", while China views Russia as a western anchor for its efforts to secure its interests in Asia' (Tennenbaum, 2002).

For the United States, Russia's partnership with China and India poses a Cold War-type problem. If Russia, India and China become friendlier, the alliance between the United States and its traditional European allies will be weakened. This has serious political implications, and the US must stop the strengthening of the triangular relationship.

Ethnic tensions

Ethnic relations, both within Russia and with its neighbors, are extremely tense. The war in Chechnya has strained relations with neighbors such as Georgia. In fact, after the fall of the Soviet Union, Russian minorities have been dispersed everywhere (comprising more than 30 percent of the population in Latvia and Estonia, 38 percent in Kazakhstan, 22 percent in Ukraine and 13 percent in both Moldova and Belarus) and are problematic as well. Taken altogether, these ethnic compositions represent an explosive mixture (Kranz and Bush, 2004).

Ethnic tensions may lead Russia to adopt drastic measures to safeguard its territory and regional influence. This will put the United States in a difficult position, since siding with the minorities would strain relations with Russia. On the other hand, the United States cannot permit Russia unilaterally to spread its hegemony over the region.

Economic Outlook and Challenges

Conventional wisdom suggests that the Russian economy has turned the corner and will achieve impressive growth in coming years, while many other states of the former Soviet Union remain stuck in an economic quagmire. Such optimistic predictions have been proposed in the past but proved false. However, the emerging economic scenario is based on more solid evidence although some doubts still remain. In addition to the growth prospects above the global average, Russia presents a number of other positive trends. For example, inflation has been falling and the state budget has been showing surplus. Overall, Russia seems genuinely interested in shaking its Soviet past and appears capable of doing so. The nation shows determination to take its place among the top international economies.

Humanpower

If past accomplishment says anything for future potential, it is conceivable that Russia will again become the superpower it once was. The country still boasts a literacy rate of 99.6 percent, comparable to if not greater than that of most developed nations (Sharma, 2004). Such a high literacy rate, despite the economic and political turmoil within the country, suggests a nation that places extreme value on education, which is the key to the development of a highly skilled and productive workforce. Arguably, once the economic policies and the political arena are stable, the potential (and volume) of the labor force will generate exceptional returns. As it is, different types of design and development projects in the United States are outsourced to Russia, where the standard of living (and thus required salaries) is significantly lower. As Russia continues to attract more ventures requiring the labor forces' high skill level, the employees will not only begin to earn higher wages, but will also learn critical skills that will enable them to replicate the achievements that the economic leaders of the world have experienced, and perhaps improve the country's current processes.

Economic growth in Russia will provide new investment and trade opportunities for American companies, which will be a welcome development. But outsourcing of technical projects to Russia may amount to transferring strategic knowledge to a country which was hitherto an unfriendly state. Thus, the US government must alert American firms to be discrete in engaging Russian talent for their work.

Natural resources

The high literacy rate is only one of the striking features that allow Russia to attract business propositions. Although the educated workforce is crucial to develop sectors outside of base natural resource production, the country encompasses extremely valuable assets within the confines of its extensive borders. A scarce and critical resource, oil has charmed the interests of key players such as BP and ConocoPhyllips in the American and international arenas. Russian oil output has been declining dramatically as technological improvements in the equipment have stagnated. However, BP and other Western oil tycoons, with more advanced technology, were not only able to pump the oil faster, but also concluded that the country's oil reserves had been severely underestimated. In fact, the new oil forecasts raise its placement in the hierarchy from seventh to second, behind only Saudi Arabia. The multinational collaboration is part of the reason for the 14 percent increase in production expected at Samotlor this year, the biggest the field has seen since its heyday in the 1970s. As more natural resources are explored, more business opportunities for foreign investments become evident (White, 2004). While the sophisticated technologies available to the developed world seep into and replace Russia's archaic equipment, the need for collaboration becomes clear, as it will not only help the Russian companies produce exponentially more oil, but also provide an exceptional return on investments as business relationships are forged.

Russia's emergence as the world's largest oil producer outside the Organization of Petroleum Exporting Countries (OPEC) has been a major contributor to Moscow's heightened international clout. There are also several other factors that have highlighted Russia's presence on the international stage (Lucas, 2005). One such factor includes extensive diamond production, which allowed Russia to become a major world player via organizations such as the Kimberley Process, a plan by the United Nations to curb 'conflict diamonds'. The world's recognition of Russia as a large player in the diamond market has presented yet another opportunity for foreign investors to partner with, and perhaps improve, current diamond quests.

Russia offers a timely opportunity for the United States to reduce its dependence on oil from Islamic nations. But the United States must develop policies to deal with Russia on terms that are mutually beneficial and that do not permit the latter to exploit the situation to only their advantage.

Revival of the internal market
In the early years of the new century, Russia experienced an approximation to a normal investment cycle, that is, increased demand, raising production which in turn led to increased investment and higher wages, again boosting demand. In other words, the Russian economy began to incorporate a real mechanism of development. At the same time, the economy moved away from the economic model based on export of primary energy and raw materials to the potential of its own internal market.

As the consumer demand continues to increase, Russia would offer tremendous export opportunities for consumer as well as industrial goods. Russia, however, is not going to be a captive market for the US. Both India and China would compete head-to-head to seek opportunities in the emerging Russian market. Western Europe would pose tremendous challenges as well (Council on Foreign Relations, 2001). After all, European Union nations have been doing business with the Soviet Union for a long time, albeit selectively, and they know how to deal with Russians.

All said, any market – provided there are no legal barriers – belongs to those firms that compete well. American companies need to divert their attention from their traditional markets and formulate strategies to become significant in the Russian market.

Embedded cultural beliefs

The Communist regime has had a lasting effect on the Russian way of doing business. There exists a deeply embedded cultural belief that no one should earn substantially more than anyone else. Serious hostility can occur when a foreign businessperson appears to be a profiteer at the expense of the flawed Russian enterprise system. Western concepts of leadership and empowerment are difficult to grasp because of the absence of a strong work ethic and merit-based professionalism during the Communist regime. For this reason, many Russians are mistrustful or resentful of those business people who are overly determined, progressive or materialistic, as Russians may view them as suspicious and potentially dangerous to the much less ambitious Russian way of life. It is important to remember that while Russians do not want to be treated as inferiors in the business world, they are still adjusting to a recent and dramatic transformation in their government and way of life. This means that while they are still holding onto many of their old communist views of the free enterprise business world, they are beginning to create a new vision of what Russian businesses can become in a free market (Shleifer, 2000). It is for this reason that foreign business people must be particularly sensitive and understanding to both the old traditions and newly emerging traditions of the Russian culture.

Dealing with corruption

This is Russia's greatest weakness. It is known that nothing is done in Russia without giving bribes to self-appointed intermediaries. The Mafia is still very powerful in the country. President Putin is trying to fight against corruption, but he faces difficult challenges. Some even suspect that he is a part of the Mafia (*Financial Times*, 2005). However, the fact remains that it is impossible for a firm to enter the Russian market without being close to a Mafia. In fact, security is controlled primarily by Mafia although the public security sector also expects its piece of the cake. Because of this security problem, there is a huge problem of piracy of intellectual properties.

The bottom line is that doing business in Russia is more risky than say, China, India or Brazil, yet US companies ignore the booming Russian market at their own peril. US firms must develop new business models to enter Russia, which would entail gaining new knowledge, enhancing negotiation skills, and judging results according to a long time-frame.

The partnership between the US and Russia exists largely in the realm of declarations. US intellectuals and politicians readily advise Russia to seek stability in both politics and the economy. If Russia aspires to make the country a truly competitive player in today's global economy, it must undo in a fundamental way the gigantic mistakes of the Soviet past. But this is a tremendous challenge. Institutions and traditions established over 50 years cannot be discarded in a span of ten years. Change has to evolve over time. More wrenching change and dislocation could lead to insurmountable instability, which the leadership wants to avoid. Russia professes to keep people in place and employ technical fixes to make the Soviet legacy more manageable and efficient, and, finally, to change the entire system (Metzer et al., 2002). To the Americans, this model of change is slow, time-consuming and inefficient. With that attitude, the US government and companies wait and hope to get involved with Russia once conditions have improved.

Meanwhile, Europe, China and India are actively bidding for Russia's attention and allegiance. China is seriously negotiating a free-trade pact with Russia, as is India. The fourth generation of leadership in China sees the strengthening of ties with Moscow as a priority in its foreign policy. India always had close ties with the Soviet Union, and now wants to build a firmer relationship with Russia to their mutual advantage. These relationships are supported not only by shared security concerns, but also by concrete economic benefits.

Not to be outdone, the European Union has also moved forward with a vision of a 'wider Europe' that encompasses Russia. For example, it has been predicted that by 2008, two-thirds of all Russian exports will be absorbed by the EU. Currently, EU nations account for about 62 percent of all foreign direct investment in Russia.

The United States must rethink its relations with Russia. The time is ripe to understand Russia's political standing and plan to participate in a booming economy.

No doubt, Russia's budding capitalist system would be even better off within a more democratic framework and without the power battles that are an integral part of Russia's history. Democracy in the country is a revolutionary concept, especially since the society has little experience with it.

Even the president's powers are kept in check by the country's complicated structure. In as much as the nation has tasted the benefits of economic freedom, there is no question of regression. President Putin's popularity lies in the fact that he is delivering on the economic front. He deserves credit for being a proponent of the notion that good economics makes good politics.

US firms have not been enthusiastic about emerging Russia. This is unfortunate, since Russia has been one of the best-performing markets over the past few years. Forward-looking companies would do well to partner with one of the fastest-expanding economies in the world.

INDIA

India is another nation emerging as a hub for globalization both politically and economically. India has caught on in the world's investment community. Nowadays, the Western press rarely mentions the giant of world trade, China, without adding 'and India'. This is so because India as a nation has developed a mindset needed for a player in a globally integrated economy. If properly channeled, such a spirit can be an enormous strength for the global role. Thus, in some ways, India is well prepared to be a hub. It is a multicultural, multi-ethnic society with a vibrant democracy and a press that readily exposes shortcomings. The rule of law prevails. The highest elected office of the country is open to any Indian without reference to caste, creed, religion or national origin. This reflects a willingness to assimilate, and work with, that which is foreign in the broadest sense of the term. But on the economic front, India has a long way to go. It is still not open to foreign goods and services, labor or knowledge, as is necessary to be a global player. On the International Monetary Fund's (IMF) trade restrictiveness index, India scored 8, placing it among the most restrictive nations.

India has the will and strength to play a key role internationally in all spheres. But it must adopt bold policy measures to turn that potential into reality. The United States can be of help in India's endeavors if India will make the first move.

Geopolitics

Politically speaking, the secular, democratic India is more like the United States than any other nation in the world. But the West merely pays lipservice without actually considering it a stronger ally. India's democratic political system has been the ultimate source of the state's legitimacy, the major avenue of group mobility, and the main ingredient in the glue that has kept the country together.

India has a well-established, vibrant, desirable democracy. Despite an electorate of over 600 million, Indian general elections are held on time, and are generally fair and free. The average turnout in Indian parliamentary elections has been 57 percent of all adults, as compared to an average turnout of 56.5 percent of only registered voters in the US presidential elections since 1948. Indian voters have repeatedly demonstrated their independence and sophistication (*The Economist*, 2005b).

Despite the heightened achievement of India as a democratic, secular state, it does face chronic political problems. The first of these problems is the Kashmir issue. The second problem relates to the Nuclear Non-Proliferation Treaty (NPT).

The Kashmir problem

After decades of strife, India and Pakistan are trying to normalize their relations. However, in the past these have been only or merely symbolic gestures toward resolving the problem, similar to a cricket match between the two countries. Such prickly displays, reminiscent of a stand-off between peacocks, are a symbol of kinship between the two countries that used to be one. But it is also a reminder that their bloody partition, their three wars and their continuing quarrel over Kashmir remain unforgotten. For the United States, it is important that the Kashmir dispute is resolved peacefully and quickly. The United States must maintain good relations with both India and Pakistan.

India is a growing economy that promises a great potential opportunity for US companies. Pakistan is a nation strategically located to assist America in its war against terrorism. Looking ahead, India, with its large manpower reserves, could be of great help to the US if ever there is a stand-off between the US and China. Therefore, from the US perspective, it is imperative that a solution, mutually agreeable to India and Pakistan, be found over Kashmir. At one time, India and Pakistan, particularly the former, considered the Kashmir problem to be an internal matter and they refused any offers of help from a third nation. Times have changed, however. Although they may not explicitly say so, both nations want the Kashmir problem resolved and are willing to seek the help of a friendly country in this matter. The United States faces the challenge of working out a fair deal acceptable to both nations.

War-weariness in both Pakistan and India make the time propitious for a resolution of the conflict in Kashmir. Pakistan's industrial and entrepreneurial class is interested in economic ties with India. Following China's lead, India wants to augment its market presence so as to expand its influence in world affairs. To fully accentuate the energies toward this goal, India wants the conflict in Kashmir to be out of its way. Both India and

Pakistan could cut defense spending and convert defense industries to more productive civilian lines if the conflict in Kashmir were to be resolved. Almost 30 percent of Pakistan's and 15 percent of India's federal spending goes on defense (*Business Week*, 2005b).

A possible solution to resolving the Kashmir conflict would be the acceptance of the 'line of control' as the boundary between the two nations. Both nations might find this solution acceptable, although a lot of politicking and give and take would be needed to satisfy different constituencies in both countries.

India's nuclear ambitions

Another geopolitical issue relative to India is its refusal to sign the Nuclear Non-Proliferation Treaty (NPT). Since its inception in 1968, the NPT represented a bargain: states that did not possess nuclear weapons were not to develop or acquire them, while the states that did have nuclear weapons (the United States, the UK, France, Russia and China), were to work toward their eventual destruction. One hundred and eighty-two non-nuclear weapons states plus Taiwan and five nuclear weapon states joined the NPT. Four states: India, Pakistan, Israel and Cuba, refused to sign the NPT. India's nuclear test in 1998 spurred immediate global condemnation. Two weeks later, Pakistan followed with its own nuclear tests. The United States asserts that India's action has encouraged Pakistan to join the nuclear weapons race and it might still encourage other states to acquire nuclear weapons (*The Economist*, 2001).

As it is, the United States would want India to abandon completely its nuclear weapons program. India, however, claims that it has always been committed to non-proliferation of nuclear weapons, but its growing perception of a security threat from China and Pakistan has led the country to perform nuclear tests.

India claims, with documentary evidence, that China's security assistance to Pakistan during the 1990s, especially in the realms of nuclear weapons design and ballistic missile technology, made Pakistan a virtual strategic surrogate for China in its backyard.

In the matter of non-proliferation, the United States' challenge is to develop a new policy prescription as an alternative to the prevailing wisdom. For example, the United States may pursue a differentiated policy that explicitly takes into account the particular security concerns of India and Pakistan, as well as of Israel. India developed nuclear weapons to counter security threats from China, and secondarily Pakistan. Pakistan, in turn, acquired its nuclear arsenal to cope with India's overwhelming conventional superiority. If other nations follow their example, they will do so for their own reasons, not because the South Asian neighbors have done it.

The real geopolitical challenge that the United States faces is the status of Pakistan. Pakistan's woes matter not just to the Indian subcontinent, but to America as well. Pakistan is a nuclear-armed state with crushing economic problems, a burgeoning population, and few effective civilian institutions. It abuts two regions of the world: the Persian Gulf and Central Asia, which are flash-points in America's battles over oil, terrorism and drugs. Pakistan wields major influence in the growing Islamic movement in Central Asia with the surrounding regions. If Pakistan collapses, refugees would flood into India and Iran, and Afghanistan's stability would be further undermined. Worse yet, it could leave Pakistan's nuclear arsenal vulnerable to terrorists.

Economic Issues

Although long overdue, the reform process initiated in 1991 brought far-reaching change to India's creaky, largely state-controlled economy in just four years. The removal of the 'license raj' system that stifled domestic business and the reduction of taxes and tariffs, as well as new openness to foreign investment, generated rapid growth. India's economy, which had lumbered along at 3–5 percent growth rate per year from 1950 to 1980 (which critics deemed the 'Hindu state of growth'), increased to 5.5 percent in the 1980s and averaged 7 percent growth in the 1990s. Some claimed that India had joined the ranks of Asia's 'tiger economics'.

Assuming the economic reforms move along, India will continue to endure as a viable market for a variety of goods and services. In turn, many business opportunities will surface for Western firms, particularly US companies. But to conduct business successfully in India, the companies will need to formulate innovative strategies that might be different to their strategies in the US and Western markets. Below are the major challenges that the foreign enterprises will face in the growing Indian economy.

Product and process innovation
Western products with minor adaptations are not suitable for the Indian market. The mass market in India remains considerably poorer than that in the US. For this reason, most Western output is too expensive or complex for the Indian market. Thus, new product concepts are needed to fill the needs of this market. This will require products that are cheaper in price, yet intact in quality. In the process, the foreign enterprises will find Indian companies to be tough competitors; the latter are adept in developing products that adequately meet the market need (Huang, 2003).

Take the case of automobiles. In 2006, the cheapest car in India was Suzuki's $5000 Maruti compact. Even this price is too high for middle-class buyers, most of whom use motorbikes. To tap this market, there is a need for a car that sells for $2000–$2500. How many Western auto companies are willing to design a car that could be sold at such a meager price? But an Indian company, Tata Motors, is just doing that. By the end of 2006, Tata's 'Peoples Car' will be on the market to be followed by an export model for the rest of the developing world.

Tata has already developed the Indica, a compact hatchback that retails for $6600 and is exported to Europe. In the process, Tata engineers figured out how to use the skilled but cheap local labor instead of the industrial robots that would have been used in Japan or the US on a car like the Indica. That decision shaved roughly $1 billion off the design and production costs. As a result, the Indica can break even on an output of 80 000 vehicles, about 30 percent less than the volume that global auto companies need to profit from such a car (*Business Week*, 2005b).

The standard economy car, the new Tata compact, pushes the envelope on cost even further than the Indica does. For example, the company is experimenting with cost-saving manufacturing techniques. Instead of welded bodies, Tata is considering bolted or glued panels. The company is also planning to outsource about 80 percent of component manufacturing to inexpensive Indian suppliers.

Tata is also considering a new business model for the distribution of cars. The car will be distributed not only from the factory near Bombay, but also in unassembled kits, to franchises across the country. The franchises will assemble the new auto in mini-factories, as well as sell it, creating thousands of local jobs. That will save Tata millions since it is easier to ship kits than fully loaded cars and the savings will show up in the car's price.

The Tata car is innovative on an industrial scale. But mass-market techniques, Indian style, can be applied to health care too. The Aravind Eye Care Center in the city of Madurai has developed inexpensive cataract surgery for $50 to $300 compared with over $2000 in the US. The procedure's price even includes the cost of a locally made intraocular lens, inserted during surgery to restore sight.

The key to keeping costs down is the huge volume of operations and the efficient system the doctors have developed. At Aravind's three hospitals, doctors perform 50 operations a day. Clearly, it is a process innovation that is a critical step in making products and services affordable for the average person.

The challenge for Western companies is to innovate new technology answers that make sense in a developing country. In India, the cost of doing innovative technology is very low. The capability of India is its people. Chinese do an admirable job, but Indians are better. India has ingenuity. India has its fair share of intelligent, hard-working people, great raw materials and assets, and now they are learning how to use them.

Transformation of Indian farming

Great opportunities are available in India for foreign enterprises' involvement to transform Indian farming. India is the world's second-largest producer of fresh fruit and vegetables, yet it hardly exports them. The experience of a joint venture between the Rothschild family and an Indian company, Bharti, conglomerate called Field Fresh Foods is relevant here (*Business Week*, 2005a). The joint venture aims to supply high-quality and low-cost fresh fruit and vegetables to markets in Europe by exploiting high-volume farm production in several north Indian states.

India's farm sector, which supports 65 percent of the 1.1 billion population, has long been gripped by a belief that the welfare of the rural poor was linked to agricultural protection. But slowly, with companies like Field Fresh Foods taking the lead, the attitudes are beginning to change. There is ample opportunity for foreign firms to earn respectable returns by investing in modernizing agriculture-based operations in India. Most local fruit and vegetable crops are of poor quality, and modern storage and refrigeration facilities are rare. The result is that up to 40 percent of fruit and vegetable production in India goes to waste because of such limited infrastructure. Foreign direct investment can play an important role in building the infrastructure, which, in turn, would boost agricultural production quality and the distribution of farm products. The net result would be the increase in the farmers' income.

Organized retailing

Indian shopping habits are slowly becoming more Westernized. But the retailing sector remains outdated and inefficient. Currently, organized retailers account for 2 percent of India's market, compared with 15–20 percent in China, and 81 percent in Taiwan. India is a late starter, but the opportunity is tremendous for firms interested in establishing a foothold in this market (Mellon, 2005).

In recent years, a number of Indian companies have started expanding into retailing. New and fashionable shopping malls are being built to cater to the needs of the 'aspiration class' of Indian consumers, representing a market of about 30 million people, forecasted to rise to 50 million by 2009. For now, this overhaul of Indian shopping habits is a purely domestic affair. Although India is a global sourcing base for retailers, as a retail market it remains out of bounds for foreign investors such as WalMart and Carrefour. But the reform permitting foreign direct investment in retailing is on the horizon.

Taking advantage of India's manpower strength

Inspired by the revolution in IT, several Indian drug companies have set out on an ambitious game plan. By tapping the same low-cost pool of

English-speaking scientists, they want pharmaceuticals to become the next phase in the shift to service industries to India. The big pharmaceutical companies claim it costs them at least $800 million to develop a new drug, while Indian companies claim they can do it for $50 million. It will be fascinating to see how far the globalization of drug development can be pushed.

But the fact remains that India has a large pool of highly trained people in different areas, the cost of whom is less than one-tenth of that of their counterparts in developed countries. Besides, they all speak English and have substantial knowledge of their field, since they read Western books and literature. This means any 'brain' work can be done in India. The challenge is for US firms to figure out what processes can be outsourced from India. The outsourcing does not have to be at the same level as in the IT business. The energy industry is different and new business models can be created by multinationals to link with India. As an example, Ranbaxy, an Indian drug company, has entered into an alliance with GlaxoSmithKline (GSK), the UK multinational, allowing the former to benefit from GSK's extensive research infrastructure. GSK has invested billions of dollars in an early-stage discovery process that produces hundreds of possible ideas for drugs every year. Ranbaxy gets access to some of those leads, and, if they prove viable in smaller trials, GSK conducts the late-stage trials. Ranbaxy gets a royalty on sales (Dyer, 2004). Such alliances are mutually beneficial.

Opportunities for foreign direct investment
Compared to other developing nations of its size, India has not attracted as much foreign direct investment (FDI). Much has been said and written as to why India does not get its share of FDI. Areas of improvements have been identified for the Indian government to create a favorable environment to encourage FDI inflow. From the perspective of the multinational enterprises, despite shortcomings of different sorts, India is a fast-growing market which no firm can afford to ignore (Mckinsey Global Institute, 2005).

Time is ripe right now for the US firms to make direct investments in India. If they fail to act, in a few years they would find competitors from Europe and Asia have already entered the market and have established themselves there.

The 1991 reforms have launched India in the direction that most Indians want: toward more widely shared prosperity and a position of influence in the world. The momentum is not reversible. The new direction is all set, but proper initiatives along the path will make reaching the goal more rapidly feasible.

India's coming of age raises new geopolitical as well as economic challenges for the US. The thinking in political circles and among business people on India must change. It is emerging into a global leader with the third-largest GDP. Politically, accommodations must be made to welcome India into the big league. The US government should try to gain insights into India's security concerns relative to the resolution of the Kashmir issue, and in the matter of the NPT. US multinationals should look at India as a large and lucrative market, and not as a nation with restrictive policies. Business alliances with India may be difficult to negotiate, but they are bound to be beneficial.

CHINA

China's dramatic recent rise to power raises many questions. Will it become an economic giant, surpassing even the United States? Will it try to achieve hegemony in the region? Will its development be derailed by domestic political problems and/or AIDS and environmental devastation? According to a Goldman Sachs study, China will eventually be a larger economy than the US, but not until 2040. Meanwhile, it will continue to grow, overtaking Japan in 2016. Even if the Chinese economy slows sharply over the next few years, its long-term prospects remain bright. Most of China's growth over the past 20 years is attributed to high rates of investment and migration of workers from subsistence farming – where they added little economic value – to more productive jobs in industry. But China's growth is not based entirely on inexpensive labor. It is also due to good infrastructure, an educated cadre of workers, a high rate of savings for investment, and an open economy. Both tariff and non-tariff barriers have fallen significantly. In addition, China welcomes foreign investment, which has helped growth by increasing the stock of fixed capital and by providing new technology and managerial skills. No wonder joint ventures with foreign firms account for 27 percent of China's industrial output (*Business Week*, 2005a).

The relationship between China and the United States will be an important matter in the twenty-first century. It will have critical ramifications for the two nations as well as the international community.

The geopolitical significance of China's rise requires careful analysis. The issue with the greatest potential to provoke a major Sino-American conflict is China's territorial ambitions in Asia. There is a feeling in some quarters that China's integration into the world economy will make it more moderate and cautious in its foreign policy and more open and democratic at home. An alternative view sees China becoming more aggressive as a consequence of its growing economic and military strength. Already there are signs that China's emerging economic influence is giving it the power to enhance authoritarianism at home, resist international dissatisfaction with its policies and practices, and expand its power and prestige abroad in ways hostile to American interests.

The United States needs to understand the economic and political significance of China. It can no longer operate on the assumption that an economically strong China will become an agreeable partner in dealing with global issues. In sum, the United States needs a policy for managing a rising power and potential rival. The policy should be built on the assumption that expanded economic relations and official dialogues on security issues, human rights and the global commons will maximize the prospect that China will use power in a manner conducive to US interests.

Geopolitical Challenges

Economically, China is emerging as a great power. The question is, how do its economic achievements affect its geopolitical behavior? In what way do China's geopolitical ambitions conflict with the United States' objectives in Asia and elsewhere in the world? Some scholars believe that China ultimately aims to surpass the United States, becoming the world's most powerful nation. Others look at China more optimistically in the hope that the game of international relations has changed and China would adopt policies that are friendlier and more accommodating. In any event, summarized below are the geopolitical challenges that the United States faces with reference to China's rise into economic prominence.

Status of Taiwan Strait

China wants to unite all its parts to form a greater Chinese nation. This ambition was expunged by Hong Kong's return in 1997 and Macaw's in 1999. However, the topic is not finished until Taiwan is fully integrated with the motherland. China considers Taiwan as an internal matter and refuses to accept any mediation even by an impartial, largely ethnic Chinese state such as Singapore.

China may one day decide to annihilate Taiwan by force, leading to unthinkable international consequences. Chances are high that the United States would defend Taiwan without formally declaring war against China. At the same time, Japan's economy will face tremendous challenges if it were denied access to the South China Sea. East Asian nations would be equally impacted by the stand-off in the Taiwan Strait (Chandler, 2004). That probably would be the end of the Asian economic miracle.

Military operations in the Taiwan Strait, far away from home, would mean tremendous economic loss for the United States. Not only would it slow the US economy, but the entire global economy may come to a standstill.

America finds itself in a difficult position regarding Taiwan. While it acknowledges that there is only one China, it refuses to accept China's claim on Taiwan as an internal matter. China's neighbors on this matter are aligned with the United States. They raised no objection when the United States sent its aircraft carriers to the region in response to China's missile tests in 1996. Tensions in the region eased fairly quickly. But the problem is unresolved and may surface again in the future.

Territorial disputes in the region

There are a number of territories in the region to which China lays its claim. In the South China Sea, the Spratly and Parcel islands are claimed by China as well as by Taiwan and Vietnam. (Spratly Island is claimed by Malaysia and the Philippines as well.) The islands are suspected to cover significant oil reserves, leading each nation to justify its claim. A global concern, shared by the United States, is that China will use the islands as military bases to establish hegemony over the South China Sea and the waterway's important shipping lanes. Dispute has also risen in the past over a set of islands in the East China Sea called Diaoyu in China and Seukaku in Japan (Council on Foreign Relations, 2002). But thus far, this problem has been contained.

From time to time, questions have arisen about the status of these islands. Fortunately, the disputes have been successfully handled under the aegis of the Association of South East Asian Nations (ASEAN). But as China establishes its hegemony, it may raise the issue in the future with greater force.

China's nuclear ambitions

China does not share the perspectives of its nuclear power. The US government has done some analysis of China's arsenal, but it is classified. Therefore, not much is known about China's nuclear standing. China conducted its first nuclear test in October 1964, and its first hydrogen bomb followed shortly thereafter. In all, China has conducted 45 tests in 41 years. This is less than the number of tests conducted by the British and far less than was performed by the US, which has conducted 1 030 tests. In 1996, China signed the Comprehensive Test Ban Treaty (CTBT) agreeing not to engage itself in any nuclear weapon modernization.

Unfortunately, advanced Russian technologies are conveniently available to China. Using these technologies, it would like to modernize its missile force to improve payload, accuracy and survivability (*Financial Times*, 2004). China's goal is to be better able to penetrate enemy defenses, to have more advanced command, control and communication systems, and to gain the ability to attack space-based assets.

In the past, the Soviet Union and the United States were China's main concern in strengthening its nuclear program. Today, however, in addition to Russia and the US, India's emerging nuclear and missile capabilities have become a new headache. So far, China has maintained that India's nuclear capabilities will not lead to any change in its nuclear posture. But this is not easy to accept. If India's Agni missile is deployed on mobile systems, which is quite likely, and if India decides to build a substantial number of warheads, China will want to modernize its own arsenal.

China is also concerned about Japan joining the United States to confront China in launching nuclear attacks. Thus, any deployment of missile defenses in Japan could provoke China to modernize and enhance its nuclear program. China, in addition, does not trust either Japan or the United States about their professed commitment to de-emphasizing nuclear weapons in their own defense policies. China, therefore, does not want to be surprised by the pre-emptive use of nuclear weapons by any nation.

The challenge for the United States is to examine its nuclear and missile defense policies, keeping in mind China's future perspectives. At the same time, the United States should reach an understanding with the Chinese in addressing nuclear proliferation in the Korean Peninsula, South Asia and the Middle East. Lastly, American policy-makers, as a matter of last resort, should make contingency plans to pursue an adequate response to Chinese actions for the sake of its own security.

A related issue is China's close military cooperation with other states in the region, such as North Korea, and in the Middle East with Iran and with Pakistan in South Asia. After all, Pakistan would not have a nuclear arms capability without Chinese help. Both Iran and North Korea have boosted their nuclear capabilities by acquiring technology from China.

China's staying power as a nation

China presents a new model of state control. Politically, the government remains Communist, while in economic matters, it has adopted the capitalistic model. The question is whether such an arrangement is workable in the long run. Western thinkers feel that as the economic growth continues, the Chinese people will develop new tendencies to force the state to loosen political control. The Tiananmen Square demonstrations are mentioned as a case in point. But the Chinese government, instead of providing freedom, has instituted stricter control over the country's intellectuals and dissenters. China's harsh, outdated and impractical political arrangements are not helpful. Even in ordinary times, the Communist apparatus is monstrously hard to handle. But the coming years will be no ordinary time. Future events may spark a popular challenge to the leadership in Beijing.

Even from inside the party, such popular protests have the potential to destroy the party's unity.

Sooner or later, tensions are bound to arise between state and society due to the sweeping economic liberalization that has been occurring for more than two decades. People are frustrated with widespread corruption. Further, the Communist party is gradually losing its popularity, especially among the new generation. While the outside world may not know it, Chinese society is in deep flux and the political system is struggling to keep up. As the rigid political system weakens, China may surmount ethnic separation in different regions, such as from Muslim Highurs and Tibetans. Political troubles in China will deeply impact the global economic system. The United States is especially vulnerable, considering its larger-scale trade and business with China.

Diplomatic efforts by the United States are required in order to make the Chinese aware of the need to introduce political reforms to satisfy economic gains. A stable China is a prerequisite for peace in Asia. On the other hand, China may never become a democratic country. This is contrary to its political culture. China, throughout her history, has always been ruled by a self-selected and self-perpetuating clique, regarding and treating opposition as traitors. Thus, the concept of individual rights, governmental responsibility to citizens, independent media and judiciary are unknown to the Chinese. Such interpretation makes things uncertain. No plans can be made for such an eventuality. The world must wait and see.

China's power play

China is a large country both geographically and in terms of population. With its economy booming, where is China headed? What role and status does it perceive for itself in the world at large and in Asia in particular? Does China want to achieve paramount status in Asia? If it does, it conflicts with the American objective in the region to prevent China from asserting her hegemony there.

Countries in the region are equally concerned about China's dominant power. They do not want China to resume the imperial status that it wielded centuries ago. They are uneasy about being treated as vassal nations who must send tribute to China.

America, as the formidable global power, faces difficult choices with regard to China. Should it consider China as a strategic friend or a long-term adversary? Further, the United States cannot prevent Chinese hegemony in Asia without forming a coalition with Japan and India. These two nations have their own concerns. How far they are willing to work with the United States to stop China's influence in Asia requires influence and judgement.

Perhaps India might be more willing than Japan. Either way, governments in India and Japan will face strong reaction in their countries, leading
to anti-American opposition, if they join the United States in constraining
China from spreading its influence in the Asian theatre. Finding ways to
align India and Japan with the purpose of preventing China from achieving hegemonic status in Asia will be an important task for American diplomacy in coming years.

Economic Challenges

Only a few years ago, the term 'world economy' was used as shorthand for
the economies of the developed world. China would at best rate a brief
mention. But now it is too big to ignore. It was largely thanks to China's
robust growth that the world as a whole escaped recession after America's
stock market bubble burst in 2000–2001. But its recent boom is also responsible for much of the surge in the global energy demand that has pushed up
oil prices. China's massive purchases of American treasury bonds explain
why the dollar has not fallen further or bond yields risen more sharply even
though America's huge current-account deficit continues to widen. Last
but not least, many people blame the sickly state of America's job markets
on imports from China.

Napoleon once remarked: 'Let China sleep, for when she awakes she will
shake the world.' Perhaps Napoleon was ahead of his time. But now the
dragon is certainly stirring. Since 1978, when the country first set out on the
path of economic reforms, its GDP has grown by an average of 9.65 percent
annually, three times the rate in the United States, and faster than in any
other nation.

China's was the largest economy for much of recorded history. Until the
fifteenth century, China had the highest income per head and was the technology leader. But then it suddenly turned its back on the world. Its rulers
imposed strict limits on international trade and tightened their control on
new technology. Measured by GDP per person, it was overtaken by Europe
by 1500, but it remained the world's biggest economy for long thereafter. In
1820, it still accounted for 30 percent of world GDP. However, by 1950,
after a century of anarchy, warlordism, foreign suppression, civil war and
conflict with Japan, its share of world output had fallen to less than 5
percent. Now China is making up lost ground (*Financial Times*, 2003).
Even if the economy slows sharply over the next couple of years, its long-
term prospects remain bright.

There are many ways in which China's rapid economic development will
affect the United States, ranging from jobs and growth to oil prices and
inflation. The integration of China's 1.3 billion people will be momentous

for the world economy. China could make growth more volatile, but in the long run it will be a powerful engine of global growth, and export vitality to the world economy.

Disproportionate use of world resources

Since 1978, when China introduced economic reforms, 250 million people have been lifted out of poverty. This is an unprecedented achievement in economic history. Still, 800 million people in China live in rural areas. China must pull them out of the countryside, where they are engaged in unproductive labor, into the cities and provide them jobs in factories. Chinese leaders plan to move out about 400 million into the cities in the next 25 years. It will be a Herculean task, since it would put tremendous pressure on the infrastructure in urban areas in terms of buses, roads, schools, railways, sewage systems and power plants (Gilboy, 2004). Where will the government find resources and materials to develop the infrastructure? As an example, China is the world's largest producer of steel (in 2003, China produced 220 million tonnes of steel which is more than the combined steel production of the US and Japan), yet in 2003, it imported 40 million tonnes of steel. For China to continue its economic boom, it must use a disproportionate share of the world's resources. This will deprive other nations of sufficient resources, creating an imbalance in the global economy. In other words, the long-term growth of China raises significant questions for the United States as a global power. What could be done so that China's fast growth does not hinder growth in other nations?

China: the trading giant

China has become a global trading colossus with total two-way trade in 2003 amounting to $857 billion. This was first a boon, then a bang to many nations. US consumers saved $600 billion through cheap Chinese imports. But the US gain came at the expense of rival exporters. Many nations have lost their markets in developed countries, since China is more competitive than these nations. Consider the case of textile notes. Since 1 January 2005, China has been providing almost 50 percent of textile goods worldwide. Many, many small nations earned their valuable foreign exchange through exporting textiles to developed markets. But they cannot compete with China. Thus, China's rise will leave many third-world nations in acute poverty. While this may not affect the US directly, the reduction of global poverty has been an important goal of the US government in the post-9/11 period. Poverty in the poorer countries may lead to terrorism, which the civilized world wants to avoid (*The Economist*, 2004b). How to deal with China so that the smaller developing countries are not hurt economically is an important challenge for the US.

If the present growth rate continues, China may emerge as an economic, technological and military threat to the United States. Through the incorporation of market reforms, China has opened up the economy to foreign firms. However, political and social reforms have lagged behind. For example, China has encouraged state-owned enterprises at the cost of the independent private sector through giving the former preferential access to capital, technology and markets. Thus, China has inefficient public-sector enterprises, increasingly efficient foreign enterprises, and an inefficient private sector. Further, lack of political reforms in China has led Chinese managers to develop an industrial strategic culture that focuses on short-term profits, local autonomy and excessive dissatisfaction. Consequently, China has limited ability to wield technological gains, mainly depending on foreign technology. China must implement structural reforms in the political sphere if it wants to be a global competitor. Free markets and greater foreign investment alone are not sufficient. It is in the common interest of the United States and China for the latter to continue developing its economy and liberalizing its politics. The United States can help in this endeavor through strategic engagement. This will require the US simultaneously to strengthen its technological and manufacturing leadership and promote US exports, investment and liberal values abroad.

Adverse economic impact on the United States
China's model of economic growth has worked well for it, while creating economic problems in the US. American capital, technology and managerial skills are transferred to China by American firms. There they are able to manufacture goods cheaply, using inexpensive Chinese labor. They export the output to the US to be consumed by the American public and industry. In the process, American factories are closed, laying off millions of workers. This is tolerable to an extent since America is a large economy. But a point may be reached where the American manufacturing sector is completely destroyed (Gao, 2002).

Proponents of free trade often mention the service sector as a growing opportunity for the laid-off workers. But service sector jobs usually pay less and often do not provide the kind of fringe benefits that manufacturing does.

Granted, there are upscale service jobs too. But with the trend toward offshore outsourcing of elite service jobs to China and other developing nations (particularly India), low-wage service jobs will become the last resort of employment for Middle America.

A scenario of this nature raises difficult questions for the US. Economically speaking, what kind of American will exist in the middle of the twenty-first century? If things continue in their present form, we may end up with a two-tiered nation: an upper-class segment with vast resources, and a working class, mostly employed in service jobs. The tasks that the middle-income wage earners currently perform would probably be outsourced to other nations. It is easy to ignore the impact of the rise of China on US jobs since the effect becomes noticeable only in the long run. But the problems are apt and important.

Emergence as a global economic leader

It has been predicated that by 2040, China's GDP will be higher than the GDP of the United States. In other words, in about 35 years, China will be the world's largest economy, surpassing the United States. Of course, the US per capita income will still be higher, yet it will be ranked as the number 2 economy of the world (*Financial Times*, 2004).

Currently, the US plays the dominant role globally in economic matters. With China's rise to the number one position, the US will have to accept a lesser role for itself relative to global economic issues. The challenge that the US faces is how to avoid such a situation. This requires the US either to outpace China's growth or to prevent China from superseding it (Vanhonacker, 1997). China is bound to grow. Nothing can stop it. However, the United States can adopt strategies to grow faster, which is feasible by staying in the forefront of research and development in order to come out with new and innovative products, and by developing innovative processes.

CONCLUSION

The potential ascendancy of BRICs raises the question, what must America do to maintain its dominant position? After the fall of the former Soviet Union, the United States remained the single superpower of the world. The transformation of BRICs into economic powerhouses will make it necessary for the US to share economic power with Brazil, Russia, India and China, particularly the last two nations. This is not going to be easy, but America may not have a choice. It has been estimated that China could surpass the US as the world's largest economy by mid-century. China and India combined will account for about half the global GDP. Thus, the United States must formulate new strategies to flourish by sharing power and leadership with the BRICs.

The new strategy focus requires that America encourage and support innovations which lead to new products and services for the world market. Through designing, producing and marketing high-margin products (for example, aircraft and construction equipment), branded consumer products (for example, Coca-cola and Ipods), and intellectual properties (movies, drugs) United States could continue to be a leader in the global marketplace.

But bringing out innovations is not the prerogative of the US. The BRICs have the skills and commitment that underlie America's success in this front. For example, China and India together graduate about 500 000 engineers and scientists a year as against 60 000 in the US. A similar situation exists in the life sciences. Granted, the United States has the best higher education in the world in practically all fields, but BRICs are fast improving their educational standards which in some cases are already better than the US. In addition, they have a cost advantage over the US. As has been said: 'the sheer amount of low-cost brainpower that China and India will have at their disposal will eventually give them an edge'. Both federal government and state governments should tap their resources to set more rigorous standards for instruction in such key areas as science and math. US students should aim to outperform students from BRICs.

Some critics may claim that economically BRICs will never rise as predicted. The four nations have fundamental problems that would have destabilizing effects on their economic progress. But it would be foolhardy to count on BRICs to falter, which by default, would permit the US to maintain her global hegemony. Even if all the four nations among the BRICs, do not move ahead as predicted, the progress in China and India is likely to continue as anticipated. The Chindia (China and India) have unique strategies such as cheap skilled labor, capital-friendly governments and huge domestic markets which are potent factors that almost guarantee their economic emergence.

The rise of the BRICs is a wake-up call for America. By ignoring their challenge, America risks becoming like the old Europe.

REFERENCES

Baptista, Jolanda E. Yogosse (2004), *The Brazilian Economy*, New York: FGV-SP Economics Department.
Business Week (2005a), 'China and India: The Challenge and the Opportunity', 22–29 August, 51.
Business Week (2005b), 'The Ties That Bind Delhi and Washington', 21 March, 52.
Chandler, Clay (2004), 'Inside New China', *Fortune*, 4 October, 84.
Council on Foreign Relations (2002), *The Rise of China*, New York: W.W. Norton & Company.
Dyer, Geoff (2004), 'How India Hopes to Reshape the World Drug Industry', *Financial Times*, 18 August, 9.
The Economist (2001), 'A Survey of India', 2 June.
The Economist (2004a), 'Brazil's Trade Diplomacy: Looking South, North, or Both', 5 February, 18.

The Economist (2005a), 'Brazil's Economy', 8 February, 34.

The Economist (2003), 'Make or Break', 20 February, 24.

The Economist (2004b), 'The Dragon and the Eagle', 2 October, 3.

The Economist (2005b), 'The Tiger in Front', 5 March.

Financial Times (2003), 'Historical Shifts: Asia's Impact', 22 September, 13.

Financial Times (2004), 'FT China: Special Report', 7 December.

Financial Times (2005), 'FT Russia: Special Report', 5 April.

Gao, Paul (2002), 'A Tune-up for Chinese Auto Industry', *McKinsey Quarterly*, **1**, 144–55.

Gilboy, George J. (2004), 'The Myth Behind China's Miracle', *Foreign Affairs*, (July/August), 33–48.

Hakim, Peter (2001), 'The Uneasy Americas', *Foreign Affairs*, (March/April), 44–56.

Huang, Yasheng and Tarun Khanna (2003), 'Can India Overtake China', *Foreign Policy*, (July/August), 74–81.

Khanna, Tarun, Krishna G. Palepu and Jayant Sinha (2005), 'Strategies that Fit Emerging Markets', *Harvard Business Review*, (June), 63–76.

Kranz, Patricia and Jason Bush (2004), 'Putin's Game', *Business Week*, 7 June, 54.

Lapper, Richard (2005), 'Latin Lessons: The US Faces a Loss of Leadership in a Troubled Region', *Financial Times*, 17 May, 13.

Lucas, Edward (2005), 'Putin's Choice', *The Economist*, 14 February.

McKinsey Global Institute (2005), *Learning From China to Unlock India's Manufacturing Potential*, Washington, DC: McKinsey Global Institute.

Mellon, George (2005), 'The Courtship of Mother India', *Wall Street Journal*, 19 April, A21.

Metzger, Dean, Richard Bloom and K. Ratnikov (2002), 'A New Russian Revolution: Corporate Governance Reform,' *International Financial Law Review*, **1**, 21–27.

Onis, Juan de (2000), 'Brazil's New Capitalism,' *Foreign Affairs*, (May/June 2000), 48–55.

Sharma, Ruchir (2004), 'Russia: A Few Words Conveying a Lot', *Newsweek*, 28 June, 49.

Shleifer, A and D. Treisman (2000), *Without a map: Political Tactics and Economic Reform in Russia*, Cambridge, MA: MIT Press.

Sotero, Paulo (2004), 'Common Market for the Southern Cone: The Promise of the Mercosur', *Foreign Policy*, (January–February), 17–25.

Tennenbaum, Jonathan (2002), 'Russia's Economy: Strong Growth', *Executive Intelligence Review*, 1 February, 4.

The United States and Russia (2001), New York: Council on Foreign Relations.

Vanhonacker, Wilfried (1997), 'Entering China: An Unconventional Approach', *Harvard Business Review*, (March–April), 130–40.

Weidenbaum, Murray (2004), 'The Uncertain Prospects for the Russian Economy', *Vital Speeches of the Day*, **70**(22), 681–83.

White, Gregory L. (2004), 'As Westerners Move into Russia, Its Vast Oil Wealth Keeps Growing', *Wall Street Journal*, 30 November, A.1.

Wilson, Dominic and Roopa Purushothaman (2003), 'Dreaming with BRICs: The Path to 2050', Global Economics Paper No. 99, New York: Goldman Sachs.

PART VI

Conclusion

19. Peaks and pits with the BRICs: accommodations with the West

Jack N. Behrman

That the BRICs would join the world economy has been a hope and goal of the US and Europe since World War II. But each opted for a more isolationist policy, in both economic development and national security. Now all intend to become full members of a globalizing world as soon as feasible, and their success requires that both the BRICs and the West make a series of accommodations. But the West is seemingly less eager than the BRICs. A successful accommodation would bring a new peak in global growth but also a number of strains – not the least on the world's resources. At the same time, there are many pitfalls on the path to economic integration for both the BRICs and the West, dependent mainly on the policies each adopt, but also on their divergent traditions, cultures and socio-economic-political development. To simplify the argument herein, the US will stand for the West, and Brazil will not be assessed in detail because it plays a lesser role in establishing any new international order or hierarchy.

THREE SCENARIOS

There are three quite different scenarios which the US could adopt as its role in the world economy.

In one view, held by many Americans, the BRICs are seen as merely historical extensions of their past conditions, requiring no change in US policies under which each is treated unilaterally or bilaterally, and downplaying the role of intergovernmental institutions:

1. China is seen as a potential strategic and economic challenger;
2. Russia is viewed as imperialist, authoritarian and a potential enemy;
3. India is a continuingly poverty-stricken mass of peoples, subject to disasters and always needing humanitarian assistance.
4. Brazil is viewed as having a bright future – and always will be.

This is a world of 'fear and insecurity' with an objective of US dominance and deterrent power to prevent challenges. This imperial worldview is unacceptable to the BRICs and is no longer available to the US as it loses its hegemony and legitimacy of leadership. Loss of American leadership is seen in the loss of its followership around the world – evidenced by potential collaborators (and foreign media) turned critics. Their condemnations include: adventurism, arrogance, corruption, deceit, expediency over principle, fiscal and financial irresponsibility, hypocrisy, militaristic foreign policy, secrecy, unilateralism, uninvited interference abroad, violence (crime), weakened industrial competitiveness, zealotry – and, above all, rejection of its value foundations – so that it is no longer trustworthy. Domestic critics of the American economic condition focus on a degraded environment, deteriorating infrastructure and education, excessive consumption and inadequate savings, and extreme inequities in wealth and income.

If it is to remain even an influential player in a process of globalization that would include the BRICs, the US has much to change, including its worldview and policy of forcing freedom and democracy on the world.

A second and more hopeful scenario would be based on a worldview aimed at developing an international 'community of interest' for peace and progress:

1. America would become an example of open democracy and ethical private enterprise and government, demonstrating both equity and justice through responsible governance.
2. Leading nations would shift from 'conflict competition' to 'cooperative competition and collaboration'.
3. The US would accept the role of 'a declining first among equals' – and assist the BRICs to take, at least *ad hoc*, leadership roles.
4. The BRICs would be admitted into a new 'G12' – along with the US, Canada, Japan, the EU, Germany, Britain, France and Australia.
5. All would support multilateral institutions to develop a world community that would pursue progress through globalization and be concerned to mitigate the conditions causing or associated with poverty, ignorance, squalor, disease and environmental degradation.
6. The US would efficiently and effectively assist all countries adopting responsible policies in the process of globalization, fostering economic progress with equity and stability, while interdicting disrupting speculative movements of finance and other asset exchanges.
7. All would recognize that the most effective foundation for peace is economic integration through FDI, with democracy second (NB: China & Russia). Deep economic integration leads to an interdependence that counsels against destructive conflict and fosters democracy.

8. All would buttress these initiatives with an effective and efficient peace-keeping force to oppose domestic tyranny and cross-border conflicts.

Such a world is too much to expect in the near future, but it can become an accepted goal. Even so, it will involve a drastic shift in cross-cultural understanding and influences, with the West harmonizing its values with those emanating from the BRICs, whose origins – from religion and ethnicity to history and geo-location – are different from those of the West and even among themselves.

Some Western values have been absorbed by the BRICs, but unfortunately they are not always the most elevated. (America has become the best example of the fears of the eighteenth-century philosophic radicals, who sought a free society with democracy and capitalism, that individualism would give rise to a general pursuit of the lusts of power, greed and licentiousness.) The rest of the world would like our material standard of living but not our culture, though they have adopted a good bit through consumerism and entertainment.

At the same time, their longer and deeper value-sets will also permeate others, forming a 'complex hybrid'.[1] Even the Western concepts of a 'civil society' will be modified, and the merged concepts will reflect the growing self-confidence of these advancing societies, presenting the West with alternatives that may become attractive to some of its citizens, many of which are recent immigrants.

The tight extended family traditions in the BRICs have supported privacy, secrecy and differential treatment of the 'foreigner'. This, plus the dominant role of the state, has brought 'information-less societies' with little transparency or accountability; consequently, official data cannot be validated or considered reliable.

The continuation of traditional mores (including superstition in China and the caste system in India), and the burden of thousands of years of history, bring striking differences in lifestyles and concepts of identity. Americans constantly need to ask who they are and reinvent themselves according to fads or examples from celebrities; the Chinese have no such problem, for they know that they are citizens of the 'Middle Kingdom', standing between Heaven and Earth and, therefore, above others.

These self-views conflict with the pervasive spirituality of India, and the messianic spirituality of the Slav opposed to the pervasive materialism of the West. Thus, an accommodation of cultures will be significant in determining the shape of any new community of interest.

In the near-term, a third, realistic scenario would be founded on a world-view that mankind and nations are imperfect and not perfectible from the top down or by force; but would focus on the foundations of political and economic freedom, leaving the fundamental shift to the more hopeful scenario above to the inner transformation of man, which is its prerequisite. The proximate foundations include:

1. building a significant middle class, with an equitable distribution of income and wealth, through equality of opportunity;
2. recognizing the need for attention to both inner and outer development, requiring initiatives from and responsible actions by individuals and from diverse sources in addressing the specific external problems and situations;
3. promoting more ethical behavior through self-regulation, and acceptance that government or state regulation will continue to be necessary; seeking harmonization and gradual reduction of these restraints;
4. promoting appropriate regional associations as steps toward a global community; relying on the BRICs to become the hubs for their regions;
5. encouraging expansion of intra-regional FDI to ensure that these regions do not engage in conflict-competition and that capital is moved to labor where feasible, rather than vice versa;
6. making the UN Specialized Agencies effective promoters of functional harmony among nations – dealing with human rights, environment, trade, intellectual property, international law, labor conditions, impacts of mobile industries and services, and (im)migration;
7. helping to establish the basic institutions underlying a private enterprise system and civil society, so that integration will be founded on similar modes of business behavior.

The World Economic Forum at Davos, Switzerland in January 2005 concluded:

> The analysis of 2004 shows that few in either the public or the private sector are doing anywhere near what is necessary to get the world on track. In a series of scores using a zero-to-ten scale, the world has earned failing grades. In all issue areas, from education to hunger to peace to human rights, humanity is doing less than half of what is needed to build a more stable, prosperous world.

Its report proposed a Global Governance Initiative by business to change the world – by developing products and services affordable to the poor and finding profitable ways to supply them; business – NGO cooperation; public–private partnerships; corporate philanthropy; and public policy dialogue on rule-making and institution-building.

In opposition, *The Economist* (22 January 2005), in a review of corporate social responsibility, argued that MNCs and corporations in general should 'stick to their last' and let governments set and guide development policies. As with others urging the Classical tenets, its editors are uncomfortable with business taking initiatives or making inroads in public policy. They argue that there has been too much profiteering when business and government mix – as evidenced particularly in the BRICs. An appropriate separation requires private enterprise to pursue efficiency in production and distribution under ethical constraints and in competitive markets and governments to provide the 'favorable climate' for investment by firms operating ethically in a private enterprise system.

But governments, responding to competing interests, have not shown themselves capable of setting the rules for progress so that it is equitable among citizens, and business generally does not take implementing initiatives in social responsibility in the absence of government mandates. Both will require encouragement to play more effective roles. One encouragement would be to find ways of internalizing in corporate costs the externalities that burden social and economic progress, which are not adequately measured by GNP.

Socio-economic progress includes recognition that 'The health of nations is more important than the wealth of nations' (Will Durant). It involves a number of elements of development other than GNP: education, access to health care, family and social cohesion, environmental protection, recreation, infrastructure, energy availability, equal opportunity in employment, cultural advance, community relations, human rights, the dignity of individuals, political participation, encouragement of creativity, and the fuller use of individual talents. Most of these are not calibrated in the market, and market-based GNP may, in fact, drain resources from them.

PROSPECTS FOR ACCOMMODATION

Where is the US (as surrogate for the West) in its willingness to accommodate the entry of the BRICs into the global economy? And where are the BRICs in their readiness to establish the requisite institutions and constraints to achieve civil societies with private enterprise systems?

US Attitude

Despite the fact that the US has sought in the past to help all four BRICs join the world economy – though Russia was given aid only in the past few years and China only through private channels – its policies indicate that it has not really welcomed their advance. Instead, it has continued policies that constrain their trade in agriculture – the litmus test posed by the developing world under the WTO – and charged them with unfair competitive practices and undervalued exchange rates. It has claimed that their rise in industry, services and finance has had adverse impacts on employment and wages in the US – through exceedingly low prices as a result of what used to be called 'social dumping' (that is, wages below the poverty level and poor working conditions), government subsidies, lack of environmental regulations, poor health care, and violations of intellectual property rights.

Complaints in the US are intensified by the continuing decline in competitiveness of key industry sectors and services, leading to outsourcing of component manufacture, assembly, services and entire product lines. But such offshore movements should have been anticipated as developing economies opened to the world markets, and they will increase both extensively and intensively, with a gradual rise in wages, incomes, living standards, capabilities in science and technology, and competitiveness in host countries. The continuing transfer of technology will raise the quality of production and service in the BRICs, and the rise in productivity and wages – even faster now in China than in Japan in the 40 years after World War II – will gradually tend to reduce their competitive pressures.

An even greater threat to the US than increased competitiveness from the BRICs is the volume of dollar reserves held by them and other countries. Asian countries hold $2 trillion in reserves, and 50 percent of US treasuries are held abroad. Any significant drop even in the rate of buying of dollars or treasuries – at $2 billion per day to finance the twin US deficits – can accelerate the decline in the dollar, force a rise in interest rates, and cause bankruptcies in mortgages, and a decline in consumption means recession. It is to the interest of Asia to keep the dollar high to stimulate their exports and reduce unemployment, but the decline in the dollar is making this policy increasingly costly now and in the future; that is, it is unsustainable.

To play a leading role within such a complex world, the US must change itself by:

- putting its financial house in order, for America is strong when the dollar is strong;
- achieving greater cross-cultural sensitivity, including foreign languages, and giving up its expectation that progress in other countries will move them closer to American values and culture;
- cooperating in multilateral organizations;
- providing effective assistance – namely people-to-people rather than grants or unproductive loans, and FDI rather than speculative capital flows;

- shifting from a 'money-grubbing' approach in business careers to one of service and productive contributions in the market;
- achieving a higher order of ethics in all political and economic affairs – one that underpins freedom of individual choice through the social virtues of trust, promise, honesty, integrity, self-responsibility; plus accountability, transparency and reciprocity in business affairs;
- buttressing these over the long term with improved educational programs that also include an appreciation of the key role of values in society; and, finally,
- leading by example through internal reform and by closer integration with the EU; and then, encouraging the BRICs to accept responsible leadership roles within their regions even though the results may not accord with American values or objectives.

It is not at all clear that the US is prepared to reform itself in order to be an acceptable partner in leadership. And, a major caveat in accepting the US as the surrogate for the West in dealing with the BRICs is that American hegemony is being challenged by both the EU and the BRICs. Its role in setting terms of entry is declining. The process of accommodation is, therefore, becoming more complex, requiring more participants, closer cooperation and firmer commitments than in the past, hopefully reducing uncertainty.

Common Obstacles in the BRICs

It is not clear what worldview is held by each of the BRICs. But it is clear that they have some significant obstacles to achieving a cohesive view both within and among themselves. At least 18 internal difficulties exist that impede their joining fully in a global economy:

- Obstreperous parliaments, with members putting personal careers above the future of their country.
- Strong left-wing constituencies that make moves to a private enterprise system difficult and slow.
- Inability to provide leadership within their region as a model of economic integration, which would be a strong signal of willingness to take a responsible role within the world economy.
- Absence of social integration and loyalty to the nation (except in extremis), reflecting multiple languages and sub-cultures: 'China is a mountain of loose sand' (Sun-yat Sen).
- Corruption, with government officials and judges often directly involved.

- Government bureaucracies that stifle and drain intellectual and economic resources, including ineffective and uncertain judicial systems.
- Only partial 'rule of law' providing necessary protections of intellectual property, ownership of land, and contract, and assuring appropriate corporate governance.
- Continuing presence of state-owned enterprises restricting the domestic market open to the private sector, creating unfair competition for resources and capital.
- Market signals not accepted as the fundamental method of decision-making; non-market agreements often sought (for example India and China in agreement with OPEC to stabilize oil purchases and prices).
- Serious environmental pollution, with weak efforts at clean-up, which if increased will decrease investment for growth.
- Lack of financial and fiscal rectitude; large fiscal deficits, partly due to tax evasion.
- Inefficient agricultural sectors with underemployment, and rural populations ranging from 40 to 70 percent of the total, with outmigration to cities.
- Deterioration of urban infrastructure in mega-cities, taxing both public and private resources; in 1950, 10 percent lived in cities; now nearly 50 percent, going to 60 percent in ten years.
- Deficiencies in infrastructure (education, transport and communications), impeding growth.
- Uncertain moves toward privatization.
- Absence of an integrated national economy and polity, with states, provinces and oblasts pulling away from the center; plus competition among major cities for economic and political prominence and tax revenue.
- Unbalanced growth geographically: Russia's and China's east and west are not integrated, nor is Brazil's coast and hinterland, or India's north and south.
- Finally, each has a self-view or orientation that requires modification to move toward integration with the West: Russia and China consider they deserve 'great nation' status; Brazil that it deserves dominance in South America and a place with Western nations without earning either; and India seeks to lead in Asia without solving major problems of leadership within.

Of course, some of these apply also to Western countries, inhibiting their eagerness to accommodate the entry of the BRICs.

WHAT ARE THE BRICs DOING TO ADJUST?

Autarky in Russia and China has ended in failure, and Brazil and India have determined that their past efforts to protect their domestic economies and constrain FDI are inadequate for growth. In Brazil, Lula has turned from socialism and populism and is seeking to attract FDI with an offer of public–private partnerships, but this initiative has not yet gelled; and it may not, given the obstacles noted above. All four countries have opened their economies – some more than others; growth rates are at peaks and FDI flows are increasing rapidly. But three of the BRICs contain pitfalls in addition to the above obstacles, creating still more uncertainty as to their future roles.

Russia

Russia's first concern is security; its second is growth to join the world economy as a 'great power', again. Its proximate objectives are Putin's: to achieve democracy, civil society and the rule of law. Before him, Yeltsin, speaking to the US Congress, said: 'Our principles are the supremacy of democracy, human rights, liberties, loyalty, and morality'; '[we] seek to join the world community of civilized societies'. But it is not clear that this vision is shared by the Duma or the military; many prefer the 'old-style' great power status. And there is uncertainty as to how Putin intends to gain a place in the 'multi-polar world' he promotes.

Initiatives
Internally, Putin is moving cautiously to prevent the opposition from gaining political power; this has required control over the governors of the oblasts, over the oligarchs in industry, and over the military. To achieve these, he has turned to his colleagues in the former KGB. This authoritarianism will not scare FDI away – witness China – but instability and uncertainty will, even in a democracy, as in India. And recent moves by Putin have restricted foreign ownership and bidding privileges of joint ventures with over 49 percent foreign ownership.

Russia's long-term ability to enter the world economy depends on development from the bottom up, diversification through SMEs and FDI. Putin's short-term strategy, however, is to concentrate on the development and export of energy, relying on foreign partnerships for technology exploration and delivery. He sees this as enhancing Russia's influence in the G8 and hastening its entry into the WTO, which is a reason for regaining state control.

SMEs have coalesced to insist on the elimination of corruption and the freeing of enterprise from confusing, conflicting and constraining regulations (which foster bribes to the ministries). But the Russian culture still contains a higher priority for Self and family over the 'common good'; the Russian culture was seen by Gorbachev as unalterable even within a generation or two.

Putin is taking tough initiatives to hasten cultural change:

1. encouraging a private sector apart from energy and supporting growth of SMEs and their associations;
2. seeking to remedy the ills of the 'Mafia economy';
3. reforming the judicial system;
4. reducing corruption – especially in ministries – a 50-year task;
5. dominating the Duma, media and oblasts to force compliance;
6. attempting to institute democracy, partly for security: 'Democracies don't fight each other' (Putin);
7. refusing to accept the criticism of the West, which has never understood the culture and behavior of Russians; 'Russia is a riddle, wrapped in a mystery, in an enigma' (Churchill);
8. seeking to mollify the military while not bankrupting the country through an enlarged military;
9. trying to prevent further break-up of Russia, while easing out of Chechnya with EU assistance;
10. addressing the environmental degradation of the past;
11. accepting loss of the 'near abroad', but initiating a Common Economic Space agreement with Belarus, Kazakhstan and Ukraine;
12. opening the domestic market to private enterprise, FDI and joint ventures, with an average of $7 billion FDI in 2003–2004, less than half of China's but 50 percent above India's;
13. introducing financial rectitude and raising Russia's creditworthiness to a sound ranking by amassing exchange reserves and repaying debt;
14. establishing strategic partnerships with or buying major US companies to cement long-term relationships, obtain technology, and ease Russia's entry into the world economy;

Pitfalls

Besides the 18 deficiencies and obstacles in common with other BRICs, Russia faces additional pitfalls:

- absence of a strong community of interest – evidenced among the oblasts; antagonism toward control from the center; jealousy between St Petersburg and Moscow; growing xenophobia and anti-Semitism;
- agony of leaders over loss of empire, plus weakened military and loss of prestige from its positions on Palestine, Chechnya and Ukraine;

- continuing paranoia over the West's objectives;
- population declining to 150 million by 2050;
- interference by oligarchs and regional governors in large companies, Russian and foreign;
- uncertainty over state ownership of industry, especially energy, with resulting decline in investment in other sectors and potential drag on overall growth.

The total American investment in the Russian Federation is around $6 billion, while Russian investors have put some $1 billion in the American economy. Future American investment in Russia could be jeopardized if concerns over the Putin government's increasingly autocratic style are not allayed. However, FDI is often attracted by strong governments, if they provide a favorable climate for local business. But uncertainty about Russian policies and the pervasive corruption leaves Russia behind China in competition for foreign investment funds.

India

India's major concern since independence has been to raise the populace out of abject poverty. Per capita income has risen from $50 per year in the early 1960s to over $350, but the population is rising so fast that it will be larger than China's before 2050, holding down per capita growth. India sought growth internally and with little help from MNCs.

Initiatives
This attitude has now changed, and the rapid growth of services with the stimulus of outsourcing has raised middle-class incomes. India is now seeking to reduce poverty with the skills and information available from IT, using it in medical diagnosis and providing information to the agriculture sector. But IT employs only 1 million of the 470 million labor pool, and is expected to rise to only 2 million; and IT output amounts to only 1 percent of GDP. Total services amounts to over 50 percent of GDP, with industrial output actually shrinking as a percentage over the 1990s – meaning jobless growth for the economy and doing little to relieve poverty.

India sees itself in direct competition with China for international and regional prominence – at the same time it is in continuing talks with Chinese officials to establish close cooperation in economic and defense matters. Areas of friction in defense revolve around Tibet, border disputes, and China's assistance to Pakistan. On domestic progress, India sees itself behind China in infrastructure, enterprise development, inward FDI and energy security – 'I find China ahead of us in planning for the future . . .. We can no longer be complacent and must learn to think strategically, to think ahead and to act swiftly and decisively' (Prime Minister Manmohan Singh). The gap keeps widening at present, but some investors see India as a long-term better bet as a result of its stable democracy and long-term accommodation with the West.

The US sees India as an ally and has assisted it as a counter to both Russia and China, but now US FDI goes more to China, despite an authoritarian government versus a democratic one in India, and despite the facts that India is moving more quickly to offer protection to intellectual property, has a functioning capital market, a stable financial system (though a large fiscal deficit), and substantial economic ties to the West. In China FDI is 3.2 percent of GDP; in India it is only 1.1 percent, with portfolio (speculative) inflows twice the level of FDI. India is projecting annual FDI inflows of $10 billion, compared to China's $60 billion annual inflow of FDI and less than $5 billion portfolio due to an undeveloped stock market. (China's investment in infrastructure is seen in its Maglev train, traversing 30 km from the Pudong SEZ to Shanghai airport in 7 minutes, compared with the same distance from Mumbai in India to the airport that requires 45 minutes to an hour.)

India is not yet a significant source of FDI outflow, despite foreign exchange reserves of $130 billion. These funds should be available for capital goods imports for infrastructure and encouragement of FDI. But such priorities are not agreed by the parliament and the leftists.

PM Manmohan believes FDI is the key to India's progress as an economic powerhouse. But he has hit roadblocks from the left-wing parties which are a key coalition partner and on whose support the government survives. He announced the setting up of a regulatory framework for infrastructure to create the necessary environment to attract $150 billion FDI over a decade to achieve 7–8 percent annual growth based on public–private partnership. And caps on FDI in some manufacturing, retail, and banking are being raised. But Manmohan has to mitigate the objections of the left-wing parties by funding some projects in rural development, health and education. Foreign aid for these purposes would mitigate the obstacles from the left.

India is far ahead of China in IT, support of foreign companies outsourcing in the country, and general services. It is moving to maintain this lead but at the same time strengthen and expand both manufacturing and banking to gain a more balanced economy and offer diverse jobs. Its progress has brought investment from Indians residing abroad and a return of many technically skilled workers to help in the advance.

In 2005 it began discussion of a strategic partnership with the EU, which is the source of over 20 percent of India's trade. It would join the

US, Canada, Japan, China and Russia, which have similar agreements with the EU.

Pitfalls

India is a country in which economics security is a primary concern in jobs and for companies and banks (versus foreign competition). Workers prefer jobs in government, next in high-tech. This concern is being mitigated by the rapid rise in wages and salaries; for example, in the software sector, from 2000 to 2004, wages rose 50 percent and salaries of project managers rose 150 percent. In addition to the 18 obstacles noted above for all BRICs, India faces the following:

- Domestic market still small compared to its population, despite a rising middle class.
- Judicial cases taking a decade or more to be heard.
- Endemic corruption within state governments, which are largely incompetent as well – illustrated by the staggering estimate that a third to a half of India's electricity is stolen every year.
- Labor laws constituting a de facto social security safety net, decreeing that businesses with more than 300 workers cannot close down without government approval, and workers employed more than six months are effectively immune from firing.
- Old industries – machine tools, textiles and engineering – still inefficient and protected.
- An unbalanced tax system: 35 million pay personal tax in a population of 1070 million. India's manufacturers account for just 17 per cent of annual economic output but pay 80 per cent of taxes; tax evasion is widespread so that the budget deficit has averaged 10 percent of GDP for the past several years and is projected to continue.
- Larger assistance to the rural sector restrained by the need to accelerate investment in industry and infrastructure.
- Half of the children considered undernourished, requiring more funding from New Delhi and the states, already in deficits.
- Relative lack of understanding of the history, culture, politics and economics of other countries in South and Southeast Asia, preventing assumption of a leadership role.
- Lack of adequate education for children, offset by focus on higher education in science and technology; new Indian School of Business seeking world status – a 'global brand' similar to INSEAD, but complete with spirituality. Dean Mahajan: 'A global brand from India without spirituality would be a flawed brand.'
- Continuing drain of the conflict over Kashmir.

China

China has been highly concerned about employment, requiring continued high growth. The population has risen from 600 million in 1960 to 1.3 billion in 2005 and is expected to add 10 million a year for the next decade. China wants to be acknowledged as a global power, and has been relying on export-led growth to achieve that goal. But the US government (and Japan) is opposed if its power is based on military strength. Economic progress is welcomed – to a point – and democracy would be encouraged by America, along with human rights. The major challenges are market competition, population and unemployment, and the military.

Initiatives

In 2003, China exported $130 billion in electronic and information technology goods worldwide, and this production is projected to grow to $207 billion by 2007. China's entrance into knowledge-based industries has infringed upon the advantage that the US retained when competing with other developing nations. Research and development operations of numerous companies are opening offices in China; for example, Beijing and Shanghai have major stem-cell research centers; and overseas patients with life-threatening illnesses are traveling to China for experimental treatments using stem cells.

The security issues about China in the international debate relate to how a rising China will behave toward other countries. Will China seek military might to match its economic strength? Will it seek to dominate the region? Will it attract most of the FDI going into the region to the detriment of other Asian countries?

One scenario shows China to be so dedicated to economic growth that a confrontational foreign policy would be too disruptive, damaging so many Chinese that the Communist Party's hold on power would be threatened. Contrarily, China is seen by neo-conservatives in the US as likely to escalate economic competition into war, because great powers seek to maximize their share of world power and eventually want to dominate the system. In this case, an attempt would be made to dominate Southeast Asia and then force the US to leave the region. But, such a policy would lead to confrontation with the US and Japan, with the latter likely arming itself with nuclear weapons – neither of which China wants – at least until its level of development matches the US or the EU. Further, if China sought to expand in the region, New Zealand and Australia would feel the effects directly and would have to respond.

Moving toward entry into the global economy, it has embraced multilateralism and promoted a number of regional agreements. It has become a major buyer of the products of Southeast Asian countries, helping to assuage the fear that the inflow of FDI will damage the interests of its neighbors. China has reversed course on its Confucian culture and is seeking to explain it to the rest of the world, indicating a desire for others to understand a more peaceful, community-oriented China.[2]

But, even if China progresses peacefully, its potential economic size and competitive strength through low-cost and skilled labor pose a significant challenge to all countries. With government encouragement, Chinese companies are integrating with foreign countries through outward FDI – amounting to $3.6 billion in 2004 and with $1 billion projected out of Guangdong Province alone. Accelerated entry into high-tech ventures is being encouraged, along with domestic venture capital firms.

Given its market orientation, export surplus, access to world resources and drive for technology, there is virtually no industry or service that China cannot enter successfully. And Western multinationals are planning still larger investments to serve both export and local markets. To encourage FDI inflows, it is inserting the protection of private property into the Constitution; and in the service sector, in which China lags behind India, it is offering tax incentives and Special Economic Zones (SEZs) dedicated to IT for outsourcing by foreign firms. Most recently, it has opened up the sectors of power, rail, oil, aviation and defense for local and foreign investors.

The government has also encouraged outward FDI, especially in acquisitions of resource- and technology-based companies – half of the $4 billion total outflow in the former. It expects to move more rapidly up the learning curve of management and marketing. And the growth of its industry abroad is no threat to the government or its SOEs. It is following the path of Japan and South Korea, and the result should be the same – a more benign relationship and reduction of any strategic threat. It is unlikely to try to hold US investors hostage, given its counterbalancing FDI abroad.

Pitfalls
Events that would upset a peaceful stance in China include:

- conflict over Taiwan and continuing tensions with Japan;
- serious domestic instability resulting from internal migration, bank failures, a massive influx of North Korean refugees, or internal revolution (similar to Ukraine).

In addition to the common obstacles facing BRICs, some events that would slow its economic progress include:

- inability of cities attracting FDI to provide promised incentives;
- lack of profitability for FDI affiliates;
- expansion of conflict between JV partners;
- serious misallocation of capital: preference to SOEs in funding and markets; preference for FDI over domestic investment sources;
- continued high FDI and local investment, leading to excess capacity and a 'rough' and unbalanced economic expansion;
- absence of reform in its stock market, dominated by state enterprises;
- lack of means to maintain high grain production and farm income;
- bottlenecks in energy supply and generalized inflation.

INTEGRATION INITIATIVES AMONG THE BRICS

International economic integration by the BRICs is not restricted to the West but in important measures encompasses initiatives in trade and investment among themselves – principally bilaterally but also with a regional focus.

China and India

Trade is the main integrating activity between China and India at present, with bilateral trade rising from less than $2 billion in 2001 to over $13 billion in 2004; China is expected to become India's largest trading partner during 2006. To facilitate this, direct flights have risen from zero in 2002 to five a week in 2004, with more expected.

Although FDI is small between them, nearly 100 Indian companies now have offices in China – mostly software and IT. Only a few Chinese companies have an operating presence in India, as yet. Both see mutual benefits from opportunities to cooperate, but India will remain behind China until it opens its economy wider and invests in infrastructure. Even so, they are beginning to cooperate in joint buying agreements with suppliers of needed commodities (notably oil – even partnering with foreign producers), enhancing the bargaining power of each. And they take similar positions within the WTO. If they can overcome the historic fear of each other through greater economic integration, they will jointly dominate the world economy.

China and Brazil

China is seeking a regional presence in Latin America, having $50 billion in trade and investments there. Argentina, Brazil, Chile, Mexico and Panama are leading trading partners, with China as Brazil's third-largest export market, more than doubling since 1995 to 2004. Brazil was also offered some $7 billion for port and RR investments. Recent discussions at the highest policy level suggest a lessening of Brazil's orientation to the north and redirection both east to Europe and west to Asia – buttressing a 'multi-polar' world order.

On a regional basis, wider consultations are occurring through the China–Latin America forum, China–South American Common Market talks, and the China–Andean Community. President Hu visited several countries in November 2004, signing 39 agreements on trade, investment, space exploration, tourism and education. He stressed the benefits of mutual economic growth, through FDI and technology.

China and Brazil are a good fit for both FDI and trade, and the Latin American region more so, given China's thirst for oil. China's demand for resources means stiffer competition with the US in Latin America, and its diplomacy and economic agreements betoken even wider competition, as China seeks to become a global power.

China and Russia

Trade between Russia and China was $12 billion (including over $2 billion in arms) in 2004 (plus cross-border smuggling) but is expected to rise to between $60 and $80 billion in five years. China is hungry for Russian commodities, especially oil. Some FDI is exchanged between them – for example, China's loan to a Russian oil company. The two countries take similar positions in the UN and seek to contain the influence of the US through a strategic partnership aimed at creating a multi-polar world and facilitated by direct communication networks. Both countries see the US as a strategic opponent, eager to contain both. Thus, their economic ties have a strategic objective.

Regional cooperation exists through the Shanghai Cooperation Organization encompassing Russia, China, Kazakhstan, Kyrgyzstan, Tajikistan and Uzbekistan. Some observers expect that Russia and China will agree on a means of addressing security issues jointly and eventually invite India and Brazil to join a NATO-type entity and a consultative unit similar to the G7 on economic matters (*India Daily*, 3 February 2005). India is added to these two states in their fight against terrorism, the push for a multi-polar world, and respect for sovereignty with respect to separatist movements in Chechnya, Kashmir and Taiwan. And all three have made progress in resolving their border disputes.

Russia and India

Trade and people contacts between Russia and India are relatively slight, dominated by the supply of high-quality military equipment from Russia, constituting 70 percent, of India's weaponry, including tanks, aircraft and carriers, and cruise missiles. Energy cooperation is a primary objective of both countries, with Indian firms cooperating in projects on Sakhalin and the Caspian, and Russia assisting with hydro- and thermoelectric projects in India. They also are planning collaboration in the development of more advanced technologies. The visit by Putin to India in late 2004 produced a joint declaration on strategic cooperation plus ten memoranda and coope-rative agreements on exploration of space, navigation, banking and visa services to encourage exchanges. These, and potential further collabor-ations, are a consequence of a common view that the US has not paid sufficient attention to the regional and global aspirations and potential of each country.

Russia and Brazil

Trade between Brazil and Russia amounts to only $2 billion annually but is expected to increase two to three times in the near future. Putin, on a visit with Lula in November 2004, said that Russia was ready to promote joint efforts in technology – including space, military, airplane building and energy – leading to a technology 'alliance'. The longer-term objective seems to be to set up a coalition of the BRICs to challenge the US and the EU. All four are opposed to a dominant influence of the West; Brazil lies in the American sphere and can oppose most directly. Putin seeks to establish a long-term Russian foothold in Latin America, expanding its global influence. For its part, Brazil is attracted by the mutual support offered in economic development, trade, diplomacy and security, based on a collec-tive population of three-fourths of the world, dominance in natural resources, and a commanding build-up of science and technology (S&T) skills. If achieved, this coalition would change the balance within the United Nations, where Russia and China are permanent members of the Security Council and both India and Brazil are seeking the same status.

India and Brazil

Brazil, India and China are leading members of the G20 group of devel-oping countries, as well as of the G77 of 132 underdeveloped economies. The invitation to these three to meet with the G8 in 2006, to be chaired by Russia, is recognition by the West that the patterns of economic develop-ment and cross-border integration are no longer represented in existing groupings.

Both India and Brazil are more tightly integrated with either China or Russia than with each other, but they are close within the wider groups. In

2002, they set up an India–Brazil Commercial Council to discuss future trade and technology transfers. In 2003, Brazil, India and South Africa formed a G3 to strengthen the influence of southern states and agreed to support each other's initiatives in international organizations.

A January 2004 visit by Lula to India produced a preferential trade agreement between India and Mercosur, in which Brazil is dominant, and an agreement for cooperation in space programs. But trade and investment remain small between these two members of the BRICs, remaining under $1.5 billion of exports and imports in 2004. Higher levels are expected as they cooperate in aircraft, military equipment, space satellites, agriculture and pharmaceuticals. Joint R&D projects are also under development.

PROSPECTS FOR ACCOMMODATION

Eagerness of the BRICs to enter progressively into a global economy and a welcome by the West are tempered by a number of concerns:

1. Catalyzed by numerous scandals of fraud and corruption in their own countries and among MNCs, attention has turned to corporate behavior and governance. This leads to a concern over ethics, transparency and accountability. None of these is yet satisfactory in the BRICs – nor, for that matter, in the West.
2. The distribution of benefits has become a priority as FDI penetrates more deeply into the local economies, leading to the constraints on FDI noted above.
3. Major issues under negotiation between the BRICs, the US and the EU include environmental protection, global warming, human rights, transparency, intellectual property, movement of people, accounting standards, nuclear weapons, export subsidies, tax harmonization, exchange rates, anti-competition regulations, and others.

The approach to these negotiations has generally been to focus on each issue separately, with NGOs taking a prominent role in raising awareness – such as pesticide use, child labor, working conditions and wages, AIDS, and so on. Separate negotiations may lead to some collective action on single issues, but they are unlikely to lead to overall accommodations among nations leading to an acceptable worldview supporting economic integration with appropriate roles for MNCs.

If the world is to move further along the path of economic and socio-political integration, means must be found for making trade-offs and compromises among these issues as well. Such trade-offs will require holistic and systemic approaches to MNC roles in the development of regional associations or a global economy – a cooperative agreement embodying the processes by which individual issues are brought forth and resolution negotiated.

The wider and closer integration that will result from the fuller inclusion of the BRICs requires moves toward a 'community of interest' that permits, on a regional or global scale, the types of accommodations and compromises found within nation-states. To achieve this 'community of interest' requires adjustments that few nation-states or ethnic groups are yet willing to make – viz., the European Community and ASEAN. A priority is the development of wider cross-cultural understanding, sensitivity and tolerance.

Yet one of the greatest obstacles to formation of such a community is – as seen in Europe especially – the concept of identity. Every person and nation feels the necessity to distinguish themselves in some way from certain others and to identify with those who have some basic similarities – ethnicity, beliefs, dress, pursuits, careers or character traits. The need to 'belong' is evidence of the desire to know 'who we are'.

The effort to become European has been difficult enough; to seek to become a world citizen, in fact rather than as an ideal, is even more difficult. Yet, such a new worldview will eventually be a part of any global economy, if and when it is achieved.

A community of interest buttressing economic integration among the West and the BRICs will involve priorities for the foundations of private enterprise systems:

- economic efficiency for productivity and progress;
- socio-economic equity in benefits and burdens, plus equality of opportunity;
- political participation under appropriate democratic institutions;
- cultural diversity;
- venues for creativity at all levels of society;
- civil societies, encompassing the 'rule of law' plus ethical foundations, including accountability and transparency, and the protection of human rights.

MNCs are, along with all enterprises, involved in the implementation of socio-economic change to establish civil societies the world over. This requires a much higher degree of ethical behavior than evident in the BRICs. Unfortunately, individual and corporate freedom is often sought without the necessary accompanying responsibility. Responsibility involves not only ethical and law-abiding behavior but also self-regulation, accountability, transparency and compliance with government regulations – aspects of management not insisted upon even within American business schools.

VALUE FOUNDATIONS

If freedom is a primary value in the pursuit of globalization, responsibility (both public and private, collective and individual) must be its complement. Both are based on value foundations. The necessary community of interest is also set upon agreed values. But, it is not necessary for regional or global integration that the value-set be unified – that is, the same. It is sufficient for it to be harmonized, which can imply standardization or mere acceptance of known differences. Harmonization implies a lack of dissonance or conflict among the value-sets of different cultures. Therefore, there is no necessity for international law or global government in order to achieve a community of interest. All that is required is agreement on the necessary similarities and the acceptable differences – so that such differences do not lead to conflict.

The values involved are both communal (societal ethics) and individual (morals). Ethics, in fact, are 'morals in action'. Morals are involved in 'intent', which is a spiritual matter. Ethics can be derived from traditions, mores and customs, but these are generally based on some concept of 'the good'. Fortunately for the development of a community of interest, the fundamental moral lessons are the same in all major religions. It is in the dogma and organizational practices and structures that differences arise and lend themselves to zealous fundamentalism. The 'Masters' in each religion practiced and advocated tolerance of differences in the Paths to Truth and the absence of zealotry and control.

Building a community of interest will require a change in worldview and in the individual's view of Self, leading to a merger of the 'small Self' into the larger Self of the community. Such a transformation in human and institutional (organizational) relationships will require a strong act of will. From whence might it come? Only from each individual; and as has been noted: 'If the people lead, the leaders will follow' – evidenced in the Velvet Revolution in Czechoslovakia, and the Orange Revolution in Ukraine.

The CIBERs are presumably involved in all facets of the issues ahead – dealing with research, education and outreach to business. To lead within business schools, they need actively to encompass these issues and management's responsibility to help implement the desired changes. This would be a revolution in academic circles, for there is little in terms of curricula or publication requirements that lead to holistic or systemic analysis, much less to action, implementation and service in the public domain.

The present need is to demonstrate the requirements in public and corporate policies for including the BRICs in the global market and to educate managers to be able to take appropriate initiatives or respond effectively to the concerns (protests) that will arise if equity and participation do not accompany efficiency and if trust, promise and honesty are not the bases of communication and contract.

If values are not the foundation on which enterprise systems are erected, governments will be involved in more closely monitoring and supervising business to achieve socio-economic goals. And the public will focus on the pervasive involvement of business through concern for good corporate governance, requiring it to participate intelligently and responsibly in the identification of problems, analysis of potential solutions, development of appropriate means, and generation of the will to action, which is the supposed hallmark of management.

NOTES

1. In early December, to prepare the grounds for the strategic talks, a seminar was held at the Institute for Peace and Conflict Studies (IPCS) in New Delhi. Zhang Guihong, the deputy director of the Institute of International Studies, at Zhejiang University in Hangzhou, pointed out that China and India could play a major role in regional affairs. He grouped China and India with Pakistan (nuclear), Japan (economic), Russia (multipolar), and United States (strategic) to form respective triangles, basically to affirm the two countries' important place in the world. He also grouped the two with the Association of South East Asian Nations (ASEAN) and Central Asia, to discuss the benefits of a triangular relationship.
2. An example: 'American cars are all about ego, but [new Chinese cars] are friendly and neighborly. They're all about getting along; not getting away.' (*Wired*, April 2005, p. 111).

REFERENCES

Adler, Solomon, 2004, *The Chinese Economy.* London: Routledge Curzon.

Alexandroff, Alan, Sylvia Ostry and Rafael Gomez (eds) (2004), *China and the Long March to Global Trade: The Accession of China to the World Trade Organization*, London: Routledge.

Behrman, Jack N. (2002), 'Moral Buttresses and Obstacles in the Globalization Process', *Futures Research Quarterly*, **18**(4), 57–89.

Bjorkman, Tom (2003), *Russia's Road to Deeper Democracy*, Washington, DC: Brookings Institution

Buckley, Peter (2004), 'The Role of China in the Global Strategy of Multinational Enterprises', *Journal of Chinese Economics and Business Studies*, (January), 1–25.

Bugajski, Janusz and Marek Michalewski (2002), *Toward an Understanding of Russia*, New York: Council on Foreign Relations.

Cohen, S.P. (2001), *India: Emerging Power*, Washington, DC: Brookings Institution.

Dunning, John H. (2003), *Making Globalization Good*, New York: Oxford University Press.

Dyson, Tim, R. Cassen and L. Visaria (2004), *Twenty-First Century India: the Population, Economy, Human Development, and the Environment*, New York: Oxford University Press.

Eswar, Prasad (2004), 'China's Growth and Integration into the World Economy: Prospects and Challenges', Occasional Paper, Washington, DC: International Monetary Fund.

Fishman, Ted C. (2005), *China, Inc.: How the Rise of the Next Superpower Challenges America and the World*, New York: Scribner.

Gaidar, Y. (translated by Jane Anne Miller) (2003), *State and Evolution: Russia's Search for a Free Market*, Seattle: University of Washington Press.

Gao, Shangquan (2004), *China's Economic Reform*, NY: St Martin's Press.

Goldgeier, James M. and Michael A. McFaul (2003), *Power and Purpose: US Policy toward Russia After the Cold War*, Washington, DC: Brookings Institution Press

Gordon, Lincoln (2001), *Brazil's Second Chance: En Route toward the First World*, Washington, DC: Brookings Institution.

Hoge, James F., Jr. and Gideon Rose (2002), *Globalization: Challenge and Opportunity*, (*Foreign Affairs* Anthology), New York: Council on Foreign Relations.

Hoge, James F., Jr. and Gideon Rose, (2002), *The Rise of China* (*Foreign Affairs* Anthology), NY: Council on Foreign Relations.

Hough, Jerry F. (2001), *The Logic of Economic Reform in Russia*, Washington, DC: Brookings Institution.

Hussain, Athar (2005), *China: Transition to a Market Economy*, London: Routledge.

Jha, Prem Shankar (2003), *The Perilous Road to the Market – the Political Economy of Reform in Russia, India, and China*, London: Pluto Press.

Kupchan, Charles A. (2002), *The End of the American Era: US Foreign Policy and the Geopolitics of the Twenty-First Century*, NY: Alfred A. Knopf.

Lardy, Nicholas R. (2001), *Integrating China into the World Economy*, Washington, DC: Brookings Institution.

Li-Hua, Richard (2004), *Technology and Knowledge Transfer in China*, London: Ashgate Press.

Malmgren, K. Phillippa (2004), 'China's Secret Ambition: to Compete with America in America', *International Economy*, 22 September, 20–21, 88.

Nakamae, Tadashi (2004), 'Can the Earth Support Chinese Growth?', *International Economy*, 22 September, 10–13, 88.

Pei, Minxin (2002), 'China's Governance Crisis', *Foreign Affairs*, Sept/Oct, 96–109.

Segal, Adam (2002), *Digital Dragon: High-Technology Enterprises in China*, Ithaca, NY: Cornell University Press.

Shenkar, Oded (2004), *The Chinese Century: The Rising Chinese Economy and Its Impact on the Global Economy, the Balance of Power and Your Job*, Upper Saddle River, NJ: Wharton School Publishing.

Srinivasan, T.N. and Suresh D. Tendulkar (2003), *Re-integrating India with the World Economy*, Washington, DC: Institute for International Economics.

Wehrheim, Peter (2003), *Modeling Russia's Economy in Transition*, London: Ashgate Press.

Yao, Shujie and Xiaming Liu (eds) (2004), *Sustaining China's Economic Growth in the Twenty-first Century*, London: Routledge.

Current Media

Asia Wall Street Journal; *Boston Globe*; *British Standard*; *Business Standard (India)*; *Business Week* – U.S.; *China Daily*; *The Economist* (London); *Financial Express* (Bombay); *Financial Times* (London); *Globe and Mail* – Canada; *Guardian* (British); *Hindu*- India; *Indian Express*; *Interfax*-Russia; *Financial Express* – India; *Moscow Times*; *MOSNEWS* – Russia; *Navhind Times* – India; *New Kerala* – India; *Press Information Bureau* (India); *Los Angeles Times*; *New York Times*; *Reuters* – India; *RIA Novosti* – Russia; *Times of India*; *Wall Street Journal*; *Washington Post*; *Washington Times*; *Xinhua* (China)

Index